MW01114266

Here's what people say about author Brian J. Smith:

"Brian J. Smith is much more than your typical software expert. He's a
man with a mission to engage and enlighten his readers in direct,
understandable language. Smith is one of those rare technical writers
who cares more about teaching than about showing off his considerable
technical prowess."
— **Dave Kalman, Publisher, *DBMS* magazine and *Internet***
***Systems* magazine**

"Brian explains the components of PowerBuilder in a
logical, clear, and concise way."
— **Adonna Roelke, Consultant, PowerPartners**
Consulting

"Brian Smith's application development insights have
influenced the work of thousands of programmers. His latest
book will show you the best way to get jump-started with
PowerBuilder."
— **Dian Schaffhauser, Editorial Director,**
Pinnacle Publishing

"Brian Smith has the rare ability to convey exactly the right
amount and type of information for a person to grasp the topic
at hand comfortably. Many authors jump between information
that is too general to be of any use and low-level technical
details that are inappropriate and difficult to understand.
Brian, on the other hand, leaves you feeling good about what
you learned and able to actually use what you learned!"
— **Steve West, System Specialist, Bergen Brunswig**
Corporation

"I've known Brian Smith for years, and he is one of the best
consultants and trainers in the software industry. Undoubtedly, your
PowerBuilder productivity will improve to amazing levels with Brian's
tips and tricks, so that you can keep up with today's high paced
client/server application development."
— **Ken Hertzler-Walters, Director of Windows Products,**
Mercury Interactive

"Great job. Your class and book were extremely
instrumental in jump starting the team into
PowerBuilder and client/server. I am grateful for the
fine contribution you made toward our increasing
success in developing applications that add value to our
business."
— **Bob Kealing, Manager of Application**
Development, Prudential Healthcare

"Having observed Brian as a technical writer and trainer on
both sides of the Atlantic, I heartily commend his book. Brian
is a master communicator. I know of no other individual with
his gift for presenting complicated technical concepts with
such clarity. His extraordinary knowledge and user friendly
approach will benefit novice and expert alike."
— **Carolyn Custis James, Consultant,**
ABBA Systems, Inc.

"Brian Smith's new PowerBuilder book reflects his
exceptional teaching skills and ability to make complex
subjects easy to understand. His refreshing pragmatic
approach helps the reader to stay focused on learning the
essentials of PowerBuilder. Brian's innovative style should
help readers learn PowerBuilder much quicker and with
more confidence than ever before."
— **Phil Hauser, PowerBuilder Developer and**
Recruiter, Omnikron Systems, Inc.

FOUNDATIONS™ *of*

PowerBuilder® 5.0

PROGRAMMING

FOUNDATIONS™ *of*

PowerBuilder® 5.0
PROGRAMMING

Brian J. Smith

Gordon W. Schaad

Richard Castler

Jon E. Bruce

Azita Gandjei

John Miller

IDG
BOOKS
WORLDWIDE

Foundations™ of PowerBuilder® 5.0 Programming
Published by
IDG Books Worldwide, Inc.
An International Data Group Company
919 E. Hillsdale Blvd.
Suite 400
Foster City, CA 94404

Library of Congress Catalog Card No.: 95-77585
ISBN: 1-56884-302-X
Printed in the United States of America
10 9 8 7 6 5 4 3 2 1
IB/RZ/QY/ZW/FC
Distributed in the United States by IDG Books Worldwide, Inc.
Distributed by Macmillan Canada for Canada; by Contemporanea de Ediciones for Venezuela; by Distribuidora Cuspide for Argentina; by CITEC for Brazil; by Ediciones ZETA S.C.R. Ltda. for Peru; by Editorial Limusa SA for Mexico; by Transworld Publishers Limited in the United Kingdom and Europe; by Academic Bookshop for Egypt; by Levant Distributors S.A.R.L. for Lebanon; by Al Jassim for Saudi Arabia; by Simron Pty. Ltd. for South Africa; by Pustak Mahal for India; by The Computer Bookshop for India; by Toppan Company Ltd. for Japan; by Addison Wesley Publishing Company for Korea; by Longman Singapore Publishers Ltd. for Singapore, Malaysia, Thailand, and Indonesia; by Unalis Corporation for Taiwan; by WS Computer Publishing Company, Inc. for the Philippines; by WoodsLane Pty. Ltd. for Australia; by WoodsLane Enterprises Ltd. for New Zealand. Authorized Sales Agent: Anthony Rudkin Associates for the Middle East and North Africa.
For general information on IDG Books Worldwide's books in the U.S., please call our Consumer Customer Service department at 800-762-2974. For reseller information, including discounts and premium sales, please call our Reseller Customer Service department at 800-434-3422.
For information on where to purchase IDG Books Worldwide's books outside the U.S., please contact our International Sales department at 415-655-3172 or fax 415-655-3295.
For information on foreign language translations, please contact our Foreign & Subsidiary Rights department at 415-655-3021 or fax 415-655-3281.
For sales inquiries and special prices for bulk quantities, please contact our Sales department at 415-655-3200 or write to the address above.
For information on using IDG Books Worldwide's books in the classroom or for ordering examination copies, please contact our Educational Sales department at 800-434-2086 or fax 817-251-8174.
For authorization to photocopy items for corporate, personal, or educational use, please contact Copyright Clearance Center, 222 Rosewood Drive, Danvers, MA 01923, or fax 508-750-4470.

is a trademark under exclusive
license to IDG Books Worldwide, Inc.,
from International Data Group, Inc.

Welcome to the world of IDG Books Worldwide.

IDG Books Worldwide, Inc., is a subsidiary of International Data Group, the world's largest publisher of computer-related information and the leading global provider of information services on information technology. IDG was founded more than 25 years ago and now employs more than 8,500 people worldwide. IDG publishes more than 270 computer publications in over 75 countries (see listing below). More than 90 million people read one or more IDG publications each month.

Launched in 1990, IDG Books Worldwide is today the #1 publisher of best-selling computer books in the United States. We are proud to have received eight awards from the Computer Press Association in recognition of editorial excellence and three from *Computer Currents'* First Annual Readers' Choice Awards. Our best-selling *...For Dummies®* series has more than 25 million copies in print with translations in 30 languages. IDG Books Worldwide, through a joint venture with IDG's Hi-Tech Beijing, became the first U.S. publisher to publish a computer book in the People's Republic of China. In record time, IDG Books Worldwide has become the first choice for millions of readers around the world who want to learn how to better manage their businesses.

Our mission is simple: Every one of our books is designed to bring extra value and skill-building instructions to the reader. Our books are written by experts who understand and care about our readers. The knowledge base of our editorial staff comes from years of experience in publishing, education, and journalism — experience which we use to produce books for the '90s. In short, we care about books, so we attract the best people. We devote special attention to details such as audience, interior design, use of icons, and illustrations. And because we use an efficient process of authoring, editing, and desktop publishing our books electronically, we can spend more time ensuring superior content and spend less time on the technicalities of making books.

You can count on our commitment to deliver high-quality books at competitive prices on topics you want to read about. At IDG Books Worldwide, we continue in the IDG tradition of delivering quality for more than 25 years. You'll find no better book on a subject than one from IDG Books Worldwide.

John J. Kilcullen

John Kilcullen
President and CEO
IDG Books Worldwide, Inc.

Credits

ABOUT THE AUTHORS

Brian J. Smith is President of Brian J. Smith and Associates, Inc., a consulting and training company in Los Angeles. He has worked as a systems development professional since 1974, first as a programmer, then as a systems manager, then as a management consultant, and finally as president of his company. He and his company have developed business systems for hundreds of companies, including Bank of America, Twentieth Century Fox, UCLA, Kaiser Permanente, Southern California Edison, and Toyota.

Brian is a prolific author and lecturer. He is a contributing editor to *Data Based Advisor* magazine, where his articles have appeared since 1987. His most recent features have been about three-tiered/multitiered architecture. He has taught programming seminars on four continents, attracting audiences of four hundred people and more. He was the Chairman of the second Borland International Developers Conference.

Brian began using PowerBuilder in 1994, with version 3.0. The following year, he began an ongoing series of PowerBuilder lectures for the Los Angeles and Orange County (California) PowerBuilder Users Groups. He holds a Bachelor of Science in Mathematics from the California Institute of Technology, and is a Certified PowerBuilder Developer (CPD).

Gordon W. Schaad is a well-known lecturer, writer, programmer, and consultant. He has developed business systems for many companies, chiefly in the banking and health care industries. His expertise encompasses a variety of application development tools, including, of course, PowerBuilder.

Gordon has delivered technical presentations at a number of developer conferences. For five years he was the editor-in-chief and frequent contributor to *Instant Scripts*, the newsletter of the LAPALS Paradox User Group. His training courses for Paradox, Microsoft Access, and Lotus Approach are in use by corporations and training organizations nationwide.

Gordon earned his Bachelor's degree in Mathematics from New York University, where he was elected to Phi Beta Kappa.

Richard Castler has over twenty years experience as a programmer, consultant, and manager. He has given lectures at developers' conferences on such topics as data security, performance tuning, and event-driven programming. Richard is the Vice President of Brian J. Smith and Associates, Inc., and holds a B.S. degree in Computer Science and an M.S. in Operations Research. He is a Certified PowerBuilder Developer (CPD).

Jon Bruce is a Managing Consultant with the Deloitte and Touche Consulting Group — DRT Systems. He began using PowerBuilder with release 2.0. He specializes in the design and implementation of large client/server systems for Fortune 500-level companies. Jon was the principal organizer and first president of the Orange County PowerBuilder Users Group. He designed and teaches the course "Developing Client/Server Applications" for the University of California, Irvine Extension department.

Azita Gandjei is a computer consultant specializing in designing and developing database applications for major corporations. An expert in several major database programming languages, she has led many software training classes and given several technical presentations to software developers at professional meetings and software industry conferences.

John Miller has worked in the computer industry for over ten years. He has written several academic papers on client/server technology and is an expert on relational databases. Receiving his Master of Science in Computer Science from the University of California at Los Angeles, Mr. Miller has taught courses in database management, programming languages, and mathematics. He is currently a database consultant with Brian J. Smith & Associates.

To my wife Cindy. Thank you for ten wonderful years together. I look forward to the next fifty. — BJS

To Jane. — GWS

Foreword

I read somewhere fairly recently that 95 percent of all database application development from 1995 to 2000 will be on a client/server platform. Clearly, the war is over, and client/server has won. (How would you like to be product manager for CA-COBOL right now? How about dBase for Windows?) This pronouncement seems fairly obvious at this point, but David Litwack, the President of Powersoft (when it was just Powersoft), and now the Executive Vice President of the tools division of Sybase, made this same prediction way back in 1990. PowerBuilder 1.0, a completely client/server-centric development tool was released in June, 1991. At the time, the competition was Gupta's SQL Windows, Knowledgeware (where have you gone, Fran Tarkenton?), and some quickly forgotten names such as Easel and Omnis 7. Last time I looked, only SQL Windows was still around, and Powersoft stopped being concerned with them as serious competition years ago.

So Powersoft did what every student is taught to do in Marketing 101. It got into the market early with a good product, a well-defined message, and a strong management team. They also had plenty of venture capital and a very strong IPO, followed by a purchase by Sybase that valued them at close to a billion dollars in 1994. Great story — build a product in 1991 and sell the company three years later for a billion or so. Actually, this is the business model I designed for my own company, give or take 990 million dollars.

What does this mean to you, assuming you are a programmer who bought this book to learn PowerBuilder? Well, for one thing it means that you have made a good decision. Learning PowerBuilder isn't just another professional requirement, it can be a quantum leap in your career because strong client/server developers are extremely difficult to find. I know. I spend a large portion of my life interviewing and recruiting developers for my company. Take a look in the Sunday newspaper — PowerBuilder and client/server dominate the employment ads. Someone who is fluent in PowerBuilder with strong Sybase, Oracle, Informix, or SQL Server skills can literally write his or her own ticket. One friend of mine is traveling around the world over the next few years, financing his way by taking contract programming jobs in PowerBuilder as he travels. There is so much demand that he just picks a city, posts an Internet classified ad, and is employed as soon as he reaches his destination. So far he has traveled across the U.S. and is currently in Australia. He plans to make it back to North Carolina sometime in 1998.

And the great thing is, PowerBuilder is really a simple language. Assuming you have some basic computer programming skills, PowerBuilder is about as easy as a language gets. If you really work at it and study the examples and knowledge in this book, you can probably be about 50 percent fluent in a few weeks, which is plenty to get a PowerBuilder programming job. Once you are on the job, you can continue to learn (and get paid for it — a nice combination) and study the advanced sections of *Foundations of PowerBuilder 5.0 Programming*. By the end of a year you will be a PowerBuilder guru, your life's work will be assured, and you will finally be able to buy that beach condo in Malibu. Well, maybe the Malibu condo is an exaggeration, but the career is in the bag.

As you know, if you browsed the local bookstore shelves, there are a ton of PowerBuilder books out there, some of them by good friends of mine. So I had some trepidation when I agreed to write a foreword for Brian's book, even though I have known of and respected Brian's writing for a long time. Luckily, the fears dissipated as soon as I started reading. Brian's writing is clear, concise, accurate, and his explanations of technical issues are extremely accessible. I am very enamored of writing that gets directly to the point. (I once had a business professor that told me if I couldn't get the point across in a one page brief, my thinking was too cloudy. I often revisit that sentiment.) Brian is economical while still managing to be thorough. This is a book that will serve its audience well. Welcome to the world of PowerBuilder programming; I'm sure you will enjoy having *Foundations of PowerBuilder 5.0 Programming* as your roadmap.

Michael Horwith
Editor, *PowerBuilder Advisor* magazine
Partner, Financial Dynamics;
Raleigh, North Carolina

Preface

Welcome to the world of PowerBuilder 5.0!

In the past few years, PowerBuilder has emerged as the leading product for Rapid Application Development (RAD) of client/server application systems. It has succeeded for good reason. PowerBuilder offers a unique and powerful blend of development tools, including easy-to-use interactive screen painters, modern object-oriented technology, and an impressive set of database connectivity features.

The purpose of this book is to transform you into a professional PowerBuilder developer, even though at the outset you may not know anything about the product other than its name.

Who Should Read This Book?

This book is for several types of readers: experienced programmers, not-so-experienced programmers, MIS managers, and even people who have already used PowerBuilder somewhat. In any case, I assume an understanding of basic programming concepts, such as variables, arrays, do-loops, and the construction of program logic. Since I assume that you know nothing about PowerBuilder, one goal is to show you how to do ordinary programming things, things that you already understand, with PowerBuilder.

PowerBuilder relies heavily on features such as graphical (e.g., Windows) user interface design, client/server, SQL, object-oriented programming, and event-driven programming. Many people, especially those coming from the mainframe or PC-DOS worlds, are new to these ideas. If these ideas are new to you, you'll be happy to find here an introduction to each of them — sometimes, entire chapters.

Each chapter begins with simple definitions and explanations and then proceeds to more complex information. With some topics, such as with DataWindows and with object-oriented programming, several chapters carry a concept from the basics, through the detailed how-to's, and on to the advanced techniques.

Some people, especially managers, could get by with just the beginnings of each chapter. Others, who have some knowledge already and are looking to expand it, might skip directly to the more advanced stuff. I hope, of course, that most of you will want to read the entire book.

This is a book about version 5.0 of PowerBuilder, not 4.0 or any earlier version. If you already know PowerBuilder 4.0, and are looking for what's new in 5.0, begin by reading Appendix A, which compares the two versions. If you are new to PowerBuilder but have been assigned to update a 4.0 application to 5.0, keep an eye on Appendix A while reading the other chapters.

Is Another PowerBuilder Book Really Necessary?

We know that there are many PowerBuilder books out there to choose from. Therefore, we have spent a lot of time and effort to make sure that this book will be more valuable to you than any other.

Many of you might wonder whether you need any book at all. After all, PowerBuilder itself comes with plenty of documentation. Most of it is on CD-ROM, unless you special-order hard copy books. Shouldn't this documentation teach you everything you need to know? The answer is that the PowerBuilder documentation is an excellent reference, but it doesn't help much as a learning guide. And it suffers from a common failing of software vendor literature, which is that it shows how to solve the problems that the product can do easily, but it carefully skirts most of the thornier problems.

Then there are the typical beginner books about PowerBuilder. Most of them seem to be watered-down recaps of the product manuals. I've never found them very helpful. In spite of their thickness, they don't scratch very deep below the surface, and they always leave me with more questions than answers. In general, I've made much better progress by trying out PowerBuilder on my own and researching the on-line documentation, and so the beginner books spend most of the time on the shelf. The more advanced PowerBuilder books are better, but only if you already know the product.

My co-authors and I have taken a different approach than the authors of the typical beginner and advanced books. We are practical, down-to-earth people. We've been developing systems for many years — decades even — and we have worked with many tools and in many environments. When we began learning PowerBuilder, our biggest concern was how to build the kinds of complete application systems that our customers expect. (We have customers in just about every industry, so we have a firm understanding of what business systems in general require.)

It was not necessarily our goal to learn every feature in PowerBuilder. But it was critical that we discover and thoroughly master the essential elements for standard business applications. We also wanted to learn these essential elements as quickly as possible. We succeeded, and our findings became the groundwork for this book.

We didn't pull any punches in this book. If PowerBuilder is missing an essential feature, we tell you. If an important technique requires coding that's more complex than it ought to be, we show you the complex code. That's what we'd want someone to tell us, so that's what we tell you.

A side-effect of our practical writing style is that the sample applications in this book have a very plain look. We've concentrated on the internal functionality, and that's where we want you to concentrate too. Yes, I think your applications should look prettier than ours. But I also think you can learn pretty on your own. If not, Chapter 14 refers you to some good interface design books. That leaves more room in this book to tackle the trickier technical issues.

What are the topics that set this book apart? Here are a few examples:

- Every book teaches how to create a DataWindow, and so do we. But I believe only this book explains how to program important data entry functionality, such as complex field validation, updating related tables, and building one-to-many forms such as a classic order entry form.
- Every book covers object orientation, but few show you the kinds of objects that all the best PowerBuilder pros build for their toolkits.
- Every other book assumes you have connected PowerBuilder to your database, but no one else tells you where to investigate when your first attempts at connecting fail (which they will).

How to Write About a Big Product

PowerBuilder is an enormous product. It's perhaps the most feature-rich software that I've ever worked with. Every dialog box is loaded with options. Besides that, there are usually several ways to do any given task. If you click a toolbar button to do something, for example, there's probably a function key and also a menu choice or two that do exactly the same thing.

With so much to work with, we have not attempted to give a comprehensive description of every part of PowerBuilder. That would be a much, much bigger book. After all, the PowerBuilder documentation set, which does attempt to be comprehensive, is over 7000 pages altogether. Instead, we have focused on those features that we have found to be valuable in our own work.

Should You Do the Exercises?

All of the sample programs and exercises described in this book are on the accompanying CD-ROM. In fact, the CD-ROM often contains more detailed programming and more alternative solutions than you'll find in the book, since we can fit so much more on the CD-ROM than on printed pages. Please refer to the appendix, "How to Use the CD-ROM," and to the CD-ROM's README.TXT file for instructions and more information.

As you begin each chapter, you will find it helpful to copy the chapter's CD-ROM directory onto your computer so that you can inspect the sample files as you read. Another approach is that you could develop your own samples from scratch, following the instructions in the book, and refer to the CD-ROM if you get stuck. Either way, you'll get the benefit of hands-on experience as you learn.

Having said all that, I must confess that I'm one of those people who never touches the CD-ROM or diskette that comes with a book. Yes, I'm sure that I'd learn more if I did, and I'd get more for my money. But it's just not my style. I tend to read computer books only in easy chairs, at the lunch table, and on airplanes.

(Yes, I carry a laptop on flights, but doing exercises with a big book and a laptop on a tray table is not my idea of air travel.)

So I've made sure that this book stands perfectly well on its own. It's loaded with screen shots and diagrams so that you can picture what's going on. This should satisfy the "read-only" people like me.

ABOUT WINDOWS 95 AND OTHER OPERATING SYSTEMS

The screen images in this book are all from Windows 95 so they have the Windows 95 look and feel. Since PowerBuilder is a cross-platform product, everything should work just fine with other operating systems. We've cross-tested most of the examples under Windows 3.1, just to be sure.

Where there are differences between Windows 95, 3.1, and NT, we've noted them in the text. We have not made a big effort to address Apple Macintosh or UNIX PowerBuilder issues. For one thing, the Mac and UNIX versions of PowerBuilder 5.0 are not available at the time that this is being written.

THE BONUS CHAPTERS

This book has 21 chapters, although you'll find only 16 of them on paper. The other five are "bonus chapters" and you will find them on the CD-ROM. The bonus chapters cover topics of specialized importance, such as advanced DataWindows and an introduction to SQL. Please refer to the README.TXT file on the CD-ROM for more information about the bonus chapters and instructions on how to access them.

"I" IS "WE"

Throughout the book there are many comments such as "I have found that…" and "I believe that…" To give credit where it's due, please recognize that this book was a collaborative effort, with each of the co-authors contributing material. So "I" most often is Brian, but "I" could also be Gordon, Richard, Azita, John, or Jon. Some might argue that "we" would be more accurate, but "we" consider that too impersonal.

(In this introduction, however, "I" is Brian and "we" are we.)

WHERE TO SEND YOUR COMMENTS

If you have any comments, criticisms, or questions, we'd love to hear from you. My e-mail address is 75530.332@compuserve.com.

Thank you for your interest in this book! We hope that you enjoy it and that your PowerBuilder efforts are successful and rewarding!

Acknowledgments

During the year and a half it took this book to evolve from concept to reality, we have been fortunate to receive help from many talented people. I'd like to thank each of them.

The book got its start thanks to Trudy Neuhaus. It was at a Comdex convention that I mentioned my interest in writing about PowerBuilder to Trudy, who at the time was Publishing Director for IDG Programmers Press. Trudy followed through immediately and, before I knew it, a book contract was in place with IDG. Thanks, Trudy!

The people at Powersoft Corporation were always very generous with their support. Richard Dill, Alex Whitney, and Bill Rabkin gave excellent answers to every technical question, no matter how odd. Cecile Roux, Rachel Stockton, Michelle Murray, and Susan Donahue helped to open every door when we came knocking.

Thanks also to the project team at IDG Books Worldwide: Jim Markham, Amy Pedersen, Ken Brown, Katharine Dvorak, Ann Marie Walker, and Jill Reinemann. Amy and Ken, in particular, provided excellent guidance and never took their eyes off the target.

Mark Jordan, the technical editor, was meticulous in insuring the accuracy of every sentence in this book. Bob Campbell, the manuscript editor, was equally meticulous in keeping the text readable and the style consistent. Both did a fine job.

Special thanks go to the men and women of the Los Angeles and Orange County PowerBuilder User Groups. These groups allowed me to visit them and deliver lectures based on the rough drafts of this work. Their feedback was very valuable in polishing the material. Thanks to Victor Reinhart, George Hays, Phil Hauser, and Helen Wang for setting up the lectures, and to all the members who attended.

Thanks also to David Kodama, Mike Horwith, Michael Kells, David Kalman, Dian Schaffhauser, Bob Kealing, Aaron Stockser, and Mary Adkins for your support, advice, and efforts during this project.

The biggest thank you of all goes to Nancy Kelly, the Administrative Assistant at Brian J. Smith and Associates. While all of us were tied up with writing, Nancy kept the office afloat. She also spent innumerable hours pasting figures into draft documents and printing and photocopying chapters. Thank you, Nancy, for a job well done!

Brian J. Smith

Contents Overview

Table of Contents

I The Foundations

1

A First Look at PowerBuilder

*T*his chapter offers an overview of PowerBuilder, its features, and the type of applications you can develop with it. It's a high-level orientation, to show you the lay of the land and give you some idea about where we'll be going in the course of this book. You won't find any detailed "how-to" instructions in this chapter. Those will begin in Chapter 2.

What Is PowerBuilder?

PowerBuilder is a development tool, primarily for the development of client/server applications.

With PowerBuilder, development is a very visual process. Suppose that you want to design a window to display some data on the screen. (PowerBuilder calls these displays "windows." Other products you've used may have called them "screens" or "forms.") Much of your design time is spent painting the window, using the mouse and keyboard to draw it. You don't write program code to describe the layout. If you come from a non-visual programming environment such as COBOL, where you tend to create visual displays by writing a ton of program code, the painting aspect of PowerBuilder will be one of the first major concepts for you to assimilate. On the other hand, if you have experience with visual development tools, especially such Windows-based ones as Visual Basic, this part of PowerBuilder will be quite familiar to you.

This is not to say that you don't write any program code with PowerBuilder. You have to write at least a little, and for complex applications you'll write a lot. In PowerBuilder, program modules are called *scripts* and you write them in a proprietary language called "PowerScript." For example, you might write a script to perform calculations on a data value as the user types it in. Even here, however, you may be able to avoid coding, since PowerBuilder offers many tools for specifying data handling without the need for programming. The point is that you will find yourself writing a lot less code, with much more attractive results, than you would with an older-style development tool. This is what is meant by the term "Rapid Application Development."

The PowerBuilder Environment

As you develop your application using PowerBuilder, you will switch between two modes:

- **The Development Environment** — Pictured in Figure 1-1, this is the PowerBuilder program itself, with all the tools necessary to design the application's components, write its scripts, and so forth. Figure 1-1 is pretty busy; it shows what the screen might look like after you've been at work for a while. When you first start the PowerBuilder program, the screen is much emptier, with just the menu bar, the toolbar, and no child windows.

- **Run mode** — With a click of a button in the development environment, you can run the application. The development environment hides, and you see the application exactly as it will look and operate for the end user, as in Figure 1-2. When you close the window (or windows, since in some cases the application may open more than one), the application terminates and the development environment reappears.

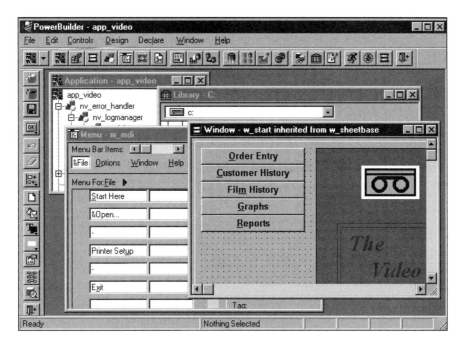

Figure 1-1

The PowerBuilder development environment.

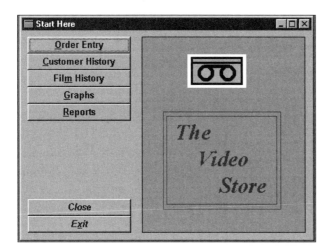

Figure 1-2

Running the application.

Thus the process of developing a PowerBuilder application involves designing the application in the development environment, switching to run mode to test it, switching back to the development environment to fix bugs and add new features, running it again, and so on back and forth.

The Video Store Application

Figure 1-2 shows the startup window for a simple application named "The Video Store." This application, or variations of it, will be used as an example throughout this book. It's a system you might develop if you owned a video store. It keeps track of customers and films, including which customers rent which films. When a customer visits the store and makes a rental, that's when order entry takes place. The application also displays graphs and prints various reports.

The startup window consists of seven buttons — Order Entry, Customer History, and so on. Clicking a button opens another window that leads to one of the various components of the application. Clicking Order Entry, for example, opens the Order Entry Form, which is another window. The right half of the startup window, with the words "The Video Store" and the cassette tape graphic above it, doesn't do anything. It's just there to look good. (I hope that you have more artistic talent than I do!)

To terminate the application, click the Exit button or close the Video Store Application window. (In Windows 95, you close a window by clicking its close button, which is in the top-right corner.) If you started the application from the development environment, you will return to the development environment.

Figure 1-1 shows the Video Store application in the development environment. Most of the screen is occupied by the four overlapping child windows, each showing the design of some component. The one in the lower right is the startup window itself, the same one shown running in Figure 1-2, as it appears in the development environment.

SDI and MDI

Many of the sample applications you'll encounter in the chapters to follow require only one window to be open at a time. Therefore, as each window opens in these simple applications, the one before it closes. In the Microsoft Windows world, this style is called a "Single Document Interface," or SDI. More ambitious applications, such as the Video Store application, offer a "Multiple Document Interface," or MDI. In MDI, one large parent window, called the *frame*, contains many smaller child windows. You can open any number of child windows at once, and you can move and resize them in any arrangement. For example, you could open an order entry window, a customer history window, and a film history window, and you could place them side by side to do some research. You could likewise open multiple copies of the order entry window to review more than one order at a time.

The PowerBuilder development environment itself is an MDI application, as you can tell from Figure 1-1.

Our goal is for almost every application to be MDI. But we must cover a lot of ground first. In Chapter 14 I will show you how to set up an MDI version of the Video Store application, and the chapters that follow will build on that model.

DEPLOYING THE APPLICATION

When you have completed the development and testing of your application, you *deploy* it. That is, you place it into production. In PowerBuilder, deployment involves converting the application to an executable version and making it available to the user. When the end user runs the application, it will look just as it did when you ran it from the development environment. (It had better look the same!) And, of course, the end user will have no ability to switch into the development environment. When the user terminates the application, that's the end of it.

PowerBuilder lets you organize your executable version in a variety of ways. The major choice is to generate a compiled version, in which your application is converted to machine language instructions, or a "p-code" version, in which the instructions are in a proprietary form that is not machine language. The compiled version runs faster, but it takes longer to generate.

CLIENT/SERVER

I mentioned at the outset that PowerBuilder's purpose is to develop client/server applications. This means that a typical PowerBuilder application has two components: the *client* and the *server.* The client is the user interface part: the windows, menus, buttons, and other things that the user sees and interacts with, along with the programming that drives them. The server is the database part. It manages the data, storing and retrieving information as the client requires.

In a typical setting, the client and server run on separate machines, communicating with each other across a network. The client is your PowerBuilder application, running on each user's workstation on the desktop. The server is a separate product, usually running on a single, more powerful machine, the database server. The server might be the Sybase SQL Anywhere product bundled with PowerBuilder, or Sybase System 11, or the Oracle server, or any of dozens of other possibilities. You could say that PowerBuilder is a "multilingual client," since it works perfectly well with any of them.

Client/server may be new to you and therefore seem somewhat mysterious. There's not much to it though, really. Even on a single machine, it's always been a good idea to separate an application's user interface logic from its database management logic. Client/server simply formalizes that separation. The most important new thing to learn, if you haven't already, is SQL, the Structured Query Language. This is the language that your PowerBuilder application, or any client application for that matter, uses to communicate with the database server. It's fairly English-like. For example, here's how to ask, "Who are all the customers who live in San Francisco?" in SQL. This query searches the customer table for this information and returns the customers' first and last names:

```
SELECT firstname, lastname FROM customer WHERE city='San Francisco'
```

PowerBuilder does an excellent job of handling the lower-level complexities of client/server, such as communication protocols. That lets you concentrate on what you do best, which is developing the application.

Earlier, when I was describing the PowerBuilder development environment, running the application, and deploying it, I was describing the client side of client/server. With PowerBuilder, you develop the client application, which communicates with the server as needed for database work. However, the PowerBuilder development environment provides tools, most notably the Database Painter, for working directly with your database on the server. And PowerBuilder has many special features that simplify the task of integrating your application with the server, making PowerBuilder a better tool than many of its competitors, and maybe all of them, for client/server development.

THREE-TIER AND OTHER ARCHITECTURES

Other architectures exist that are extensions of client/server. I described client/server as typically running on two machines. In a *three-tier archi-tecture* there are typically three machines involved:

- **The client** — which presents the user interface and runs the pro-gramming that drives it
- **The business process server (the "middle tier")** — which receives requests from the client and runs the programming to process them
- **The database server** — which stores and manages the data

In a three-tier application, the client does not communicate directly with the database server. (I suppose it could, but it typically doesn't.) Instead, it talks to the business process server, which in turn talks to the database server. One benefit of this approach is that the client can ask higher-level questions. It can ask the business process server, "Run a credit check on customer #1234" or "Deduct 3 from inventory for product A-333." (Actually, these would be formulated as procedure calls.) The client doesn't have to express these requests in terms of SQL commands, because the business process server takes care of that. The other major benefit is that you can off-load a great deal of the client's processing onto the middle tier, reducing the cost of hardware needed for every end user's desktop.

I have described three-tier architecture as running on three indepen-dent machines, because it's convenient to picture it that way. In reality, the number of machines has nothing to do with it. The business process serv-er and the database server could be independent processes sharing the same machine, for example. Or you could distribute the business processing and database management across many machines. There are plenty of variations, which lead some in the industry to prefer terms such as "n-tier" or "tierless" architecture. The important thing is the separation of the application into three independent functions — user interface, business logic, and database management — which communicate with one another to carry out their duties.

The remaining question is, how does PowerBuilder support three-tier architecture, or whatever you choose to call it? Certainly you can use PowerBuilder to develop the client tier. You can also use its "Distributed PowerBuilder" capabilities to develop the middle tier. Regardless of whether the middle tier is developed using PowerBuilder or using some other tool such as C++, a PowerBuilder client can communicate with it, just as it can communicate with a database server. However, in most cases where the middle tier is non-PowerBuilder, you will need to acquire or develop additional interface software.

Working in the Development Environment

The PowerBuilder development environment is a collection of *painters*. Each painter is a module for developing one type of application component. For example, there is a Window Painter for designing windows, and there is a Menu Painter for designing menus. At every point in the development process, you are working in one of the painters. There are over twenty painters in the entire product. These are the major ones:

1. Application Painter — for designing the "application object," the home of scripts that control the overall application

2. Project Painter — for converting an application to an executable

3. Window Painter — for designing windows

4. User Object Painter — for designing user objects, reusable units each consisting of a visual layout (optional), variables, and programming

5. Menu Painter — for designing the application's menus

6. Structure Painter — for designing structures, which are complex user-defined variable types

7. Function Painter — for defining functions, which are program modules callable from scripts and from other functions

8. DataWindow Painter — for designing DataWindows, the primary tool in PowerBuilder for data display and data entry

9. Query Painter — a visual tool for constructing SQL queries interactively without programming

10. Data Pipeline Painter — for defining and running a data pipeline, a tool for quickly and easily transferring data from one database to another

11. Table Painter — for reviewing and modifying the structure of a database table

12. Database Painter — for connecting to a database server, and for reviewing and modifying the database contents

13. Library Painter — for managing libraries, the files in which the other application components are stored

14. PowerScript Painter, or Script Painter — a specialized editor for writing scripts in the PowerScript language

The purposes of some of these painters should be clear just from their names. Others require more explanation. In the chapters to follow, we will look at each of them in detail.

To open a painter, click its button on the PowerBar, which is a *toolbar,* a collection of buttons located, usually, just below the menu. You can see it near the top of Figure 1-1. Figure 1-3 identifies each PowerBar button. To open the Window Painter, for example, click the Window button.

Figure 1-3

The PowerBar.

As you can see from Figure 1-3, the PowerBar contains a button for opening each of the major painters except the Script Painter. You open the Script Painter from within other painters: the Application, Window, Menu, and User Object Painters. The PowerBar also has a few buttons that do not open painters: Text Editor, which opens a text-file editor similar to Windows Notepad; Run, which runs the application; and Debug, for debugging the application. As I will explain shortly, you can customize the PowerBar to add, delete, or rearrange buttons.

To see even more PowerBar buttons, click the dropdown button to the right of the first button. A "dropdown palette" appears, with some of the same buttons as the PowerBar plus some additional choices. This is pictured in Figure 1-4. As you will see, many PowerBuilder toolbars include dropdown palettes like this one that provide extra features.

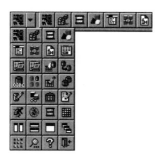

Figure 1-4
The PowerBar's Dropdown Palette.

The PowerBar is always available in PowerBuilder, so you can click it at any time to open a painter. You can open any number of painters at once. You can even open the same painter more than once, in order to design several windows at a time, for example. Each time you open a painter, it opens in its own window, in the MDI style described earlier. Figure 1-1 shows the development environment with Window, Menu, Library, and Application Painter windows open.

When you first open a painter window, PowerBuilder by default opens it to a size that fills the entire screen. Thus, it hides any other open windows behind the new one, and you may not realize that they are still open back there. By moving the windows with the mouse, or by making menu selections such as Window|Cascade, you can rearrange the windows to see them all.

THE MENU

There is a menu at the top of the PowerBuilder screen at all times. The choices in the menu vary depending on which painter is active. In Figure 1-1, you see the Window Painter menu choices, because the Window Painter window is the active one, with the other three windows underneath it inactive.

The underlined letter in each menu choice is its "hot key," an alternative to clicking it with the mouse. For example, to select File from the menu, you can press Alt+F on the keyboard. Other keyboard shortcuts are available, which you will see next to menu choices as you explore. For example, Ctrl+R is a shortcut for File|Run. One that is not listed, but that is generally well known, is Alt+F4 as a shortcut for File|Exit, which shuts down PowerBuilder.

TOOLBARS

Initially, the PowerBar appears just below the menu. I say "initially" because you can move it or hide it. To move it, click and drag it with the mouse. Alternatively, right-click it (that is, click it with the right mouse button), and make choices from the pop-up menu that appears. For example, choose Bottom from the menu to move it to the bottom of the screen. Click PowerBar1 to switch it between invisible and visible.

As you open painters, other toolbars will appear. Most of them are called "PainterBars." The Window Painter's PainterBar appears along the left edge of the screen in Figure 1-1. It contains window design buttons, such as one to place buttons and other controls on the window and another to open the Script Painter. You can move and hide all of these toolbars just as you can move and hide the PowerBar.

You can customize a toolbar — that is, add, delete, or rearrange its buttons — by right-clicking it and selecting Customize from the pop-up menu. Select New to design an entirely new toolbar.

There's one more toolbar trick: Right-click it and pick Show Text from the menu. The buttons get bigger, and a descriptive label appears within each. Figure 1-5 shows part of the PowerBar, with Show Text turned on. This feature is convenient when you're first learning the buttons. But it has a couple of drawbacks: The larger buttons leave less screen space for the painter windows, and some of the buttons may get pushed out of sight off the screen. In most of the figures in this book, I do not show the button text, except in small pictures of individual buttons.

Figure 1-5
Part of the PowerBar, with Show Text.

THE DOCUMENTATION

PowerBuilder comes with an extensive and comprehensive set of manuals. Most of them are in electronic format on the installation CD-ROM. Having them there, instead of on paper, can be inconvenient, especially when you are first learning the product. For an extra fee, you can order the printed versions from Powersoft. I made that investment, and it has been very worthwhile.

Although I believe that this book provides a better introduction to PowerBuilder than the manuals do and digs much deeper into critical topics, I won't pretend that this book is a complete substitute for the manuals. For one thing, the manuals have ten times as many pages, and my writing style isn't *that* concise! The manuals are the ultimate source for detailed reference information. Therefore, I will refer you to them from time to time for additional information.

THE ONLINE HELP

At any time in PowerBuilder, online help is not far away. Unlike the manuals, the online help is installed on your hard drive during installation; it does not reside on the CD-ROM.

The help system is standard Windows help. I'll assume you're familiar with Windows help from your experience with other products, or that you'll pick it up quickly. If you are new to it, here's a crash course: To get started, press the F1 key or select one of the choices under Help in the menu. This opens help, with an index or table of contents displayed. Pick a topic to display its documentation. Various buttons and menu choices in help take you to other topics. Also, clicking any green text within a topic pops up a definition or an entire screen explaining it. Help and PowerBuilder are independent programs, so you can keep them both open and toggle between them by pressing Alt+Tab or by other means. To close help, select File|Exit from its menu.

In general, the help is quite good and contains much of the important material from the manuals. The function reference is especially comprehensive. It does have some weaknesses. I consider the index poorly organized, and the cross-referencing between topics is weak.

What's Next?

This chapter has been a lot of talk, but no action. Be prepared in the next chapter to jump in with both feet — and with both hands, too — to do some hands-on exercises!

2

Your First Application, Up and Running

*T*he best way to start learning PowerBuilder, or any other computer product in my opinion, is to *do something* with it right away. Get hands-on experience building something that really works. Once you have a quick success under your belt, you will have a solid foundation on which to add all the details that follow later. You will become confident that, as you continue to learn more features, you can be successful with them, too.

In this chapter, you will build a small application, run it, and see that it works. The application is very simple, but it will teach you many of the basic "how-to's" that you will rely on for the rest of your PowerBuilder career.

This chapter is very detailed and precise in instructing you what to do, step by step — "first press this key, then click that button." Since everything is new to you at this point, I will make everything as crystal clear as possible to avoid mistakes. Later chapters will not be so meticulous, because by then you will have mastered so many of the basic techniques.

I recommend that you actually sit down at your computer and do the steps as you read along. I also suggest that you not stray off on your own while doing the exercises for now. If you get lost, sometimes getting back on track can be tricky. And by the time you do find your way back, you may have introduced small differences between your application and mine that will cause trouble later. So do each exercise exactly as instructed the first time through. After you've completed it, by all means, explore to your heart's content!

You'll realize early on just how elementary these exercises are. Left to your own devices, you might have tried something more sophisticated, more like a "real application," that you intend to build with PowerBuilder. That can be a big mistake, and it's a mistake I myself made a few years ago. Setting out to learn a brand new development tool (not PowerBuilder), I threw a lot of complex features into my very first exercise: complex data relationships, detailed screens, clever programming. I never got it to work! It was too much "newness" at once! That well-intentioned error set me back a month in learning that product. I finally threw away the complex exercise and started fresh with the simplest application I could think of: a window, a box, and a button. With that, I scored a quick success, and from there I was able to master the product quickly, by stepping from one small success to the next.

The formula that led to success for me — a window, a box, and a button — is the same formula that will lead to success for you.

A Simple Application

If you've ever studied the C programming language, you know that most books about it start out with a program to display the message "Hello, world!" I think a PowerBuilder book should begin with something just as simple but a little more visual.

Our first application will display the window shown in Figure 2-1. In the window are a button and a box. When you push the button, the box turns blue. It takes only two lines of program code to implement this example. But in addition to writing those two lines, you must undertake a certain number of other tasks, such as creating the window, drawing the button, and drawing the box.

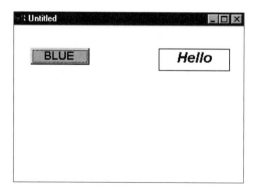

Figure 2-1
The finished product—click the button, the box turns blue.

THE FOUR ESSENTIAL COMPONENTS

In order to get anything, even the simplest window, up and running in
PowerBuilder, you need to create at least four components:

1. **One application object** — created using the Application Painter

2. **At least one window** — created using the Window Painter

3. **At least one event script** — created using the PowerScript Painter.
   An event script is a program module. This script must instruct the
   application to open the window.

4. **At least one library file** — created using the Library Painter or (as
   we will do it) using the Application Painter as a by-product of creating
   the application object. The library is a physical file on your disk with
   the extension .PBL (pronounced "pibble") that stores the application,
   the window, and the script.

The four components are illustrated in Figure 2-2.

Technically, only three of the four components — the application, the
event script, and the library — are absolutely required. The window is
optional. You could have an application with an event script but no window. When you would run such an application, the script would execute
and might do something useful. But almost all applications have at least
one window, because windows provide the user interface. There are such
things as applications without user interfaces, but they are rare.

CREATING THE "BLUE BUTTON" APPLICATION: STEP BY STEP

Here are step-by-step instructions for creating and executing the "turn the
box blue" window by starting from the very beginning and building the
four components.

STEP 1. START POWERBUILDER

In Windows 95, select PowerBuilder 5.0 from the Start button menu. In
other Windows versions, double-click the PowerBuilder 5.0 icon in the
Windows Program Manager.

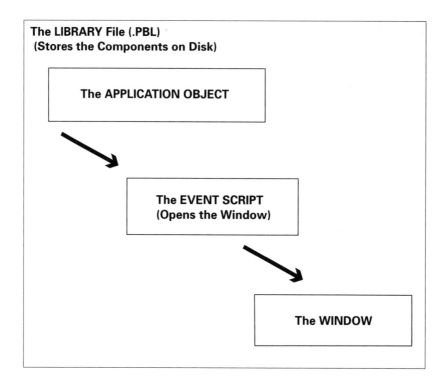

Figure 2-2

The four essential components of an application.

When PowerBuilder starts, it always insists on loading an application. By default, it's the application that you worked on in your previous session. If there was no previous session, PowerBuilder requires that you create a new application. Thus, on startup, one of three things will happen:

Scenario #1: You may see the screen shown in Figure 2-3, with an empty workspace and no error message. In this case, PowerBuilder has started normally — that is, the way it will start for you most of the time. It has located an application for you to modify. This may be one of the sample applications that comes with PowerBuilder, if you installed them, or some application you were working with previously. The name of that application appears on the PowerBuilder title bar at the top of the screen. In any event, you are going to create a brand new application right now, not work on an old one. So proceed with step 2.

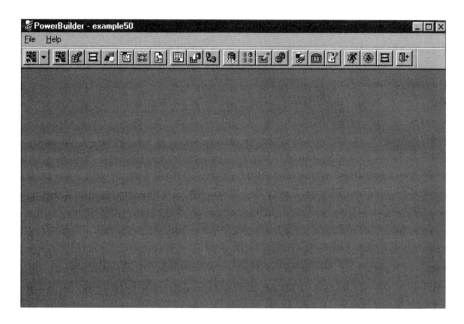

Figure 2-3

The PowerBuilder screen at start-up, if there is an existing application.

Scenario #2: You may see the screen shown in Figure 2-4, saying that "PowerBuilder requires an application." If so, then this is probably the first time you have ever started PowerBuilder since you installed it, and you did not install the sample applications that come with it. No problem, because you are about to create a brand new application anyway. Click the New button and proceed with step 4.

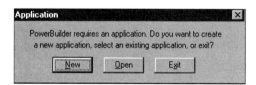

Figure 2-4

The PowerBuilder screen at start-up, if there is no application.

Scenario #3: You may see the Select Application Library dialog box, shown in Figure 2-5. (Figure 2-5 shows the Windows 95 version of the dialog box. If you are running Windows 3.1 or Windows NT, its layout will be somewhat different.) In this case, PowerBuilder tried to find the application that you worked on last time, but for some reason it's missing. So PowerBuilder is asking you to select a library from those that do exist. Since you want to create a new library, click Cancel, which displays Figure 2-4. Then click New and proceed with step 4.

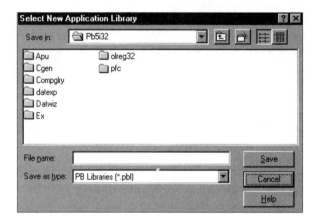

Figure 2-5
The PowerBuilder screen at start-up, if the library is missing.

STEP 2. OPEN THE APPLICATION PAINTER

Open the Application Painter by clicking the Application button on the PowerBar. As I explained in Chapter 1, the PowerBar is the toolbar, or row of icon buttons. Unless you've customized it, the PowerBar should be right underneath the menu bar at the top of the PowerBuilder screen, and the Application button should be the second button from the left.

STEP 3. SWITCH FROM AN OLD APPLICATION TO A NEW ONE

At this point, you will see an application window open inside the PowerBuilder window. In it, PowerBuilder is showing whatever application you have worked on most recently, or the sample application. But we want to create a new application, not modify an old one. Select File|New from the menu. This opens the Select New Application Library dialog box, shown in Figure 2-6.

Identifying Toolbar Buttons

On the PowerBar and other toolbars, it's easy to tell what each button is. Just move the mouse pointer on top of a button for a second. A yellow message pops up with the name of the button. This is called a "PowerTip." For example, when you touch the mouse to the first button on the PowerBar, the PowerTip "Application" appears.

At the bottom of the screen, a longer description appears. This is called MicroHelp. The MicroHelp for the Application button is "Run Application Painter."

If you left-click a toolbar button, it performs its function when you let go of the mouse button — the Application Painter opens, for example. To avoid that, drag the mouse pointer away from the button before letting go. You can always use this trick in Windows whenever you click a button by mistake.

You can also add labels directly to the buttons: Right-click the toolbar and select Show Text from the pop-up menu. This makes the buttons bigger and adds a label to each, beneath its icon. The label for the Application button is "Appl." I don't care for this style myself, because it runs some of the buttons off the screen. But many people prefer it until they learn to recognize the buttons from their icons alone.

In this book I use the Show Text style whenever I show a picture of a single toolbar button.

STEP 4. CREATE THE LIBRARY

The Select New Application Library dialog box is asking you to type in a file name and a directory to create a new PowerBuilder library (.PBL) file. For the directory, the dialog box may suggest the one where you have installed PowerBuilder, which will typically be something like "c:\ProgramFiles\ Powersoft\PowerBuilder 5.0" or "c:\pwrs\pb5" or "c:\pwrs\pb5i32," but I don't recommend putting your application files there. You should select some other directory, or take a moment to create one. In Windows 95, they are now called "folders," not "directories." Nevertheless, I'll continue to refer to them as "directories" throughout this book.

If you have installed the sample files that come with this book, you ought to have a directory named C:\FOUNDPB, and this would be a good one to select. In the "File name" space, type "TEST2" or "TEST2.PBL," as you see in Figure 2-6. (Figure 2-6 shows the Windows 95 version of the dialog box. If you are running Windows 3.1 or Windows NT, its layout will be somewhat different.) If you omit the .PBL extension, PowerBuilder will add it. Click the Save button (Windows 95) or the OK button (Windows 3.1 or NT).

(It's true that there never was a TEST1.PBL. I chose the name TEST2 to indicate "the library for testing Chapter 2.")

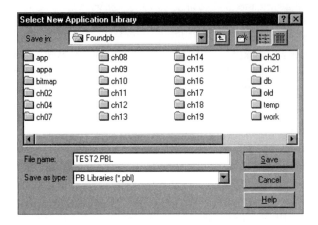

Figure 2-6
Fill in the dialog box to create the library file.

STEP 5. CREATE THE APPLICATION

Next, the Save Application dialog box appears. (See Figure 2-7.) This asks you to describe the application that you are adding to TEST2.PBL. Type "app2" in the space below the word "Applications." Click to the Comments space and type in "Created while following Chapter 2 by" and your name. The box in between Applications and Comments is blank for now but later will show the name of this application and any others stored in this .PBL file. Click OK.

(As with the library name, the "2" in "app2" refers to "Chapter 2." There never was an "app1.")

Figure 2-7
Fill in the dialog box to create the application.

PowerBuilder displays the box shown in Figure 2-8, which offers to generate an Application template. If you were to click Yes, PowerBuilder would add a certain number of windows and other objects to your new application to help get you underway. This option may be handy in the future, and I will further describe it in Chapter 16. But it doesn't help for this first simple application, so please decline the offer by clicking No.

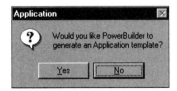

Figure 2-8
For a new application, PowerBuilder offers to generate a template for you.

STEP 6. ENTER THE APPLICATION PAINTER
PowerBuilder creates the "app2" application and shows it to you in a window labeled "Application - app2." (See Figure 2-9.) You are now in the

Application Painter, the part of PowerBuilder used for defining and modifying an application object. While you are in the Application Painter, a second toolbar appears, either beneath the PowerBar or along the left edge of the screen, unless you've customized it. In Figure 2-9, it's beneath the PowerBar. This is the Application PainterBar. It has buttons for various application-building functions.

If your PainterBar is not beneath the PowerBar, please move it there: Right-click anywhere within the PainterBar, and click Top on the pop-up menu. All the figures and descriptions in this chapter assume a top-of-the-screen PainterBar, so you will now be able to follow along more accurately.

Having created the application object, we're done with our work in the Application Painter for now. We'll return to it soon, but right now we will switch to another painter, the Window Painter.

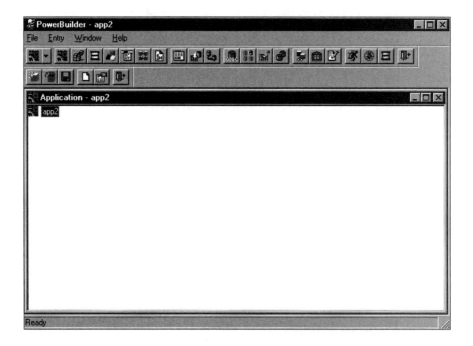

Figure 2-9
The Application Painter, with the newly created "app2" application.

STEP 7. CREATE THE NEW WINDOW

Click the Window button, the fourth button on the PowerBar. Remember, the PowerBar is the upper toolbar in Figure 2-9, not the lower one.

PowerBuilder, thinking that you want to open an existing window, displays the Select Window dialog box, shown in Figure 2-10. This dialog box shows the list of windows in the library. Right now it looks pretty empty, since you have no windows yet. Click the New button to create a new window.

Figure 2-10
Click the New button in the Select Window dialog box.

STEP 8. ENTER THE WINDOW PAINTER

PowerBuilder opens the Window Painter and shows you a new window, labeled "Window - (Untitled)," as in Figure 2-11. While you are in the Window Painter, the Window PainterBar appears at the top of the screen, below the PowerBar. It is similar to the Application PainterBar that you saw while in the Application Painter. The Window PainterBar is a toolbar with buttons for various window-drawing functions.

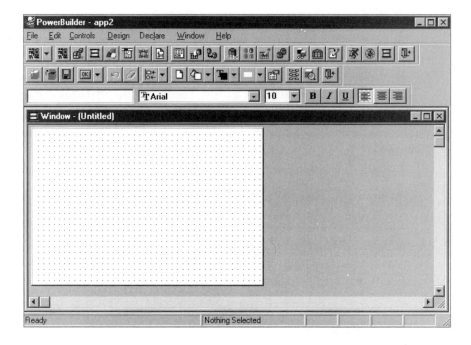

Figure 2-11
The Window Painter, with the new window.

At this point, much of the screen is occupied by a box with a dotted grid inside it. This box is the window that you are drawing. When, in a moment, you run the application or when you deliver the application to the users and they run it, this window is what they will see. They won't see the dots, which are just a drawing aid for you while you are designing the window.

Once again, let's take a moment to make sure that our configurations match — especially if you don't see any dotted grid inside your window. Select Design|Options from the menu. In the Options dialog box that pops up, click Snap to Grid and Show Grid, if necessary, to place check marks in front of them both. Set both X and Y to 8. Show Grid makes the grid visible. X and Y determine the spacing between the dots. Snap to Grid means that each element we place on the window will be aligned to the grid dots, making it easier for us to control its size. Click OK to implement these settings.

STEP 9. DRAW A TEXT BOX ON THE WINDOW

There are several dropdown buttons on the PainterBar. A *dropdown button* is a button with a downward-pointing triangle. When you click any of these, a palette of additional toolbar buttons appears.

Click the leftmost dropdown button to open the "dropdown control palette" pictured in Figure 2-12. This palette has a button for each type of control. A *control* is the general term given to anything you can place on a window, such as a button, a box, or text.

Figure 2-12
The dropdown control palette.

Click the StaticText button on the palette. This button has the big letter "A" on it. Let go of the mouse button. (Some people have a habit of clicking and dragging at this point, while depressing the mouse button, as you do with some other drawing products. You don't do it that way in PowerBuilder! Let go of the mouse button.) Move the mouse into the design window. Click anywhere, and the word "none" appears there. (See Figure 2-13.) This is what is properly called a "StaticText Control" — an object (control) on the window that displays unchanging (static) text. I will call it simply a "text box."

STEP 10. MOVE AND STRETCH THE TEXT BOX

You can move the text box around by clicking inside it and dragging it somewhere else. You can stretch it by clicking and dragging any of the four black dots at its corners, or anywhere along the edge of the box. Move and stretch to approximately the position shown in Figure 2-13.

Clicking and Dragging, for New Windows Users

If you are new to Microsoft Windows, "clicking and dragging" can be tricky at first. Let me explain it and offer a helpful tip.

"Click and drag" means this: (1) Move the mouse pointer on top of something on the screen, such as on top of one of the black dots in Figure 2-13. (2) Depress the left mouse button to "click." (3) While keeping the button depressed, "drag" the mouse to a new position. (4) Let go of the mouse button. In general, this is how you move something or stretch something using the mouse.

To stretch something, for example to make a box bigger, first find the "hot spot" along the edge of the object where you click and drag. In the case of the text box in Figure 2-13, the hot spots are the four dots at its corners or anywhere along the border of the box. Click one of the corner dots and drag it (while keeping the left mouse button down) to stretch the box.

Now here's the tip: Finding the "hot spot" takes some practice, but you can tell when you are on a hot spot for stretching because the mouse pointer changes appearance. In the case of the four corner dots in Figure 2-13, the mouse pointer will change to a double-tipped arrow. When you see the double-tipped arrow, that's the time to click. Keep your hand steady. If you don't see the double-tipped arrow, don't bother clicking, and certainly don't click and drag — you're not pointing to the right place, and who knows what you will do instead (probably move the box instead of stretching it). Keep moving the mouse around slowly until it changes to the double-tipped arrow, then click, holding steady, and then drag. This technique applies to stretching boxes, windows, and just about everything else.

If you are an experienced Microsoft Windows user, all of this is very familiar to you, of course. In fact, it's automatic and intuitive. I'm pointing it out for the benefit of those of you who are new to Windows.

STEP 11. NAME THE TEXT BOX, CHANGE ITS TEXT, ADD A BORDER

Move the mouse into the middle of the box and double-click — that is, click the left mouse button twice rapidly. This brings up the property sheet for the StaticText control, shown in Figure 2-14. If you have trouble double-clicking, refer to the "Property Sheets" sidebar for other ways to open it.

This dialog box shows the many properties of the control. There are so many, in fact, that the dialog box is organized into a series of tab pages — General, Font, Position, and so on. Figure 2-14 shows the General tab page.

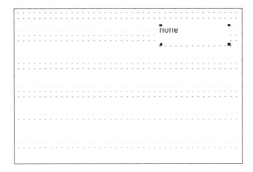

Figure 2-13

Create the text box object.

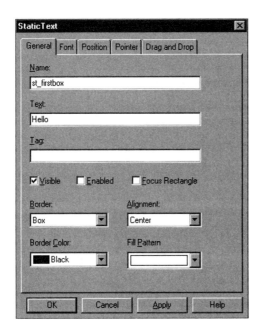

Figure 2-14

Fill in the StaticText property sheet to name and modify the text box.

Fill in the dialog box as shown in Figure 2-14. Type in "st_firstbox" for the Name. Originally, PowerBuilder named the control "st_1," meaning "the first StaticText control." It's common practice to give controls your own names instead of staying with the PowerBuilder-supplied names.

Type in "Hello" for the Text. Change the Border from None to Box by clicking the dropdown button next to the word "None" and clicking Box

Property Sheets

A *property sheet* is a dialog box in which you can view and change the properties of an item. Property sheets are pervasive throughout PowerBuilder, and you will encounter many of them. Figures 2-14 and 2-27 show two property sheets that play a role in this chapter.

Rather than repeating the instructions for property sheets every time we see one, let's just review the instructions once, right now.

There are usually several ways to open an item's property sheet:

- Double-click the item.
- Right-click the item and select "Properties" from its pop-up menu.

- Single-click the item and click the Properties button on the PainterBar.
- Single-click the item and select Edit|Properties from the menu.

Depending on where you are in PowerBuilder and what the item is, some of these options might not be available.

Most property sheets, like the one in Figure 2-14, have tab pages, with different properties on each page. You can visit the pages by clicking the tabs, and on each page you can view and change property settings. For more information about the properties, click the Help button.

When you are done, click the OK button to apply your changes and close the property sheet. Click the Apply button to apply the changes without closing the sheet. If you make a mistake, click Cancel to close the sheet without applying the changes.

Property sheets are not a PowerBuilder invention. Many Windows 95 products, and Windows 95 itself, make heavy use of them. They work exactly the same throughout Windows 95 as they do in PowerBuilder. By offering property sheets, therefore, PowerBuilder is conforming to the latest Windows user interface standards.

from the list. Change Alignment to Center by clicking its dropdown button. Leave everything else as it is, and click OK.

The word "Hello" now appears in the box that used to read "none." The name "st_firstbox" will come into play in a moment, when we write the script to turn the box blue. Notice that PowerBuilder displays the name, "Name: st_firstbox," at the bottom of the screen whenever you click the box, to make it easy to remember the object's name.

STEP 12. CHANGE THE FONT STYLE OF THE TEXT

Notice that there is a third toolbar just below the PainterBar. It looks very much like toolbars found in many word processing products, with buttons for changing the style of text. In PowerBuilder, it is called the "StyleBar."

Click the B button on the StyleBar, and the word "Hello" becomes boldface. Click the I button, and it becomes italic. Click the dropdown button next to the number 10 and pick 16 from the list, making the text larger. If necessary, stretch the box again if the bigger text no longer fits within it. Feel free to experiment with the other tools on this toolbar to see what they do.

If this isn't working for you, you may need to click the text box first to select it. Once you select it, black dots will appear at its four corners, and the message "Name: st_firstbox" will appear at the bottom of the screen. Now the toolbar buttons should work as I've described. The toolbar operates on the currently selected control, which is generally the control clicked most recently.

By clicking the first cell on the StyleBar and typing, you can change the text to something other than "Hello." We saw just a moment ago that you can make the same change from the property sheet (Figure 2-14). There are many points in PowerBuilder where there is more than one way to do the same thing.

STEP 13. PLACE A BUTTON ON THE WINDOW

Now add a second control on the window: a button. Once again, click the dropdown button on the PainterBar that displays the dropdown control palette (Figure 2-12). Click the CommandButton button, which is near the top of the palette, and then click somewhere inside the window to place the new button there. If you have been following my directions closely, the label on the button, "none," will be 16-point bold italic, the same as the text box. Use the StyleBar, as you did in the previous step, to change the button label to 12-point bold but not italic. Change its label from "none" to "BLUE." Stretch the button a little bigger and move it so that your button matches the one in Figure 2-15.

Button Hot Keys

When you type in a button's label, such as "BLUE," you can also designate a hot key for the button. If you type "&BLUE" instead of "BLUE", then Alt+B will be the button's hot key. When you run the application, pressing Alt+B on the keyboard will be the same as clicking the button with the mouse. This is convenient for people who prefer to use the keyboard.

The use of the ampersand (&) in this way follows a common windows convention for button labels and for menu choices. The ampersand does not appear in the window. Instead, the letter following it — in this case, the "B" — is underlined. The Alt key plus that letter form the hot key.

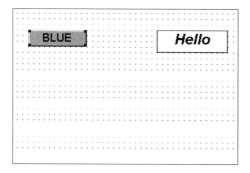

Figure 2-15
Draw the button.

STEP 14. SAVE YOUR WORK UP TO THIS POINT

So far, we've created the application and the window, but we're still not ready to run it. For one thing, the button isn't smart enough to figure out that its label, "BLUE," means, "Turn the box blue." We have to write a script for that!

Before going further, however, let's save the work we've done up to this point. That way, if something goes wrong in the next few steps, or if there is a power failure, you won't lose everything and be forced to start over from the beginning. The rules about when to save your work are the same with PowerBuilder as with every other computer product: You should save your work any time that you've gotten it to a point that would be too painful to lose. For me, that means saving every five or ten minutes, especially with a new product.

Here's what to do: From the menu, select File|Save. Because you are working in the Window Painter, PowerBuilder understands File|Save to mean that you want to save the window you have drawn. The Save Window dialog box, shown in Figure 2-16, appears. Under Windows, type in "w_boxcolor," which is the name we will give to it. Click to the Comments space, and type in something like this: "Created while following Chapter 2 by" and your name. Then click OK.

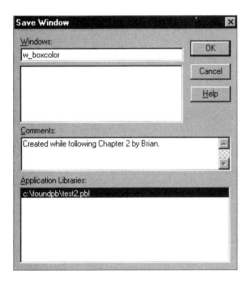

Figure 2-16
Name and save the window.

PowerBuilder saves the window to the disk. It does not ask you for a filename, because it places it within TEST2.PBL, the library file that we created earlier. On the screen, the title of the Window Painter now says, "Window - w_boxcolor" where it used to say, "Window - (Untitled)."

There are conventions that most PowerBuilder developers follow in naming things. For example, I begin all window names with the prefix "w_". Chapter 4 details the naming conventions that my company follows, which are very similar to the conventions followed in the PowerBuilder documentation.

If You Make a Mistake . . .

If you make a mistake, such as deleting a control from the window or moving a control to the wrong place, try selecting Edit|Undo from the menu. It reverses many of the most serious goofs. Sometimes there is an Undo button on the PainterBar that does the same thing.

If you get into really big trouble and want to throw all your work away, select File|Close from the menu and click No when PowerBuilder offers to save your changes. When you don't save changes, your window will remain the way it was the last time you saved it. Let's hope you saved it at a recent "good" point and haven't lost too much work.

Since the window is now saved to disk, from this point on you can take a break at any time and come back later to pick up where you left off. Anytime something goes wrong, you can recover your work back to your last save point. If you're familiar with how to do this with other Windows products, you'll find that PowerBuilder is no different. If not, the instructions are in the sidebar "Saving, Closing, and Reopening Your Work," later in this chapter.

Now let's proceed to the programming. . . .

STEP 15. CREATE THE SCRIPT FOR THE BLUE BUTTON

Click the BLUE button to select it (it may already be selected), and then click the Script button on the PainterBar. This button lets you write a script (a program module) for the button.

STEP 16. ENTER THE SCRIPT PAINTER

PowerBuilder opens the Script Painter and shows you a new window. Figure 2-17 shows the Script Painter, with a line of code typed into it. While you are in the Script Painter, the Script PainterBar appears at the top of the screen below the PowerBar. It has buttons for things that are useful for text editing, such as cut, copy, and paste. Many of them are disabled until you begin typing or until you mark a block of text.

The title of the Script Painter window, "Script - clicked for cb_1," means, "This is the script that will execute when you click cb_1," which is the name of the BLUE button. It is the default name given by PowerBuilder and is short for "Command Button #1." We have not renamed the button as we have done for the text box.

STEP 17. TYPE IN THE SCRIPT

The Script Painter is a text editor window. I'll describe some of its capabilities in Chapter 4. For now, type this one-line Script into the window:

```
st_firstbox.BackColor = 0
```

In English, this line says, "Set the background color of st_firstbox to zero." What's st_firstbox? It's the text box you created in step 9. What's the BackColor? It's the background color of the text box, as opposed to its text color (TextColor) or border color (BorderColor). What's zero? In Microsoft Windows, every color is assigned a number. Zero is the number for black. The trouble is, we want blue.

Microsoft Windows and the VGA monitor can display over 16 million different colors. The color is a 24-bit unsigned integer. Zero is black, and 16777215, the maximum, is white. All the other colors, blends, and shades fall somewhere in between. Blue is 16711680. So to turn the box blue, you could change the script to this:

```
st_firstbox.BackColor = 16711680
```

There's an easier way to deal with colors than reading and typing such large numbers. It's better to call the RGB function, a PowerBuilder function that calculates color numbers. You call the function with three parameters: the amounts of red, green, and blue you want in the color (hence the initials RGB). Each parameter is a number between 0, for none of that color, and 255, for the maximum dosage of that color. The color blue is no red, no green, and all blue. So here's how the RGB function calculates it:

```
st_firstbox.BackColor = RGB(0,0,255)      // turn the box blue
```

Go ahead and change the line you typed to call the RGB function. The "//" begins a comment — PowerBuilder ignores anything to the right of it. Figure 2-17 shows how the screen should look at this point.

I will go into detail about the PowerScript syntax in Chapters 3 and 4, which will include an explanation of the dot notation for changing and reading properties, as well as where to look up lists of features such as BackColor and RGB.

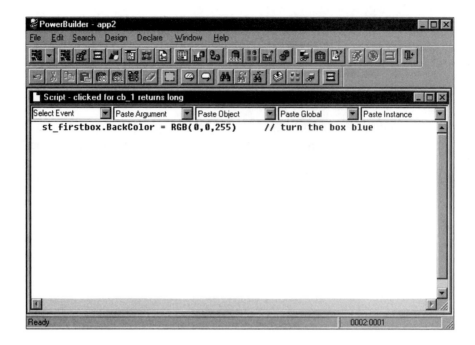

Figure 2-17

Type in the script to turn the box blue.

STEP 18. COMPILE THE SCRIPT

Click the Compile button on the PainterBar. PowerBuilder makes sure that the script has the correct syntax, that the object st_firstbox exists, and that the keywords "BackColor" and "RGB" are understood. If a compiler error message pops up, then correct your script and try again until you get no errors.

STEP 19. RETURN TO THE WINDOW PAINTER

Click the Return (to Window Painter) button, which is the last button on the Script PainterBar. This closes the Script Painter and displays the Window Painter once again. Our turn-the-box-blue script is complete.

The Return button may not be visible. If you're using the toolbar's Show Text option, the buttons may be so large that they shove the Return button off the screen. If so, there are other easy ways to close the Script Painter and return to the Window Painter. The most common of these is to close the Script Painter window by clicking the close button at its top-right corner (in Windows 95) or double-clicking the control button at its top-left corner (in any version of Windows). You can also select File|Return or File|Close from the menu or press Ctrl+F4 on the keyboard. If a message pops up asking whether to save changes, click Yes.

STEP 20. SAVE YOUR WORK UP TO THIS POINT

Select File|Save from the menu to save your work up to this point.

There is one last task before you can run the application and try it out: You must write a script that tells the application "app2" to open and display the window w_boxcolor upon executing. If you try to run the application right now by clicking the Run button on the PowerBar, you will get an error message: "This application needs a script for its open event." So our next step is to write that script.

STEP 21. RETURN TO THE APPLICATION PAINTER

Select Window|1 Application - app2 from the menu to return to the Application Painter window. This window has been open all along, ever since we last saw it way back in step 6 (Figure 2-9), and it looks the same now as it did then. It has been hiding behind the Window Painter window the whole time. In PowerBuilder, as with most Windows products, you can have several windows open at once. You can stack them one on top of another, rearrange them, minimize or maximize them, or do just about anything to lay them out in a particular arrangement. Right now we have brought the Application Painter window to the top, and the Window Painter window is hiding underneath it.

STEP 22. CREATE THE OPEN SCRIPT FOR THE APPLICATION

Click the Script button on the Application PainterBar. This opens up the Script Painter once again. But this time you are writing the Open script for app2 — the script that will execute when the application first opens. The other script you wrote earlier was clicked for cb_1 — it was the script that will execute when cb_1 (the BLUE button) is clicked.

STEP 23. TYPE IN THE SCRIPT

Type this one-line script into the window, as shown in Figure 2-18:

```
Open(w_boxcolor)     // when the app opens, it opens w_boxcolor
```

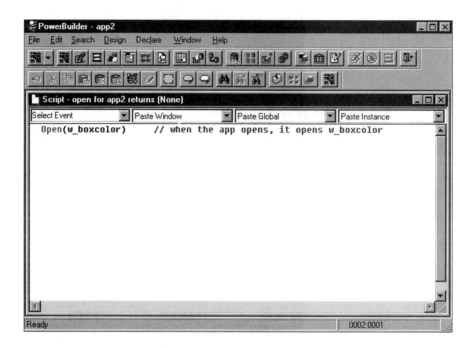

Figure 2-18

Type in the script to open the w_boxcolor window.

This script, when it executes, will open our w_boxcolor window, so you will be able to see it and click the BLUE button. The script calls the Open function, which opens a window.

STEP 24. COMPILE THE SCRIPT

Click the Compile button on the PainterBar to compile the script. Or select Design|Compile Script from the menu, or press Ctrl+L, which all do the same thing. If you have syntax errors, correct them and try again until it comes up clean.

STEP 25. RETURN TO THE APPLICATION PAINTER

Click the Return (to Application Painter) button on the Script PainterBar. The Script Painter closes, and the Application Painter reappears.

STEP 26. RUN THE APPLICATION

At last, we're ready to go. Click the Run button on the PowerBar to run the application. First, PowerBuilder asks if you want to save your changes to TEST2.PBL. Click Yes. (We could have avoided this interruption by doing a File|Save prior to clicking Run.)

The PowerBuilder development environment launches the application app2 and disappears. The application opens the window w_boxcolor and displays it to you. What you see is shown in Figure 2-19.

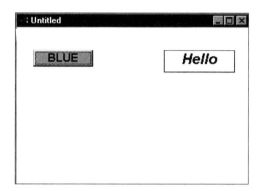

Figure 2-19
The finished product: Click the button, the box turns blue.

STEP 27. CLICK THE BLUE BUTTON
Click the BLUE button. The box turns blue!

STEP 28. CLOSE THE APPLICATION, RETURN TO POWERBUILDER
After you've clicked the button, there's not much more that the application does at this point. Accordingly, close the window by clicking its close button (the "x" button in the window's top-right corner, in Windows 95), by double-clicking its control button (the button in the top-left corner of the window in any version of Windows), or by pressing Alt+F4 on the keyboard. Whichever way you do it, the window closes, the application stops running, and the PowerBuilder development environment reappears. You can now modify the application, its window, or its scripts, and you can click the Run button to run it again at any time.

STEP 29. ALL DONE
For now, that's the end of the exercise. We'll be doing more work on the application soon. You can either select File|Exit from the menu to close PowerBuilder or leave it running until the next exercise.

Saving, Closing, and Reopening Your Work

It's easy to save your work at the end of a PowerBuilder session. When you come back next time, it's just as easy to pick up where you left off.

The simplest way to close PowerBuilder and save your work is to select File|Exit from the menu. If you have any unsaved work, PowerBuilder will ask you if you want to save it first and walk you through any steps, such as naming new windows, necessary to write everything safely to disk.

To restart PowerBuilder in Windows 95, select PowerBuilder 5.0 from the Start|Programs menu. In other Windows versions, double-click the PowerBuilder 5.0 icon in the Windows Program Manager. When PowerBuilder appears, click the Application button on the PowerBar. The Application Painter should open and show your application, the same one you were working on previously. If it shows you a different application — which could happen, for example, in the case of a power failure — or if you want to work on a different application, select File|Open from the menu and then respond to the dialog boxes to select the library (the .PBL file) and the application.

If you are working on the app2 sample application described in this chapter and you want to reopen one of its windows, such as the w_boxcolor window, that you have saved, click the Window button on the PowerBar and then select the window from the Select Window dialog box. Upon starting PowerBuilder, you can open the window immediately — you don't have to open the Application Painter first, unless PowerBuilder has brought you into the wrong application.

For a shortcut, select File from the menu bar. At the bottom of its dropdown menu, you will see a list of recently opened objects. Your window is likely to be on this list, and you can select it to open it.

How do you recover from a crash? If PowerBuilder or some other program terminates abnormally with an error, but Microsoft Windows stays up and running, it's a good idea to shut down and restart Microsoft Windows right away, to avoid any domino effect by which the crash might trigger more trouble down the line. If your computer freezes altogether, reboot it or power it off and on. When you restart Windows and then restart PowerBuilder, everything should be as it was the last time you saved it. Open your application, your windows, and your other objects as you would normally. Any work done since your last save will be lost.

LESSONS LEARNED FROM THE "BLUE BUTTON" EXERCISE

You have now developed your first PowerBuilder application. Figure 2-20 shows its components and how they relate to one other. Compare this figure to Figure 2-2.

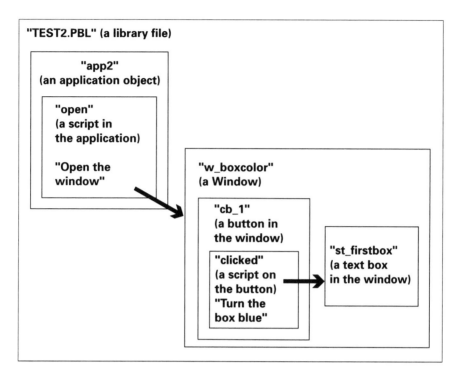

Figure 2-20
The components of the completed application.

The application is a simple one, too simple to be called a "real world" application. But in the course of creating it, we covered a lot of ground that *is* practical:

- You worked with three of the most important and fundamental painters: the Application Painter, the Window Painter, and the Script Painter.

- You saw how all the components — the application, the window, the scripts — are stored in a single library file, TEST2.PBL.

- You practiced drawing objects on a window and altering their appearance.

- You may have noticed how scripts are attached to objects, such as to the application and the button. Furthermore, scripts run in response to *events* that occur to those objects: When the application opens, a script runs. When the button is clicked, a script runs. This *event-driven* style of programming is very important. I'll talk about it more in the next chapter, and it will come up again and again throughout the book.

- You wrote a couple of lines of PowerScript code, giving you a first glimpse of what the language looks like. Chapter 4 covers the PowerScript language in more detail.

It's striking how little programming was necessary for this application: only two lines of code! Most of your effort was spent working with the painter tools, creating and drawing objects. Certainly you can expect that your real applications will require much more programming than this. But it is important to realize that with PowerBuilder, the painting process is at least as important as the programming. You will quickly learn that because of its painters, PowerBuilder allows you to get applications up and running much faster and more easily than do traditional, nonvisual, programming-intensive products. This is one reason why PowerBuilder is known as a "Rapid Application Development (RAD)" tool.

Having gone through this exercise, you may be rather concerned because there were 28 steps to it and the final application doesn't do all that much. If you followed along carefully, doing the steps yourself while reading along in the book, it probably took an hour or two. This may seem like a lot of work for what I billed as a "simple" exercise!

Don't worry! You actually spent most of your time reading my explanations, not doing the work. If you don't believe me, try the exercise again without reading the book, just peeking at it when you get stuck. Once you can do it without mistakes, which shouldn't take more than a couple more practice runs, you'll see that the whole run-through doesn't take more than a minute or two. "Rapid application development" is a reality!

The Library Painter: a Quick Peek

So far, we've seen three painters: the Application Painter, the Window Painter, and the Script (or PowerScript) Painter. There is a fourth painter that you should become familiar with in your first days with PowerBuilder: the Library Painter.

The Library Painter, of course, helps you to manage libraries, such as the TEST2.PBL library you created in step 4 of the BLUE button exercise. Furthermore, it shows you the contents of the library — the application, windows, and other objects within it — and provides tools for managing them as well.

To open the Library Painter, click the Library button on the PowerBar. As you can see in Figure 2-21, the Library Painter displays the contents of your hard drive in a tree diagram, similar to the Windows File Manager or the Windows Explorer. By double-clicking items, you can expand and contract parts of the tree. When you double-click a .PBL file, the painter expands it to show its contents. In Figure 2-21, you can see the PowerBuilder library TEST2.PBL, in the directory C:\FOUNDPB. You can see that TEST2.PBL contains two objects: the application app2 and the window w_boxcolor.

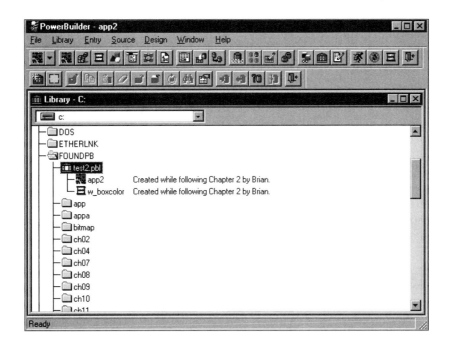

Figure 2-21
The Library Painter.

The Library Painter provides a convenient alternative to the PowerBar for launching painters. For example, if you double-click on w_boxcolor in

Figure 2-21, PowerBuilder opens the Window Painter and opens the w_boxcolor window within it.

There are some common maintenance functions that you can do only in the Library Painter. For example, only in the Library Painter can you delete a window or other object or change its comments. To do these things, right-click the item in the Library Painter display and make choices from the pop-up menu that appears.

I will describe the Library Painter in detail in Chapter 16. However, if you embark on a full-scale development project before you read that far, you will want to get in the habit of using the Library Painter right away.

More Simple Scripts

To follow up on our success with the "BLUE button" exercise, let's add a few more buttons and a little more programming to the w_boxcolor window. The new examples will introduce further simple PowerBuilder techniques.

From here on, I will not provide such detailed step-by-step instructions as I gave in the first exercise. I'll assume that you've learned those basics and are eager to focus on what's new and different in the coming examples. To get started, you may want to read the sidebar earlier in this chapter titled "Saving, Closing, and Reopening Your Work," if you haven't already. It may also help if you practice switching between the Application Painter, the Window Painter, and the Script Painter, to get a clear picture of how to navigate from one to the other. That will be our starting point.

THE SECOND EXAMPLE: SIMPLE ARITHMETIC

The "BLUE button" example didn't do anything with arithmetic, but many of your scripts will. So let's work through a very simple arithmetic example.

Open the Window Painter on the w_boxcolor window. Add another button to the window, like the BLUE button, by clicking the CommandButton button on the PainterBar's dropdown control palette

(Figure 2-12) and then clicking a site for it on the window. Change the new button's label to "Arithmetic" and change the font and size of the button to be similar to the BLUE button. This brings you to Figure 2-22.

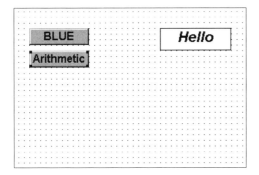

Figure 2-22
Draw the Arithmetic button on the window.

Click the Arithmetic button to select it. Then click the Script button on the PainterBar to write a script for it, as you did for the BLUE button. This brings you into the Script Painter.

Type in this script for the new button:

```
Integer i,j,k
i = 22
j = 33
k = i + j
st_firstbox.Text = String(k)
```

Click the Compile button on the PainterBar to make sure you have no errors, select File|Return on the menu (which is the same as clicking the Return PainterBar button) to return to the Window Painter, and click the Run PowerBar button to run the application. Click Yes when PowerBuilder asks whether to save changes. The application runs, and the window opens.

When you click the Arithmetic button on the running window, the script executes: It creates three variables, *i*, *j*, and *k*, which the Integer statement has declared to be integers. The script sets *i* to 22 and *j* to 33. It sets *k* to 55 by adding *i* plus *j*. And finally, it changes the text in the text box from "Hello" to the value of *k*, which is "55." The result is shown in Figure 2-23.

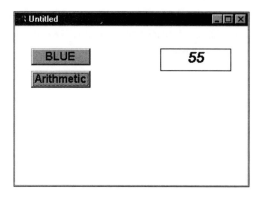

Figure 2-23
Click the Arithmetic button to display the value of 22 + 33.

The String(*k*) function call is important because it converts the integer 55 to the two-character string of text "55." You can set the text value of st_firstbox only to a text string, not to a number. Otherwise you will get a compiler error.

THE THIRD EXAMPLE: SIMPLE ARITHMETIC WITH USER INPUT

The Arithmetic button example was simple enough, but it would be better to let the user specify values for *i* and *j*, rather than hard-coding them into the script. Let's add another button to do it that way.

Once again open the w_boxcolor window in the Window Painter. Don't add a third button to the window yet. First add a SingleLineEdit control: Click the SingleLineEdit button on the PainterBar's dropdown control palette (Figure 2-12) and then click the window just below the "Hello" text box, to place the SingleLineEdit control there. Repeat the process to add a second SingleLineEdit control beneath the first one. Figure 2-24 shows the two new controls.

A SingleLineEdit control is a field in which the user can type a single line of text. We will use the two controls for the input of *i* and *j* for our arithmetic.

Change the name of each SingleLineEdit control by double-clicking it. Change the name of the first control from sle_1 to sle_inputi and the name of the second control from sle_2 to sle_inputj.

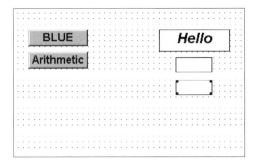

Figure 2-24
Draw two SingleLineEdit controls on the window.

Draw StaticText controls to the left of sle_inputi and sle_inputj, to serve as labels for them. Follow the same procedure used to create the st_firstbox text box in the first exercise. Change the text labels to "I=" and "J=," as shown in Figure 2-25.

Now that the input fields are ready, it's time to add the new button that will do the arithmetic to add the two fields. Rather than create this button from scratch, as we did with the other two buttons, let's create it by making a copy of the Arithmetic button, since the new button will be so similar.

Right-click the Arithmetic button to bring up its pop-up menu. Select Duplicate from the menu. This adds a new Arithmetic button to the window, identical to the first one. Change the label on the new button from "Arithmetic" to "Add I+J." The window should now look like Figure 2-25.

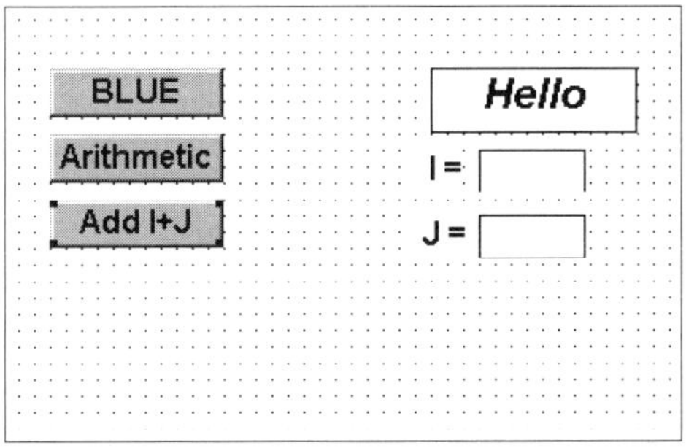

Figure 2-25
Create the "Add I+J" button by duplicating the Arithmetic button.

Duplicate, Copy and Paste, and Inherit

In the Window Painter, there are three ways to make a copy of a control, such as a button, so that you have a second control that looks identical to the first. Each of the three techniques differs from the others in how "identical" the copy is:

1. **Duplicate** — This is the technique recommended in the exercise in this chapter for creating the "Add I+J" button as a copy of the Arithmetic button: Right-click on the original control and select Duplicate from the pop-up menu. This makes a duplicate of the control and places it right below the original. The two controls look identical, but the new one has no scripts. The Duplicate option does not copy the scripts.

2. **Copy and Paste, using the clipboard** — Click the control to select it, and select Edit I Copy from the menu. This action passes a copy of the control to the clipboard, a work area shared by all Microsoft Windows programs. Then select Edit I Paste from the menu. PowerBuilder places a copy of the control onto the window. It's hard to tell at first, because the program places the new control right smack on top of the first one, but if you move the control aside, you'll see the original underneath it. The copy and paste technique has a big advantage over Duplicate, because it copies the control's PowerScript code to the new control.

3. **Inheritance** — This is a technique in which you duplicate a control but the copy maintains a connection back to the original. Any changes you make to the original get passed along to its copies. Inheritance is one of PowerBuilder's most powerful features; it will be explained in detail in Chapter 13.

Open the Script Painter on the new button by selecting it and clicking the Script button on the PainterBar. The script for the new button is empty, because Duplicate duplicates only the appearance of the old button, not its programming. (The "copy and paste" technique would have duplicated the programming.) Type in this script:

```
Integer i,j,k
i = Integer(sle_inputi.Text)
j = Integer(sle_inputj.Text)
k = i + j
st_firstbox.Text = String(k)
```

The next steps are the same as for the other button scripts: Compile the script, return to the Window Painter, and run the application. When the application runs and the window opens, type numbers into the I= and J= fields and click the Add I+J button. The sum of I and J should appear in the st_firstbox text box. (See Figure 2-26.)

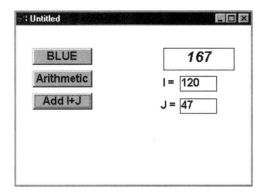

Figure 2-26
Click the Add I+J button to display the sum of I and J.

This script could use a little polish. If you type something into I or J that is not a number, such as "abc," the script treats it as zero. This is not necessarily bad, but maybe you'd prefer that the script display an error message instead. If you type in values outside the range of integer variables, which is –32768 to +32767, or values that yield a sum outside that range, you get a wrong result. Modifications should be made to the script to deal with these problems.

THE FOURTH EXAMPLE: A CLOSE BUTTON

The next example is a simple exercise to add a Close button to the window. When you click the button, the window will close. Up until now, you have been closing the window in other ways, such as by pressing Alt+F4. You will still be able to close the window in those ways, but the Close button will be more convenient and more obvious to inexperienced end users of your application.

Open the Window Painter on the w_boxcolor window. Add another button to the window, but this time click PictureButton on the PainterBar's dropdown control palette instead of CommandButton. Then click somewhere inside the window to place the button where you have some empty space. Be careful to click PictureButton, near the top of the dropdown palette, and not Picture, which is farther down. These are two similar buttons, a fact that can be confusing at first.

A PictureButton is almost exactly the same as a CommandButton, except that a PictureButton has a picture on it, as well as an optional text label.

Double-click the new button to open its property sheet. Under Enabled File Name, specify the path of any Windows Bitmap (.BMP) file. You should find one named TUTEXIT.BMP in your PowerBuilder directory (usually c:\Program Files\Powersoft\powerBuilder 5.0 or c:\pwrs\pb5, or c:\pwrs\pb5i32). It is a picture of an exit door. If you can't find it there, try the directory C:\FOUNDPB\BITMAP, or the BITMAP subdirectory wherever you have installed this book's sample files.

Other things to do in the property sheet, as shown in Figure 2-27: Erase the word "none" that appears in the Text box by clicking it and pressing the Del or Backspace keys. (Thus, the button will have a picture but no label. If you prefer to have a label, type it into Text.) Then click Original Size to place a check mark in front of it. Finally, click OK.

Although the file name reference in Figure 2-27 includes a full path name for the .BMP file, it is a better idea to exclude the path name. As I will explain in detail in Chapter 16, including the path name makes your application more difficult to place into production. If you omit the path name, so that the file name is simply "TUTEXIT.BMP," the application will be more transportable. However, you must make sure the the directory containing TUTEXIT.BMP is in your DOS search path.

Now click the Script button on the PainterBar to open the Script Painter for the PictureButton. Type in this script:

```
Close(Parent)
```

This script will close the window w_boxcolor. The word "Parent" is a reference to w_boxcolor, because that window is the parent (container) of the new button.

Click Return on the PainterBar. Back in the Window Painter, move the new picture button to the lower-right corner of the window, as you see in Figure 2-28. When you run the application, you can now click this button to close the window.

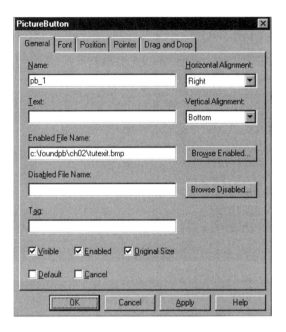

Figure 2-27
Fill in the PictureButton's property sheet.

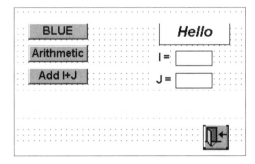

Figure 2-28
Move the Picture Button to the lower-right corner of the window.

CHANGING THE TAB ORDER

When you run the application and press the Tab key on the keyboard, the *focus* moves from control to control. When a button has focus, a faint dotted box appears around its label. When a field has focus, an insertion cursor (or "I-bar") appears in it.

The *tab order* for a window is the sequence in which controls are visited as you press Tab. On our window, the tab order is not ideal. If you have laid out the controls on the window more or less as in Figure 2-28, you are likely to find that tabbing travels through the following zigzag sequence:

1. BLUE button
2. Arithmetic button
3. I field
4. Add I+J button
5. J field
6. Close button

A more intuitive tab order would be to visit each of the buttons on the left first, from top to bottom, then the fields on the right, and then the Close button:

1. BLUE button
2. Arithmetic button
3. Add I+J button
4. I field
5. J field
6. Close button

You can change the tab order while designing the window. In the Window Painter, select Design|Tab Order from the menu or click Tab Order on the PainterBar. When you do, red numbers pop up on the controls. (See Figure 2-29.) The numbers indicate the sequence that tabbing will follow. Zeros indicate controls that are not tabbed to — in other words, that never get focus.

To change the tab order of a control, simply click its red number and change it. When you have made all your changes, select Design|Tab Order once again to return to regular window design.

PREVIEWING THE WINDOW

You can try out your revised tab order, and test the look and feel of the window in general, by selecting Design|Preview from the menu or clicking Preview on the PainterBar. This displays the window the way it will appear during execution a lot quicker than by running the entire application. During Window Preview, the buttons, fields, and other controls behave normally, but no scripts execute.

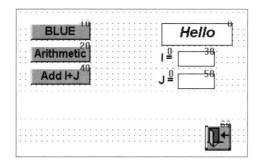

Figure 2-29
Change the numbers on the controls to alter the tab order.

To return from Window Preview back to the Window Painter, close the window, by pressing Alt+F4 for example, or select Design|Preview from the menu once again.

You get a more powerful form of Window Preview when you click the Run Window button on the PowerBar. This runs a fully functioning version of the window, with working scripts and all, essentially by running the application and opening this particular window. It works great for the simple window we have created so far. Unfortunately, the more sophisticated windows in most applications often can't be run this way, because they rely on application initialization that Run Window bypasses.

DEFAULT AND CLOSE BUTTON PROPERTIES

To be true to the Microsoft Windows standards for window design, it should be possible to click most of the buttons by using the keyboard as an alternative to the mouse. For example, on many windows pressing

Enter clicks the OK button and pressing Esc clicks the Cancel button. On a window with many buttons, you can usually press Tab to pass focus from one button to another, and pressing the Spacebar clicks the button in focus.

At first, a button you've added to a PowerBuilder window can be clicked only with the mouse, not the keyboard. You can change this in the Window Painter by double-clicking the button to bring up its property sheet. In the property sheet,

- Select the Default check box to allow the button to be clicked by pressing Enter when it has focus or when no other button has focus.
- Select the Cancel check box to allow the button to be clicked by pressing Esc.

You can see the Default and Cancel check boxes in Figure 2-27. For the w_boxcolor window we've been designing, turn on Default for the BLUE button and Cancel for the Close button. Then run the application and experiment with the Tab, Enter, Spacebar, and Esc keys.

You Are Now a PowerBuilder Developer!

Only two chapters into this book, you have already learned many of the essential techniques and concepts necessary to master PowerBuilder. The examples in this chapter were simple, but we covered a lot of ground. If you have performed all of the exercises in this chapter, here is what you have achieved:

- You developed an application and got it up and running.
- You designed a window to serve as the user interface to the application.
- You wrote many small scripts in the PowerScript language to control the behavior of the application.

Of course, there is still plenty more to learn! But now that you have some successes under your belt, you are well on your way. Much of what you do with PowerBuilder going forward is just an extension of what you have already accomplished.

I have certainly left many questions unanswered. The next chapter goes into a lot more detail, exploring the techniques used so far.

Events, Properties, and Functions

*I*n Chapter 2, you developed a simple application with a window, a few buttons, and some scripts. The first script you wrote was typical of the work you did. It was called the "clicked event script for the CommandButton cb_1," and it was a single line of code:

```
st_firstbox.BackColor = RGB(0,0,255)
```

I explained how this line turns the background color (BackColor) of a box (st_firstbox) to blue (using the RGB function to calculate the number for the color blue). You tried it and it worked.

But even this simple exercise raises many questions that I have not answered yet. Questions such as these:

- What is the "clicked event script"? What's an event? Are there other event scripts besides "clicked"?

- What is the "dot notation" in st_firstbox.BackColor all about? When do I use it in PowerBuilder?

- We've seen a couple of types of controls. For example, cb_1 is a CommandButton control and st_firstbox is a StaticText control. What other types of controls are there? Can I use "dot notation" with all of them? Do they all have the BackColor property?

- What properties are there besides BackColor? Where can I find a list of them?

This chapter has all the answers.
In particular, this chapter covers these topics:

- **Event-driven programming** — PowerBuilder's style of programming, which is quite different from traditional programming

- **Controls** — buttons, boxes, and all the other objects that you can place on a window

- **Events, properties, and functions** — the major features for manipulating controls, windows, and other objects

We will be building on the sample application constructed in the previous chapter. If you would like to do the exercises yourself as you follow along, be sure that you have completed the exercises from Chapter 2 first.

Event-Driven Programming

One of the major things that distinguishes PowerBuilder from traditional programming languages that you may have used in the past, such as COBOL, BASIC, or C, is that with PowerBuilder you do *event-driven programming*. This means that in PowerBuilder you write scripts that run in response to events. Some examples of events are the user clicking a button, the user typing a number into a field, or the application opening when you first run it.

Traditional programming languages are not event-driven. You write a single, monolithic program that controls everything, including all user interaction. This structure is illustrated in Figure 3-1. When you run the one program, it takes control of the entire environment. It reads every keystroke, detects every mouse action, does all the writing to the screen, and so on. That one program does it all.

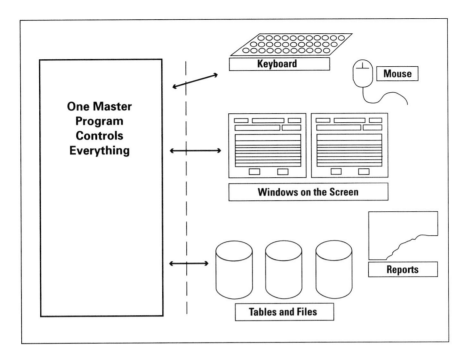

Figure 3-1

Traditional programs are monolithic. They are not event-driven; the one pro-gram controls everything.

With an event-driven programming tool such as PowerBuilder, the situation is much different. There is no concept in PowerBuilder of a single, large, do-it-all program. In PowerBuilder, your programming consists of tiny code modules — scripts — attached to buttons, fields, and other places on your windows. This structure is shown in Figure 3-2. Most of the time the scripts are dormant, waiting for an event to occur. When the event does occur, a script runs. For example, when the user clicks a button, the "clicked" script on that button runs. Usually the script is short, and after it accomplishes its small task it returns to dormancy. You are then back in the state where all the scripts are quietly waiting for the next event.

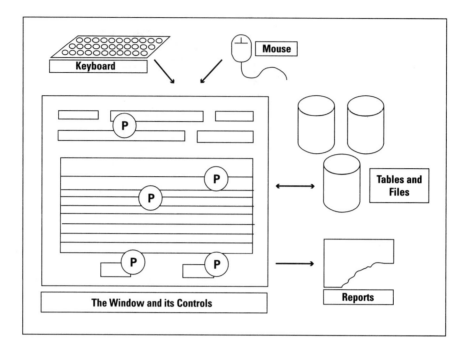

Figure 3-2
In an event-driven system, the programming lies dormant on the surface of your application, waiting for an event to occur.

Most of the time, therefore, no programming is running at all. At least, not any of your programming. PowerBuilder and Microsoft Windows are always running, and these two programs manage the user's interactions with the keyboard, the mouse, and the screen. When PowerBuilder detects that the user has done something that constitutes an event, PowerBuilder runs your script associated with that event, if there is one.

If you have worked only with traditional programming in the past, PowerBuilder may seem "inside out" to you. Event-driven programming is a very different approach.

Why is PowerBuilder forcing us to learn this entirely new way of programming? The reason is, event-driven programming is the best way to write programs for the modern, graphical Windows environment. In Windows, there are too many things going on at once for the traditional monolithic program to handle effectively. Event-driven programming is the current state of the art and, therefore all the modern programming languages are moving in that direction. PowerBuilder just happens to be one of the first to arrive.

Consider the script you wrote to turn the box blue. It was only one line of code:

```
st_firstbox.BackColor = RGB(0,0,255)    // turn the box blue
```

This code was attached to a button and set to respond to the clicked event for the button. When you click the button, the event fires, the script runs, and the box turns blue. All this requires only one line of code!

To accomplish the same thing in the traditional environment would take a lot more programming. One line of code might still be enough to turn the box blue, but leading up to that would be hundreds or thousands of lines of code controlling the user's interaction with the mouse, the keyboard, and the screen. Did the user click the mouse? Was it the left or right button? Where is the mouse pointing? Is it pointing to a button? Which button? All of this and more would be up to the programmer to control, all adding up to an enormous programming job. With PowerBuilder, you are freed from all that tedious work. PowerBuilder manages the mundane parts of the user interaction. You need to program only the exceptions. Thousands of lines of programming are reduced to only one or two.

There is nothing limiting about the event-driven approach. You can still do everything you can do with the traditional languages, but probably a lot more easily. If you insist on writing a single large, monolithic program, you can. Just make your giant program the open event script for the application. When the application starts, the script runs. This might be okay for a "batch" job, with no user interface and a lot of disk processing. The script can also take complete control of the mouse and keyboard, as a traditional program would — but I don't know why you'd want it to.

LOOKING FOR THE EVENTS

In order for event-driven programming to work, PowerBuilder has to provide us developers with a set of events, built into its environment, where we can hang our program code. And PowerBuilder does. In our examples so far, we have seen only a couple: The clicked event on a button and the open event on the application. There are many, many others.

Every object in your application has its set of events — the application has events, each window has its events, every button, field, and other control on a window has events. Anywhere there is an object or control, there are events. And anywhere there is an event, you can attach a script.

Let's go look.

CONTINUING THE EXERCISE

This exercise continues from where you left off at the end of Chapter 2. Once again, open the window w_boxcolor in the library TEST2.PBL.

Click the text box st_firstbox (where the word "Hello" is) and click the Script button on the PainterBar. We've done this before for the buttons, but never before for st_firstbox. Clicking opens the Script Painter so that we can attach a script to the text box. But if you look closely, you'll see that it's not just *any* script for the text box. It is the script for the clicked event for the text box, and it will run when you click (left-click) the box with the mouse. That's what is meant by "Script - clicked for st_firstbox" at the top of the Script window.

Rather than program the clicked event, let's program a different event for the box. Click the dropdown button near the top left of the window, to the right of the words "Select Event." This button drops down a list of every event for the box, as you see in Figure 3-3. There are twelve of them. "Clicked," at the top of the list, is the default. (It's at the top because the list is alphabetical, not because it's the default.)

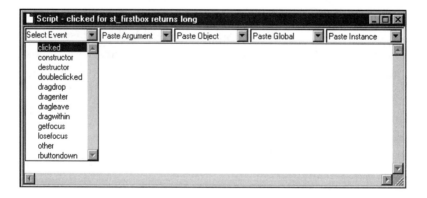

Figure 3-3

Select an event for st_firstbox.

Select "rbuttondown" from the list. This is the "right-button-down" event, which fires when you right-click the box. Notice that the window title changes to "Script - rbuttondown for st_firstbox."

Type in this one-line script:

```
This.BackColor = RGB(0,255,0)    // turn the text box green
```

When you right-click the text box, it will turn itself green. *This* is a "pronoun" that means "this control to which the script is attached." You could use the name of the control, st_firstbox, instead of *This*. But *This* is more flexible in case you change the name of the control or copy this script onto a different control.

You can also remove "This." altogether. If PowerBuilder sees an attribute such as BackColor standing alone, it assumes you mean "This." However, I always prefer to use the dot notation to avoid confusion.

Click the Compile button on the PainterBar to compile the script and make sure there are no errors.

Now let's write a similar script for the text box's clicked (that is, left-clicked) event. Click the dropdown button next to Select Event. This time, select "clicked" from the list. Now you are about to write the "clicked" script for st_firstbox. Here is the script to type in:

```
This.BackColor = RGB(255,0,0)    // turn the text box red
```

When you left-click the box, it will turn red. When you right-click the box, it will turn green. Two events, two scripts.

Click the Compile button on the PainterBar and if there are no errors, click the Return button on the PainterBar.

You must do one extra thing to the text box to get these events working. Double-click the text box to open its property sheet and then check-mark its Enabled property. Enabled means that the box is able to respond to mouse-clicks. Click OK to close the property sheet.

If you like, you may run the application now and try it out. Or you can continue on.

EVENTS ON THE WINDOW

The window itself has events, just as the controls on the window do. To get to the window events, click somewhere on the window (in the dotted grid) where there are no controls. Make sure the status line at the bottom of the screen says "Nothing Selected." If not, try clicking somewhere else. Now click the Script button on the PainterBar and once again you are in the Script Painter, but this time you are attaching a script to the window, not to a control.

The Script Painter opens the open event for the window w_boxcolor, as you will see from the script title bar. Any code you type here will run when the window first opens. Click the dropdown list for Select Event to see what other window events are available. There are 29 events for a window, many more than there were for a text box control.

Select the activate event from the list. This event fires when the window becomes active, which is when you first open it, and also when you come back to it after visiting some other window. Type in this script, and click the Compile button on the PainterBar to check it:

```
This.BackColor = RGB(255,255,0)  // turn the window yellow
This.Title = "Here I Am!"    // change the window's title
```

The first line changes the window's background color to yellow. The second line changes the window's title.

Now click the Select Event dropdown button again and select "deactivate." The deactivate event fires when the window becomes inactive, for instance, when you press Alt+Tab to switch to another program in Microsoft Windows. Type in this script, and click the Compile button on the PainterBar to check it:

```
This.BackColor = RGB(255,0,255)  // turn the window magenta
This.Title = "I'll Be Back!"   // change the window's title
```

Once again, click the dropdown button for Select Event, just to look at it. See Figure 3-4. Notice the Script icon next to "activate" and "deactivate." These flags indicate which events have scripts written for them.

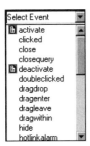

Figure 3-4

The events with scripts written are marked.

Click the Return button on the PainterBar to close the Script Painter and return to the Window Painter. Select File|Save from the menu to save your work. Now run the application and try it out.

EVENTS ON THE APPLICATION

The application object also has events, and programming them is not a whole lot different than programming the events for window objects and controls.

Click Application on the PowerBar to switch to the Application Painter for app2. Click the Script button on the PainterBar to open the Script Painter for the application.

You were here once before, when you programmed the open event in step 22 of last chapter's exercise, and it is the "open" script that you see now. Click the Select Event dropdown button. The application object has six events. You should see an icon next to "open," indicating that it has been programmed.

Select "close" from the list. Type in this script, and click the Compile button on the PainterBar to check it:

```
MessageBox("Goodbye","Thanks for visiting")
```

When the you close the application, the MessageBox function will display the dialog box shown in Figure 3-5.

Figure 3-5
The "Goodbye" dialog box.

Here's a variation on the close script. It displays the message shown in Figure 3-6, informing you how long the application was running:

```
Long  t
String s
t = CPU( )/1000
s = "Thanks for visiting for " + String(t) + " seconds"
MessageBox("Goodbye",s)
```

The CPU function returns the number of milliseconds the application has been running. Divide that by 1000 and you get *t*, the number of seconds. I could have written this script without the variables *t* or *s* and just placed all the arithmetic in MessageBox as the second parameter, but I broke it up this way to make it easier to read.

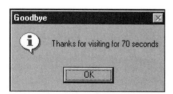

Figure 3-6
The "Goodbye" dialog box, with run time.

Now let's try everything out. Click Return (to the Application Painter) on the PainterBar to close the Script Painter. Click Run on the PowerBar. Click Yes when asked to save changes. When the application opens the w_boxcolor window, it should be yellow and say "Here I Am!" at the top, as shown in Figure 3-8.

The MessageBox Function

The MessageBox function used in this exercise is an easy and frequently used PowerBuilder function, especially for beginners. With a single line of code, MessageBox can pop up a dialog box to give the user information, to alert the user about an error, or to ask the user a question.

MessageBox has two required parameters in its argument list, as well as optional third, fourth, and fifth parameters:

```
MessageBox(title, text, icon, button, default)
```

The first two parameters, title and text, are the title to appear at the top of the dialog box and the text to be displayed within it. This call to MessageBox displays the dialog box shown in Figure 3-5:

```
MessageBox("Goodbye","Thanks for visiting")
```

The third parameter, icon, indicates an icon to use in place of the default "i" (information) icon seen in Figure 3-5. The fourth parameter, button, indicates which button or buttons you want on the dialog box instead of the one OK button. The fifth parameter, default, indicates which button is the default (the one that is clicked if you press the Enter key) when there is more than one button. This example uses all five parameters:

```
i = MessageBox("Warning: You Have Unsaved Work",        &
        "Do you want to save your work before exiting?", &
        question!, yesnocancel!, 2)
```

This call pops up the dialog box shown in Figure 3-7. It has a question mark icon because the third parameter is question! Other possibilities for this parameter include information! (the "i" icon) and stopsign! The dialog box in Figure 3-7 has three buttons — Yes, No, and Cancel — because the fourth parameter is yesnocancel! Other possibilities include ok!, yesno!, and abortretryignore! Because the fifth parameter is 2, the second button, No, is the default. The "&" at the end of the first two lines is the continuation character in PowerScript, used when a single command extends across more than one line. The items with exclamation points — "question!" and "yesnocancel!" — are called *enumerated data types*. In the next chapter I will explain them and how to look them up in the online help.

continued

continued

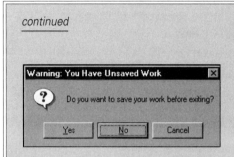

Figure 3-7
The "Yes/No/Cancel" message box.

The MessageBox function returns a numeric value — into the variable *i*, in this case — depending on which button the user clicks: 1 for Yes, 2 for No, or 3 for Cancel. The script then proceeds to test *i* to determine what action to take. In the first example in Figure 3-5, which had only an OK button, there was no need to capture the function's return value, because with only one button the value will always be 1. Although all PowerScript functions return a value, you are not required to make use of it.

You will probably use MessageBox a lot while learning PowerBuilder. Many people replace it with other techniques as they get more sophisticated, however. For example, rather than call MessageBox every time an error occurs, you should probably develop and call a centralized error handling procedure. In Chapter 17, I will show you how to do that.

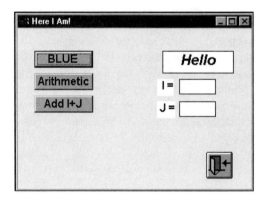

Figure 3-8
Run the application.

Try each of the events that you have programmed:

- Right-click the Hello box. It turns green.

- Left-click the Hello box. It turns red.

- Click the BLUE button. The Hello box turns blue.

- Resize this window and some other window, such as the Windows Program Manager, so that you can see them side by side, with no overlap.

- Click to the other window. The w_boxcolor window turns magenta, and its title changes to "I'll Be Back!"

- Click back to the w_boxcolor window. Once again it becomes yellow, and its title returns to "Here I Am!"

- Close the window, and the message box shown in Figure 3-5 or Figure 3-6 pops up. Click OK. The application closes, and you are back in the PowerBuilder development environment.

Working with Controls

The exercises in this chapter have done simple things, mostly working with *controls*. A *control* is an object that you place on a window, such as a button, a SingleLineEdit field, or a StaticText text box. You have now had a little bit of practice drawing controls on a window, moving and stretching them, and changing their properties. You have also had a little bit of practice writing scripts that manipulate controls, such as the script that turns the text box blue and the script that changes its text to "55."

Controls, as you can see, are the key to developing the user-friendly interface that PowerBuilder applications are known for. The rest of this chapter takes a broader look at how you work with controls in PowerBuilder.

TYPES OF CONTROLS

In a PowerBuilder application, you can use controls in only two places: in windows, as you already know, and in user objects, as you will learn in Chapter 12.

There are 28 types of controls, and you can draw each of them while designing a window with the Window Painter. The four types that we have drawn in the exercises so far are the CommandButton, the PictureButton, the StaticText, and the SingleLineEdit. The complete list of 28 is given in Table 3-1.

Table 3-1

Types of Controls

Type of Control	Description
CommandButton PictureButton	Push-button controls
StaticText SingleLineEdit EditMask MultiLineEdit RichTextEdit	Text and field controls: Display text and (except with StaticText) allow the typing in of text
ListBox PictureListBox CheckBox RadioButton DropDownListBox DropDownPictureListBox ListView TreeView	Pick-list controls: Display items or lists of items and let the user pick an item with the mouse
Tab GroupBox	Container controls: Collect other controls for easier viewing or easier access
HScrollBar VScrollBar	Stand-alone horizontal and vertical scroll-bar controls
Picture Graph OLE 2.0	Graphical controls: Display pictures, graphs, and documents from other Windows products
Line Oval Rectangle RoundRectangle	Drawing controls: These help make your window more attractive
DataWindow UserObject	Complex controls: Chapter 8 explains DataWindow controls, and Chapter 12 explains User Object controls

CREATING A CONTROL IN THE WINDOW PAINTER

There are two ways to place a control on a window. The first is to use the Window PainterBar. As you know from the last chapter, the PainterBar has a button for each of the 28 control types (Figure 2-12). To place a control, first click the PainterBar button for it and then click a point on the window.

The other way is to select Controls from the menu. This pops up a list of the 28 control types, shown in Figure 3-9. Select a control type from the menu, then click the window to place the control on the window.

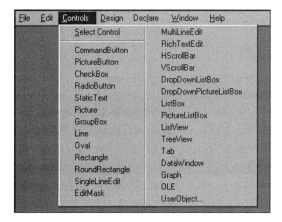

Figure 3-9
The Controls menu.

If you click a PainterBar button to draw a control and then change your mind, click the Selection button on the PainterBar or choose Controls|Select Control from the menu.

MANIPULATING A CONTROL IN THE WINDOW PAINTER

After you have placed a control on a window, there are several ways to change its appearance and other characteristics:

1. **Direct manipulation with the mouse** — Using the mouse, you can click and drag a control to a new location or change its size by stretching its edges and corners.

2. **The StyleBar** — This toolbar is shown in Figure 3-10 in its floating position, although I usually keep it docked at the top of the screen. It has tools for changing the fonts and values of a text control, such as the boldface button and the italic button, and for changing the text displayed on a control, such as a button label.

Figure 3-10
The Text Style Toolbar or "StyleBar."

3. **The property sheet** — When you double-click a control or click the Property button on the PainterBar, the control's property sheet pops up. The property sheet is a tabbed dialog box displaying most of the characteristics of the control.

4. **The pop-up menu for the control** — This menu pops up when you right-click a control. All of its choices are available elsewhere in the Window Painter, but you may find the pop-up menu a more convenient way to get to them. For example, the Script... and Properties... menu choices are the same as the Script and Properties PainterBar buttons. The other choices, such as Cut and Send to Back, are also found under Edit in the main menu.

5. **Setting the tab order** — The tab order is the sequence in which focus hops from one control to another as you press the Tab key. As explained in the previous chapter (Figure 2-29), you can assign a sequence number to each control to specify its tab order by clicking the Tab Order PainterBar button or by selecting Design|Tab Order from the menu.

6. **To delete a control** — Click it to select it. Then press the Del key on the keyboard, or click the Clear button on the PainterBar. If you regret deleting it and haven't done anything else yet, Edit|Undo from the menu will bring it back.

A Small Piece of the Object-Oriented Puzzle

In this chapter, I describe events, properties, and functions as features of window controls. However, this is just a small piece of a much bigger picture: object-oriented development techniques. A control is just one type of object. Other objects include application objects, windows, and other things that we have yet to see. Almost all types of PowerBuilder objects have events, properties, and functions.

Chapter 11 of this book begins an in-depth look at object orientation. It's not necessary for you to understand that topic yet, but it may be helpful to know that it's coming.

Manipulating a Control in a Script: Events, Properties, and Functions

PowerBuilder gives you, as the programmer, extensive powers to respond to, inspect, and alter controls from a script while the application is running. The first script we wrote in the last chapter, which turns a text box blue, is an example of a script altering a control.

There are certainly a minimum number of features that would be required of any visual development tool like PowerBuilder, just to be practical. You must be able to write a script to respond to a button click, to inspect the value of an input field on a window, and to change the value of a field. PowerBuilder goes far beyond these basics, giving the programmer power over virtually every aspect of every control at runtime.

To manipulate controls with programming, every type of control has three sets of features accessible from the PowerScript language:

- Events
- Properties
- Functions

Events, properties, and functions on controls and on other objects are so important that one of the manuals in the PowerBuilder documentation set, the *Objects and Controls* guide, is dedicated entirely to documenting them.

EVENTS

I have already described events at some length earlier in this chapter, in the section about "Event-Driven Programming." Events will play a role in almost every script written in your applications and in the remainder of this book.

Of the 28 types of controls, 5 of them do not have events: the GroupBox control and the four drawing controls. The other 23 types have between 8 and 31 events. Many commonly used controls, such as buttons and fields, have about a dozen events. In addition to the documented events that are built into every PowerBuilder control, you can also invent new events of your own. They are called *user events*, and Chapter 12 will explain how to define them.

An event is something that happens to the control — usually something that the user does to the control — while the application is running. We, as programmers, get to write a script that responds to the event. So if a control has, say, 12 events, that means you can attach as many as 12 different scripts to the control, one for each event.

As explained earlier, you see the list of events for a control while in the Script Painter by clicking the Select Event dropdown button (Figure 3-3). Events are documented in the *Objects and Controls* manual and in the online help.

Here are examples of a few commonly used events:

- **Clicked** — The user has clicked the control with the left mouse button. This event is especially important for CommandButton and PictureButton controls, but the "clicked" event is available for most other types of controls as well.

- **RButtonDown** — The user has clicked the right mouse button on the control. Use this event if you want to implement right-clicking.

- **Modified** — The user has typed a new value into a field-type control (SingleLineEdit, EditMask, MultiLineEdit, ListBox, or DropDown-ListBox). Use this event to validate the new value or use it in calculations.

- **Constructor** — This event fires on each control while the window is opening, just before the window open event. Use this event to initialize variables and properties associated with a control.

- **Destructor** — This event fires on each event while the window is closing, just after the window close event. Use this event to handle any loose ends that need tying up before the control ceases to exist.

PROPERTIES

The *properties* for a control are such things as its color, its size, and its position on the window — in general, properties are the visual or behavioral characteristics of the control. In the Window Painter, you inspect and modify properties by double-clicking a control to pop up its property sheet.

Properties = Attributes

Prior to version 5.0 of PowerBuilder, properties were called "attributes." You may still see the term "attribute" pop up in the documentation or in the online help from time to time. However, as of version 5.0, the preferred term is "property."

In the sample scripts in Chapter 2, we made use of properties a number of times. Here are a few examples from the previous exercises:

```
st_firstbox.BackColor = RGB(0,0,255) // change the "BackColor" prop.
st_firstbox.Text = String(k)        // change the "Text" property
x = Integer(sle_inputx.Text)        // read the "Text" property
```

In PowerScript, you use the *dot notation* for a property. The syntax is always:

```
controlName.PropertyName
```

You can use a property anywhere in a script where you can use a variable. In particular, you can place it to the right of an "=" to read a property's value, or to the left of an "=" to change it:

```
var1 = st_firstbox.BackColor  // read the BackColor property
st_firstbox.BackColor = var1  // change the BackColor property
```

Thus, properties are simple and direct tools for manipulating the user interface.

Browser

Each of the 28 types of controls has its set of properties. Properties are documented in the *Objects and Controls* manual and in the online help.

To get a list of properties for a control while you are typing in a script, click the Browser button on the PowerBar. In the next exercise we'll look at this feature and how to use it.

Here are examples of a few commonly used properties:

- **Text** — the text displayed in or on a control. If the control is a field (a SingleLineEdit, EditMask, or MultiLineEdit control), text is the value displayed in the field, which has been typed in by the user or filled in by PowerBuilder. Many other controls have the text property as well. For example, a button's text is the label on the button. You can use this property to change a button's label dynamically, such as by changing it from "On" to "Off" when the user clicks the button.

- **BackColor** — the background color of a control

- **TextColor** — the color of the text in a control

- **BorderColor** — the color of a control's border

- **Width** and **Height** — the size of the control

- **X** and **Y** — a control's position in the window (the x and y coordinates of the upper-left corner of the control)

- **Visible** — true or false, whether a control is visible

- **Enabled** — true or false, whether a control such as a button responds to mouse-clicks

FUNCTIONS

A *function* in the PowerScript language is not unlike a function in any other programming language. In fact, it's not unlike a function in spreadsheet software for that matter: A function is a subprogram you can call from your script that performs an operation and returns a result.

Many of the sample scripts in the previous chapter relied on functions. For example, this script calls the RGB function:

```
st_firstbox.BackColor = RGB(0,0,255)
```

There are various types of functions. I will go into more detail about them in the next chapter. Right now, I am going to focus on one particular type: *functions on controls*.

A *function on a control* uses dot notation, similar to the syntax for a property:

```
controlName.FunctionName ( parameters )
```

The addition of "controlName." preceding the function call indicates that this is a function that operates on a control.

For example, there is a function Resize that changes the size of a control:

```
st_firstbox.Resize(300,500)
```

When this statement executes, it changes the size of the StaticText control st_firstbox to 300 wide and 500 tall. 300 and 500 are in "PowerBuilder Units," which are explained in the sidebar.

As with properties, each of the 28 types of controls has its set of functions. Functions on controls are listed by control type in the *Objects and Controls* manual, and they are described alphabetically in the "PowerScript Functions" chapter of the *Powerscript Reference* manual. You can also look them up in the "Functions for Controls" topic of the PowerBuilder help.

As with properties, you can get a list of functions for a control by clicking the Browser button on the PowerBar. This feature will be demonstrated in the exercise that follows.

THE FINAL EXERCISE: THE JIGGLE BUTTON

In this final hands-on exercise, you will add one more button to the w_boxcolor window. When you click the button, it will jiggle the text box st_firstbox up and down. The programming illustrates the use of a function for a control.

Once again, open the w_boxcolor window in the window painter and draw a CommandButton on the window. Change the label of the button to "Jiggle," and stretch and move it as shown in Figure 3-11.

PowerBuilder Units

In the function call "st_firstbox.Resize(300,500)," the parameters 300 and 500 are in "PowerBuilder Units." This special unit of measure is used throughout PowerBuilder for almost all on-screen measurements.

The PowerBuilder Unit is a flexible measurement, so I can't make a precise statement like "there are 280 PowerBuilder Units to an inch." The value of the unit is dependent on how your system is configured. For example, if you have a typical video screen, with Windows configured for VGA display, 640 × 480 pixels on the screen, and you are using the standard system font, one PowerBuilder Unit will probably be somewhere between 1/300 and 1/250 of an on-screen inch. And a vertical PowerBuilder Unit will be a little bit bigger than a horizontal PowerBuilder Unit! If you switch any of these system settings — for example, if you switch to an 800 × 600 display — the size of the PowerBuilder unit will be quite different.

There is wisdom to this seemingly fluid way of measuring things. PowerBuilder units are highly transportable as you move your application to different platforms. For example, a box that looks square on a Windows 640 × 480 screen will still look square on an 800 × 600 screen or an EGA screen or a Macintosh. This is not possible if you use more conventional units of measure such as pixels.

Thus, in the statement

```
st_firstbox.Resize(300,500)
```

the result is a box that is, perhaps, approximately one inch wide and two inches tall, depending on your configuration.

You will find more information about PowerBuilder units in the "Defining Windows" chapter of the *PowerBuilder User's Guide*.

Click Script on the PainterBar to open the Jiggle button's clicked event script. Here is the script to type in:

```
Integer i,j,n
Integer li_how_many_times, li_how_far
li_how_many_times = 20
li_how_far = 40
i = st_firstbox.X
j = st_firstbox.Y
FOR n = 1 TO li_how_many_times
  st_firstbox.Move(i,j+li_how_far)
  st_firstbox.Move(i,j)
NEXT
```

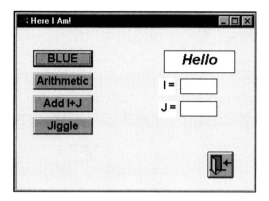

Figure 3-11
The final version of the w_boxcolor window, with the Jiggle button.

The script uses the Move function to move the st_firstbox control a little bit in the "y" direction — that is, vertically. This statement moves the box down slightly:

```
st_firstbox.Move(i,j+li_how_far)
```

The variables *i* and *j* are the original x and y coordinates of the box. They were captured by reading the X and Y properties of the control, in the two lines of code just above the FOR statement. The position *j+li_how_far* is a little bit lower than *j*. Vertical coordinates begin with y = 0 at the top of the window and grow as you move down from there. So the bigger the y value of a point, the farther down it is.

This statement moves the box back up to its original position:

```
st_firstbox.Move(i,j)
```

The two Move function calls are enclosed within a FOR...NEXT loop. The next chapter will describe loops in more detail. The loop causes the Move functions to be performed repeatedly, while the loop counts from 1 to *li_how_many_times*, which is to say from 1 to 20. So the box moves down and then up again twenty times during the course of the script.

PASTE OBJECT

While typing in this script, take some time to explore the online lists of properties, functions, and other PowerScript features available while you are in the Script Painter. For starters, when you get to the fifth line of code, type in just the beginning of it:

```
i =
```

Now let's say you've forgotten the name of the "Hello" text box. Click the Paste Object dropdown button at the top of the Script Painter window and, as shown in Figure 3-12, you'll see a list of all the controls in the window.

Figure 3-12

In the Script Painter, the names of all controls are just one click away.

Click st_firstbox on the list, and PowerBuilder types it into the script, right where you left off typing:

```
i = st_firstbox
```

Now type the ".X" that follows:

```
i = st_firstbox.X
```

THE BROWSER

To type the next line, let's use another helpful, and much more comprehensive, feature, the Browser. First, type this much of the line:

```
j =
```

The Browser will fill in the rest of the line for you. Click the Browse Object button on the the PainterBar, or click the Browser button on the PowerBar, or select Design|Browse Object from the menu. Each of these techniques opens the Browser (Figure 3-13), which is a gold mine of information.

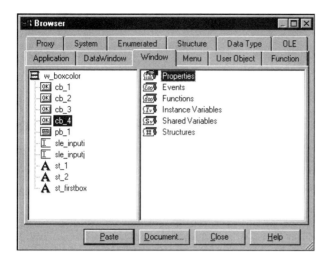

Figure 3-13
The Browser.

The Browser lists objects on the left and their properties, events, functions, and other features on the right. The tabs along the top take you to lists of other types of objects, which I will describe in later chapters. The Document button creates a Rich Text Format (RTF) version of the Browser's display, which you may then print, export to a document file, or copy to the clipboard.

Initially, the Browser highlights the current object. This is the Jiggle button which, if you've been following the exercise closely, is named cb_4, the fourth CommandButton. Click st_firstbox to select it on the list. On the right-side list double-click Properties. The list expands to show all the properties of this control.

Scroll down to "Integer y" (Figure 3-14), click it to select it, and click the Paste button. PowerBuilder types the "st_firstbox.y" into your script:

```
j = st_firstbox.y
```

Okay, I admit that was a lot to go through to avoid typing the letter "y"! But you'll learn to appreciate the Browser when you start using properties like "legenddispattr," "linkupdateoptions," and "toolbarpopmenutext"!

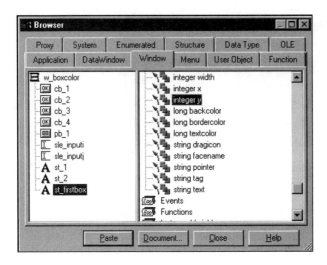

Figure 3-14
Select the property "y" from the Browser.

You should type in the next line, the FOR statement, by hand. There is a way to look it up and have PowerBuilder type it for you, and I'll show that in the next chapter.

That brings you to this line:

```
st_firstbox.Move(i,j+li_how_far)
```

Use the Browser to help type in this line. Click the Browse Object button on the PainterBar. As before, click st_firstbox from the Browser's left-side list of controls. On the right, double-click Functions. Scroll down to the Move function (see Figure 3-15), click it, and click the Paste button. PowerBuilder types this line into your script:

```
st_firstbox.move ( integer x, integer y )
```

Replace the PowerBuilder parameters, "(integer x, integer y)," with your parameters, "*(i,j+li_how_far)*."

Now type in the rest of the script.

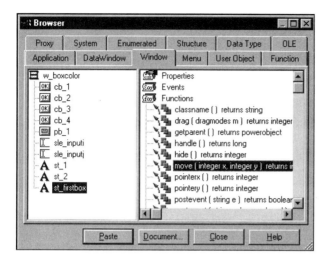

Figure 3-15
Select the function move from the Browser.

To save and run the script, click the Return to Window Painter button, select File|Save from the menu to save your work, and click the Run button to run the application. The window opens as shown in Figure 3-11.

When you click the Jiggle button, the box jiggles up and down twenty times.

Events, Properties, and Functions for Other Objects

Windows and applications, being PowerBuilder objects, have events, properties, and functions, just as controls do. You use them very much like you do for controls. For example, properties and functions all require the same dot notation syntax. And they are documented in the same places, such as in the *Objects and Controls* manual and in the Browser dialog box.

We have seen some examples of events and properties on these objects already in this chapter and the previous one:

- **Application events** — Open and Close
- **Window events** — Activate and Deactivate
- **Window properties** — BackColor and Title

We shall see many more examples in future chapters.

4

The PowerScript Language

*I*n the previous chapter you saw some basic examples of the PowerScript language. This chapter describes the language in more detail.

Elements of the PowerScript Language

Every line of code must be one of these language elements:

- Variable declaration
- Assignment statement
- Program control statement
- Function call
- Embedded SQL statement
- Comment or blank line, which is not executed

During the course of this chapter I'll cover all of these, except for embedded SQL, which is the topic of Chapter 7. To start with, let's look at assignment statements.

Assignment Statements

Assignment statements in PowerScript are pretty much what they are in any other programming language:

```
something = some value
```

In other words, "Set something equal to some value." The "something" on the left of the "=" is often a variable:

```
x = 27
```

But it could be other things, such as a control property, as we've seen in previous chapters:

```
st_firstbox.BackColor = RGB(0,0,255)
```

The "some value" on the right of the "=" could be a literal value, a variable, a function call, an arithmetic expression combining these elements, or any of a number of other things, as long as it results in a value.

For example:

```
i = 3            // literal value
d2 = d1          // variable
s1 = String(i1)  // function call
i = i1 + i2      // arithmetic expression
```

A *literal* is just what it sounds like — an exact number, string, date, or time value such as 123, "John Adams," 1996-12-25, or 10:46:23.

An arithmetic expression can include any of the following operators:

- **Arithmetic** — addition (+), subtraction (−), multiplication (*), division (/), and exponentiation (^)

- **Logical** — Not, And, and Or

- **Relational** — equals (=), greater than (>), less than (<), not equal to (<>), greater than or equal to (>=), and less than or equal to (<=)

- **Concatenation** of strings (+)

As in other languages, you can use parentheses to indicate the order of evaluation.

Here are some examples of assignment statements:

```
i = i2 + i3 * 2        // i, i2, and i3 are integer variables
b = Not (i2 = i3)      // b will be True or False
b = i2 > i3            // b will be True or False
s = s1 + "Smith"       // s and s1 are string variables
```

PowerScript offers a few shortcuts for the assignment statement. They have slight performance advantages over their equivalents. Here are some common examples:

```
i ++            // increment i by one      …same as  i = i + 1
i --            // decrement i by one      …same as  i = i - 1
i += i2         // add i2 to i             …same as  i = i + i2
i -= i2         // subtract i2 from i      …same as  i = i - i2
s += "Smith"    // concatenate Smith to s …same as   s = s + "Smith"
```

Unlike some programming languages, such as C, PowerScript does not allow a regular assignment to be mixed with an assignment shortcut. For example, this is not allowed:

```
i1 = i2 ++    // increment i2 and assign its value to i1 (illegal)
```

Programming Style

PowerScript is quite flexible when it comes to how you type in your script. Here are some conventions:

WHITE SPACE

You may have any number of blank spaces or tabs between the elements of a statement and any number of blank lines between two statement lines. You can indent any line as much as you wish.

CAPITALIZATION

The use of upper- or lowercase makes no difference. You can type a script all in uppercase, or all in lowercase, or in a mixture. You can name a variable *ABC* in one place and refer to it as *abc* or *Abc* elsewhere.

Adopting Programming Standards

Although PowerScript is flexible about programming style, you should adopt standards and follow them. For example, you should have standards for where to use white space, when to use upper- and lowercase, and how to name variables.

Powersoft has devised and documented such standards, which they have used throughout their examples and documentation. Most developers follow the same or similar standards.

The section "PowerScript Programming Standards" at the end of this chapter describes the standards that our development team follows in our work and in this book. It is based closely on the Powersoft standards.

About the only place where case matters is inside literal text strings, especially in searching and assignments. For example, these two statements are different:

```
s1 = "Hello"
s1 = "hello"
```

MULTIPLE LINES PER STATEMENT

You may break a single statement into more than one line if it is too long to fit, or even if you just like it that way. To continue a statement to another line, place an ampersand (&) at the end of the first line. For example:

```
s = "This is a long string " +          &
    "created by concatenating   " +     &
    "three smaller strings"
```

MULTIPLE STATEMENTS PER LINE

You may place two or more short statements onto a single line. Sometimes this makes a script more concise and readable, especially if the statements are related. Use a semicolon (;) to separate multiple statements on the same line. Here is a line that contains three statements:

```
i ++;   s1[i] = "abc";   s2[i] = "xyz"
```

COMMENTS

A *comment* is text in your script that PowerScript completely ignores. You can add comments to your code in one of two ways:

- Any text to the right of a double slash (//) is a comment.
- Any text in between a slash followed by an asterisk (/*) and an asterisk followed by a slash (*/) is a comment, even if it extends across multiple lines.

The next two examples illustrate the use of the // comment method:

```
s1 = s2 + " " + s3    // concatenate strings, with a space in between
// Concatenate strings, with a space in between
s1 = s2 + " " + s3
```

Here is an example of the /* method:

```
/* In the following section we concatenate the
 first and last names. This creates a more
 readable format for forms and reports.*/
```

Our programming standards prohibit the use of the /* method for a multiline comment. It's too hard to tell which lines are comments and which are not. Instead, we begin each line of a multiline comment with //.

The PowerScript Painter

The PowerScript Painter, or Script Painter, is the part of PowerBuilder in which you type in and edit most of your source code. As you know from Chapter 2, the easiest way to open the PowerScript Painter is to click the Script button on the toolbar. This button appears in the PainterBar for the Application Painter, the Window Painter, and many other painters.

There are other ways to open the Script Painter. For example:

- In the Window Painter, right-click the window or a control in the window and select Script from the pop-up menu that appears. In the User Object Painter, the technique is similar.

- In the Application, select Entry|Script from the menu.
- In the Menu Painter, select Edit|Script from the menu.
- In any of these painters, press Ctrl+K.

You also use the Script Painter to write the code for user-defined functions, which I will describe later in this chapter.

Figure 4-1 shows the PowerScript Painter open on the "clicked" script for a button named cb_if1.

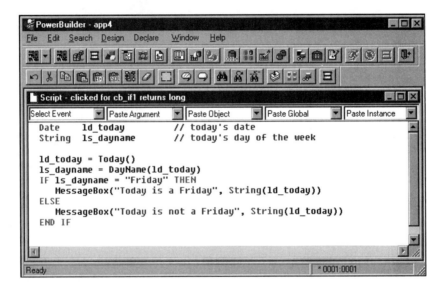

Figure 4-1

A script in the PowerScript Painter.

ELEMENTS OF THE POWERSCRIPT PAINTER

The PowerScript Painter is a text editor that can be navigated via Windows-standard keystrokes, mouse clicks, and scroll bars. PowerBuilder color codes the text as you type it, making it easy to spot misspelled keywords, unmatched quotes, and other mistakes.

DROPDOWN LIST BOXES

Beneath the painter's title bar is a row of dropdown list boxes. They make it easy for you to find the names of things, and with a mouse click, to paste a name into your script.

Depending on your configuration and the type of object, some combination of these seven lists will appear. By default, the first five appear when you are editing a script for a window or control:

1. **Select Event** — the events that can occur to the current object. For each class of object, PowerBuilder assumes that there is a *default event*, for example the "clicked" event for a CommandButton. Whenever you open the PowerScript Painter on an object for the first time, the default event's script will appear. Thereafter, the most recently edited event's script will appear.

   You can move to another script for the current object if you select another script from this dropdown list. The list is alphabetical, with an icon marking events that you have already programmed.

2. **Paste Argument** — the argument variables (parameters) passed to this script by whoever calls it. An event, like a function, has parameters passed to it. Function arguments are described later in this chapter. Event script arguments will be described in Chapter 12.

   With Paste Argument, or with any of the other Paste dropdowns, when you click an item on the list, PowerBuilder immediately copies it into your script at the current insertion point.

3. **Paste Object** — the objects that are in the current window, application, user object, or menu.

4. **Paste Global** — the global variables, both system- and user-defined, that are visible to the current object.

5. **Paste Instance** — the instance variables that are visible to the current object. I will discuss global, instance, and shared variables later in this chapter.

6. **Paste Shared** — the shared variables that are visible to the current object.

7. **Paste Window** — the windows in the application.

You can select which of the seven should appear, and you can rearrange their order. Choose Design|Options from the menu to open the PowerScript property sheet and click its Dropdowns tab.

THE MENU AND PAINTERBAR

The other elements of the PowerScript Painter are its menu and PainterBar. As with all other PowerBuilder menus and PainterBars, these elements include selections and buttons specific to the current context — in this case script editing. The PainterBar buttons are all shortcuts for menu choices. For example, the Paste Statement button is equivalent to the Edit|Paste Statement menu selection.

The menu and PainterBar include these choices:

- **Undo, Cut, Copy, Paste, Clear** — which are operations common to Windows editors and word processors.

- **Select All** — which marks the entire script, prior to an operation such as Cut, Copy, Clear, or Comment.

- **Comment** — which inserts double slashes at the beginning of the current script line or the selected range of lines.

- **Uncomment** — which removes double slashes from a line or range of lines.

- **Paste SQL** — which allows you to select and insert an SQL statement into your script. Chapters 7 and 21 will introduce SQL and its role in scripts.

- **Paste Statement** — which allows you to select and insert an entire program control statement structure, such as *IF...THEN...ELSE* or *CHOOSE...CASE*, into your script. I'll discuss this option in more detail in a later section.

- **Browse Object** — which opens the Browser, a quick reference to all sorts of PowerScript program elements. We walked through an exercise with the Browser in Chapter 3, and it will appear again later in this chapter and in future chapters.

Online Help for PowerScript

PowerBuilder online help offers complete documentation for all PowerScript features, such as functions and reserved words. Search for any function or other topic in the help index. If the name is already in your script, there's an even faster way to get help for it: Click the word to move the insertion point into it and press Shift+F1.

Variables

We've used variables in many examples already. Now let's take a closer look at them.

As in any programming language, a PowerScript variable is a named storage location in your computer's memory. You store a value in the variable, and later you can read and work with the variable's value or change the value to something else.

You can store many different types of data in a PowerScript variable. This script creates six variables, using six of the most commonly used data types, and assigns a value to each:

```
String  s
Integer i
Decimal c
Date    d
Time    t
Boolean b
s = "John Adams"  // string
i = 123           // integer
c = 123.456       // decimal
d = 1995-12-25    // date
t = 23:01:01      // time
b = False         // boolean
```

As you can see, in PowerScript you place quote marks — either single (') or double (") — around literal strings. There are two ways place a quote inside of quotes: Precede the inner quote with a tilde (~) or use the other kind of quote (that is, single or double) to enclose the string. Examples:

```
s = "He said ~"Win one for The Gipper.~""
s = 'He said "Win one for The Gipper."'
s = "He said 'Win one for The Gipper.'"
```

Literal dates and times require a special format: *yyyy-mm-dd* and *hh:mm:ss*, respectively. Literal numbers (123.456) and booleans (True or False) you simply express as is. PowerBuilder understands that anything in the precise format ####-##-## (where each # is a digit), such as 1995-12-25, is a literal date and not integer subtraction.

NULL VALUES

In addition to the values you would normally expect a variable to have, a variable can also value a value of NULL. NULL means "having no value." You can also think of it as meaning "undefined" or "unknown." It is not the same as an empty string or zero or False. A common way for a variable to get a NULL value is when you retrieve its value from a database column that has never been filled in — a missing zip code for a customer, for example.

Any variable, regardless of its type, can be set to NULL using the PowerScript SetNull function. For example, this line of code sets string variable *i1* to NULL:

```
SetNull(i1)
```

Whenever you use a NULL variable in arithmetic, the result of the expression is NULL. For example, suppose that the variable *i1* is NULL:

```
i2 = 7 + i1
```

The result, *i2*, will be NULL. After all, seven plus an unknown value is unknown, not seven. If you want NULL to be treated like zero, extra coding is required. The IsNull function tests whether a value is null:

```
IF IsNull(i1) THEN      // if i1 is null, then
    i2 = 7 + 0          // treat null like zero
ELSE                    // if i1 is not null, then
    i2 = 7 + i1         // use it in the expression
END IF
```

Because of their special behavior, you must always anticipate that null values may be encountered by your script. Make sure that your script deals with nulls effectively!

Chapter 7 will address the topic of NULL values further and demonstrate how to deal with NULL values in a database.

NAMING A VARIABLE

So far I have used only one- and two-character variable names, such as *i*, *i2*, and *s*. But I don't want you to think that no more are allowed, and that PowerScript is therefore restricted to no more than a few dozen possible variable names!

A variable name can be as long as 40 characters. You can choose just about any name you want, as long as the first character is a letter and the remaining characters are letters, digits, or the punctuation characters underscore (_), dollar sign ($), number sign (#), or percent (%).

By default, PowerBuilder also allows you to use dashes (-) in variable names. This means that when you use the subtraction operator (-) or the decrement operator (--) in a script, you must surround it with spaces. To disallow dashes in variable names (which is my preference), select Design|Options from the menu to open the PowerScript property sheet. In the General tab, remove the check mark from "Allow Dashes in Identifiers."

Variable names are not sensitive to case. For example, *PARTNUMBER*, *PartNumber*, *Partnumber*, and *partnumber* all reference the same variable.

DECLARING VARIABLES

The PowerScript compiler requires that every variable be declared. *Declaring variables* means notifying PowerBuilder up front about the names of the variables that your scripts will use and what type of data each will hold.

You can declare variables in either of two places:

- Anywhere within the script. Use this method to declare local variables. By convention, we prefer to place the declarations at the beginning of the script before the first executable statement.

- From the Declare menu in the Window, User Object, Menu, or PowerScript painter. Use this method to declare global, instance, and shared variables.

Global, *instance*, *shared*, and *local* variables are defined under "Variable Scope" later in this chapter.

To declare a variable, enter the data type followed by one or more spaces and the variable name:

```
String  ls_custname
Integer li_counter
```

You can declare multiple variables of the same data type on one line. Use commas between variable names:

```
String ls_name, ls_addr, ls_phone
```

The naming convention that Powersoft follows, and that we also follow, uses a prefix to identify the variable's scope and type. The prefix *ls_* means "local string." The prefix *li_* means "local integer." The tables at the end of this chapter give a complete list of prefixes and describe how to use them.

DATA TYPES

Every variable in a PowerBuilder application must have a specific *data type*. The data type specifies the kind of data that a specific variable can contain, such as a string, an integer, or a date. There are four major categories of data types in the PowerScript language:

1. Standard

2. Enumerated

3. Object class

4. Structure

As you will see, each category contains many data types. In addition, you can define your own class and structure data types.

STANDARD DATA TYPES

There are 15 standard data types supported in PowerScript. They are listed in Table 4-1.

Table 4-1

Standard Data Types

Data Type	Description	Examples
String	A text string of up to 60,000 characters	s = "Hello"
Character or Char	A single character	c = "H"
Integer or Int	A short integer, or more precisely a 16-bit signed integer; a whole number with no fraction in the range −32768 to +32767	i1 = 32000 i2 = -32000
UnsignedInteger, UnsignedInt, or UInt	A 16-bit unsigned integer, in the range 0 to 65535	ui1 = 0 ui2 = 60000
Long	A long integer; a 32-bit signed integer, in the range −2,147,483,648 to +2,147,483,647	l1 = 1000000 l2 = −1000000
UnsignedLong or Ulong	A 32-bit unsigned integer, in the range 0 to 4,294,967,295	ul = 1000000
Decimal or Dec	A signed decimal number of up to 18 digits, with a decimal point anywhere within the 18 digits	dec = 123.45
Real	A signed 32-bit floating-point number with approximately six digits of accuracy and a range from approximately $1.17E{-}38$ to $3.4E{+}38$	r = 123.456
Double	A signed floating-point number with approximately 15 digits of accuracy and a range from approximately $2.2E{-}308$ to $1.7E{+}308$.	dbl = 123.456
Date	A date, with year, month, and day, in the range 1000-01-01 through 3000-12-31	d = 1996-12-25
Time	A time of day, with hour, minute, second, and up to six digits of fractional second, in the range 00:00:00 to 23:59:59.999999	t = 13:50:00
DateTime	A date and time combined in a single variable; PowerScript does not support arithmetic on a DateTime variable, but you can use the Date and Time functions to separate it into separate date and time variables to perform arithmetic; the main use for DateTime is to hold a value of this type retrieved from a database	
Boolean	True or False	b = True
Blob	A Binary Large OBject, used to store an unlimited amount of data such as a large amount of text or a graphic; in some cases, PowerBuilder does not know how to interpret the data and is storing just a large collection of bits and bytes; in other cases, built-in functions, such as BlobEdit and BlobMid, can convert blob data to and from other data types	
Any	A generic data type capable of holding any of the other types of values	

All PowerScript variables declared with a standard data type are assigned an initial value, either by you in their declarations or by PowerBuilder. An initial value is the value that a variable contains when it first comes into existence.

The variable declarations we have seen so far don't specify an initial value. Therefore PowerBuilder assigns them for us based on the data type. For instance, strings are initialized as empty strings(""); integers, decimals, and other numbers as 0; and booleans as False. If you want to override PowerBuilder's initial value for a variable, just include a new value in the variable declaration, as in these examples:

```
String   ls_name     = "Megan"
Date     ld_birthdate = 1986-09-04
Integer  li_age      = 10
```

ENUMERATED DATA TYPES

An *enumerated data type* is a data type with a limited set of special values. For example, "Alignment" is an enumerated data type. A variable of the Alignment type can have one of these four values: center!, justify!, left!, or right! Here's an example of such a variable:

```
Alignment   a  // declare "a" to be an Alignment-type variable
a = left!       // assign one of the four possible values to the var.
st_thetext.Alignment = a    // change a control's property
```

You could make this example even simpler by doing away with the variable and changing the property directly:

```
st_thetext.Alignment = left!
```

In fact, you'll probably use enumerated values such as left! in this way, directly assigning them to properties, much more often than you'll declare variables to hold them. But it's good to know about the possibility of using a variable. You could use one, for example, to shift every text control in a window to a user-specified alignment.

Another common use for enumerated data values is as function arguments, when the function's documentation calls for them. For example, the third argument of the MessageBox function must be an "icon," which is an enumerated variable type with one of five values: exclamation!, information!, none!, question!, or stopsign! It designates which icon should appear in the message box. This example displays an error message with a stop sign symbol in it:

Constants

If you assign an initial value to a variable that will not change during execution, you should consider making the variable a *constant*. A *constant* is essentially a read-only variable. Just add the word "Constant" to the beginning of its declaration:

```
Constant Integer li_age = 10
```

The PowerScript compiler flags any subsequent attempt to change the constant's value as an error. The compiler also replaces all references to the constant with its value at compile time, not at runtime, which typically yields a slight performance improvement over a nonconstant variable.

The data type for a constant must be either a standard data type or an enumerated data type.

```
MessageBox("Warning", "An error has occurred", stopsign!)
```

Since you can always replace a hard-coded value with a variable as a function argument, as long as the variable has the right type, this longer (and less practical) script would do the same thing:

```
Icon  i
i = stopsign!
MessageBox("Warning", "An error has occurred", i)
```

As you can see, every enumerated value ends with an exclamation point (!), which is commonly called a "bang." So stopsign! is pronounced "stop sign bang."

You can see the enumerated data types and their values in the Browser. Click the Browse Object button in the Script PainterBar to open the Browser. Click its Enumerated tab. The left side of the Browser lists the enumerated data types. Double-click Properties in the right-side list to display the values for a given type. This procedure is illustrated in Figure 4-11, later in this chapter.

OBJECT CLASS DATA TYPES

A variable declared with an *object class* data type can be used to reference an object. This subject is somewhat abstract, and I'll postpone a thorough explanation until Chapter 11. In the meantime, here's a brief example.

I have already disclosed that every control within a window is an object, and so is the window itself. Suppose that you have two StaticText controls, st_firstbox and st_secondbox, in a window. They are both objects — StaticText objects — and this script will turn them both red:

```
st_firstbox.BackColor  = 255
st_secondbox.BackColor = 255
```

As an alternative, you can declare a StaticText variable and use it as a reference to these StaticText objects. So this script also turns both controls red:

```
StaticText  st        // declare "st" to be a StaticText variable
st = st_firstbox      // point the variable to the first control
st.BackColor = 255    // turn it red
st = st_secondbox     // point the variable to the second control
st.BackColor = 255    // turn it red
```

Every object type, such as StaticText, is also an object class data type. In other words, you can use it to declare variables.

An important use of object class data types is to declare and create instances of nonvisual objects, especially for user-defined object classes. But now I'm delving deep into object-oriented terminology and concepts! Chapter 11 will provide the definitions and examples.

STRUCTURE DATA TYPES

A *structure* is a programmer-defined variable type. A single structure variable can hold multiple values, somewhat like an array. I will explain structures, and also arrays, later in this chapter.

VARIABLE SCOPE

Whenever you declare a variable, you are specifying not only its name and data type but also its *scope*. The scope of a variable determines two characteristics:

1. **Lifespan** — When does the variable come into existence, how long will it survive, and when will it cease to exist?

2. **Visibility** — What scripts can see, share, and change the variable?

You determine the scope of a variable by deciding where to declare it. Every variable must be declared somewhere within an application. But there are four different places to declare a variable, and the *declaration site* determines the variable's scope. There are four options: local, instance, shared, and global. Table 4-2 summarizes the four options.

Table 4-2
Variable Scope

Variable Scope	Declaration Site	Visibility	Lifespan
Local	Script	To only the script in which it is declared	Until the script terminates
Instance	"Declare Instance Variables" dialog box	To all scripts within a single instance of the object in which it is declared and, optionally, to the entire application (see later)	Until the instance of the object closes
Shared	"Declare Shared Variables" dialog box	To all scripts within all instances of the object in which it is declared	Until the application terminates
Global	"Declare Global Variables" dialog box	To all scripts in an application	Until the application terminates

OPTION #1: LOCAL VARIABLES

One place you can declare variables is within a script. Any variable declared in this manner is a *local* variable. The variable's visibility is restricted: It is visible only to this one script. The variable's lifespan is temporary: It is erased from memory and ceases to exist as soon as the script terminates.

Consider this script, on the clicked event for a button, which adds 1 to a local variable *li_count* and displays its value in a StaticText control:

```
Integer li_count     // local variable
li_count ++
st_local.Text = String(li_count)
```

The prefix *li_* means "local integer." In the programming conventions followed in this book and documented at the end of this chapter, the first letter of a variable identifies its scope: *l* for local, *i* for instance, *s* for shared, or *g* for global.

Since *li_count* ceases to exist when the script terminates, every time you click the button and run the script again, *li_count* is recreated from scratch, with a zero value. And since *li_count* always starts out zero, the statement *li_count* ++ always sets it to 1. So the StaticText control st_local will always display the value 1.

Other variables may have the same name, *li_count*, elsewhere in the application, and they may even exist at the same time. But they have no relation whatsoever to this *li_count* nor to one another. Every *li_count* is a separate and independent variable, with its own separate location in memory, and PowerBuilder keeps track of each one and determines which scripts reference which.

Although this is not a very practical example, local variables are very useful. I find that in my work I declare many more local variables than any of the other three types. In fact, all the variables we have seen in sample scripts up to this point have been local.

Figure 4-2 illustrates the visibility of local variables in relation to scripts. There are two scripts, s1 and s2, in the window w1. Each script declares a local variable *v*. Even though both variables have the same name, they are distinct and independent from each other.

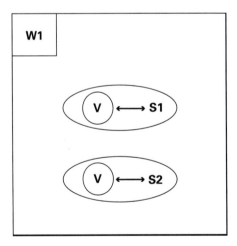

Figure 4-2
Local variables.

OPTION #2: INSTANCE VARIABLES

An *instance variable* is one that belongs to an object such as a window and is visible to all scripts within the object.

For example, if you design a window and attach an instance variable to it, that variable will be available to every script in that window, including the scripts for the window's controls. As long as the window stays open, the variable continues to exist. As soon as the window closes, the variable disappears. If you open the window a second time, a new copy of the variable (which is to say, a new "instance" of it) comes into existence. If you open the window twice at the same time (two "instances" of the window), there are two separate copies of the variable, one for each window. This scenario is illustrated in Figure 4-3. In this figure, the variable *v* is declared as an instance variable for the window w1. All scripts in the window, such as s1 and s2, see the same *v*. But each window has its own *v*, separate and distinct from the other window's.

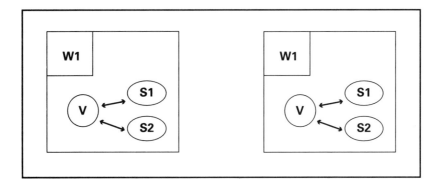

Figure 4-3
Instance variables.

Objects Taking Instance Variables

The preceding example describes a window with an instance variable. Any of these types of objects can have instance variables:

- Applications
- Windows
- Menus
- User objects

Notice that controls do not have instance variables of their own. Instead, controls use the instance variables for the window that contains them. If you need to limit the scope of an instance variable to a single control or group of controls, you can do this through the use of a user object. I will explain this in Chapter 12.

You declare instance variables in the Declare Instance Variables dialog box. The menu choice Declare|Instance Variables, which is available in the PowerScript Painter and in several of the other painters, displays this dialog box.

Access Levels

You can further refine the visibility of an instance variable by specifying one of three *access levels* for it: *public, private,* or *protected.* A private or protected instance variable is visible only to scripts within the object. A public instance variable is visible to the entire application, much like the object's properties. I'll explain these in Chapter 12.

OPTION #3: SHARED VARIABLES

A *shared variable,* like an instance variable, is seen and shared by all the scripts within a window or other object. Unlike an instance variable, there is only one copy of a shared variable no matter how many copies of that object you open. That single variable is seen and shared by all the instances of the object.

Figure 4-4 depicts this relationship. The variable *v* is declared as a shared variable for the window w1. Another *v* is a shared variable for the window w2. These two *v*'s are distinct and independent. However, all the instances of w1, whether open at the same time or open at different times, share the same w1-version of *v*. All instances of w2 would share the other *v*.

A shared variable's lifespan is fairly permanent. It comes into existence when the first instance of its window (or whatever object) opens. However, it does not cease to exist when its window/object closes. It retains its value and remains available the next time an instance of the same window opens, or until the application terminates.

As with instance variables, the following types of objects can have shared variables:

- Applications
- Windows
- Menus
- User objects

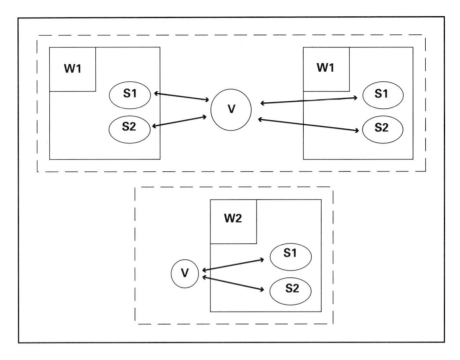

Figure 4-4
Shared variables.

You declare shared variables in the Declare Shared Variables dialog box. The menu choice Declare|Shared Variables displays this dialog box.

OPTION #4: GLOBAL VARIABLES

A *global variable* is a variable that is seen and shared by all scripts attached in all objects in an application. Its lifespan is the same as the lifespan of the application: It comes into existence when the application opens, continues to exist while the application is running, and ceases to exist when the application is closed. In Figure 4-5, *v* is declared as a global variable. Every script in every window in the application sees and shares the same *v*.

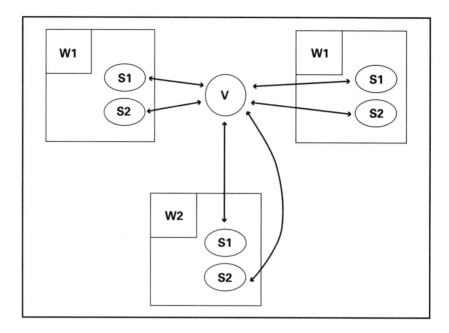

Figure 4-5
Global variables.

Every global variable is associated with the entire application. There is no such thing as a global variable for a window, menu, or user object.

You declare global variables in the Declare Global Variables dialog box. The menu choice Declare|Global Variables opens this dialog box.

Program Control Statements

The scripts we have written so far have a pretty simple flow to them. In most of them, PowerBuilder executes the PowerScript statements one at a time in exactly the order you wrote them.

Programming starts to get a lot more interesting when you alter this one-way, top-to-bottom program flow and introduce blocks of statements that may execute once, or many times, or not at all. To modify the program flow, you use *program control statements* such as IF...END IF and DO...LOOP.

IF...END IF

The simplest program control statement is the IF...END IF statement. Here is an example which, as usual, is the clicked event script for a command button in a window:

```
Date    ld_today        // today's date
String  ls_dayname      // today's day of the week

ld_today = Today()
ls_dayname = DayName(ld_today)
IF ls_dayname = "Friday" THEN
    MessageBox("Today is a Friday", String(ld_today))
ELSE
    MessageBox("Today is not a Friday", String(ld_today))
END IF
```

The overall result of this script is to display one of two dialog boxes, depending on whether today is a Friday. The dialog box also displays today's date and a single OK button.

In between THEN and ELSE, and also between ELSE and END IF, you can put a block of statements, as many as you want, pages and pages of them if need be. Either the first block of statements or the second block, but not both, will execute, depending on whether the condition following the IF is true. Following an IF, the THEN segment is required, but the ELSE segment is optional.

You may place an entire IF...THEN conditional construct on a single line if it fits. In this case you do not terminate the line with END IF:

```
IF ls_dayname = "Friday" THEN i = 0 ELSE i ++
```

To do something when a condition is false, add the word "not" before the condition. The PowerScript compiler may also require that you place parentheses around the condition for clarity:

```
IF not (ls_dayname = "Friday") THEN
    MessageBox("Today is not a Friday", String(ld_today))
END IF
```

Here's another way to do the same thing, using "<>" instead of "not." It does not require parentheses:

```
IF ls_dayname <> "Friday" THEN
    MessageBox("Today is not a Friday", String(ld_today))
END IF
```

A slightly more complex form of the IF...END IF statement is the IF...ELSEIF...ELSE...END IF construct. In the example that follows, the script executes one of four possible blocks of code, depending on whether it's Monday, Wednesday, Friday, or any other day:

```
Date    ld_today        // today's date
String  ls_dayname      // today's day of the week
ld_today = Today()
ls_dayname = DayName(ld_today)
IF ls_dayname = "Monday" THEN
    MessageBox("Today is a Monday", String(ld_today))
ELSEIF ls_dayname = "Wednesday" THEN
    MessageBox("Today is a Wednesday", String(ld_today))
ELSEIF ls_dayname = "Friday" THEN
    MessageBox("Today is a Friday", String(ld_today))
ELSE
    MessageBox("Today is not a Monday, Wednesday, or Friday", &
                String(ld_today))
END IF
```

CHOOSE CASE...END CHOOSE

In PowerScript you can nest one IF...END IF inside another, inside another, to any level, to deal with complex conditions. A simple case is one in which you need to test among many alternatives. You can also use the IF...ELSEIF...ELSE...END IF construct, with any number of ELSEIFs, for the same purpose.

Another approach to the situation in which you must locate the first among many alternatives is to use the CHOOSE CASE...END CHOOSE statement. Here is a script that performs exactly the same function as the previous IF...ELSEIF...ELSE...END IF example. It is a little easier to follow because the variable *ls_dayname* is not repeated for each condition:

```
Date    ld_today        // today's date
String  ls_dayname      // today's day of the week
ld_today = Today()
ls_dayname = DayName(ld_today)
CHOOSE CASE ls_dayname
CASE "Monday"
```

```
      MessageBox("Today is a Monday", String(ld_today))
CASE "Wednesday"
      MessageBox("Today is a Wednesday", String(ld_today))
CASE "Friday"
      MessageBox("Today is a Friday", String(ld_today))
CASE ELSE
      MessageBox("Today is not a Monday, Wednesday, or Friday", &
                 String(ld_today))
END CHOOSE
```

Any number of statements can follow immediately after a CASE line. Only the block of statements after the first CASE condition that is true will be executed. If they are all false, then the statements after CASE ELSE will be executed. The CASE ELSE segment is optional, just as the ELSE segment is optional in IF...END IF.

There are several ways on the CASE line to specify a list of values or a range of values. Examples:

```
CASE 1, 2, 3, 4                 // if it's 1 or 2 or 3 or 4...
CASE 1 TO 4                     // if it's between 1 and 4...
CASE IS < 4                     // if it's less than 4...
CASE 1, 2, 3, 10 TO 15, IS > 50 // if it's 1, 2, or 3,
                                // or between 10 and 15,
                                // or greater than 50...
```

DO...LOOP

With the IF...END IF and CHOOSE CASE...END CHOOSE statements you can make a block of code run either once or not at all. The DO...LOOP statement is a *looping* statement: It causes a block of code to execute over and over repeatedly, any number of times.

The DO...LOOP construct has four different syntaxes, each of which functions slightly differently from the others. These syntaxes are

- DO ... LOOP WHILE <condition>

- DO ... LOOP UNTIL <condition>

- DO WHILE <condition> ... LOOP

- DO UNTIL <condition> ... LOOP

DO...LOOP WHILE

DO...LOOP WHILE *<condition>* repeatedly executes the block of code within the loop while *condition* is true. The condition is not checked until the end of each loop iteration, so the script will always execute the code within the loop at least once.

As an example, here is a script that simulates a baseball game. The standard game length is nine innings. If the score is tied after nine innings, extra innings are played until one team has the lead at the end of an inning. The loop iterates once per inning.

```
Integer li_score1      = 0      // visiting team's score
Integer li_score2      = 0      // home team's score
Integer li_inning_no   = 0      // current inning #
DO
   li_inning_no ++
   li_score1 = li_score1 + Max(0, Rand(24) - 20)
   li_score2 = li_score2 + Max(0, Rand(24) - 20)
LOOP WHILE li_inning_no < 9 OR li_score1 = li_score2
MessageBox("The final score, after "               + &
           String(li_inning_no) + " innings is:",     &
           "Visitors: " + String(li_score1)        + &
           ",  Home: " + String(li_score2))
```

The LOOP WHILE condition in this script says, "loop while we're still in the first eight innings, or (if it's the ninth inning or later) while the two teams have the same score." Within each loop, the score of each team is increased by a random number between 0 and 4, but usually 4. The Rand(24) function returns a random number between 0 and 24. The Max(0,something) function returns either 0 or "something," whichever is greater, thereby ensuring a non-negative result.

Since I've introduced the Rand function here, I should make an important point: When you call Rand repeatedly in a script, it returns a random sequence of numbers, as you would expect. However, if you close the application and run it again, it returns exactly the same sequence! To get a truly random sequence — that is, a different sequence for every run of the application — you must call another function, Randomize, before the first call to Rand. Randomize initializes the Rand function to a random starting point based on the system clock. This is called "providing a seed" to the random number generator.

DO...LOOP UNTIL

DO...LOOP UNTIL *<condition>* is similar to DO...LOOP WHILE *<condition>*, except that it repeatedly executes the block of code within the loop *until* the condition is true. Thus it is equivalent to DO...LOOP WHILE NOT *<condition>*. In the preceding example, we can achieve the same result by replacing this line of code:

```
LOOP WHILE li_inning_no < 9 OR li_score1 = li_score2
```

with this:

```
LOOP UNTIL li_inning_no >= 9 AND li_score1 <> li_score2
```

DO WHILE...LOOP

DO WHILE *<condition>*...LOOP repeatedly executes the block of code within the loop while *condition* is true. The condition is checked at the beginning of each loop iteration, and so the script may not execute the code within the loop at all.

The next script is similar to the previous "baseball game" example. The difference is that this version of the game simulation executes a loop for extra innings only. The two teams' nine-inning scores are obtained via two additional calls to Rand placed before the loop. If one team has more runs after nine innings, the condition *li_score1 = li_score2* will evaluate to False, and the loop will be skipped entirely. Otherwise, as before, the loop will iterate once for each extra inning until one team has more runs than the other.

```
Integer li_score1 = 0    // visiting team's score
Integer li_score2 = 0    // home team's score
Integer li_inning_no = 9 // current inning #
li_score1 = Rand(7) - 1
li_score2 = Rand(7) - 1
DO WHILE li_score1 = li_score2
   li_score1 = li_score1 + Max(0, Rand(24) - 20)
   li_score2 = li_score2 + Max(0, Rand(24) - 20)
   li_inning_no ++
LOOP
MessageBox("The final score, after "             + &
           String(li_inning_no) + " innings is:",    &
           "Visitors: " + String(li_score1)     + &
           ",  Home: " + String(li_score2))
```

DO UNTIL...LOOP

DO UNTIL *<condition>*...LOOP is similar to DO WHILE
<condition>...LOOP, except that it repeatedly executes the block of code
within the loop *until* the condition is true. Thus it is equivalent to DO
WHILE NOT *<condition>*...LOOP.

FOR...NEXT

The FOR...NEXT statement is another looping command, like DO...LOOP.
The latter is somewhat open-ended; it loops an undetermined number of
times, until some condition changes. FOR...NEXT is more precise: It loops
a predetermined number of times and counts the loops as it goes.

Here is another variation on the baseball game example, played
between persnickety teams whose players refuse to play more than nine
innings:

```
Integer li_score1 = 0    // visiting team's score
Integer li_score2 = 0    // home team's score
Integer li_inning_no     // current inning #
FOR li_inning_no = 1 TO 9
    li_score1 = li_score1 + Max(0, Rand(24) - 20)
    li_score2 = li_score2 + Max(0, Rand(24) - 20)
NEXT
MessageBox("The score after 9 innings is:",       &
           "Visitors: " + String(li_score1)    + &
           ",  Home: " + String(li_score2))
```

The FOR statement in this case, FOR *li_inning_no* = 1 TO 9, instructs
PowerBuilder to perform the loop while counting from 1 to 9. So the loop
will be executed exactly nine times, which is once for each inning.

In this statement, *li_inning_no* supplies PowerBuilder with a *counter
variable* — a variable that is used to count the loops. Thus in the first
pass, *li_inning_no* will be 1, in the second pass it will be 2, and so on.

EXIT

Sometimes you may want your script to detect a situation in the middle of
a DO...LOOP or FOR...NEXT that requires the looping to be terminated

prematurely. In this case, you can issue the EXIT command. This special command jumps control out of the loop and continues with whatever statement follows the end of the loop.

For example, here is an enhancement to the DO...LOOP WHILE example shown earlier. I have added an IF...THEN EXIT inside the loop. The result is that control will jump out of the loop under a certain condition. (The condition is that if the home team has the higher score before their turn to play in the ninth inning, then the game ends early.)

```
Integer li_score1 = 0     // visiting team's score
Integer li_score2 = 0     // home team's score
Integer li_inning_no = 0  // current inning #
DO
    li_inning_no ++
    li_score1 = li_score1 + Max(0, Rand(24) - 20)
    IF (li_inning_no = 9) AND (li_score1 < li_score2) THEN EXIT
    li_score2 = li_score2 + Max(0, Rand(24) - 20)
LOOP WHILE li_inning_no < 9 or li_score1 = li_score2
MessageBox("The final score, after "              + &
           String(li_inning_no) + " innings is:",   &
           "Visitors: " + String(li_score1)        + &
           ",  Home: " + String(li_score2))
```

CONTINUE

The CONTINUE command, like EXIT, interrupts a loop in progress, but it is not as extreme as EXIT. Whereas EXIT terminates all remaining iterations of the loop, CONTINUE terminates only the current iteration; it continues with the next iteration, if there are more to do.

Here is a variation on the previous example that utilizes the CONTINUE statement. At the start of each loop iteration it evaluates boolean variable *lb_game_over* to decide whether to perform another iteration (or inning). The last statement in the loop sets *lb_game_over* to True if we've played nine or more innings. However, the previous statement executes a CONTINUE — immediately forcing another loop iteration regardless of the inning number — if the score is tied.

```
Integer li_score1 = 0         // visiting team's score
Integer li_score2 = 0         // home team's score
Integer li_inning_no = 0      // current inning #
Boolean lb_game_over = False  // True, if the game is over
DO UNTIL lb_game_over
```

```
        li_inning_no ++
        li_score1 = li_score1 + Max(0, Rand(24) - 20)
        IF (li_inning_no = 9) AND (li_score1 < li_score2) THEN EXIT
        li_score2 = li_score2 + Max(0, Rand(24) - 20)
        IF li_score1 = li_score2 THEN CONTINUE
        lb_game_over = (li_inning_no >= 9)
LOOP
MessageBox("The final score, after "                    + &
            String(li_inning_no) + " innings is:",      &
            "Visitors: " + String(li_score1)            + &
            ",  Home: " + String(li_score2))
```

The EXIT and CONTINUE statements can be placed only inside loops.
Because of their dramatic effect upon the loop, the only practical place
for either of them is inside an IF or CHOOSE CASE statement nested within the loop.

RETURN

The RETURN statement terminates the script or function, returning control to whatever called it. If it's an event script, RETURN typically returns
control to PowerBuilder.

If the script or function returns a value, as you will see in the section
on user-defined functions later in this chapter, the RETURN statement
must include the value.

HALT

The HALT statement unconditionally terminates the application. Some
people use HALT as their preferred way of handling errors. I prefer friendlier error recovery, however, and so I rarely use HALT.

HALT CLOSE

The HALT CLOSE statement, like HALT, unconditionally terminates the application. But first it executes the application's close script, if there is one.

GOTO

PowerScript includes a GOTO statement that jumps control from one statement to another within a script. Like many people, I recommend avoiding GOTO, because it makes program flow difficult to follow. I do make one exception, allowing a limited use of GOTO to streamline error handling. I will describe this technique in Chapter 17 on the CD-ROM.

Arrays

A traditional variable, such as the ones we've seen so far, is a single storage location in memory that can hold no more than one value at a time. However, PowerScript provides a few special types of variables that can store multiple values. The best known of these is the *array*.

An array is a special variable that holds many storage locations, not just one. Thus, in a single array, you could store, for example, all the presidents' names, or all their birthdays, or all the Friday the thirteenths in this century.

An array can be single- or multidimensional. Single-dimensional arrays can have a fixed size or a variable size, whereas multidimensional arrays must have a fixed size. Arrays may be of any data type and are declared in a manner similar to single-value variables.

To create an array, follow the array name in its declaration statement with a pair of square brackets. If the brackets contain one or more numbers, it is a fixed-size array. If the brackets are empty, it is a variable-size array:

```
String ls_presname[42]      // fixed-sized array
Date   ld_fri13th[]         // variable-sized array
Dec    ldec_wktemp[7,24]    // two-dimensional fixed-sized array
Dec    ldec_daytemp[0 to 23]  // one-dimensional fixed-sized array
```

To place or use a specific element within an array, you must follow the array name with an *index*, in square brackets. The index must contain as many integers, separated by commas, as there are dimensions to the array. In the case of fixed-size arrays, that index must be within the range or size specified in the declaration.

Here are some examples of valid array element specifications, based on the array declarations just given:

```
ls_presname[1]     = "George Washington"
ls_presname[16]    = "Abraham Lincoln"
ld_fri13th[14]     = 1996-12-13
ld_fri13th[60000]  = 2234-09-13
ldec_wktemp[3,24]  = 57.3
ldec_daytemp[0]    = 48.9
```

In these examples, every array index is an integer constant. However, any array index can also be an integer variable, for instance:

```
Integer i
String  ls_the_name
i = 16
ls_the_name = ls_presname[i]
```

Or it can be an arithmetic expression that results in an integer:

```
ls_the_name = ls_presname[i+1]
```

An index for a fixed-size array must be within the *bounds*, or allowable range, defined by the array declaration. For a variable-size array, the index must be at least 1 and cannot be above its largest assigned value or below its lowest assigned value. These are examples of invalid or possibly invalid array element specifications, based on the declarations earlier in this section:

```
ls_presname[0]     = "None"            // valid range is 1 to 42
ls_presname[43]    = "None yet"        // valid range is 1 to 42
ld_fri13th[0]      = 1900-01-13        // valid range starts at 1
d                  = ld_fri13th[60001] // may be a problem if we've only
                                       // assigned up to dFri13th[60000]
ldec_wktemp[3,25]  = 57.3              // valid range is [1,1] to [7,24]
ldec_daytemp[-1]   = 48.9              // valid range is 0 to 23
```

If an index value is outside the allowable range for its array — a common programming bug, especially when the index is a variable — you will get an error. The error is caught while you are running the application, not while you are compiling or saving the script. Figure 4-6 shows the error dialog box that is displayed if you click the Bad Array Elements button in this chapter's sample application.

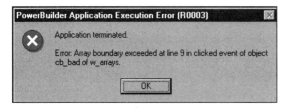

Figure 4-6
An "Array boundary exceeded" error.

Is there a limit to how big an array can be? Yes, but it's a pretty benign limit! A single-dimensional array can hold approximately two gigabytes of elements. Note that this is the total amount of data, not the number of elements. Each dimension of a multidimensional array can have two gigabytes of elements. However, you should be aware that these are PowerBuilder's limits. In reality you'll probably run out of hardware resources long before you reach that limit.

As with single-value variables, you can assign initial values to arrays when you declare them. Place the initial values in curly braces as shown in these examples:

```
String ls_strings[3] = {"Larry","Curly","Moe"}
Date ld_dates[4] =    {1949-07-25, &
                       1953-08-21, &
                       1955-06-04, &
                       1954-12-08}
Int li_primes[] =      {2,5,7,11,13,17,23,29}
```

Structures

Arrays are not the only variables that can hold multiple storage values. Another such variable is the *structure*. Unlike an array, which has a single variable name and a range of numeric index values, a structure is composed of many variable names that are related in some way. These variables may be of different data types.

Here is any example of a structure whose variables describe a fruit:

```
lstr_fruit.s_name = "Apple"
```

```
lstr_fruit.s_color = "Red"
lstr_fruit.b_ha._seeds = True
```

In this example, *s_name*, *s_color*, and *b_has_seeds* are the three variables that make up the structure. *lstr_fruit* is the "structure instance" and is itself a variable, like an array. You might describe a structure as a "variable composed of variables."

Creating a structure is a two-step process. Step 1 is to define the structure data type; that is, define the list of variables that the structure contains, and give a name to this type of structure. Step 2 is to declare the structure variable.

To define a structure data type, open the Structure Painter, shown in Figure 4-7, by clicking the Structure button on the PowerBar. In this painter, type in the names and data types of the variables that make up the structure. Then save the structure with a name that is unique for the application. The rules for naming variables and objects apply to these names. My convention is to begin the name of each variable with a prefix identifying its type, such as *s_* for string and *d_* for date, and to begin the structure data type with the prefix *s_*.

Figure 4-7 shows a structure data type named s_president as it looks in the Structure Painter. This structure contains four variables: three strings (last name, first name, and party) and one date (birthdate).

Var Insert	Variable Name	Type		Decimal
	s_lastname	string	▼	
	s_firstname	string	▼	
	d_birthdate	date	▼	
	s_party	string	▼	
			▼	

Structure - s_president

Figure 4-7
The s_president structure.

At this point, the structure you have painted, such as s_president, is actually a new variable data type, a "programmer-defined" data type. You use it to declare one or more variables ("instances" of the structure) in your application, in the same way that you declare any variable. This statement declares *lstr_pres* to be a variable of type s_president:

Global and Local Structure Definitions

You can make a structure definition, such as the one in Figure 4-7, either global to the entire application or local to a single window (or other object). To make the structure definition global, click the Structure button on the PowerBar. To make it local, select Declare|Window Structures from the Window Painter menu.

Declaring a structure instance is just like declaring any variable, and you have the same four scope options: local, instance, shared, or global. It makes sense that you can only declare a structure instance in a place where its structure definition is visible. For example, you can't use one window's local structure definitions in another window's variable declarations.

```
s_president  lstr_pres    // presidential structure
```

I use the prefix *lstr_* for "local structure variable."

Once the structure variable *lstr_pres* is declared, use dot notation to refer to its elements:

```
lstr_pres.s_lastname    = "Washington"
lstr_pres.s_firstname   = "George"
lstr_pres.d_birthdate   = 1732-02-22
lstr_pres.s_party       = "Federalist"
```

The structure definition s_president is a global structure definition, similar in scope to a global variable. You can also define structure data types that are available only to the scripts within one object such as a window. While in the Script Painter for a script in a window, select Declare|Window Structures from the menu to define a structure that will be available only to that window.

In Chapter 7, I will show an example of how to use a structure to retrieve all the rows and columns of a database table into a single variable in memory.

Copying Arrays and Structures

A powerful, and easily overlooked, PowerScript feature is the ability to copy all elements of an array or structure to another array or structure with a single assignment statement. Here is an example of an assignment statement that copies structure elements:

```
s_president lstr_pres, lstr_pres2 // two structures of the same type
lstr_pres.s_lastname    = "Washington"
lstr_pres.s_firstname   = "George"
lstr_pres.d_birthdate   = 1732-02-22
lstr_pres.s_party       = "Federalist"
lstr_pres2 = lstr_pres              // copy the first structure into the second
```

Assuming that s_president contains only the four variables shown, the last line of this script is equivalent to these four lines, which copy each element one by one:

```
lstr_pres2.s_lastname    = lstr_pres.s_lastname
lstr_pres2.s_firstname   = lstr_pres.s_firstname
lstr_pres2.d_birthdate   = lstr_pres.d_birthdate
lstr_pres2.s_party       = lstr_pres.s_party
```

You can copy array elements in a similar manner. For instance, in this script:

```
String s1[3], s2[3]
s1[1]   = "Alpha"
s1[2]   = "Beta"
s1[3]   = "Gamma"
s2      = s1
```

the last line is equivalent to

```
s2[1]   = s1[1]
s2[2]   = s1[2]
s2[3]   = s1[3]
```

Pronouns: *This, Parent, ParentWindow, and Super*

The PowerScript language includes four special words called the *pronouns*. You use them in scripts to make general references to objects, in place of hard-coding the actual names of those objects. The PowerScript pronouns are:

- ***This*** — The pronoun *This* refers to the object that contains the script. For example, the following code in the clicked event for a CommandButton slides the button to the right:

```
This.X = This.X + 50
```

- ***Parent*** — When you use *Parent* in a script for a control, it refers to the window that contains the control. For example, the following line of code in the "clicked" script for a CommandButton closes the window that contains the button:

```
Close(Parent)
```

There are other uses for Parent: In a script for a control in a user object, Parent refers to the user object. In a script for a menu item, Parent refers to the next higher menu item.

- ***ParentWindow*** — You use *ParentWindow* only in scripts for MenuItems, which are the individual choices within a menu. As you will learn in Chapter 15, you design a menu for your application by defining its MenuItems and associating it with a window. The *ParentWindow* pronoun refers to that window. Here is the script for a File|Close MenuItem, which closes the window:

```
Close(ParentWindow)
```

- ***Super*** — The pronoun *Super* is used in conjunction with inheritance, a concept I'll explain in detail in Chapter 13. It allows a descendant object to reference its ancestor.

Functions

A *function* is a subprogram, a program module that is defined once and called from many places in your application. It's smart programming to call a function rather than to replicate many copies of the same program code.

There are three types of functions in PowerBuilder:

- Built-in functions
- External functions
- User-defined functions

BUILT-IN FUNCTIONS

The PowerScript language comes with approximately 400 *built-in func-tions* that perform such diverse operations as converting data types, manipulating objects, communicating with databases, and controlling data window behavior. You have already seen a number of examples of built-in functions in this book. For example:

- **MessageBox** — displays a system MessageBox with a title, text and at least one button.
- **String** — converts a date, time, or number to a string.
- **DayName** — determines the name of the day of the week for a date; for example, DayName*(1994-07-03)* returns "Monday".
- **Rand** — generates a random number between 1 and a specified upper limit.

You use a built-in function in your script by making a *function call*. A *function call* is simply the name of the function with its parameters in parentheses. Here are some examples:

- A function call as its own line of code:

```
MessageBox("Greetings", "Hello World")
```

- A function call as an expression in an assignment statement:

```
ls_dayname = DayName(ld_todays_date)
```

- A function call embedded as a parameter within another function call:

```
MessageBox("Today is", String(ld_todays_date))
```

The built-in PowerScript functions come in two varieties:

- **System functions** — which are independent of any object
- **Object functions** — which operate on a specific object

Let's look at system functions first, and then object functions.

SYSTEM FUNCTIONS

The syntax for a system function call is

```
<function name>(<parameter list>)
```

where

- ***Function name*** is the name of the built-in function; for example: MessageBox, DayName.
- ***Parameter list*** is a list of variables, constants, and expressions, separated by commas. Each built-in function expects a specific number of required parameters and optional parameters — either number may be zero. The parameters, also called *arguments*, must be listed in a specific order as specified in the "PowerScript Functions" chapter of the *PowerScript Reference* manual. For example:

  MessageBox expects two required parameters (*title* and *text*) and up to three optional parameters (*icon*, *button*, *default*).

  DayName expects one required parameter (*date*) and no optional parameters.

In addition, every built-in system function has a *return value*, that is, a value that can be retrieved by the calling script after the function has executed. In your script, you can use the return value in several ways, such as these:

- Storing it in a variable:

```
ls_dayname = DayName(ld_today)
```

- Embedding it in an expression, as part of an assignment or program control statement:

```
ls_today_message = "Today is " + String(ld_today)
IF DayName(ld_today) = "Sunday" THEN ls_status = "Closed"
```

- Ignoring it completely, by calling the function as a standalone statement:

```
MessageBox("It's Sunday", "The store is closed.")
```

The data type for the return value is function-dependent. For example:

- **String,** as you might expect, returns a string.
- **MessageBox** returns an integer indicating the number of the button that was clicked by the user, or –1 if an error occurs. In the simple one-button scenario, which is the default, MessageBox returns 1.

Other functions return different data types — including dates, booleans, and enumerated data types. Each function's return value is described in the "PowerScript Functions" chapter of the *PowerScript Reference* manual.

OBJECT FUNCTIONS

Object functions were described in Chapter 3. Their syntax is

```
<object name>.<function name>(<parameter list>)
```

Like system functions, object functions have a name, a parameter list, and a return value. The new element in this type of function call is the *object name*, which is the name of an object of a class specific to the function.

For example, in Chapter 3 I described an object function Resize that changes the size of a control:

```
st_FirstBox.Resize(300,500)
```

When this statement executes, it changes the static text control st_firstbox to be 300 PowerBuilder Units wide and 500 units tall. And in terms of the syntax that I've been discussing

- *st_firstbox* is the object name.

- *Resize* is the function name.

- *(300,500)* is the parameter list.

- The **return value** is an integer: 1 if the function call succeeds, –1 if an error occurs. I've chosen to ignore it in this instance, but only because I know that PowerBuilder won't have any problems handling the number of units that I've specified.

EXTERNAL FUNCTIONS

PowerScript can call functions written in another language such as C++ and stored in Dynamic Link Libraries (DLLs). From PowerScript's perspective, these are called *external functions*.

In order to use an external function, you must first declare it and specify its calling syntax. Use the menu choice Declare|Global External Functions, available in many painters, to declare it and make it available to all scripts in your application. Use Declare|Local External Functions, also available to many painters, to declare it and associate it with a window or other object, similar to the object functions just described. Once an external function is declared, you call it in much the same way as a built-in function.

Refer to the *PowerScript Reference* manual for more information.

USER-DEFINED FUNCTIONS

User-defined functions are functions that you, the programmer, create within your application. Like a built-in function, a user-defined function is called from within a script, expects a specific number of parameters, and returns a value. The return value is optional. You can define a function to be global to the entire application, or you can associate it with a window or other object.

Suppose that you want to create a user-defined function named "f_add3" that adds three integers together and returns their sum:

```
i = f_add3(1, 2, 3)    // this should return i = 6
```

Func

To create this as a global function, click the Function button on the PowerBar. Click New on the Select Function dialog that appears to open the New Function dialog box shown in Figure 4-8. In this dialog, describe the syntax of the function:

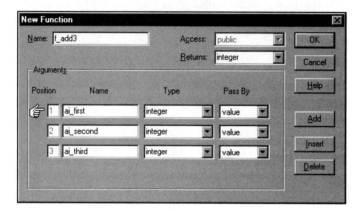

Figure 4-8

The New Function dialog box.

- **Name** —Type in the name of the function; in this case, "f_add3."

- **Access** —This is not used for a global function, but only for an object-oriented, user-defined function of a type that is described in the next section.

- **Returns** —Type in the data type returned by the function, or choose it from the dropdown list. If the function does not return a value, choose "(None)," which you will find at the bottom of the list. The f_add3 function returns an integer.

- **Arguments** — Describe each argument to be passed to the function. Use the Add and Insert buttons to add arguments to the list and the Delete button to remove them.

- **Argument Name** —Type in a name for each argument. I've chosen to name f_add3's arguments *ai_first*, *ai_second*, and *ai_third*. The prefix *ai_* means "integer argument."

- **Argument Type** — Specify the type for each argument. Each of the three arguments for f_add3 is an integer.

- **Argument Pass By** — Select one of three possible values:
  - **Value** — One-way argument passing: The calling script passes a copy of the argument value into the function. Changes the function makes to the argument value are not passed back to the caller.
  - **Reference** — Two-way argument passing: Changes the function makes to the argument value are passed back to the caller.
  - **Read-only** — One-way, that read-only argument passing: The function treats the argument value as a constant that cannot be changed.

(At a deeper level, here's how value, reference, and read-only work: With a value argument, PowerBuilder makes a copy of the value into a new variable, and that variable is local to the function's program code; since it's a separate variable, changes made by the function have no effect on the caller. With a reference argument, PowerBuilder passes the memory address of the caller's variable into the function, so the function has access to and can change the caller's variable. A read-only argument is the same as a reference argument, except that PowerBuilder does not let the function's program code change its value.)

For the Returns and Argument Type choices, you are not limited to the choices on the dropdown lists, which include the standard data types such as integer, string, and date, along with a few object class types such as window. You may also type in other data types, such as enumerated data types, structures, and other user-defined object class types.

After you supply this information, as shown in Figure 4-8, click OK to open the Function Painter, which is essentially the Script Painter with a few minor differences. The Function Painter has a dropdown list for pasting the names of the function's arguments into the script. It also has an Edit Function Declaration button on the PainterBar and an equivalent Design|Function Declaration menu choice, which displays the function declaration syntax (Figure 4-8) again for review and modification.

You type in the program code for a function just as you would for any script. You can use its arguments as variables. If the function returns a value, you must include a RETURN statement to pass the value back.

Here is the script for the f_add3 function:

```
Integer i1, i2
i1 = ai_first + ai_second
i2 = i1 + ai_third
RETURN i2
```

This script is longer than it needs to be. But it does illustrate how a function script is no different than the event scripts we have written up to now. If you prefer, you can write this one-line script that accomplishes the same result:

```
RETURN ai_first + ai_second + ai_third
```

OBJECT-ORIENTED, USER-DEFINED FUNCTIONS

Because we used the Function button on the PowerBar to define it, the f_add3 function is a global function. It is not tied to any particular object, and you can call it from anywhere in the application.

You can also create user-defined functions that are tied to a specific object: a window, a user object, a menu, or the application object. To do this from the Window Painter, for example, select Declare|Window Functions from the menu. After that, the process is the same as for a global function.

Any script within the object can call the function just as if it were global. Scripts outside the object may or may not be able to call the function using dot notation, depending on the Access you specify in the New Function dialog box (Figure 4-8).

I will describe object-oriented, user-defined functions in detail in Chapter 12.

More PowerScript Painter Features

Now that I've covered all the PowerScript language elements, let's revisit a couple of features of the PowerScript Painter that I mentioned earlier: Paste Statement, Paste Function, and the Browser. With each of these features, you can browse PowerScript language elements and review their syntax. You can also paste the selected element, such as an IF...END IF statement or a function call, into your script.

PASTE STATEMENT

When you click the Paste Statement button on the PainterBar or choose Edit|Paste Statement from the menu, the Paste Statement dialog box opens. (See Figure 4-9.) It displays the various program control statements that I described earlier in this chapter. You can paste a prototype of one of these statements, such as an IF...THEN...ELSE...END IF construct, into your script by clicking its radio button and then the OK button.

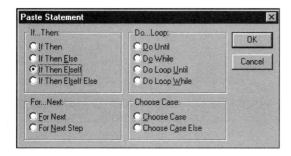

Figure 4-9
The Paste Statement dialog box.

PASTE FUNCTION

Click Paste Function on the PainterBar or select Edit|Paste Function from the menu to pop up the list of functions shown in Figure 4-10. It can display all types of functions: built-in (system and object), user-defined (only global, not object-oriented), and external (only global, not local). When you select a function and click OK, PowerBuilder pastes it and a description of its arguments into your script.

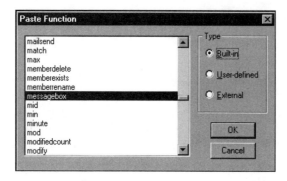

Figure 4-10
The Paste Function dialog box.

THE BROWSER

Click Browser on the PowerBar, click Browse Object on the PainterBar, or select Design|Browse Object from the menu to open the Browser. The Browser provides the most extensive lists of PowerBuilder elements.

Figure 4-11 shows the Browser, listing the enumerated data types on the left, and the values (called "Properties" here) for the alignment type on the right. Some of the elements are arranged in a tree structure. Double-click an element to expand or contract the tree below it. Click the Paste button to paste a selected element into your script. Clicking Paste in Figure 4-11 would paste "left!" into the script.

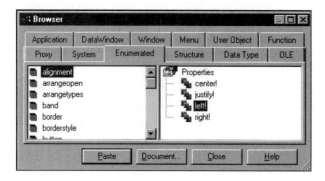

Figure 4-11
The Browser.

Each tab across the top of the Browser displays a different set of PowerBuilder elements:

- **Application** — the application object, with its properties, events, functions, and so on.

- **DataWindow** — the DataWindow objects that you've developed, with their properties and functions.

- **Window** — the windows that you've developed, with their properties, events, functions, instance variables, shared variables, and structures. Double-click a window to see the controls it contains.

- **Menu** — the menus that you've developed, with their properties, events, functions, and so on. Double-click a menu to expand its menu tree, displaying the MenuItems it contains one level at a time.

- **User Object** — the user objects that you've developed, with their properties, events, functions, and so on. Double-click a user object to see the controls it contains.

- **Function** — the global user-defined functions that you've developed. To see object-oriented, user-defined functions, click the object's tab — for example, click the Window tab to see a window's functions.

- **Proxy** — the proxies that you've developed as part of a distributed PowerBuilder application.

- **System** — a list of the most commonly used PowerBuilder object classes, such as the types of controls, with their properties and functions.

- **Enumerated** — a list of the enumerated data types and their values.

- **Structure** — the structure data types that you've developed, and the variables that they contain.

- **Data Type** — a list of the standard data types, such as string, integer, and date.

- **OLE** — the list of OLE objects available to your application.

In the System tab and some of the others, you can right-click an element on the left-hand list and pick Show Hierarchy from the pop-up menu to switch to an object-oriented display. In this style of display, the list is arranged into a tree of ancestor objects and their descendants. We'll explore this arrangement in the chapters on object-oriented programming, beginning with Chapter 11.

For an exercise that uses the Browser to paste elements into a script, refer back to Chapter 3. (See Figures 3-13, 3-14, and 3-15.)

POWERSCRIPT PAINTER CONVENTIONS

You should note that the PowerScript Painter's tools for pasting elements into scripts, such as Paste Statement and the Browser, follow specific conventions in terms of upper- and lowercase. For example:

- Paste Statement inserts everything in uppercase.
- Paste Function and the Browser paste everything in lowercase.

There is no way to modify these conventions. For example, if you prefer "Choose Case" or "choose case," Paste Statement won't be too useful for you, since it always pastes "CHOOSE CASE." For that reason, most PowerBuilder users adopt a personal coding style consistent in most cases with these tools.

The PowerScript Compiler

Before you can run your PowerScript source code in an application, PowerBuilder compiles it into lower-level instructions, which it executes at runtime. When you run the application for development, the lower-level code (or *p-code*) is not the machine language object code that some language compilers generate, but it is nevertheless quite fast. When you deploy your application into production, as I will show in Chapter 16, you have a choice of compiling into p-code or into object code.

After you write or modify an event script or function, PowerBuilder will compile it before it is executed. It compiles your script at one of two times, whichever comes first:

1. When you click the Compile PainterBar button, select Design|Compile Script from the PowerScript Painter menu, or press Ctrl+L

2. When you close the PowerScript Painter window. In this case, PowerBuilder compiles only if the script is new or has been modified.

The PowerScript compiler checks your script for errors. These errors, called *compiler errors*, could be such things as a misspelled variable name or a DO without a matching LOOP. Any errors detected by the compiler are listed at the bottom of the PowerScript Painter window under the heading Errors. As long as there is a compiler error, PowerBuilder will not allow you to save your script.

For each error, the following information is displayed: script line number, error code, and error description. You can move quickly to an offending line in your script if you click its entry in the *Errors* section.

A long list of errors can seem overwhelming, but often it's caused by a single mistake in your script. For instance, if you forget to declare a variable, or if you misspell the variable name in the declaration, the compiler will flag every line that references it. By simply declaring the variable or correcting its spelling in the declaration, you can make all of these errors disappear.

You can turn off some compiler error messages if they are distracting. Select Design|Options from the menu to open the PowerScript property sheet. Its General tab has various check boxes that control error messages. For example, uncheck the Display Compiler Warnings option to eliminate messages about undeclared variables. Later, checkmark Display Compiler Warnings again to restore these messages.

Documenting Your Scripts

Since scripts and variable declarations are scattered all around your application, how do you ever find everything? How do you print them out all in one place for documentation?

First of all, while you are in the PowerScript Painter editing a script, you can identify all the other scripts for that same object. Click the Select Event dropdown list at the top of the editor window. As we've already explained, those scripts containing code will have an icon beside their names.

To obtain a printout of an open script, select File|Print from the PowerScript Painter menu. Even better, you can document all the source code associated with a window if you select File|Print from the Window Painter menu. The resulting listing is quite comprehensive, including these features:

- .PBL path name, last update date/time, and a picture of the window
- Window properties, shared and instance variable declarations
- For each object: properties and script listings

To produce this printout for all objects in the library (.PBL file), follow these steps:

1. Open the Library Painter.
2. Double-click the .PBL name, if necessary, to display the list of objects within it.
3. Select Library|Select All to mark the list of objects.
4. Select Entry|Print to produce the printout. A dialog box will allow you select which information to include.

PowerScript Programming Standards

Every programming team, even if that team is only one person, should adopt programming standards: naming conventions, rules for source code layout, and so forth. The standards that my group has adopted, and that you see followed throughout this book, are very similar to those recommended and used by Powersoft itself.

SCRIPT LAYOUT

The "script layout" conventions enforce a common appearance for all scripts: how to document each script in its "header section," where to declare variables, where to put comments, how use white space, and whether to use GOTO.

THE HEADER SECTION

Begin each script or function with a block of comments describing the function's purpose, revision history, arguments, and return value. Declare the local variables at the end of this block of comments before the first line of executable code. Listing 4-1 shows an outline of this header section.

Listing 4-1
The script or function header section

```
//  Function Name:  f_ThisFunction

//  This comment describes the purpose of this
//  function.  It may take several lines to fully describe.

//  Revision History:
//     mm/dd/yy — Person's name
//                   Brief description of the revision

//  Arguments:
//     as_text      // description of argument as_text
//     ai_num       // description of argument ai_num

//  Return Values:
//     True         // description of condition that returns True
//     False        // description of condition that returns False

//  Local Variables:
Boolean  lb_ok      // description of local variable lb_ok
Integer  li_count   // description of local variable li_count
String   ls_name    // description of local variable ls_name
```

VARIABLE DECLARATIONS

Declare each variable on a separate line. Add an in-line comment to each declaration line describing the variable, as shown in the last three lines of Listing 4-1.

When declaring public instance variables, explicitly declare them as "Public:" just as you would declare them private or protected. Don't rely on the fact that public is the default.

WHITE SPACE AND LINE LENGTH

Place at least one space on each side of an operator (+, -, *, /, =, <=, and so on).

Use indentation for the lines of code within control blocks such as IF...END IF and DO...WHILE. Use tabs to indent. In the PowerScript Painter, a tab indents three spaces.

No line of code should be longer than 68 characters. This allows you to read the line in the PowerScript Painter without horizontal scrolling, with a standard Painter configuration and a 640 x 480–resolution VGA monitor. (Exception: an in-line comment may extend farther to the right.)

Use the continuation character (&), if necessary, to wrap a long statement onto multiple lines. Indent a continuation line at least three spaces.

COMMENTS

Use in-line comments liberally to describe individual lines of code.

Break long scripts and functions into sections. Precede each section with a full-line comment, explaining the section's purpose. Add a blank line above and below the comment so that the beginning of the section is easy to see.

Do not indent full-line comments, even when they fall within an indented block of code.

Do not use the /* comment symbol to extend a single comment across more than one line. This practice makes it too hard to determine what's a comment and what isn't. Instead, precede each line with the // comment symbol.

GOTO

Do not use the GOTO command, because it makes program flow difficult to follow, leading to bugs and maintenance headaches. There is one exception: We allow GOTO in order to jump to the bottom of a script or a function when a fatal error has occurred. For example:

```
... <the script begins here> ...
IF <an error has occurred> THEN
    ls_errormessage = "An error occurred when <doing something>"
    GOTO ErrorHandler
END IF
... <if there is no error, the script continues>
RETURN    // successful completion

//  Error handling

ErrorHandler:
MessageBox("Error", ls_errormessage, stopsign!)  // display error
```

The GOTO labels should always begin with the prefix "Error." A GOTO should always jump down, never up. In particular, a GOTO should never jump from the error handling block back up into the main body of the script.

UPPER- AND LOWERCASE

Table 4-3 lists the conventions for when to use uppercase and when to use lowercase.

Table 4-3

Upper- and Lowercase Conventions

Language Element	Case	Example
Property	Leading cap	sle_1.BackColor
Boolean values	Leading cap	True, False
Comment - full-line	Leading cap	// This is a comment
Comment - in-line	Lower	i = 0 // initialize it
Data type, in a declaration	Leading caps	Integer i DateTime dt
Enumerated data type	Leading caps	Alignment!, DwBuffer!, Pointer!
Enumerated data value	Lower	center!, primary!, hourglass!
Event	Lower	clicked
Function - built-in	Leading caps	MessageBox(...)
Function - user-defined	Lower	(see "Naming Conventions" later)
Instance variable access level	Leading cap	Public:
Keyword in PowerScript	All caps	IF, THEN, DO, RETURN

Keyword in SQL	All caps	SELECT custid
		    FROM customer
		      WHERE city = 'Omaha'

Object or control	Lower	(see "Naming Conventions" later)
Pronoun	Leading cap	This, Parent
Structure	Lower	(see "Naming Conventions" later)
Variable	Lower	(see "Naming Conventions" later)
Variable - default global	Lower	sqlca, error, message

AN ALTERNATIVE CONVENTION

The case conventions in Table 4-3 make for attractive program code. Of course this is subjective, and beauty is in the eye of the beholder. However, some organizations adopt a different and simpler standard, which is this:

Follow the case conventions used by the many "Paste" features in the PowerScript Painter. For example, the "Paste Statement" feature uses all uppercase for PowerBuilder keywords (such as IF, THEN, DO, and RETURN). The "Paste Function" feature uses all lowercase for functions (such as messagebox).

The "Paste" features follow a very simple rule: Keywords are all uppercase, and everything else is entirely lowercase. To make it easier to use these features, you may wish to adopt this alternative convention.

NAMING CONVENTIONS

In developing a PowerBuilder application, you assign a variety of names:

- Object and control names
- Variable names
- Names for user-defined functions, structures, and events

Begin every name with a prefix, identifying the type of thing it is, and perhaps its scope. Thus, you should not use simple names like these:

```
order              // order entry form (a window)
cancelbutton       // "Cancel" button (a CommandButton control)
counter            // row counter (a local integer variable)
numcustomers       // # of customers (a global integer variable)
docalcs(a,b,c)     // do calculations (a user-defined function)
```

Instead, every name has a prefix followed by an underscore:

```
w_order // order entry form (a window)
cb_cancelbutton    // "Cancel" button (a CommandButton control)
li_counter         // row counter (a local integer variable)
gi_num_customers   // # of customers (a global integer variable)
f_docalcs(a,b,c)   // do calculations (a user-defined function)
```

Tables 4-4 through 4-8 show the prefix conventions that we follow. For example, suppose you design a window. According to Table 4-5, its prefix is "w_":

```
w_order         // order entry form (a window)
```

Later in a script, you might declare a window variable to open the window. Its prefix depends on its scope. For example, if it's a local variable, its prefix should be "lw_", according to Table 4-5:

```
w_order lw_order    // w_order is the object class,
                    // lw_order is the variable
Open(lw_order)      // open the window
```

VARIABLE SCOPE PREFIX

Every variable has a scope: local, instance, shared, global, or argument (that is, a function parameter). The first letter of the variable's prefix indicates its scope:

- **l** — is the prefix for a local variable.
- **i** — is the prefix for an instance variable.
- **s** — is the prefix for a shared variable.
- **g** — is the prefix for a global variable.
- **a** — is the prefix for a function argument variable.

Examples:

```
ld_yesterday        // local date variable
id_yesterday        // instance date variable
sd_yesterday        // shared date variable
gd_yesterday        // global date variable
ad_yesterday        // argument date variable
```

Tables 4-4 through 4-7 show only the local and instance prefixes. You can easily convert them to shared, global, and argument prefixes by replacing the *l* or *i* with *s*, *g*, or *a*.

For a variable that is part of a structure definition, use a prefix indicating data type (such as *d_* for date) but no character to indicate scope.

GLOBAL AND OBJECT-BASED FUNCTIONS AND STRUCTURES

User-defined functions and structures can be global to the entire application, or they can be local to a particular object. Every global user-defined function name begins with the prefix *f_*, and every global structure name, with *s_*. You create these by clicking the Function Painter and Structure Painter buttons on the PowerBar.

For functions and structures local to an object, an additional prefix letter identifies the object: application, menu, user object, or window. (There is one other possibility: a structure local to a function.) You create these functions and structures in the various painters. For example, in the Window Painter, you create a window-object function by selecting Declare|Window Functions from the menu.

Table 4-8 lists the prefix combinations. Here are some examples of function names:

```
f_docalcs(a,b,c)         // global function
appf_docalcs(a,b,c)      // application-object function
mf_docalcs(a,b,c)        // menu-object function
uf_docalcs(a,b,c)        // user-object function
wf_docalcs(a,b,c)        // window-object function
```

STRUCTURE PREFIXES

The previous paragraphs address the prefix to be used for a structure definition's name, such as "*s_*" for a global structure definition. For an element within the structure, the prefix indicates the element's type, with no scope letter. For an instance declared from the structure definition, the prefix begins with the scope letter (such as "g" for global) followed by "str_". For example:

```
s_people lstr_boy      // declare local instance of global structure
lstr_boy.s_name = "Matthew"        // string variable in structure
lstr_boy.d_birthday = 1989-03-28   // date variable in structure
```

ADDITIONAL UNDERSCORES FOR MULTIPLE-WORD NAMES

You may add more underscores for longer names, in addition to the underscore that follows the prefix. You should add underscores when it will make the name easier to read and understand. For example, either of these names is acceptable, but the second one is preferred:

```
li_howmanytimes        // local integer variable
li_how_many_times      // local integer variable
```

POWERBUILDER-ENFORCED RULES

In addition to these naming conventions, PowerBuilder itself enforces certain rules about names, and of course you have no choice but to follow them. For example, a name may be no longer than 40 characters and must begin with a letter.

Although PowerBuilder allows hyphens (-) in a name — a carryover from COBOL, I suppose — don't ever use one. It is too easily confused with subtraction.

SHORTCUT NAMES FOR LOCAL VARIABLES

Local variables have a very short lifespan. If a local variable is particularly short-lived, spanning no more than a few lines of code, it may have a "shortcut name." There are two kinds of shortcut names:

A shortcut name can be the variable's standard prefix, which is often a single letter, possibly followed by a number:

```
Integer      i
Integer      i1, i2, i3
DateTime     dt1, dt2, dt3
String       s, s1, s2
Transaction  trans1
```

The letters *j, k, m,* and *n* can be used as shortcut names for local integer-type variables. The letters *x, y,* and *z* can be used for local floating-point-type variables:

```
Integer (or Long or Unsigned)  j, j1, j2, j3, etc.
Integer (or Long or Unsigned)  k, k1, k2, k3, etc.
Integer (or Long or Unsigned)  m, m1, m2, m3, etc.
Integer (or Long or Unsigned)  n, n1, n2, n3, etc.
Real (or Double or Decimal)    x, x1, x2, x3, etc.
Real (or Double or Decimal)    y, y1, y2, y3, etc.
Real (or Double or Decimal)    z, z1, z2, z3, etc.
```

USER OBJECT NAMES

An application can have a great diversity of user objects, and that diversity is reflected in more elaborate naming conventions for them. Here are some of the most common examples:

Visual User Objects — Standard and Custom

Visual user objects come in several varieties. The most common are "standard" and "custom." Use the prefix *u_* for them. Add a second prefix to the name of standard visual user object, indicating the control type that it is derived from:

```
u_progressmeter    // custom
u_pb_closebutton   // standard (derived from PictureButton)
u_dw_smart         // standard (derived from DataWindow)
```

When you place the user object in a window (or in another custom user object), PowerBuilder will give it a name such as uo_1, pb_1, or dw_1. Retain or add the "uo_" prefix, to distinguish the control (uo_) from the object (u_), but change the name, preferably to match the object name:

```
uo_progressmeter    // custom U.O. control
uo_pb_closebutton   // standard U.O. control (PictureButton)
uo_dw_smart         // standard U.O. control (DataWindow)
```

If you need to declare a variable that will refer to one of these controls, the variable name should follow the same rules, but with an extra leading character to indicate its scope:

```
u_pb_closebutton    lu_pb_closebutton    // local
u_pb_closebutton    iu_pb_closebutton    // instance
u_pb_closebutton    su_pb_closebutton    // shared
u_pb_closebutton    gu_pb_closebutton    // global
u_pb_closebutton    au_pb_closebutton    // function argument
```

This script declares and uses the local variable *lu_pb_closebutton*:

```
u_pb_closebutton   lu_pb_closebutton
lu_pb_closebutton = uo_pb_closebutton
lu_pb_closebutton.Hide()
```

In this example, the variable, the control, and the object all have the same suffix — closebutton. It is not required that the suffix always be the same.

Nonvisual User Objects — Standard and Custom

Nonvisual user objects are also called "custom class user objects" in PowerBuilder. Like visual user objects, they too come in "standard" and "custom" varieties. Therefore, they follow similar naming conventions.

Use the prefix *nv_* instead of *u_* for nonvisual objects. For a standard object, a second prefix identifies the class it is derived from:

```
nv_usagetrack        // custom
nv_trans_smart       // standard (derived from Transaction)
```

To use a nonvisual object, you must declare a variable for it and use the CREATE command to instantiate it. The variable name has the same prefix, but with an extra leading character to indicate its scope:

```
nv_usagetrack    lnv_usagetrack    // local
nv_usagetrack    inv_usagetrack    // instance
nv_usagetrack    snv_usagetrack    // shared
nv_usagetrack    gnv_usagetrack    // global
nv_usagetrack    anv_usagetrack    // function argument
```

This script declares, instantiates, and uses two local variables based on nonvisual user objects:

```
nv_usagetrack  lnv_usagetrack  // custom nonvisual object var
nv_trans_smart lnv_trans_smart // std. nonvisual obj. var (Trans.)
lnv_usagetrack  = CREATE nv_usagetrack
lnv_trans_smart = CREATE nv_trans_smart
lnv_usagetrack.Intialize()
lnv_trans_smart.DBMS = "Video Store DB"
```

In this example, the object and its variable have the same suffix — usagetrack or smart — but that is not required.

POWERSOFT PREFIXES

I mentioned at the outset that our conventions are similar to those published by Powersoft, but they are not identical. The Powersoft conventions have evolved and changed over the years. Comparing the latest published version (late 1995) of Powersoft's conventions to mine, I find most of the differences are with a few of the prefixes. For example:

- **Object-Based Functions and Structures** — We use appf_, mf_, uf_, and wf_ for object-based function names. Powersoft uses of_ in all cases. We use apps_, ms_, us_, and ws_ for object-based structure names. Powersoft uses os_ in all cases.

- **Shortcut Names for Local Variables** — We allow shortcut names for variables, like *i* or *i1* for an integer. Powersoft does not.

- **Nonvisual Objects** — We use nv_ for nonvisual objects. Powersoft uses n_.

- **Data Types, Controls, and Objects** — There are differences for a few of the prefixes in Tables 4-4 through 4-7. For example, I use "any" and "blob" in the prefix for "any" and "blob" variables. Powersoft uses "a" for "any" and "blb" for "blob."

Table 4-4

Prefix Conventions for Variable and Object Names—Standard Data Types

Type of Variable or Object	Object Prefix	Variable Prefix Local	Instance
STANDARD DATA TYPES			
Any		lany_	iany_
Blob		lblob_	iblob_
Boolean		lb_	ib_
Character		lc	ic_
Date		ld_	id_
DateTime		ldt_	idt_
Decimal		ldec_	idec_
Double		ldbl_	idbl_
Integer		li_	ii_
Long		ll_	il_
Real		lr_	ir_
String		ls_	is_
Time		lt_	it_
UnsignedInteger		lui_	iui_
UnsignedLong		lul_	iul_

Table 4-5

Prefix Conventions for Variable and Object Names—Controls and Library Objects

Type of Variable or Object	Object Prefix	Variable Prefix	
		Local	Instance
CONTROLS			
CheckBox	cbx_	lcbx_	icbx_
CommandButton	cb_	lcb_	icb_
DataWindow	dw_	ldw_	idw_
DropDownListBox	ddlb_	lddlb_	iddlb_
DropDownPictureListBox	ddplb_	lddplb_	iddplb_
EditMask	em_	lem_	iem_
Graph	gr_	lgr_	igr_
GroupBox	gb_	lgb_	igb_
HScrollBar	hsb_	lhsb_	ihsb_
Line	ln_	lln_	iln_
ListBox	lb_	llb_	ilb_
ListView	lv_	llv_	ilv_
OLEControl	ole_	lole_	iole_
Oval	oval_	loval_	ioval_
Picture	p_	lp_	ip_
PictureButton	pb_	lpb_	ipb_
PictureListBox	plb_	lplb_	iplb_
RadioButton	rb_	lrb_	irb_
Rectangle	r_	lr_	ir_
RichTextEdit	rte_	lrte_	irte_
RoundRectangle	rr_	lrr_	irr_
SingleLineEdit	sle_	lsle_	isle_
StaticText	st_	lst_	ist_
Tab	tab_	ltab_	itab_
TreeView	tv_	ltv_	itv_
UserObject	uo_	luo_	iuo_
VScrollBar	vsb_	lvsb_	ivsb_

continued

Table 4-5 (continued)

Type of Variable or Object	Object Prefix	Variable Prefix	
		Local	Instance
LIBRARY OBJECTS			
Application	app_	lapp_	iapp_
DataWindow Object	d_		
Function	f_	lfo_	ifo_
Menu	m_	lm_	im_
Pipeline	pipe_	lpipe_	ipipe_
Project	proj_		
Proxy	proxy_		
Query	q_		
Structure	s_	lstr_	istr_
User Object	u_ or nv_		
Window	w_	lw_	iw_

Table 4-6

Prefix Conventions for Variable and Object Names—Object Hierarchy

Type of Variable or Object	Object Prefix	Variable Prefix	
		Local	Instance
OBJECT HIERARCHY			
PowerObject		lpo_	ipo_
.Application	app_	lapp_	iapp_
.Function_Object	f_	lfo_	ifo_
.GraphicObject		lgo_	igo_
..Menu	m_	lm_	im_
..Window	w_	lw_	iw_
..WindowObject		lwo_	iwo_
...DragObject		ldrag_	idrag_
...DrawObject		ldraw_	idraw_
...MDIClient	mdi_	lmdi_	imdi_
.GrAxis		lgrax_	igrax_

continued

Table 4-6 (continued)

Type of Variable or Object	Object Prefix	Variable Prefix	
		Local	Instance
.GrDispAttr		lgrda_	igrda_
.NonVisualObject		lnv_	inv_
..ConnectObject		lco_	ico_
...Connection		lconn_	iconn_
...Transport		ltport_	itport_
..CPlusPlus		lcpp_	icpp_
..DataStore		lds_	ids_
..DynamicDescriptionArea		ldda_	idda_
..DynamicStagingArea		ldsa_	idsa_
..Error		lerr_	ierr_
..ExtObject		lexto_	iexto_
...DWObject	d_	ld_	id_
...OMObject		lomo_	iomo_
....OLEObject		loo_	ioo_
...RTEObject		lrteo_	irteo_
..MailSession		lms_	ims_
..Message		lmsg_	imsg_
..OMStorage		lomsto_	iomsto_
...OLEStorage		losto_	iosto_
..OMStream		lomstr_	iomstr_
...OLEStream		lostr_	iostr_
..Pipeline	pipe_	lpipe_	ipipe_
..RemoteObject		lro_	iro_
..Transaction		ltrans_	itrans_
.Structure	s_	lstr_	istr_
..ConnectionInfo		lcinfo_	icinfo_
..DataWindowChild		ldwc_	idwc_
..Environment		lenv_	ienv_
..ListViewItem		llvi_	ilvi_
..MailFileDescription		lmfd_	imfd_

continued

Table 4-6 (continued)

Type of Variable or Object	Object Prefix	Variable Prefix	
		Local	Instance
..MailMessage		lmmsg_	immsg_
..MailRecipient		lmrcp_	imrcp_
..TreeViewItem		ltvi_	itvi_

Table 4-7

Prefix Conventions for Variable and Object Names—User Objects and Database Variables

Type of Variable or Object	Object Prefix	Variable Prefix	
		Local	Instance
USER OBJECTS			
Visual Custom	u_		
Visual Standard	u_<type>_		
Visual External	u_ext_		
Visual VBX	u_vbx_		
Nonvisual Custom	nv_	lnv_	inv_
Nonvisual Standard	nv_<type>_	l<type>_	i<type>_
Nonvisual C++	nv_cpp_	lcpp_	icpp_
Structure Variable		lstr_	istr_
DATABASE VARIABLES			
Cursor		lcur_	icur_
Stored Procedure	sp_	lsp_	isp_

Table 4-8

Prefix Conventions for User-Defined Function, Structure, and Event Names

	Global	App.	Menu	User Object	Window	Function
Function	f_	appf_	mf_	uf_	wf_	
Structure	s_	apps_	ms_	us_	ws_	fs_
User Event—Custom				ue	ue	
User Event—Windows Message				<name>	<name>	

Summary

In this chapter, you have seen how PowerBuilder programming uses many constructs that will be familiar from other modern programming languages — variables, operators, assignment statements, function calls with arguments, and so on. We have covered PowerBuilder programming style, including small variations between the naming conventions found in this book and Powersoft's own conventions in their current forms. The PowerScript Painter in particular has many features to aid you in constructing error-free code.

II Working With Data

5 Databases

*C*reating applications and windows with PowerBuilder and writing scripts for them make up an important part of the development process, but for even the simplest practical application you need one more major component: *data*.

Your application's data will live in a database, or perhaps in more than one database. Even while your application is in the development phase, PowerBuilder provides a powerful tool for working with your database: the Database Painter. Using the Database Painter, you can see and modify your data, set properties for how your database should behave, and much more — basically, you can prepare your database for the application that will rely upon it.

In order to do all these wonderful things with the Database Painter, you must first "connect" it to your database. Connecting to a database in the Database Painter is the same sort of thing as opening an application in the Application Painter or opening a window in the Window Painter, both of which we did in Chapter 2. Connecting to a database is not quite so straightforward, however, because the database is not created by PowerBuilder but by some other product. Accordingly, this chapter contains quite a bit of preliminary information about the nature of those outside data sources and how PowerBuilder connects to them. The major topics in this chapter are

- Databases from PowerBuilder's point of view

- The information (called *database profiles* and *data source configurations*) that PowerBuilder requires before it can connect to a database

- How to connect to a database in the Database Painter

■ How to use the Database Painter to work with a database

Beyond the Database Painter, the critical issue remains of how to integrate database access into a PowerBuilder application and into the application's scripts — these are topics to be dealt with in Chapters 7–10.

Database Terminology

Before going any farther, let's define the basic terms. The concepts are probably familiar to you from other products, but the terminology can differ somewhat from one product to another.

DATABASES, TABLES, ROWS, AND COLUMNS

A *database* is an organized collection of all the information you would need for a particular purpose, such as an application. The example used throughout this book is a video store application. If you owned a video store, your database would consist of information about the films you have available for renting, the customers who rent them, and the orders placed by customers when they rent the films.

A *relational* database is a collection of *tables*. Each table contains only one type of data. The Video Store database includes a film table, a customer table, an order table, and probably other tables. The customer table — or part of it, anyway — is shown in Figure 5-1. This is the way the table looks using the Data Manipulation Painter in PowerBuilder. The customer table contains information about all the customers. All the information about customers is in the customer table, and no information about customers is in any other table.

A table is composed of *rows* and *columns*. In the customer table in Figure 5-1, it's pretty obvious what the rows and columns are. Each row is the information about one customer. The first row is about Paul Jackson, the second is about Matthew Cooper, and so on. The columns are Custid, Lastname, Firstname, and so on.

In some products, rows are called *records* or *tuples* and columns are called *fields* or *attributes*. But, throughout PowerBuilder, the only terms

Custid	Lastname	Firstname	Address1	Address2	City	State	Zip
1010	Jackson	Paul	514 Topaz Street		Los Angeles	CA	90017
1011	Cooper	Matthew	4 Lucia Avenue		Portland	OR	97227
1032	Gray	Gina	5540 16-th Street		Seattle	WA	98104
1040	Newman	Bill & Kathleen	4098 Emerald Street		Sacramento	CA	95814
1088	De Carlo	Frank	873 Catalina Avenue		San Francisco	CA	94103
1100	Williams	Adam	241 Maria Avenue	Apt. 3	Tacoma	WA	98402
1200	Green	Diana	68 Irena Avenue		Portland	OR	97220
1300	Carpenter	Heather	637 Agate Street		San Diego	CA	92101
1400	Cooper	Victor	44 Avenue C		Los Angeles	CA	90015
1424	Cole	Hector	5346 Beryl Street		Seattle	WA	98121

Figure 5-1

The customer table in the Video Store database.

used are *rows* and *columns*. This is true even when the data is displayed in a way that no longer looks like rows and columns, such as Paul Jackson's name and address as it would appear on a mailing label:

> Paul Jackson
> 514 Topaz Street
> Los Angeles, CA 90017

Even though this looks like three rows, we'll still refer to this as "one row" from the customer table. It consists of six columns from that one row: Firstname, Lastname, Address1, City, State, and Zip.

Although I said earlier that one database contains all the data for an application, some applications need to draw data from more than one database. For example, an accounting application might rely on an accounting database but also tap into a sales database for some of the data it needs.

WHAT IS CLIENT/SERVER?

Client/Server is the term for an application software environment in which the application is split into two components: the *client*, also called the *front end*, which is the user interface half of the application; and the *server*, also called the *database server* or *back end*, which controls access to the data. This relationship is illustrated in Figure 5-2. The client and the server are two separate pieces of software, often running on two different computers linked through a network.

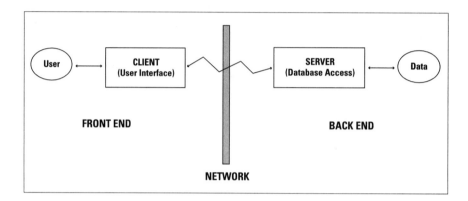

Figure 5-2

A client/server application has two parts: The client (front end) and the server (back end).

In a nonclient/server system, the application is a single program that handles both the user interface and the database access. All the logic necessary to access the data right down to the disk I/O level is in the program. This logic may take the form of library procedures that the programmer binds into the program. In a client/server system, the programmer of the client software might also use library procedures to access the data, but these procedures get the data by communicating with the database server to ask for it, not by doing the disk I/O themselves.

Client/server systems have many advantages over nonclient/server systems. Some of the most important benefits are

- **"Best of Breed" software** — You can pick the product that best matches your needs for client software (PowerBuilder, presumably) and the best database server product. You do not have to find a single product that is the best at both.

- **Transportability** — With little reconfiguration and little or no reprogramming, you can connect the same client application to any of a number of different database server products. This assumption holds true, however, only if the various servers provide the same interface to the client. The ODBC and SQL interfaces, which will be discussed shortly, address this issue.

■ **Scalability** — As your business grows and so do the amount of data and the number of concurrent users you must handle, you can increase the capacity and throughput of your system by upgrading only the database server hardware or database server software. There is no need to upgrade the client hardware or software for all the end users, an approach that could be significantly more expensive.

PowerBuilder is strictly a "client" product. You will use PowerBuilder to develop the front end of an application. The database server will be some other product, and your PowerBuilder application will connect to it.

PowerBuilder Database Connections

PowerBuilder can connect to a large number of database products, which are listed in Table 5-1. Please refer to the PowerBuilder documentation for the latest information about which versions of each product are supported. Also, in some cases you may need to purchase additional third-party software, such as the MicroDecisionware Gateway or Sybase Net-Gateway Interface for DB2.

Table 5-1

PowerBuilder Database Server Connections

Data Source	PowerBuilder Desktop	PowerBuilder Professional	PowerBuilder Enterprise
ODBC Data Sources			
SQL Anywhere (Watcom)	X	X	X
Btrieve	X	X	X
dBASE, Clipper, FoxPro	X	X	X
Excel	X	X	X

continued

Table 5-1 *(continued)*

Data Source	PowerBuilder Desktop	PowerBuilder Professional	PowerBuilder Enterprise
Paradox	X	X	X
Scalable SQL (Win 3.1 only)	X	X	X
Text File	X	X	X
Other ODBC Data Sources		X	X
Native Databases			
IBM DB2			X
INFORMIX			X
Microsoft SQL Server			X
ORACLE			X
Sybase SQL Server			X

As you can see from the table, not all connections are available from all PowerBuilder products. The major difference between the Desktop and Enterprise editions is that only Enterprise can connect to what are rightfully called client/server databases, whereas Desktop connects only to desktop and LAN-based databases via ODBC.

The "ODBC Data Sources" use Microsoft's Open Database Connectivity (ODBC) application programming interface (API), which provides a uniform interface from a client product such as PowerBuilder to a diverse collection of database products. Besides the ODBC connections listed in the table, which are bundled with all editions of PowerBuilder, you can connect with other database products via ODBC if you are using the Professional or Enterprise edition, and if there is ODBC interface software available for the product, usually from its vendor or from a third party.

For each of the "Native Databases," PowerBuilder Enterprise includes a non-ODBC programming interface to connect to the database server. The interfaces were developed by Powersoft, usually in cooperation with the database vendor.

Have You Installed SQL Anywhere? How to Tell

If you are not sure whether or not SQL Anywhere support is installed with your copy of PowerBuilder, here are some of the things to check for. On your system, there should be:

- A directory named SQLANY50, perhaps C:\SQLANY50. Some subdirectory of it, such as C:\SQLANY50\WIN32, should contain files such as DBENG50.EXE and should be part of your system path.
- An icon for SQL Anywhere Interactive in the Powersoft 5.0 folder in the Windows Start Menu or the Program Manager
- The file WOD50T.DLL in your SQL Anywhere directory (typically, C:\SQLANY50\WIN32)
- The file ODBC.DLL or ODBC32.DLL in your Windows system directory
- The file PBODB050.DLL in your PowerBuilder shared directory (typically, C:\PWRS\SYS, C:\PWRS\SYS32, or C:\ProgramFiles\Common Files\PowersoftShared)

If any of these elements are missing, then most likely SQL Anywhere is not installed or should be reinstalled. Run the PowerBuilder setup program (for most of us, that's SETUP.EXE on the PowerBuilder CD-ROM) and select the following from the PowerBuilder custom setup options:

- "SQL Anywhere" (installs C:\SQLANY50 and the Start Menu icon)
- The "SQL Anywhere ODBC" option under "ODBC Drivers" (installs WOD50T.DLL and related files)
- The "Powersoft ODBC Interface" option under "Native Database Drivers" (installs ODBC.DLL or ODBC32.DLL, PBODB050.DLL, and related files)

SQL ANYWHERE

Of all the database products on the list, SQL Anywhere is special. Everything you need to connect PowerBuilder to SQL Anywhere is included with every edition of PowerBuilder. All the sample applications that come with PowerBuilder use SQL Anywhere as their data source.

(Prior to 1996, SQL Anywhere was called "Watcom SQL." Same product, updated version, different name.)

Thus SQL Anywhere is the easiest database to get started with, and it is the common denominator that all PowerBuilder users share. For that reason, we have used SQL Anywhere as the primary database for the sample applications in this book. While writing the book, we constructed a

Microsoft SQL Server version of the database, in order to perform parallel testing of the sample applications. Other than occasional references, however, all of the database examples shown in this book were developed and tested using SQL Anywhere.

If you did not select SQL Anywhere for installation when you first installed PowerBuilder, however, you may want to run the PowerBuilder setup program again and install SQL Anywhere now, so that you can follow along with the exercises in this book. If you are not sure whether you have SQL Anywhere installed or how to install it, refer to the sidebar "Have You Installed SQL Anywhere? How to Tell" in this chapter.

THE LINKS IN THE CONNECTION CHAIN

In order to connect PowerBuilder to any database successfully, especially if you plan to connect to more than one database, it is very helpful to understand the software links that are involved. Figure 5-3 shows the four main components:

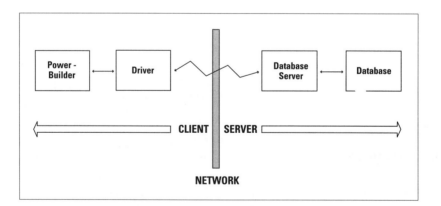

Figure 5-3
The links connecting PowerBuilder to a database.

1. **PowerBuilder** — the client software which, by itself, is database independent

2. **The driver software** — which consists of one or more software

library modules. In Microsoft Windows, the drivers are Dynamic Link Libraries, "DLLs," which reside on the client machine. From the Windows point of view, the driver is not a separate program from PowerBuilder. PowerBuilder is the program that is running, and it is making subroutine calls to the modules in the driver DLLs. *Database Interface* is another term for "driver," especially for a non-ODBC connection.

3. **The network** — which is the medium across which the client and server communicate.

4. **The database server software** — which is a program running on the database server machine. The client and the server run independently from one another and communicate by sending messages · – across the network, if they are on two different machines. In this chapter, I will tend to use the following terms interchangeably, as if they were synonyms:

   - Database server
   - Database product
   - Database engine

   Actually, there are some differences among these terms. The "product" is what you purchase from the database software vendor, such as the System 11 product purchased from Sybase. But you can have any number of copies of the product up and running across your network, perhaps on different machines. In this case you would have multiple "database servers" but only one database product. So you might have several Sybase System 11 Servers, with names like "Accounting Server," "Marketing Server," and so forth. The "database engine" is the part of the server software that handles the physical I/O with the database.

5. **The Database** — which is the physical storage place for your data. Typically, but not always, it is a collection of one or more files on the disk drive of the computer that is running the database server software. The database is the only one of the four components in Figure 5-3 that is not software.

   A database, especially an ODBC database, is often called a *data source*, as are spreadsheets and text files to which you can connect via ODBC.

SIMPLE CONFIGURATIONS

Although Figure 5-3 illustrates a typical PowerBuilder-to-database connection — and this is what most people picture when you mention PowerBuilder and client/server — a real configuration could very well be less complicated or more complicated.

In the direction of "less complicated," the four components collapse down to three for many of the ODBC connections. If you connect PowerBuilder to a local dBASE database on your local C: drive, for example, everything will be on one computer — there is no separation between client and server. And there is no database server component, because the driver software contains within it the database engine that does all the I/O on dBASE files.

When you use the single-user SQL Anywhere server that is installed with PowerBuilder, all the components usually reside on a single machine, but it's one step more complex than dBASE. There are two independent programs running under Windows: (1) the PowerBuilder program, along with its SQL Anywhere driver DLLs, and (2) the SQL Anywhere database server program.

COMPLEX CONFIGURATIONS

In the direction of "more complicated," the configuration in Figure 5-3 can grow more complex in many ways. An obvious case is what would happen if you were to have many of the server products listed in Table 5-1, and several databases for each server. The result is Figure 5-4.

DATABASE PROFILES AND DATA SOURCES

Before you can connect PowerBuilder (in particular, the PowerBuilder Database Painter) to a database, you must do one thing first:

1. Create a *database profile* for the database.

   If it's an ODBC database, then a second step is required:

2. Create a *data source configuration* for the database.

   It turns out that if step 2 is required, then you must do it before step 1, but it's easier to explain database profiles first and data source configurations second.

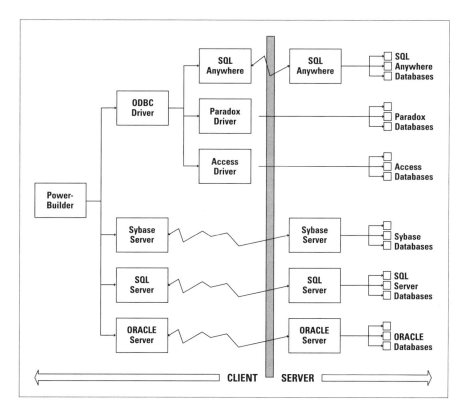

Figure 5-4

Connecting PowerBuilder to many drivers, many servers, and many databases.

DATABASE PROFILES (PB.INI)

A *database profile* is simply a set of parameters that identify a database. It tells PowerBuilder everything it needs to know about how to connect to that database.

For example, I have created a version of the Video Store sample database (used as an example throughout this book) with Microsoft SQL Server. To connect PowerBuilder to it, I created a database profile. In the profile, I named the database "Video Store (SQL Server)," even though in SQL Server its name is "VideoSqlServer." The database profile name does not have to match the actual database name.

I created the database profile by filling out the Database Profile Setup dialog box shown in Figure 5-5. You reach this dialog box by selecting File|Connect|Setup from the Database Painter menu and clicking New or Edit on the Database Profiles dialog that appears. (I will describe these Database Painter menu choices shortly.)

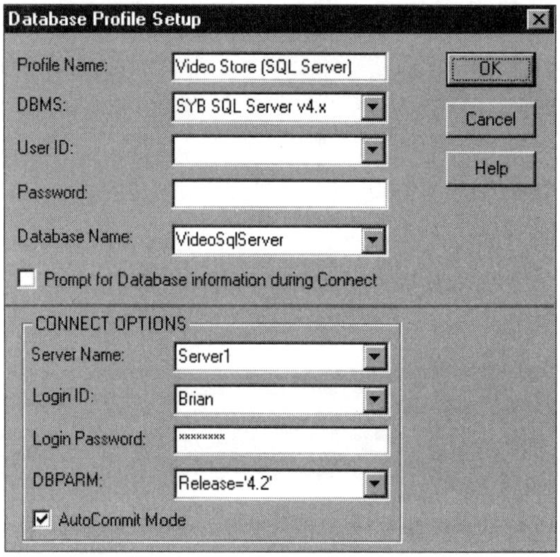

Figure 5-5
This Database Profile Setup dialog box describes the database profile for the SQL Server version of the Video Store database.

For information about how to complete the database profile setup for your database, refer to the *Connecting to Your Database* manual in the PowerBuilder documentation set. It has a section about every server product. You can find similar information online, by looking up "database, connecting to" in the help index.

In the dialog box in Figure 5-5, the Profile Name, "Video Store (SQL Server)," is the unique identifier for this database to PowerBuilder, and it is the name that PowerBuilder will use to connect to it. The DBMS, "SYB SQL Server v4.x," identifies the database server to be SQL Server. User ID and Password are not used for SQL Server profiles, so I left them blank. The Database Name, "VideoSQLServer," is SQL Server's name for the database. The database must already exist before you can create the database profile.

PB.INI

Many Microsoft Windows applications store parameters to control their execution in configuration settings files — that is, files with the extension .INI. For example, WIN.INI contains general Windows parameters, SYSTEM.INI describes the system configuration, and PB.INI contains PowerBuilder parameters. Many INI files reside in your Windows directory, typically C:\WINDOWS. PB.INI lives in the PowerBuilder directory, which is usually named C:\PWRS\PB5, C:\PWRS\PB5132, or C:\ProgramFiles\Powersoft\PowerBuilder5.0.

An INI file is a text file, so you can read and modify it with any text editor, such as Notepad. The file is divided into sections, and each section contains parameters, like so:

```
[Section 1]
Parameter1=value
Parameter2=value
Parameter3=value

[Section 2]
Parameter1=value
Parameter2=value
Parameter3=value
```

As far as I know, there is no limit to the number of sections and parameters.

PB.INI contains many parameters about your PowerBuilder configuration. For example, there are sections for many of the painters, describing your preferences for their operation, and there is a section for every database profile.

The PowerScript language has functions for reading and writing INI file information. This call to the function ProfileString shows how to fetch the Database parameter from the Profile Video Store (SQL Server) section of PB.INI:

```
ls_param = ProfileString("PB.INI",                  &
            "Profile Video Store (SQL Server)",     &
            "Database", "")
```

Given the fragment of PB.INI shown in Listing 5-1, this line of code would place the value "VideoStore1" into the variable *ls_param*. There is a companion function, SetProfileString, that writes a parameter to an INI file.

Although you can modify PB.INI, or any other INI file, with a text editor, it's usually not a good idea to do so, unless there is vendor documentation explaining exactly what to do.

continued

continued

Unexpected side effects may arise when you rely on guesswork to change a parameter. In PowerBuilder, every PB.INI parameter appears in some dialog box somewhere. If you want to change a parameter, it's wiser to locate its dialog box and change it there.

You might consider creating an INI file for every application that you create. You can store programmer-defined parameters and user-defined preferences there, rather than hard-coding them in the programming. We have a VIDEO.INI file for the Video Store application that accompanies this book. An application is not required to have an INI file, but you'll find that it's a very useful technique.

"Server1" is the name of the database server running in my office. The Login ID "Brian" and the Login Password, which echo as asterisks, show how I log in to the server. For tighter security, you can leave the Login ID and Login Password blank, and PowerBuilder will prompt you for them every time you connect to this database. DBPARM is used to specify server-specific parameters. In this case, "Release='4.2'" informs PowerBuilder that the server is release 4.2 of SQL Server, so that PowerBuilder can take advantage of special features in that version.

PowerBuilder stores all the database profiles that you have created in PB.INI (described in the accompanying sidebar). Listing 5-1 shows the section of my PB.INI file with the "Video Store (SQL Server)" profile. Notice how the information in PB.INI corresponds to the information in the Database Profile Setup dialog box in Figure 5-5.

Listing 5-1
The Profile section for "Video Store (SQL Server)" in PB.INI

```
[Profile Video Store (SQL Server)]
DBMS=SYB SQL Server v4.x
Database=VideoStore1
ServerName=Server1
UserId=
DatabasePassword=
LogId=Brian
LogPassword=whatever
Lock=
DbParm=Release='4.2'
Prompt=0
AutoCommit=1
```

Whenever you want to open a database in a painter, you provide PowerBuilder with the database's profile name. PowerBuilder locates the name in PB.INI, reads the profile, and uses it to load the driver, connect to the server, and open the database. Figure 5-6 illustrates how key information from the database profile forges the link from PowerBuilder to the database.

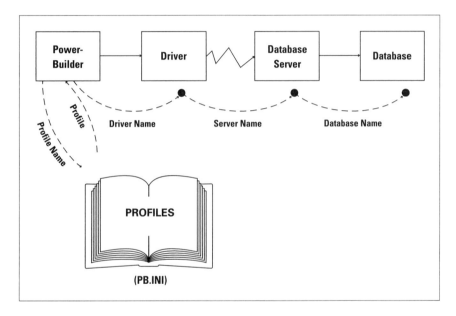

Figure 5-6
PowerBuilder uses the database profile in PB.INI to connect to a database.

In the PowerBuilder development environment, painters such as the Database Painter use database profiles and PB.INI to make their connections. However, a running application might or might not rely on database profiles and an INI file. As I will explain in Chapter 7, you must write a script to connect your application to the database, and you, as the application developer, decide how to supply that script's connection parameters.

DATA SOURCE CONFIGURATIONS (ODBC.INI)

Connecting to an ODBC data source adds one more link to the chain: the ODBC driver. And it adds one more step to set up: You must "configure the data source" in addition to defining the database profile.

Figure 5-7 illustrates the connection from PowerBuilder to SQL Anywhere. Rather than PowerBuilder calling the SQL Anywhere driver directly, as would occur with a non-ODBC database connection, PowerBuilder calls the ODBC driver, which in turn calls the SQL Anywhere driver. (There is actually one more driver, a minor one, not shown in the figure: PBODB050.DLL, provided with PowerBuilder, that connects PowerBuilder to the ODBC driver. Also, there are several SQL Anywhere server programs available for various kinds of connections; DBENG50.EXE, shown in the diagram, is just one of them.)

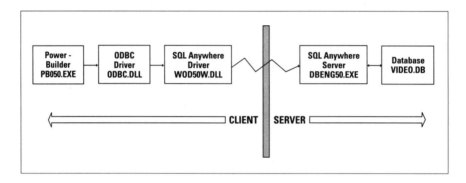

Figure 5-7

Connecting PowerBuilder to a SQL Anywhere database using ODBC.

The ODBC driver, named ODBC.DLL or ODBC32.DLL depending on your Windows version, is a Microsoft product. You may already have installed a copy of it on your Windows system, quite possibly without realizing it, in conjunction with some Windows product other than PowerBuilder. If not, a version of it is bundled with PowerBuilder and installs automatically when you install PowerBuilder.

The goal of ODBC is to provide a universal application programming interface (API) between any client product and any database server product. As you have seen from Table 5-1, PowerBuilder does not rely on ODBC for its "native database" connections, but it does use ODBC for all the others, including SQL Anywhere.

ODBC does not know anything about PowerBuilder. Therefore, ODBC does not know anything about the database profiles in PB.INI and the parameters there that define a database connection. Instead, ODBC must maintain its own set of database profiles, which go by the name *data source configurations* and are stored in the Windows registry for Windows 95 and Windows NT, or in ODBC.INI for Windows 3.1. Setting one up is known as "configuring a data source."

Configuring a data source is very similar to defining a database profile. Figure 5-8 shows the screen for configuring Video Store DB, an SQL Anywhere data source. This screen resembles the Database Profile Setup dialog box in Figure 5-5. The data source configuration dialog differs for each brand of server, so for a database other than SQL Anywhere it would look somewhat different.

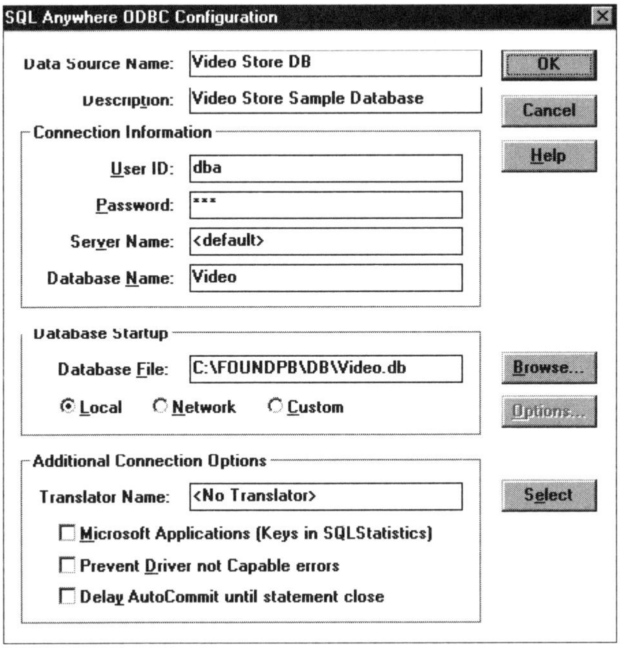

Figure 5-8
This SQL Anywhere ODBC Configuration dialog box is used by ODBC to define the Video Store DB data source, which is an SQL Anywhere database.

In comparing Figures 5-5 and 5-8, notice that the key identifier is called the "Profile Name" in one and the "Data Source Name" in the other. Notice that for SQL Anywhere, you supply an actual DOS path and file-name for the database. For SQL Server, I used "VideoSqlServer" as the database name, a name that is meaningful only to the SQL Server "Server1."

Also notice that the DBMS field in Figure 5-5 identifies the server type as SQL Server but that there is no corresponding field in the Figure 5-8 dialog identifying its server type as SQL Anywhere. The reason is that before you get to Figure 5-8, you have already specified the server type (in this case, SQL Anywhere 5.0) in an earlier dialog box. I will show that part of the process in a moment. The title of the dialog in Figure 5-8 demonstrates that PowerBuilder and ODBC already know that this is an SQL Anywhere data source.

To avoid confusion I should point out that the Video Store (SQL Server) database described in Figure 5-5 and the Video Store DB database in Figure 5-8 are not the same database, in spite of their similar names. The former is an SQL Server database accessible only through SQL Server. It happens to be part of a file named DEV27.DB in a directory on my Windows NT network. The latter is an SQL Anywhere 5.0 database, accessible only through SQL Anywhere. It is the file C:\FOUNDPB\DB\VIDEO.DB on a local C: drive. Nevertheless, I built the two of them with the same tables and the same make-believe video store data so that I could test the multiple-database handling capabilities of PowerBuilder.

ODBC stores its data source configurations in the Windows registry for Windows 95 or Windows NT, or in ODBC.INI for Windows 3.1. The information there is very similar to the Database Profile sections of PB.INI, with one section for each data source. Figure 5-9 shows my Windows 95 registry data for the Video Store DB key. Listing 5-2 is the section in my Windows 3.1 ODBC.INI for the Video Store DB data source.

Listing 5-2

The Profile section for Video Store DB in ODBC.INI (Windows 3.1)

```
[Video Store DB]
Driver=c:\windows\system\WOD40W.DLL
UID=dba
PWD=sql
Description=Video Store Sample Database
Database=C:\FOUNDPB\DB\VIDEO.DB
Start=db32w
DatabaseFile=C:\FOUNDPB\DB\VIDEO.DB
DatabaseName=Video
AutoStop=yes
Driver32=c:\sqlany50\win32\WOD50T.DLL
```

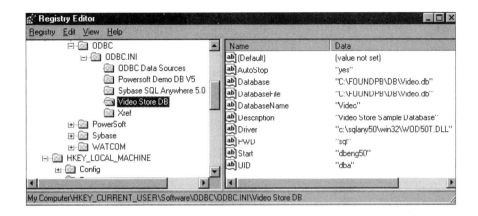

Figure 5-9

Windows 95 registry information for the Video Store DB key found in HKEY_CURRENT_USER/SOFTWARE/ODBC/ODBC.INI.

Although the data source information in ODBC.INI may be sufficient for the ODBC driver to make the connection, the PowerBuilder program nevertheless requires a database profile for this same database in PB.INI. Fortunately, when you configure an ODBC Data Source, as in Figure 5-8, PowerBuilder automatically creates the database profile for you, saving you that extra step. (This assumes that you use PowerBuilder to configure the Data Source. If you use some other ODBC front-end product, which is not unusual, you must create the database profile yourself, in PowerBuilder.)

You can review the PowerBuilder database profile for an ODBC Data Source at any time. Figure 5-10 shows the Database Profile Setup dialog box (the same one shown in Figure 5-5) for the SQL Anywhere database Video Store DB. Listing 5-3 shows the corresponding section in PB.INI.

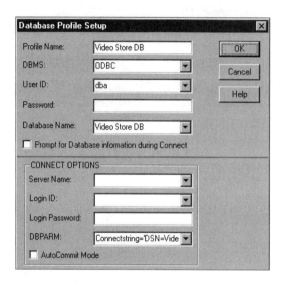

Figure 5-10
This is the database profile for the SQL Anywhere (ODBC) database Video Store DB.

Listing 5-3
The Profile section for the SQL Anywhere (ODBC) database Video Store DB in PB.INI

```
[PROFILE Video Store DB]
DBMS=ODBC
Database=Video Store DB
UserId=dba
DatabasePassword=
LogPassword=
ServerName=
LogId=
Lock=
DbParm=Connectstring='DSN=Video Store DB'
AutoCommit=0
Prompt=0
```

It's interesting to note (and it makes sense when you think about it) that the database profile for Video Store DB in PB.INI does not need to know that this is a SQL Anywhere database. It needs only to know that it's an ODBC database, as is shown by the "DBMS=ODBC" parameter, and the name of this data source in ODBC, which is the "DSN=..." parameter. "DSN" stands for "Data Source Name." Usually the profile name and the data source name will be the same, but they are not required to be. Once PowerBuilder uses the PB.INI profile to connect to ODBC, ODBC can use its information in the Windows registry (or ODBC.INI) to extend the connection all the way to the SQL Anywhere database.

Figure 5-11 illustrates how both PB.INI and the Windows registry (or ODBC.INI) are used to make a connection from PowerBuilder through ODBC to a database. Compare this to Figure 5-6, the non-ODBC scenario.

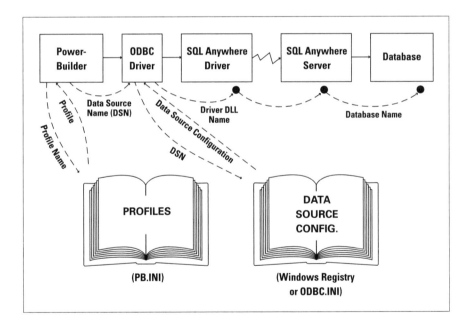

Figure 5-11

PowerBuilder uses the database profile in PB.INI to connect to ODBC. ODBC uses the data source configuration in the Windows registry or ODBC.INI to connect to the SQL Anywhere driver, the server, and the database.

When the Database Painter Won't Open

The Database Painter, when you open it, is very insistent about connecting the "default" database, whose profile name is recorded in PB.INI. If there is some problem — the database no longer exists, or its server is not available, or whatever — the painter pops up a stream of error messages. It's very cranky about it.

When this situation arises, here is a formula that has always allowed me to deal with this situation: Close each dialog box that pops up by clicking its Cancel button or, if it has no Cancel button, its OK button. After several messages, this should bring you to

a state where the Database Painter is open but no database is connected. From here you can create or connect to a valid database using File|Connect|Setup, File|Create Database, or File|Configure ODBC.

If that formula does not work, exit from PowerBuilder and edit PB.INI using Notepad. In the [DBMS_PROFILES] section, delete the line for "CURRENT=." In the [Database] section, delete the line for "DBMS=." Start PowerBuilder again and run through the formula. This time you should make progress.

One more issue about the Windows registry and ODBC.INI: Many products besides PowerBuilder may connect to ODBC on your system. There is only one ODBC.INI registry key or file, and it contains all of the ODBC data source configurations required by all of your client products. This fact makes it even riskier to alter the Windows registry or ODBC.INI using an editor than it is to edit PB.INI. Who knows what damage you could cause to a connection from a non-PowerBuilder product to its databases.

Defining and Connecting to Databases in the Database Painter

In PowerBuilder development, the Database Painter is the primary place to work with your databases. Before you can do anything else with a database, such as display one of its tables or change a table's definition, you must connect to the database. The Database Painter has menu choices for connecting to a database and also tools for creating and editing database profiles and data source configurations, among other things.

To open the Database Painter, click the Database button on the PowerBar. When the Database Painter first opens, it connects to the same database that you were connected to in your previous session.

THE FILE MENU IN THE DATABASE PAINTER

In the Database Painter, the File menu (Figure 5-12) contains four choices pertaining to database connection:

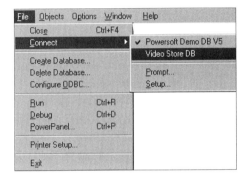

Figure 5-12
The File menu in the Database Painter.

- **File | Connect** — which leads to three features:
  - **File | Connect | <*profile name*>** — Connect to a database by picking an existing database profile.
  - **File | Connect | Prompt** — Connect to a database without using or creating a database profile.
  - **File | Connect | Setup** — View and edit database profiles, or create a new database profile.
- **File | Create Database** — Create a new SQL Anywhere database.
- **File | Delete Database** — Delete an SQL Anywhere database.
- **File | Configure ODBC** — View and edit data source configurations, or create a new one.

These menu choices are not arranged in the order in which you will probably need to visit them when you are first getting underway. Which one you need to visit first depends on your situation. The following paragraphs describe the general sequence of steps.

INSTALLING THE SERVER AND DRIVER SOFTWARE

A prerequisite for any attempt to connect to a database is to

- Make sure the database server software is installed, up and running, and accessible to your client workstation.
- Install the driver software on your client workstation necessary to connect PowerBuilder to it.

For SQL Anywhere, these steps are all options when you install PowerBuilder. For other database products and their drivers, you set up the server separately from PowerBuilder. The drivers may or may not be included with PowerBuilder. If they are, you install them as an option during PowerBuilder installation. The *Connecting to Your Database* manual can give you guidance about what driver software you need for your database and where to get it. For software not supplied with PowerBuilder, you must follow the instructions that come with those products to install them.

File|Create Database — Creating an SQL Anywhere Database

If you plan to create an SQL Anywhere database from scratch, select File|Create Database to display the dialog box shown in Figure 5-13. (Actually, PowerBuilder first displays a shortened version of the dialog box, with a More>> button on it. When you click the More>> button, the dialog box expands to what is shown in the figure.) An SQL Anywhere database is a DOS file with the extension .DB. The figure shows what you might type in to create a database named DBNEW in your C:\FOUNDPB directory

When you click OK, PowerBuilder not only creates the database but also

- Creates the ODBC data source configuration for it
- Creates the database profile for it
- Connects to it

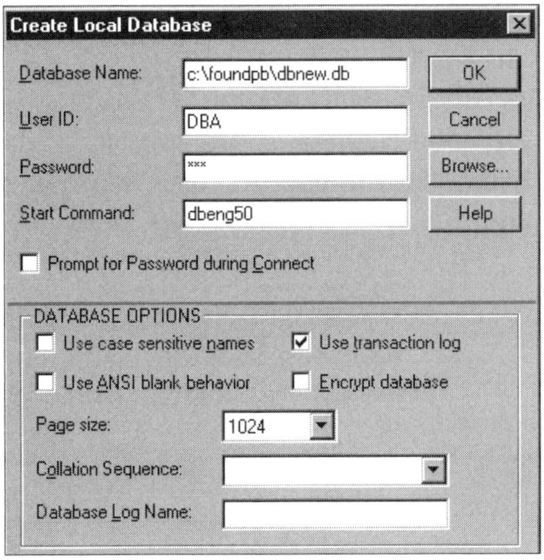

Figure 5-13
The Create Local Database dialog can create a new SQL Anywhere database.

File|Delete Database — Deleting an SQL Anywhere Database

The File|Delete Database choice allows you to delete an SQL Anywhere database. It also deletes the database's database profile and ODBC data source configuration automatically.

Creating and Deleting a Non–SQL Anywhere Database

PowerBuilder has no direct ability to create a new database or delete an old database, unless it's SQL Anywhere. Therefore, all non–SQL Anywhere databases must be created or deleted externally, typically by using the tools provided by the database vendor or some third-party provider.

In some cases, it may be possible to run such a tool from within a script and thereby create or delete a database when you run your application. For example if the tool is an .EXE file with a command-line interface, you could run it using the PowerScript function RUN.

File|Configure ODBC|Create — Creating an ODBC Data Source Configuration

Suppose that you have an ODBC database already on your system, but PowerBuilder does not yet know about it. For example, maybe you have copied an SQL Anywhere or dBASE database onto your C: drive from another system. To set up access to it from PowerBuilder, you need to create its ODBC data source configuration in ODBC.INI.

Select File|Configure ODBC from the menu. This displays the Configure ODBC dialog box shown in Figure 5-14. The top half of the dialog box displays the ODBC drivers that you have installed. When you click one of the driver names, the bottom half of the dialog box shows the data source configurations, if any, for that driver.

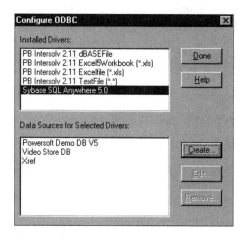

Figure 5-14

The Configure ODBC dialog displays your ODBC drivers and data sources.

To create a new data source configuration, click a driver and then click the Create button. The Data Source Configuration dialog box for the selected driver appears. Each driver has its own product-specific dialog box. Figure 5-15 shows the one for an SQL Anywhere data source, which we have seen once before earlier in this chapter. (Apparently, the scene in Figure 5-15 took place before the one in Figure 5-14, since the Configure ODBC dialog shows the Video Store DB data source as already existing.)

When you create a new data source configuration, PowerBuilder automatically creates the database profile for it.

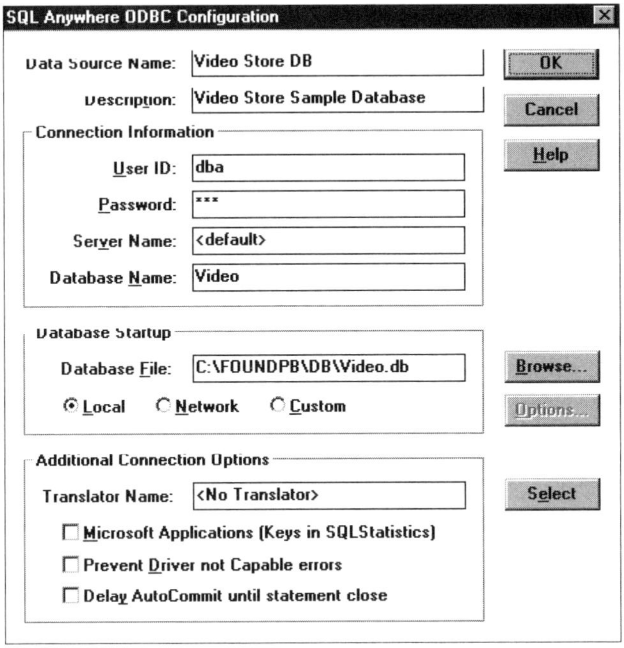

Figure 5-15
The Data Source Configuration dialog box for an SQL Anywhere database.

FILE|CONFIGURE ODBC — EDITING OR REMOVING AN ODBC DATA SOURCE CONFIGURATION

The Configure ODBC dialog box also has buttons to edit the parameters for a data source and to remove a data source, as you can see from Figure 5-14. Clicking the Remove button deletes the selected data source's configuration information from the Windows registry (or ODBC.INI) but has no effect on the physical database, which will continue to exist even if this particular PowerBuilder client no longer knows about it.

FILE|CONNECT|SETUP|NEW — CREATING A DATABASE PROFILE

Whether your database is ODBC or non-ODBC, it must have a database profile in PB.INI before you can connect to it. If you have used the "Create Database" process to create the database (it would be SQL Anywhere in that case) or the "Configure ODBC" process to configure it as an ODBC data source, PowerBuilder has already created the database profile for you, and so you are ready to connect. That leaves two other possibilities, in which the database would exist but its database profile would not:

- It is a non-ODBC database.
- It is an ODBC database whose data source configuration in the Windows registry (or ODBC.INI) already exists, but that configuration was done outside PowerBuilder, so PB.INI has no database profile for it.

In either of these cases, you must create a database profile. You begin the process by selecting File|Connect|Setup from the Database Painter menu. This pops up the database profiles dialog box shown in Figure 5-16. The dialog box shows the database profiles that already exist in your PB.INI. Since your database has no profile yet, you will not see it on the list, so click the New button.

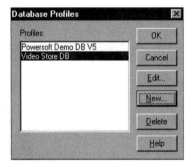

Figure 5-16
The Database Profiles dialog box lists your profiles. Click the New button to create a new profile.

Clicking New calls up the Database Profile Setup dialog box. We've seen this twice already: Figure 5-5 shows it for a non-ODBC database, and Figure 5-10 shows it for an ODBC database. (Actually, a shorter version of the dialog box first appears. The short version has a More>> button, which expands the dialog box to what you see in the figures.)

When you fill out the Database Profile Setup and click OK, you return to the Database Profiles dialog box in Figure 5-16. But now your new profile is on the list and is the highlighted entry. Click OK and the Database Painter connects to the database.

FILE|CONNECT|SETUP — CONNECTING TO, EDITING, AND DELETING A DATABASE PROFILE

There are other buttons on the Database Profiles dialog box (see Figure 5-16):

- **OK** — Connect to a database using the selected profile.
- **Cancel** — Close the dialog box.
- **Edit** — Display the Database Profile Setup dialog box for the selected profile so that you can modify its parameters.
- **Delete** — Delete the selected profile from PB.INI (but do not delete the physical database, nor its ODBC data source configuration, if any). Be careful: There is no confirmation step!

FILE|CONNECT — CONNECTING TO A DATABASE

To connect to a database that already has a database profile, make the menu choice File|Connect. This leads to a submenu, shown back in Figure 5-12, the top part of which lists your database profiles. This is the same list you would see if you were to click Setup and open the Database Profiles dialog box. PowerBuilder gets this list from PB.INI, the "PROFILES=" parameter of the [DBMS_PROFILES] section.

On the menu, the checkmarked item is the currently connected database. To connect to a different database (or to disconnect from and reconnect to the current one), select its profile name from the menu.

FILE|CONNECT|PROMPT — CONNECTING TO A DATABASE WITHOUT A PROFILE

I have stated that you must have a database profile before you can connect to a database. But it turns out that there is a way to connect without a profile and without creating one. Select File|Connect|Prompt from the menu. PowerBuilder displays several dialog boxes that you use to specify the database, and then it connects to it.

This may be useful for a database you plan to connect to only once. But for a database that you plan to visit repeatedly, you should use File|Connect|Setup to create a profile for it. It is much less work to connect to a database with a profile than to go through the much longer File|Connect|Prompt process.

CONNECTING TO THE VIDEO STORE DATABASE

The CD-ROM that accompanies this book contains a copy of the Video Store database that I use throughout the book, along with a procedure to install it. If you plan to follow along "hands-on" with the exercises in the chapters to follow, you should now connect to this database:

1. If you have not done so already, you should follow the instructions in the README.TXT file on the CD-ROM for installing the sample files onto your system. That process creates a subdirectory DB in a directory of your choice — C:\FOUNDPB by default — and places the SQL Anywhere database file VIDEO.DB into it: C:\FOUNDPB\DB\VIDEO.DB. Use Windows 95 Explorer, the Windows 3.1 File Manager, or some similar tool to confirm that this file exists.

2. Start PowerBuilder and click Database on the PowerBar to open the Database Painter. If you have trouble, refer to the sidebar to this chapter "When the Database Painter Won't Open."

3. Configure the Video Store database as an ODBC Data Source: Select File|Configure ODBC from the menu. This brings up the Configure ODBC dialog box. Scroll through the list of "Installed Drivers," if need be, and click "Sybase SQL Anywhere 5.0" to highlight it. Depending on what ODBC drivers you've installed, your screen should look more or less like Figure 5-14, except that "Video Store DB" will not yet appear on the "Data Sources for Selected Drivers" list. (If it does appear, you can click Done and skip this step, or you can click "Video Store DB" and click the Remove button, if you would like to continue with this exercise.)

Click the Create button to open the SQL Anywhere ODBC Configuration dialog box. Fill it in as shown in Figure 5-15. The password, which echoes as "***," is "sql," which is the default for new SQL Anywhere databases. If you installed the sample files in a directory other than C:\FOUNDPB, type in your directory name followed by "\db\video.db" in the Database File field.

Click OK to create the data source configuration. This takes you back to the Configure ODBC dialog box. Note that "Video Store DB" is now on the list of data sources. Click Close to close the dialog box.

4. Confirm that PowerBuilder has created a database profile for the database, as a result of your configuring the ODBC Data Source: Select

File|Connect|Setup from the menu. The Database Profiles dialog box pops up. It should look like Figure 5-16, although your list of profiles will probably be different than mine. But you should see "Video Store Db" on the list. (If you don't, then something went wrong with step 3, so click Cancel, go back, and try it again.)

Click "Video Store Db" to select it and click the Edit button. Click the More>> button to expand the Database Profile Setup dialog box that appears. It should look like Figure 5-10.

Actually, it will be slightly different. For some reason, PowerBuilder has converted the "B" in "Video Store DB" to lowercase. You can come back to this dialog box later to change the "Db" to "DB." But for now, just leave it as is.

Click the Cancel button to close this Database Profile Setup dialog box. Click Cancel to close the Database Profiles dialog box.

5. Connect to the Video Store database: From the menu, select File|Connect|Video Store Db to connect to the database. (You could have done the same thing by clicking the OK button on the Database Profiles dialog box in the previous step.) Upon connecting, PowerBuilder opens the Select Tables dialog for the database, which is shown in Figure 6-1 in the next chapter.

You are now connected! That brings us to the next topic.

WHAT HAPPENS WHEN YOU CONNECT TO A DATABASE?

When you connect to a database in the Database Painter, two things happen:

1. The Select Tables dialog box pops up. (This is shown in Figure 6-1 in the next chapter.) It lists the tables in the newly connected database. (For a new database with no tables yet, the list will be empty.) In most cases, you will click on one or more tables on the list and click Open, which is how you begin working with tables in the Database Painter. Or you can click Cancel, which closes the dialog box but leaves you connected to the database. You can bring back the Select Tables dialog box at any time by clicking the Open button on the PainterBar or by right-clicking in the Database window and choosing Select Tables from the pop-up menu.

Tools for Troubleshooting Database Connections

For combating serious trouble with a database connection, PowerBuilder offers two troubleshooting tools: the "Database Trace" tool, which writes internal database commands to a log file as they occur, and the "ODBC Driver Manager Trace" tool, which does the same thing for ODBC commands. Refer to the *Connecting to Your Database* guide for instructions on how to use these tools.

---

2. PowerBuilder modifies PB.INI to store the name of the currently connected database. After connecting to the Video Store database, you will have these entries in PB.INI:

```
[DBMS_PROFILES]
CURRENT=Video Store DB
```

PowerBuilder uses this information to connect to the same database every time you open the Database Painter, until you connect to a different database.

Summary

The Database Painter is the key to the critical task of connecting your PowerBuilder client to a database. In this chapter, after a quick review of database terminology in a PowerBuilder context, we have detailed how to make such a connection and work through it, especially in the context of SQL Anywhere databases such as our sample, which PowerBuilder richly supports.

6

The Database Painter

*N*ow that we've explored the ins and outs of connecting to a database, let's look at what else you can do in the Database Painter. The primary purpose of the Database Painter is to allow you to view and modify the database and its tables.

In the course of describing the Database Painter, this chapter will also cover other related painters. The two most important are these:

- **The Data Manipulation Painter**, in which you can view and change the actual data within a table

- **The Table Painter**, in which you can view and change a table's structure (for example, add a new column to it) and other properties and features.

You can launch these painters from the Database Painter to carry out their special tasks.

The previous chapter explained in detail how to open the Database Painter. This chapter picks up where we left off.

Selecting Tables in the Database Painter

When you first open the Database Painter or first connect it to a database, the Select Tables dialog box appears. (See Figure 6-1.) It lists the tables in the database. Most of your work in the Database Painter will be to manipulate one or more of these tables, so in this dialog you should click one or more table names to select them and then click the Open button. If for some reason you don't want to work with a table, click Cancel. As for the New button, it's for creating a new table, and I'll talk about it later.

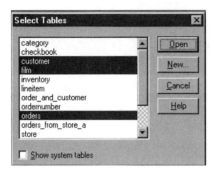

Figure 6-1
Select the tables to open.

After you have clicked Open or Cancel to close the Select Tables dialog box, you can pop it back up again at any time to select more tables by clicking the Open button on the PainterBar or by right-clicking somewhere within the Database Painter window and choosing Select Tables from the pop-up menu.

When you have selected some tables, they appear in the Database Painter window. Figure 6-2 shows the Painter window after selecting three tables: customer, orders, film.

(I ought to take a moment here to direct your attention to the table name "orders." My preference is to give every table a name that is singular, not plural. But "order" is a bad name for a table because ORDER is an SQL keyword. Not only can a table named "order" cause confusion, but some servers, such as SQL Server, don't allow such a name at all.)

In Figure 6-2, you see a box for each of the three tables. Each box lists the columns in the table. You can move or stretch a box by clicking and dragging with the mouse. There are also key symbols attached to each box. They indicate a table's primary key, index keys, and foreign keys, which are topics covered later in this chapter. You might also see a comment to the right of each column, which is not shown in Figure 6-2 but which makes the table boxes much wider.

If you would like to see more information or less information about each table, right-click anywhere in the Database Painter window outside of the table boxes. The menu shown in Figure 6-3 pops up. The first choice on this menu is another way to bring back the Select Tables dialog box. The other choices change the amount of detail shown. For example, if you select Show Comments, PowerBuilder makes each table's box wider and displays the comments for every table and column.

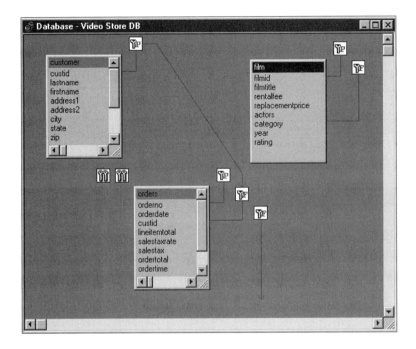

Figure 6-2

The Database Painter — After you select tables, PowerBuilder displays an information box about each table.

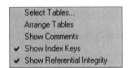

Figure 6-3

The pop-up menu for the Database Painter window.

To remove a table from the Database Painter display, right-click the table's name at the top of its information box and select Close from the pop-up menu that appears.

The Data Manipulation Painter

The most interesting thing to do with a table is to look at its data. To do that, click a table's information box in the Database Painter window — that selects it. Then click the Data Manipulation (grid) button on the PainterBar. This launches a new painter, the Data Manipulation Painter, which presents the rows and columns of the table. Two other PainterBar buttons also open the table in the Data Manipulation Painter — the Data Manipulation (tabular) button and the Data Manipulation (freeform) button — but they present it in a different style:.

Figure 6-4 shows the customer table in the Data Manipulation Painter. In this painter, you can not only look at and scroll through the customer data, you can also modify it.

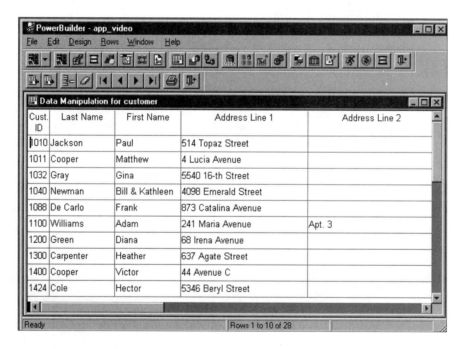

Figure 6-4

When you click the Data Manipulation (grid) button on the Database PainterBar, the Data Manipulation Painter displays the selected table in a grid style.

The PainterBar buttons let you retrieve data from the database, write changes you've made to the database, insert and delete rows, and navigate up and down through the rows. If you make changes, none of them are made to the physical database unless you click Save Changes on the PainterBar. If you want to throw away your changes and read a fresh set of rows from the database, click Retrieve on the PainterBar.

OTHER DATA MANIPULATION FEATURES

The Data Manipulation Painter incorporates many other useful features, including these:

- The File|Print menu selection prints the table.

- The File|Save Rows As menu selection exports the table to an external format. Twelve export formats are supported, including Text, dBASE, and SQL INSERT statements.

- The Rows|Import menu selection imports rows into the table from an external file. The import file can be either a tab-separated ASCII text file (.TXT extension) or a dBase II or III data file (.DBF extension).

- The Rows|Filter menu selection lets you limit the data to a subset of the table's rows by specifying selection criteria.

- The Rows|Sort menu selection lets you sort the data in the painter windows by one or more columns. Without sorting, the Data Manipulation Painter (like SQL database products in general) retrieves rows in no particular order.

- You can widen or shrink columns by clicking and dragging the border lines that separate them.

- You can rearrange the columns into a different sequence by clicking and dragging a column name left or right to a new location.

- You can open more instances of the Data Manipulation Painter to view more than one table at a time or to view different parts of the same table. To do this, just return to the Database Painter without closing the Data Manipulation Painter. (Selecting Window|Database - <*database name*> from the menu is one way to do that.) In the Database Painter, click another table and then click Preview. That opens the Data Manipulation Painter again in a new window. To see the windows side by side, use menu choices such as Window|Vertical.

CLOSING THE DATA MANIPULATION PAINTER

To close the Data Manipulation Painter, click the Close button on the PainterBar. This returns you to the Database Painter. If you have made data changes, a dialog box pops up first asking whether you want to save them.

The Table Painter

The Database Painter (Figure 6-2) can present all the tables in a database. It also shows you a little bit of information about each table's columns and properties. Various toolbar buttons and menu choices in the Database Painter can show you more. But the Table Painter goes much further and provides the most comprehensive look at a table. Figure 6-5 shows the Table Painter opened on the customer table.

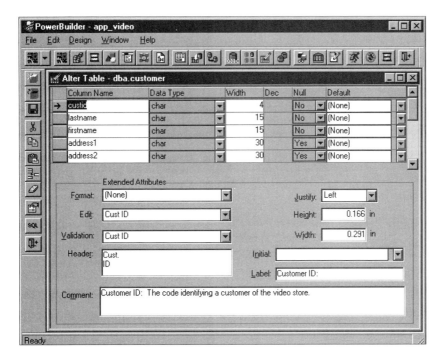

Figure 6-5
The Table Painter for the customer table.

OPENING THE TABLE PAINTER

There are many ways to open the Table Painter. Whether or not the Database Painter is open, you can always click the Table button on the PowerBar. An Open Table dialog opens, almost identical to the Select Table dialog in Figure 6-1. Pick a table and click Open, or click New to add a new table to the database.

If the Database Painter is already open, there are several convenient ways to launch the Table Painter on an existing table. First, click any table information box (such as the customer, orders, or film box in Figure 6-2) to select that table. Then do one of the following:

- Double-click the table information box

Deleting a Table

To delete a table from the database, open the table in the Database Painter, right-click the table name in its table information box, and select Drop Table from the pop-up menu. You can also click the Drop button on the PainterBar. A dialog box pops up asking if you are sure. Since deleting a table required by an application will make that application dysfunctional, you should approach this operation with caution.

- Right-click the table information box and select Alter Table or Definition from its pop-up menu
- Click the Edit Selected Object button on the PainterBar
- Select Object|Edit Object from the menu.

To create a new table from the Database Painter:

- Click the Create Table button on the PainterBar
- Click the New button on the Select Tables dialog box in Figure 6-1
- Select Object|New|Table from the menu.

When you open the Table Painter on an existing table, its title bar will say "Alter Table," as it does in Figure 6-5. When you open it to create a new table, its title bar will say "Create Table."

You can alter or create two or more tables at the same time by opening more copies of the Table Painter. The easiest way to open another copy is to click the Table button on the PowerBar.

THE TABLE PAINTER'S TWO SECTIONS

As you can see in Figure 6-5, the Table Painter window has two sections:

- **The top half** — a list of the table's column names and their data types displayed in a grid.

- **The bottom half** — the "extended column attributes" section, which contains additional characteristics of a column, presented for one column at a time. An arrow in the top half points to the column described by the bottom half.

THE LIST OF COLUMNS

The title of the Table Painter window includes the name of the table preceded by its owner in the example, "dba.customer." With most database server products, one user is designated as a table's owner. You can change the name of a table, but some of the database objects that reference the old table name, such as views and queries, will not be changed.

Each row in the scrolling list of columns is a column in the table — custid, lastname, firstname, and so forth in Figure 6-5. Click the Insert Column button to add a new column or the Delete Column button to delete the current one.

The columns have the following information:

- **Column Name** — the name of the column.

- **Data Type** — the column's data type, such as "char," "numeric," or "date."

- **Width** — the number of characters or digits allocated to the column. This applies to some data types, such as "char," but not to others, such as "integer."

- **Dec** — the number of decimal digits allocated. This applies only to a few data types, such as the SQL Anywhere "numeric" type.

- **Null** — whether null values are allowed in the column.

- **Default** — the default value, if any, for the column. Depending upon your database product, the dropdown list lets you pick such defaults as current date and time, user name, autoincrement, and null.

All of this information comes directly from the database's table definition, and your ability to change it depends entirely on the database server product. Also, the data types differ from one database product to another.

An Alternative Way to See and Change a Column's Extended Attributes

The Table Painter shows you the extended attributes for all the columns in a table all in one place. In the Database Painter, there is another way to get to the extended attributes of a single column. Right-click a column name in a table's information box and select Properties from the pop-up menu. This opens a tabbed dialog box of extended column attributes.

EXTENDED COLUMN ATTRIBUTES

The lower part of the Table Painter window displays the ten *extended attributes* for a column. When you click on or scroll to a column in the column list, that column's extended attributes are displayed. An arrow indicates the current column. In Figure 6-5, it's pointing to the custid column, so you are seeing the extended attributes for custid.

The extended column attributes are PowerBuilder-specific information. PowerBuilder is enhancing the basic description of each column that the database maintains. PowerBuilder will use this information to make it easier for you and me to develop DataWindows and reports. But the database server itself, although it is storing this information (more on this later), does not know what it is or how to interpret it. Only PowerBuilder and, perhaps, you as the developer, know how to make use of it.

The extended column attributes are these:

- **Format** — the format for displaying the column's values. A format could determine, for example, whether you want a dollar sign and commas in a number.

- **Edit** — an edit mask controlling the characters typed into a column. For example, an edit mask might show the placement of hyphens and parentheses in a phone number.

- **Validation** — a rule for validating the column's values. For example, an integer year column may have a validation rule to force the value to be between 1900 and 2001.

Formats, edit masks, and validation rules require a longer explanation, which I'll provide later in this chapter.

- **Header** — the default heading for the column in a grid or tabular display. You can enter multiple header lines by pressing Enter at the end of each line.

- **Label** — the default label for the column in a free-form display

- **Justify** — whether to left-, right-, or center-justify the column's value in a display cell

- **Height** — the height for the column in inches

- **Width** — the width for the column in inches

The heading, justification, height, width, and label control the appearance of the column in the Data Manipulation Painter. They are also the default settings for the column when you create a new DataWindow.

- **Initial** — the initial value (default value) for the column. For example, "CA" (California) might be the initial value for the state column.

  For some data types, the "Initial" field includes a dropdown list box with some special initial values. For instance, a "char" column has these three selections: "Fill With Spaces," "Set To Null," and "Set To Empty String."

- **Comment** — a description of the column, for documentation purposes

THE TABLE PROPERTY SHEET

Still more information is available in the Table Painter, and you'll find it in the table property sheet, shown in Figure 6-6. To open it, click the Properties button on the Table PainterBar.

As with any property sheet, this one is organized into tab pages:

- **General** — the table name and a description of the table for documentation purposes.

- **Data Font, Heading Font, Label Font** — the default display font, style, and size for the data, headings, and labels in the table.

- **Indexes**, **Primary Key**, and **Foreign Keys** — the table's indexes, primary key, and foreign keys. These will be described later in this chapter.

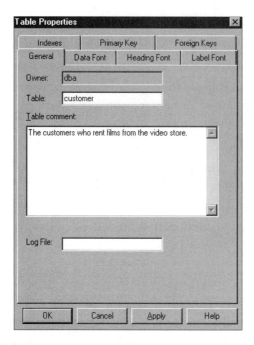

Figure 6-6
The property sheet for the customer table.

SAVING YOUR WORK

PowerBuilder does not apply the changes you make in the Table Painter
— to columns, extended column attributes, and table properties — to the
database until you select File|Save from the menu or click Save Changes
on the PainterBar. If you close the Table Painter without doing this,
PowerBuilder will ask whether you want to save changes first.

If you are creating a new table, PowerBuilder will pop up a dialog box
asking for its name when you select File|Save.

VIEWING THE SQL

PowerBuilder makes the changes by constructing a series of SQL commands and transmitting them to the database server. You can inspect the

pending SQL commands at any time prior to performing the File|Save by clicking the SQL Syntax View button on the PainterBar. When you see the pending changes, you can select File|Print from the menu to print them. The SQL Syntax View button button is a toggle, so click it again to return to the Table Painter.

Display Formats, Edit Styles, and Validation Rules

In describing the extended column attributes in the Table Painter, I mentioned three important attributes: *display formats*, *edit styles*, and *validation rules*. Using each of these attributes is a two-step process:

1. In the Database Painter, use the three choices near the middle of the Design menu (Figure 6-7) to define the attributes, making them available to the database. PowerBuilder defines some automatically, so you might be able to skip this step.

2. In the Table Painter, assign the attributes to columns in the database.

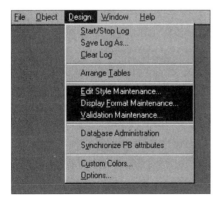

Figure 6-7

The Database Painter's Design menu. Notice the three choices near the middle for defining edit styles, display formats, and validation rules.

DISPLAY FORMATS

A *display format* specifies how a string, number, date, or time should be displayed. You might want the number –1234.5, for example, to be shown as "($1,234.50)." That's what a display format is for.

In PowerBuilder you use a symbolic language to define display formats. For example:

- **$#,##0.00;($#,##0.00)** — This display format converts a number into a currency display. In English it says, "Add a leading dollar sign, commas, a decimal point, and two decimal places. Enclose negative numbers in parentheses." The semicolon separates the format for a positive number from the format for a negative number. Each "0" will be replaced by a digit (0-9) when a value is displayed. Each "#" will be replaced by a digit, too, except that leading zeroes will not appear.

- **m/d/yy h:mm** — This defines how to display a "datetime" (a date and a time) value. It will display such a value as, for example, "7/4/96 1:42."

IN THE DATABASE PAINTER . . .

When you create a database or first connect to it, PowerBuilder adds a certain number of display formats to it for you to use. The formats "$#,##0.00;($#,##0.00)" and "m/d/yy h:mm" are among them. You can review the definition of these, or add new formats of your own, by selecting Design|Display Format Maintenance from the menu to pop up the Display Formats dialog box shown in Figure 6-8. Pick a format and click Edit to review it, or click New to create a new one. This step opens the Display Format Definition dialog box shown in Figure 6-9.

In the Display Format Definition dialog, you can assign a display, format a name, type in its format string, and test it by typing in a "Test Value" and clicking Test. For assistance in typing in the format string, click Help.

IN THE TABLE PAINTER . . .

Figure 6-10 shows part of the Table Painter window as it might appear while you are in the process of picking a display format ("Format") from the dropdown list to apply to a numeric column. The choice "[None]," near the bottom of the list, is the default.

Figure 6-8

When you select Design I Display Format Maintenance from the Database Painter menu, the Display Formats dialog box appears.

Figure 6-9

The Display Format Definition dialog box.

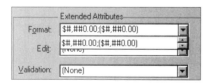

Figure 6-10

Assigning a display format to a numeric database column in the Table Painter.

EDIT STYLES

An *edit style* controls how the user types a value into a column. This is different than a display format, which controls how the value is displayed after it is typed in. For example:

- You can allow users to type a ten-digit phone number such as "714-555-6666" without requiring them to enter the dashes, yet the dashes will display on the screen.
- You can allow users to enter dates in a format other than the standard "mm/dd/yy" format — for example, "24-JUL-96" instead of "7/24/96."
- You can limit entry in a column to a small set of acceptable values by assigning it a dropdown list, check box, radio button, or dropdown DataWindow style.

Defining an edit style and assigning it to a column follows the same process that I described for display formats.

IN THE DATABASE PAINTER . . .

If you want to review the definition of an edit style or add a new edit style, select Design | Edit Style Maintenance from the Database Painter menu. This selection pops up the Edit Styles dialog box shown in Figure 6-11. Each type of edit style is identified by a different icon preceding the style name. For example, in Figure 6-11, "Film Rating" is a DropDownListBox, "Phone" is an EditMask, and "Yes or No" is a CheckBox. You can pick a style from the list and click the Edit button.

To define a new edit style, click the New button to open the Edit Style dialog box. There are six types of edit styles and hence six items in the Style dropdown list. Select the one you want, and the Options panel changes to display the appropriate items for that style (see Figure 6-12):

- "Edit" controls the characters that the user can type into a field. You can use it, for example, to make sure that only digits can be typed in.
- "EditMask" is an extension of "Edit"; it defines an edit mask for entering data that has a format containing fixed characters, such as a phone number.

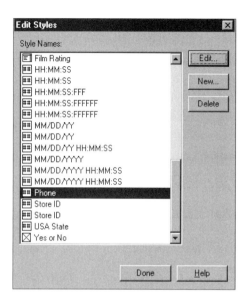

Figure 6-11

The Edit Styles dialog box.

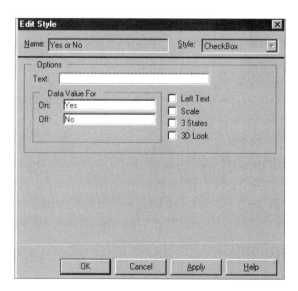

Figure 6-12

The Edit Style dialog options for a "CheckBox" style.

■ The "CheckBox" style displays a column as a check box. This style is appropriate where a column can take only one, two, or three values. In the video store database, the ispaidup column in the customer table can have only two values — "Yes" and "No." Therefore, it's a good candidate for the "CheckBox" edit style. (See Figure 6-13.)

Cust. ID	Last Name	First Name	Paid Up?
1040	Newman	Bill & Kathleen	☐
1088	De Carlo	Frank	☑
1100	Williams	Adam	☐
1200	Green	Diana	☐
1300	Carpenter	Heather	☑
1400	Cooper	Victor	☑

Figure 6-13
Using the "CheckBox" style to indicate whether a customer is paid up.

■ "RadioButton" displays a column as a group of radio buttons. Like "DropDownListBox" and "CheckBox," it's useful for columns that have a limited number of allowable values. (See Figure 6-14.)

Film ID	Film Title	Rating
A-137	Forrest Gump	○ G ○ R ● PG ○ NC-17 ○ PG-13 ○ NR
A-155	Schindler's List	○ G ● R ○ PG ○ NC-17 ○ PG-13 ○ NR
A-400	Jurassic Park	○ G ○ R ○ PG ○ NC-17 ● PG-13 ○ NR

Figure 6-14
Using the "RadioButton" style to select a film rating.

■ "DropDownListBox" lets the user pick column values from a drop-down list. In the Video Store database, for example, we use this style for the film rating, as shown in Figure 6-15.

Film ID	Film Title	Rating
A-130	The Maltese Falcon	NR
A-137	Forrest Gump	PG
A-155	Schindler's List	R
A-400	Jurassic Park	PG-13 ⬇
B-201	A Little Princess	G
B-202	Beethoven	PG
		PG-13
B-203	Pocahontas	R
C-500	Bringing Up Baby	NC-17
		NR
C-520	The Mask	PG
C-682	Return of the Jedi	PG

Figure 6-15
Using the "DropDownListBox" style to select a film rating.

- "DropDownDataWindow" is a more complex form of "DropDownListBox." You can use a DataWindow of your own design in place of the standard dropdown list, for a more elaborate appearance. Since this edit style requires the use of DataWindows, I'll show an example of it in Chapter 9.

IN THE TABLE PAINTER . . .

Figure 6-16 shows how to assign an edit style to a column in the Table Painter by picking it from a dropdown list.

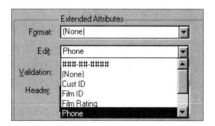

Figure 6-16
Assigning an edit style to a column in the Table Painter.

VALIDATION RULES

A *validation rule* is a rule that PowerBuilder uses to make sure that a
value is valid. The rule is tested after the user finishes typing in the value.
For example:

- You can test that a zip code has been entered in either five-digit or
  "zip plus four" format.
- You can enforce a rule that a date may not be a Sunday.

Defining a validation rule and assigning it to a column follows the
same process that I described for display formats and edit styles.

IN THE DATABASE PAINTER . . .

Unlike display formats and edit styles, PowerBuilder does not create any
validation rules automatically. So you must set up every validation rule
yourself, by selecting Design | Validation Maintenance from the Database
Painter menu and clicking New on the Validation Rules dialog box shown
in Figure 6-17. To review or modify a validation rule that you set up previously, pick a rule from the list and click Edit. Clicking either New or Edit
opens the Input Validation dialog box shown in Figure 6-18.

Figure 6-17
The Validation Rules dialog box.

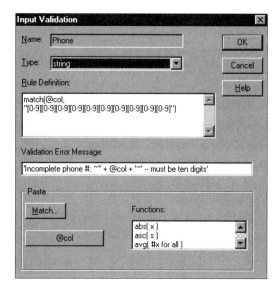

Figure 6-18

The Input Validation dialog box.

The major elements of the Input Validation dialog box are these:

- **Name** — the name of the validation rule. You should use descriptive names, such as "Phone" or "Zip Code."

- **Type** — the type of value being validated: string, number, date, time, or datetime.

- **Rule Definition** — a PowerScript expression that evaluates to true or false, indicating whether or not the value is valid. The rule definition will frequently rely on PowerScript functions, which is why a list of functions is available on this dialog box.

- **Validation Error Message** — the error message to be displayed if the validation rule is violated.

In the rule definition and error message, "@col" represents the value that is being validated.

IN THE TABLE PAINTER . . .

Figure 6-19 shows how to assign a validation rule to a column in the Table Painter by picking it from a dropdown list.

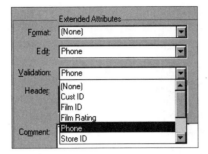

Figure 6-19
Assigning a validation rule to a column in the Table Painter.

WHO USES DISPLAY FORMATS, EDIT STYLES, AND VALIDATION RULES?

I have explained how to create display formats, edit styles, and validation rules. When do they come into play?

- They are used and enforced by the Data Manipulation Painter as it displays columns and you edit them.

- When you design a new DataWindow, they are copied into it. When you run the DataWindow, they are used and enforced. In the DataWindow Painter, you can override the display format, edit style, or validation rule of a column to make it something other than what it picks up from its database source, or you can remove them altogether.

- Any SQL commands, in particular UPDATE and INSERT commands that you execute from a script, ignore validation rules.

Where the Extended Definitions Live: the PowerBuilder Repository

All of the table and column properties we've discussed so far must be stored somewhere in the database. After all, if this were not the case, all of the PowerBuilder users of the database would not be able to see and share the same properties. But no database server product has built-in support for these extended properties. To resolve this problem, PowerBuilder creates five special tables in the database and stores the extended properties there. These tables are called the *PowerBuilder System Tables* or the *PowerBuilder Repository*.

The first time you use PowerBuilder to connect to, say, an SQL Server database, PowerBuilder adds these tables to it. From the database server's point of view, these tables are no different than any others in the database. But from PowerBuilder's point of view, they are special.

The five tables are these:

- **pbcattbl** — extended properties of every table
- **pbcatcol** — extended attributes of every column
- **pbcatfmt** — the display formats
- **pbcatedt** — the edit styles
- **pbcatvld** — the validation rules

PowerBuilder creates these tables in a database the first time you connect to it. (It's important, therefore, that the first connection be by a user with sufficient security rights to create tables with public read/write privileges.) The contents of the tables is documented in the appendix of the *PowerBuilder User's Guide*.

When you first open the Select Tables dialog box, you will not see these tables listed. As system tables, they are hidden. Clicking the Show System Tables check box displays them. (See Figure 6-20.) From here, you can open them and do anything to them that you can do to any other table. For safety, however, you should not modify them directly — let PowerBuilder manage them.

Besides the five repository tables, your database probably contains other system tables. These are created and managed by the database server for its own purposes. Exactly what these tables are and how they are used depend on your server product. For a Sybase SQL Anywhere database, they begin with the prefix "sys" — you can see some of them in Figure 6-20 — and are documented in the SQL Anywhere manual. Although PowerBuilder uses the term "system tables" to refer to both the repository tables and the database-specific system tables, from the database server's point of view, only the latter are "system tables."

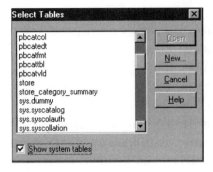

Figure 6-20
Check Show System Tables to see system tables in the Select Tables dialog box.

Keys and Indexes

Tables in a relational database will often have *primary keys, foreign keys,* and *indexes* to enhance their usefulness and performance.

PRIMARY KEYS

A *primary key* is a column or a set of columns that contain a unique, non-null identifier for each row in the table. For example, an employee table might have an employee number column as its primary key. Each employee must have an employee number, and no two employees can share the same number. The database server will enforce the uniqueness rule on the primary key.

A table can have only one primary key, which can be one or more columns. Although a primary key is not required, it is a rule of good database design that every table should have one. The primary key columns do not have to be the first columns in the table, although that is where most database designers put them.

In the Video Store database, five of the seven tables have a single column as their primary key. The other two — lineitem and inventory —

have two primary key columns each. When you open tables in the
Database Painter, the primary keys are indicated by a key icon with the
letter "P" pointing to each key column. (You can see them in Figure 6-2.)
If you cannot see them in your own Database Painter window, try right-
clicking the window and turning on the Show Referential Integrity
option.

Tbl Prop

To define, review, or change the primary key for a table, using the
Database Painter or the Table Painter: Open the table's property sheet by
clicking the Table Properties button on the PainterBar. Click the Primary
Key tab, which is shown in Figure 6-21 for the lineitem table. Specify the
key fields by clicking them in the Table Columns list, which adds them to
the Key Columns list.

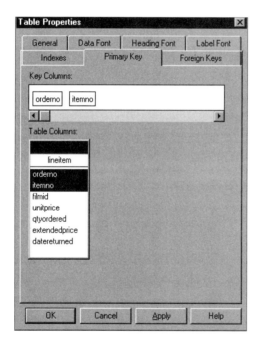

Figure 6-21
The Primary Key page of the lineitem table's property sheet.

FOREIGN KEYS

When a table contains a column that references the primary key of another table, you can define a *foreign key*. A foreign key establishes a *dependency* between the two tables, also known as a *referential integrity relationship*. Not all database products support foreign keys and referential integrity.

An example of a referential integrity relationship is the one between the orders and customer tables. The primary key of customer is the column custid. Orders also has a custid column, although it is not its primary key. However, we would like to enforce the rule that every custid value in orders must always exist in customer. This rule is what is known as referential integrity. We establish the rule by declaring custid in orders to be a foreign key to customer.

When you open tables in the Database Painter, the foreign keys are indicated by a key icon with the letter "F" pointing to the key columns and linking the pair of tables. You can see the link from customer to orders in Figure 6-2. If you cannot see them in your own Database Painter window, try right-clicking the window and turning on the Show Referential Integrity option. (Figure 6-2 also indicates that orders has a second foreign key. It happens to be to the store table, which is not open.)

There are several ways to define, review, or change a foreign key:

- From the Database Painter, select a table and click Create Foreign Key on the PainterBar to define a new foreign key.

- From the Database Painter, double-click a foreign key icon attached to a table box to review or change the foreign key.

- From the Table Painter, open the table's property sheet and click the Foreign Keys tab. As Figure 6-22 shows, this displays a list of the table's foreign keys. To view or change a key's definition, select it from the list and click the Edit button. To define a new foreign key, click the New button.

All of these procedures open the Foreign Key Definition dialog box. Figure 6-23 shows this dialog box for the foreign key linking orders to customer. Fill in this dialog and click OK to create or modify the foreign key.

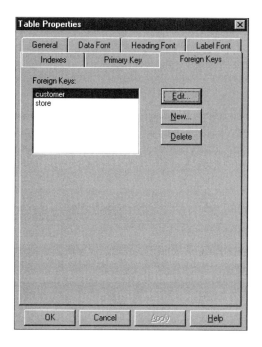

Figure 6-22
The Foreign Key page of the order table's property sheet.

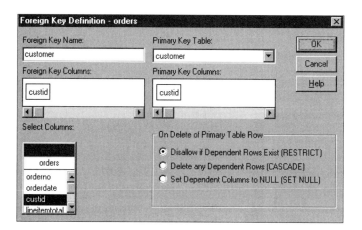

Figure 6-23
The Foreign Key Definition dialog for the orders table's foreign key to the customer table.

INDEXES

A table may have one or more *indexes*. Like primary keys and foreign keys, indexes are composed of one or more columns in the table. The main purpose of an index is to increase the speed of searches and sorts. You should consider creating an index to support any column, or combination of columns, that is frequently used in searching or sorting. The columns that make up an index are called the index's *key*.

An index in a table is very much like an index in a book, and it gives the same kind of speed improvement. A book index is provided so that the reader doesn't have to search through every page to find a topic. Similarly, a table index eliminates the need for the database server to search an entire table for rows that contain a value.

In Figure 6-2, the two key icons to the left of the orders table indicate indexes. To review an index's structure, double-click one of these icons. A double-key icon indicates the index allows duplicate key values. A single-key icon, which is less common and not shown here, would indicate an index requiring every key value to be unique.

As with foreign keys, there are several ways to define, review, or change an index:

- From the Database Painter, select a table and click Create Index on the PainterBar to define a new index.

- From the Database Painter, double-click an index icon attached to a table box to review the index.

- From the Table Painter, open the table's property sheet and click the Indexes tab. This displays a list of the table's indexes. To view or change an index's definition, select it from the list and click the Edit button. To define a new index, click the New button.

Any of these procedures opens the Create Index dialog box, shown in Figure 6-24. The operation of this dialog box is very similar to the one for creating primary keys, with some extra options applicable to indexes.

REMOVING KEYS AND INDEXES

To remove a primary key, foreign key, or index from a table using the Database Painter: Open the table. If necessary, adjust the Database Painter settings so that the key or index icon becomes visible. Click the icon to select it and click the Drop button on the PainterBar. PowerBuilder will ask for confirmation.

To remove a foreign key or index from a table, using the Table Painter: Open the table's property sheet, select the foreign key or index on its tab page, and click the Delete button. To delete the primary key, switch to the property sheet's Primary Key tab and click each highlighted item in the "Table Columns" list to deselect it.

Figure 6-24

The Create Index dialog box for filmindex on the lineitem table.

Views

A *view* might also be called a "virtual table." From the point of view of an end user or an application developer, a view looks no different than any other table in the database. But, in reality, it has no rows or columns of its own. When the database server shows you the rows and columns that appear to be in the view, it is actually fetching them from other tables — real tables in the database.

In the Video Store database, I have created seven tables and three views. One of the views is named order_and_customer. When you preview it in the Data Manipulation Painter, you see the rows and columns shown in Figure 6-25, which certainly look like a typical table. But this information is not actually stored in the order_and_customer view. Instead, the database has combined data from the orders table (Figure 6-26) and the customer table (which was shown back in Figure 6-3) into a single integrated view. If you make a change to either of those tables and then re-retrieve the data for order_and_customer, the change will be reflected in the view. So the view is a virtual table whose data is assembled dynamically by the database server from other sources.

Order No.	Order Date	Cust. ID	Last Name	First Name	Order Time	Store ID	Order Total
101	12/28/95	1424	Cole	Hector	06:30:00	B	$7.03
102	12/28/95	1040	Newman	Bill & Kathleen	09:00:00	A	$30.31
103	12/28/95	5001	Miller	Kay	12:00:00	A	$12.72
104	12/28/95	5002	DeCamp	Julia	07:30:00	A	$7.31
105	12/28/95	5957	Staebell	Alice	02:00:00	A	$2.17
106	12/29/95	1200	Green	Diana	09:00:00	B	$6.22

Figure 6-25
The order_and_customer view.

Order No.	Order Date	Cust. ID	Line Item Total	Sales Tax Rate	Sales Tax	Order Total	Order Time	Store ID	Paid?
101	12/28/95	1424	$6.50	8.20%	$0.53	$7.03	06:30:00	B	☐
102	12/28/95	1040	$28.00	8.25%	$2.31	$30.31	09:00:00	A	☐
103	12/28/95	5001	$11.75	8.25%	$0.97	$12.72	12:00:00	A	☐
104	12/28/95	5002	$6.75	8.25%	$0.56	$7.31	07:30:00	A	☐
105	12/28/95	5957	$2.00	8.25%	$0.17	$2.17	02:00:00	A	☐
106	12/29/95	1200	$5.75	8.20%	$0.47	$6.22	09:00:00	B	☐

Figure 6-26
The orders table is one source for the order_and_customer view.

THE PURPOSE OF VIEWS

Using a view instead of real tables has many advantages, including convenience and security. Here are a few more of them:

- If a view represents the result of a complex query retrieval from one or more tables that you perform frequently, it is much easier to refer to the view than to restate the complex query every time.

- A view can give an end user a restricted view of a table, showing only certain rows and columns. It's easy to control users' access to data by giving them access rights to the view, but not to the underlying table.

- You can give the view and its columns more user-friendly names than its source tables may have.

DEFINING A VIEW

All of the major database server products support views. Instead of defining a view as a collection of columns with attributes, as you do for a table, you define the view in terms of a query: "What rows and columns from what tables (or other views) are the source of this view's data?" In SQL terms, this query is a SELECT statement.

This is the SQL command CREATE VIEW that created the order_and_customer view. Notice the SELECT command embedded within it:

```
CREATE VIEW order_and_customer AS
    SELECT orders.orderno, orders.orderdate, orders.custid,
        customer.lastname, customer.firstname,
        orders.ordertime, orders.storeid, orders.ordertotal
    FROM orders,customer
    WHERE customer.custid = orders.custid
```

The SELECT command asks the question, "What are all the rows from the orders and customer tables, where the orders and customer rows match (have the same custid value)? From the orders table, show these columns: orderno, orderdate, custid, ordertime, storeid, ordertotal. From the customer table, show these columns: lastname, firstname."

If you're new to SQL, I'm putting the cart before the horse here. Chapter 21 is an introduction to SQL, so please read it first and then come back.

When you preview order_and_customer, or do anything else that forces the database server to retrieve its data, the database server performs the query and returns its result rows as if they were from a real table.

WORKING WITH A VIEW IN THE DATABASE PAINTER

In the Database Painter, a view is treated just like a table. In the Select Tables dialog box (Figure 6-1), the list of names includes both tables and views, with no indication of which are which. When you open a view, its information box lists its name and its columns, as you would see for any table. Click a Data manipulation button, and PowerBuilder displays the view as if it were a table, as we've seen in Figure 6-25.

The big differences begin when you double-click a view's information box in the Database Painter. Instead of the Table Painter opening, the View dialog box appears, as shown in Figure 6-27. This dialog box presents the SELECT statement that defines the view.

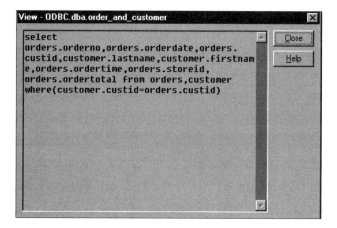

Figure 6-27

The View dialog box for the order_and_customer view.

CREATING A VIEW IN THE DATABASE PAINTER

To define a new view for your database, click the Create View button on the PainterBar. This launches another painter, the View Painter. First you'll see the Select Tables dialog box. In it, select the tables that will be the source for the new view, such as film, lineitem, orders, and store, as shown in Figure 6-28. Then click Open.

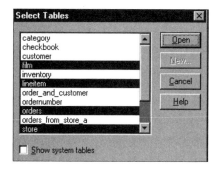

Figure 6-28

Use the Select Tables dialog box to select the source tables for a new view.

Figure 6-29 shows the View Painter in the process of defining what will become the store_category_summary view. The operation of the View Painter is nearly identical to that of the Query Painter described in Chapter 21. So rather than explain it in detail here, I refer you to that chapter for instructions.

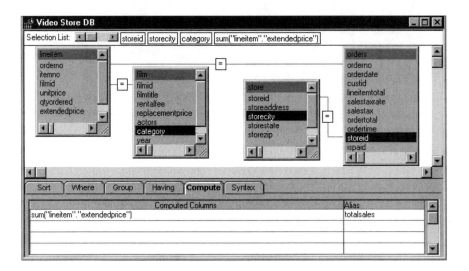

Figure 6-29

The View Painter, in the process of defining the store_category_summary view.

UPDATEABLE VIEWS

The data in the view might be read-only or might be partially or entirely updateable. This depends on the degree to which your database server product supports updateable views, and usually on the nature of the SELECT statement defining the view. If a view is updateable, you can modify it using SQL commands such as UPDATE, INSERT, and DELETE.

Regardless of whether a view is updateable or not, in the Data Manipulation Painter it is always read-only.

OTHER VIEWS

There are three views in the Video Store database. One of them, order_and_customer, we've already seen. Here are the other two:

1. **The orders_from_store_a view** — This view, shown in Figure 6-30, is drawn from the orders table. It is almost identical to the orders table, except that it does not show all of its rows. It shows only the orders from store "A." (The database covers a chain of four video stores, with the stores identified as A, B, C, and D). This SQL command created the view:

```
CREATE VIEW orders_from_store_a AS
    SELECT orderno, orderdate, custid, lineitemtotal,
        salestaxrate, salestax, ordertotal, ordertime, ispaid
    FROM orders
    WHERE storeid=3D'A'
```

Order No.	Order Date	Cust. ID	Line Item Total	Sales Tax Rate	Sales Tax	Order Total	Order Time	Paid?
102	12/28/95	1040	$28.00	8.25%	$2.31	$30.31	09:00:00	☐
103	12/28/95	5001	$11.75	8.25%	$0.97	$12.72	12:00:00	☐
104	12/28/95	5002	$6.75	8.25%	$0.56	$7.31	07:30:00	☐
105	12/28/95	5957	$2.00	8.25%	$0.17	$2.17	02:00:00	☐
112	1/1/96	1100	$14.00	8.25%	$1.16	$15.16	07:00:00	☐
113	1/1/96	1424	$9.00	8.25%	$0.74	$9.74	07:30:00	☒

Figure 6-30
The orders_from_store_a view.

This view is beneficial for security reasons. You could grant the clerks in store A rights to view and modify this view, but remove all rights to the orders table itself. In this way, the clerks have access to the orders for their own store and no access to other stores' orders.

2. **The store_category_summary view** — This view, shown in Figure 6-31, draws information from four tables and summarizes it to answer this question: What are the total sales for each category of film in each store? I defined the view using the View Painter, as shown in Figure 6-29, which in turn generated this SQL command:

```
CREATE VIEW store_category_summary
    (storeid, storecity, category, totalsales) AS
    SELECT orders.storeid, store.storecity, film.category,
        sum(lineitem.extendedprice)
    FROM orders, store, film, lineitem
    WHERE (store.storeid = orders.storeid)
      AND (film.filmid = lineitem.filmid)
      AND (orders.orderno = lineitem.orderno)
    GROUP BY orders.storeid, film.category, store.storecity
```

Store ID	Store City	Category	Total Sales
A	Los Angeles	Classics	$46.00
A	Los Angeles	Comedy	$118.50
A	Los Angeles	Horror	$21.00
A	Los Angeles	Sci-Fi	$35.70
B	Seattle	Classics	$50.00
B	Seattle	Comedy	$61.50
B	Seattle	Horror	$15.00
B	Seattle	Musical	$3.00
B	Seattle	Sci-Fi	$29.10
C	Portland	Classics	$24.00
C	Portland	Comedy	$48.00
C	Portland	Horror	$6.00
C	Portland	Sci-Fi	$8.40

Figure 6-31
The store_category_summary view.

The benefit of this view is that it makes using a complex query as simple as opening a table.

DELETING VIEWS

To delete a view from the database, open and select it in the Database Painter. Then click the PainterBar's Drop button.

Summary

This chapter has continued our look at the PowerBuilder Database Painter, including two closely related painters: The Data Manipulation Painter, as its name implies, allows you to work directly with the data in a database and with the organization of its tables. The Table Painter lets you work with the data in a table at a greater depth of detail, including display formats, edit styles, and validation rules. The Database and Table Painters are also critical for defining or changing a table's primary or foreign keys and its indexes.

The Database Painter itself is the means for designing *views*, "virtual tables" that can assemble data from real tables in a user-friendly fashion.

7 SQL in PowerScript

*T*here are two principal ways in which a PowerBuilder application connects to and manipulates a database. The first is the subject of this chapter: writing scripts in the PowerScript language that execute SQL commands. The other way, using PowerBuilder's DataWindow feature, will be the subject of the next three chapters.

The sample scripts in this chapter perform what is still called "batch" processing, a carryover term from mainframe data processing. The script performs its task, which might take milliseconds or might take hours, with little or no user interaction. For "data entry" processing, where there is a lot of user interaction with the data, you should use DataWindows instead.

It should be no surprise that your application performs all database processing using SQL. In PowerScript, the ways of issuing SQL commands fall into two categories:

- **Embedded SQL** — embedding an SQL command directly in a script, intermingled with regular PowerScript statements
- **Dynamic SQL** — constructing an SQL command in a string variable and then transmitting that variable to the database for execution

Embedded SQL is certainly the simpler and more direct of the two approaches, so we'll cover that first. Dynamic SQL is more powerful and flexible, since it allows you to build commands based on parameters that might not be known until runtime.

From your database product's point of view, PowerScript is a *host language.* That is, PowerScript is a programming language with embedded and dynamic SQL capabilities. Many languages, such as popular dialects of COBOL, C, and Pascal, have similar host language capabilities.

The ANSI SQL 92 standard, published by the American National Standards Institute (ANSI) in 1992, has guidelines for how a host language should support embedded and dynamic SQL. PowerScript adheres to these guidelines quite closely.

Embedding SQL in PowerScript: A First Example

Listing 7-1 is an example of a script with embedded SQL. The four lines beginning "UPDATE customer" are an embedded SQL statement. The "CONNECT USING trans1" and "DISCONNECT USING trans1" lines are also embedded SQL statements. The remainder of the script is standard PowerScript.

Listing 7-1
A script with an embedded UPDATE statement.

```
Transaction      trans1
trans1 = CREATE Transaction
trans1.DBMS        = "ODBC"
trans1.Database    = "Video Store DB"
trans1.UserId      = "dba"
trans1.DBParm      = "Connectstring='DSN=Video Store DB'"
CONNECT USING trans1;
UPDATE customer
    SET address1='123 Main Street'
    WHERE firstname='Gina' and lastname='Gray'
    USING trans1;
DISCONNECT USING trans1;
DESTROY trans1
```

It's unlikely you'll ever write a script exactly like this one in a real application. For one thing, you'll usually place the CONNECT, UPDATE, and DISCONNECT statements in different event scripts within the application, not all together in a single script. Also, if you use a special variable named *sqlca* in place of *trans1*, you can eliminate a few lines of code. A little later I'll show how to transform this script so that it's suitable for the "real world." For now, however, this script is a good starting point because it's a complete, self-contained example.

The UPDATE statement should be familiar from your knowledge of the SQL language. It locates the row (or rows) for the customer named Gina Gray and changes her address to 123 Main Street. (If you need a quick lesson on SQL, refer to Chapter 21, a bonus chapter that you will find on the CD-ROM.) The terrific thing about embedded SQL is that you don't have to learn any new database commands — PowerScript understands and accepts your database's standard SQL.

There are syntax differences between SQL statements and PowerScript statements. Two important differences are:

- SQL statements must end with a semicolon; PowerScript statements do not.

- PowerScript statements must use the character "&" if they extend to extra lines; SQL statements do not.

Nevertheless, you will have no problem intermixing SQL and PowerScript in a single piece of code.

The example in Listing 7-1 is self-contained. Everything that you need to connect to the database and do the UPDATE is here in a single script. There are several things about this script that are not "the typical way to do it." For example, it's typical to divide the CONNECT, the UPDATE, and the DISCONNECT into separate scripts responding to different events. So please don't start pasting Listing 7-1 into your live applications until you've read a bit further.

THE TRANSACTION OBJECT

Listing 7-1 makes heavy use of a variable named *trans1*. In most applications you will name this variable *sqlca*, which is a special built-in PowerBuilder variable that lets you skip a couple of steps. I'll introduce *sqlca* soon. But I think it's important to learn the big picture first before learning the shortcuts.

The variable *trans1* is the name of a *transaction object*. A transaction object is a complex variable, very much like a structure (Chapter 4), that stores information about a database connection. Transaction objects play a role in all interaction between a PowerBuilder application and a database.

DECLARING, CREATING, AND DESTROYING THE TRANSACTION OBJECT

The first line declares the variable *trans1* to be a "Transaction" type variable. It looks like variable declarations we have seen earlier:

```
Transaction    trans1
```

The next line "creates" the transaction object — that is, it assigns *trans1* to a location in memory and initializes its values. This is a necessary first step before you can begin using *trans1*:

```
trans1 = CREATE Transaction
```

The DESTROY command in the last line of the script is the opposite of CREATE:

```
DESTROY trans1
```

It removes the transaction object from memory as if it never existed, freeing the memory for other uses. Of course, no further references to *trans1* are allowed after that, unless you issue another CREATE.

TRANSACTION OBJECT CONNECTION PROPERTIES

Several lines in the script assign values to the elements, or *properties*, of *trans1*:

```
trans1.DBMS      = "ODBC"
trans1.Database  = "Video Store DB"
trans1.UserId    = "dba"
trans1.DBParm    = "Connectstring='DSN=Video Store DB'"
```

The syntax of these statements is the same as that for assigning values to structure variables, which we did in Chapter 4. Actually, *trans1* is not a structure; it is something more sophisticated called a "nonvisual object," which I will define in Chapter 11. Until then, it should be okay to think of *trans1* as a structure.

The transaction object has fifteen properties, four of which are used in Listing 7-1. Ten of the properties are the parameters for connecting to the database:

- **DBMS** = the type of database server, such as "ODBC" or "SYB SQL Server v4.x"

- **ServerName** = the name of the database server

- **Database** = the name of the database, such as "Video Store DB"

- **UserID** = the user's database ID

- **DBPass** = the user's database password (in PB.INI, this is the "DatabasePassword" parameter)

- **LogID** = the user's server-login ID

- **LogPass** = the user's server-login password (in PB.INI, this is the "LogPassword" parameter)

- **Lock** = the "isolation level," which determines how locking is performed during transactions

- **DBParm** = additional connection parameters specific to the database product

- **AutoCommit** = whether or not to automatically commit each statement after executing it (explained later in this chapter)

All of these properties are string values except AutoCommit, which is Boolean. Besides these ten, there are five others, which return error codes and other information following a SQL statement. I'll list them shortly, in the section on error handling.

We encountered these same connection properties in Chapter 5, when connecting to databases interactively. In Chapter 5, the PowerBuilder Database Painter presented dialog boxes to us so that we could supply values for them or review them. PowerBuilder stored the values in PB.INI. In PB.INI, the parameters have the same names as the transaction object properties, with two slight differences: "DBPass" is "DatabasePassword," and "LogPass" is "LogPassword."

In an application, you have several options for how to set the values of the connection properties: You can hard-code them, as Listing 7-1 does; you can ask the user to supply them in a dialog box, which is especially appropriate for IDs and passwords; you can retrieve them from PB.INI or some other "INI" file; or you can do a combination of all three. Later in this chapter I'll show how to retrieve them from PB.INI. Chapter 14 will show the dialog box approach.

In Listing 7-1, it is necessary to set only two of the ten connection parameters, DBMS and DBParm. the Video Store database is a simple Sybase SQL Anywhere database without password security, so the other parameters are not needed.

EMBEDDING THE SQL

These three statements in Listing 7-1 are embedded SQL:

```
CONNECT USING trans1;
UPDATE customer
    SET address1='123 Main Street'
    WHERE firstname='Gina' and lastname='Gray'
    USING trans1;
DISCONNECT USING trans1;
```

The CONNECT statement connects to the database. It is the same as the File|Connect menu choice in the Database Painter. The UPDATE statement updates the customer table, changing Gina Gray's address. The DISCONNECT statement is the opposite of CONNECT. It ends the connection with the database, so that no other SQL can be done without another CONNECT.

THE USING CLAUSE IN EMBEDDED SQL

As you can see, each of these three statements ends with the clause "USING trans1." Once you have declared and initialized a transaction object variable, such as *trans1*, you must add it to the end of every embedded SQL statement in a USING clause.

The USING clause is required so that PowerBuilder will transmit the SQL statements to the right database. If your application connects to several databases, you will declare a separate transaction object variable for each of them. The USING clause avoids ambiguity.

SQL Embedding Tips

Since the SQL that you'll embed in scripts is very similar to the SQL you create in the Database Administration Painter or the Query Painter, you can copy and paste statements from either of these painters into the PowerScript Painter. This lets you test the SQL interactively before adding it to your script.

For Listing 7-1 you would test just the UPDATE command in the Database Administration Painter.

```
UPDATE customer
    SET address1='123 Main Street'
    WHERE firstname='Gina' and lastname='Gray' ;
```

Assuming that you've already connected to the database you want to manipulate, you don't need to include CONNECT, USING, or DISCONNECT in your test SQL code. CREATE and DESTROY are PowerScript statement keywords, not SQL commands, so don't include them either.

When the SQL works the way you want it to, copy it to your script.

 Another approach is to use the SQL Painter that is built into the PowerScript Painter. Click the Paste SQL button in the PowerScript PainterBar. In the SQL Statement Type dialog box (Figure 7-1), double-click the icon for the type of SQL statement you want to create. To produce an UPDATE statement similar to the one we've been looking at, use the Non-Cursor Update icon. This leads to an interactive SQL Painter very much like the Query Painter described in Chapter 21. When you're done defining the SQL statement, return to the PowerScript Painter. PowerBuilder will type the SQL statement into your script.

The USING clause is not required if you use the special name *sqlca* for your transaction object. "USING sqlca" is the default. I'll talk more about *sqlca* in the pages ahead.

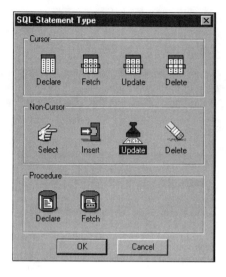

Figure 7-1
Open the SQL Statement Painter by double-clicking an icon.

Creating a Real-World Example

The Listing 7-1 script works as a simple first example, and it illustrates the essentials of embedded SQL. But there are several ways in which it differs from typical real-world programming:

- The script lacks error handling.
- It is more convenient to use *sqlca*, the predefined transaction object, than a special one like *trans1*.
- Rather than CONNECT to and DISCONNECT from the database in every script, it makes more sense to do a single CONNECT when the application opens and leave the database connected throughout.
- The script supplies hard-coded values for the transaction object's properties. The application will be more flexible to manage if it reads the values from PB.INI or some other "INI" file.

The next few sections transform the simple script into a real-world example.

ERROR HANDLING

The Listing 7-1 script is woefully optimistic. The CONNECT, UPDATE, and DISCONNECT statements might fail. But the script does nothing to detect an error, nor to display an error messages to the user, nor to cancel the script if there is an error.

In PowerScript, SQL error handling relies on the transaction object, the script's *trans1* variable. The transaction object has five properties that return error information and other information following a SQL command. The name of each begins with the prefix "Sql:"

- **SqlCode** — a code indicating success or failure: 0 for no error, –1 for an error, 100 if no rows were processed
- **SqlNRows** — the number of rows processed
- **SqlDBCode** — a database-specific error code
- **SqlErrText** — the error message, if any, returned by the database
- **SqlReturnData** — an informative message returned from the database (used only by Informix, Oracle, and some ODBC database products)

SqlCode, SqlNRows, and SqlDBCode are longs (32-bit signed integers). SqlErrText and SqlReturnData are strings.

After every SQL statement, you should test the value of SqlCode. If it is not zero, and especially if it is –1, something has probably gone wrong. If it is –1, use SqlDBCode and SqlErrText to learn more about the problem.

In Listing 7-1, you could add error handling after the UPDATE statement like so:

```
UPDATE customer
   SET address1='123 Main Street'
   WHERE firstname='Gina' and lastname='Gray'
   USING trans1;
IF trans1.SqlCode <> 0 THEN
   MessageBox("Error on Update",                    &
       "Error Code: " + String(trans1.SqlDbCode) +  &
       "~nError Message= " + trans1.SqlErrText,      &
       StopSign!)
   RETURN
END IF
```

The IF...THEN block handles an error by displaying SqlDBCode and

---

Do As I Say, Not As I Do

In many of the programming examples in this book, I do not show the error handling code. I have eliminated it for brevity, to make it easier to focus on the issue at hand. However, you must always include error handling in your applications. To see the complete error handling for the examples, refer to the sample applications that accompany this book on CD-ROM. I have included the complete programming, including error handling, there.

SqlErrText to the user using MessageBox and then terminating the script with RETURN. Similar blocks of code should follow the CONNECT and DISCONNECT statements.

You can go much further with error handling than this simple example does. Maybe you want to add special handling for certain SqlDbCode values; maybe you want to write all error messages to a log file as well as display them to the user; maybe you want to replace the SqlErrText error message, which is usually very user-unfriendly, with a message in your own words. All of these decisions depend on your application requirements. Chapter 17 (a bonus chapter on the CD-ROM) will talk about error handling in more detail. The important thing is to do something when errors occur and not to ignore them.

USING *sqlca* — THE SQL COMMUNICATIONS AREA

PowerBuilder automatically declares and creates a global transaction object variable, *sqlca*. Using *sqlca* instead of the *trans1* that we have been using up to now has two advantages:

- There is no need to declare *sqlca*, nor to CREATE or DESTROY it. PowerBuilder does these things automatically.

- There is no need for a USING clause at the end of every SQL statement. PowerBuilder assumes "USING sqlca" by default.

Thus, if you use *sqlca*, you can write less code.

The only time that you must use transaction objects other than *sqlca*, such as *trans1*, is when you must have more than one database connection open at the same time. Each connection requires its own transaction object. So if you need three connections, for example, you'll need to declare *trans1*, *trans2*, and *trans3* — or whatever you choose to name them. Or you could use *sqlca* for the first and *trans1* and *trans2* for the other two.

By replacing *trans1* with *sqlca*, the Listing 7-1 script reduces to this:

```
sqlca.DBMS       = "ODBC"
sqlca.Database   = "Video Store DB"
sqlca.UserId     = "dba"
sqlca.DBParm     = "Connectstring='DSN=Video Store DB'"
CONNECT;
UPDATE customer
    SET address1='123 Main Street'
    WHERE firstname='Gina' and lastname='Gray';
DISCONNECT;
```

(It's still necessary to add error handling.)

From this point on, I'll use *sqlca* for all examples.

Opening a Global Connection

Typically, you'll want an application to remain connected to the database as long as it's running. Therefore, a good place to CONNECT is in the application's "open" event script:

```
sqlca.DBMS       = "ODBC"
sqlca.Database   = "Video Store DB"
sqlca.UserId     = "dba"
sqlca.DBParm     = "Connectstring='DSN=Video Store DB'"
sqlca.AutoCommit = True
CONNECT;
IF sqlca.SqlCode <> 0 THEN
...
```

A good place to DISCONNECT is in the application's "close" event script:

```
DISCONNECT;
IF sqlca.SqlCode <> 0 THEN
...
```

Once you've done this, there is no need to have CONNECT or DISCON-NECT in any other script. In fact, you typically should avoid them. CON-NECT is a fairly slow operation on most servers, so the fewer the better.

READING CONNECTION PARAMETERS FROM AN .INI FILE

Rather than hard-coding the values of transaction properties in scripts, which is too inflexible for most real-world applications, you'll want your scripts to read some or all of them from an .INI file. You could use PB.INI, if you make sure that each user has such a file. Or you could have an application-specific file of your own design, such as VIDEO.INI for the Video Store application. In Chapter 17 I'll talk more about application .INI files.

Listing 7-2 shows the section of PB.INI defining the connection parameters for the Video Store database. This was explained in detail in Chapter 5.

Listing 7-2
The PROFILE section of PB.INI

```
[PROFILE Video Store DB]
DBMS=ODBC
Database=Video Store DB
UserId=
DatabasePassword=
LogPassword=
ServerName=
LogId=
Lock=
DbParm=Connectstring='DSN=Video Store DB;UID=dba'
AutoCommit=0
Prompt=0
```

Listing 7-3 shows how to retrieve the parameters from PB.INI and store them in the properties of *sqlca*. PowerBuilder provides the function ProfileString for the very purpose of reading .INI parameters.

Listing 7-3
Reading transaction properties from PB.INI

```
String ls_inifile, ls_section, ls_dbms

ls_inifile = "PB.INI"
```

```
ls_section = "PROFILE Video Store DB"

ls_dbms = ProfileString(ls_inifile,ls_section,"DBMS","")
IF ls_dbms = "" THEN
   MessageBox("Error on Connect to Video Store DB",  &
      "Unable to read DBMS vendor from the "      + &
      ls_section + " section of the INI file "    + &
      ls_inifile,                                 &
      stopsign!)
   RETURN
END IF

sqlca.Database   = &
   ProfileString(ls_inifile,ls_section,"Database","")
sqlca.ServerName = &
   ProfileString(ls_inifile,ls_section,"ServerName","")
sqlca.UserId     = &
   ProfileString(ls_inifile,ls_section,"UserId","")
sqlca.DBPass     = &
   ProfileString(ls_inifile,ls_section,"DatabasePassword","")
sqlca.LogId      = &
   ProfileString(ls_inifile,ls_section,"LogId","")
sqlca.LogPass    = &
   ProfileString(ls_inifile,ls_section,"LogPassword","")
sqlca.Lock       = &
   ProfileString(ls_inifile,ls_section,"Lock","")
sqlca.DBParm     = &
   ProfileString(ls_inifile,ls_section,"DbParm","")
sqlca.DBMS       = ls_dbms
CONNECT;
```

More Embedded SQL Commands

So far we've seen three embedded SQL commands: CONNECT, UPDATE, and DISCONNECT. There are fifteen embedded SQL commands in all:

CLOSE	COMMIT	CONNECT
DECLARE	DELETE	DISCONNECT
EXECUTE	FETCH	INSERT
OPEN	ROLLBACK	SELECT
SELECTBLOB	UPDATE	UPDATEBLOB

I'll explain SELECTBLOB and UPDATEBLOB in Chapter 19. As for the others, you'll see at least one example of each of them during the course of this chapter.

This set of commands does not represent the sum total of what you can do with SQL using PowerScript. You can, for example, issue the SQL command CREATE TABLE from PowerScript, even though CREATE TABLE is not on the list. *Dynamic SQL*, covered in the last half of this chapter, is the alternative to embedded SQL. Dynamic SQL allows you to execute virtually any SQL command from PowerScript.

INSERT AND DELETE

This script inserts one new row into the customer table:

```
INSERT INTO customer
    (custid, lastname, firstname, address1, city, state)
    VALUES ('9999', 'Johnson', 'Janet',
            '123 Main Street', 'Los Angeles', 'CA');
IF sqlca.SqlCode <> 0 THEN
    MessageBox("Error on Insert",                          &
        "Error Code: " + String(sqlca.SqlDbCode)+          &
        "~nError Message= " + sqlca.SqlErrText,            &
        stopsign!)
    RETURN
END IF
```

Since the customer table has a primary key, the INSERT will fail if there's already a row with custid = 9999 (among other reasons). In this case, SqlCode will be –1 and you'll see the error message. The values of SqlDbCode and SqlErrText depend, as always, on the database product. For Sybase SQL Anywhere SqlDbCode will be –193.

This script deletes all the Janet Johnson rows from the customer table:

```
DELETE FROM customer
    WHERE firstname='Janet' and lastname='Johnson';
IF sqlca.SqlCode <> 0 THEN
    MessageBox("Error on Delete",                     &
        "Error Code: " + String(sqlca.SqlDbCode) +    &
        "~nError Message= " + sqlca.SqlErrText,       &
        stopsign!)
    RETURN
END IF
```

Embedded SQL and the PowerScript Compiler

The PowerScript compiler tests the syntax of your embedded SQL by transmitting it to the current database server for parsing and validation. The current database server is the one connected in the Database Painter or, if the Database Painter is not open, the one listed as the default database in PB.INI.

If your embedded SQL references an unknown table or column name, you may get a "database warning" from the compiler. This will be likely if the current database server is not the one your application plans to use. The database warnings are harmless. You can ignore them and proceed to save and run your application.

The best way to get rid of the warning messages is to use the Database Painter to connect to your application's database, or a test version of it, before checking syntax on a script. This won't eliminate all such warnings, though, if a single script has embedded SQL statements for more than one database.

The easiest way to get rid of the warning messages is to turn off the "Display Database Warnings" option in the PowerScript editor property sheet. (Select Design|Options from the menu while in the editor, and look in the General tab page.) Of course, ignoring the warnings might lead to trouble at runtime.

If there are no matches for the WHERE condition — that is, if there are no Janet Johnsons — then SqlCode = 0. Even though no rows are deleted, SQL does not consider this to be an error, but you might. If you want to flag "no rows deleted" as an error, there is an easy way to do it. The property SqlNRows tells how many rows were deleted, so you can test it for zero by adding this code:

```
IF sqlca.SqlNRows = 0 THEN
    MessageBox("Error on Delete",                    &
                "No rows were deleted.", stopsign!)
    RETURN
END IF
MessageBox("All Done",                               &
            "# of Rows Successfully Deleted: " +  &
            String(sqlca.SqlNRows))
```

The SqlNRows value might be useful after other SQL statements as well. Following a successful INSERT, for example, it will be the number of new rows.

USING VARIABLES IN A SQL STATEMENT

In the examples so far, I have used hard-coded literal strings like "Janet" in the SQL WHERE, SET, and VALUES clauses. Often you need to use variables instead, because the values are not known until runtime. To insert a PowerScript variable in a SQL statement, precede it with a colon (:). Here's an example of an INSERT statement with variables:

```
String s1,s2,s3
s1 = "9999"
s2 = "Johnson"
s3 = "Janet"
INSERT INTO customer
    (custid, lastname, firstname)
    VALUES (:s1, :s2, :s3);
```

Here's an example of variables in a DELETE statement:

```
String s1, s2
s1 = "Janet"
s2 = "Johnson"
DELETE FROM customer
    WHERE firstname= :s1 and lastname= :s2;
```

In PowerScript, you can use "control.properties" such as "st_firstbox.BackColor" anywhere that you can use a variable. (Controls and properties were described in Chapter 3.) So if you have placed fields ("SingleLineEdit" controls) on your window for the customer's ID, last name, and first name, and if the user has typed values into them, you can use the field values in place of variables:

```
INSERT INTO customer
    (custid, lastname, firstname)
    VALUES (:sle_custid.Text, :sle_lastname.Text,
            :sle_firstname.Text);
```

Don't forget the colons!

There are severe restrictions on where you can use ":" variables. You can use them only in place of literal values, as I have shown, and in INTO clauses, which are coming up in examples soon. You cannot use them in place of table names, column names, keywords (such as UPDATE and WHERE), or anywhere else.

This example will not work, because it's an attempt to insert a variable in place of a column name:

```
String ls_columnname
ls_columnname = "address1"
UPDATE customer
   SET :ls_columnname = '2020 Lincoln Street'  // this will NOT work
   WHERE firstname='Gina' and lastname='Gray';
```

If you need this kind of flexibility, you must resort to dynamic SQL, which gives you total flexibility.

SELECT

An embedded SQL SELECT statement can read a single row from the database:

```
String s1,s2
SELECT custid, address1
   INTO :s1, :s2
   FROM customer
   WHERE firstname='Gina' and lastname='Gray';
```

By adding an INTO clause to the SELECT, you can store the retrieved column values in PowerScript variables. In the example above, the variables *s1* and *s2* are set to Gina Gray's customer ID and address.

Following the SELECT, sqlca.SqlCode will be

- 0 if one row was selected
- 100 if no rows were selected
- –1 if there was an error, or if more than one row was selected

SELECTing More Than One Row

If you need to retrieve more than one row with a SELECT, the SELECT...INTO technique is not adequate. Instead, you should use "Cursors," which are explained later in this chapter.

If you simply want to know how many rows match a criterion, that's simple enough. Use the "Count(*)" function, which counts matching rows:

```
Long ll_howmany
SELECT Count(*)
   INTO :ll_howmany
   FROM customer
   WHERE lastname = :sle_lastname.Text;
```

Dealing with Null Values

As you saw in previous chapters, columns in a database table may contain null values. A null is not the same as an empty string or the number zero. Often you must add special handling for nulls in your PowerScript programming.

In the SQL WHERE clause, the expression IS NULL can select null values, and IS NOT NULL can select non-null values. For example, to count the number of customers with a null in the *address2* column and place the count into the variable *ll_howmany*:

```
Long ll_howmany
SELECT Count(*)
   INTO :ll_howmany
   FROM customer
   WHERE address2 IS NULL;
```

In an INSERT statement, you can set a column to null simply by omitting the column from the column list, or by specifying NULL as its value:

```
INSERT INTO customer
   (custid, lastname, firstname, address1, address2,
        city, state, zip)
   VALUES ('9999', 'Adams', 'John', NULL, NULL,
        'Braintree', 'MA', NULL);
```

You can also use the NULL value in an UPDATE statement:

```
UPDATE customer
   SET address2 = NULL
   WHERE lastname= 'Gray';
```

NULL VARIABLES IN POWERSCRIPT ARITHMETIC

When a SELECT statement retrieves a null column value into a PowerScript variable, then the variable will be null — that is, it will contain a null value. To use that variable, you should be aware of how PowerScript handles nulls, especially in arithmetic. The PowerScript function IsNull, which tests for null values, can help.

Suppose that customer 8888 has null city and null open balance, and that you retrieve them with this SELECT statement:

```
String  ls_city
Real    lr_openbal, r2
SELECT city, openbalance
   INTO :ls_city, :lr_openbal
   FROM customer
   WHERE custid = '8888';
```

Now the variables *ls_city* and *lr_openbal* contain null values.

Any arithmetic with null values gives a null result. So what is the result of this addition, if *lr_openbal* is null?

```
r2 = lr_openbal + 10
```

You might expect *r2* = 10. Instead, *r2* will be null. If you want nulls treated like zero, something like this is required:

```
IF IsNull(lr_openbal) THEN
   r2 = 10
ELSE
   r2 = lr_openbal + 10
END IF
```

Similar null handling is necessary for arithmetic if the variables are strings or any other type.

NULL VARIABLES AND CONTROL PROPERTIES

Another thing to watch out for is attempting to set the Text property of a SingleLineEdit control, or some similar type of field control, to a null:

```
sle_city.Text = ls_city
```

What happens is that the statement is ignored, and the control's text remains unchanged. If you want a null value to cause the control to be blanked out, you need to add something like this:

```
IF IsNull(ls_city) THEN
    sle_city.Text = ""
ELSE
    sle_city.Text = ls_city
END IF
```

NULL VALUES IN SQL ARITHMETIC

You can do arithmetic in SQL statements, and SQL handles null values in the same way as PowerScript: If any part of the expression is null, the result of the entire expression is null.

For example, this query will set the totalamount column to null in all rows where pretaxamount or salestax is null:

```
UPDATE invoice
    SET totalamount = pretaxamount + salestax;
```

Assuming that you want nulls to be treated like zeros, you should rewrite the UPDATE statement like this:

```
UPDATE invoice
    SET totalamount = IsNull(pretaxamount,0) + IsNull(salestax,0);
```

The IsNull function in SQL is not at all like the IsNull function in PowerScript. What it does is return the first parameter that is not null. So "IsNull(x,0)" returns x if x is not null or zero if x is null. So either way, a non-null value is placed into the expression. The IsNull function is a feature of Sybase SQL Anywhere but may not be available for other SQL dialects.

INDICATOR VARIABLES

The easiest way to detect a null value retrieved into a variable is to use the IsNull function, as we've already seen:

```
SELECT city, openbalance
   INTO :ls_city, :lr_openbal
   FROM customer
   WHERE custid = '8888';

IF IsNull(ls_city) THEN ...        // null city

IF IsNull(lr_openbal) THEN ...     // null open balance
```

Another alternative is to use an *indicator variable*. This is a separate variable that you can place in an INTO statement next to a value. The indicator variable returns 0 if a value is not null, –1 if it is null, and –2 if there is a data conversion error.

```
SELECT city, openbalance
   INTO :ls_city       :indvar_city,
        :lr_openbal    :indvar_openbal
   FROM customer
   WHERE custid = '8888';

IF indvar_city = -1 THEN ...       // null city

IF indvar_openbal = -1 THEN ...    // null open balance
```

The SQL parser can tell the difference between an indicator variable and a regular INTO variable because there is no comma separating the indicator variable from the variable before it.

Indicator variables are part of the SQL standard and, therefore, it is appropriate that PowerBuilder support them. However, I don't find them as convenient to use as the IsNull technique.

Transactions: Commit and Rollback

A *transaction* is a group of SQL statements that must succeed or fail as a unit. For example, suppose that every time you INSERT a new row into the lineitem table, you must also UPDATE the inventory table to change the "quantity on hand" column of the corresponding item. Both SQL statements, the INSERT and the UPDATE, must succeed in order for the database to retain its integrity. If either one fails, then the other one should fail also.

All SQL products (or all the ones that PowerBuilder can connect to, at least) support transactions, and they make it easy for you to control whether and when a transaction should be committed to the database. Some variation exists in the syntax from one server to another. In ANSI-standard SQL, a transaction begins with the first command, such as INSERT or UPDATE, that affects the database, and you must conclude the transaction by issuing the command COMMIT or ROLLBACK:

```
execute multiple SQL statements here
IF everything worked THEN
    COMMIT;
ELSE
    ROLLBACK;
END IF
```

COMMIT causes all the database changes made by the SQL statements to become permanent. ROLLBACK causes all of them to be undone. In either case, this transaction is finished. The next SQL statement, such as INSERT or UPDATE, will begin a new transaction.

PowerBuilder supports COMMIT and ROLLBACK as embedded SQL statements. So you can include them in a script as shown above, with a USING clause if necessary.

As you can see, transactions are essential for making multiple related updates to the database.

AutoCommit

A PowerScript transaction object has a property, AutoCommit, which can have an important effect on transactions. AutoCommit is a boolean value (True or False). You can set it either before or after you CONNECT to the database. For example:

```
sqlca.AutoCommit = False
CONNECT;
```

For some database products, AutoCommit has no effect, as I'll explain in a moment. But for those database products for which AutoCommit is implemented, here's what it does:

- If you set AutoCommit = False, all SQL commands are part of a transaction and you must issue COMMIT and ROLLBACK commands from time to time to complete your work.

- If AutoCommit = True, there are no transactions, and each SQL command is immediately committed. In this case, explicit COMMIT and ROLLBACK commands in a script have no effect.

AutoCommit is one of the transaction object properties. You can set it just like the others:

```
sqlca.DBMS        = "ODBC"
sqlca.Database    = "Video Store DB"
sqlca.UserId      = "dba"
sqlca.DBParm      = "Connectstring='DSN=Video Store DB'"
sqlca.AutoCommit  = False
CONNECT;
```

The default value for AutoCommit is True.

You can change the value of AutoCommit any number of times in your application. Thus you can turn transaction processing on or off as it suits you. For example, you might set AutoCommit = True at the beginning of simple modules and set AutoCommit = False at the beginning of more complex modules. There is no need to DISCONNECT and re-CONNECT in order to change AutoCommit.

Exactly how PowerBuilder and the database server implement AutoCommit depends on the server product:

- **For SQL Anywhere and certain other ODBC databases.** These products provide an AutoCommit feature that works just as I've described. That is, if AutoCommit is True, the server commits each SQL command immediately, and if AutoCommit is False, the server waits until you issue a COMMIT or ROLLBACK to conclude the transaction. Therefore, PowerBuilder simply passes your AutoCommit setting to the server.

- **For Sybase and Microsoft SQL Server, and for the Sybase Net-Gateway Interface for DB2.** These products automatically commit each SQL command immediately by default, which corresponds to PowerBuilder's AutoCommit = True behavior. To initiate a multicommand transaction, the server must receive a special command, BEGIN

TRANSACTION. All commands between a BEGIN TRANSACTION and a COMMIT or ROLLBACK form a transaction. If you set AutoCommit = False in your application, PowerBuilder issues BEGIN TRANSACTION commands behind the scenes whenever necessary. For example, it issues one when you CONNECT, and also after each COMMIT or ROLLBACK. If AutoCommit = True, PowerBuilder has no need to issue any BEGIN TRANSACTION commands.

- **For all other database products, such as Oracle.** These products have no equivalent to PowerBuilder's AutoCommit = True behavior and no BEGIN TRANSACTION command. All SQL commands belong to transactions, and you must always conclude them with COMMIT or ROLLBACK. For these products, therefore, AutoCommit is ignored, and your application's behavior will always be as if you set it to False.

AN EXAMPLE OF TRANSACTION MANAGEMENT: INVENTORY UPDATE

Listing 7-4 is a script that updates two tables, lineitem and update, as part of a single transaction. Within the transaction the script executes three SQL commands:

1. **INSERT** — Add a new row to the lineitem table. The row describes the rental of some number of units (qtyordered) of a certain film (filmid) from the video store.

2. **UPDATE** — Update a row in the inventory table. The row is the one containing the quantity on hand (qytonhand) for the item being ordered. The line item quantity is subtracted from quantity on hand.

3. **SELECT** — The inventory row just updated is reread in order to test whether the new quantity on hand has become negative. If so, there is not enough inventory to support the new line item. Negative inventory is a business rule error, not a database error, but it must be treated as a fatal error all the same.

At the conclusion, the script issues a COMMIT if no error has occurred or a ROLLBACK if there has been an error. An error occurs if any of the three SQL commands fail, or if the inventory quantity goes negative. In the script, the string variable *ls_error* is the error message. If *ls_error* is an empty string, there is no error.

Listing 7-4
Processing a transaction that consists of inserting a lineitem row and updating the related inventory row.

```
// Local Variables:
Integer  li_newqtyonhand    // the new inventory quantity,
String   ls_error = ""      // error message, if any, that occurs

//  INSERT the new row into the lineitem table

INSERT INTO lineitem
   (orderno, itemno, filmid, unitprice, qtyordered, extendedprice)
   VALUES (101, 1001, 'B201', 2.50, 3, 7.50);
IF sqlca.SqlCode <> 0 THEN      // did the INSERT cause an error?
   ls_error = "Error on INSERT."
END IF

//  If the INSERT succeeded, then UPDATE the inventory table

IF ls_error = "" THEN    // no error yet - INSERT succeeded
   UPDATE inventory
      SET qtyonhand = qtyonhand - 3
      WHERE (filmid = 'B201') and (storeid = 'A');
   IF sqlca.SqlCode <> 0 THEN      // did the UPDATE cause an error?
      ls_error = "Error on UPDATE."
   ELSEIF sqlca.SqlNRows = 0 THEN
      ls_error = "Error on UPDATE: No row for film B201 at store A"
   END IF
END IF

//  If the UPDATE succeeded, then re-SELECT it and test its qty

IF ls_error = "" THEN  // no error yet - INSERT and UPDATE succeeded
   SELECT qtyonhand
      INTO :li_newqtyonhand
      FROM inventory
      WHERE (filmid = 'B201') and (storeid = 'A');
   IF sqlca.SqlCode <> 0 THEN      // did the SELECT cause an error?
      ls_error = "Error on SELECT."
   ELSEIF li_newqtyonhand < 0 THEN // trans makes inventory negative
      ls_error = "Insufficient inventory on hand."
   END IF
END IF

//  Successful completion:  Do the COMMIT

IF ls_error = "" THEN      // no error occurred
   COMMIT;                 // commit the transaction
```

```
      //  An error occurred:  ROLLBACK and display the error message

   ELSE                            // an error occurred
      ls_error = ls_error                                        + &
              "~nError Code: " + String(sqlca.SqlDbCode)     + &
              "~nError Message= " + sqlca.SqlErrText
      ROLLBACK;                    // roll back the transaction
      MessageBox("Error", ls_error, stopsign!)
   END IF
```

In this script the film ID is hard-coded ("B201"), and so is the quantity ordered (3). It would be a simple matter to replace them with variables set by user input. The sample application on the CD-ROM has a more extensive version of the script that implements this and other enhancements.

Because this script relies on COMMIT and ROLLBACK to work effectively, sqlca.AutoCommit must be set to False at some earlier point in time if you are connected to a server that supports AutoCommit. In this case, you will find this command in the window's open script:

```
   sqlca.AutoCommit = False
```

Keep Your Transactions Short!

During the course of a transaction, the database server locks the sections of the database that you are modifying so that other users cannot make changes that would conflict with yours. Therefore, you should design your transactions to execute as quickly as possible and avoid needless delays. Another user's application encountering your lock will get an error message or be forced to wait, depending on the configuration.

An easy trap to fall into is writing your script so that it waits for user input during the transaction. This is a killer! Notice, at the bottom of Listing 7-4, how I call the MessageBox function after the ROLLBACK. What if I were to move the MessageBox call up, above the ROLLBACK? Big mistake! The user would see a dialog box while the transaction is still in progress and while database sections are still locked. Until the user clicks OK, those locks remain in place, causing other users to freeze or fail. How long does the transaction take? If the user goes to lunch or departs on a holiday before clicking OK, it could be a very long time. This is not very friendly to the other users!

Cursors

The SELECT...INTO... examples shown earlier are practical only for SELECT commands that return exactly one row. They have no capability to retrieve values from the second row, third row, or any later row. For that you need a *cursor*.

Two-Phase Commit

The transactions I've been describing often affect more than one table in a database, as shown in Listing 7-4. However, they do not span more than one *database*. If you must update two or more databases and ensure an all-or-nothing conclusion, you must begin a separate transaction for each database and conclude the transactions with what is known as a *two-phase commit*.

In PowerScript, you'll need a transaction object variable for each database. You can use sqlca for one and declare the others as transaction object variables as you saw at the beginning of this chapter.

The conclusion of the transaction requires the two-phase commit:

- **Phase one** — Issue a special command on each database to ensure that the upcoming COMMIT will be successful. For SQL Anywhere, this command is PREPARE TO COMMIT. For Microsoft SQL Server, it's PREPARE TRANSACTION. For other products it might be something else, or it might not exist at all, which will be a problem. You will need to use dynamic SQL for this command, since it is not an embedded SQL command.

- **Phase two** — Issue the COMMIT command for each database.

You should read the documentation for your database product to determine how it handles a two-phase commit.

A *cursor* is a pointer into the result set of a SQL SELECT statement. It provides the means to navigate among and work with multiple rows, one at a time.

The following embedded SQL commands implement and use a cursor:

- **DECLARE** — specifies the cursor's SELECT statement.
- **OPEN** — executes the cursor's SELECT statement.
- **FETCH** — retrieves values from one row of the cursor.
- **UPDATE WHERE CURRENT OF *cursor*** — updates the fetched row.
- **DELETE WHERE CURRENT OF *cursor*** — deletes the fetched row.
- **CLOSE** — terminates cursor processing.

You can think of a cursor as a fancy variable, which you operate upon with special commands. Figure 7-2 illustrates a cursor and the key commands in the process, OPEN and FETCH.

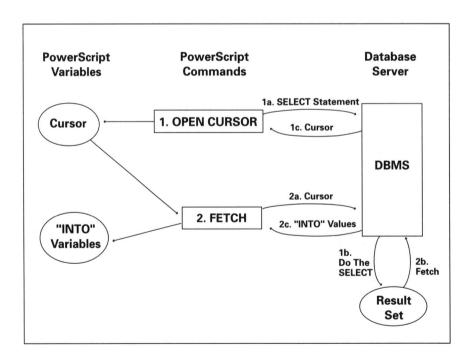

Figure 7-2

Fetching data from the database into variables by means of a cursor.

You must perform the cursor-related tasks in the following sequence:

1. DECLARE

Just as you must declare all variables, you must declare a cursor before you can use it:

```
DECLARE cursor1 CURSOR FOR
    SELECT payment, deposit
        FROM checkbook
        ORDER BY checkdate, checkno;
```

The cursor declaration must include a SQL SELECT statement. DECLARE is not an executable statement in the same way that variable declarations are not executable. Therefore, DECLARE does not set the error properties, such as SqlCode and SqlErrText, of the transaction object.

2. OPEN

After you have declared the cursor, you must open it before you can use it. OPEN executes the SQL SELECT statement specified in the DECLARE statement for the cursor:

```
OPEN cursor1;
IF sqlca.SqlCode <> 0 THEN ...
```

Since executing the SELECT might succeed or fail, you should check SqlCode after the OPEN, as you would do after any executable embedded SQL statement.

3. FETCH

After you've successfully opened the cursor, FETCH retrieves a single row into variables. The OPEN statement positions the cursor before the first row. FETCH, by default, retrieves the next row. Typically, you will place the FETCH statement in a loop to execute repeatedly until the "not found" error occurs:

```
DO
    FETCH cursor1 INTO :decPayment, :decDeposit;
    IF sqlca.SqlCode = 100 THEN EXIT   // no more rows — all done

    ... (process the row here) ...

LOOP WHILE True
```

4. UPDATE AND DELETE

After you've fetched a row, you may use UPDATE or DELETE with the WHERE CURRENT OF cursor clause to update or delete the row to which the cursor points.

```
UPDATE checkbook
    SET balance = :decBalance
    WHERE CURRENT OF cursor1;
IF sqlca.SqlCode <> 0 THEN ...
```

Of course, there is no obligation to use UPDATE or DELETE if your intention is simply to read rows.

5. CLOSE

When you're through with the cursor, CLOSE it:

```
CLOSE cursor1;
```

It is not always necessary to close the cursor. COMMIT and DISCONNECT close it automatically.

EXAMPLE: USING A CURSOR TO READ ROWS INTO A STRUCTURE

The script in Listing 7-5 uses a cursor to fetch each row from the store table. The store table describes each store in the chain of video stores. Rather than fetch columns into individual variables, the script fetches them into a structure.

The cursor, named *icur_store*, is declared as an instance variable.
Select Declare|Instance Variables from the menu to see it (Figure 7-3). The
structure, *ws_storerow*, shown in Figure 7-4, is defined with the
Declare|Window Structures menu choice. It has an element for each col-
umn in the cursor's SELECT statement. The script uses an instance of the
structure named *lstr_storerow*, which it declares on the second line of
Listing 7-5.

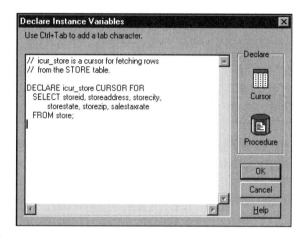

Figure 7-3

The declaration for the cursor icur_store.

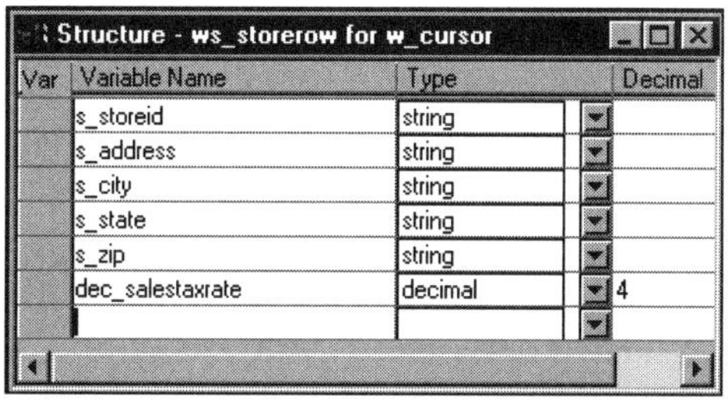

Figure 7-4

The declaration for the structure ws_storerow.

Listing 7-5

Reading each row from the store table into a structure, with error trapping removed for brevity.

```
Integer li_rows              // # of rows fetched
Ws_storerow  lstr_storerow // a structure to hold one row
OPEN icur_store;             // open the cursor
li_rows = 0                  // no rows fetched yet
DO                           // fetch each row into the structure
   FETCH icur_store INTO
      :lstr_storerow.s_storeid, :lstr_storerow.s_address,
      :lstr_storerow.s_city, :lstr_storerow.s_state,
      :lstr_storerow.s_zip, :lstr_storerow.dec_salestaxrate;
   IF sqlca.SqlCode = 100 THEN EXIT   // no more rows — all done
   li_rows ++    // one more row has been read
   MessageBox ("Store Row # " + String(li_rows),       &
      "Store ID:    ~t" + lstr_storerow.s_storeid   + &
      "~nAddress :  ~t" + lstr_storerow.s_address   + &
      "~nCity:    ~t~t" + lstr_storerow.s_city      + &
      "~nState:   ~t~t" + lstr_storerow.s_state     + &
      "~nZip:     ~t~t" + lstr_storerow.s_zip       + &
      "~nSales Tax: ~t" + String(lstr_storerow.dec_salestaxrate))
LOOP WHILE True
CLOSE icur_store;            // close the cursor
```

The script goes through the steps described earlier: Open the cursor, loop to process each row, fetch the row, exit when sqlca.SqlCode = 100, and close the cursor. Once fetched, the script does nothing more with the structure than display it using MessageBox. But you could, of course, add any amount of additional processing here.

The benefit of using a structure is that a structure keeps all the values together in a single place, which makes it easier for you as the programmer to keep track of them. Furthermore, you can pass a single structure as a parameter in a user-defined function instead of many individual parameters.

You can extend this script further and retrieve the entire table — all its rows and columns — into a single variable by declaring an array of structures.

```
Ws_storerow  lstr_storerows[] // a structure array to hold all rows
```

The FETCH loop fetches each row into an element of the array. Thereafter, if you want to know the third row's city, for example, it would be

```
lstr_storerows[3].s_city
```

This technique would be useful for fetching a table into memory once and referring to it many times. It would be faster than making many retrievals from the database. However, I'd recommend it only for small tables that don't change. Please refer to the CD-ROM for the complete example.

CURSORS AND TRANSACTIONS

All cursor activity occurring between the OPEN and CLOSE statements belong to a single transaction. In fact, a COMMIT will automatically close any open cursors.

Earlier I urged you to keep your transactions short, because commands within a transaction typically lock sections of the database, making them inaccessible to other users. It follows, then, that you should keep your cursor processing short as well. Construct your FETCH loop to run as quickly as possible, and defer any extraneous processing until after the CLOSE and COMMIT.

Quick cursor scripts are probably important even if you are not changing the data with UPDATE or DELETE, only reading it with FETCH. The reason is that FETCH itself might lock sections of the database to ensure that no one else changes a row while you're working with it. The locks remain in place until a COMMIT or ROLLBACK occurs. (Whether or not locks are set upon reading a row depends on the value you've set for the database connection's "isolation level." Please consult your database documentation for details.)

The script in Listing 7-5, although useful as a practice exercise, violates the "make it quick" rule. The MessageBox call turns control over to the user in the middle of the loop. So there will be an arbitrarily long delay while locks are being held. That's something to avoid!

CURSOR SCOPE: LOCAL, INSTANCE, SHARED, AND GLOBAL

As with any variable, when you declare a cursor you also establish its scope: local, instance, shared, or global. The scope rules that I described in Chapter 4 apply to cursors as well as variables.

Figure 7-3 shows the declaration for an instance cursor. If this declaration were within the Listing 7-5 script itself, the cursor would be local to that script. By declaring the cursor as an instance variable, you enable any script in the window to open and use it without the need to redeclare it in each one. However, you need to be careful that two scripts don't attempt to perform separate FETCH loops using the same cursor at the same time.

THE CURSOR PAINTER

You can type the DECLARE CURSOR statement by hand, or you can get assistance by using the Cursor Painter. Since declaring a cursor is primarily constructing a SELECT statement, the Cursor Painter is virtually identical to the Query Painter described in Chapter 21.

To reach the Cursor Painter for a locally declared cursor, click the Paste SQL button on the Script Painter's PainterBar. Then double-click on the Cursor|Declare icon in the SQL Statement Type dialog, which was shown earlier, in Figure 7-1. You will also notice icons to help you construct cursor FETCH, UPDATE, and DELETE statements.

To reach the Cursor Painter for a global, shared, or instance cursor, first open the dialog box for declaring those variables. For example, select Declare|Instance Variables from the Script Painter menu. In the Declare Variables dialog that pops up, double-click the Declare Cursor icon, which you can see in Figure 7-3.

Stored Procedures

A *stored procedure* is SQL code that resides in the database rather than in a client application and is executed by the database server rather than a client workstation. The benefits of stored procedures are

- Speed improvement, gained by moving processing to the database server, where it can manipulate data without generating network traffic
- Standardized processing, because every client, including non-PowerBuilder clients, can call the same stored procedures

- Centralized maintenance, because by making an enhancement to the stored procedure in one place — in the database — you immediately make the enhancement available to all applications that utilize it

When you call a stored procedure, you can pass it parameters, just as you can with a PowerBuilder function. The procedure itself might return a value, again like a function does, and perhaps pass values back through its parameter list.

Unlike PowerBuilder functions, many stored procedures return result sets: sets of values organized, like a table, into rows and columns. To retrieve a result set, a PowerBuilder script performs an exercise much like we've just seen for cursors: First, call the procedure to generate the result set. Then, issue FETCH commands in a loop to retrieve the results one row at a time. Figure 7-5 illustrates this process.

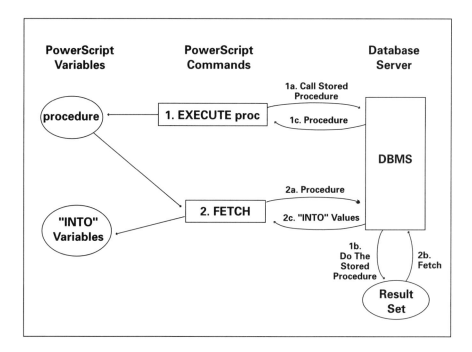

Figure 7-5

Fetching data from the database into variables by means of a stored procedure.

How you create a stored procedure depends on the database product. Each product has its own stored procedure dialect. I will return to that topic shortly.

THE STEPS FOR USING A STORED PROCEDURE

Assuming that the stored procedure is already in place, your PowerBuilder script will use the following embedded SQL commands to work with it:

1. **DECLARE PROCEDURE** — specifies a procedure to reference the stored procedure and its parameters.
2. **EXECUTE** — executes (calls) the stored procedure.
3. **FETCH** — retrieves values from one row of the procedure's result set.
4. **CLOSE** — terminates procedure processing.

If this list looks very similar to the cursor commands, it's no coincidence. From PowerBuilder's point of view, a stored procedure is very much like a cursor. Once it's opened, (executed), it returns a stream of multivalued rows, one row for each FETCH.

EXAMPLE: USING A STORED PROCEDURE TO CALCULATE SALES TAX

Listing 7-6 is a script that calls a stored procedure to calculate sales tax. In the database, the procedure is named sp_SalesTax. If it were a PowerBuilder function, you would call it with two parameters, like this:

```
sp_SalesTax ("B", 20.00)
```

The first parameter, "B," identifies a store in the video store chain. Each store, being in a different county, has a different sales tax rate. The second parameter, $20.00, is the dollar amount on which to calculate the tax.

The sp_SalesTax procedure returns a result set consisting of one row with two columns: the tax rate, such as 0.08, and the tax amount, such as $1.60.

The script declares a "procedure variable" named *lsp_tax* for the pro-

cedure sp_SalesTax. As with a cursor, you perform all procedure operations using this variable. Notice the use of ":" variables to identify the procedure's parameters. The EXECUTE statement calls the procedure. The
FETCH statement returns the result row, copying its values into two variables. Since this procedure returns only one row, there is no need to
enclose the FETCH in a loop.

Listing 7-6

Executing the stored procedure that calculates sales tax.

```
Decimal{2}  ldec_amount, ldec_tax
Decimal{3}  ldec_taxpct
Real        lr_taxrate
String      ls_store
DECLARE lsp_tax PROCEDURE FOR sp_SalesTax
    :ls_store, :ldec_amount;
ls_store    = "B"
ldec_amount = 20.00
EXECUTE lsp_tax;
FETCH lsp_tax INTO :lr_taxrate, :ldec_tax;
ldec_taxpct = lr_taxrate * 100
MessageBox("Successful Stored Procedure Call",          &
            "Store:        ~t"   + ls_store              + &
            "~n$ Amount:   ~t"   + String(ldec_amount)   + &
            "~nTax Rate:   ~t"   + String(ldec_taxpct)  + "%" + &
            "~nTax $ Amount:~t"  + String(ldec_tax))
CLOSE lsp_tax;
```

CREATING A STORED PROCEDURE

In larger organizations, creating a stored procedure will be the database
administrator's responsibility. But whether you are creating them or only
calling them, it is useful to understand the creation process.

There is no standard for the syntax of a stored procedure language, as
there are for other elements of SQL. Each vendor has implemented its
own dialect and feature set. Some products do not implement stored procedures at all. The example in this chapter uses Sybase SQL Anywhere.
Doing the same exercise with any other database product would certainly
be different. (The CD-ROM also contains a SQL Server version.) This is the
CREATE PROCEDURE command that creates the sp_SalesTax procedure

in a Sybase SQL Anywhere database:

```
CREATE PROCEDURE sp_SalesTax
                (IN thestore   CHAR(1),
                 IN theamount DECIMAL)
    RESULT (salestaxrate REAL, salestax DECIMAL)
    BEGIN
       SELECT salestaxrate,
               salestaxrate * theamount
          FROM store
          WHERE storeid = thestore;
    END
```

You could create the procedure from a PowerScript script by issuing this as a dynamic SQL command — the sample application for this chapter has a button that does exactly that. However, it's more common to develop a stored procedure using the database administration tools that come with the database server product.

The executable part of this stored procedure, which is enclosed between BEGIN and END, is nothing more than a SELECT statement. It turns out that you can calculate the procedure's two return values by doing a query on the video store's store table. It is not unusual for a stored procedure to use SELECT to do its work. However, many dialects also offer regular programming language elements such as variables, loops, and IF-THEN-ELSE structures so that you can write more complex procedures.

STORED PROCEDURE PAINTERS

Just as you saw earlier with cursors, you can declare a procedure, such as *lsp_tax* in Listing 7-6, so that its scope is local (from the PowerScript Painter), or so that its scope is global, shared, or instance (from the Declare menu). Furthermore, you can type the DECLARE PROCEDURE statement by hand, but PowerBuilder also provides a Stored Procedure Painter to help you through the process.

To paint a local procedure declaration, click the Paste SQL button on the PowerScript PainterBar. The SQL Statement Type dialog box, shown earlier in Figure 7-1, pops up. Double-click the Declare icon in the Procedure group to paint a local DECLARE PROCEDURE statement into your script. This same dialog box has assistance for the construction of FETCH commands. Double-clicking the Declare Procedure icon opens the Select Procedure dialog box shown in Figure 7-6.

To paint a DECLARE PROCEDURE with global, shared, or instance scope, select the appropriate choice from the Declare menu. For example, select Declare | Instance Variables for the instance scope. The dialog box that appears has a Declare Procedure icon, as you can see in Figure 7-3. Double-click the icon to reach the Select Procedure dialog box shown in Figure 7-6.

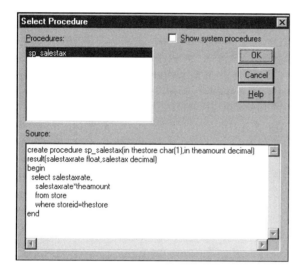

Figure 7-6

Selecting a stored procedure.

In the Select Procedure dialog box, PowerBuilder lists all stored procedures in the currently connected database. In Figure 7-6 only one stored procedure is listed: sp_SalesTax. When you click a procedure on the list, the dialog box displays its source code. Select the procedure that you want to incorporate into your script and click OK. This pops up the Parameters dialog box in Figure 7-7.

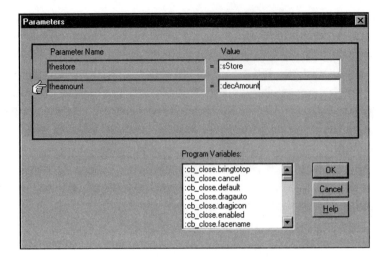

Figure 7-7

Specifying parameters for the procedure declaration.

The Parameters dialog lists the stored procedure's parameters, which it has retrieved from the procedure's definition in the database. You must assign a PowerScript variable, with a ":" prefix, to each parameter, as shown in Figure 7-7. Once you click OK, a Save Declare Procedure dialog box appears. Type in a name for the procedure variable, such as *lsp_tax*, and click Yes. PowerBuilder returns you to the Script Painter, or to the variable declarations dialog box, with the DECLARE PROCEDURE statement pasted in. For example:

```
DECLARE lsp_tax PROCEDURE FOR sp_SalesTax
    :ls_store, :ldec_amount;
```

TRIGGERS

A *trigger* is SQL code associated with a particular database event. Like stored procedures, triggers reside in the database. The database server executes the trigger automatically when an event occurs, such as INSERT, DELETE, or UPDATE on a table.

You might create a trigger that assigns a sequential number to a table's primary key column whenever a new row is inserted, or perhaps one that generates an error when a user attempts to delete a row that was inserted after a certain date. Triggers are good for enforcing business rules.

PowerBuilder does not control or communicate with triggers directly. But, like any client of the database, your PowerBuilder application might cause triggers to execute whenever it changes the database.

The implementation of triggers depends on the database product. Refer to the documentation for your product to determine how to create and use them.

Dynamic SQL

So far in this chapter we have shown how to use "embedded SQL" in your scripts. The remainder of this chapter describes the second type of SQL supported in PowerScript, "dynamic SQL."

With embedded SQL, the SQL statement is hard-coded in the script. Its structure, including the names of tables and columns, is fixed and unchangeable at runtime. The only capability to alter the statement at runtime is through the insertion of ":" variables to supply values, such as:

```
DELETE FROM customer
   WHERE firstname= :s1 and lastname= :s2;
```

With dynamic SQL, the SQL statement is contained in a string variable. You construct the string variable at runtime, so everything about it is flexible and under your control.

Here are the most common reasons why you might choose dynamic SQL instead of embedded SQL:

- You don't know the precise SQL statement at programming time — you will know it only at runtime. For example, you might develop a flexible query interface where the user will select the table and column names and other characteristics at runtime, and your script must construct a dynamic SQL string in response.

- You need to issue a SQL command that is not supported by PowerScript embedded SQL, such as CREATE TABLE.

- You need to issue a server-specific variation of a SQL command in which the command itself is supported by PowerScript embedded SQL, but the variation is not. For example, although PowerScript supports the FETCH command for a cursor, in Sybase SQL Anywhere there is an optional FOR UPDATE clause for FETCH. PowerScript embedded SQL does not accept FETCH ... FOR UPDATE.

- You are developing an application that must work with more than one database server product, and you need to accommodate differences in their SQL dialects.

THE FOUR FORMATS OF DYNAMIC SQL

The explanation of dynamic SQL ranges from the very simple to the very complex. There are four different procedures for using dynamic SQL, which PowerBuilder calls the "four formats." In order of increasing difficulty, they are

Format 1: EXECUTE IMMEDIATE

Format 2: PREPARE and EXECUTE

Format 3: Dynamic Cursor/Procedure (without DESCRIBE)

Format 4: Dynamic Cursor/Procedure with DESCRIBE

EXECUTE IMMEDIATE (FORMAT 1)

The simplest form of dynamic SQL is this:

```
EXECUTE IMMEDIATE :stringVariable;
```

You can use it as long as you do not need to work with input parameters or returned values.

PowerBuilder makes no attempt to interpret or validate the string. (That's true for all forms of Dynamic SQL.) PowerBuilder transmits the string directly to the server for execution, as shown in Figure 7-8. You can send any string at all to the server, but it had better be a valid command and not nonsense, or else you'll get an error message back.

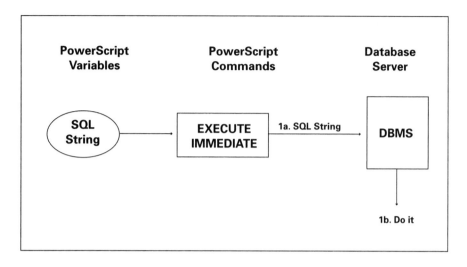

Figure 7-8
EXECUTE IMMEDIATE.

The script in Listing 7-7 constructs a SQL statement in the string variable *ls_sql* and then executes it with EXECUTE IMMEDIATE. In the SQL statement, the table name, the column name, and the column values come from variables. In the script, the variables are assigned hard-coded values, such as "customer" for *ls_tablename*. In a real-world application, the values might come from user input or some other source.

Listing 7-7
Using Dynamic SQL to update a table.

```
String ls_sql, ls_tablename, ls_columnname, ls_oldvalue, ls_newvalue

ls_tablename  = "customer"
ls_columnname = "lastname"
ls_oldvalue   = "Gray"
ls_newvalue   = "Grant"

ls_sql =  "UPDATE "   + ls_tablename +        &
          " SET "     + ls_columnname +       &
          " = '"      + ls_newvalue   + "' " + &
          " WHERE "   + ls_columnname +       &
          " = '"      + ls_oldvalue   + "' "

EXECUTE IMMEDIATE :ls_sql;
IF sqlca.SqlCode <> 0 THEN ...  // test for an error
```

This is the constructed SQL string, as it ends up in the variable *ls_sql*:

```
UPDATE customer SET lastname = 'Grant' WHERE lastname = 'Gray'
```

Another use for EXECUTE IMMEDIATE is to execute SQL statements that are not allowed by embedded SQL, such as CREATE TABLE. Here is a CREATE TABLE command:

```
CREATE TABLE temp1
    (field1 char(10) NOT NULL,
     field2 char(10) NOT NULL,
     field3 char(10) NOT NULL)
```

Here is the script that executes it:

```
String  ls_sql          // the dynamic SQL statement
ls_sql = "CREATE TABLE temp1 "              + &
         "  (field1 char(10) NOT NULL, "    + &
         "   field2 char(10) NOT NULL, "    + &
         "   field3 char(10) NOT NULL)"
EXECUTE IMMEDIATE :ls_sql;
IF sqlca.SqlCode <> 0 THEN ...  // test for an error
```

Having shown this CREATE TABLE example, I must point out that it would be very unusual for an application to create a table, except for temporary use. Permanent tables should be created during system development, not at runtime.

If you plan to display or print the *ls_sql* SQL string, it may look funny because it is one long run-on line of text:

```
CREATE TABLE temp1   (field1 char(10) NOT NULL,    field2 char(10) NOT
NULL,    field3 char(10) NOT NULL)
```

You may want to add "~n" (newline) characters to the string, to break it up more neatly onto multiple lines when it is displayed:

```
ls_sql = "CREATE TABLE temp1 "              + &
         "~n  (field1 char(10) NOT NULL, "  + &
         "~n   field2 char(10) NOT NULL, "  + &
         "~n   field3 char(10) NOT NULL)"
```

You can place a literal string, instead of a ":" variable, in an EXECUTE IMMEDIATE statement:

```
EXECUTE IMMEDIATE
   "DROP TABLE temp1";
```

However, there is a rather severe restriction to this approach: The SQL statement must consist of just one quoted literal, not an expression, and it must fit on a single line in your script. So "DROP TABLE temp1" fits, but the CREATE TABLE and UPDATE statements shown earlier do not. That rules out most of my SQL statements!

You cannot use ":" variables within a dynamic SQL string, as you can with embedded SQL:

```
SELECT ...etc... WHERE lastname = :ls_oldvalue
```

But who needs them? Since you're constructing the SQL string programmatically, it's a simple matter to concatenate the value of the variable *ls_oldvalue* directly into the string, as in the Listing 7-7 script.

Actually, there is one place where ":" variables would be nice — as part of the INTO clause in a SELECT statement, to retrieve returned values:

```
SELECT lastname, firstname INTO :s1, :s2 ...etc...
```

INTO clauses are not allowed in EXECUTE IMMEDIATE statements. This is the one feature of embedded SQL that EXECUTE IMMEDIATE cannot duplicate. But don't worry! As you will see, formats 3 and 4 of dynamic SQL achieve the same end result through other means.

PREPARE AND EXECUTE (FORMAT 2)

If you plan to execute a dynamic SQL statement that requires input parameters, you will probably find format 2 of dynamic SQL most convenient. This format involves two commands: first a PREPARE command, which transmits a SQL statement with input parameter placeholders to the server, and then an EXECUTE command, which passes parameter values to the server and executes the SQL statement.

Listing 7-8 is a script that PREPAREs a SQL statement, and Listing 7-9 is a script that EXECUTEs that statement. This is the SQL statement, which is constructed in the variable *ls_sql* in the PREPARE script:

```
UPDATE customer
   SET lastname = ?, firstname = ?
   WHERE lastname = ? AND firstname = ?
```

In prepared SQL statements, you use "?" to indicate parameters that will be replaced at execution time. This is similar to the use of ":" variables in embedded SQL, but remember: There are no ":" variables inside dynamic SQL strings.

Listing 7-8

PREPARE-ing an SQL statement with four input parameters

```
String  ls_sql          // the dynamic SQL statement
ls_sql = "UPDATE customer " + &
        "~n   SET lastname = ?, firstname = ? " + &
        "~n   WHERE lastname = ? AND firstname = ? "
PREPARE sqlsa FROM :ls_sql;
IF sqlca.SqlCode <> 0 THEN ...  // test for an error
```

Listing 7-9

EXECUTE-ing the prepared SQL statement

```
String  ls_oldfirst, ls_oldlast, ls_newfirst, ls_newlast

ls_oldfirst = sle_oldfirst.Text
ls_oldlast  = sle_oldlast.Text
ls_newfirst = sle_newfirst.Text
ls_newlast  = sle_newlast.Text

EXECUTE sqlsa USING :ls_newlast, :ls_newfirst, &
                    :ls_oldlast, :ls_oldfirst;
IF sqlca.SqlCode <> 0 THEN ...  // test for an error
```

When you EXECUTE the SQL command, you must supply a value for each "?" parameter. The values go into a USING clause in the EXECUTE statement. The Listing 7-9 script supplies the four values as ":" variables. Those variables, in turn, get their values from fields on the currently open window, where the user has typed in values. For example, the window has an "Old Last Name" field, which is a SingleLineEdit control named sle_old-last. If the user types "Smith" into that field, that value will be placed into the *ls_oldlast* variable and inserted into the EXECUTE statement.

Curiously, when the EXECUTE command extends onto two or more lines, it requires the "&" continuation symbol at the end of each line, like a non-SQL PowerScript statement. But it also requires a ";" to conclude it, like embedded SQL:

```
EXECUTE sqlsa USING :ls_newlast, :ls_newfirst,  &
                    :ls_oldlast, :ls_oldfirst;
```

THE *sqlsa* VARIABLE AND OTHER DYNAMICSTAGINGAREA VARIABLES

There is one more variable that plays a role in the process: *sqlsa*, which appears in both the PREPARE and the EXECUTE commands. It is what is called a "DynamicStagingArea" variable. Its purpose is illustrated in Figure 7-9.

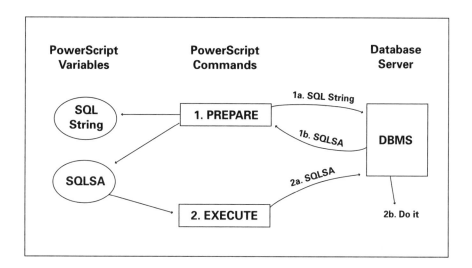

Figure 7-9
The PREPARE-EXECUTE process.

The PREPARE command passes the SQL string to the database server to be parsed but not executed. The server creates a special parsed version of the SQL statement and passes it back to the client, where it is stored in *sqlsa*. The EXECUTE command sends *sqlsa* back to the database server for execution.

There is no way to see the actual contents of *sqlsa*. Whatever they are, they are database-product specific. I think of *sqlsa* as the "compiled" version of the SQL.

Like *sqlca*, *sqlsa* is a global variable that is automatically defined. Whereas *sqlca* is a Transaction-type variable, *sqlsa* is a Dynamic-StagingArea-type variable.

You can declare your own DynamicStagingArea variables and use them instead of, or in addition to, *sqlsa*. You'll need to do this if you have more than one dynamic SQL command prepared and awaiting EXECUTE at a time.

This line declares a DynamicStagingArea variable named *dsa1*:

```
DynamicStagingArea dsa1
```

Before you can use *dsa1,* you must create it. We saw the same requirement for the *trans1* transaction object variable at the beginning of this chapter.

```
dsa1 = CREATE DynamicStagingArea
```

If you are using *sqlsa*, there is no need for the CREATE step. PowerBuilder automatically declares and creates it for you.

Now you can use *dsa1* in PREPARE and EXECUTE commands, as the scripts in Listing 7-8 and Listing 7-9 did with *sqlsa*:

```
PREPARE dsa1 FROM :ls_sql;
EXECUTE dsa1 USING :ls_newlast, :ls_newfirst, &
                   :ls_oldlast, :ls_oldfirst;
```

DYNAMIC CURSORS (FORMAT 3)

The first two formats of dynamic SQL are not suitable for SELECT statements, because they cannot handle result sets. In embedded SQL, the three techniques for retrieving result sets are the INTO clause, cursors, and procedures. In dynamic SQL, you may not use an INTO clause. But you can use *dynamic cursors* and *dynamic procedures*. This section describes dynamic cursors.

The script in Listing 7-10 shows the use of a dynamic cursor. It is essentially the combination of two techniques shown previously: the cursor technique from Listing 7-5, and the PREPARE-and-EXECUTE technique from Listing 7-8 and Listing 7-9.

Listing 7-10

Using a dynamic cursor to FETCH values INTO PowerScript variables

```
String   ls_sql                                  // SQL statement
String   ls_value1, ls_value2                    // input values
String   ls_custid, ls_lastname, ls_firstname    // fetched values
String   ls_city, ls_state                       // more fetched values
Dec{2}   ldec_openbal                            // fetched $ value

DECLARE cursor1 DYNAMIC CURSOR FOR sqlsa;

ls_sql = "SELECT custid, lastname, firstname, " + &
         "~n      city, state, openbalance "    + &
         "~n    FROM   customer"                 + &
         "~n    WHERE city = ? AND state = ?"
PREPARE sqlsa FROM :ls_sql;    // prepare the dynamic SQL statement
IF sqlca.SqlCode <> 0 THEN ...  // test for an error

ls_value1 = sle_value1.Text
ls_value2 = sle_value2.Text

OPEN DYNAMIC cursor1 USING :ls_value1, :ls_value2;
IF sqlca.SqlCode <> 0 THEN ...  // test for an error

DO
   FETCH cursor1 INTO
         :ls_custid, :ls_lastname, :ls_firstname,
         :ls_city, :ls_state, :ldec_openbal;
   IF sqlca.SqlCode = 100 THEN EXIT // no more rows - all done
   IF sqlca.SqlCode <> 0 THEN ...    // test for an error

   ... etc ...  // processing of the row's fetched values goes here

LOOP WHILE True
CLOSE cursor1;     // close the cursor
IF sqlca.SqlCode <> 0 THEN ...  // test for an error
```

These are the key steps in the script:

1. **DECLARE DYNAMIC CURSOR** — Declare the cursor and associate it with the DynamicStagingArea variable *sqlsa*. You associate a regular cursor with a SELECT statement. You associate a dynamic cursor with a DynamicStagingArea variable, which will soon hold a parsed SELECT statement.

2. **PREPARE** — Send the SELECT statement to the server, and store the result in *sqlsa*. This is the same as in the example for format 2.

3. **OPEN DYNAMIC CURSOR** — Execute the SELECT statement stored in *sqlsa*, create a result set, and prepare the cursor to fetch rows from it. The OPEN DYNAMIC CURSOR command replaces the EXECUTE command in the format 2 example. Like EXECUTE, the OPEN DYNAMIC CURSOR command must provide variables in its USING clause to provide values for the "?" parameters in the SELECT.

4. **FETCH** — Retrieve values from one row of the dynamic cursor. Since this is in a loop that will terminate when FETCH returns sqlca.SqlCode = 100, FETCH will retrieve each row in the result set, one at a time.

5. **CLOSE** — Terminate cursor processing.

Figure 7-10 illustrates the process.

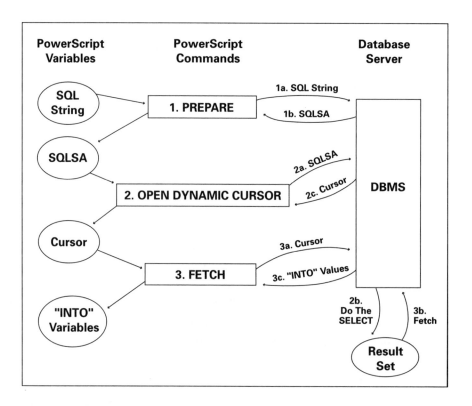

Figure 7-10

The dynamic cursor process.

Although the example doesn't show it, you can also use the commands UPDATE WHERE CURRENT OF CURSOR and DELETE WHERE CURRENT OF CURSOR to update or delete FETCHed rows.

DYNAMIC CURSOR WITH DESCRIBE (FORMAT 4)

The fourth and final format of dynamic SQL is by far the most complex. But it is necessary in order to complete the transition from the "hard-coded" style of embedded SQL to the "on-the-fly" style of dynamic SQL.

The dynamic SQL techniques shown so far would permit you to construct *almost* every element of every possible SQL statement "on-the-fly" through programming. However, two exceptions remain:

- The USING clause in the EXECUTE and OPEN DYNAMIC statements requires that you hard-code a fixed number of parameters. Therefore, you are restricted to a precise number of "?" input parameters in the dynamic SQL statement.

- Similarly, the INTO clause in the FETCH statement requires a fixed, hard-coded number of result variables. Therefore to use it, you are restricted to the exact number of columns and expressions returned by the dynamic SELECT statement.

Format 4 dynamic SQL overcomes both of these limitations. It introduces one more special variable, the Dynamic Description Area, and a command to build it, DESCRIBE.

AN EXAMPLE OF FORMAT 4 DYNAMIC SQL

Some applications include an ad hoc query feature, which allows the end user to construct and execute queries in a rather free-form way. The programming behind the scenes translates the user's specifications into a SELECT statement and executes it.

The most free-form ad hoc query that I can imagine would be to present users with a box and let them type in any SELECT statement at all. This is shown in Figure 7-11. The SELECT statement can even include "?" parameters.

The application must figure out how many parameters there are and prompt the user to supply values for them. You can see this in Figure 7-12. Now the application has what it needs to execute the query and fetch the rows of the result set.

The number of values returned by the SELECT, and their datatypes, are unknown to the application until it fetches the first row. But once the first row is fetched, the application can display the columns and their datatypes. This is shown in Figure 7-13. (I admit that the presentation style could be prettied up somewhat. I have to leave something for the reader to do!)

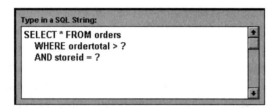

Figure 7-11
A free-form query box. The user types in a SELECT statement.

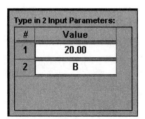

Figure 7-12
Typing in the input parameters.

One Row Fetched. - # of Columns: 10		
#	Value	Type
1	133	Long
2	1/6/96	Date
3	5002	String
4	20.45	Decimal
5	0.08	Decimal
6	1.68	Decimal
7	22.13	Decimal
8	10:00:00	Time
9	B	String
10	Yes	String

Figure 7-13

Presenting the first fetched row.

Granted, this example is a little bit contrived. Why would the user want to type "?" into the SELECT and immediately thereafter type in the values? Wouldn't it be easier to type the values directly into the SELECT? Nevertheless, more sophisticated query systems could very well contain variations on each of the elements in this example.

Formats 1, 2, and 3 cannot accomplish the tasks in this example. Format 1 cannot deal with "?" variables. Formats 1 and 2 cannot deal with result sets. None of these formats can deal with an unknown number of input values or result values. But format 4 can do all of these things.

Here is a step-by-step walk-through of the PowerScript programming. Figure 7-14 is a diagram of the key points. You will find the completed version in the sample application on the CD-ROM.

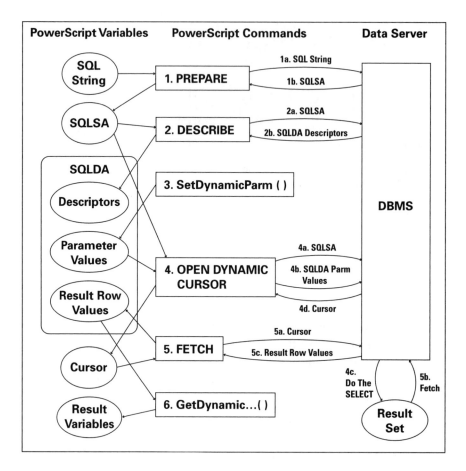

Figure 7-14
Format 4 of dynamic SQL — the dynamic cursor with DESCRIBE.

1. **Declare variables** — In addition to regular variables, we need to declare a DynamicStagingArea, a DynamicDescriptionArea, and a dynamic cursor:

```
DynamicStagingArea      idsa1
DynamicDescriptionArea  idda1
DECLARE icur1 DYNAMIC CURSOR FOR idsa1;
idsa1 = CREATE DynamicStagingArea
idda1 = CREATE DynamicDescriptionArea
```

The DynamicStagingArea, *idsa1*, was described in the section on format 3 dynamic SQL, and it will play the same role here. The

DynamicDescriptionArea, *idda1*, is new to format 4, and I will explain it as we go along. I could have used the predefined PowerBuilder variables *sqlsa* and *sqlda* instead of *idsa1* and *idda1*. That would save the trouble of declaring and creating them. But this time around, I've chosen to use declared variables.

The DECLARE DYNAMIC CURSOR statement was described in the format 3 example earlier. It must reference the DynamicStagingArea variable, *idsa1*.

2. **PREPARE** — The PREPARE statement is much the same as in the format 3 example:

```
PREPARE idsa1 FROM :mle_sqlstring.Text;
```

It transmits the SQL SELECT statement in mle_sqlstring.Text to the server. The server parses it and sends back *idsa1*. (This is number 1 in Figure 7-14.)

Previous examples supplied the SQL SELECT statement in a variable, *ls_sql*. This example shows that you can also supply a control property. mle_sqlstring is the field (MultiLineEdit control) shown in Figure 7-11.

3. **DESCRIBE** — This is the first step that's new in format 4 dynamic SQL:

```
DESCRIBE idsa1 INTO idda1;
```

The DESCRIBE command sends the parsed SELECT statement, *idsa1*, back to the server. The server "describes" the SELECT and sends the description back to *idda1*, the DynamicDescriptionArea variable. (This is number 2 in Figure 7-14.) You might think of the DynamicDescriptionArea as a packet of information. It holds such information as the number of input parameters and output items, their data types, and their values.

4. **Get the number of parameters and ask the user to provide values** — The DynamicDescriptionArea variable has properties and functions that set or return the information it contains. For example, it has a property "NumInputs," which is the number of "?" parameters in the SELECT statement:

```
li_params = idda1.NumInputs
```

You might think it is odd that a variable has properties and functions. We have already seen, in Chapter 2, that window controls have them. But so do certain complex variables. This is a common feature of object-oriented programming languages, and I will describe it in detail in Chapter 11.

Now that the script knows the number of input parameters — for the SELECT in Figure 7-11, there are two — it can ask the user to type in that many values.

5. **Type in values** — The user types in the input values, as shown in Figure 7-12. The device shown in Figure 7-12 is a DataWindow. The design and programming of DataWindows will be described beginning in the next chapter.

6. **SETDYNAMICPARM( )** — This FOR loop transfers the input values into the DynamicDescriptionArea:

```
FOR i = 1 TO li_params
    ls_param = dw_params.GetItemString(i, "ParamValue")
    idda1.SetDynamicParm(i, ls_param)
NEXT
```

The key is the function SetDynamicParm. The Dynamic-DescriptionArea, *idda1*, contains an array of input values. The call to SetDynamicParm places the value *ls_param* into the *i*th input value in *idda1*. (This is number 3 in Figure 7-14.) When $i = 1$, *ls_param* is 20.00. When $i = 2$, *ls_param* is "B." *ls_param* is set by calling GetItemString, a function that retrieves a value from a row in a DataWindow.

At this point, the script knows everything necessary to execute the SELECT and get a result set.

7. **OPEN DYNAMIC CURSOR** — We saw an OPEN DYNAMIC CURSOR in the format 3 example. In format 4 dynamic SQL, it's a little bit different:

```
OPEN DYNAMIC icur1 USING DESCRIPTOR idda1;
```

This command tells the database server to execute the SELECT statement and prepare the cursor, *icur1*, to fetch rows from the result set.

(This is number 4 in Figure 7-14.) The "USING DESCRIPTOR idda1" clause says that input parameter values should be retrieved from *idda1*, which is where we stored them in the previous step.

8. **FETCH** — The FETCH statement must be a little different than what we've seen in the past. The usual version — "FETCH cursor INTO var1, var2, ..." — doesn't work, because we don't know how many variables are needed for the INTO list. Therefore, the format 4 FETCH command goes like this:

```
FETCH icur1 USING DESCRIPTOR idda1;
```

This says, "Use the cursor *icur1* to fetch the next row from the result set. Store the fetched values in the DynamicDescriptionArea *idda1*." (This is number 5 in Figure 7-14.) The next step will deal with getting the values out of *idda1* so that we can display them.

As we have seen before, you usually place the FETCH statement in a loop to fetch every SELECTed row:

```
DO
    FETCH icur1 USING DESCRIPTOR idda1;
    IF sqlca.SqlCode = 100 THEN EXIT  // no more rows - all done
    IF sqlca.SqlCode <> 0 THEN ...  // test for an error

    ... etc ...  // processing of the row's fetched values goes here

LOOP WHILE True
```

9. **GETDYNAMIC...( )** — This FOR loop, which would follow each FETCH, retrieves each result value from the DynamicDescriptionArea (this is number 6 in Figure 7-14), converts it to a string, and places it into the DataWindow shown in Figure 7-13:

```
li_values = idda1.NumOutputs
FOR i = 1 TO li_values
    CHOOSE CASE idda1.outParmType[i]
        CASE typestring!
            ls_value = idda1.GetDynamicString(i)
        CASE typedate!
            ls_value = String(idda1.GetDynamicDate(i))

        ... etc... (other Cases for the other possible datatypes)

    END CHOOSE
```

```
    dw_fetched.SetItem(i, "FetchedValue", ls_value)
NEXT
```

The NumOutputs property of *idda1* is the number of output values (result set values) retrieved from the most recent FETCH. In our example, the number is 10, since there are ten columns in the order table. The FOR loop, therefore, will repeat ten times, once for each value.

The outParmType property of *idda1* is an array identifying the datatype of each of the ten output values. In our example, the first value, 133, is a long integer, the second value, 1/6/96, is a date, the third value, "5002," is a string, and so on. The outParmType array elements are enumerated datatypes, with values such as typelong!, typedate!, and typestring! There are twelve types in all, and the processing is a little different for each, so the CHOOSE CASE statement is followed by twelve CASEs, of which I have shown only the first two here.

This line transfers the *i*th output value into the string variable *ls_value*:

```
ls_value = idda1.GetDynamicString(i)
```

Unfortunately, the GetDynamicString function works only if the output value is a string. There are six such functions, and you have to use the correct one for the output value's data type: GetDynamicString, GetDynamicNumber, GetDynamicDate, GetDynamicTime, and GetDynamicDateTime. That's the reason for the CHOOSE CASE (which I consider tedious).

The dw_fetched.SetItem function places the output value *ls_value*, in the "Value" column of the *i*th row of the DataWindow (Figure 7-13). There is other programming code that I am not showing here, such as the code that fills in the "Type" column.

10. **CLOSE CURSOR** — After all the rows have been FETCHed, close the cursor:

```
CLOSE icur1;
```

If you have no further need for the DynamicStagingArea and DynamicDescriptionArea variables, you should destroy them to free up memory:

```
Destroy idsal
Destroy iddal
```

Don't destroy the system variables *sqlsa* or *sqlda*.

DYNAMIC PROCEDURES

As I mentioned earlier, there are also "dynamic procedures." They provide a more flexible way to call stored procedures than the regular approach, in the same way that dynamic cursors provide a more flexible way to fetch a result set than regular cursors. Refer to the documentation for the EXECUTE DYNAMIC PROCEDURE command in the *PowerScript Reference Manual* for more information.

Temporary Tables

During some complex processing, you may need a place to accumulate interim results. A *temporary table* provides an ideal repository for this type of data. The term is something of a misnomer, though; the table itself is no more temporary than any other table, but its rows are.

LIFESPAN AND VISIBILITY OF TEMPORARY TABLE ROWS

Once you've created a temporary table, it remains in the database unless you DROP it. The rows of a temporary table, however, never live longer than the duration of a connection to the database. DISCONNECT deletes all rows inserted during the connection. Furthermore, the rows inserted during one connection will be invisible to any other connections that may be using the same temporary table — each connection's rows are private to that connection. This characteristic makes a temporary table perfect for situations where different users may be doing the same operation — a complex report, for example — but with different data that must not intermingle.

You can control the lifespan of temporary table rows somewhat — before DISCONNECT deletes them — by specifying whether COMMIT should also delete them.

CREATING A TEMPORARY TABLE

You create a temporary table, like any table, with the CREATE TABLE command. The requirements and syntax for CREATE TABLE vary somewhat among database products, so you should always consult your database documentation and also the PowerBuilder documentation relating to that product. With SQL Server, you must set AutoCommit = True before executing CREATE TABLE or any other DDL command. With Sybase SQL Anywhere, on the other hand, CREATE TABLE does an automatic COMMIT regardless of the value of AutoCommit.

This script, which is appropriate for Sybase SQL Anywhere, creates a temporary table named temp1:

```
ls_sql = "CREATE GLOBAL TEMPORARY TABLE temp1 "        + &
      "~n  (storeid        char(1)      NOT NULL, "     + &
      "~n   storecity      char(13)     NOT NULL, "     + &
      "~n   category       char(9)      NOT NULL, "     + &
      "~n   totalsales     numeric(7,2) NOT NULL) "     + &
      "~n    ON COMMIT " + ls_oncommit + " ROWS"
EXECUTE IMMEDIATE :ls_sql;
IF sqlca.SqlCode <> 0 THEN ...  // test for an error
```

The GLOBAL TEMPORARY clause identifies the table as temporary. The ON COMMIT clause determines whether the rows will be deleted or preserved by COMMIT. The variable *ls_oncommit* has "DELETE" or "PRESERVE" as its value (set elsewhere).

Once you've successfully created the temporary table, you'll populate its rows in the usual way — that is, with INSERT commands. For example, the following embedded SQL code performs a summary calculation and INSERTs the resulting rows:

```
INSERT INTO temp1
   (storeid, storecity, category, totalsales)
   SELECT orders.storeid,
          store.storecity,
          film.category,
          sum(lineitem.extendedprice)
      FROM orders, store, film, lineitem
      WHERE (store.storeid=orders.storeid)
```

```
        AND (film.filmid=lineitem.filmid)
        AND (orders.orderno=lineitem.orderno)
        GROUP BY orders.storeid, film.category,
                  store.storecity;
IF sqlca.SqlCode <> 0 THEN ...  // test for an error
```

If the process for which you've created the temporary table will occur repeatedly, there's no need to delete the table itself. Each connection can continue to use its own separate rows in the table, as needed. However, if the entire table is no longer necessary, you can DROP it:

```
ls_sql = "DROP TABLE temp1"
EXECUTE IMMEDIATE :ls_sql;
IF sqlca.SqlCode <> 0 THEN ...  // test for an error
```

Summary: SQL and PowerScript

In this chapter, you learned how to use SQL in conjunction with PowerScript programming to work with data:

- You learned how to use the transaction object to establish a connection to a database.

- You discovered some techniques to use when embedding SQL — how to make sure that errors don't derail your scripts and how to use PowerScript variables together with SQL.

- You gained insight into the workings of a transaction — how it starts and ends and how you can control it.

- You learned how cursors and stored procedures let you work with multiple rows.

- You learned about the four formats of dynamic SQL and how they give you tremendous flexibility in building SQL statements that can change as needed.

- You saw how temporary tables can function as private work spaces during complex processing.

Now that you're comfortable combining PowerScript and SQL, you're ready to explore PowerBuilder's DataWindow objects — where the data meets the eye.

8

DataWindows

*M*any people call the DataWindow the most important feature in PowerBuilder, and I have to agree. It is certainly the richest, packing more functionality per square inch than you'll find anywhere else.

The DataWindow is how your applications will present database data, and maybe even nondatabase data, to the end user. Whether it's an inquiry screen, a data entry form, or a printed report — all of these are DataWindows.

The DataWindow topic is so large that this book dedicates several chapters to it. In this chapter, you'll learn how to create a DataWindow and integrate it into an application. In the next chapter, you'll learn how to use the DataWindow Painter, and you'll learn a lot about how DataWindows operate. Chapter 10 describes how to solve common data entry problems with DataWindows and PowerScript. Chapter 18 talks about using DataWindows for printing reports. Chapter 19 covers advanced DataWindow techniques.

There's a lot to learn! As always, let's start with the basics.

What Is a DataWindow?

A *DataWindow* is just what its name says: a window with data. Figure 8-1 shows a DataWindow that is presenting a row from the Video Store's customer table.

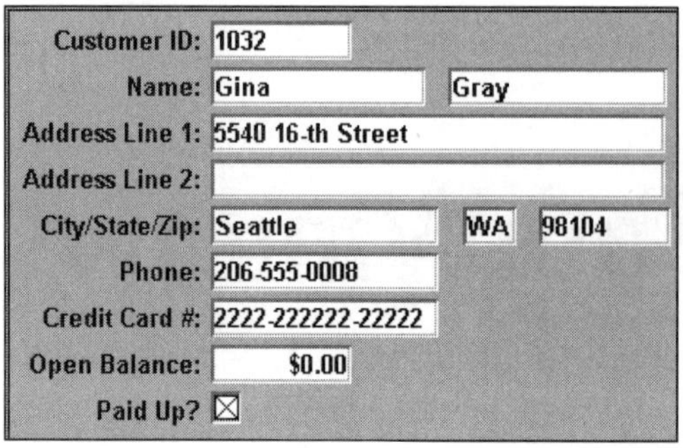

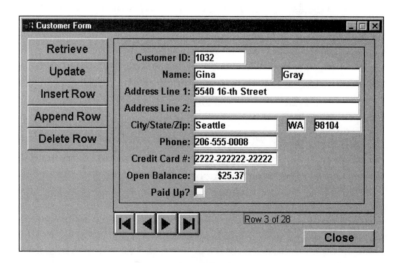

Figure 8-1
A DataWindow.

In a running PowerBuilder application, a DataWindow never stands alone, as the one in Figure 8-1 appears to do. A DataWindow must be embedded within a regular window, as shown in Figure 8-2.

Figure 8-2
The DataWindow in a regular window.

In the design of the DataWindow, three objects come into play:

1. **The DataWindow Object** — This is what is pictured in Figure 8-1. You create it with the DataWindow Painter. Later you embed it within the DataWindow control on the window.

2. **The Window** — This is what is pictured in Figure 8-2. You create this with the Window Painter. It is the container for everything else.

3. **The DataWindow Control** — You place this on the window using the Window Painter. A DataWindow control is not unlike other window controls that we've already worked with, such as Command-Button controls. The DataWindow control is the container for the DataWindow object.

Figure 8-3 illustrates these relationships.

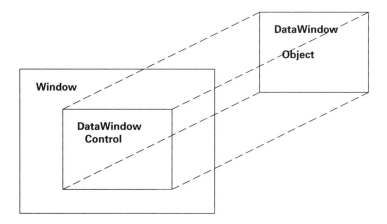

Figure 8-3
The window, the DataWindow control, and the DataWindow object.

At first, the distinction between the DataWindow control and the DataWindow object may be confusing. The control and the object are two very different things, and each plays a separate and important role. It's important to keep them straight in your mind.

This analogy may help: Think of a painting in a frame, hanging on a wall. The DataWindow object is like the painting, the DataWindow control is like the frame, and the window is like the wall. The frame and the painting are two different things, and although you may think the frame is not very important, you can't hang the painting on the wall without it.

Getting Your First DataWindow Up and Running Quickly

A minimum number of components are required to get a typical DataWindow up and running in an application. The components, which are illustrated in Figure 8-4, are these:

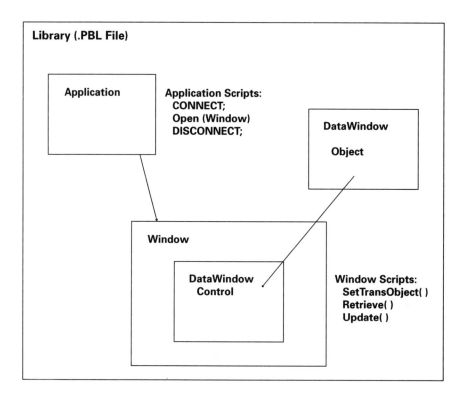

Figure 8-4

Minimum components for a functioning DataWindow in an application.

1. **An application** — In Chapter 2, I explained that an application requires at least

   - An application object
   - A window
   - A script on the application's open event that opens the window

- A library (.PBL file) in which to store everything

2. **A DataWindow Object** — created with the DataWindow painter

3. **A DataWindow Control** — placed on the window, containing the DataWindow object

4. **PowerScript Commands** — to prepare and manipulate the database and the DataWindow control. These commands will be contained in application's and window's event scripts:

   - A CONNECT command and related commands, to connect to the database. Typically, you issue CONNECT from the application's open script.

   - A DISCONNECT command, to disconnect from the database when done. Typically, you issue DISCONNECT from the application's close script.

   - A SetTransObject function call, to associate the transaction object (typically sqlca) with the DataWindow control. Typically, you call SetTransObject from the window's open script or the DataWindow control's constructor script.

   - A Retrieve function call, to read rows from the database and display them in the DataWindow. Typically, you call Retrieve from the window's open script, the DataWindow control's constructor script, a button's clicked script, or a menu item's script.

   - An Update function call, to write changed rows back to the database, if your window allows users to make changes. There are many places where you might call the Update function — for example, the window's close script, or the DataWindow control's destructor script, or a button's clicked script, or a menu item's script.

STEP BY STEP: A FIRST DATAWINDOW EXERCISE

Chapter 2 walked you through a tutorial-style exercise to develop your first application. Here is a similar exercise to develop your first DataWindow application. At the end of the exercise, the application will display the "minimal" window/DataWindow pictured in Figure 8-5.

Figure 8-5

A "minimal" DataWindow application, the end result of the first exercise.

STEP 1. CONNECT TO THE VIDEO STORE DATABASE

This exercise requires you to have installed Video Store DB, the SQL
Anywhere database that is included on the CD-ROM that accompanies
this book. If you have not yet installed it, please do so by following the
instructions in the CD-ROM's README.TXT file.

The DataWindow Painter steps in this exercise will connect to Video
Store DB. It's best to test that connection now, before going further.

Click the Database button on the PowerBar to open the Database
Painter. Click Cancel when the Select Tables dialog box appears. Select
File|Connect|Video Store DB from the menu. If the Select Tables dialog
box appears, and if it lists the tables shown in Figure 8-6, then you're in
business. Click Cancel to close the dialog box, and then select File|Close
to close the Database Painter. Even though you close the painter,
PowerBuilder will remain connected to the Video Store database.

If Video Store DB is not a choice in the File|Connect menu, you must
install the database from the CD-ROM. If it is a choice, but tables are missing from the Select Tables list, you need to rebuild the database. Follow
the instructions in the CD-ROM's README.TXT file. If you have other connection problems, please review Chapter 5.

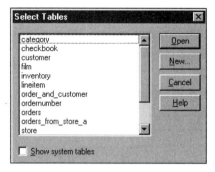

Figure 8-6
The Select Tables dialog box, as it should appear when you connect to "Video Store DB."

STEP 2. CREATE THE LIBRARY, APPLICATION, AND WINDOW

Open the Application Painter and create a new application, named "appdw," in a new library, TESTDW.PBL. You can place the library in any directory. You may have a directory C:\FOUNDPB from earlier exercises; this would be a good place for it. Answer "No" when asked, "Would you like PowerBuilder to generate an Application template?"

Open the Window Painter and create a new window. Don't place any controls on the window yet. Select File|Save and save the window with the name "w_first." Close the Window Painter.

If you have trouble with this procedure, please refer to steps 2–8 in Chapter 2.

STEP 3. WRITE THE OPEN SCRIPT FOR THE APPLICATION

After you close the Window Painter, you will return to the Application Painter. If not, then return to the Application Painter by clicking the Application button on the PowerBar.

Open the open event script for the Application by clicking the Script button on the PainterBar. In the Script Painter, type in this script:

```
//  Connect to the SQL Anywhere Video Store Database

sqlca.DBMS       = "ODBC"
sqlca.Database   = "Video Store DB"
sqlca.UserId     = "dba"
sqlca.DBParm     = "Connectstring='DSN=Video Store DB'"
sqlca.AutoCommit = True
```

```
CONNECT;
IF sqlca.SqlCode <> 0 THEN
   MessageBox("Error on Connect to Video Store DB", &
      "Error Code: " + String(sqlca.SqlDbCode) +    &
      "~nError Message= " + sqlca.SqlErrText,        &
      StopSign!)
   HALT
END IF

// Open the window

Open(w_first)
```

This script does two things: First, it connects to Video Store DB, a SQL Anywhere database. Second, it opens the window w_first. Chapter 7 explained the database-connection programming in detail. Since there is no USING clause in the CONNECT statement, this application will use the default transaction object, *sqlca*.

Select Design|Compile Script from the menu to check the syntax of the script. If there are errors, correct them and try again.

STEP 4. WRITE THE CLOSE SCRIPT FOR THE APPLICATION

While still in the Script Painter for the application, switch to the close script by picking "close" from the Select Event dropdown list. Type in this one-line close script:

```
DISCONNECT;
```

When the application closes, this script will disconnect from the Video Store database.

Select Design|Compile Script from the menu to check the syntax of the script. If there are errors, correct them and try again.

Select File|Close from the menu to close the Script Painter and return to the Application Painter. Answer "Yes" to the question about saving changes to the script. Select File|Close to close the Application Painter, and answer "Yes" to the question about saving changes to the application. At this point, you should have no painter windows open. If you do, close them.

If you like, you can run the application at this point. If it works, it will open the empty "Untitled" window, which you can then close to return to the PowerBuilder development environment. If you get an error message, perhaps like the one in Figure 8-7, it indicates that the CONNECT failed. (In my case, I misspelled "Video.") Double-check your application open script, or return to step 1 and test the connection from the Database Painter.

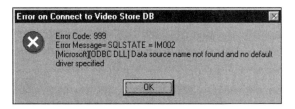

Figure 8-7
When the CONNECT command fails, the application halts with an error message.

STEP 5. CREATE THE NEW DATAWINDOW OBJECT

Click the DataWindow button on the PowerBar to open the DataWindow Painter. A delay may occur while PowerBuilder starts up the SQL Anywhere server and connects to the video store database. Then the Select DataWindow dialog appears (Figure 8-8). Organized much like the Select Window dialog that opens the Window Painter, it lists the DataWindow objects in the library. Of course there are none yet, but in the future you will see a list and be able to pick one for editing. For now, click the New button. PowerBuilder opens the New DataWindow dialog box, shown in Figure 8-9.

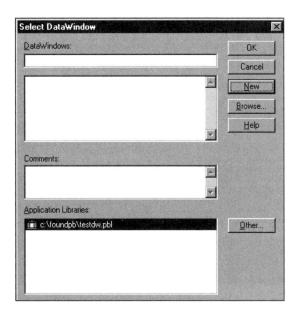

Figure 8-8
The Select DataWindow dialog box.

STEP 6. SELECT A DATA SOURCE AND A PRESENTATION STYLE

To get the new DataWindow started, PowerBuilder asks you to select one of five "Data Sources" and one of eleven "Presentation Styles." The Data Source specifies how PowerBuilder should get the data, and the Presentation Style specifies how PowerBuilder should arrange the data.

At the end of Chapter 9, I'll describe each option. For now, to keep this first exercise moving along, click Quick Select and Grid as shown in Figure 8-9. They are the simplest options. Then click OK.

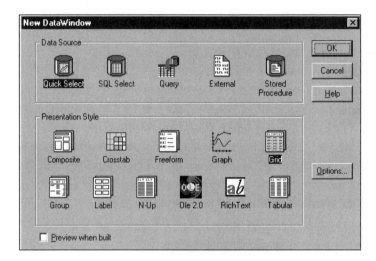

Figure 8-9
The New DataWindow dialog box.

STEP 7. SELECT TABLES AND COLUMNS

Because you chose the Quick Select data source, the Quick Select dialog box appears. (See Figure 8-10.) In this dialog box, pick a table, pick some columns, and away you go. It's quick!

Click "film" in the list of tables. The list changes to show you tables related to the film table, allowing you to pick columns from multiple tables. In the right-hand list, PowerBuilder displays the columns in the film table. Select "filmid," "filmtitle," "rentalfee," and "category." If you wanted to select all columns, which you don't for this exercise, you could click the Add All button. Figure 8-11 shows the selections you should make.

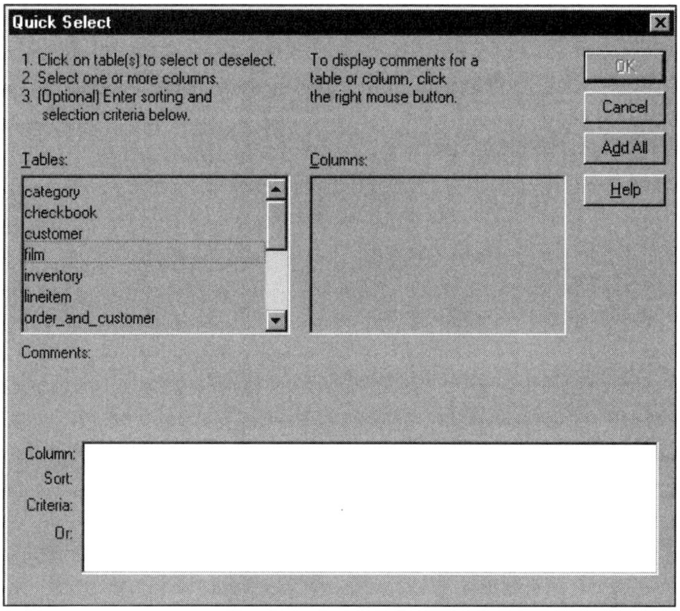

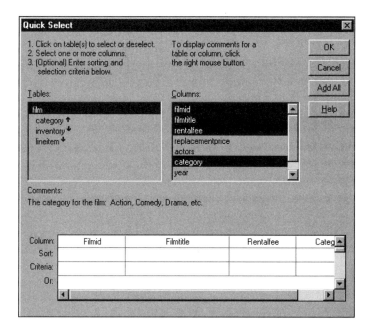

Figure 8-10

The Quick Select dialog box.

Figure 8-11

Select the film table and four columns.

Behind the scenes, PowerBuilder will construct a SQL SELECT statement based on your choices. In the grid at the bottom of the dialog box, which you should leave blank, you have the opportunity to specify a sort sequence, which becomes an ORDER BY clause, and selection criteria, which produce a WHERE clause.

Click OK. This concludes the preliminaries, and now PowerBuilder drops you into the DataWindow Painter.

STEP 8. SEE THE LAYOUT IN THE DATAWINDOW PAINTER

Based on the selections you've made, PowerBuilder populates the new DataWindow with the four film-table columns arranged in a grid style. In the DataWindow Painter, the layout looks like Figure 8-12. You can see from Figure 8-5 how it will look when you run it and display data.

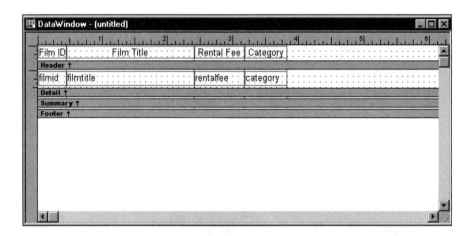

Figure 8-12
The DataWindow Painter.

The DataWindow Painter is a "banded report designer," representing a popular approach found in many report- and screen-design products. The Painter is divided into four regions by the horizontal bands labeled Header, Detail, Summary, and Footer. Anything in the Header band appears at the top of the DataWindow when you run it, as column headings. The Detail band layout determines how data will be arranged in the body of the running DataWindow. In a grid-style DataWindow like this one, the Detail band shows only one data row in the painter, but it will multiply into many rows when you run it.

The column headings are not exactly the same as the field names. For example, the "Film ID" column heading in the DataWindow is for the filmid column the film table. The column headings come from the database repository, that is, the extra attributes for database columns, including user-friendly labels, that you set up in the Database Painter. This process was explained in Chapter 6.

STEP 9. CLOSE THE DATAWINDOW PAINTER

It would be fun to play around in the DataWindow Painter — resizing things, changing fonts and colors, and so forth. We'll come back and do those things later. For now, close the Painter and save the DataWindow: Select File|Close from the menu. Answer "Yes" when asked whether to save changes. Type in the name "d_filmgrid" in the Save DataWindow dialog box (Figure 8-13) and click OK. PowerBuilder saves the new DataWindow object in the library, testdw.PBL.

Figure 8-13
Save the DataWindow Object.

STEP 10. REOPEN THE WINDOW PAINTER

Click the Window button on the PowerBar and reopen the window w_first. So far, it's just an empty window.

STEP 11. PLACE A DATAWINDOW CONTROL IN THE WINDOW

Placing a DataWindow control in the window is very much like placing a button, or any other type of control: Click the DataWindow button on the PainterBar's dropdown control palette (Figure 8-14). Then click somewhere inside the window to place the control there. Initially, it will look like a plain white box (Figure 8-15).

Be careful! The DataWindow PainterBar button, for placing a control, is identical in appearance to the DataWindow PowerBar button, which opens a painter. Don't click the wrong one.

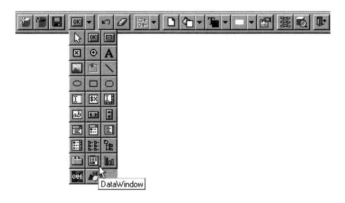

Figure 8-14
The DataWindow control button on the dropdown palette.

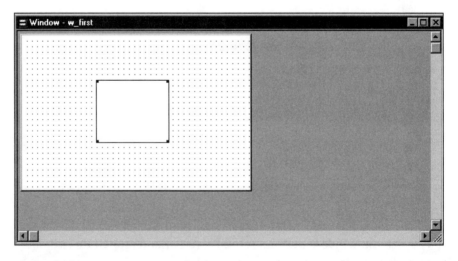

Figure 8-15
The DataWindow control in the window.

STEP 12. ASSOCIATE THE DataWindow OBJECT WITH THE DataWindow CONTROL

Double-click the DataWindow control. Its property sheet pops up where, among other things, you can pick a DataWindow object to associate with the control. Type in "d_filmgrid" for the DataWindow Object Name, as shown in Figure 8-16. Alternatively, you can click the Browse button and select "d_filmgrid" from a list. (See Figure 8-17.)

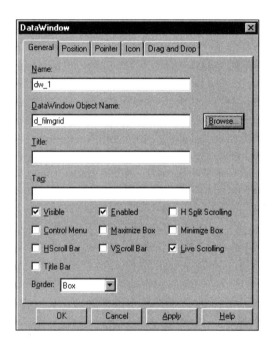

Figure 8-16

The Property Sheet for the DataWindow Control.

Figure 8-17

Select a DataWindow object to associate with the DataWindow control.

Notice in Figure 8-16 that PowerBuilder has named the DataWindow control "dw_1," even though the DataWindow object's name is d_filmgrid. The control and the object will typically have different names. Click OK. You will now see the DataWindow object — or a little piece of it anyway — in the DataWindow control.

STEP 13. STRETCH THE WINDOW AND THE DATAWINDOW CONTROL

Use the mouse to stretch the window and the DataWindow control until the entire DataWindow object is visible. Figure 8-18 shows the result. Although the DataWindow shows only two data rows, and they are empty, don't worry. When you run the application, you will see as many rows as will fit, and they will be full of data.

About DataWindow Control Names

Although PowerBuilder assigns a name like "dw_1" or "cb_1" to every control as you place it on a window, I usually change the names to something more descriptive, such as "dw_filmgrid" or "cb_close." It makes the programming and documentation more self-explanatory.

For this book, however, I have chosen to retain "dw_1" as the name of almost all

DataWindow controls. I've done this because I want to make the distinction between DataWindow controls and DataWindow objects as clear as possible. In real life, I might name the control "dw_filmgrid" and the object "d_filmgrid." In the book, it will be "dw_1" and "d_filmgrid" so that you can distinguish between the two more quickly.

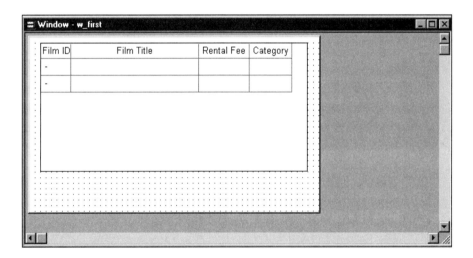

Figure 8-18
Stretch the window and the DataWindow control.

STEP 14. CHANGE THE WINDOW'S TITLE

We can change the title of the window in the window's property sheet. To open the property sheet, double-click the window in the Window Painter, somewhere outside the DataWindow control. Type in "The First DataWindow Exercise" for the title and click OK.

STEP 15. WRITE THE WINDOW'S OPEN SCRIPT

The window requires a script for its open event to initialize the DataWindow at runtime. (As an alternative, you could use the DataWindow control's constructor event instead.) First, click the window in the Window Painter, somewhere outside the DataWindow control. This will select the window as the current object. Next, click the Script button on the PainterBar to open the Script Painter.

Type in the following two-line open script:

```
dw_1.SetTransObject(sqlca)
dw_1.Retrieve()
```

Select Design|Compile Script and correct any errors that appear.

The syntax of these two lines of code should be familiar. They are object function calls on dw_1, the DataWindow control.

The SetTransObject function associates the transaction object variable *sqlca* with the DataWindow control. Whenever the DataWindow needs to send a SQL command to a database — to issue a SELECT to retrieve some rows or an UPDATE to change a row, for example — it will send the command to the database to which *sqlca* is connected. The CONNECT command, which you wrote in step 3, connected *sqlca* to the Video Store database. So the SetTransObject function ties the DataWindow to the Video Store database.

There is an alternative to SetTransObject: the similarly-named SetTrans function. It is rarely used because it performs a CONNECT and DISCONNECT for every SQL operation, greatly slowing down processing.

The Retrieve function retrieves a set of rows into the DataWindow. It issues an unseen SELECT command to the database server (in the next chapter I'll show you how you can see the command):

```
SELECT filmid, filmtitle, rentalfee, category
  FROM film
```

If you do not call the Retrieve function when the window opens, the DataWindow will be empty. Because of the Retrieve, the DataWindow will now contain rows of data.

Close the Script Painter by selecting File|Return from the menu or by clicking Return to Window Painter on the PainterBar.

STEP 16. RUN THE APPLICATION

At this point, you have a workable DataWindow application. So let's run it! Click the Run button on the PowerBar and answer "Yes" when PowerBuilder asks whether to save the window.

When the application starts running, it connects to the database and opens the window. When the window opens, it associates the DataWindow with the *sqlca* transaction object and retrieves data. What you see are the first six or so rows of the film table, as pictured in Figure 8-19.

Film ID	Film Title	Rental Fee	Category
A-130	The Maltese Falcon	$2.00	Classics
A-137	Forrest Gump	$3.00	Comedy
A-155	Schindler's List	$3.00	Drama
A-400	Jurassic Park	$3.00	Sci-Fi
B-201	A Little Princess	$2.00	Children
B-202	Beethoven	$2.00	Children

The First DataWindow Exercise

Figure 8-19

Running the application.

You can scroll up and down through the rows in the film table (there are 36 of them) by pressing keys such as Page Up and Page Down on the keyboard. You can also make changes, such as changing a film title. But the changes never get written to the database, because the window never does an UPDATE. We have to add a little more PowerScript programming for that.

When you are done scrolling around, close the window. This also closes the application, returning you to the Window Painter.

STEP 17. ADD AN UPDATE BUTTON

Now we'll add two buttons to the window, an Update button and a Retrieve button, as pictured in Figure 8-20. In a real-world application, you might prefer to place buttons like these on a toolbar. I'll show you how to do that in Chapter 15. For now, however, it's easier to place the buttons inside the window.

Add the first button to the window in the usual way: Click CommandButton on the PainterBar's dropdown control palette, and then click a spot in the window for the button to appear. Change the button's text label from "none" to "Update."

Next, click the Script button on the PainterBar and type in this one-line script:

```
dw_1.Update()
```

This line asks the DataWindow control to update the database with all the changes that you have made on-screen. For example, if you change film A130's title from "The Maltese Falcon" to "The Big Sleep," PowerBuilder will issue this SQL command, or one like it, when your script calls dw_1.Update():

```
UPDATE film
    SET filmtitle = 'The Big Sleep'
    WHERE filmid  = 'A130'
```

How PowerBuilder converts your changes to a series of INSERT, UPDATE, and DELETE SQL commands is very interesting. I'll describe the process in the next two chapters.

No COMMIT command is needed after the UPDATE, because you set sqlca.AutoCommit to True during the CONNECT process in step 3.

Select Design|Compile Script from the menu to make sure there are no errors. Select File|Return to close the Script Painter and return to the Window Painter.

STEP 18. ADD A RETRIEVE BUTTON

Add another button to the window. Follow the same steps as you did for the Update button, with two differences: (1) Change its text to "Retrieve." (2) Write the following script for it:

```
dw_1.Retrieve()
```

This same command appears in the window's open script (step 15). It retrieves film rows from the database and displays them in the DataWindow. The reasons for having it on a button as well are

1. To refresh the DataWindow with the latest database data, to see any changes made by other users

2. To throw away all the changes you've made to rows in the DataWindow without writing them to the database, and to refill the DataWindow with freshly read rows

STEP 19. RUN THE APPLICATION

Once again, click the Run button on the PowerBar to run the application, clicking "Yes" to save the window when asked. Figure 8-20 shows the running window, with its two new buttons.

Film ID	Film Title	Rental Fee	Category
A-130	The Maltese Falcon	$2.00	Classics
A-137	Forrest Gump	$3.00	Comedy
A-155	Schindler's List	$3.00	Drama
A-400	Jurassic Park	$3.00	Sci-Fi
B-201	A Little Princess	$2.00	Children
B-202	Beethoven	$2.00	Children

The First DataWindow Exercise

Retrieve   Update

Figure 8-20
Running the application, with the Retrieve and Update buttons.

Try updating the database: Change a few fields and click Retrieve. Your changes disappear, replaced with newly retrieved rows with the original data. Change a few more fields and click Update. Although nothing visual happens, the script writes the changes to the database. Click Retrieve. Nothing changes, because the newly retrieved rows reflect your updates. Try a few more experiments to become comfortable with how Retrieve and Update work.

When you have finished, close the window to return to the PowerBuilder development environment.

This concludes the exercise.

Are the Retrieve and Update Buttons Really Necessary?

You may consider it inconvenient or confusing for end users to have Retrieve and Update buttons on the window. Shouldn't the application be smart enough to retrieve and update automatically, when needed?

Well, you can certainly make it that smart and do away with the buttons. Whether that's an improvement depends on the application. PowerBuilder requires that the Retrieve and Update functions be called somewhere, but there are plenty of events whose scripts could call them. We've already used the window open event for Retrieve. You could use the window close event for Update. The CloseQuery event, as I'll show in the next chapter, is even better than the close event for Update. The DataWindow control has a RowFocusChanged event, which, with a little work, could update each changed row as you move off it.

Most of the sample DataWindows in this book have explicit Retrieve and Update buttons. For learning PowerBuilder, you will find that these buttons make it easier to precisely control the DataWindow. But I will also introduce the more automatic techniques as we proceed.

LESSONS LEARNED FROM THE "FILM GRID DATAWINDOW" EXERCISE

By going through this exercise, you have learned how to get a reasonably functional DataWindow up and running. Notice how it brings together the window-building techniques of Chapter 2 and the database management techniques of the last few chapters.

In addition to the objects you create — the application, the window, the DataWindow object, and the DataWindow control — some programming is also required: most notably, the CONNECT command and the function calls SetTransObject, Retrieve, and Update.

I hope that the distinction between a DataWindow object and a DataWindow control is becoming clearer. In this exercise, d_filmgrid is the object, created with DataWindow painter; dw_1 is the control, placed on the window with the Window Painter.

You may have noticed that all the scripts that act upon the DataWindow address the control, dw_1, and never the object, d_filmgrid. This is always the case. Scripts never address a DataWindow object directly; they always go through the DataWindow control. This means that the DataWindow control will play a more important role than might first be apparent. It is more than just a picture frame!

Although you have already accomplished a lot, we have only begun to scratch the surface of DataWindows.

Polishing the Window

Although the film-grid window does work, I wouldn't consider it "ready for the public" yet. It needs at least a few more ingredients: in particular, navigation controls and error handling.

NAVIGATION CONTROLS

Figure 8-21 shows the film-grid window after adding a few navigation controls. By "navigation controls," I am referring to:

- The six VCR-like buttons, with arrow-head icons, for scrolling through the DataWindow.
- The "row counter" control, at the lower-right corner of the DataWindow. It displays the location of the current row, such as "Row 2 of 36."
- The Insert Row, Append Row, and Delete Row buttons.
- The vertical scroll bar on the DataWindow.

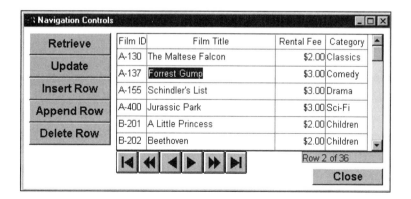

Figure 8-21

Navigation controls.

VCR BUTTONS

Each of the six VCR buttons is a PictureButton with a simple script for its clicked event. Table 8-1 shows the script for each button. For your convenience, the CD-ROM contains a set of the six icons (.BMP files) in the subdirectory "\foundpb\bitmap" that you can paste onto PictureButtons of your own.

Technically, you could do without these buttons and still scroll through the DataWindow. Keys on the keyboard, such as Page Down, do the same thing. But your users will certainly appreciate the buttons. In fact, they will probably insist on them.

Table 8-1
VCR Button Scripts

Button	Function	Script
◀|	Scroll to the first row	dw_1.ScrollToRow(1) dw_1.SetFocus()
◀◀	Scroll to the previous page	dw_1.ScrollPriorPage() dw_1.SetFocus()
◀	Scroll to the previous row	dw_1.ScrollPriorRow() dw_1.SetFocus()
▶	Scroll to the next row	dw_1.ScrollNextRow() dw_1.SetFocus()
▶▶	Scroll to the next page	dw_1.ScrollNextPage() dw_1.SetFocus()
|▶	Scroll to the last row	Long n n = dw_1.RowCount() dw_1.ScrollToRow(n) dw_1.SetFocus()

Almost every script line is a call to a function on dw_1, the DataWindow control. For example, the line

Printing the DataWindow as a Report

By adding a Print button to the window, you can print the contents of the DataWindow as a report. The Print button's clicked script needs only a single line of code:

```
dw_1.Print()
```

When the DataWindow prints, it adjusts itself to the size of the paper. So you'll see many more rows of data on each page than the few that fit within the window in Figure 8-21.

This is the jumping-off point for the way all printed reports are produced in a PowerBuilder application: tabular reports with totals and subtotals, mailing labels, form letters, envelopes, and all others. They are all DataWindows. There is a lot to be said about report design, and Chapter 18 addresses the topic in detail.

```
dw_1.ScrollNextRow()
```

commands the DataWindow to scroll to the next row. Each script concludes with this statement:

```
dw_1.SetFocus()
```

This statement sets the focus on the DataWindow. In Figure 8-21 the DataWindow has focus. In particular, the "Forrest Gump" cell within the DataWindow grid has focus, as the highlight indicates. After users click a VCR button, they expect to be able to begin typing into the row that they have scrolled to. For them to do that, the DataWindow must get focus. If you remove the SetFocus statement, focus is likely to remain on some other control — most likely, it will be on the button just clicked. That would confuse users.

The script to scroll to the last row is the only one that's more than two lines long. There is no "ScrollToLastRow" function, so two steps are needed: (1) Call the RowCount function, which returns the number of rows in the DataWindow, and (2) Call the ScrollToRow function, which jumps to the row number that's passed as a parameter.

THE ROW COUNTER

The "Row Counter" control, which displays the message "Row 2 of 36" in Figure 8-21, is a nice touch. It's also very easy to implement. It is a StaticText control whose Text property is changed by a script. The script is the DataWindow control's RowFocusChanged event script. DataWindow controls have many interesting events, and we'll explore many of them in Chapter 10. The RowFocusChanged event fires any time the user moves from one row to another in the DataWindow. Here's the script:

```
Long i,n
i = This.GetRow()
n = This.RowCount()
st_rowcount.Text = "Row " + String(i) + " of " + String(n)
```

The GetRow function returns the current row number. The RowCount function returns the number of rows in the DataWindow, and "st_rowcount" is the name of the row counter control.

INSERT ROW, APPEND ROW, AND DELETE ROW

The scripts for these three buttons resemble those for the VCR buttons, as you can see from Table 8-2.

Table 8-2
Scripts for Insert Row, Append Row, and Delete Row

Button	Function	Script
Insert Row	Add a new row above the current row	Long n n = dw_1.GetRow() n = dw_1.InsertRow(n) dw_1.ScrollToRow(n) dw_1.SetFocus()
Append Row	Add a new row below the last row	Long n n = dw_1.InsertRow(0) dw_1.ScrollToRow(n) dw_1.SetFocus()
Delete Row	Delete the current row	dw_1.DeleteRow(0) dw_1.EVENT RowFocusChanged(0) dw_1.SetFocus()

The Insert Row and Append Row buttons have almost identical scripts. Both rely on the InsertRow function, which inserts a new empty row into the DataWindow. The parameter for this function — which is *n* for Insert Row and 0 (zero) for Append Row — specifies where to insert the row: above the *n*th row if the value is greater than zero, or below the last row if the value is zero. The InsertRow function does not scroll the DataWindow to the new row, which is why the ScrollToRow function must be called.

Although this window has both Insert Row and Append Row buttons, many windows will probably need only one or the other, or neither.

The Delete Row script uses the DeleteRow function. The parameter passed to this function is zero to delete the current row or a value *n* greater than zero to delete the *n*th row. For the button, we want to delete the current row, so zero is used.

The Delete Row script includes this interesting line:

```
dw_1.EVENT RowFocusChanged(0)
```

This command forces dw_1's RowFocusChanged event to fire. Why is it needed? So that the RowFocusChanged script, which updates the row counter, will run. When you delete a row, the row counter should change — from "2 of 36" to "2 of 35," for example. The functions used on the other button scripts, such as ScrollToRow and ScrollNextPage, fire RowFocusChanged automatically. But the DeleteRow function does not. I guess PowerBuilder figures that, because the row number does not change when you delete a row, there is no need to fire RowFocusChanged. Therefore you must force the event to run, and the call to the RowFocusChanged event does exactly that.

THE SCROLL BAR

The vertical scroll bar on the DataWindow, like the VCR buttons, gives you a quick and easy way to scroll up and down through the DataWindow rows using the mouse.

The scroll bar on the DataWindow is not a separate control. It is a property of the DataWindow control itself. To add it to a DataWindow, double-click the DataWindow control in the Window Painter (not the DataWindow Painter). In the property sheet (Figure 8-16), checkmark "VScroll Bar" and click OK.

When you add a vertical scroll bar, you should also give some thought to the "Live Scrolling" option, which you also see in the property sheet. When Live Scrolling is on, the rows scroll while you drag the scroll bar button. When Live Scrolling is off, scrolling occurs only when you release the button in its new position. If your DataWindow displays a large number of rows, you will probably be happier with Live Scrolling turned off.

There is one trait of the scroll bar that you may not like: When you scroll, the same row retains focus even though that row may not remain visible. So if you start from row 2 of 36 and scroll to the bottom, you'll see the last rows — rows 31–36. But row 2, although unseen, still has focus. If you start typing, the display jumps back to row 2, which is disconcerting (although it's standard Windows behavior and it's better than leaving the row unseen).

ERROR HANDLING

Every function described so far, such as Retrieve, ScrollNextRow, and InsertRow, returns a value to indicate success or failure. The scripts I've shown ignore the return values, even though they shouldn't. Your applications should always perform some sort of error checking.

The codes returned vary somewhat from one function to another, as shown in Table 8-3. So you should consult the documentation or online help before using one. For this set of functions (but not for all functions in PowerScript), –1 indicates an error.

Table 8-3

Error Codes and Success Codes Returned by DataWindow Control Functions

Function	Error Code	Success Code
SetTransObject	−1	1
Retrieve	−1	# of rows retrieved
Update	−1	1
InsertRow	−1	row #
DeleteRow	−1	1
ScrollToRow	−1	1

continued

Table 8-3 (continued)

Function	Error Code	Success Code
ScrollPriorPage	−1	row #
ScrollPriorRow	−1	row #
ScrollNextRow	−1	row #
ScrollNextPage	−1	row #
SetFocus	−1	1
GetRow	−1 for error	row #
	0 for no current row	
RowCount	−1	# of rows

Here is how you could revise the window open script, which calls SetTransObject and Retrieve, to detect and deal with errors:

```
Long ll_count               // # of rows retrieved
IF dw_1.SetTransObject(sqlca) <> 1 THEN   // connect DW to sqlca
    MessageBox("Error on SetTransObject",              &
               "Unable to associate the DataWindow " + &
               "the transaction object.",              &
               StopSign!)
    Close(This)             // after a fatal error, close the window
    RETURN
END IF
ll_count = dw_1.Retrieve() // retrieve rows into the DataWindow
If ll_count < 0 Then        // error flag (-1)
    MessageBox("Error", "Unable to Retrieve Rows", StopSign!)
    Close(This)             // after a fatal error, close the window
    RETURN
ELSEIF ll_count = 0 Then    // no rows were retrieved
    MessageBox("Warning", "No Rows to Retrieve", StopSign!)
    RETURN
END IF
```

When an error is detected, the script displays a message to the user (MessageBox) and terminates itself (RETURN). Since this is a window open event and the window shouldn't remain open on a severe error, some errors also call the Close function. Unlike what you might expect, the script continues to run even after you call the Close function, so it is necessary to follow Close with Return. Some people prefer the Halt command, which terminates the entire application, but I consider that unduly harsh.

The Pessimist's Approach to Error Checking

I take a pessimistic approach to error code checking. Some developers would detect an error on SetTransObject, for example, like this:

```
IF dw_1.SetTransObject(sqlca) = -1 THEN...
```

I do it a little bit differently:

```
IF dw_1.SetTransObject(sqlca) <> 1 THEN...
```

In practice, the two ought to be equivalent, since, according to the documentation –1 and 1 are the only two possible return values. But as I say, I'm a pessimist, and I worry about things like, "What if someone goofed and the function returns a weird value like 57 some day? Should that be treated as an error?" I think it should. So you'll see my scripts written so as to trap unexpected values as errors.

Here is the script for the "Scroll to the Next Row" VCR button, enhanced to handle errors:

```
Long ll_origrow,ll_newrow
ll_origrow = dw_1.GetRow()        // what row do we start at?
IF dw_1.ScrollNextRow() < 0 THEN   // try to scroll
   MessageBox("Error", "Can't Move in That Direction", StopSign!)
   RETURN
END IF
ll_newrow = dw_1.GetRow()             // what row are we at now?
IF ll_newrow = ll_origrow THEN Beep(1)  // we haven't moved
IF dw_1.SetFocus() <> 1 THEN
   MessageBox("Error", "DataWindow SetFocus Failed", StopSign!)
   RETURN
END IF
```

If you are at the last row and try to scroll to the next row, the ScrollNextRow function succeeds — that is, it does not return an error code. By keeping track of the old and new row numbers, your code can detect this situation and beep, which is the purpose of this line:

```
IF ll_newrow = ll_origrow THEN Beep(1)
```

THE DBERROR EVENT

If the Retrieve or Update function causes an error, it's almost certain to be a database error — that is, an indication that your database server had trouble with the SQL command. PowerBuilder handles the database errors in a special way. The Retrieve or Update function itself might return a –1 to indicate failure — or it might not! What's more important is that PowerBuilder does fire a special event, DBError, on the DataWindow control when a database error occurs. If you want to detect the error, interpret it, and manage its response yourself, you need to write a script for the DBError event.

If you don't write a DBError script, PowerBuilder will automatically display an error message when a database error occurs during Retrieve or Update. Figure 8-22 shows an example.

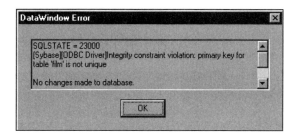

Figure 8-22

An error message that PowerBuilder might display, if there is no DBError script.

Here is a simple DBError script:

```
Long   ll_errorcode     // the error code
String ls_errormessage  // the error message
ll_errorcode    = sqldbcode      // sqldbcode is an event argument
ls_errormessage = sqlerrtext     // sqlerrtext is an event argument
MessageBox("There Has Been a Database Error",        &
           "The error code is " + String(ll_errorCode) +  &
           "~nThe error message is "              +  &
           "~n" + ls_errormessage,                    &
           StopSign!)
RETURN 1
```

This script produces the error message shown in Figure 8-23 instead of the one in Figure 8-22. It's a little more user-friendly. If you don't think so, you can add a more code to make it still friendlier.

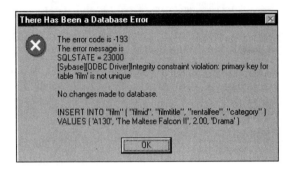

Figure 8-23

An error message that the DBError script might display.

PowerBuilder passes two arguments to the event DBError script: *sqldbcode* and *sqlerrtext*. These two arguments are the error code number and the error message text, respectively. We will learn a lot more about event script arguments in Chapters 10 and 12. Just like function arguments, they contain values passed into the script from whoever calls it and within the script they behave as variables.

The script transfers the argument values to two local variables, which the MessageBox function call displays. The RETURN 1 that concludes the script prevents the default error message, the one in Figure 8-22, from popping up. The alternative, RETURN 0, would cause the default message to appear (in this case, it would appear after your custom message).

Even though the DBError script captures many of the errors that might result from a Retrieve or Update function call, it does not capture all of them. It is still necessary to test the return values for these functions. For example:

```
IF dw_1.Update() <> 1 THEN
    MessageBox("Error", "The Update Failed", StopSign!)
    RETURN
END IF
```

The DBError event is just one of several dozen available for the DataWindow control. Many of them rely on event arguments and RETURN values, as DBError does. The more complex your DataWindow application gets, the more you will be writing scripts like this one. The entire Chapter 10 is dedicated to this topic, and it will explore all of these features in depth.

Summary

This chapter has covered the basics of DataWindows:

- The relationship between a DataWindow object, a DataWindow control, and a window
- The steps to design a DataWindow and add it to an application
- How to implement commonplace features, such as navigation controls
- How to detect and handle DataWindow errors.

There is still much more to say about DataWindows! Several more chapters in this book are dedicated to them. In the next chapter, we explore the DataWindow Painter in more detail.

The DataWindow Painter

*T*he last chapter gave a quick demo of how to create a DataWindow object, but most of that chapter focused on how to integrate it into an application. This chapter provides a much more in-depth look at the process of designing a DataWindow object and how it functions.

In particular, we will cover these topics:

- **How to use the DataWindow Painter** — The first part of this chapter is a survey of the DataWindow Painter: how to open the painter, where to find its major features, and how to perform basic design operations.

- **How to control and change DataWindow properties at run-time** — Using the DataWindow Painter, you have extensive ability to set the properties of each part of the DataWindow. For example, you can set the color and font style of each text box and column. These settings don't have to stay frozen at runtime, however. I will show you two ways to change DataWindow object properties at runtime: DataWindow painter expressions and referencing properties in PowerScript code.

- **The SQL behind the scenes** — The DataWindow uses ordinary SQL commands, such as SELECT and UPDATE, to transfer data to and from the database. PowerBuilder constructs and executes the the SQL automatically, based on the DataWindow design, but it also gives you extraordinary control over this process if you choose to exercise it.

- **Data sources and presentation styles** — When you design a new DataWindow, you can choose from among five different data sources, such as SQL Select or stored procedures. You can also also choose from among eleven different presentation styles, such as grid, tabular, or freeform. This section describes these many choices.

- **DropDownDataWindows** — One special purpose for a DataWindow is that it can serve as a dropdown list for a column in a table or a column in another DataWindow. I introduced dropdown lists back in Chapter 6. Here you will learn how to create a DropDownDataWindow.

Even after covering all this material, there will still be more to say about DataWindows. Chapter 18, for example, will look at the techniques for designing printed reports with the DataWindow Painter.

How to Use the DataWindow Painter

So far we have visited the DataWindow Painter only briefly, to create the DataWindow object d_filmgrid. Let's return to it now and look at its most important features.

OPENING THE DATAWINDOW PAINTER

The most direct way to open the DataWindow Painter, of course, is to click the DataWindow button on the PowerBar. You can also get there from the Window Painter. While working on a window with a DataWindow in it, such as the one in Figure 8-18 in Chapter 8, right-click the DataWindow control and select Modify DataWindow from the pop-up menu. This opens the DataWindow Painter and loads the DataWindow object that is embedded in the window.

Figure 9-1 shows the DataWindow Painter and the d_filmgrid DataWindow, as we created it in the last chapter's exercise.

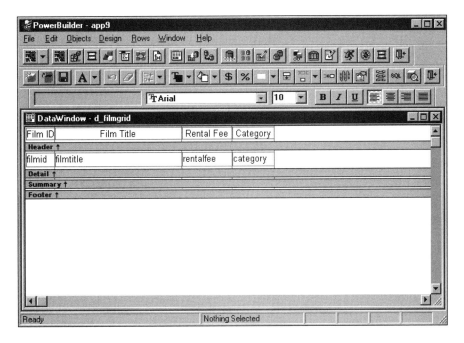

Figure 9-1
The "film grid" DataWindow object, d_filmgrid, before modification.

COMPARING THE DATAWINDOW PAINTER TO THE WINDOW PAINTER

In quite a few ways, the DataWindow Painter resembles the Window Painter. You can use either to design a GUI layout that the user will see at runtime. Both have a PainterBar full of tools for adding new objects to the design. You manipulate objects directly with the mouse or pop up their property sheets to change such of their properties as color and font.

In other ways, the DataWindow Painter is quite different from the Window Painter. The former has no event scripts. Except in one limited way—"DataWindow painter expressions," described shortly—you do not attach PowerScript program code to the DataWindow or to its component objects. (You can, and do, write event scripts for the DataWindow control that houses the DataWindow object.) And the objects you place on the DataWindow are quite different than the objects used on a Window: Instead of CommandButtons, PictureButtons, and CheckBoxes, you'll find computed fields, sums, and graphs.

Your experience with the Window Painter will help you get started with the DataWindow Painter, but soon you will discover that they are very different animals.

THE BANDS

The DataWindow design (Figure 9-1) is separated into a series of bands, which run horizontally across it.

- **The Header band** — contains the column headings, the report titles, and anything else you want to appear at the top of the DataWindow when displayed or printed.

- **The Detail band** — is the main body of the DataWindow. Most of the detail data, such as column values retrieved from a table and calculations based on them, appear in the detail band. With a grid-style window, and several of the other styles, you design the layout for one row, and at runtime that design replicates into enough rows to fill the entire DataWindow control or printed page.

- **The Summary band** — is for totals and other information that appear at the end of the report following the last line of detail data.

- **The Footer band** — is for information that appears at the bottom of the DataWindow on-screen, or at the bottom of each printed page.

In Figure 9-1, the Summary and Footer bands are empty, but you can pull them down with the mouse to open up space for them and begin adding objects to them. You can also add more bands than these original four. For example, you can add bands for group headers and footers that are convenient places for such things as subtotals. Chapter 18 will cover these topics.

PREVIEW

To preview your DataWindow running "live" with real data, click the Preview button on the PainterBar to open the DataWindow Preview Painter. You may also enter preview mode by selecting Design|Preview or pressing Ctrl+Shift+P. (See Figure 9-2.)

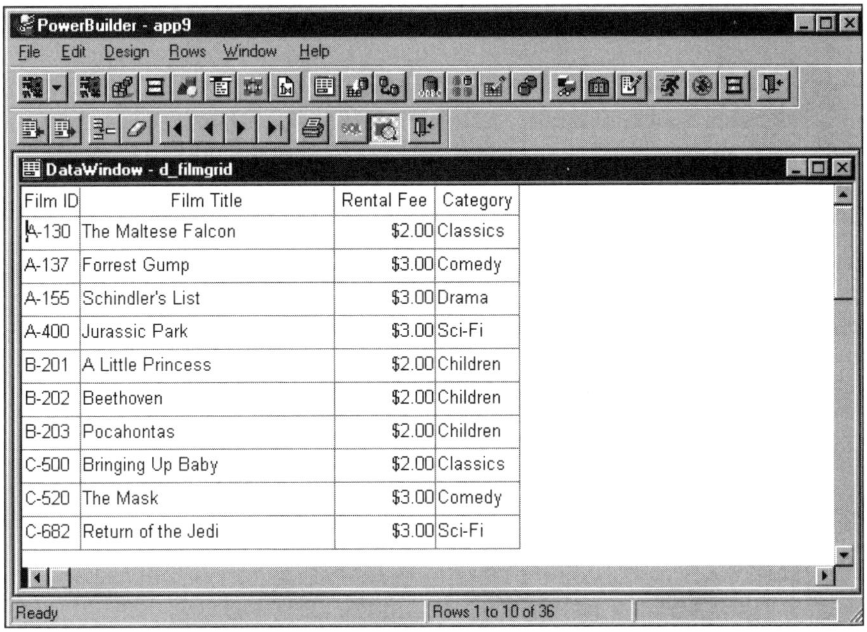

Figure 9-2
The DataWindow Preview Painter.

The Preview Painter is a variation of the Data Manipulation Painter described in Chapter 6. You can scroll through and change the data. The PainterBar provides buttons with now-familiar functionality: Retrieve, Save Changes (Update), Insert Row, Delete Row, Print Rows, and VCR-style buttons for scrolling. Be careful about changing the data and clicking Save Changes. This is your live data, and you will be updating your live database.

When you are done previewing, click the Preview button on the PainterBar to return to the design mode of the DataWindow Painter. The Preview button is a toggle that stays pushed in while you are previewing and pops out when you return to design. During DataWindow design, you will find it convenient to toggle to the Previewer often to see how your work is progressing.

BASIC DATAWINDOW PAINTER OPERATIONS

Here are some of the basic DataWindow Painter operations, which are similar to the Window Painter operations that you have already learned:

- **Selecting, moving, stretching** — Click an object, such as a column heading or a detail-band column, to select it. Click and drag to move it. Click and drag an edge to stretch it. (In a grid-style DataWindow you can't move the columns, because that would disrupt the grid. With other styles, you can move objects more freely.)

- **Using property sheets** — Pop up an object's property sheet to view and change most of its properties. Figure 9-3 shows the property sheet for the "filmtitle" detail-band column. Some of the choices are familiar, such as border, name, and tag. There are tabs that can be selected to set other options. The most important of these options will be described in the pages and chapters to come.

There are several ways to open a property sheet: You can double-click an object, single-click it and click the Properties button on the PainterBar, or right-click it and pick Properties from its pop-up menu.

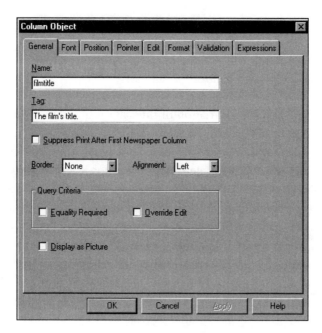

Figure 9-3
The Property Sheet for a detail-band column.

- **Placing objects from the Objects menu or PainterBar** — Use the Objects menu to select objects such as Text or Computed Field, and then click a spot in the design window to place something new in the DataWindow. (Again, the grid style has rigid rules about where you can place things, but other styles are more flexible.)

As an alternative to the Objects menu, you can select objects from the PainterBar's dropdown object palette, shown in Figure 9-4.

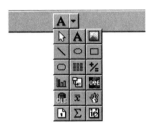

Figure 9-4
The DataWindow PainterBar's dropdown object palette.

ADDING ANOTHER COLUMN

Adding another column to the DataWindow is a three-step process: First, add the column to the SQL SELECT statement that serves as the DataWindow's data source. Second, adjust the column's properties. Third, set the column's tab order. Here are the steps to add the film table's year column to the DataWindow.

STEP 1. MODIFY THE SQL SELECT STATEMENT

Click the SQL (Data Source) button on the DataWindow PainterBar. It opens the DataWindow Select Painter in Figure 9-5, which is very similar to the Query Painter described in Chapter 21. When you select the Syntax tab in the bottom part of the screen, it displays the SELECT statement that PowerBuilder constructed when we created the DataWindow (back in Step 7 of the exercise in the previous chapter):

```
SELECT "film"."filmid",
       "film"."filmtitle",
       "film"."rentalfee",
       "film"."category"
    FROM "film"
```

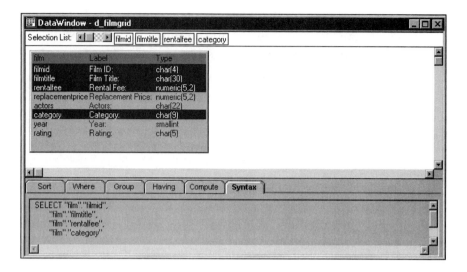

Figure 9-5

The DataWindow Select Painter.

The box in the middle of the window lists the columns in the film table, with four of them selected. Click "Year" on the list to add it to the SELECT statement. Then click the SQL Select button on the PainterBar to pop it out and return to DataWindow design mode.

STEP 2. ADJUST THE COLUMN'S PROPERTIES

When you return to the DataWindow Design, PowerBuilder will automatically add the newly selected year column and its column heading to the grid. Adjust its width and other properties with the mouse.

STEP 3. SET THE TAB ORDER

One more modification is necessary. PowerBuilder assigns the new column a zero tab order, so when you run the DataWindow you cannot tab to the column or change it. In fact, strange things will happen if you attempt to do so. (For more about tab order, refer to Chapter 2.)

To fix that, click the Tab Order button on the PainterBar. Change the year's tab order from 0 to 50—since the other four columns have 10, 20, 30, and 40—as depicted in Figure 9-6. Then click the Tab Order button again to pop it out and return to Design mode.

The Four Modes of the DataWindow Painter

The DataWindow Select Painter (Figure 9-5) is not a separate painter from the DataWindow Painter in the way that, say, the PowerScript Painter is separate but associated with the Window Painter. Powersoft has chosen to implement the DataWindow Select Painter as a different mode of the DataWindow Painter itself.

If you experiment, you will discover that the DataWindow Painter has four modes:

- Design mode, pictured in Figure 9-1
- Preview mode, pictured in Figure 9-2
- SQL Select mode, pictured in Figure 9-5
- Tab Order mode, pictured in Figure 9-6

If these four were separate painters, PowerBuilder would open a new window when you switched to any one of them. Instead, because they are modes, they are implemented as a single window. As you switch between the modes, PowerBuilder changes what is displayed in that window.

One ramification of the multimode feature, and one that trips me up all the time, is this: If you select File|Close from the menu while in, let's say, Preview mode, you'll probably expect to return to Design mode. But what you've actually done is to close the DataWindow Painter itself.

Figure 9-7 shows the end result, in preview.

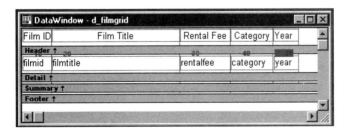

Figure 9-6
Changing the tab order.

DataWindow - d_filmgrid				
Film ID	Film Title	Rental Fee	Category	Year
A-130	The Maltese Falcon	$2.00	Classics	1941
A-137	Forrest Gump	$3.00	Comedy	1994
A-155	Schindler's List	$3.00	Drama	1993
A-400	Jurassic Park	$3.00	Sci-Fi	1993
B-201	A Little Princess	$2.00	Children	1995
B-202	Beethoven	$2.00	Children	1992
B-203	Pocahontas	$2.00	Children	1995
C-500	Bringing Up Baby	$2.00	Classics	1938

Figure 9-7
The DataWindow after adding the year column.

DELETING AND RE-ADDING A COLUMN

If a column is already in the SQL SELECT statement, you can add it any number of times to the DataWindow. And, of course, you can delete a column from the DataWindow.

Deleting a column is easy: Click the column in the detail band to select it and press the Delete key on the keyboard. Both the column and its column heading disappear. After deleting the column from the DataWindow, you should also consider whether to remove it from the SELECT statement using the Select Painter.

To add or re-add a column that's already in the SQL SELECT: Click the Column button on the PainterBar's dropdown object palette, and then click a point in the detail band where you want the column to appear. The Select Column dialog box appears, showing the columns from the SELECT statement (Figure 9-8). Click a column and click OK. PowerBuilder places the column in the DataWindow. In a grid-style DataWindow, it makes room for the new column between two others or places it to the right of the others.

After adding the column, you must also set its tab order, as described earlier.

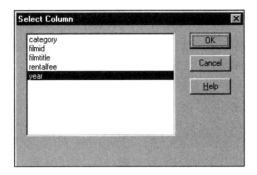

Figure 9-8
Selecting a column to place on the DataWindow.

ADDING A COMPUTED FIELD

A *computed field* is a field on a DataWindow displaying a value calculated from other fields. To place one on the DataWindow, click the Compute button on the PainterBar's dropdown object palette, and then click a location for it in the detail band.

PowerBuilder pops up the Computed Object dialog box. Type in an expression for the field in the Expression box, or click More to pop up the Modify Expression dialog box shown in Figure 9-9. That figure shows how to define a field named "discountfee," calculated as "round(rentalfee*0.85,2),"—that is, 85 percent of the Rental Fee amount, rounded to the nearest penny. To assist you in building the expression, the buttons and lists at the bottom of the dialog box show the arithmetic operators, functions, and column names that you can use.

There are a few more steps to pretty things up. First, create a column heading for the new computed field: Click the Text button on the PainterBar's dropdown object palette, click the space in the header band where the heading should appear, and type in "Fee with 15% Discount." Make the new column wider: Click the computed field in the detail band and stretch it wide enough for the column heading. Change the computed field's format: Double-click the computed field, select the Format tab on the property sheet, and select the format "$#,##0.00;($#,##0.00)."

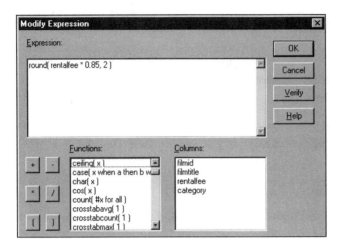

Figure 9-9
The Modify Expression dialog box.

The end result, previewed, is shown in Figure 9-10.

Film ID	Film Title	Rental Fee	Category	Year	Fee with 15% Discount
A-130	The Maltese Falcon	$2.00	Classics	1941	$1.70
A-137	Forrest Gump	$3.00	Comedy	1994	$2.55
A-155	Schindler's List	$3.00	Drama	1993	$2.55
A-400	Jurassic Park	$3.00	Sci-Fi	1993	$2.55
B-201	A Little Princess	$2.00	Children	1995	$1.70
B-202	Beethoven	$2.00	Children	1992	$1.70
B-203	Pocahontas	$2.00	Children	1995	$1.70
C-500	Bringing Up Baby	$2.00	Classics	1938	$1.70

Figure 9-10
The DataWindow with the computed field.

EXTENDED ATTRIBUTES: FORMATS, EDIT STYLES, AND VALIDATION RULES

Chapter 6 described display formats, edit styles, and validation rules. They
are the "extended attributes" that you can assign to a column in a database

table, using the Database Painter. When you first create the DataWindow, PowerBuilder copies these extended attributes from the database to every column in the DataWindow. In the DataWindow Painter, you can inspect or override them.

For example, pop up the property sheet for the Film ID column in the DataWindow detail band (Figure 9-1) and click its Edit tab. As you can see in Figure 9-11, the column uses an edit mask named "FilmID," whose mask, "!-###," requires the Film ID to be an uppercase letter, a hyphen, and three digits. From here, you can pick a different edit mask, if there is an appropriate alternative. Or you can pick a different style, such as a DropDownListBox, for the column. In most cases, you won't modify the formats, edit styles, and validation rules in the DataWindow Painter. You'll stick with the settings that you defined in the Database Painter.

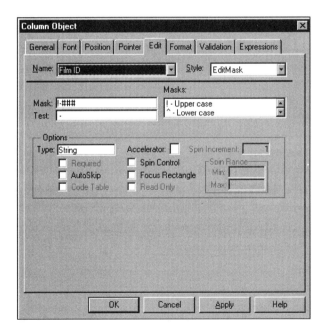

Figure 9-11
The "Edit Mask" style, one of the possible alternatives for a column's edit style.

UPDATING FORMATS, EDIT STYLES, AND VALIDATION RULES: THE DWEAS UTILITY

Here's some bad news: Although PowerBuilder automatically copies formats, edit styles, and validation rules from the database to the DataWindow when you first create the DataWindow, it isn't very helpful as things change. In particular:

- When you add a new column to an existing DataWindow, PowerBuilder fetches its validation rule, but not its format or edit style, from the database.

- When you return to the Database Painter and change an extended attribute for a column, PowerBuilder does not propagate that change to existing DataWindows containing that column. The DataWindows will retain their old attributes.

You have to be on guard that your DataWindow extended attributes don't get out of date!

To deal with this problem, use the DataWindow Extended Attribute Synchronizer (DWEAS). This is one of the Advanced PowerBuilder Utilities that are part of the PowerBuilder Professional and Enterprise packages. (These utilities are not packaged with the PowerBuilder Desktop edition, but you can purchase them separately.) When you run DWEAS, it compares the columns in a DataWindow to the columns' extended attributes in the database and provides a way to update those that are out-of-date. (I find that it does a good job of finding them but an imperfect job of updating them, which is better than nothing.)

How to Control and Change DataWindow Properties at Runtime

Once you've set the properties of the various objects in a DataWindow using the DataWindow Painter, those are of course the properties you'll see when you open the DataWindow in your application. There are two techiques for changing property settings at runtime:

- DataWindow painter expressions
- Manipulation using PowerScript

DATAWINDOW PAINTER EXPRESSIONS

DataWindow objects don't have event scripts. DataWindow controls do, but DataWindow objects don't. So when you're in the DataWindow Painter, there's no way to write a script that will respond to an event that occurs in the DataWindow. This is one of the main differences between DataWindows and ordinary windows.

The closest thing to event-driven programming in DataWindow objects is a feature called "DataWindow painter expressions." They provide a way to cause DataWindow object properties to change dynamically, as the user or the application programming changes DataWindow column values at runtime.

For example, suppose you want the year column to display big numbers (that is, with a large font height) for recent years and progressively smaller numbers for older years. This effect is shown in Figure 9-12. When you change the year, PowerBuilder immediately changes its font. It may look hideous, but it's easy to do with a DataWindow painter expression.

Film ID	Film Title	Rental Fee	Category	Year
F-097	Psycho	$3.00	Horror	1960
F-488	Cries and Whispers	$2.00	Foreign	1972
F-719	Rashomon	$2.00	Foreign	1950
F-745	Sleepless in Seattle	$2.00	Comedy	1993
F-800	The Wizard Of Oz	$2.00	Classics	1939
F-801	Some Like It Hot	$2.00	Classics	1959
F-803	While You Were Sleeping	$3.00	Comedy	1995
G-001	Four Weddings and a Funeral	$3.00	Comedy	1994
G-002	Hook	$3.00	Adventure	1991
G-003	Gilligan's Island	$2.00	TV	1965
G-004	Remains Of The Day	$3.00	Drama	1993

Figure 9-12

A DataWindow painter expression changes the year's font height based on the year's value.

To set a DataWindow painter expression, open the Expressions tab on a detail-band column's property sheet, as shown in Figure 9-13.

Figure 9-13

The Expressions tab in the year column's property sheet.

This dialog box lists properties of an object, in this case the year column. They are a subset of the properties available elsewhere in the property sheet. To the right of a property, you can type in an expression for the property's value, as you can see I've done for the font.height property. At runtime, whenever the expression's value changes, so does the property. The expression can contain column names (such as "year") and DataWindow Painter functions (such as "today"). It can also call user-defined functions.

DataWindow painter expressions are a powerful extension of the usual ability to set properties. For example, if you want the background color of the year column to be red, the usual way is to select the column and pick red from the PainterBar's background color dropdown palette. But you can also fill in 255 (which is red) in the Expressions tab for the year column. Filling in a constant like 255 isn't very interesting. What makes this feature special is its ability to accept an expression.

The expression in Figure 9-13 for font.height changes the font size according to the year a film was made. The expression is

```
(year(today()) - year) / 8 - 14
```

The today function returns today's date. The expression "year(today())" is today's year, since the year function returns the year of whatever date you pass it. The "year" to the right of the minus sign is the "year" column in the DataWindow, not the "year" function. The older (less) the year column value, the greater the expression's value. The result is always a negative number between –14 and –4. For example, if today is June 1, 1996, and the year for the film "Psycho" is 1960, the expression evaluates to

```
(1996 - 1960) / 8 - 14, which is -10
```

This makes the font size 10 points. (The font height property uses negative numbers for point size. Positive numbers for a different unit of measure, which you set in the DataWindow object's property sheet, are shown in Figure 18-5 of Chapter 18.)

CHANGING A DATAWINDOW OBJECT'S PROPERTIES IN POWERSCRIPT

A DataWindow painter expression is one of two ways that you can change a DataWindow object property at runtime. The other is for a PowerScript statement in a script to change it directly. This line of code, executed in response to a button's clicked event or to any other event, will change the year column's font height to 14 point text:

```
dw_1.object.Year.Font.Height = -14
```

The first part, "dw_1.object", means "the DataWindow object associated with the DataWindow control dw_1." The next part, "Year.Font.Height" means "the Font.Height property of the Year object within that DataWindow object."

This is similar to the manipulation of window control properties that we saw in Chapter 2, such as

```
st_firstbox.BackColor = 255
```

Using this technique, you will have runtime control over most aspects of the DataWindow.

The SQL behind the Scenes

While you run an application and work with a DataWindow, PowerBuilder is busy behind the scenes doing the necessary database manipulation. All database access is done by PowerBuilder sending SQL commands to the database server. The most important commands are SELECT, INSERT, UPDATE, and DELETE. In a "retrieve" operation, PowerBuilder does a SELECT. In an "update" operation, PowerBuilder does a series of INSERTs, UPDATEs, and DELETEs.

When your application calls the Retrieve function on the film-grid window,

```
dw_1.Retrieve()
```

PowerBuilder issues this SELECT statement:

```
SELECT "film"."filmid",
       "film"."filmtitle",
       "film"."rentalfee",
       "film"."category",
       "film"."year"
   FROM "film"
```

After you've made changes to the rows in the DataWindow and your application calls the Update function on the film-grid window,

```
dw_1.Update()
```

PowerBuilder issues a series of SQL commands: a DELETE for each row you've deleted, an INSERT for each row you've added, and an UPDATE for each row you've changed. Here's an example of each:

```
DELETE FROM "film"
   WHERE "filmid" = 'A137'

INSERT INTO "film"
   ("filmid", "filmtitle", "rentalfee", "category", "year")
```

```
      VALUES ('A000', 'Toy Story', 3.00, 'Children', 1995)

UPDATE "film
   SET "rentalfee" = 3.01
   WHERE "filmid" = 'H933'
```

WHEN DOES POWERBUILDER EXECUTE THE SQL?

There's no magic to the process by which PowerBuilder translates DataWindow activity into SQL. PowerBuilder does an excellent job of making it plain for us developers, and it gives us tools to monitor and control it.

A critical point to realize is that PowerBuilder never issues a SQL command automatically. *Every* SQL statement and, therefore, all database activity, is executed in response to a command or function call in your application programming.

Other than embedded and dynamic SQL that you explicitly code into your scripts, as described in Chapter 7, there are only three other PowerBuilder functions that result in SQL being issued. All three are DataWindow control functions (assume "dw_1" is the name of the control):

- **dw_1.Retrieve( )** — causes a SQL SELECT.

- **dw_1.Update( )** — causes a series of SQL INSERTs, UPDATEs, and DELETEs.

- **dw_1.ReselectRow( )** — like the Retrieve function, does a SELECT. But it rereads only one row, previously fetched using the Retrieve function. It's useful in situations where another user may have updated the row in the database since the time you first fetched it and you want to get the most up-to-date values.

That's all—just these three functions! If your application scripts never call the Retrieve or ReselectRow function, the database will never be read. If your application never calls the Update function, the database will never be changed. (You could do it with embedded or dynamic SQL, but that would still be a case of your application scripts performing all database access. And it would be a lot more work for you!)

All other activity, such as when the user inserts, deletes, and changes rows on-screen in the DataWindow, is done strictly with local PowerBuilder buffers. No database access whatsoever happens during these periods, unless you add Retrieve and Update function calls in an event script.

HOW TO SEE AND MODIFY THE SQL

PowerBuilder provides features to let you monitor and modify the SQL commands that it generates:

- **dw_1.GetSqlSelect( )** — Call this function anytime to get the DataWindow's SQL SELECT statement.

- **dw_1.SetSqlSelect( )** — This function is a counterpart to GetSqlSelect. It lets you change the DataWindow's SQL SELECT statement, prior to the Retrieve.

- **The SQLPreview event** — SqlPreview is a DataWindow control event that fires in response to Retrieve and Update function calls. This event occurs immediately before a SQL statement is submitted to the DBMS. Its "sqlsyntax" argument can fetch the SELECT, DELETE, INSERT, or UPDATE statement just before it is executed.

  An SQL statement can be changed by assigning a new SQL statement to the "sqlsyntax" argument.

- **The database trace** — This feature, described in the *Connecting to Your Database* PowerBuilder documentation, writes every SQL command to a text file as PowerBuilder transmits it to the database server. To use it, simply modify the value of sqlca.DBMS, before doing the CONNECT, adding the word "trace" to the beginning of it:

```
sqlca.DBMS = "trace ODBC"
CONNECT;
```

HOW TO CONTROL THE SQL

The DataWindow Painter includes a number of options that control how PowerBuilder translates DataWindow activity into SQL statements.

THE DATAWINDOW SELECT PAINTER

By clicking the SQL Select button on the DataWindow PainterBar or by selecting Design|Data Source from the DataWindow menu, you launch the Select Painter. It is similar to the Query Painter described in Chapter 21 on the CD-ROM. You can see and modify the DataWindow's SELECT statement. We visited this painter earlier, during the exercise that added the year column to the DataWindow.

Figure 9-14 shows the DataWindow Select Painter in the process of adding a WHERE clause to the SELECT statement. The DataWindow's new SELECT statement will be

```
SELECT "film"."filmid",
       "film"."filmtitle",
       "film"."rentalfee",
       "film"."category",
       "film"."year"
   FROM "film"
   WHERE "film"."category" = 'Comedy'
```

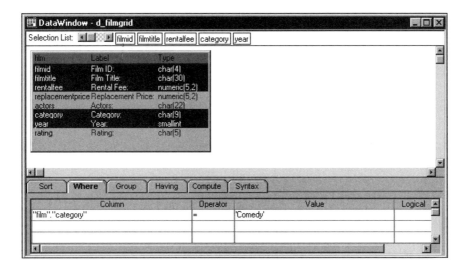

Figure 9-14
The DataWindow Select Painter.

ROWS|PROMPT FOR CRITERIA

A DataWindow utilizing the "Prompt for Criteria" feature expects criteria to be supplied for its WHERE clause every time the Retrieve function is called.

To set it up, select Rows|Prompt for Criteria from the DataWindow menu. The Prompt for Criteria dialog displays the DataWindow's SELECT columns, asking which ones should play a role in the criteria-setting process. Figure 9-15 shows this dialog, with the category and year columns selected.

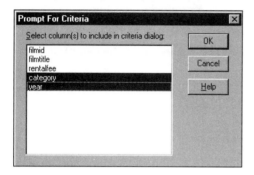

Figure 9-15

The Prompt for Criteria dialog box.

From this point forward, whenever you call the Retrieve function on this DataWindow, or whenever you open the DataWindow Previewer on it, PowerBuilder will prompt you for category and year criteria. Figure 9-16 shows how you would specify "all adventures or comedies from 1994 or 1989" in this dialog box. Each row in the dialog becomes a condition in the SELECT statement's WHERE clause:

```
SELECT  "film"."filmid",
            "film"."filmtitle",
            "film"."rentalfee",
            "film"."category",
            "film"."year"
   FROM "film"
   WHERE ("film"."category" = 'Adventure' AND "film"."year" = 1994)
      OR ("film"."category" = 'Adventure' AND "film"."year" = 1989)
      OR ("film"."category" = 'Comedy'    AND "film"."year" = 1994)
      OR ("film"."category" = 'Comedy'    AND "film"."year" = 1989)
```

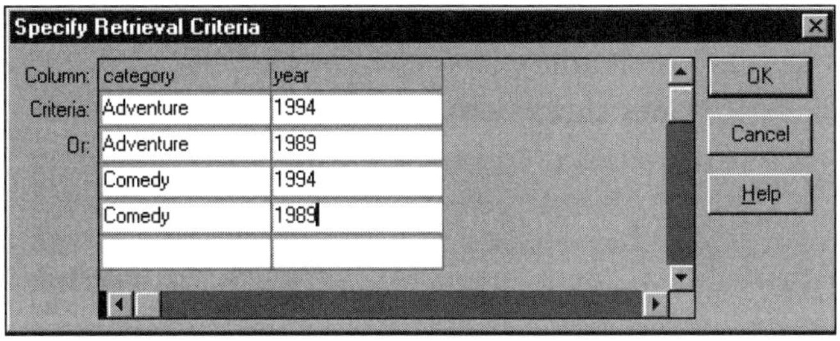

Figure 9-16
Prompting for criteria.

There is similar feature, "Retrieval Arguments," that I will describe shortly. It is somewhat more powerful than the Prompt for Criteria feature.

Rows|Retrieve|Rows As Needed

I've described how the Retrieve function call executes a SELECT command, but there is more to it than that. PowerBuilder actually declares a cursor, opens it with the SELECT, and then issues a series of FETCH commands to retrieve the result into the DataWindow one row at a time. In particular, PowerBuilder uses the "Dynamic Cursor with DESCRIBE" technique, also known as "Dynamic SQL Format 4," explained in Chapter 7. I also defined cursors, FETCH, and Dynamic SQL Format 4 in that chapter.

Since PowerBuilder is doing FETCHes, it can read as many or as few rows as it wants to after issuing the SELECT. You can control how many it does FETCH by selecting Rows|Retrieve|Rows As Needed from the DataWindow Painter menu.

Rows|Retrieve|Rows As Needed is a checkmark menu choice. Every time you choose it, you toggle it on or off. When it is turned off, which is the default, the Retrieve function does the SELECT and immediately FETCHes all rows from the result set into the DataWindow. Some are displayed on-screen, but all rows are available in memory buffers waiting for you to scroll to them. If Rows|Retrieve|Rows To Disk is checked, your data will be stored on disk if necessary.

When Retrieve|Rows As Needed is turned on, the Retrieve function does the SELECT but performs only as many FETCHes as needed to fill the DataWindow on-screen. Other FETCHes are performed later as needed, as you scroll downward through the DataWindow.

If you are working with a very large result set, but the user works with only a few rows at a time, it might at first seem reasonable to turn on Rows|Retrieve|Rows As Needed. Why make the user wait for all those unneeded FETCHes? But beware! In Chapter 7 I warned you not to interrupt a FETCH loop, because FETCH typically locks sections of the database, restricting the access of other users. Turning on Rows|Retrieve|Rows As Needed causes exactly the same problem.

Here is the most common way to use "Retrieve Rows As Needed": Turn it on initially; call Retrieve to fill the screen so the user sees some data quickly; then immediately turn off the feature using PowerScript so that the remaining FETCHes occur.

Under some situations, PowerBuilder ignores the "Retrieve Rows As Needed" setting and treats it as turned off. These situations are when you select Rows|Sort or add aggregate functions such as sum( ) to the DataWindow. PowerBuilder can implement these features only by retrieving all rows.

Rows|Retrieve|Rows To Disk

Rows|Retrieve|Rows To Disk is another checkmark menu choice, which you toggle on or off. It is available only with the 32-bit versions of PowerBuilder. When it is turned on, the Retrieve function can store rows in a temporary disk file. This allows the DataWindow to retrieve more rows, since when the feature is turned off, the number of rows is limited by the amount of available RAM memory.

Rows|Data

The Rows|Data menu choice allows you to type in a set of data rows that PowerBuilder stores in the DataWindow object in the .PBL file. When you run the DataWindow, these rows will appear immediately, before you call the Retrieve function.

You probably won't use this feature with most DataWindows, which must be populated with the latest database data using Retrieve. The feature does come in handy in for a couple of purposes: During development, it's a quick and easy way to fill the DataWindow with test data. Also, it's a convenient way initialize a DataWindow whose data source is "external."

ROWS|UPDATE PROPERTIES

The menu choice Rows|Update Properties in the DataWindow Painter is very important. It determines how PowerBuilder translates DataWindow activity into DELETEs and UPDATEs.

When you select Rows|Update Properties, the Specify Update Properties dialog box appears. Figure 9-17 shows this dialog box, with the default settings PowerBuilder supplied for the film-grid DataWindow.

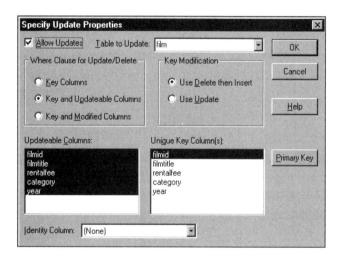

Figure 9-17
The Rows|Update Properties dialog box.

Every setting in this dialog box is very powerful. To understand the impact of each, consider this scenario: In the window pictured in Figure 9-18, you make two changes. On the first row, you change the film title from "The Maltese Falcon" to "The Big Sleep." Then you delete the second row, for film A-137. Then you click the Update button, which calls the Update function. PowerBuilder constructs and executes two SQL commands: an UPDATE for the first row and a DELETE for the second. The Rows|Update Properties settings determine exactly what the clauses in the UPDATE and DELETE statements will be.

Figure 9-18

Using the film-grid DataWindow.

Allow Updates

If you clear the Allow Updates box, PowerBuilder will do no INSERTs, UPDATEs, and DELETEs. The DataWindow cannot change the database. If you have an Update button (why would you?) and it calls the Update function, PowerBuilder displays an error message: "DataWindow does not have UPDATE capability."

Table to Update

If your DataWindow SELECT is a multitable join, PowerBuilder allows only one of the tables to be updated. The other tables are read-only. The Table to Update selection specifies which table is the updatable one, for which PowerBuilder will generate INSERTs, UPDATEs, and DELETEs. In the film-grid DataWindow, the film table is the only choice.

Updatable Columns

This is the list of the columns in the DataWindow's SELECT. Marked (black) columns can be updated, and unmarked (white) columns may not be updated. Click a column with the mouse to toggle it marked to unmarked.

Unique Key Column(s)

In this list of the columns in the DataWindow, marked (black) columns are the table's key. Click a column with the mouse to toggle it from marked to unmarked.

Making a Column Truly Nonupdatable

In the Rows|Update Properties dialog box, the precise effect of marking a column nonupdatable is to omit it from the SET clause of UPDATE commands. That certainly makes it impossible to update, because there's no way to change a column that can never be in a SET clause. However, the overall behavior of the DataWindow might not be what you'd expect. On screen, PowerBuilder actually does permit the user to change the column's value. It's just that PowerBuilder will never write the change to the database.

Assuming that you want the column to be truly nonupdatable, on the DataWindow as well as in the database, here's what you must do:

In addition to unmarking the column in the Rows|Update Properties dialog box, you must also change the column's "protect" property in the DataWindow Painter. Open the Expressions tab in the column's property sheet, and set the "protect" property to 1. When protect = 1, the user cannot tab to the column and, therefore, cannot modify it.

For the purpose of this dialog box, the "key" is the set of columns used in the WHERE clause of UPDATE and DELETE commands. In almost all cases, that should be the table's primary key, which PowerBuilder will determine from the database definition. You can specify a different key if you need to, but that would be unusual. To restore the key to be the primary key from the database, click the Primary Key button.

Where Clause for Update/Delete

Every DataWindow UPDATE or DELETE command affects only one row in the table. To ensure this, PowerBuilder includes the table's key column(s) in the WHERE clause:

```
WHERE filmid = 'A130'
```

Because the key value A130 is unique, only one row will be affected. However, it's actually more precise to say that "at most" only one row will be affected.

There are serious issues to consider regarding changes other users might make to this row at the same time that you are in the process of changing it. You are changing a snapshot of the row, as pictured in Figure 9-18, the way it looked in the database when you retrieved it. Now that you're updating it, what if another user has changed or deleted it in the database in the meantime? How can you detect this situation, and how should you deal with it?

The way you detect it is to select one of the three options under "Where Clause for Update/Delete." Your choice determines what PowerBuilder puts into the WHERE clause in addition to the key column. Your decision is based on how cautious you need to be about other users' changes. These are the three options (listed in order of increasing caution, not in the order they appear on the screen):

1. **Key Columns** — You are not very cautious. You want PowerBuilder to include only the key column(s) in the WHERE clause:

```
UPDATE film
   SET filmtitle = 'The Big Sleep'
   WHERE filmid = 'A130'

DELETE FROM "film"
   WHERE "filmid" = 'A137'
```

   The SQL command will fail if someone else has deleted the row or changed its key value. If someone else has changed the row's nonkey columns, your SET clause changes will overwrite theirs. This might not be so bad for a film title change. But it's very bad policy to ignore the changes of others for more critical data, such as account balances or inventory quantities. (Of course, it would not be a problem in a single-user system.)

2. **Key and Modified Columns** — You are moderately cautious. You want PowerBuilder to include in the WHERE clause not only the key column(s), but also any columns you've modified:

```
UPDATE film
   SET filmtitle = 'The Big Sleep'
   WHERE filmid = 'A130'
     AND filmtitle = 'The Maltese Falcon'
```

   The UPDATE will fail if someone else has changed the film title before you do, because no row matching the WHERE clause will be found.

   Curiously, if you change a column in a row before deleting it, PowerBuilder includes the changed column in the DELETE's WHERE clause:

```
DELETE FROM "film"
   WHERE "filmid" = 'A137'
     AND filmtitle = 'Forrest Gump'
```

Although this is consistent with UPDATE behavior, there's no good reason for it. Modifications to a deleted row are always irrelevant. Typically the user does not change a row before deleting it, and so only the key will be included in the WHERE clause, which is how it should be:

```
DELETE FROM "film"
   WHERE "filmid" = 'A137'
```

3. **Key and Updateable Columns** — You are most cautious. You want PowerBuilder to include in the WHERE clause not only the key column(s), and not only any columns you've modified, but all columns that the DataWindow can modify, whether they are in fact modified or not:

```
UPDATE film
   SET filmtitle = 'The Big Sleep'
   WHERE filmid = 'A130'
     AND filmtitle = 'The Maltese Falcon'
     AND rentalfee = 2.00
     AND category  = 'Classics'
     AND year      = 1941

DELETE FROM "film"
   WHERE "filmid" = 'A137'
     AND filmtitle = 'Forrest Gump'
     AND rentalfee = 3.00
     AND category  = 'Comedy'
     AND year      = 1994
```

The UPDATE or DELETE will fail if someone else has changed any of these five columns in the row before you do, because no row matching the WHERE clause will be found.

If you are using one of the last two options and the UPDATE or DELETE produces an error, how do you handle it? Here's a good approach: Display an error message to the user, and offer to retrieve the most up-to-date version of the row, by calling the ReselectRow function. If

ReselectRow fails, then most likely the row was deleted by someone else; issue an embedded SELECT to be sure that it's deleted, and notify the user. If the ReselectRow succeeds, then offer to let the user see and modify the refreshed version, and also provide an option to make the user's original changes on top of it automatically.

Key Modification

This is a set of two options for what to do when the user modifies a key column value—for example, if you change Jurassic Park's key from A-400 to Z-999 in Figure 9-18. The simpler option is, obviously, to do an UPDATE:

```
UPDATE film
   SET filmid   = 'Z999'
   WHERE filmid = 'A400'
```

The other option is to DELETE the record and then INSERT it again with the new key:

```
DELETE film
   WHERE filmid = 'A400'

INSERT INTO film
   (filmid, filmtitle, rentalfee, category, year)
   VALUES ('Z999', 'Jurassic Park', 3.00, 'Sci-Fi', 1993)
```

The DELETE/INSERT option usually executes more slowly, but it is more accurate than the UPDATE option in one situation: Suppose you change the keys of many rows in the DataWindow, and you change them in such a way that there is overlap between old and new key values. For example, you change 1 to 2, and 2 to 3, and 3 to 4, and 4 to 5. Then the UPDATE approach will probably cause a duplicate-key error at every step of the way. But the DELETE/INSERT approach works perfectly, because PowerBuilder performs all the DELETEs first, then all the INSERTs. On the other hand, if your database has delete triggers (stored procedures that run when you delete a row) or other triggers, the DELETE/INSERT approach could cause unexpected side effects.

Making the Key Column Nonupdatable

I described a little earlier how to make a column nonupdatable by setting its "protect" property to 1. You can use the same means to make a key column nonupdatable, but usually a slightly different technique is called for.

Do you really want to make the key nonupdatable always, or nonupdatable only for existing rows? When you are inserting a new row, in many applications the key should not only be updatable but also be required. So how do you protect the key in existing rows, but not in new rows?

The solution is to use this expression for the key column's "protect" property, in the dialog box on the Expressions tab on the property sheet:

```
If(IsRowNew(), 0, 1)
```

This expression sets protect = 0 (not protected) if the row is new and sets protect = 1 (protected) if the row is not new. The IsRowNew function returns True or False, whether or not the row is new. The If function, like in many spreadsheet products, takes three parameters: a Boolean and two numbers. If the Boolean is True, the function returns the first number; otherwise it returns the second number.

This is a cute trick, but I must confess I didn't invent it myself. It's from the PowerBuilder online help!

RETRIEVAL ARGUMENTS

Retrieval arguments are special variables that you can insert into the WHERE clause of a SQL statement. You specify the values for the retrieval arguments at runtime. Thus, retrieval arguments are a simple technique for making an SQL statement flexible. In PowerBuilder, you can add retrieval arguments to a query using the Query Painter (Chapter 21) and to a DataWindow's SQL SELECT. With a DataWindow, the retrieval argument values can be supplied either by the user or by a script. With a Query, the only option is for the user to supply them.

To implement retrieval arguments for a DataWindow, click SQL Select from the DataWindow PainterBar to open the DataWindow Select Painter. (See Figure 9-14.) Select Design | Retrieval Arguments from the menu. Fill in the names and data types of the retrieval arguments, as in Figure 9-19, and click OK. In the toolbox's Where tab, or in other tabs, you can use a retrieval argument in place of a value by preceding its name with a colon

(Figure 9-20). The SELECT statement has ":" variables in it; you will recall from Chapter 7 that the ":" means that the variables' values will be inserted into the query at runtime:

```
SELECT "film"."filmid",
       "film"."filmtitle",
       "film"."rentalfee",
       "film"."category",
       "film"."year"
  FROM "film"
 WHERE ( "film"."category" = :Category )
   AND ( "film"."year" between :FromYear and :ToYear )
```

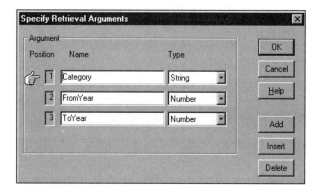

Figure 9-19

Specifying retrieval arguments.

Sort	**Where**	Group	Having	Compute	Syntax		
Column			Operator		Value		Logical
"film"."category"			=		:Category		And
"film"."year"			between		:FromYear and :ToYear		

Figure 9-20

Adding retrieval arguments as WHERE-clause values.

When you run the application and call the Retrieve function on the DataWindow, it will pop up a dialog box asking you to supply values for the retrieval arguments, as shown in Figure 9-21. After you type in values and click OK, PowerBuilder plugs them into the SELECT statement and then executes it in the usual way to fetch rows into the DataWindow.

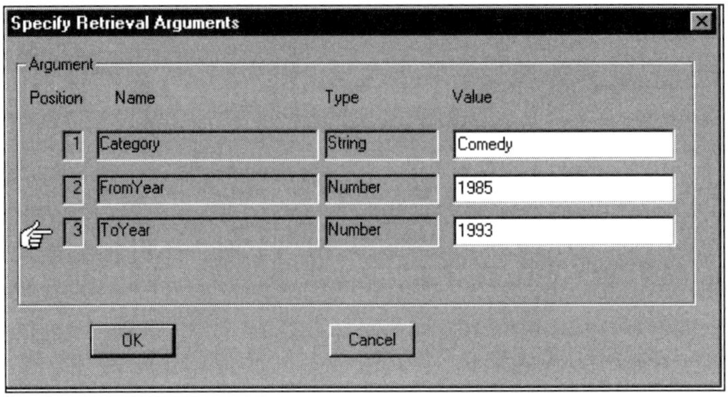

Figure 9-21
Supplying values for the retrieval arguments.

Alternatively, your Retrieve function call can supply the values and avoid the dialog box. To cause this to happen, insert the retrieval argument values as parameters when you call the Retrieve function:

```
dw_1.Retrieve("Comedy", 1985, 1993)
```

Passing arguments to the Retrieve call is useful if you want to present a dialog box of your own design instead of presenting the PowerBuilder-designed one in Figure 9-21.

SORTING AND FILTERING

Sorting and filtering are two processes that the DataWindow can perform on retrieved data before displaying it. Sorting determines the sequence in which rows are displayed, similar to the ORDER BY clause in the SQL SELECT statement. Filtering selects a subset of rows for display, similar to the WHERE clause.

There is, however, a major difference between sorting and ORDER BY, and between filtering and WHERE: Sorting and filtering are performed by the client workstation after it fetches all the rows from the database server. ORDER BY and WHERE are performed by the server, as it carries out the SELECT and builds the result set.

Whether you should use sorting instead of ORDER BY, or filtering instead of WHERE, depends on many factors in your application and environment: the size of the result set, the speed and capacity of the server and client workstations, the number of workstations, whether there is a communication traffic bottleneck, and so forth.

RowslSort

Use the menu choice Rows|Sort in the DataWindow Painter to specify a sort. Figure 9-22 shows the dialog that pops up. Use the mouse to drag columns from the list on the left to the list on the right to specify the sort order. In Figure 9-22, the sort order is by category (ascending) and by year (descending). PowerBuilder can also sort on arithmetic expressions. Double-click an item in the right-side list to convert it from a column to an expression.

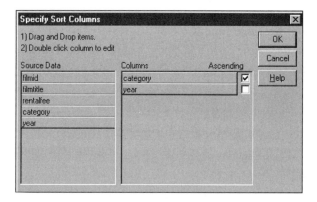

Figure 9-22
Specifying the sort columns.

RowslFilter

Use the menu choice Rows|Filter in the DataWindow Painter to specify a filter. Figure 9-23 shows the dialog that pops up. You must type in an expression. This dialog box is very similar to the one for a computed field expression (Figure 9-9), except that, for a filter, the expression must evaluate to True or False. The expression in Figure 9-23 will select comedy films released between 1986 and 1993. In the DataWindow, only rows that match the filter expression will be displayed.

DataWindow Painter Functions

Another benefit of using a filter instead of a SQL WHERE clause is that the filter expression can include "DataWindow Painter functions." These are a set of over one hundred functions developed for use in DataWindow expressions. DataWindow Painter functions are not the same as the PowerScript functions, which are used in scripts, although the two sets do share many functions in common.

We have already seen several examples of DataWindow Painter functions in this chapter: The computed field example used the

Round function in its expression. The DataWindow painter expression example included the Year and Today functions. The discussion of key columns showed an example using the IsRowNew function.

As you can see, DataWindow Painter functions can be used in any of the places in a DataWindow that you can type in an expression. That includes in filters and in sort expressions. This capability goes well beyond what your database's SQL dialect offers.

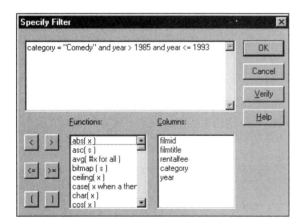

Figure 9-23
Specifying the filter.

SORTING AND FILTERING IN POWERSCRIPT

PowerScript provides functions for sorting and filtering at runtime. This script sets the same sort and filter as the previous examples did interactively:

```
dw_1.SetSort("category A, year D")
dw_1.Sort()
dw_1.SetFilter("category='Comedy' and year>=1986 and year<=1993")
dw_1.Filter()
```

The SetSort and SetFilter functions set up the specifications for the
DataWindow, and the Sort and Filter functions perform them.

To clear the settings, use empty strings:

```
dw_1.SetSort("")
dw_1.Sort()
dw_1.SetFilter("")
dw_1.Filter()
```

To present the dialog boxes shown in Figure 9-22 and Figure 9-23,
supply null string arguments:

```
String ls_null                        // the null string
SetNull(ls_null)                      // make the string null
IF dw_1.SetSort(ls_null)  1 THEN   // show "Specify Sort" dialog
    RETURN                            // user clicked "Cancel"
END IF
dw_1.Sort()                           // apply the new sort
IF dw_1.SetFilter(ls_null)  1 THEN // show "Specify Filter" dialog
    RETURN                            // user clicked "Cancel"
END IF
dw_1.Filter()                         // apply the new filter
```

To retrieve the current sort and filter settings into string variables in
order to display or analyze them, use the DataWindow property expresions:

```
String ls_sort, ls_filter
ls_sort = dw_1.object.DataWindow.Table.Sort
MessageBox("Sort", ls_sort)
ls_filter = dw_1.object.DataWindow.Table.Filter
MessageBox("Filter", ls_filter)
```

COUNTING ROWS

Several PowerScript functions provide statistics about the rows in the
DataWindow. Each returns a long integer:

```
n = dw_1.RowCount()      // # of rows being displayed
n = dw_1.FilteredCount() // # of filtered-out rows
```

```
n = dw_1.ModifiedCount()  // # of modified rows (new and existing)
n = dw_1.DeletedCount( )  // # of deleted rows
```

MAKING SURE ALL UPDATES OCCUR

The windows in this chapter all contain an Update button, and the user is supposed to click it from time to time. If the user forgets and closes the window without clicking Update, all changes are lost.

To make sure that an update occurs before the window closes, you need to write a CloseQuery script. The CloseQuery event fires on a window just before it closes; this event has the ability (unlike a Close script) to set a flag to keep the window open. If the update fails, we want the window to stay open.

Here's the script:

```
Long ll_modified, ll_deleted    // # rows modified, # rows deleted
IF dw_1.AcceptText()<>1 THEN    // is the latest column change ok?
   RETURN 1                     // don't let the window close
END IF
ll_modified = dw_1.ModifiedCount()       // how many modified rows?
ll_deleted  = dw_1.DeletedCount()        // how many deleted rows?
IF ll_modified > 0 OR ll_deleted > 0 THEN  // an Update is needed
   IF dw_1.Update()<>1 THEN              // do the Update
      MessageBox("Error", "The Update Failed", StopSign!) // error
      RETURN 1                           // don't let the window close
   END IF
END IF
```

If the user has just finished typing a value into a column, then AcceptText makes sure the value is valid. I'll talk more about AcceptText and other related functions in the next chapter.

If either the ModifiedCount function or the DeletedCount function returns a nonzero value, then the user has made changes to rows in the DataWindow that have not yet been applied to the database. In that case, the script calls the Update function.

If either AcceptText or Update fails, the "RETURN 1" command prevents the window from closing. If the script ends without a RETURN command, or with a "RETURN 0," the window closes. The CloseQuery event script is one of several in PowerBuilder in which you return a value to indicate what PowerBuilder should do next. We will see others, such as the ItemChanged event script, in the next chapter.

Data Sources

When you create a new DataWindow, PowerBuilder asks you to pick a "data source" and a "presentation style" in the dialog box shown in Figure 9-24. We've covered a lot of ground in this chapter using only the simplest options: "quick select" and "grid." Now I'd like to describe the other choices, beginning with the data sources.

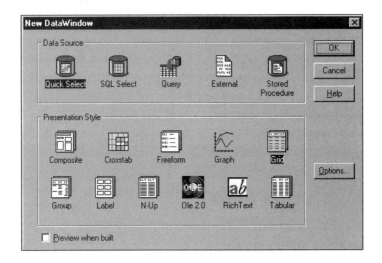

Figure 9-24
The New DataWindow dialog box.

The term "data source" in this chapter is not the same as the "data source" described in Chapter 5, which is the name of a connection to an ODBC database. This term is used in two different ways in PowerBuilder.

In a DataWindow, the "data source" determines how the DataWindow gets its data. There are five options, as you can see in Figure 9-24. The first three are ways to specify a SQL SELECT. The other two are non-SELECT sources.

1. **Quick Select** — This is the choice we made for the film-grid DataWindow exercise. It leads to the Quick Select dialog box, which we walked through in the last chapter. Based on your choices, PowerBuilder constructs a SQL SELECT statement. Once in the

DataWindow Painter, you can see and modify the statement using the Select Painter.

2. **SQL Select** — This choice drops you directly into the Select Painter (Figure 9-14) so that you can build the SELECT before proceeding to the DataWindow Painter.

The end result is the same for both Quick Select and SQL Select—it's a SELECT statement. Quick Select is easier; SQL Select is more powerful.

3. **Query** — When you make this choice, PowerBuilder shows you a list of queries and asks you to pick one. In an earlier step, you must have created the query with the Query Painter (Chapter 21), named it, and saved it in a .PBL file. When you pick a query, which is essentially nothing more than a SELECT statement with a name, PowerBuilder copies and uses it as the DataWindow's SELECT source. Once in the DataWindow Painter, you can see and modify the statement using the Select Painter.

So the end result of the Query option is also a SELECT statement, just as it is for the other two options.

PowerBuilder makes a copy of the query's SELECT; it does not link the DataWindow to the query. Therefore, if you change the query, that change is not reflected in the DataWindow, nor vice versa.

4. **External** — This is the do-it-yourself option. Rather than tell PowerBuilder how to fetch the data, it is up to you as the developer to write code to populate and manipulate the DataWindow.

Since the external-source DataWindow has no direct connection to a database, you do not manage it with the SetTransObject, Retrieve, and Update functions. Typically, special functions are used to populate an external-source DataWindow. ImportString and ImportFile import multiple rows into a DataWindow in one operation.

The External option has several useful applications. One is to connect a DataWindow to a non-SQL source, such as a business-process server in a three-tier architecture. Another is to present program-generated data to the user in an attractive DataWindow format and let the user modify it. I used two external-source DataWindows for this purpose in the example of Format 4 dynamic SQL in Chapter 7.

5. **Stored Procedure** — With this option, the DataWindow retrieves rows by calling a database-stored procedure. I explained in Chapter 7 that many stored procedures return result sets, similar to those returned by SELECT statements. The data that it returns might be drawn from a table in the database or might be some other kind of data — that's up to the person who created the stored procedure. But to the DataWindow, they look like the rows and columns that might be fetched from a table. When you select the "Stored Procedure" option, PowerBuilder displays the stored procedures in the database, and you pick one from the list.

Presentation Styles

A DataWindow must be based upon one of the eleven presentation styles depicted in the New DataWindow dialog box (Figure 9-24). So far we have worked mostly with a grid-style DataWindow. You can use each style to design DataWindows for on-screen data display or for printing reports. Some styles are more suitable for one task than the other.

Rather than show an example of each style here, I will refer you to other chapters in this book where you will find examples.

In the dialog box, the eleven styles are listed alphabetically. I will describe them in order of complexity, starting with the simplest:

1. **Grid** — The film-grid DataWindow that we've used throughout this chapter is a grid-style DataWindow. In the grid style, PowerBuilder arranges the data into a rigid matrix of rows and columns. It is suitable for either data entry or reporting. It is functional but not very attractive.

2. **Free-Form** — In the free-form style, PowerBuilder lays the columns out vertically, but you can rearrange them into any configuration. Figure 8-1 at the beginning of the previous chapter is a free-form DataWindow. Because you can put anything anywhere with this style, it has many diverse uses, including form letters and envelopes, as we'll see in Chapter 18 on the CD-ROM. We'll also be seeing a lot of the free-form style in Chapter 10.

3. **Tabular** — As in the grid style, in the tabular style data are arranged into rows and columns. It is more flexible than the grid style, making it easier to develop attractive designs. It is a very popular style for reports and is also good for data entry DataWindows. Chapter 18 goes into detail about the tabular style.

4. **Group** — The group style is actually the same as the tabular style. PowerBuilder just gives you some extra help with setting up titles, groups, subtotals, and grand totals. This makes it easier to get a more complex report design underway. See Chapter 18 for more information.

5. **Label** — Use this style is to design and print mailing labels. See Chapter 18.

6. **N-Up** — This is a variation of the tabular style, in which the layout is divided into two or more columns, like a newspaper page, for a more compact display of data.

7. **Graph** — A graph is a pictorial representation of your numeric data: a pie chart, a bar graph, or the like. Graphs will be covered in Chapter 19.

8. **CrossTab** — A crosstab ("cross-tabulation") is the summarization of your numeric data into a matrix. In several ways, a crosstab is similar to a graph, except that one is numeric and the other is pictorial. Chapter 19 describes them both.

9. **Composite** — With the composite style, you take any number of other DataWindows and paste them together into a single design. This style is useful for management reports, and you can also use it for data display and data entry. There will be an example in Chapter 18.

10. **Rich Text** — Using a rich text DataWindow, you can create letters or other documents by merging information in your database into a formatted DataWindow master. Word processing–oriented features such as headers, footers, and multiple fonts are available in an easy-to-use format. In Chapter 18 we'll use the rich text style to design a form letter.

11. **OLE 2.0** — Using a process called uniform data transfer, information from PowerBuilder-supported data sources can be sent to an OLE 2 server application. The OLE 2 compliant application uses the PowerBuilder-supplied data to formulate a graph, a map, a spreadsheet, or the like to be displayed in the DataWindow.

DropDownDataWindows

A DropDownDataWindow (DDDW), also known a "child DataWindow," is a DataWindow put to a special purpose: It serves as the dropdown list for a column on another DataWindow.

Figure 9-25 shows an example. It is an order form—that is, a window containing a free-form DataWindow based on the order table. One field on the form, "Cust. ID," has a dropdown list. In Figure 9-25 the dropdown button has just been clicked so the list is visible, but most of the time the list is hidden.

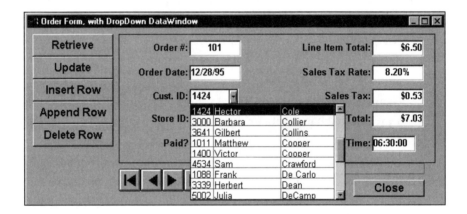

Figure 9-25
The customer field on this order-table DataWindow has a DropDownDataWindow based on the customer table.

PowerBuilder supports two dropdown list styles for DataWindow columns: the DropDownListBox and the DropDownDataWindow. Both look the same to the end user, but the DropDownDataWindow is more sophisticated. In a DropDownListBox, which I described in Chapter 6, you hand-code the choices on the list when you design it, or you populate the list programatically at runtime. A DropDownDataWindow is actually a DataWindow and, therefore, it retrieves its choices from the database.

To use a DropDownDataWindow, first design it in the DataWindow painter and then assign it to a column in the parent DataWindow.

Figure 9-26 shows the DataWindow d_customerdropdown, which is destined to become the DDDW. It is a simple grid-style DataWindow, with three detail-band columns and no header. Figure 9-27 shows it in the Previewer.

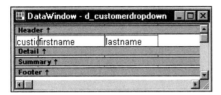

Figure 9-26
The DropDownDataWindow, in the DataWindow Painter.

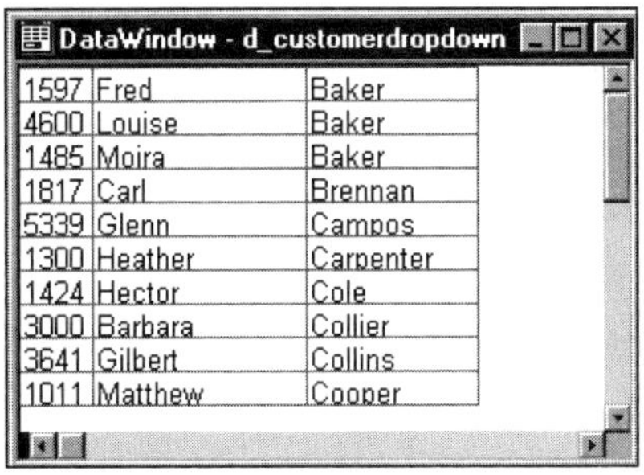

Figure 9-27
The DropDownDataWindow, in the DataWindow Previewer.

After d_customerdropdown is designed and saved, open the order form, d_orderform, in the DataWindow Painter, as you see in Figure 9-28. It is a free-form DataWindow. Open the custid column's property sheet, and select its Edit tab. Select "DropDownDW" from the "Style" list. This changes the layout of the property sheet as pictured in Figure 9-29. The most important thing in this dialog box is specifying the name of the DataWindow, d_customerdropdown. It might take some trial and error to come up with the right number for "Width of DropDown," which determines how wide the DDDW will be when displayed and is expressed as a percentage of the width of the field to which the DDDW is attached.

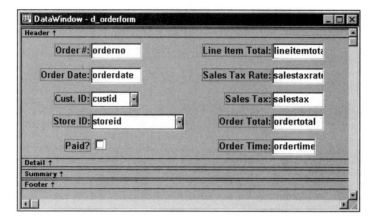

Figure 9-28
The order form, in the DataWindow Painter.

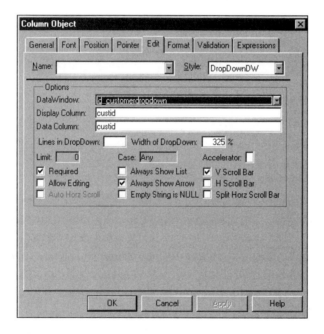

Figure 9-29
Specifying the DropDownDataWindow edit style.

A great thing about DropDownDataWindows is that no PowerScript programming is required to implement one.

Summary: DataWindows up to This Point

This chapter has shown the fundamentals of creating DataWindows and how they work:

- The difference between a DataWindow object and a DataWindow control
- The minimal requirements for implementing a DataWindow to an application
- Essential functionality: retrieve, update, navigation controls, and error handling
- How to use the DataWindow Painter
- DataWindow painter expressions
- The SQL that PowerBuilder assembles and executes in response to DataWindow activity, and how you can monitor and control it
- The options for data sources and presentation styles

This is quite a broad foundation. The next chapters will concentrate on more specific and sophisticated DataWindow issues.

10 Data Entry Programming

When you design a DataWindow for the purpose of data entry, it's often necessary to add programming to it. The programming may assist the end users as they type in the data, and it may also keep them out of trouble. There are many common data entry programming tasks. A few that we cover in this chapter are special validations, special calculations, and updating related tables.

This chapter concentrates on critical data integrity issues — making sure that only "clean data" is written to the database and that all inter-table relationships remain in balance. The programming can be tricky, and it requires care and precision.

The Order Form: w_orders

Figure 10-1 shows the window that we will be working with for most of this chapter. Its name is "w_orders," and it is an order entry form. The DataWindow contained in the window shows one row from the orders table. The staff of the video store can use it to browse through orders and to add, delete, and change orders.

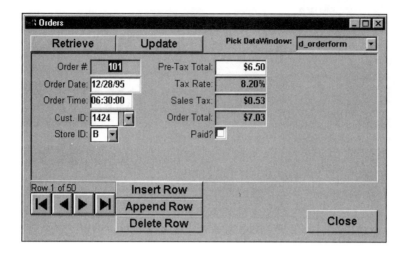

Figure 10-1

The order entry form, w_orders, with a free-form DataWindow.

In a completed Video Store application, the real order form window would be more complex than Figure 10-1. It would be a "one-to-many" form, showing one order and many line items (films rented). Figure 10-1 is sufficient for our needs in this chapter. Chapter 19 will introduce the one-to-many version.

The buttons in Figure 10-1, such as Retrieve and Insert Row, are the same ones that I presented in Chapter 8. There's nothing different about them here. What is new in this window is something that can't be seen: complex event scripts attached to the DataWindow control, monitoring and controlling the user's data entry activity.

In the top right of w_orders is a DropDownListBox control. Using it, you can change the DataWindow object from d_orderform, the free-form DataWindow shown in Figure 10-1, to d_ordergrid, the grid-style DataWindow shown in Figure 10-2. Both show the same columns from the orders table. The d_ordergrid DataWindow, being a grid, shows multiple rows.

It would be unusual to have a DropDownListBox like this one in a real-world order form. But for the discussion in this chapter, it's convenient to switch to the form shown in Figure 10-2 whenever we're working on a multiple-row operation. You can do all the same operations, no matter whether you're using the Figure 10-1 or the Figure 10-2 configuration, but sometimes Figure 10-2 makes them easier to visualize.

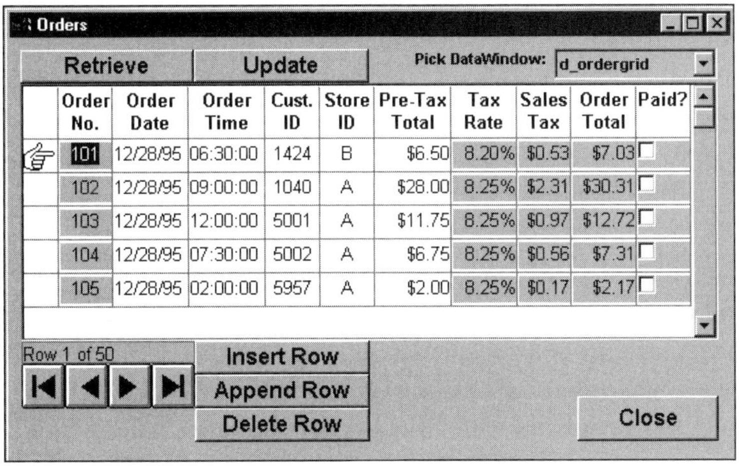

Figure 10-2
The order entry form, with a grid-style DataWindow.

The programming on the DropDownListBox is very simple:

```
dw_1.DataObject = This.Text
```

This script says: "Change the DataWindow object contained in dw_1 (the DataWindow control) to the DropDownListBox's text." The text is "d_orderform" or "d_ordergrid," the names of the two DataWindow objects.

Regardless of which DataWindow object is displayed, all of the other scripts in the window work exactly the same. Nothing in this window or its PowerScript programming is sensitive to which DataWindow object is in use.

Data Entry Programming: the Tasks at Hand

Three data entry programming techniques are critical to master:

- **Field-oriented processing** — When the user types a value into a field, an event script performs special validations and calculations on it. For example, when the user fills in a customer ID in Figure 10-1, a script performs a credit check to make sure the customer is paid up.

- **Row-oriented processing** — When the user has finished typing values into a row, an event script performs special validations and calculations on it. For example, after the user inserts a new row in Figure 10-2 and fills in values, a script makes sure that the user hasn't left a required field empty.

- **Update-oriented processing** — When the user clicks the Update button, a script updates the database, adding, deleting, and updating rows in the orders table. At the same time, other processing must take place. For example, a script must update the open balance, which is a column in the customer table, to reflect the new or changed order amounts.

Most of this chapter is dedicated to the ins and outs of these three techniques. Along the way we'll explain the DataWindow buffers, where PowerBuilder stores the data in a DataWindow.

Field-Oriented Processing

All data entry programming techniques rely upon the events, properties, and functions of the DataWindow control. In Chapter 3, I explained events, properties, and functions for simple controls such as Command-Buttons. It should be no surprise that the DataWindow control has many more events, properties, and functions than any other type of control, since it is the most sophisticated of all controls.

What Is a Field?

In this book, I use the term *field* more loosely than the PowerBuilder documentation does. My definition of a *field* is the same as it is for most people: "A place on the screen for seeing and typing in a data value." In PowerBuilder, a field can be one of three things:

1. A control in a window, such as a SingleLineEdit control, for presenting or entering a data value. We saw a number of these in Chapter 2.

2. A column in a DataWindow, such as the order # column and order date column in Figure 10-1 and Figure 10-2.

3. A "computed field" in a DataWindow, which displays a value that is calculated from other fields.

In the PowerBuilder documentation, the term *field* is used primarily when referring to the third item, a computed field. It is occasionally used for the other two, but not often.

In this chapter, when I talk about "field-oriented processing," for example, I am using the term in the context of the second item: a column in a DataWindow.

Tables 10-1 and 10-2 list the events and functions that play special roles in field-oriented processing.

Table 10-1
Events for Field-Oriented Processing

Events	Arguments	RETURN Values
EditChanged	row	(none)
	dwo	
	data	
ItemChanged	row	RETURN 0: Accept
	dwo	RETURN 1: Reject
	data	RETURN 2: Restore old
		value and change focus
ItemFocusChanged	row	(none)
	dwo	

continued

Table 10-1 *(continued)*

Events	Arguments	RETURN Values
ItemError	row	RETURN 0: Reject data,
	dwo	Display message
	data	RETURN 1: Reject data,
		don't display message
		RETURN 2: Accept data
		RETURN 3: Restore old
		value and change focus

Table 10-2

Functions for Field-Oriented Processing

Functions	GetItem Functions
AcceptText	GetItemDate
CanUndo	GetItemDateTime
GetColumn	GetItemDecimal
GetColumnName	GetItemNumber
GetText	GetItemString
SetColumn	GetItemTime
SetItem	
SetText	
Undo	

Arguments and Return Values in Event Scripts

Just like a function, an event script can have arguments passed into it and return a value. DataWindow event scripts make heavy use of these features, as you can see from Table 10-1 and other tables in this chapter.

For example, PowerBuilder passes three arguments into an ItemChanged script: *row*, *dwo*, and *data*. (I'll explain the ItemChanged event and these three arguments shortly.) In your event script, you use them like variables. PowerBuilder stuffs values into them (such as the current row number into *row*) before calling the script so that your script can inspect the values to determine what the event is all about. In some cases, you can change their values to pass information back to PowerBuilder.

You can also pass a return value back to PowerBuilder by executing the RETURN command, followed by the number to pass back. For example, you can terminate your ItemChanged script with RETURN 0, RETURN 1, or RETURN 2. As Table 10-1 shows, the value you choose instructs PowerBuilder how to handle the item value.

Here's a simple ItemChanged event script that rejects any data value that is "xyz" and accepts all others:

```
IF data = "xyz" THEN     // inspect the data argument
    RETURN 1             // reject it
ELSE
    RETURN 0             // accept it
END IF
```

FIELD-ORIENTED PROCESSING: AN EXERCISE

The order form in Figure 10-1 performs four types of field-oriented processing:

1. **Validating the customer ID** — Make sure that the customer ID exists in the customer table.

2. **Customer credit check** — Before accepting a customer ID, make sure that the customer does not owe us money.

3. **Filling in the sales tax rate** — Fill in the sales tax rate by looking it up in the store table, based on the order's store ID.

4. **Calculating the sales tax and order total** — Calculate the sales tax and order total after the user has filled in the pretax total and the sales tax rate.

Each of these tasks relies on a field: the customer ID field, the store ID field, or the order total. Calculating the sales tax and order total relies on two fields: pretax total and sales tax rate.

The first two tasks are examples of field-oriented validations. The last two are examples of field-oriented calculations.

THE ITEMCHANGED AND ITEMERROR EVENTS

The ItemChanged and ItemError events are the key to most field-oriented processing. When the user finishes placing a value into a field, PowerBuilder fires ItemChanged. If the field is invalid, PowerBuilder fires ItemError.

The Edit Control

DataWindows use something called an "edit control" during the data entry process. This is illustrated in Figure 10-3. Until you start making changes, the fields in a DataWindow display values retrieved from the database. As you type characters into a field, PowerBuilder first places them into the "edit control." When you've finished typing in a value — typically, when you tab out of the field — PowerBuilder validates it and, if it's okay, copies it from the edit control into the DataWindow itself.

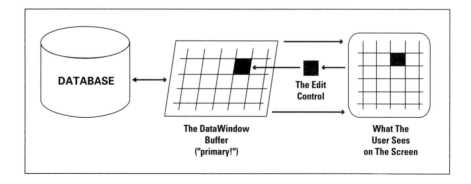

Figure 10-3
The edit control.

The edit control sits on top of whatever DataWindow field has focus. As you tab from field to field, the edit control moves with you. The edit control is what the user *sees* in the field. The buffer is what's actually *in* the field.

This concept of an edit control is not important to an end user, but it is important to you as the programmer. In PowerScript, the technique to read or change the edit control's value is not the same as the technique for the field's value. If you choose the wrong technique, your script will work with the wrong value.

For example, suppose the field storeid contains "A." The user has typed in "B" but has not yet tabbed out of the field. This "dot notation" reads the field value, which is still "A":

```
s = dw_1.object.storeid[row]      // this returns "A"
```

In an ItemChanged and ItemError event script, the *data* argument contains edit control's value, which is "B":

```
s = data                          // this returns "B"
```

Other scripts and functions don't have a *data* argument, but you can always call the GetText function, which also returns the edit control's value:

```
s = dw_1.GetText()                // this also returns "B"
```

The Field-Validation Process

PowerBuilder validates a new field value by making sure it's the correct data type and by testing it against the field's validation rule, if it has one. If the value is okay, PowerBuilder then fires the ItemChanged event, giving you a chance to validate it further using PowerScript. You conclude the ItemChanged script with a RETURN command, which passes a code back to PowerBuilder to indicate success or failure.

If anything goes wrong — that is, if PowerBuilder or your Item-Changed script rejects the value — PowerBuilder fires the ItemError event and displays an error message to the user.

If everything goes okay and no ItemError occurs, then PowerBuilder transfers the new value from the edit control to the DataWindow field. In most cases, focus then jumps to the next field, because the user has clicked that field or pressed the Tab or Enter key, the action that set the whole field-validation process off in the first place.

When focus arrives at a new field in the DataWindow, PowerBuilder transfers the new field's value to the edit control so that the user can modify it and fires the event ItemFocusChanged.

VALIDATING THE CUSTOMER ID

If you type an invalid number into the customer ID field on the order form and attempt to leave the field, the ItemChanged script must detect the error. A customer ID is invalid if it is not found in the customer table. The ItemError script must pop up the error message shown in Figure 10-4.

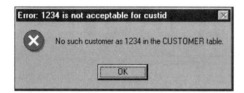

Figure 10-4

An error message about the customer ID.

Why Validate the Customer ID in a Script?

You might think that it shouldn't be necessary to write a script to validate the customer ID. It seems like something PowerBuilder should be able to do automatically. After all, you might think, doesn't the dropdown list on the field (Figure 10-5) force a valid customer to be picked? And, if not, won't the database's referential integrity rules reject an invalid customer ID? The answer to the first question is "No." The answer to the second question is "Yes, but not in a way that will be acceptable to most users."

First of all, here's what's wrong with the dropdown list: Even though customer ID has a DropDownDataWindow based on the customer table, as you see in Figure 10-5, it does not restrict you to values in the list. You may type in any four-digit value. That's because, in the DataWindow Painter, I checkmarked the "Allow Editing" option in the Edit tab of the field's property sheet. (See Figure 9-29 in Chapter 9.)

Fields in Windows and Fields in DataWindows

A field in a DataWindow, such as the customer ID in the order form, closely resembles a field in a window, such as the SingleLineEdit control named "sle_inputx" that we created back in Chapter 2. (See Figure 2-24, for example.) Therefore, you might expect the PowerScript language to let you manipulate both types of fields in pretty much the same way. And this is the case (thanks mostly to a feature that is new with version 5.0), although with DataWindows, it's a little wordier.

A field in a window is a *control*, and like all window controls, it has events, properties, and functions. Most manipulation of a control is done using the "control.property" dot notation syntax, which is very direct. For example, this four-line script reads and changes the value (text property) and background color (BackColor property) of a field named "sle_inputx" in a window:

```
s = sle_inputx.Text              // get the value
sle_inputx.Text = "A"            // change the value to "A"
n = sle_inputx.BackColor         // get the color
sle_inputx.BackColor = 255       // change the color to red
```

A field in a DataWindow is not called a "control." It is called a "column" or a "computed field," and it is an object contained within the DataWindow object, which in turn is planted into a DataWindow control in a window. Since the field is not a control, it does not have events or functions. The DataWindow control does have events and functions, and some of them deal with the field objects inside it. The ItemChanged event is an example of one such event.

A field object in a DataWindow does have properties, and you can use dot notation syntax to manipulate them. Here is how you get and change the value and background color of a field object in a DataWindow using dot notation (dw_1 is the DataWindow control, and storeid is a field within it):

```
r = dw_1.GetRow()                          // the next 2 lines need the
                                           // current row #
s = dw_1.object.storeid[r]                 // get the value
dw_1.object.storeid[r] = "A"               // change the value
n = dw_1.object.storeid.Background.Color   // get the color
dw_1.object.storeid.Background.Color = 255 // change the color
```

Handling events on a DataWindow field, however, is not as direct: PowerBuilder actually fires the event on the DataWindow control, not directly on the field. In the field-processing exercise, we rely on the ItemChanged event to detect when the user has changed a field value. You write a script for the DataWindow control to respond to the event, but the first thing your script has to do is figure out which field within the control is affected by the event.

If you turn off "Allow Editing," it becomes impossible to type in a four-digit customer number. PowerBuilder forces you to scroll through the dropdown list and pick from it. This is slow and inconvenient if you know the number and don't need to look it up.

(Microsoft Windows has a convention for dropdown lists: If the dropdown button is slightly separated from the field, you are not forced to pick a value from the list; you may type in any value. If the dropdown button touches the field, you must pick from the list. In the DataWindow Painter, the "Allow Editing" option sets that distinction.)

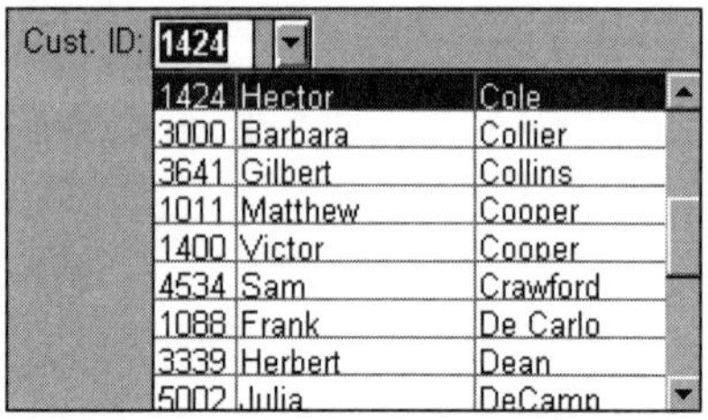

Figure 10-5
A DropDownDataWindow for the customer ID.

What about referential integrity? It's true that the database server will not allow an invalid customer ID in the orders table. That's because in the Database Painter, I created a foreign-key link between the customer ID field in the orders table and the same field in the customer table. So now the database (SQL Anywhere or whatever) will enforce referential integrity.

However, if we rely on referential integrity, the error handling will not be to the liking of most end users. The trouble is that the error does not occur until you click the Update button. That might be minutes (or hours) after the user typed in the invalid customer number. Most users prefer not to wait that long, especially after they've wasted time typing in the rest of the order. They want an instant response: Type in a bad customer, get an error message right away. That requires ItemChanged event programming.

The ItemChanged Script

The ItemChanged script, like almost every script in this chapter, is attached to dw_1, the order form's DataWindow control. Whenever the user changes any field's value, the ItemChanged script runs. The first thing that almost any ItemChanged script must do is figure out, "Which field has changed? Is it one that I'm interested in?"

PowerBuilder passes three arguments into the ItemChanged script to help you determine what's going on:

- **row** (a long integer) — the current row number
- **dwo** (an object) — the current column
- **data** (a string) — the newly typed-in data value

The *dwo* argument is an "object class variable," a type we'll see more of in Chapters 11–13. It has properties and functions, which you reference using dot notation, similar to Chapter 2's *st_firstbox.BackColor*. The *dwo.Name* property gives you the name of the current field:

```
ls_colname = dwo.Name          // what is the current column?
```

The ItemChanged script usually begins by fetching the current field's name and follows with a CHOOSE-CASE statement with the processing required for each field:

```
String ls_colname                 // the name of the current column
ls_colname = dwo.Name             // what is the current column?
CHOOSE CASE ls_colname            // processing depends on column
   CASE "custid"                  // it's the customer ID column
      ...etc...                   // customer ID processing goes here
   CASE "storeid"                 // it's the store ID column
      ...etc...                   // store ID processing goes here
   CASE "lineitemtotal"           // it's the lineitemtotal column
      ...etc...                   // lineitemtotal proc. goes here
END CHOOSE
```

You don't need a CASE line for every DataWindow field, but you do need one for every field requiring special processing.

Under the CASE line for "custid," this is the code that validates the customer ID:

```
ls_custid = data                 // get the newly entered customer ID
SELECT ispaidup, openbalance
   INTO :ls_ispaidup, :ldec_openbal
   FROM customer
   WHERE custid = :ls_custid;
IF sqlca.SqlCode = 100 THEN   // 100 indicates zero rows selected
```

```
        is_itemerror = "No such customer as "    + ls_custid              + &
                  " in the CUSTOMER table."
    RETURN 1                // tell PowerBuilder to do ItemError event
END IF
IF sqlca.SqlCode <> 0 THEN    // -1 indicates an error
    is_itemerror = "Error reading customer " + ls_custid                 + &
                  " from the CUSTOMER table."                            + &
                  "~nError Code: "           + String(sqlca.SqlDbCode)   + &
                  "~nError Message: "        + sqlca.SqlErrText
    RETURN 1
END IF
```

The *data* event argument provides the edit control value, which is the new value that needs validating, and places it into *ls_custid*, a string variable.

The SELECT statement searches the database for a customer row with *ls_custid* as the customer ID. It retrieves two columns, ispaidup and open-balance, which we will need for a later field-processing operation, but which are not relevant to the current task.

SELECT, like many embedded SQL statements, returns 0 for success, –1 for a database error, and 100 if no row is found. The IF statement handles these possibilities.

If the script detects an error, it must do two things:

- Place an error message into *is_itemerror*, an instance variable. The ItemError script will display the message.

- Use the statement "RETURN 1" to terminate the script execution. There's no need for ItemChanged to do more processing if the customer ID is not valid. The return value "1" signals PowerBuilder that an error has occurred. After the script concludes, PowerBuilder will retain focus on the current field and run the ItemError script.

If no error occurs, then the script issues this statement:

```
RETURN 0
```

This is the last line of the script, after all validation has concluded successfully. The return value "0" signals PowerBuilder that everything is okay.

The Completed Script

Most of the scripts in this chapter are quite long, so I have broken them into fragments to describe them more easily. You will find the completed versions in the sample application for this chapter on the book's CD-ROM.

The ItemError Script

Here is the DataWindow control's ItemError script:

```
String ls_errortitle          // title of the error message
IF is_itemerror <> "" THEN     // there is an error message
    ls_errortitle = "Error: " + data +    &
                    " is not acceptable for " + dwo.Name
    MessageBox(ls_errortitle, is_itemerror, stopsign!)
    is_itemerror = ""          // clear error message for next time
    RETURN 1                   // disable PowerBuilder error message
ELSE
    RETURN 0                   // enable PowerBuilder error message
END IF
```

The ItemError event will occur either because the ItemChanged script detected an error or because PowerBuilder itself detected an error. You handle the two cases differently, which is the reason for the IF-THEN-ELSE.

If the instance variable *is_itemerror* is not an empty string, then it must contain the error message placed into it by the ItemChanged script. In that case, the script calls MessageBox to display the error message, which might be the one shown in Figure 10-4.

If *is_itemerror* is an empty string, then the error was detected by PowerBuilder. In this case, the script returns 0, signaling PowerBuilder to display its own error message. Figure 10-6 shows an example, which results from a validation rule I placed on the field using the Database Painter.

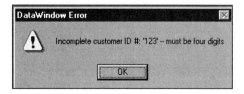

Figure 10-6
A PowerBuilder-detected error message.

In the ItemError script, you should always return one of these values:

0 = Reject the item value and display PowerBuilder's error message.

1 = Reject the item value but don't display the PowerBuilder error message, presumably because the script displays a custom error message.

2 = Cancel the error and accept the item value after all.

3 = Cancel the error but replace the bad value with the field's original value.

CHECKING THE CUSTOMER'S CREDIT

Credit checking is a classic feature of order entry systems. If any customers owe us too much money, we don't let them place any new orders.

In the Video Store application, credit checking depends on two columns in the customer table: ispaidup, which indicates whether the customer has an open balance due ("Yes" or "No"); and openbalance, which is the amount owed.

The SELECT statement in the ItemChanged script that validated the customer ID also retrieved these two column values into variables:

```
SELECT ispaidup, openbalance
   INTO :ls_ispaidup, :ldec_openbal ...
```

From here it's a simple task to test the customer's credit. In the ItemChanged script, these lines of code follow the customer ID test shown earlier:

```
IF ls_ispaidup = "No" THEN      // customer is not paid up
   IF ldec_openbal >= 10 THEN    // $10 credit limit
      li_yesno = MessageBox (                          &
         "Deadbeat Customer Alert!",                   &
         "This customer owes us "              + &
         String(ldec_openbal, "$#,##0.00") + "."   + &
         "~nAre you sure you want this "           + &
         "customer to have a new order?",              &
         stopsign!, yesno!, 2)
      IF li_yesno <> 1 THEN      // user said "No"
         is_itemerror = "No more orders for customer " + &
                        ls_custid          + " until they pay
                                                       up!"
         RETURN 1               // causes ItemError event to fire
```

```
        END IF
      END IF
    END IF
```

If the customer's balance is more than ten dollars, the script displays the dialog box shown in Figure 10-7. If the user clicks No, the script triggers an error in the same way we did earlier: by placing an error message in a variable and returning 1.

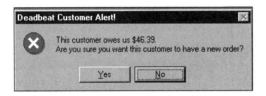

Figure 10-7

Customer credit check notification.

INACTIVE CUSTOMERS

Although I did not implement it in the Video Store application, it is usually helpful to have an "inactive" status for customers. An inactive customer remains in the database but may not be used for new orders. You implement this by adding an "inactive" column to the customer table and setting it to "Yes" or "No" (or Y or N, or 1 or 0, or whatever you prefer) for inactive customers. Then add code to the ItemChanged script, very similar to the credit-check code, to disallow a customer if inactive is "Yes."

FILLING IN THE SALES TAX RATE FROM THE STORE TABLE

In the order form, four fields are protected from user modification: order #, tax rate, sales tax, and order total. For each of them, I have turned on its "Display Only" edit property using the DataWindow Painter and, as a convention, changed its color to gray. These fields are, however, required columns in the orders table, so PowerScript programming must place values into them before a new row can be inserted into the database.

After the user fills in the store ID field, the ItemChanged script fills in the tax rate. This code follows the CASE line for "storeid" in the ItemChanged script's CHOOSE CASE:

```
ls_storeid = data        // get the newly entered store ID
SELECT salestaxrate
   INTO :ldec_taxrate
   FROM store
   WHERE storeid = :ls_storeid;
This.object.salestaxrate[row] = ldec_taxrate
```

The use of the data and row arguments and the SELECT statement are similar to the script's handling of the customer ID, which I showed earlier. The assignment statement on the last line places a value into a DataWindow field. In this case, it places the value of the variable *ldec_taxrate* into the salestaxrate field in the current row (*row*). The final version of this code includes error handling, not shown here, for the SELECT statement.

CALCULATING THE SALES TAX AND ORDER TOTAL

The calculations of sales tax and order total occur after the user has filled in two fields: store ID and pre-tax total. Because the CHOOSE-CASE in the ItemChanged script is set up to handle only single-field cases, a two-field case such as this must follow the END CHOOSE:

```
IF ls_colname     = "storeid" or ls_colname = "lineitemtotal" THEN
   IF ls_colname     = "storeid" THEN
      ldec_pretax   = This.object.lineitemtotal[row]
   ELSE          // ls_colname = "lineitemtotal"
      ldec_pretax   = Dec(data)
      ldec_taxrate = This.object.salestaxrate[row]
   END IF
   ldec_tax    = ldec_pretax * ldec_taxrate
   ldec_total  = ldec_pretax + ldec_tax
   This.object.salestax[row]    = ldec_tax
   This.object.ordertotal[row] = ldec_total
END IF
```

The field labeled "Pre-Tax Total" in the DataWindow is actually named lineitemtotal.

The script sets two variables prior to doing the calculations: *ldec_pretax* and *ldec_taxrate*. How these two variables are set depends on what the current field is: You must use the *data* argument if the edit control is on the field or use the "datawindow.object" syntax otherwise. So if the current field (which the user has just filled in) is the store ID, the script uses *This.object.lineitemtotal[row]* to fetch *ldec_pretax* from the lineitemtotal field in the DataWindow. As for *ldec_taxrate*, it was set by the SELECT command on the store table, shown in the previous section. If the current field is the lineitemtotal field, the script uses the event argument, *data*, to retrieve *ldec_pretax* and *This.object.salestaxrate[row]* to fetch *ldec_taxrate*.

The calculations for sales tax and order total are simple arithmetic: multiplication and addition. The last two assignment statements use "datawindow.object" to place the values into the DataWindow fields.

WHAT ABOUT COMPUTED FIELDS?

Writing a script to calculate the sales tax and order total might seem to be unnecessary work. You might ask, "Wouldn't this be easier to do with DataWindow computed fields? They don't require any PowerScript programming to implement!"

Unfortunately, the answer is "No." Sales tax and order total are not only DataWindow fields, they are also columns in the orders table. A DataWindow field can be a computed field, or it can be a table column, but it can't be both.

If you try to set these two fields up as computed fields, yes, you can do away with the PowerScript calculations. But then you'd have to add some different PowerScript somewhere else to copy those computed values into the orders table. I think it's simpler to follow the approach that I've shown.

OTHER FIELD-ORIENTED EVENTS AND FUNCTIONS

Back in Tables 10-1 and 10-2, I listed the events and functions that support field-oriented processing. In the programming examples that have followed, I've shown how to use most of them. Here is a brief description of the others:

- **The EditChanged event** — fires while the user types characters into a field (into the edit control, actually), with each keystroke firing the event.

- **The ItemFocusChanged event** — fires when a field gets focus, usually because the user has tabbed into it from another field.

- **The AcceptText function** — forces PowerBuilder to transfer the edit control value into the DataWindow field beneath it, validating it and firing ItemChanged on it. The field retains focus. Since Power-Builder will do all of that automatically when you tab out of the field or when you call the Update function, you need to call AcceptText only in some special situations. For example, if you have a button that performs a calculation, its script should probably begin by calling the AcceptText function. Otherwise, the calculation will operate on old values in the DataWindow, and not on the new value in the edit control.

    AcceptText is an important function to know, and you will see examples later in this chapter.

- **The GetColumn function** — is like the GetColumnName function, except that it returns the number of the current column, instead of its name.

- **The SetColumn function** — moves focus to a specified field. You supply the field's column number or column name as a parameter.

- **The SetText function** — places a value into the edit control — the reverse of the GetText function.

- **The Undo function** — undoes the most recent change to the edit control value. If you are typing in a value, it will undo only the last keystroke, not the entire value.

- **The CanUndo function** — predicts whether the Undo function will, in fact, undo anything.

- **The SetText and GetText functions** — change or retrieve the value in the edit control. These functions were necessary in earlier versions of PowerBuilder. The introduction of the "data" argument for the ItemChanged event script in version 5.0 makes these functions virtually obsolete.

- **The SetItem, GetItemString, and other "GetItem..." functions** — change or retrieve a field value. Like SetText and GetText, these functions were necessary in earlier versions of PowerBuilder, but in version 5.0 they are rarely needed. The "datawindow.object" syntax, introduced in version 5.0, is usually easier to use.

Entering a Null Value into a Field

If you intend to allow the user to change a field value to null — that is, by selecting the field and pressing the Delete key to erase its contents — then you'd better turn on the Empty String Is Null option in the field's Edit Style dialog in the DataWindow Painter. If you don't, and if the field is a number or date or other nonstring type, then any attempt to change the value to null will result in an error message.

The PowerScript Functions chapter of the *PowerScript Reference* manual gives an alternative technique, a long script that avoids the error message. But I think that whoever wrote it just didn't know about the "Empty String Is Null" feature!

The DataWindow Buffers: Primary, Filter, Delete, and Original

Before proceeding to row-oriented and update-oriented processing, you must understand the DataWindow buffers and more about how PowerBuilder manages DataWindows behind the scenes.

When your application retrieves rows from the database into a DataWindow, PowerBuilder stores those rows in buffers. The buffers typically reside in the client computer's RAM. The buffers hold not just the rows that appear on the screen but all the rows fetched using the DataWindow's SELECT command. And there is not just one buffer, there are four buffers, named primary, filter, delete, and original.

- **The primary buffer** — contains the rows that you see and can scroll through in the DataWindow. These are the rows that you think of as being "in the DataWindow right now."

- **The filter buffer** — contains rows that were SELECTed but have been filtered out using the "Filter" feature, described in the last chapter.

- **The delete buffer** — contains rows that once were in the primary buffer but have been deleted using the DeleteRow function.

- **The original buffer** — contains the rows as they appeared when they were originally fetched by the Retrieve function, before the user began to modify them.

Figure 10-8 illustrates the four buffers and their relation to the database and to the DataWindow.

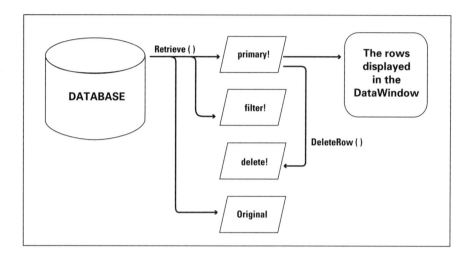

Figure 10-8
The DataWindow buffers.

PowerBuilder makes it easy to manipulate the DataWindow buffers directly. The functions are listed in Table 10-3.

Table 10-3
Functions for Manipulating the DataWindow Buffers

Functions		
DeletedCount	ModifiedCount	RowsDiscard
DeleteRow	ReselectRow	RowsMove
Filter	Reset	SetFilter
FilteredCount	ResetUpdate	SetItemStatus
GetItemStatus	RowCount	SetSort
InsertRow	RowsCopy	Sort

GETTING AND SETTING FIELD VALUES IN POWERSCRIPT

Earlier, I described the "datawindow.object" syntax that you can use to read values from the DataWindow. It's apparent that it operates on the primary buffer by default. But it also has extensions to operate on the other buffers.

Here, once again, is how to get a value from the primary buffer. Assume v is a string variable, r is a row number in the buffer, and custid is the name of a string-type column:

```
v = dw_1.object.custid[r]
```

The "[r]" is nothing more than an array index. *dw_1.object.custid* is actually an array, with one element for every row in the primary buffer. Therefore, *dw_1.object.custid[r]* is the *r*th element in that array.

If you prefer to use the column number — let's say it's stored in the integer variable c — instead of the name, then do this:

```
v = dw_1.object.data[r,c]
```

dw_1.object.data is a two-dimensional array, containing the value of every row and column in the primary buffer.

To retrieve a value from the filter or delete buffer, add an extra ".filter" or ".delete":

```
v = dw_1.object.custid.filter[r]
v = dw_1.object.data.filter[r,c]
v = dw_1.object.custid.delete[r]
v = dw_1.object.data.delete[r,c]
```

To fetch values from the original buffer, add ".original" to the syntax:

```
v = dw_1.object.custid.original[r]
v = dw_1.object.data.original[r,c]
v = dw_1.object.custid.filter.original[r]
v = dw_1.object.data.filter.original[r,c]
v = dw_1.object.custid.delete.original[r]
v = dw_1.object.data.delete.original[r,c]
```

So, for example, this,

```
v = dw_1.object.custid.filter.original[8]
```

means "set v equal to the custid field's original value from the eighth row of the Filter buffer." PowerBuilder fetches the value from the Original buffer (in which it is probably not the eighth row).

By moving the syntax to the left side of the "=," you can change any value in any buffer:

```
dw_1.object.custid[r] = v
dw_1.object.data[r,c] = v
dw_1.object.custid.filter[r] = v
dw_1.object.data.filter[r,c] = v
dw_1.object.custid.delete[r] = v
dw_1.object.data.delete[r,c] = v
dw_1.object.custid.original[r] = v
dw_1.object.data.original[r,c] = v
dw_1.object.custid.filter.original[r] = v
dw_1.object.data.filter.original[r,c] = v
dw_1.object.custid.delete.original[r] = v
dw_1.object.data.delete.original[r,c] = v
```

ITEM STATUS AND ROW STATUS

For every field in every row in every buffer (except the original buffer), PowerBuilder maintains a status flag. The status is one of two values:

- **notmodified!** — The field has never been modified. If it's a new row, the field has never been given a value. Otherwise, the field has the same value as when originally retrieved.

- **datamodified!** — The field has been modified.

PowerBuilder maintains a similar status flag for every row in the three buffers. The row status is one of four values:

- **notmodified!** — It is not a new row (that is, it was retrieved from the database), and it has not been modified (that is, all of its fields are still notmodified!).

- **datamodified!** — It is not a new row (that is, it was retrieved from the database), and it has been modified (that is, at least one of its fields is datamodified!).

- **new!** — It is a new row (that is, inserted, not retrieved), but nothing has been filled in yet (that is, all of its fields are still notmodified!).

- **newmodified!** — It is a new row (that is, inserted, not retrieved), and it has been at least partially filled in (that is, at least one of its fields is datamodified!).

The status flags play an essential role in constructing the INSERT, UPDATE, and DELETE commands that update the database. They also help your scripts determine what's been changed and what hasn't.

In the original buffer, rows and fields do not need status flags, because they never change. If they had status flags, they would always be not modified!

In the delete buffer, rows and fields do need status flags. Although they are marked for deletion, you are able to restore them to the primary buffer. In that case, PowerBuilder (and maybe your scripts) must know whether they have been modified.

MANIPULATING THE STATUS IN POWERSCRIPT

Two functions, GetItemStatus and SetItemStatus, read and change the status flags. This line tests whether column c in row r of the filter buffer has been modified:

```
IF dw_1.GetItemStatus(r,c,filter!) = datamodified! THEN...
```

This line changes the same item's status so that it appears to have been modified:

```
dw_1.SetItemStatus(r, c, filter!, datamodified!)
```

The same two functions work on row status as well as field status. For row status, specify zero as the column number:

```
IF dw_1.GetItemStatus(r, 0, filter!) = newmodified! THEN...
dw_1.SetItemStatus(r, 0, filter!, newmodified!)
```

You should use the SetItemStatus function with great caution, if at all, since it has a profound impact on the DataWindow's update processing.

The Life Cycle of the DataWindow Buffers

If you understand the role of each DataWindow buffer, the impact of common DataWindow operations on them is straightforward:

- **The Retrieve function** — empties the buffers; places all retrieved rows into the original buffer; places every row either into the primary buffer or into the filter buffer, depending on the filter in effect; sets the status of every row and column to notmodified!

- **The InsertRow function** — inserts a new row into the primary buffer; sets the row status to new! and every column status to notmodified!

- **The DeleteRow function** — does this: If the row is notmodified! or datamodified!, the function moves it from the primary buffer to the delete buffer; it has no effect on status flags. If the row is new! or newmodified!, it removes it from the primary buffer but does not place it into the delete buffer.

- **Changing a field value** — sets the field's status to datamodified!, changes the row's status to datamodified! if it was notmodified!, or to newmodified! if it was new!

- **The Update function** — issues a SQL DELETE command to the database for each row in the delete buffer; issues a SQL INSERT command for each newmodified! row in the primary and filter buffers; issues a SQL UPDATE command for each datamodified! row in the primary and filter buffers. In the UPDATE command, only datamodified! fields are included in the SET clause.

After executing the SQL commands, the Update function empties the delete buffer, resets all row and column statuses to notmodified! (except new! rows, which remain new!), and refreshes the original buffer with the current contents of the primary and filter buffers.

The Update function has an optional parameter to prevent the buffers and status flags from being reset. Another function, ResetUpdate, resets the buffers and status flags without issuing SQL commands. These features are useful if your application needs to exercise a finer level of control over the update process — for example, if you need to synchronize the simultaneous update of two DataWindows.

To save time, PowerBuilder's implementation of the original buffer is actually a little bit more sophisticated than I've described. The Retrieve function does not fill the original buffer with rows; it leaves it empty. PowerBuilder only copies rows into the original buffer as needed, as the user or the application begins to change them. Nevertheless, the way I've described the process above and depicted it in Figure 10-8 is a useful way to picture it, and it's accurate enough from our point of view as developers.

MANIPULATING THE BUFFERS IN POWERSCRIPT

I have already described many functions that manipulate the DataWindow buffers, such as InsertRow, DeleteRow, and GetItemStatus. Here are some others:

- **RowCount** — returns the number of rows in the primary buffer.
- **FilteredCount** — returns the number of rows in the filter buffer.
- **DeletedCount** — returns the number of rows in the delete buffer.
- **ModifiedCount** — returns the number of datamodified! and new-modified! rows in the primary and filter buffers.
- **RowsMove** — moves one or more rows from one buffer (primary, filter, or delete) to another, in the same DataWindow or in a different one.
- **RowsCopy** — works like RowsMove but copies the rows instead of moving them.
- **RowsDiscard** — removes one or more rows from a buffer (primary, filter, or delete) but, unlike DeleteRow, does not move them to the delete buffer.
- **Reset** — clears the DataWindow by emptying all buffers.

Row-Oriented Processing

Some processing cannot be done on a field-by-field basis but must occur when the user has completed work on an entire row. Consider, for example, a validation that relies on many fields: "If today is a Sunday, and the time is between 9 A.M. and 5 P.M., and the amount is greater than $10.00, and . . ." Relying on the ItemChanged event for every field is not practical. Such a validation should not be performed until the user has finished with all of the fields in the row. Otherwise the user will be bothered by fallacious error messages.

When is the user finished working on a row? This is true in a number of situations, such as these:

- Moving to a different row using the keyboard (for example, pressing the Page Up key) or the mouse (for example, clicking to another row in a grid)

- Moving to a different row by clicking a button that calls a function such as ScrollNextRow

- Inserting a row by clicking a button that calls the function InsertRow

- Saving changes to the database by clicking a button that calls the Update function

- Deleting the row by clicking a button that calls the function DeleteRow

- Throwing away the changes that have been made, for example, by closing the window or by retrieving new rows to overwrite the changed rows

The last two cases — delete and throwaway — probably don't require any row-oriented processing, especially if that processing involves validating the row. But the other cases certainly do.

Tables 10-4 and 10-5 list the events and functions that play special roles in row-oriented processing.

Table 10-4

Events for Row-Oriented Processing

Events	Arguments	RETURN Values
RowFocusChanged	currentrow	(none)
Clicked	row	RETURN 0: Proceed
	dwo	RETURN 1: Cancel
	xpos	
	ypos	
ScrollVertical	scrollpos	(none)

Table 10-5

Functions for Row-Oriented Processing

Functions
DeleteRow
GetBandAtPointer
GetRow
GroupCalc
InsertRow
ScrollToRow
SetRow

Row-oriented processing turns out to be the most difficult of the types of processing presented in this chapter. It's difficult because PowerBuilder does not provide an event that fires at quite the right time. At first glance, "RowFocusChanged" looks promising. But, as I will explain, it is not ideal.

ROW-ORIENTED PROCESSING: AN EXERCISE

The classic requirement for row-oriented processing is a validation: making sure that the user has filled in every required field in a new row.

In the order form (Figure 10-2), four fields are required: order date, customer ID, store ID, and pre-tax total. To make sure that the user fills in all of these in a new row, row-oriented PowerScript programming is required.

It might seem to you that required-field validation is such a common application feature that PowerBuilder should be able to handle it without programming. And I agree that it should. But unfortunately it doesn't. A couple of features come close:

1. The database server will reject an empty field if the column has the NOT NULL property in its table definition. (See Chapter 6.) An empty value in a NOT NULL column causes an error when the user clicks the Update button. However, since the user might enter many more rows before clicking Update, the error message is likely to be confusing. Ideally, an error should appear immediately after the user finishes with the row.

2. DataWindow fields have a "Required" property, which you set in the Edit tab of their property sheet. See, for example, Figures 9-11 and 9-29 in Chapter 9. Although this property purports to make the field required; in fact, it has a big loophole. It triggers an error only when focus passes through the empty field. Since plenty of ways exist to fill in a new row without ever giving focus to the required field, it's easy to circumvent this feature.

Given the problems with these nonprogramming approaches, the only remaining alternative is to test required fields using PowerScript.

THE RowFocusChanged EVENT

For field-oriented processing we relied on the ItemChanged event, which was perfect for most of our work. PowerBuilder fires this event when the user has finished changing a field, on the verge of departing from it. There ought to be a "RowChanged" event, a row-oriented equivalent to Item-Changed. Unfortunately, there isn't. There is a "RowFocusChanged" event. It turns out to be less than ideal for our needs, but unfortunately it is the best choice available.

RowFocusChanged fires when focus arrives at a new row. Since that usually happens immediately after focus departs from an old row, we can use RowFocusChanged for row-oriented processing with a little work.

The biggest problem with RowFocusChanged is that it fires *after* focus has changed to the new row. You need to validate the old row, the one the user has just departed from, not the new one. No functions or properties are available to a RowFocusChanged script to tell you which row you just departed from. But if you add enough program logic to other events, the RowFocusChanged script can figure it out.

Another problem with RowFocusChanged is that it doesn't fire in every situation in which row-oriented processing is needed. In particular, it doesn't fire when the user clicks the Update button. You can get around this problem, too, by adding program logic.

Table 10-4 offers two other events that might play a role in row-oriented processing: Clicked and ScrollVertical. I don't find them very useful, but I included them in Table 10-4 for your consideration.

The Clicked event fires when you depart from a row by clicking on a new row. Unfortunately, it doesn't fire when you depart by other means, such as a function key press.

ScrollVertical fires when departing from a row causes the DataWindow display to scroll. However, if the DataWindow displays multiple rows, you can move among the visible rows without ScrollVertical firing.

The only choice left is RowFocusChanged.

VALIDATING REQUIRED FIELDS IN A ROW

Let's put aside for a moment the issue of how to use RowFocusChanged, and let's look instead at how to write a script that validates a row — in particular, a script that makes sure that every required field has a value.

In the order form window, I placed the logic into a user-defined function named wf_rowprocessing. The function is shown in Listing 10-1. This function will be called from RowFocusChanged, and it returns True if the row is valid and False if it is not.

Listing 10-1
The wf_rowprocessing function, which validates a row.

```
DWItemStatus  l_rowstatus
Integer       li_col
Long          ll_row
String        ls_colname
IF il_rowmodified <= 0 THEN RETURN True   // no row to process
l_rowstatus = dw_1.GetItemStatus(il_rowmodified, 0, primary!)
IF l_rowstatus = newmodified! or l_rowstatus = datamodified! THEN
    ll_row = il_rowmodified
    li_col = 1
    dw_1.FindRequired(primary!, ll_row, li_col, ls_colname, True)
    IF ll_row = il_rowmodified THEN
```

```
        MessageBox("Error", "Field Requires a Value", stopsign!)
        dw_1.SetColumn(li_col)    // move to the empty column
        RETURN False              // failure
    END IF
END IF
il_rowmodified = 0
RETURN True                       // success
```

In the function, the instance variable *il_rowmodified* is the row number of the row that the user has just finished changing and that must be validated. Because RowFocusChanged fires after focus has moved to a different row, *il_rowmodified* is usually not the current row.

Other scripts, which I will show in a moment, place a nonzero value into *il_rowmodified* to indicate a modified row. If the variable is zero, it means that no row has been modified. This will happen if the user moves from row to row without making any changes. If so, the function does a quick return, because there's nothing to do.

The call to GetItemStatus function determines the status of the row. It will be either notmodified!, datamodified!, new!, or newmodified! The function stores the status in the variable *l_rowstatus*, which must be declared to be a special type, a "DWItemStatus variable," to hold these four special values. If the status is newmodified! or datamodified!, the row has been modified, and so the function proceeds to validate the row.

To identify whether a required column in the DataWindow is not filled in, use the convenient PowerScript function, FindRequired:

```
ll_row = il_rowmodified
li_col = 1
dw_1.FindRequired(primary!, ll_row, li_col, ls_colname, True)
```

The FindRequired function searches the primary buffer (since the first parameter is "primary!") for a column that is required and null. It begins the search with the row *ll_row* and the column *li_col,* which the script sets to *il_rowmodified* and 1 so that the modified row is searched. FindRequired tests every row in the buffer from that point on, even though we're interested only in this one row.

FindRequired uses the DataWindow columns' "Required" property, described earlier, to determine which columns are required. If the FindRequired function does find a null required column, it changes *ll_row* and *li_col* to that row and column number, and *ls_colname* to the column name. (The fifth parameter, *True*, specifies that only newmodified! or data-modified! rows should be tested, which speeds up the search.) If all fields are okay, FindRequired sets *ll_row* to zero.

So if FindRequired sets *ll_row* to *il_rowmodified*, a required value is missing in the row being tested. In that case, the wf_rowprocessing function calls MessageBox to display an error message and returns *False* to indicate failure. It also calls the SetColumn function to move focus to the missing field, for the convenience of the user. If everything is okay, the function returns *True*.

USING ROWFOCUSCHANGED TO VALIDATE A ROW

The RowFocusChanged event script will call the wf_rowprocessing function to validate the row the user has just modified and departed from. Unfortunately, the RowFocusChanged script has "forgotten" what row that was — it can tell you only what new row you have just arrived at. So some other event script, one that fires prior to RowFocusChanged, must "remember" that row for us. The ItemChanged script is the one, and it remembers by placing a row number (from its event argument, *row*, or from GetRow) into the instance variable *il_rowmodified*:

```
il_rowmodified = row
```

Anytime the user changes any field in any row, the ItemChanged script places the row number into *il_rowmodified*. By the time RowFocusChanged fires, if *il_rowmodified* is not zero, it indicates that a row has been modified.

Whenever no row has been modified, the variable *il_rowmodified* will be zero. The window initializes it to zero. The wf_rowprocessing function resets it to zero after validating a row, as you can see at the bottom of Listing 10-1.

Here is the RowFocusChanged script:

```
IF il_rowmodified > 0 THEN
    IF not wf_rowprocessing() THEN
        This.ScrollToRow(il_rowmodified)
        This.SetFocus()
    END IF
END IF
```

If there is a modified, unvalidated row, the script calls wf_rowprocessing to validate it. If that function returns False, indicating an invalid row, the ScrollToRow function returns focus to the row.

When you try this out, you will observe a "jittery" effect, but it can't be avoided. When you scroll from an old row to a new one, you will see the new row for an instant, then the error message. Then the old row reappears. It would be better if the old row remained in view throughout.

Other scripts, such as those calling the Update function, must call the wf_rowmodified function. If you want to see the completed work, take a look at the sample application for this chapter, in the book's CD-ROM.

Update-Oriented Processing

When a script calls the Update function, the DataWindow writes all the data changes to the database. In the order form, the Update button's clicked script calls the Update function. In other applications, other scripts might call it.

The process that calls Update might also have to do other processing to ensure data integrity. The classic example is updating a related table: Suppose that two tables in the database, Table A and Table B, share some sort of relationship. When the user updates Table A in the DataWindow, a script must make some change to Table B at the same time. Maybe Table B is an audit trail, whose rows describe every change made to Table A. Or maybe Table B contains summary data about Table A. In our video store example, "Table A" is the order table and "Table B" is the customer table. The customer table has a column, openbalance, which is the sum of all the unpaid order amounts.

Tables 10-6 and 10-7 list the events and functions that might play a role in update-oriented processing.

Table 10-6

Events for Update-Oriented Processing

Events	Arguments	RETURN Values
UpdateStart	(none)	RETURN 0: Proceed
		RETURN 1: Cancel
SQLPreview	request	(none)
	sqltype	
	sqlsyntax	
	buffer	
	row	
DBError	sqldbcode	RETURN 0: Display message
	sqlerrtext	RETURN 1: Don't display
	sqlsyntax	
	buffer	
	row	
UpdateEnd	rowsinserted	(none)
	rowsupdated	
	rowsdeleted	

Table 10-7

Functions for Update-Oriented Processing

Functions
GetNextModified
SetSQLSelect
Update

THE NEED FOR TRANSACTION CONTROL

A transaction, as I explained In Chapter 7, is a set of related database updates. By using commands such as COMMIT and UPDATE, you can make sure that either all or none of the updates in the transaction are committed to the database. Transaction control is an option, and in

PowerBuilder, the standard way to turn it on is with the AutoCommit property:

```
sqlca.AutoCommit = False    // turn on transaction control
```

Update-oriented processing in a DataWindow usually requires transaction control, since it often involves multiple tables or multiple rows in the same table. Since this is the case for the order entry form, its window open script sets AutoCommit to False.

As I explained in Chapter 7, AutoCommit is supported differently from one database server product to another, and some products don't support it at all. Setting AutoCommit to False works for SQL Anywhere, Sybase and Microsoft SQL Server, and various other products. For Oracle, it's not necessary to set AutoCommit because transaction processing always occurs. Please refer to Chapter 7 and to your database documentation to determine how to implement transaction processing for your environment.

Update-Oriented Processing: an Exercise

The order form performs two tasks as part of update-oriented processing:

1. **Updating the customer balance** — For each new, changed, or deleted order, locate the order's related customer table row, and add to or subtract from the openbalance column. The customer's open balance should always be the sum of all unpaid order amounts.

2. **Assigning order numbers** — A script, not the user, fills in the Order # field, which is the orders table's key. As each new order is INSERTed into the orders table, PowerScript programming must assign it the next available order number.

A couple of other features come into play in the "real" Video Store application, but I am ignoring them in this chapter for the sake of simplicity. For one thing, a column ispaid in the orders table indicates (with "Yes" or "No") whether the customer has paid the Order Amount. The real application should update the customer's openbalance only if ispaid = "No."

Transaction Control and Multirow Updates

If you allow the user to change many rows in the DataWindow, and you update them all with a single Update function call, transaction control is probably required, even if only one table is involved. Here's why:

At the conclusion of the update, PowerBuilder resets the status flag on each row and item. For example, it changes every datamodified! to notmodified! However, PowerBuilder resets the flags on all rows and items only after it has successfully updated all rows.

Without transaction control, you can fall into a trap. If updating the third row out of ten,

say, causes a database error, PowerBuilder stops the update process. The updates for the first two rows have been committed and cannot be rolled back, but PowerBuilder has not reset their status flags — and it never will. So the rows' status flags do not accurately reflect their status.

There are several ways to avoid this trap, but the most direct way is to use transaction control. At the conclusion of the multirow update, issue a COMMIT if all rows were successful (and PowerBuilder resets all status flags) or a ROLLBACK if any row was unsuccessful (and PowerBuilder does not reset any status flags).

Also, changing ispaid from "No" to "Yes," or vice versa, in an existing order should cause a change to openbalance. Another feature in the real system is the ispaidup column in the customer table. Any script that changes openbalance in a customer row should also change ispaidup. If the script sets the balance to zero or less, it should also set ispaidup to "Yes"; otherwise, it should set it to "No."

THE UPDATE CHAIN OF EVENTS: UPDATESTART, SQLPREVIEW, DBERROR, AND UPDATEEND

When a script, such as the clicked script on the Update button, calls the Update function, PowerBuilder goes through the process of generating and executing an SQL statement for every new, modified, or deleted row in the DataWindow buffers. In the course of doing this, PowerBuilder fires a sequence of events on the DataWindow, and you can write scripts for them to intercept and augment the process. These are the scripts that will carry out the update-oriented processing.

Is This a Job for Stored Procedures and Triggers?

In many applications, the two update-oriented features I've described — updating the customer table in response to changes to the orders table and assigning a unique key to every new row in orders — should be carried out by stored procedures and triggers. As I explained in Chapter 7, stored procedures and triggers are processing carried out by the database server, not by the client machine. They are written in the server's scripting language, not in PowerScript.

If you choose to use stored procedures and triggers, then this becomes a database exercise, not a PowerBuilder exercise. The techniques that I am about to describe in this chapter will not come into play. Nevertheless, in a complex application you will very likely need PowerBuilder programming techniques similar to these at some point, and they are important to understand.

Figure 10-9 illustrates the chain of events. When you call the Update function, PowerBuilder fires the UpdateStart event on the DataWindow, then a series of SQLPreview events — one for each SQL command issued — and then the UpdateEnd event. If an SQL command causes an error, the DataWindow's DBError event fires, and PowerBuilder bypasses the remaining SQL commands and SQLPreview events.

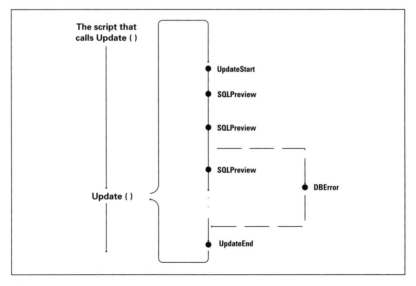

Figure 10-9
The Update chain of events.

The UpdateStart Event

The UpdateStart script is the main workhorse for update-oriented processing. It should

1. **Do row-oriented processing** — If you have a function that performs row-oriented processing, such as the wf_rowprocessing function I described earlier, the UpdateStart script must call it.

2. **Begin the transaction** — If you're doing an explicit BEGIN TRANSACTION statement, it belongs here.

3. **Issue SQL commands** — UpdateStart seems to be the best place for all SQL commands — UPDATE, INSERT, and DELETE — that you plan to do programmatically, before PowerBuilder does its DataWindow-generated SQL commands. In the order form exercise, this means the UPDATEs to the customer table.

4. **Do last-minute validation and preparation** — If any final validation or preparation of the DataWindow rows remains, it should be done now. In the order form exercise, the UpdateStart script assigns order numbers to new rows.

If anything goes wrong during UpdateStart, error-handling is a three-step process:

1. Issue a ROLLBACK, if you have executed any SQL commands.

2. Display an error message.

3. Return 1, which signals PowerBuilder to cancel the update and terminate the chain of events.

Technically, the program code in the UpdateStart script would work just as well if you moved it to the script that calls the Update function itself — in the order entry form, that would be the Update button's clicked script. If an error occurs, you simply bypass the Update call. The main argument against doing this is a question of style: Powersoft certainly invented the UpdateStart event for a reason, and therefore, you should use it to conform to the event-driven style of programming.

There are other issues, although they are small ones: Using UpdateStart avoids some duplicate code if you call the Update function from more than one place in the window. And if there is a newly entered field value, calling the Update function validates and posts it first, firing ItemChanged before UpdateStart. But if your update-processing code is in the script that calls the Update function, it should lead off by calling the AcceptText function to complete the processing of any newly entered field.

The SQLPreview Event

I have already explained how, during the update process, PowerBuilder constructs a series of INSERT, UPDATE, and DELETE SQL commands, one for each modified row. Just before executing each one of them, Power-Builder runs the SQLPreview script. Within the SQLPreview script you can read the event argument, *sqlsyntax*, to learn the SQL command about to be executed and use the function SetSqlPreview to substitute a different SQL command in its place.

You should not rely on the SQLPreview script to do validation checking, row modification, or additional SQL processing such as the customer table updates. All these tasks should be done in the UpdateStart script. The reasons are subtle: PowerBuilder has already converted the row values to an SQL command, so any change you make to the row at this point will be ignored. And I have experienced a problem under some circumstances, perhaps a bug, where executing embedded SQL within the SQLPreview script corrupts PowerBuilder's ability to convert further DataWindow rows to SQL.

If the SQLPreview script detects an error — even though, as I recommend, that should not be its purpose — it can flag an error to PowerBuilder by executing this statement (with appropriate arguments), which forces the DBError event to fire:

```
This EVENT DBError(sqlbdcode,sqlerrtext,sqlsyntax,buffer,row)
```

The DBError Event

When PowerBuilder calls the DBError script, it is signaling us that one of its SQL commands has failed and that it is about to display an error message. Although you could let PowerBuilder go about its business unobstructed, it's better to write a DBError script to force a different course of action, if transaction control is involved:

1. Set a flag (an instance variable) to notify the UpdateEnd script to do a ROLLBACK instead of a COMMIT.

2. Construct an error message, but don't display it yet.

3. Capture any other information necessary to recover from the error, such as the location (buffer and row number) of the row causing the problem.

Although DBError constructs the error message, it is important that it not display it. You must never display an error message (if it waits for the user to click OK, as most do) while a transaction is in progress, because portions of the database are locked to other users. You must defer the error message display until the UpdateEnd script, which will first execute the ROLLBACK command to end the transaction.

Alternatively, DBError could issue the ROLLBACK itself and then display the message. I prefer, however, to keep my COMMIT and ROLLBACK together in the same script. COMMIT must go in the UpdateEnd script, so I place ROLLBACK there as well.

The UpdateEnd Event

If there has been no error — that is, if DBError has not fired — then all that's left for the UpdateEnd script to do is to issue the COMMIT. If you like, it can also display a message to the user indicating successful completion and perform other tidying-up tasks.

If there has been an error, then a number of steps must be taken:

1. Execute the ROLLBACK command to undo the entire transaction and release the database locks.

2. Present whatever error message was built by the DBError script.

3. Set focus on the DataWindow row that caused the error to make it convenient for the user to inspect and correct it. If the row is in the filter or delete buffer, the script must call the RowsMove function to restore it to the primary buffer so the user can see it.

You should avoid doing any programmed SQL in the UpdateEnd script prior to the COMMIT. If something goes wrong, it's easy enough to do a ROLLBACK instead of a COMMIT, of course. But unfortunately,

PowerBuilder has already changed the status flags on all the fields and rows from DataModified! and NewModified! to NotModified!, and no function exists to undo that.

As was the case with UpdateStart, anything that you do in the UpdateEnd script could just as well be done in whatever script calls the Update function. But as a matter of style, it seems to me that if you choose UpdateStart for the preprocessing, it makes sense to choose UpdateEnd for the postprocessing.

THE UPDATESTART SCRIPT

Now that I've explained what PowerScript code goes where, let's take a look at the code itself. As always, the versions shown here are somewhat abridged, and you can find the completed scripts on the CD-ROM.

UpdateStart Initialization

The first task of the UpdateStart script is to perform the row-oriented processing. It's important to validate the current row before updating it:

```
IF il_rowmodified > 0 THEN
    IF not wf_rowprocessing() THEN
        RETURN 1
    END IF
END IF
```

For an explanation of the *il_rowmodified* variable and the wf_rowprocessing function, please refer to the previous section on row-oriented processing. The wf_rowprocessing function returns False if the row is invalid. In that case, returning 1 terminates the update process.

Another task that UpdateStart performs is to initialize some instance variables:

```
is_updateerror = ""     // no update error message yet
is_rowerror    = ""     // no update error message yet about a bad row
is_sqlcommand  = ""     // no failed SQL command yet
il_rowupdate   = 0      // no row # updated yet
ib_update      = True   // starting an update now, not retrieving
```

These variables will be set by DBError and other scripts for use in error handling.

Beginning the Transaction

PowerBuilder has no explicit BEGIN TRANSACTION command. If your database server supports AutoCommit, and if AutoCommit is False, PowerBuilder begins transactions as needed, as you issue other SQL commands. Therefore, the UpdateStart script needs no special code to begin the transaction.

You may be concerned that AutoCommit could have the wrong value, or that an incomplete transaction might remain open from another part of your application. Both problems are programming bugs and should be fixed, but you can also be cautious, toggling the value of AutoCommit, as explained in Chapter 7:

```
sqlca.AutoCommit = True    // COMMIT transaction, if there is one
sqlca.AutoCommit = False   // force a BEGIN TRANSACTION
```

Looping to Find Modified Rows

The process of updating the customer table, in response to changes the user has made to the order table, is somewhat trickier than it first appears to be. For one thing, you need a loop to locate and process every modified row in the DataWindow. Since the rows might be in three different buffers — delete, primary, and filter — a loop within a loop might make sense. It might look something like this:

```
FOR li_buffer = 1 TO 3  // 1=delete, 2=primary, 3=filter
   n = <the # of rows in the buffer>
   FOR i = 1 TO n
      <process the i-th row in the buffer>
   NEXT
NEXT
```

In the primary and filter buffers, we're interested only in modified rows. A DataWindow function, GetNextModified, speeds up the task of locating them:

```
ll_nextrow = This.GetNextModified(ll_firstrow, buf)
```

This function locates a row in a buffer that is modified — newmodified! or datamodified! It returns its row number, *ll_nextrow*, or zero if there is no such row. The first parameter, *ll_firstrow*, is the row number from which to begin searching: The first row of the buffer, if *ll_firstrow* is zero, or else the row following *ll_firstrow*. The second parameter, *buf*, is the buffer to search: primary! or filter! You could also specify delete!, but in the order entry form, we must process every row in the delete buffer, regardless of its status flag.

To utilize GetNextModified effectively, a single DO loop replaces the two nested FOR loops. It's shown in Listing 10-2.

Listing 10-2
The loop that identifies every modified row in every buffer

```
Integer  li_buffer            // buffer counter: 1=delete, 2=primary,
                              //                 3=filter
Long     ll_row               // row number
DWBuffer l_buf                // DataWindow buffer: delete!, primary!,
                              //                    filter!


li_buffer = 0                 // initialize the buffer counter
ll_row    = 0                 // initialize the row counter
DO WHILE True                 // open-ended loop
   IF ll_row = 0 THEN         // beginning a new buffer
      li_buffer ++            // count one more buffer processed
      CHOOSE CASE li_buffer   // determine the buffer
         CASE 1               // 1 = delete!
            l_buf  = delete!
         CASE 2               // 2 = primary!
            l_buf  = primary!
         CASE 3               // 3 = filter!
            l_buf  = filter!
         CASE 4               // 4 = All done with all buffers
            EXIT              // quit the DO-loop
      END CHOOSE
   END IF

   IF l_buf = delete! THEN          // if we're doing the delete! buffer
      IF ll_row >= This.DeletedCount() THEN  // we've done every row
         ll_row = 0                 // flag to begin the next buffer
         CONTINUE                   // begin the next loop
      END IF
      ll_row ++                     // do the next Deleted! row
   ELSE                             // if we're doing primary! or filter!
      ll_row = This.GetNextModified(ll_row, l_buf)
      IF ll_row <= 0 THEN CONTINUE  // no more rows in this buffer
   END IF

   <the code from Listing 10-3 goes here.>
   <the code from Listing 10-4 goes here.>
   <the code from Listing 10-5 goes here.>

LOOP
RETURN 0    // no error - let the update proceed
```

In Listing 10-2, the variable *li_buffer* counts buffers: 1 for delete, 2 for primary, 3 for filter. When *li_buffer* reaches 4, we're done. (Note the "EXIT" command following "CASE 4.") The variable *ll_row*, a long integer, counts rows. Whenever *ll_row* = 0, which it does initially and also when the last row in a buffer is reached, it indicates that *li_buffer* should be incremented and processing should begin on the next buffer.

The delete buffer is handled differently than the other two buffers. In the delete buffer, every row must be processed, so the script simply adds one to *ll_row* in each pass of the loop. When *ll_row* reaches the value returned by DeletedCount, the number of rows in that buffer, we're done with the buffer. For the primary and filter buffers, a call to GetNextModified gets *ll_row*, the next row number to process.

Determining the SQL Command: INSERT, UPDATE, or DELETE

Once you've found a modified row, the next step is to determine which SQL command PowerBuilder will generate for this row: INSERT, UPDATE, or DELETE. For a row in the delete buffer it's easy — it will always be a DELETE. In the primary or filter buffer, however, the choice depends on the row's status. A NewModified! row will be an INSERT, and a DataModified! row will be an UPDATE. Listing 10-3 shows this logic, which fits into Listing 10-2 above its closing "LOOP" line. The end result is the string variable *ls_sqlaction*, which is set to "INSERT," "UPDATE," or "DELETE."

Listing 10-3

Determining the SQL command

```
DWItemStatus l_rowstatus              // Row status: newmodified!, datamodified!
String       ls_sqlaction            // SQL command: INSERT, UPDATE, or DELETE

IF l_buf = delete! THEN               // if we're doing the delete! buffer
   ls_sqlaction = "DELETE"            // it must be a SQL DELETE command
ELSE                                  // if we're doing primary! or filter!
   l_rowstatus = This.GetItemStatus(ll_row,0,l_buf) //get row status
   CHOOSE CASE l_rowstatus            // what is the status?
      CASE newmodified!               // it's a new row
         ls_sqlaction = "INSERT"      // it must be a SQL INSERT
      CASE datamodified!              // it's a modified row
         ls_sqlaction = "UPDATE"      // it must be a SQL UPDATE
      CASE ELSE  // not INSERT/UPDATE (this should never happen)
         CONTINUE                     // skip this row
   END CHOOSE
END IF
```

Updating the Customer

At this point you've identified a modified order row, and you know how it has been modified. Now it's time to update the customer table. You need two values: custid, the column in the DataWindow that is the order's customer number; and ordertotal, the column that is the order dollar amount.

An SQL UPDATE command updates the customer row. For an INSERTed order, the UPDATE adds ordertotal to the customer's openbalance column. For a DELETEd order, it subtracts the original ordertotal. For an UPDATEd order, it adds the difference between the current and original ordertotal. All of this is carried out in Listing 10-4, which fits into Listing 10-2.

The processing for an updated order must be a little more sophisticated than Listing 10-4 shows. If the user changes the customer ID as well as the order total, the script must perform two UPDATEs: one to subtract from the original customer, and another to add to the new customer.

Listing 10-4

Updating the customer table

```
String      ls_custid      // customer ID
Decimal{2} ldec_amt        // order $ amount

CHOOSE CASE ls_sqlaction
   CASE "INSERT"
      CHOOSE CASE l_buf
         CASE primary!
            ls_custid = This.object.custid.primary[ll_row]
            ldec_amt  = This.object.ordertotal.primary[ll_row]
         CASE filter!
            ls_custid = This.object.custid.filter[ll_row]
            ldec_amt  = This.object.ordertotal.filter[ll_row]
      END CHOOSE
   CASE "DELETE"
      ls_custid = This.object.custid.original[ll_row]
      ldec_amt  = -This.object.ordertotal.original[ll_row]
   CASE "UPDATE"
      CHOOSE CASE l_buf
         CASE primary!
            ls_custid = This.object.custid.primary[ll_row]
            ldec_amt  = This.object.ordertotal.primary[ll_row]
         CASE filter!
            ls_custid = This.object.custid.filter[ll_row]
            ldec_amt  = This.object.ordertotal.filter[ll_row]
      END CHOOSE
      ldec_amt = ldec_amt - This.object.ordertotal.original[ll_row]
END CHOOSE
```

```
UPDATE customer
   SET openbalance = openbalance + :ldec_amt
   WHERE custid = :ls_custid;
```

Assigning Order Numbers

The order form automatically assigns a sequential order number to each new order row. Listing 10-5 shows how to do it. When inserted into the logic of Listings 10-2 and 10-3, identifying a new order is easy: It's any row for which *ls_sqlaction* = "INSERT."

The Video Store application maintains the highest-used order number in a table named "ordernumber," which has one row and one column. Use an UPDATE to add one to the column, whose name is highestorderno. Then use SELECT to fetch its new value. Place this value into the orderno field in the new order row in the DataWindow. Because the UPDATE and SELECT are part of a database transaction, no two users will be able to get the same order number.

Listing 10-5

Assigning the order number

```
Long ll_orderno     // new order #

IF ls_sqlaction = "INSERT" THEN
   UPDATE ordernumber
      SET highestorderno = highestorderno + 1;
   SELECT highestorderno
      INTO :ll_orderno
      FROM ordernumber;
   This.object.orderno.primary[ll_row] = ll_orderno
END IF
```

If you insert many new rows as part of a single transaction, issuing an UPDATE and SELECT on the ordernumber table for each one is needlessly slow. A more sophisticated approach is to scan the DataWindow first to count the number of new rows; do a single UPDATE to add that count to *highestordernumber*; do a single SELECT to fetch the result; and then loop through the DataWindow a second time to insert order numbers. The final version of the programming on the CD-ROM uses this approach.

Error Handling in the UpdateStart Script

I've omitted the error handling from the listings above, but of course it is essential. When the UpdateStart script detects an error, it must do a ROLL-BACK, display the error message, and return 1. Listing 10-6 shows the error handling that would follow the UPDATE in Listing 10-4.

Listing 10-6
Error handling

```
String ls_error        // error message
String ls_errortitle   // title for an error message

IF sqlca.SqlCode <> 0 THEN
    ls_errortitle = "SQL Error Updating the CUSTOMER table."
    ls_error =                                                &
        "Customer # "       + ls_custid + "."        +  &
        "~nSQL Code: "      + String(sqlca.SqlDbCode)  +  &
        "~nError Code: "    + String(sqlca.SqlDbCode)  +  &
        "~nError Message: " + sqlca.SqlErrText
    GOTO SQLErrorHandler
ELSEIF sqlca.SqlNRows = 0 THEN
    ls_errorTitle = "SQL Error Updating the CUSTOMER table."
    ls_error =                                                &
        "Customer # "       + ls_custid + "."        +  &
        "~nNo such customer # in the CUSTOMER table."
    GOTO SQLErrorHandler
END IF
```

The line, "GOTO SQLErrorHandler," jumps to a block at the end of the script that handles all SQL errors. It does a ROLLBACK first, displays the error message (always do the ROLLBACK before displaying the error message!), and then returns 1:

```
SqlErrorHandler:
ROLLBACK;                 // roll back all database changes
MessageBox(ls_errortitle, ls_error, stopsign!) // display error
RETURN 1                  // do not let the update proceed
```

The "RETURN 1" signals PowerBuilder to terminate the update process. If no error occurs, the last line of the UpdateStart script returns the code "0," telling PowerBuilder to proceed with the update:

```
RETURN 0  // let the update proceed
```

This is similar to how we signaled success and failure in the ItemChanged script.

THE SQLPREVIEW SCRIPT

The SQLPreview script doesn't have much to do in the order form. It captures the row number and the buffer of the row about to be updated. This information might be used by the DBError and UpdateEnd scripts, in case of an error. The event arguments, *row* and *buffer*, provide this information.

```
il_rowupdate = row
ibuf_update  = buffer
```

The two are declared as instance variables so that the DBError and UpdateEnd scripts can utilize them:

```
DWBuffer ibuf_update    // buffer being updated: e.g., primary!
Long     il_rowupdate   // row # being updated
```

THE DBERROR SCRIPT: HANDLING A DATABASE ERROR

When a PowerBuilder-generated SQL command causes an error, PowerBuilder runs the DBError script, shown in Listing 10-7. The most critical role of this script is to prevent PowerBuilder from displaying an error message before the UpdateEnd script has a chance to do a ROLLBACK. The RETURN 1 at the end of the script disables the PowerBuilder error message.

Listing 10-7
The DBError script

```
Long    ll_errorcode       // the error code
Long    ll_orderno         // order # being processed
String  ls_errormessage    // the error message

IF not ib_update THEN       // set true in UpdateStart
    RETURN 0 // go ahead and display the error message
END IF
ll_errorcode    = sqldbcode    // get event arguments
ls_errorMessage = sqlerrtext
is_updateerror  =                              &
    "A SQL Error has occurred."        +       &
    "~nError code: " + String(ll_errorcode) +  &
    "~nError Message: "                    + ls_errorMessage
is_sqlcommand   = sqlsyntax     // get SQL code from argument
is_rowerror     = ""
IF il_rowupdate > 0 THEN
    CHOOSE CASE ibuf_update
```

```
        CASE primary!
            ll_orderno = This.object.orderno.primary[il_rowupdate]
        CASE filter!
            ll_orderno = This.object.orderno.filter[il_rowupdate]
        CASE delete!
            ll_orderno = This.object.orderno.delete[il_rowupdate]
    END CHOOSE
    IF not IsNull(ll_orderno) THEN
        is_rowerror = "Error on order # " + String(ll_orderno)
    END IF
 END IF
RETURN 1  // disable the PowerBuilder error message
```

The SQLPreview script, which always runs just before the DBError script, identified the row number and the buffer where the error occurred; it stored that information in the instance variables *il_rowupdate* and *ibuf_update*. This is important information that will be passed on to the user in the error message.

The UpdateStart event script set the instance variable *ib_update* to True (RetrieveStart sets it to False). In the order form, I let PowerBuilder handle retrieve errors by returning 0 if *ib_update* is False.

The script places error information into several instance variables:

```
String is_sqlcommand    // SQL command causing the error
String is_updateerror   // update error message
String is_rowerror      // message describing row # with error
```

The UpdateEnd script will use these variables to display an error message to the user. The event arguments, *sqldbcode* and *sqlerrtext*, contain the error code number and message text received from the database server.

The script fetches the order number of the problem row and places it into an error message string. This will help the user determine which row caused the problem.

THE UPDATEEND SCRIPT: COMMIT OR ROLLBACK

By the time PowerBuilder runs the UpdateEnd script, either all the database commands have worked, in which case we should conclude with a COMMIT, or one has failed, in which case ROLLBACK is required. Listing 10-8 shows the UpdateEnd script.

Notice, once again, how the MessageBox must follow the ROLLBACK. The ROLLBACK undoes all SQL commands in the transaction —

not just the order table changes made by the DataWindow, but also the updates to the CUSTOMER and ORDERNUMBER tables made by the UpdateStart script.

Listing 10-8
The UpdateEnd script

```
IF is_updateerror = "" THEN   // there was no update error
    COMMIT;
    RETURN
END IF

ROLLBACK;

MessageBox("An Error Occurred During Database Update",          &
           is_rowerror + "~n" + is_updateerror              + &
           "~n~nBecause of the error,"                      + &
           " all database processing has been ROLLBACK-ed.",  &
           stopsign!)
IF is_sqlcommand <> "" THEN    // we captured the failed SQL command
    MessageBox("The SQL Command That Failed:",               &
               is_sqlcommand, stopsign!)
END IF
```

The variable *is_updateerror* identifies whether or not there has been an error. UpdateStart set it to an empty string. The DBError script, if it has run, has changed it to an error message. This variable and others set by DBError form the contents of the MessageBox messages.

UpdateEnd should do one more housekeeping task if an error has occurred. It should set focus on the row that caused the problem. If the row is in the primary buffer, this is easy to do with the SetFocus and ScrollToRow functions. If the row is in the filter or delete buffer, you must call the RowsMove function to restore it to the primary buffer. Otherwise, how can the user fix the problem?

Listing 10-9
Displaying the bad row in the UpdateEnd script

```
Long ll_targetrow                          // row # in primary! buffer
This.SetFocus()                            // give the DataWindow focus
IF il_rowupdate > 0 THEN                   // a bad row has been identified
    IF ibuf_update = filter! or ibuf_update = delete! THEN
        ll_targetrow = This.RowCount() + 1   // append row to buffer
        This.RowsMove(il_rowupdate, il_rowupdate, ibuf_update,  &
                      This, ll_targetrow, primary!)
```

```
        This.ScrollToRow(ll_targetrow)      // show the row to the user
    ELSE                                    // bad row is in primary!
        This.ScrollToRow(il_rowupdate)      // show the row to the user
    END IF
END IF
```

Other Data Entry Techniques

Although I consider field-oriented processing, row-oriented processing, and update-oriented processing to be critical data entry techniques, they are not the only data entry issues you will ever face. Here are some other issues that arise frequently.

DOING AWAY WITH THE RETRIEVE AND UPDATE BUTTONS

The presence of Retrieve and Update buttons on a data entry form (such as Figure 10-1) is confusing to many users. When should they click Retrieve? When should they click Update? These questions are easy to answer using database jargon but not always so easy to explain in user-friendly terms. It may be a good idea to remove these buttons from the window and have event scripts do the retrieves and updates automatically.

AUTOMATIC UPDATES

If you remove the Update button, then you should consider calling the update function at some or all of these times:

- Just before the window closes
- Just after the user finishes inserting or changing a row
- Just after the user deletes a row
- Just before retrieving new rows to replace the existing rows

If the DataWindow displays relatively few rows, you may not need to worry about updating after each insert, change, or deletion of a row.

Let's assume that we put the call to Update, and other related processing, into a window function named wf_update (as shown in Listing

10-10), to make it easier to call from multiple points in the window's scripts. The function returns True or False to indicate success or failure.

Listing 10-10
The wf_update function

```
IF dw_1.AcceptText() <> 1 THEN    // attempt to accept the field
   dw_1.SetFocus()
   RETURN False             // field was rejected; do not proceed
END IF
IF dw_1.ModifiedCount() <= 0 and dw_1.DeletedCount() <= 0 THEN
   RETURN True              // nothing to update
END IF
IF dw_1.Update() <> 1 THEN
   MessageBox("Error", "The Update Failed", stopsign!)
   RETURN False             // error return
END IF
RETURN True                 // successful return
```

The AcceptText function is necessary because it completes the processing of the most recently changed field, if necessary. That is, AcceptText validates the value in the edit control, calls ItemChanged, and copies the value into the field in the DataWindow buffer. If you don't call AcceptText, then the ModifiedCount function might return zero, and the Update function might not be called.

The test for ModifiedCount and DeletedCount make sure that there are, in fact, some rows to update. There's no point in calling Update otherwise. You may be able to do without this test, since calling Update when there's nothing to do is usually harmless.

To do an update just before the window closes, write this script for the window's CloseQuery event:

```
IF not wf_update() THEN    // update the database
   RETURN 1                // don't close the window
END IF
```

The CloseQuery script runs just before the window closes. It runs even in such scenarios as attempts to shut down the application or shut down Windows. This script makes sure that all changes are posted to the database first. By issuing RETURN 1 in the script, you can prevent the window from closing, which is not possible in the Close script, which also runs when the window closes.

To do an update just after the user finishes inserting or modifying a row might be tricky. What event fires at this point in time? Fortunately, I beat this subject to death earlier, in the section on row-oriented processing. The major event to use is RowFocusChanged, but it's even better to have a function, as I have described, named wf_rowprocessing, which RowFocusChanged and other events can call. The wf_rowprocessing function, if it concludes successfully, can then call the wf_update function to update the database.

To do an update just after the user deletes a row is simple, since that programming is on the Delete Row button. After successfully deleting the row, call wf_update:

```
IF dw_1.DeleteRow(0) <> 1 THEN
    MessageBox("Error", "Unable to Delete This Row", stopsign!)
    dw_1.SetFocus()
    RETURN
END IF
dw_1.SetFocus()
wf_update()
```

To provide a means to do an update just before retrieving new rows, I will in a moment propose writing a wf_retrieve function, to be called by any script that must perform a retrieve. This function should call wf_update as one of its first tasks:

```
IF not wf_Update() THEN    // do an update
    RETURN False           // the update failed - don't retrieve
END IF
dw_1.Retrieve()
  ... etc...
```

AUTOMATIC RETRIEVES

It would be easy to say that you can get rid of the Retrieve button by simply calling the Retrieve function from the window's open script. In fact, the order form window already does that. But in practical terms, there's more to consider.

The order form's DataWindow is based on a SELECT statement that retrieves all rows from the order table:

```
SELECT orderno, orderdate, ordertime, custid, storeid,
    lineitemtotal, salestaxrate, salestax, ordertotal, ispaid
    FROM orders
```

Selecting all the rows into a DataWindow works fine if you're writing a book and if your orders table has only fifty rows in it. But in real life, where tables are likely to be very much larger, it is not a good idea to fetch an entire table into a DataWindow. It would take forever, and the client workstation would probably run out of RAM (or out of disk space, if you've turned on the DataWindow's "Retrieve Rows to Disk" feature).

More likely, you will want to retrieve no more than a few rows at a time into the DataWindow. Here's a common approach: Upon opening the window, the user sees a new, blank order but cannot scroll to other orders. In other words, the DataWindow is empty, except for a single new! row. On the window are the following buttons, as shown in Figure 10-10:

- **New Order** — Finish the current order and start a new order. (This replaces the Insert Row and Append Row buttons on the order form in Figure 10-1.)

- **Find Orders** — Finish the current order and retrieve other orders for update. (This replaces the Retrieve button on the order form in Figure 10-1.)

- **Delete Order** — Delete the current order. (This is no different than the Delete Row button that we've had all along.)

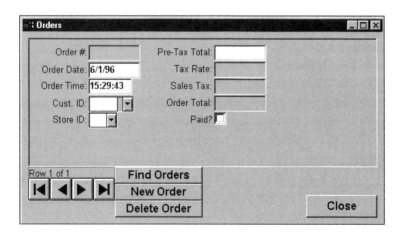

Figure 10-10
The order entry form, initialized with an empty order.

With these buttons, rarely do more than a few rows appear in the DataWindow at any given time. Either one new row is being added (after you click the New Order button), or a few existing rows are being viewed and modified (after you click the Find Orders button).

When the user clicks Find Orders, a dialog box pops up, prompting for selection criteria. The simple dialog box in Figure 10-11 asks only for an order date. I'll show more sophisticated versions in Chapter 14. When the user types in a date and clicks OK, the Find Orders script adds a WHERE clause to the DataWindow's SELECT statement. For example:

```
SELECT orderno, orderdate, ordertime, custid, storeid,
    lineitemtotal, salestaxrate, salestax, ordertotal, ispaid
    FROM orders
    WHERE orderdate = '1996-01-01'
```

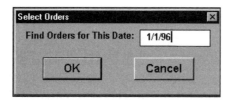

Figure 10-11

Specifying a new date for the SELECT statement.

To implement all of this, we will benefit from the wf_retrieve function shown in Listing 10-11, which initializes the DataWindow. When you call wf_retrieve, you pass it a single parameter, *ab_new*. If *ab_new* = False, the function calls Retrieve to fetch rows into the DataWindow. If *ab_new* = True, the function inserts a new empty row into the DataWindow. The function itself returns True or False to indicate success or failure.

Listing 10-11

The wf_retrieve function

```
IF not wf_Update() THEN      // do an update
    RETURN False             // the update failed - don't retrieve
END IF
dw_1.Reset()                 // empty the DataWindow
IF not ab_new THEN           // Retrieve, don't insert
```

```
    dw_1.Retrieve()              // retrieve rows from database
ELSE                             // don't retrieve
    dw_1.InsertRow(0)            // insert a new empty row
END IF
dw_1.ScrollToRow(1)              // show the first retrieved row
dw_1.SetFocus()                  // give focus to the DataWindow
RETURN True                      // successful return
```

The wf_retrieve function first calls wf_update, which was described
earlier (Listing 10-10). The wf_retrieve function is about to erase and
replace any rows already in the DataWindow, so it should first update the
database with any changed rows. After that, the call to Reset makes sure
that no rows remain from earlier work. Then, depending on the parameter
ab_new, the function calls either Retrieve or InsertRow.

When the user clicks the New Order button, this script executes:

```
wf_retrieve(True)    // insert a new empty row into the DataWindow
```

The script on the Find Orders button is more complex:

```
String ls_sql                    // the new SELECT statement
String ls_where                  // WHERE clause

Open(w_selectdate)               // display the dialog box
ls_where = " WHERE orders.orderdate = '"                  &
           + String(id_returndate,"yyyy-mm-dd") + "'"
ls_sql = is_origsql + ls_where  // build the new SELECT statement
dw_1.SetSqlSelect(ls_sql)        // assign it to the DataWindow
wf_retrieve(False)               // retrieve the rows
```

The script opens the window named w_selectdate, which is the dialog box shown in Figure 10-11. After the user types in a date and clicks
OK, the dialog box places the date into the instance variable *id_return-
date*. Chapter 14 will describe how a dialog box passes information like
this back to its parent. The script constructs a WHERE clause using this
date and appends it to the DataWindow's original SELECT statement,
which is in the instance variable *is_origsql*. The SetSqlSelect function
changes the DataWindow's SELECT statement to be the new one, and the
wf_retrieve function is shown in Listing 10-11.

The window's open script sets *is_origsql*, the DataWindow's original SELECT statement, by calling the GetSqlSelect function. It also performs the same task as the "New Order" button so that the user sees a new empty order initially:

```
is_origsql = dw_1.GetSqlSelect()
wf_retrieve(True)   // insert a new empty row into the DataWindow
```

CONTROLLING THE RETRIEVE PROCESS

Earlier I described the chain of events that occur when you call the DataWindow's Update function, shown in Figure 10-9. Calling the Retrieve function calls a similar chain of events, which is shown in Figure 10-12.

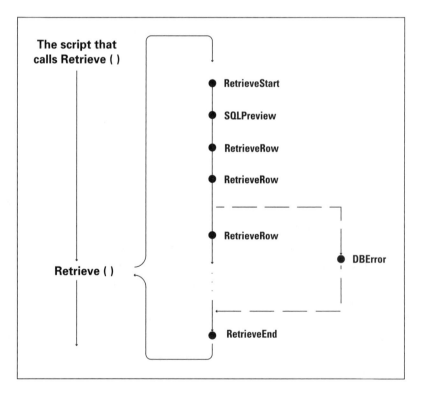

Figure 10-12
The "Retrieve" chain of events.

When you call the Retrieve function, PowerBuilder first fires the RetrieveStart event on the DataWindow. Then it fires a single SQLPreview event, just before executing the DataWindow's SELECT command. The SELECT command opens a cursor, and PowerBuilder uses a series of FETCH commands to read rows into the DataWindow one at a time. The RetrieveRow event fires after each FETCH. If anything goes wrong, PowerBuilder fires DBError and cancels the remaining FETCHes. At the conclusion of the process, PowerBuilder fires RetrieveEnd, which closes the cursor.

Tables 10-8 and 10-9 list the events and functions that play special roles in retrieve processing. We have already seen all of the functions in earlier examples in this chapter.

Table 10-8

Events for the Retrieve Process

Events	Arguments	RETURN Values
RetrieveStart	(none)	RETURN 0: Proceed
		RETURN 1: Cancel
		RETURN 2: Proceed without clearing buffers first
SQLPreview	request	(none)
	sqltype	
	sqlsyntax	
	buffer	
	row	
DBError	sqldbcode	RETURN 0: Display message
	sqlerrtext	RETURN 1: Don't display
	sqlsyntax	
	buffer	
	row	
RetrieveRow	row	RETURN 0: Proceed
		RETURN 1: Stop
RetrieveEnd	rowcount	(none)

Table 10-9

Functions for the Retrieve Process

Functions
GetSQLSelect
Retrieve
SetSQLSelect

One practical use for these events is to guard against a SELECT statement that retrieves too many rows into the DataWindow. Using the RetrieveRow script in Listing 10-12, you can display a dialog box, as shown in Figure 10-13, at program-defined intervals.

Listing 10-12

The RetrieveRow event script

```
Integer li_yesno              // 1=Yes, 2=No
il_stopretrieve --            // one less row to retrieve before stopping
IF il_stopretrieve <= 0 THEN    // we've reached the limit
   li_yesno = MessageBox ("Too Many Rows?",              &
                "You have now fetched "          + &
                String(This.RowCount())          + &
                " rows into the DataWindow."     + &
                "~n~nDo you want to keep going?",    &
                question!, yesno!, 1)
   IF li_yesno <> 1 THEN      // the user said "No"
      Return 1                // stop the retrieval
   END IF
   il_stopretrieve = 12       // reset counter - stop again later
END IF
```

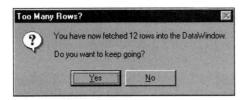

Figure 10-13

Asking the user whether to stop retrieving.

The RetrieveRow script relies on a row counter, the instance variable *il_stopretrieve*, which the RetrieveStart script initializes to count down from 12:

```
il_stopretrieve = 12  // prepare to stop retrieving after 12 rows
```

There are a couple of potential problems with using RetrieveRow that you should keep in mind. One is that it might slow down the overall Retrieve process considerably. Another is that in many cases the FETCH commands place locks on the database, so pausing for user input in the middle of the process, as Listing 10-12 does, could harm multiuser concurrency.

More DataWindow Functions

Well over one hundred PowerScript functions are available for the DataWindow control. Although I have described many in this chapter, many remain that I have not yet mentioned. The next chapter will describe functions relating to printing DataWindows. Here is a sampling of some of the others to give you an idea of the capabilities that you have available:

DESCRIBE AND MODIFY

Describe and Modify are extremely powerful functions that give you complete runtime control over the design of the DataWindow object. The Describe function can return the value of virtually any property of any part of the DataWindow, and the Modify function can modify it. They are quite complex to use, but taken to their limit they can completely transform the DataWindow design at runtime and construct, for example, ad hoc report layouts on the fly.

SELECTING TEXT

These functions operate on the text contained in the DataWindow's edit control, or on a selected portion of that text. "Selected text," in this context, means the marked (or "highlighted") portion of the text — what you get when you click and drag the mouse across part of a text string in Windows.

- **Clear** — Delete the selected text.

- **ReplaceText** — Replace the selected text with new text.

- **SelectedLength** — Return the number of selected characters.

- **SelectedStart** — Return the position of the first selected character within the text.

- **SelectedText** — Return the contents of the selected text.

- **SelectText** — Select a portion of the edit control text.

- **Cut** — Cut the selected text to the Windows clipboard.

- **Copy** — Copy the selected text to the Windows clipboard.

- **Paste** — Paste text from the Windows clipboard into the edit control.

WORKING WITH A MULTILINE TEXT FIELD

By making a string-type field tall enough in a DataWindow, you can enter and display multiple lines of text in it. These functions operate on a multi-line field.

- **LineCount** — Return the number of lines.

- **SelectedLine** — Return the line number containing the cursor.

- **TextLine** — Return the text of the line containing the cursor.

SELECTING ROWS

The SelectedRow function allows you to select (that is, mark or highlight) entire rows in much the same way that you can select fragments of text. This makes it easy to implement features that work with groups of rows. Figure 10-14 shows the grid-style DataWindow, with its odd-numbered rows selected.

Order No.	Order Date	Order Time	Cust. ID	Store ID	Pre-Tax Total	Tax Rate	Sales Tax	Order Total	Paid?
101	12/28/95	06:30:00	1424	B	$6.50	8.20%	$0.53	$7.03	☐
102	12/28/95	09:00:00	1040	A	$28.00	8.25%	$2.31	$30.31	☐
103	12/28/95	12:00:00	5001	A	$11.75	8.25%	$0.97	$12.72	☐
104	12/28/95	07:30:00	5002	A	$6.75	8.25%	$0.56	$7.31	☐
105	12/28/95	02:00:00	5957	A	$2.00	8.25%	$0.17	$2.17	☐
106	12/29/95	09:00:00	1200	B	$5.75	8.20%	$0.47	$6.22	☐

Figure 10-14
Selecting all the odd-numbered rows.

- **SelectRow** — Select or deselect a row.

- **IsSelected** — Test whether or not a row is selected.

- **GetSelectedRow** — Find the next selected row.

Example 1

This script selects all the order rows for customer 5002 and deselects all others:

```
Boolean b                              // True=select row, False=deselect
    row
Long    i                              // row counter
Long    n                              // # of rows in the DataWindow
String  ls_custid                      // customer #
n = dw_1.RowCount()                    // how many rows in the DataWindow?
FOR i = 1 TO n                         // do each row
    ls_custid = dw_1.object.custid[i]  // get the cust #
    b = (ls_custid = "5002")           // is it customer 5002?
    dw_1.SelectRow(i,b)                // select or deselect this row
NEXT
```


Example 2

This script deletes all selected rows — that is, all rows for customer 5002:

```
Long n                                 // row counter
n = 0                                  // start at the top of the d.w.
DO WHILE True                          // do each selected row
    n = dw_1.GetSelectedRow(n)         // find the next selected row
    IF n <= 0 THEN EXIT                // if n=0, no row was found - done!
    dw_1.DeleteRow(n)                  // delete the selected row
    n --                               // adjust counter for next search
LOOP
```

SEARCHING

These functions let you search for a row within the DataWindow. For example, you could use the Find function to search for the first row for customer 5002.

- **Find** — Find the first row in a group of rows that matches a condition.
- **FindGroupChange** — Find the first row in a new group. This applies to a DataWindow with groupings, which is described in Chapter 18.

SCROLLING AMONG ROWS

These functions let you scroll among the rows in a DataWindow and make a row the current row. I described most of these functions in Chapter 8.

- **GetRow** — Get the current row number.
- **RowCount** — Get the number of rows in the DataWindow.
- **SetRow** — Make a row the current row.
- **Scroll** — Scroll up or down some number of rows.
- **ScrollToRow** — Scroll to a particular row.
- **ScrollNextPage, ScrollNextRow, ScrollPriorPage, ScrollPriorRow** — Scroll in some direction.

MANAGING A VALUE LIST OR CODE TABLE

"Value Lists" and "Code Tables" are features found in several places in DataWindow design. One example is the list of stores — A, B, C, D — that appears in the dropdown list for the store field (Figure 10-15).

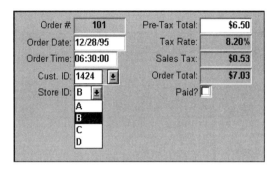

Figure 10-15
The dropdown list for the store field.

- **SetValue** — Add a value to the list or code table.
- **GetValue** — Get a value from the list or code table.
- **ClearValues** — Empty the list or code table.

Example

This script populates the dropdown list for the store ID field with the elements of an array named *ls_storeids*:

```
FOR li_store = 1 to li_nstores     // do each element in the array
   dw_1.SetValue("storeId", li_store, ls_storeids[li_store])
NEXT
```

If the values come directly from a table in the database, it's probably easier to use a DropDownDataWindow instead. (See Chapter 9.)

IMPORT AND EXPORT

These functions read (import) data into a DataWindow from an external file or write (export) data from a DataWindow to an external file. Various external file formats are supported, such as text files and dBASE files.

- **ImportFile** — Read data from a text or dBASE file.
- **ImportString** — Convert a text string into DataWindow rows.
- **SaveAs** — Export the DataWindow to a file. This function supports about a dozen different file formats.

Summary

This chapter has demonstrated several essential data entry programming techniques, with particular emphasis on these three:

- Field-oriented processing
- Row-oriented processing
- Update-oriented processing

Some of the programming was complicated. However, if you can master these techniques you are well on your way being able to solve any data entry problem.

Although this concludes the discussion of DataWindows for now, we will return to DataWindows many times in future chapters. Much of Chapter 13 shows how to apply object-oriented technology to DataWindows. Two bonus chapters on the CD-ROM are dedicated entirely to DataWindow topics: Chapter 18 ("Reports") and Chapter 19 ("More DataWindows").

III Object-Oriented Programming

11

The Object-Oriented Point of View

I first heard the term "object-oriented programming" ten or fifteen years ago. At the time, I didn't pay much attention to it. If you've been in the systems development business very long, you probably realize that this profession loves buzzwords, and that most of them sound impressive but are fairly meaningless. Like fads and fashions, the buzzwords come and go, and after they disappear our lives remain more or less unchanged. I assumed "object-oriented" was just one more meaningless buzzword.

About five years ago, I began to study object-oriented programming languages, and I discovered that I had been wrong. The trend toward object-oriented programming in recent years is a very significant one. An "object" is indeed a new milestone in the evolution of programming, unlike anything found in the languages preceding it. Object-oriented languages have become important in recent years because they are much better suited than traditional languages for developing the kind of complex, graphical systems popularized by the Apple Macintosh and Microsoft Windows.

PowerBuilder is object-oriented. If you understand objects, how they work, and the benefits they offer, your work with PowerBuilder will be much more rewarding. You are not required to understand objects — we have accomplished a lot in the earlier chapters in this book without giving any thought to them — but once you do learn objects, PowerBuilder becomes even more powerful and easy to use.

Before I adopted the object-oriented point-of-view, I could make my applications work, but too often I had to resort to the "brute force approach." It seemed that every new window and every new program posed a brand new challenge. Now that I have adopted the object-oriented point-of-view, however, application development is much easier — and a lot more fun! When I am confronted with a complex problem, I think, "What is the object-oriented way to approach this?" Usually, straightforward solutions present themselves using objects, and the solutions are unlike anything that would have occurred to me six or eight years ago.

If you have heard of object-oriented programming but PowerBuilder is your first direct exposure to it, be prepared for a treat! It is a very intriguing concept, and it will change your approach to programming.

In this chapter, I will provide a complete definition of object-oriented programming and of the terminology that goes along with it. I will start at the beginning and assume that these concepts are new to you. I will use PowerBuilder for examples, of course, but this chapter is more theoretical than practical and could apply to just about any object-oriented programming environment. The next two chapters will focus more on PowerBuilder itself and on how to use object-oriented techniques within PowerBuilder.

The Elements of Object-Oriented Programming

The precise definition of "object-oriented" depends on which book you read or expert you consult. (Unfortunately, sometimes the definition depends on what product a salesperson is trying to sell.) There is consensus, however, among the leading authorities on the major points. In this chapter, I will define a programming language (or a development environment, such as PowerBuilder) to be *object-oriented* if it has the following elements:

- **Encapsulation** — In the language, you have the ability to combine a set of variables and programming into a single unit, called an *object,* and to protect them from programming outside the object.

- **Messages** — Objects send messages to one another to do their work.

- **Object Classes and Instances** — At development time, you define classes of objects. At runtime, you can create any number of instances of any object class.

- **Object Class Hierarchy** — A relationship exists among an application's object classes. The classes form a hierarchy, with parent-child relationships among them.

- **User-Defined Classes** — The language gives you the ability to define new object classes. It might also provide an initial set of object classes.

- **Inheritance** — Any change you make to a parent class is inherited by its descendant subclasses.

- **Polymorphism** — Within an application, function names need not be unique. You can define functions with the same name for more than one object class.

- **Object Variables** — You can declare variables that represent object instances and use them in place of the object instance names in your programming.

- **Function Overloading** — You can define a function so that it can be called in more than one way, that is, with several alternative sets of arguments and return values.

PowerBuilder has every one of these features, and therefore it is object-oriented. In this chapter, I will define each of these terms in greater detail and then show how they play a role in PowerBuilder.

Let's start with the most basic question.

What Is an Object? (Encapsulation)

An *object* is a collection of variables and programming packaged together as a single, self-contained unit. This relationship is illustrated in Figure 11-1. The contents of the object are protected from the outside world. The programming inside the object can see and change the variables, but no programming outside the object can do so. The programming inside the object is similarly protected: Programming outside the object can execute the object's programming only under strictly limited conditions, which I will describe in the section about "Messages."

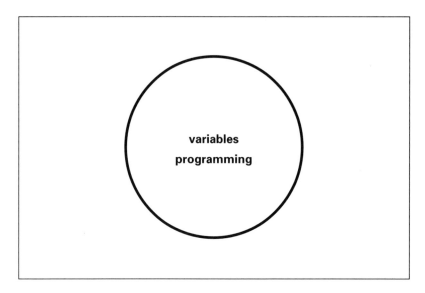

Figure 11-1
An object is an encapsulation of variables and programming.

This feature of an object — that it is a collection of variables and programming protected from the outside world — is called *encapsulation*.

Examples of Objects

In a PowerBuilder application, everything is an object. Let's consider a few examples: a window, a button, a DataWindow, and a transaction object.

A window is an object. It is an encapsulation of variables and programming. Figure 11-2 shows a PowerBuilder application with several overlapping windows. For each window, somewhere in the underlying application program is an object describing and controlling the window. The variables in the window object describe the window: its size, its position, the text in its title bar, whether it has maximize and minimize buttons, and much more. The programming in the window object can perform such tasks as maximizing, minimizing, moving, and resizing the window.

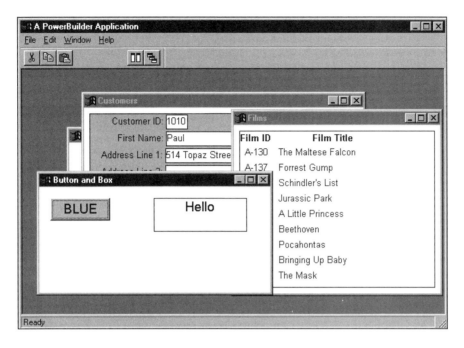

Figure 11-2

A PowerBuilder application with overlapping windows.

A button, such as the Blue button you can see in Figure 11-2, is an object. It is an encapsulation of variables and programming. The object's variables describe the button: its size and position, its text label, and so forth. Its programming performs such tasks as popping in and out when clicked. Its programming also includes the clicked script that you or I have written, telling the button what to do when clicked: It turns the text box blue — the text box is also an object, as is every control on a window.

A DataWindow is an object. Actually, there are two kinds of DataWindow objects, as I explained in Chapter 8: the object you create with the DataWindow Painter, which goes by the name "DataWindow Object," and the DataWindow Control, which is the control object on a window. Each of these two objects is an encapsulation of variables and programming, and they work together to provide the DataWindow functionality in an application.

A transaction object, such as PowerScript's *sqlca*, is an object. A transaction object is a special PowerScript variable that connects to a database and serves as the interface between your scripts and the database. Listing

11-1 is a script that was explained in detail back in Chapter 7. It uses a transaction object named *trans1*.

Listing 11-1

Using a transaction object

```
Transaction     trans1
trans1 = Create Transaction
trans1.DBMS      = "ODBC"
trans1.Database  = "Video Store DB"
trans1.UserId    = "dba"
trans1.DBParm    = "Connectstring='DSN=Video Store DB'"
CONNECT USING trans1;
UPDATE customer
    SET address1='123 Main Street'
    WHERE firstname='Gina' and lastname='Gray'
    USING trans1;
DISCONNECT USING trans1;
DESTROY trans1
```

In Chapter 7 I described the transaction object as if it were a fancy type of variable. That is not inaccurate, but it is more precise to say that it is an object. It is an encapsulation of variables and programming. The object's variables describe a database connection: the name of the database, the user ID, whether or not the connection has been made, and so forth. The object's programming can do such things as connect to the database and transmit UPDATE and other SQL statements to the database.

A transaction object is different from the other three examples in that it is a *nonvisual object*. The other examples — a window, a button, a DataWindow — are *visual objects*, because you see them on the screen. Nonvisual objects belong to the unseen application programming.

Although at first it might seem that there is a big difference between visual and nonvisual objects, from the object-oriented point of view there is no difference at all. All of these objects are nothing more than encapsulations of variables and programming.

THE BENEFITS OF ENCAPSULATION

As you will see, objects have many important features in addition to encapsulation. But even if encapsulation were their only distinctive feature, objects would still be a very important programming innovation.

In a traditional, nonobject-oriented, programming language, such as COBOL or BASIC, there are no objects. There are variables and programming, of course, but you do not encapsulate them together into objects.

If you have had formal training in a traditional programming language, you were certainly taught about modular programming: that you should divide your program into a collection of small program modules, as illustrated in Figure 11-3. Depending on the language, the modules might be called subroutines, subprograms, procedures, or functions. I will call them subroutines.

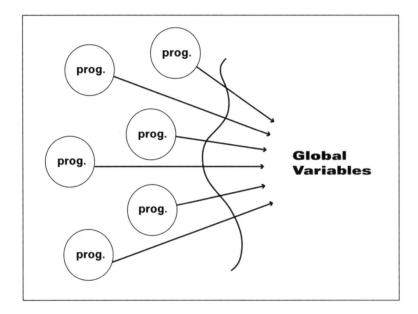

Figure 11-3

Program modules and the pool of global variables in a traditional programming language.

Modular programming is an important technique for making your application easy to develop and to modify. The premise of modular programming is this: If you test each subroutine in isolation from all the others, making sure that it produces the correct output values for all possible input values, then when you assemble the subroutines together into the total application, the application should be bug-free. Furthermore, you can modify the application simply by modifying one subroutine, or maybe a few subroutines. If the modified subroutines continue to work correctly when tested individually, the entire application will continue to work, with the modifications, when the new versions of the subroutines are plugged into it. So modular programming allows you to restrict and isolate the number of places you must modify, which simplifies the task of modifying the application.

Modular programming served us well during the COBOL and BASIC decades, but it's not good enough for the modern era. Why not? Because its premise falls apart in a graphical environment such as Windows and the Macintosh. Object-oriented programming succeeds where modular programming fails, which is why object-oriented programming has emerged as an important trend in recent years.

The problem with modular programming is that you "modularize" an application's programming into small, self-contained units. But there is no way to "modularize" the application's variables. In a nongraphical application, this is not a big problem, because the number of variables needed to control the application tends to be small. But in a graphical application, the number of variables is enormous — easily numbering in the tens of thousands — and so they become unmanageable.

The variables I am talking about are the "permanent variables" — those that need to survive for most if not all of the application's life span. In most programming languages, they are called global, common, public, or external variables. There are also temporary variables, whose life spans are transient. In PowerScript and in many other languages, temporary variables are called "local variables," and they don't play a role in this discussion, so you can ignore them for now.

In a traditional language, the permanent variables live together in a single, common pool, as shown in Figure 11-3. There is no order to them, and no access restrictions exist. Any program module is free to read or change any of them.

Consider a variable x that can take on two values: 1 or 2. You have tested the application completely, and it is bug-free for all cases where $x = 1$ and $x = 2$. Now let's suppose a new requirement arises that, under certain circumstances, $x = 3$.

The premise of modular programming suggests that you need only modify and test the one subroutine that sets the value of x. The old version sets $x = 1$ or $x = 2$, and the new version sets $x = 3$ as well. If you test the new subroutine in isolation from all the others, and it works perfectly, you should be able plug it into the application, and the application should work perfectly also, with the new three-valued x.

But, of course, that's not true. You must track down every subroutine that references x to make sure that it handles the value 3 correctly and does not crash. In a large application, that could be any number of subroutines, many of which someone else wrote and you don't know how to test. Things don't seem quite so modular anymore, do they?

In an object-oriented system, the problem is solved. Every permanent variable is encapsulated inside an object. The only programming that has access to the variable is the programming encapsulated in that object. To implement a new behavior for a variable, such as $x = 3$, you need only review the programming in that one object and test that one object. If the modified object works in isolation, it will work when you plug it into the application. The benefits of "modularity" are restored, because objects encapsulate programming and variables both.

As I have said, object-oriented programming has become important with the emergence of graphical interfaces. Graphical interfaces require tens of thousands of permanent variables to implement, and a programmer will require objects to manage that large number.

Where do I get this number, "tens of thousands?" Consider, in terms of Figure 11-2, the number of variables needed to describe just the one simple window entitled "Button and Box." If you try to enumerate every variable needed to describe this window, it's easy to count over a hundred. Among them are variables describing where the window is, how big it is, whether it has focus, and all the information necessary to redraw the window if it moves, or gets minimized, or whatever. The button and the text box in the window each have dozens of variables describing them. Then there are all the other windows and all their variables, and the menu and the toolbar. Then there are the DataWindows — they're *really* complex! I think you can see that the number of variables really adds up.

Let's say that you're responsible for writing the programming that moves that simple window across the screen. Hundreds of variables come into play as the window's position changes and the program redraws it in a new location. It's so much easier with object-oriented programming. The programming is all in the window object, and so are the variables. You don't have to deal with a single, giant pool of global variables as you would with a traditional language.

Luckily, you and I don't have to write the programming for moving windows across the screen. That programming is part of the operating system — Microsoft Windows or the Macintosh System — and you and I don't have to worry about it. The programming that you and I are called on to do in PowerBuilder, developing the functionality of our application, is (hopefully) much simpler. Even so, we too will benefit from object-oriented programming and encapsulation.

Messages

Figure 11-4 shows how an application looks to an object-oriented programmer. Everything is an object, and the contents of each object are isolated from the rest of the world.

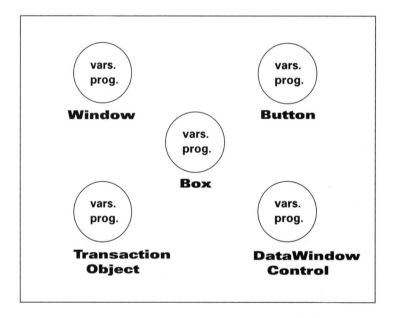

Figure 11-4

In an object-oriented system, everything is an object.

Now a big question arises: If all the programming and variables are hidden inside objects, how can anything ever happen? How can the Blue button turn the text box blue? The button and the text box are independent objects. The box's color is a variable encapsulated within the box object. The button's programming has no access to the box object's variables. How can the button change the value of the box object's color variable?

It can't. However, the button can send a message to the box, asking the box to change its color to blue. Objects work with one another by sending messages (Figure 11-5).

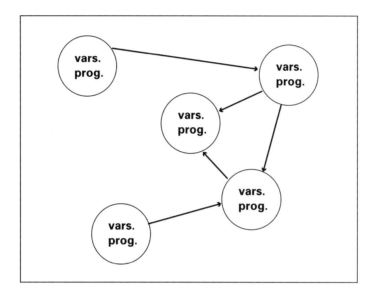

Figure 11-5
Objects send messages to other objects.

A message is a subroutine call directed at an object. In PowerBuilder, as in SmallTalk and C++, the subroutines are called *methods*, and every object has a predefined set of methods that you can call to send messages to the object. The syntax for calling a method — for sending a message — depends on the language. In C++ and in PowerBuilder, there is the dot notation:

```
object.method (parameters)
```

We have seen this syntax many times in previous chapters. In Chapter 3, for example, this script line appeared, which moved a text box named st_firstbox to a new position:

```
st_firstbox.Move(i,j+li_how_far)
```

Now that you have an object-oriented point of view, you can see that this script line is sending a message (Move) from one object (a button) to another object (st_firstbox): "Hey, st_firstbox! I'm sending you a message! Please move to these new coordinates!"

One of the terrific things about this messaging system is that the programmer who writes the "Move" instruction does not need to know how to do the move — only how to send the message. It's up to st_firstbox to carry out the instruction. The moving itself is the responsibility of st_firstbox, and of the programmer who designed the type of object known as a "StaticText control" (since st_firstbox is a StaticText control object). That programmer is somebody at Powersoft Corporation. The "Move" programming is encapsulated within st_firstbox and is probably quite complex, and so it's better to have it on the box and not on the button. As you become more comfortable with the object-oriented point of view, you will find yourself putting more of your complex programming on objects other than buttons, making them "smart objects," and putting less of your programming on buttons.

FUNCTIONS, EVENTS, AND PROPERTIES

PowerBuilder offers a little more variation to message sending. In PowerBuilder, there are three types of messages, as illustrated in Figure 11-6:

- Functions and Events, which are collectively called "methods"
- Properties

I described functions, events, and properties in detail back in Chapter 3. The next step is to redefine them from an object-oriented perspective. So far in this book, I have described only the functions, events, and properties that are built into PowerBuilder. But you can define new functions, events, and properties as well, and we'll begin doing that beginning next chapter.

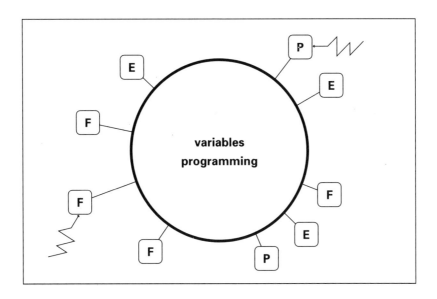

Figure 11-6

In PowerBuilder, every object has a set of functions, events, and properties for receiving messages.

FUNCTIONS

A *function* is a unit of program code that you call using dot notation. For example:

```
st_firstbox.Move(li_x,li_y+ai_howFar)
```

In this example, Move is the function and st_firstbox is the object. PowerBuilder also has functions that are not directed to an object, such as MessageBox:

```
MessageBox("Hello", "How are you?")
```

You can consider functions such as MessageBox as being outside the scope of object-orientation. Or, if you prefer to fit everything into the object-oriented point-of-view, you can think of these function calls as sending messages to PowerBuilder itself, even though you can't actually write it like this:

```
PowerBuilder.MessageBox("Hello", "How are you?")
```

"Hey, PowerBuilder! I'm sending you a message! Please display a dialog box!"

For the transaction object, you do not use the object.function syntax. Instead, you use standard SQL syntax:

```
UPDATE customer
    SET address1='123 Main Street'
    WHERE firstname='Gina' and lastname='Gray'
    USING trans1;
```

This statement sends a message to the transaction object trans1: "Hey, trans1! I'm sending you a message! Do an UPDATE!" If you were to use standard object syntax for this (which you can't), it would probably be something like

```
trans1.Update("customer SET address1=...")
```

EVENTS

Most objects have a set of *events*, which PowerBuilder can use to notify an object when something has occurred. A button object, for example, has an event called "clicked," which occurs when the user clicks the button with the mouse.

Events, like functions and properties, are types of messages. They are the technique by which PowerBuilder sends a message to one of our objects, as shown in Figure 11-7. PowerBuilder is itself a giant object, and like any object, it communicates with other objects by sending messages. "Hey, button! I'm sending you a message! You just got clicked!"

One other thing about events, which sets them apart from the functions and properties that we have seen so far, is that you get to write the programming for them. Much of your PowerScript code is in "event scripts," the programming that responds to an event. With the built-in functions and properties, you do not get to write the programming — it was written by someone at Powersoft Corporation, and you cannot see or change it but only execute it. (You can define your own functions and properties for an object, adding to the prebuilt list provided by Powersoft. I'll cover that topic later.)

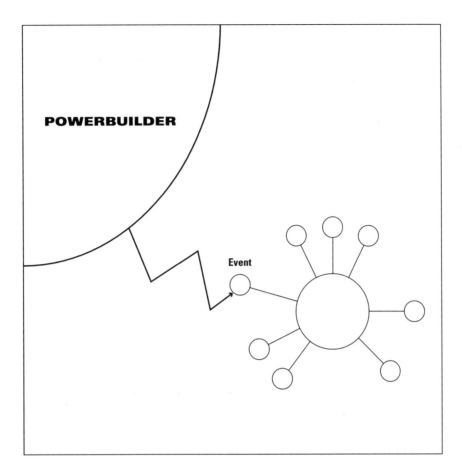

POWERBUILDER

Event

Figure 11-7

An event — PowerBuilder sending a message to an object.

I have said an event is PowerBuilder sending a message to an object. It might be more accurate to say that some events originate from PowerBuilder, but that others come directly from the operating system, such as Windows, with little or no PowerBuilder intervention. The ItemChanged event on a DataWindow control comes from PowerBuilder. But the clicked event on a button could come directly from the operating system. In general, it shouldn't matter where the event comes from, so I will tend to describe such events as originating from PowerBuilder.

FUNCTIONS = EVENTS

Although I have been emphasizing the differences between functions and events, in fact they are more alike than they are different. From an object-oriented point of view, both are *methods* — programming attached to an object that other objects can call.

Figure 11-7 shows PowerBuilder calling an event. Your own scripts, however, can call an event using an extension of the dot notation syntax used to call a function:

```
object.EVENT eventname (parameters)
```

This script, for example, fires the clicked event on the Blue button, which is the object named cb_bluebutton:

```
cb_first.EVENT clicked ()
```

When this statement executes, the button's clicked script will run, even though the user has not clicked the button.

THE EXTENDED SYNTAX FOR CALLING FUNCTIONS AND EVENTS

Adding the word EVENT to the dot syntax is just one example of an extended syntax available for calling functions or events. Here is the complete syntax:

```
object.[FUNCTION|EVENT] [STATIC|DYNAMIC] [TRIGGER|POST] method(...)
```

Between the *object* and the *method*, you can insert up to three key words, each of which is optional:

- **FUNCTION** or **EVENT,** which identifies whether the method is a function or an event of the object.

- **STATIC** or **DYNAMIC**, which specifies whether the method's existence is confirmed at compile time or at runtime. See the section on "DYNAMIC Method Calls" later in this chapter.

- **TRIGGER** or **POST**, which determines whether the method call should happen immediately (TRIGGER), or whether it should be deferred until all other pending events in the operating system's event queue have been processed (POST).

The defaults are FUNCTION, STATIC, and TRIGGER. Therefore, this way of calling the Move function:

```
st_firstbox.FUNCTION STATIC TRIGGER Move(li_x,li_y+ai_howFar)
```

is exactly the same as this familiar, and simpler, way:

```
st_firstbox.Move(li_x,li_y+ai_howFar)
```

You will probably use the simple "object.function" syntax for the vast majority of your method calls The EVENT, DYNAMIC, and POST options are necessary only for special occasions that tend to arise somewhat infrequently.

You will see functions named TriggerEvent and PostEvent in the PowerBuilder documentation. They are alternative ways to call an event in PowerScript, and were the only ways to do it in version 4.0 of PowerBuilder and earlier. The extended syntax for calling functions and events that I have just described is new to version 5.0 and supersedes the TriggerEvent and PostEvent functions. Therefore, although TriggerEvent and PostEvent still work, you should consider them obsolete and not get into the habit of using them.

PROPERTIES

Manipulating an object's property is the third type of message-sending in PowerBuilder. A *property*, as you know, is a characteristic of an object such as its color.

You manipulate a property using the dot notation —

```
object.property
```

— which you can use anywhere you can use a variable. For example, to change the background-color property of st_firstbox to red (255):

```
st_firstbox.BackColor = 255
```

To copy the same property's value into the variable *c*:

```
c = st_firstbox.BackColor
```

You can think of an object's properties as being an object's "public variables." By the rule of encapsulation, an object's variables are private and invisible to the outside world. But some of the variables — the properties — can be public, directly accessible to the outside world.

Sometimes I prefer to think of properties as a convenient shorthand for a function call. The folks who invented the PowerScript language could have eliminated properties by giving us function calls to accomplish the same tasks:

```
st_firstbox.SetBackColor (255)
c = st_firstbox.GetBackColor ()
```

The object.function syntax is a little bit clumsier than the object.property syntax, but it more accurately portrays what is happening. Changing the color of an object is more than a simple variable change. It is a process requiring some programming encapsulated within the object, since it involves redrawing a part of the screen. Nevertheless, the object.property syntax is convenient, and I am glad it is part of the PowerScript language.

Object Classes and Instances

Every object belongs to an *object class* and is called an *instance* of the class. Every window object, for example, is an instance of the "window" object class. Every transaction object is an instance of the "transaction" object class. You can think of the object class as the "prototype" or "model" for the object.

When you develop a PowerBuilder application, you design its object classes. When you run the application, the object instances come into existence (Figure 11-8). The process of creating an object instance from an object class is called *instantiation*. Instantiation always occurs at runtime. For visual objects, instantiation typically occurs when the object opens and appears on the screen.

Nonvisual objects are also instantiated at runtime. Listing 11-1 showed the use of the nonvisual object trans1. This line, which declares trans1, notifies the compiler that there will be an instance trans1 of the transaction object class:

```
Transaction    trans1
```

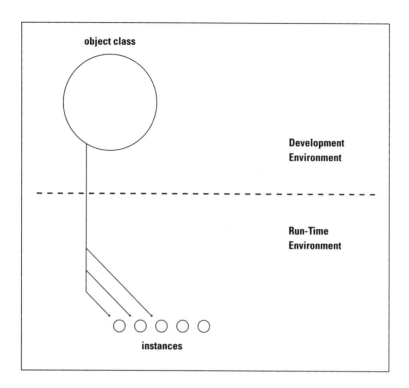

Figure 11-8

Instantiation: An object class can have any number of instances.

This line is the instantiation, causing the object instance trans1 to come into existence:

```
trans1 = CREATE Transaction
```

After trans1 is instantiated, you can begin sending it messages. These lines set some of the object's properties:

```
trans1.DBMS      = "ODBC"
trans1.Database  = "Video Store DB"
trans1.UserId    = "dba"
```

When you no longer need the instance, you can destroy it with this line:

```
DESTROY trans1
```

The Object Class Hierarchy

PowerBuilder comes equipped with 76 object classes built in. The window class and the transaction class are two of them. You can define your own object classes and add them to the list, as I will demonstrate in the pages to come. The complete list is shown in Table 11-1.

You can see the same list in the PowerBuilder Browser: Click the Browser button on the PowerBar to open the Browser, click the System tab, right-click any item on the left-side list, and click Show Hierarchy from the pop-up menu. The Browser displays the hierarchy in an expanding tree format. Double-click items to expand or contract them.

What is it that makes one object class different from another? From simple observation, it's pretty clear that a Window, a CommandButton, a DataWindow, and a Transaction are very different things, and therefore they are different classes. From a technical perspective, you can express the the distinction like so:

All instances of a single object class possess exactly the same set of variables and programming. The variable values may differ between instances, but the set of variables will be the same. If two objects have different variables or different programming, they must belong to different object classes.

So CommandButton and DataWindow must be different object classes because they have different programming. For example, a DataWindow has functions such as Retrieve and Update that a CommandButton lacks.

In Table 11-1, the indentation of the list indicates that the classes are arranged into a hierarchy, in which some classes are "subclasses" of others. A subclass has all of the features of its parent class, and more (Figure 11-9).

For example, PictureButton is a subclass of CommandButton. You might remember PictureButton and CommandButton from Chapter 2. They are very similar. Both are button controls on a window. A PictureButton has all of the features of a CommandButton and two additional features as well: a picture and more flexible positioning of its text label. As for functions, properties, and events, the PictureButton has the same set as a CommandButton, plus five more properties to support the additional features: Alignment, DisabledName, OriginalSize, PictureName, and VTextAlign.

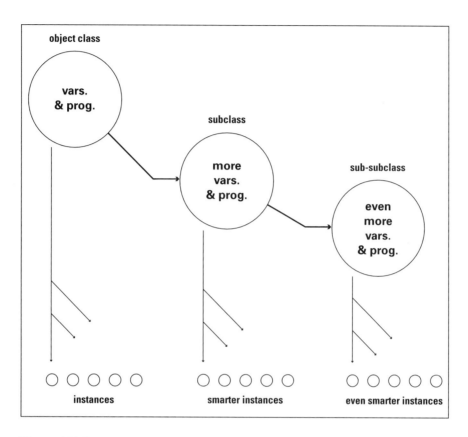

Figure 11-9

Classes and subclasses: Each subclass is "smarter" than its parent class.

Every object that we call a "control" — an object contained in a window, such as a CheckBox, CommandButton, and PictureButton — is a subclass of the WindowObject class and, more specifically, a subclass of either the DragObject class or the DrawObject class. (The MDIClient class will be explained in Chapter 14.) The WindowObject class possesses all the functions and properties common to all controls: functions such as Move and Resize and properties such as Visible. It has no events, because there is no event that every type of control possesses. Every subclass of WindowObject, such as CommandButton, DataWindow, and Rectangle, inherits all of the functions and properties from the WindowObject class and adds its own functions, properties, and events.

Table 11-1

The Object Class Hierarchy

PowerObject	Line
Application	Oval
Function_Object	Rectangle
GraphicObject	RoundRectangle
Menu	MDIClient
MenuCascade	GrAxis
Window	GrDispAttr
WindowObject	NonVisualObject
DragObject	ConnectObject
CheckBox	Connection
CommandButton	Transport
PictureButton	CPlusPlus
DataWindow	DataStore
DropDownListBox	DynamicDescriptionArea
DropDownPictureListBox	DynamicStagingArea
Graph	Error
GroupBox	ExtObjectr
HScrollBa	DWObject
ListBox	OMObject
PictureListBox	OLEObject
ListView	MailSession
MultiLineEdit	Message
EditMask	OMStorage
OMControl	OLEStorage
OMCustomControl	OMStream
OLECustomControl	OLEStream
OMEmbeddedControl	Pipeline
OLEControl	RemoteObject
Picture	Transaction
RadioButton	Structure
RichTextEdit	ConnectionInfo
SingleLineEdit	DataWindowChild
StaticText	Environment
Tab	ListViewItem
TreeView	MailFileDescription
UserObject	MailMessage
VScrollBar	MailRecipient
DrawObject	TreeViewItem

You will notice nonvisual object classes in the class hierarchy. The Transaction object class, in fact, is a subclass of a class named NonVisualObject.

At the top of the class hierarchy is the PowerObject class. This class is rarely referenced in an application. Its role is to serve as the "most general" class, the parent class for which all other object classes are subclasses.

User-Defined Object Classes

You can create your object classes and add them to the 76 provided by PowerBuilder. I will call them *user-defined object classes*. "User" in this context means you, the developer of the application, not the end user who runs the application.

A user-defined object class must fit somewhere into the class hierarchy in Table 11-1. In other words, it must be a subclass of some other class that already exists.

PowerBuilder offers several different techniques to define a new object class, depending on the class from which you plan to derive it. I will describe these techniques in the next chapter. In this chapter, I will show a couple of finished examples.

A Close Button

For a simple example of a user-defined object class, let's consider a Close button. Back in Chapter 2 we added a Close button to a window. It was a PictureButton, as shown in Figure 11-10. Its clicked script consisted of one line of code, which closes the window containing the button:

```
Close(Parent)
```

Figure 11-10
The Close button.

If you have been designing PowerBuilder windows since reading Chapter 2, chances are you placed a Close button like this one on many, if not all, of them. Did you recreate the Close button from scratch every time, by starting with a PictureButton control? Creating a user-defined object class for it makes this repetitive chore much easier.

In the object class hierarchy, the new object class would be a subclass of PictureButton:

```
PowerObject
...GraphicObject
......WindowObject
.........DragObject
............CommandButton
...............PictureButton
..................CloseButton    (the user-defined class)
```

Thus a CloseButton will have all the features of a PictureButton, plus: (1) It will always have the "closing door" picture on it, and (2) It will always contain the clicked script shown above.

When you create a new window, it's much easier to place a CloseButton object on it than to create one from scratch from the PictureButton class. In the next chapter, I will walk through the steps to create and use this CloseButton object.

Inheritance

Inheritance is an object-oriented feature that becomes important as you build an application's object class hierarchy, adding user-defined object classes to the PowerBuilder-provided object classes. The rules of inheritance are:

1. A subclass inherits all the features of its parent class. You can not remove inherited features in the subclass, but you can add to and override them.

2. If you change a feature of an object class, the change is propagated to all of its descended subclasses — except where overridden — and at runtime to all instances of this class and its descendants.

Figure 11-11 is an illustration of inheritance.

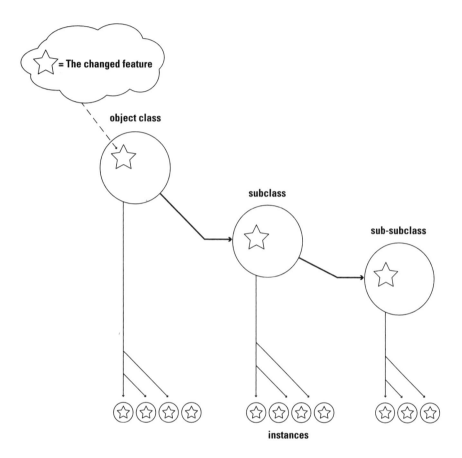

Figure 11-11

Inheritance: The features and changes to the parent class are inherited by all of its subclasses and instances.

For example, suppose that you have created a number of other sub-classes as descendants of the CloseButton class:

```
PowerObject
...GraphicObject
......WindowObject
.........DragObject
............CommandButton
...............PictureButton
..................CloseButton        (user-defined class)
....................CloseButton1     (user-defined class)
......................CloseButton1A  (user-defined class)
....................CloseButton2     (user-defined class)
```

Exactly what's different about each of the new classes isn't very important. Maybe each has a different color door in its picture. Suppose, however, that each descendant has inherited the original CloseButton's clicked event script:

```
Close(Parent)
```

Each descendant will inherit this script automatically, unless you override it with a new script in one of the subclasses.

Now suppose that you go back to the definition of the CloseButton class, which is the ancestor of all the others, and replace its clicked event script with this one:

```
Integer i    // response to the dialog box question
i = MessageBox("Close?",                                    &
               "Do you really want to close this window?", &
               Question!, YesNo!)
IF i = 1 THEN
   Close(Parent)
END IF
```

This script asks the user for confirmation before closing the window. Once you have added this script to the user-defined CloseButton object class, all of the descendant subclasses will inherit it. Therefore, all of the close buttons in all of the windows in your application — and there might be hundreds of them — will now ask for confirmation before closing a window. You have implemented an application-wide enhancement by making one simple change!

Inheritance is probably the most powerful object-oriented feature.

Because of the power of inheritance, you should plan your object class hierarchy carefully and build and acquire libraries of reusable object classes. Inheritance is so important that it merits its own chapter, and in this book it has one. Chapter 13 will go into detail about inheritance and offer many examples of how to use it.

Polymorphism

Polymorphism, which means "having many forms," is a very straightforward, object-oriented feature: In an object-oriented language, you can use the same function name more than once. (See Figure 11-12.) In a traditional language, every function name must be unique. Not so in an object-oriented language.

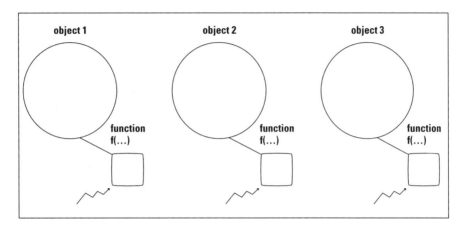

Figure 11-12

Polymorphism: Different object classes can have functions with the same name.

The main rationale for polymorphism is that situations arise in which you want to send the same kind of message to different kinds of objects and have each object respond to that message in its own unique way. Each object will have its own unique code for how it responds to that message, but it makes great sense for these messages (functions) to have the same name.

Among the functions built into PowerBuilder objects, there are many cases of polymorphism. One example is the Reset function. You can call Reset on a DataWindow control, on a ListBox or DropDownListBox control, or on a graph control:

```
dw_1.Reset()      // dw_1 is a DataWindow control
lb_1.Reset()      // lb_1 is a ListBox control
ddlb_1.Reset()    // ddlb_1 is a DropDownListBox control
gr_1.Reset(x)     // gr_1 is a graph control
```

All of these Reset functions look similar, but to each class of object, Reset means something a little bit different. For a DataWindow, Reset means to remove all the data being displayed — the opposite of the Retrieve function. For a ListBox or DropDownListBox, it means to remove all the choices from the list. For a graph, it means to delete some part of the graph (and requires a parameter to specify what part of the graph to delete).

You could create a new, user-defined object class, unrelated to any of the ones above, and define for it a function named Reset — Same function name, different functionality.

Let's look at an example of polymorphism involving user-defined object classes. Figure 11-13 shows a window with four boxes, among other things. The four boxes are named st_box1, st_box2, st_box3, and st_box4. I have defined a new function, JiggleMe, for these boxes. When you call JiggleMe on a box, it jiggles. Here is the clicked script on the "Jiggle Each Box" button, which jiggles each of the four boxes one at a time.

```
uo_st_box1.JiggleMe(20,50)
uo_st_box2.JiggleMe(20,50)
uo_st_box3.JiggleMe(20,50)
uo_st_box4.JiggleMe(20,50)
```

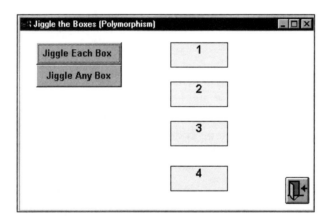

Figure 11-13
Polymorphism at work: The buttons jiggle the boxes.

The four boxes look like PowerBuilder StaticText control objects, but they are not. They belong to user-defined object classes named u_st_jigglebox, u_st_djigglebox, and u_st_hjigglebox that I created as subclasses of StaticText:

```
PowerObject
...GraphicObject
```

```
......WindowObject
.........DragObject
...........StaticText
..............u_st_jigglebox          (user-defined class)
................u_st_hjigglebox        (user-defined class)
................u_st_djigglebox        (user-defined class)
```

In the window, the first two boxes are instances of u_st_jigglebox, the third box is an instance of u_st_hjigglebox, and the fourth box is an instance of u_st_djigglebox.

All three user-defined classes have a JiggleMe function. Because of polymorphism, all the calls to JiggleMe look the same, as you can see. You always pass two parameters to JiggleMe: The first is how many times to jiggle, and the second is how far to jiggle.

But the JiggleMe functions are not the same, because each class implements JiggleMe in a different way — that is, the PowerScript programming for each class is different. Objects of the u_st_jigglebox class (the first two boxes) respond to JiggleMe by jiggling up and down. Objects of the u_st_hjigglebox class (the third box) jiggle horizontally. And objects of the u_st_djigglebox class (the fourth box) jiggle diagonally.

I will show how to create the object classes and their the JiggleMe functions in the next chapter. For now I want to focus on the concept of polymorphism. Do you start to see why polymorphism is important, and what possibilities it opens for you as a developer?

Object Variables

Often polymorphism comes into play in a general-purpose script, which can be executed to manipulate any of a large number of objects. The script knows the name of the message to send — JiggleMe, for instance — but it does not know which object should receive it.

To accomplish this, you can declare an *object variable*. For example, you can have an object variable *u* representing one of the boxes in Figure 11-13 — it doesn't matter which box, and it could be any of them at any point in time. To jiggle the box, you can say:

```
u.JiggleMe(20,50)
```

This line of code is part of the event script for "Jiggle Any Box," the button you see in Figure 11-13. Prior to this, another script line assigns a particular box object to the object variable *u*. For example:

```
u = uo_st_box1
```

So what exactly is an object variable? How you you declare it and how can you use it?

You have seen plenty of standard variables in PowerScript, which hold values such as numbers and strings. In addition to the 15 standard variable types, you may also declare a variable to be any of the 76 object classes or any of the user-defined object classes. When you use an object class to declare a variable, I call that an *object variable*. It can also be called a *reference variable*.

A transaction variable is an object variable, since transaction is one of the PowerBuilder object classes:

```
Transaction     trans1
trans1 = CREATE Transaction
trans1.DBMS       = "ODBC"
```

The transaction object is a nonvisual object, and you have seen how to use it. Now let's consider object variables declared with the visual object classes:

```
Window          w
StaticText      st
CommandButton   cb
u_st_jigglebox  u     // (user-defined object class)
```

To assign one of these variables a value, you simply assign an object instance to it. For example, if you have used the Window Painter to design a window named w_mywindow and placed controls on it named st_1, cb_1, and jiggle_1, you can do this:

```
Window          w
StaticText      st
CommandButton   cb
u_st_jigglebox  u

w  = w_mywindow
st = st_1
cb = cb_1
u  = jiggle_1
```

Thereafter, you can use the object variable in place of the object instance name anywhere in your script. This means that you can use object variables with functions, properties, and events:

```
w.Move(100,100)       // move the window
st.BackColor = 255   // make the StaticText control red
cb.Hide()            // make the CommandButton invisible
u.JiggleMe(20,50)    // jiggle the box
```

You can think of the object variable as a pointer to the physical object instance. Like any variable, an object variable can take on different values during its lifetime. For example, if you have three CommandButton controls named cb_1, cb_2, cb_3, this script uses an object variable to make all three invisible:

```
CommandButton  cb
cb = cb_1
cb.Hide()
cb = cb_2
cb.Hide()
cb = cb_3
cb.Hide()
```

This is equivalent to:

```
cb_1.Hide()
cb_2.Hide()
cb_3.Hide()
```

USING ANCESTOR-CLASS OBJECT VARIABLES

When you assign an object instance to an object variable, it is, of course, required that they be the same type. The following, for example, is illegal, because cb is a CommandButton variable but st_1 is a StaticText object:

```
CommandButton  cb
cb = st_1
```

However, you can assign an object instance to an object variable if the variable is an ancestor class of the instance. For example, all control object classes, such as CommandButton and StaticText, are descendants of the WindowObject class. You can see that in the Object Class Hierarchy:

```
PowerObject
...GraphicObject
......WindowObject
.........DragObject
............CommandButton
............StaticText
...............u_st_jigglebox                    (user-defined class)
```

Therefore, any type of control can be assigned to a WindowObject variable:

```
WindowObject wo        // a WindowObject variable
wo = st_1              // assign a StaticText object to it
wo.Hide()              // hide the StaticText object
wo = cb_1              // assign a CommandButton object to it
wo.Hide()              // hide the CommandButton object
wo = jiggle_1          // assign a "u_st_jigglebox" object to it
wo.Hide()              // hide the "u_st_jigglebox" object
```

Using an ancestor class such as WindowObject is more flexible than declaring a separate object variable for each class of control, because one variable can do the work of many.

What we have done with a WindowObject variable in this example, we could also do with DragObject. As you see in the hierarchy, DragObject is a child of WindowObject and the parent of StaticText, CommandButton, and u_st_jigglebox. The drawback to using DragObject is that you cannot assign to it any controls that are not DragObject descendants, such as oval and rectangle objects.

THE POWEROBJECT CLASS

As you see from Table 11-1, there is one object class that is the ancestor of every other object class, visual and nonvisual: the PowerObject class. You can assign controls — and any other kind of object — to a PowerObject variable:

```
PowerObject p          // a PowerObject variable
p = st_1               // assign a StaticText object to it
p = cb_1               // assign a CommandButton object to it
p = jiggle_1           // assign a "u_st_jigglebox" object to it
p = sqlca              // assign a Transaction object to it
```

DYNAMIC METHOD CALLS

When you use use PowerObject and other higher-level objects, you occasionally encounter a snag. PowerObject is not a very smart object. That is, it supports very few functions, properties, and events. In the object class hierarchy, subclasses are always smarter than their parents.

The Hide function is introduced in the GraphicObject class. Each descendant of GraphObject — WindowObject, DragObject, and all of the controls — inherits Hide from GraphObject. But PowerObject does not have Hide. Therefore, you'll get a syntax error from the PowerScript compiler if you attempt to use Hide with PowerObject:

```
PowerObject p
p = st_1          // this line works okay
p.Hide()          // this line causes a compile error
```

The solution is to use the DYNAMIC key word in the function call. As I explained earlier in this chapter, in the section on the extended syntax for calling functions and events, the "p.Hide" call is equivalent to using the key word STATIC:

```
p.STATIC Hide()    // this line causes a compile error
```

STATIC causes the PowerScript compiler to verify that the function (Hide) is acceptable for this type of object (PowerObject). Since it isn't, the compiler gives an error and you can't save or close the script.

The alternative to STATIC is DYNAMIC, and it works just fine:

```
p.DYNAMIC Hide()   // this line works
```

The DYNAMIC key word defers the verification until runtime. The PowerScript compiler does not flag the Hide function call with an error. Assuming that at runtime the variable p is associated with an object that supports the Hide function, such as a window control, the function call will be successful.

The disadvantage of DYNAMIC is that it runs a little more slowly than STATIC, since PowerBuilder must do more work at runtime to verify the function. Therefore, you should use DYNAMIC only when necessary. If possible, declare your variables with a lower-level object class, such as WindowObject, that supports calling the functions you need STATICly.

How to Manipulate All the Controls in a Window

Since all the controls in a window can be assigned, one by one, to a single WindowObject variable, is there a way to manipulate all the controls in a window? For example, can you have a button script that makes every control invisible, without the need to enumerate each control by name?

Yes you can! This script does the trick:

```
Integer  i              // control counter
Integer  nControls      // # of controls in the window
WindowObject   wo       // window object — i.e., control
nControls = UpperBound(Parent.Control)    // how many controls?
FOR i = 1 to nControls                     // do each control
   wo = Parent.Control[i]                  // get the control object
   wo.Hide()                               // make it invisible
NEXT
```

Inside the FOR...NEXT loop, each control in turn is assigned to the WindowObject variable, and the wo.Hide() function hides it.

The script relies on "Control," a property of the window object. Unlike most properties, Control is an array of values, not just a single value. To get the first control on a window named w_mywindow, for example, you can say:

```
wo = w_mywindow.Control[1]
```

If the script is on a button in the window, you can use the pronoun *Parent* in place of the window name:

```
wo = Parent.Control[1]
```

(*Parent* and other pronouns were explained in Chapter 4.)

The script uses the UpperBound function to determine nControls, the number of controls in the window. The UpperBound function gives you the highest index number of the array you pass to it. The Control array has a lowest index number of 1, so the highest index is the same as the number of elements, which is the number of controls. The value of *nControls* determines how many iterations of the FOR loop to do.

continued

continued

Within the loop, the command "wo = Parent.Control[i]" sets the WindowObject variable to the *i*th control. (The Control array is an array of WindowObjects.) Once assigned, the statement "wo.Hide()" makes the control invisible.

There are several ways to enhance this script to manipulate controls selectively, doing some and skipping others. If you want to hide only CommandButtons, for example, enclose the "wo.Hide" line in an IF...END IF:

```
IF wo.TypeOf() = CommandButton! Then    // if it's a CommandButton
   wo.Hide()                            // make it invisible
END IF
```

The TypeOf function identifies the object class of the current value of *wo*. It returns an enumerated data type, such as CommandButton!

Function Overloading

Function overloading, like polymorphism, is yet another way in which an object-oriented language makes function definition very flexible. You can define multiple versions of a function on the same object.

Each version can have (in fact, is distinguished by) a distinct calling syntax, that is, a distinct set of arguments.

The most common use for function overloading is to support optional arguments in the function call. There are plenty of examples among PowerBuilder's built-in functions. For example, the MessageBox function has two required arguments and three optional arguments. This flexibility is an example of function overloading.

To extend the "jiggle box" example, we've described the box's JiggleMe function as having two integer parameters:

```
uo_st_box.JiggleMe(20, 50)
```

You could, however, define a variation of JiggleMe that requires three parameters, the third being a string to indicate which direction to jiggle:

```
uo_st_box.JiggleMe(20, 50, "Horizontal")
```

In PowerBuilder, you implement this in just about the simplest way possible: You define the two variations as if they were two separate functions that just happen to have the same name. The PowerBuilder Function Painter lets you save both functions with the same name, as long as they have different argument lists. When you open the function painter, each variation is listed as a separate item.

Object-Oriented Programming and PowerBuilder: Theory and Practice

I have now completed my explanation of object-oriented programming. Because I have used PowerBuilder examples throughout, you have a good idea about how PowerBuilder supports the features that I have described.

The next question is, "How completely does PowerBuilder support object-orientated principles? Are there areas where PowerBuilder falls short?" These are important practical questions; they are not just theoretical musings. Any shortcomings in PowerBuilder probably point to areas where things are more difficult to do than they ought to be.

The short answer is, PowerBuilder comes very close to offering a complete implementation of object-oriented principles. Therefore you get most, if not all, of the benefits of important features such as encapsulation, inheritance, and polymorphism. There are few principles to which PowerBuilder does not completely conform, and they are relatively noncritical.

There is room for debate about where PowerBuilder does and doesn't conform. I mentioned at the outset that different people have different definitions of object-oriented principles.

Here, in my opinion, is how PowerBuilder does not conform:

1. **You can avoid object-oriented techniques** — With PowerBuilder, object-oriented techniques are an option, and you are not required to use them. If you prefer the traditional, nonobject-oriented way of doing things, you are welcome to follow that path.

   In particular, PowerBuilder lets you define global variables and functions that are not tied to any object. Global variables and functions are important traditional programming tools, but they do not belong in a purely object-oriented system.

If the benefits of encapsulation are not important to you, go ahead and use global variables and functions. If you prefer the object-oriented approach, however, you should make it a policy to avoid them.

By providing the ability to avoid object-oriented techniques, PowerBuilder is in good company. The C++ language, which is the most widely used object-oriented language, also supports such traditional nonobject-oriented features as global variables and functions.

2. **Private window variables are "too visible"** — One of the principles of encapsulation is that an object's private variables are not visible to any programming outside of the object. In PowerBuilder, an object's private variables are its private instance and shared variables. (See Chapter 4 for an explanation of instance and shared variables.) If the object is a window, its private instance and shared variables are visible to other objects: They are visible to the control objects that are contained in the window. A script on a CommandButton, for example, is free to inspect and change the private instance variables of its parent window.

I suppose the rationale is that a control is part of the window, and therefore, the control's script should have access to the window's private variables. But even though a window and a control share an obvious visual relationship to one another — anyone can see that the control is contained inside the window — they are nonetheless two different objects. If their variables are properly encapsulated, they should not be accessible to each other.

3. **Not every object class can be subclassed** — An object-oriented programming language can come with a set of predefined object classes. PowerBuilder does. An object-oriented programming language lets you define new object classes as subclasses of the original set. So does PowerBuilder. In an object-oriented programming language, you can define a new subclass of *any* class in the original set. This is not true in PowerBuilder. In the next chapter, I will list the 76 predefined object classes and show that PowerBuilder lets you define new subclasses for most, but not all, of them.

Why Will Objects Change Your Life?

If objects are new to you, and the description you have just read is your first exposure to these object-oriented concepts, I'd like to welcome you to a new way of programming. Most people discover that object-oriented programming is more than just a new set of tools. It's a whole new attitude and approach toward developing software.

I have found, personally, that the object-oriented point of view has made a dramatic change in the way that I do programming. Comparing my work to other people who take a more traditional approach, I find that I spend a lot more time encapsulating related modules of business logic into objects. I create a lot of user-defined object classes and make heavy use of object-level functions and properties. You will see many examples in the next two chapters.

A skilled object-oriented developer spends a lot of time up front carefully planning the object class hierarchy, just as a database administrator begins a new database with a careful design of tables, columns, and relationships. If you do a good job of designing new objects before becoming enmeshed in the process of writing code, you will be rewarded with applications that are cleaner, faster to develop, and easier to maintain.

Object-oriented programming is a lot of fun, too! Welcome to a whole new world!

12 User-Defined Objects

*T*his chapter explains how to create your own object classes and how to use them in your applications. You will learn how to create many different types of reusable objects, such as a Close button and other "smart buttons," complex visual objects, and nonvisual objects.

New object classes are called *user-defined object classes*. In PowerBuilder most of them are called simply "user objects." The term "user" in this context means you, the application developer. It does not mean the end user of your application, who never creates new object classes.

In the preceding chapter, I explained in detail what a user-defined object class is and why such classes are important. I demonstrated several finished examples, but I have not yet explained how to create them. In this chapter, you will get that explanation.

Classes and Subclasses

As I explained in the last chapter, PowerBuilder provides an object class hierarchy consisting of 76 classes; they are listed in Table 12-1. Any user-defined object class that you define must fit into this hierarchy some-where, as a subclass of an existing class. Of the 76 classes, PowerBuilder allows you to create subclasses for 43 of them. These are indicated with "*" in Table 12-1. For the other 33 classes, there is no way to create a subclass.

Table 12-1

The Object Class Hierarchy

You can create user-defined subclasses from those classes marked with an asterisk (*)	
PowerObject	
Application	*
Function_Object	
GraphicObject	
Menu	*
MenuCascade	
Window	*
WindowObject	
DragObject	*
CheckBox	*
CommandButton	*
PictureButton	*
DataWindow	*
DropDownListBox	*
DropDownPictureListBox	*
Graph	*
GroupBox	*
HscrollBar	*
ListBox	*
PictureListBox	*
ListView	*
MultiLineEdit	*
EditMask	*
OMControl	
OMCustomControl	
OLECustomControl	
OMEmbeddedControl	
OLEControl	*
Picture	*
RadioButton	*
RichTextEdit	*
SingleLineEdit	*
StaticText	*
Tab	*
TreeView	*
UserObject	*
VScrollBar	*
DrawObject	

continued

Table 12-1 (continued)

Line	
Oval	
Rectangle	
RoundRectangle	
MDIClient	
GrAxis	
GrDispAttr	
NonVisualObject	*
ConnectObject	
Connection	*
Transport	*
CPlusPlus	
DataStore	*
DynamicDescriptionArea	*
DynamicStagingArea	*
Error	*
ExtObject	
DWObject	
OMObject	
OLEObject	*
MailSession	*
Message	*
OMStorage	
OLEStorage	*
OMStream	
OLEStream	*
Pipeline	*
RemoteObject	*
Transaction	*
Structure	*
ConnectionInfo	
DataWindowChild	
Environment	
ListViewItem	
MailFileDescription	
MailMessage	
MailRecipient	
TreeViewItem	

How to Create a User-Defined Object Class: Take Your Pick

I wish I could tell you that there is only one procedure to create a new user-defined object class. Unfortunately, that is not so.

The procedure varies, depending on which object class is the parent of your new class. All of the procedures to derive a new subclass from a built-in PowerBuilder class are summarized in Table 12-2.

You will also want to derive subclasses from your own user-defined subclasses. To create such a sub-subclass, return to the painter in which you created the original subclass, as shown in Table 12-2. In the dialog box that pops up, you will see a New button and also an Inherit button. You clicked the New button to create the original subclass. Click the Inherit button to create a sub-subclass. There are two exceptions: You will not find an Inherit button in the Application Painter or the Structure Painter. For applications and structures, PowerBuilder does not support user-defined subclasses more than one level deep.

By the end of this chapter, I will have shown you most of these procedures. To get started, let's take one of the simpler cases — creating a subclass of a PictureButton — and walk it all the way through in detail.

Standard Visual User Objects

The simplest user-defined object to create is what PowerBuilder calls a *standard visual user object*, which is a subclass of one of the window control classes, such as CheckBox, CommandButton, or DataWindow. The last chapter's "Close button" and "jiggle box" examples were Standard Visual User Objects.

EXAMPLE: THE CLOSE BUTTON

The Close button is shown in Figure 12-1. To save you the trouble of designing a new PictureButton from scratch for every new window, you can create a new Close button object class as a subclass of the PictureButton class.

You can program this button to close a window when clicked, and then you can place instances of it on all of your windows. Here's how you do these things, step by step.

Table 12-2

How to Create a User-Defined Object Class

To Create a User-Defined Subclass of This Object Class...	First Open This Painter...	Then Click These Buttons...
Application	Application	New (on the PainterBar)
Menu	Menu	New
Window	Window	New
DragObject (external control)	User Object	1. New 2. External Visual
Standard Controls (CheckBox, CommandButton, DataWindow, DropDownListBox, DropDownPictureListBox, EditMask, Graph, GroupBox, HScrollBar, ListBox, ListView, MultiLineEdit, OLEControl, Picture, PictureButton, PictureListBox, RadioButton, RichTextEdit, SingleLineEdit, StaticText, Tab, TreeView, VScrollBar)	User Object	1. New 2. Standard Visual
UserObject	User Object	1. New 2. Custom Visual
NonVisualObject	User Object	1. New 2. Custom Class
Connection, DataStore, DynamicDescriptionArea, DynamicStagingArea, Error, MailSession, Message, OLEObject, OLEStorage, OLEStream, Pipeline, Transaction, Transport	User Object	1. New 2. Standard Class
Structure	Structure	New

Figure 12-1

The Close button.

User-Defined DataWindow Controls

The examples that follow build standard visual user objects from simple controls: a button, a StaticText. The examples are good for demonstrating the basic techniques in an elementary way.

Things get a lot more interesting when you derive a user object from the DataWindow control. The DataWindow control is the most complex of the built-in controls, and as you know from Chapter 10, you usually add a lot of additional programming to it as well. Encapsulating your programming into a DataWindow user object control packs a lot of potential. We'll walk through an example of one in the next chapter.

CREATING A NEW CUSTOM CONTROL

In PowerBuilder terminology, most user-defined object classes are called "user objects," and you create them using the User Object Painter. As you can see from Table 12-2, that is the case with the Close button, which will be a subclass of the PictureButton class.

Click the User Object button on the PowerBar to open the User Object Painter. This brings up the Select User Object dialog box shown in Figure 12-2, which is very similar to the dialog that pops up when you open the Window Painter and several other painters.

In the dialog box, the top section will list existing user objects so that you can select one for editing. If this is your first user object, as is the case in Figure 12-2, the list will be empty.

To create a new user object, click the New button. The New User Object dialog box pops up. (See Figure 12-3.)

The various buttons in the New User Object dialog are summarized in Table 12-3. Each button represents a class, or group of classes, in the PowerBuilder object class hierarchy. Click a button to create a new subclass of the class of your choice. To create a subclass of PictureButton, or of any of the other standard window controls, click Visual Standard, as shown in Figure 12-3, and then click OK.

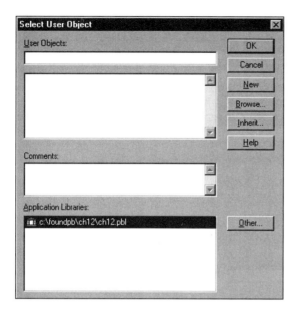

Figure 12-2
The Select User Object dialog box.

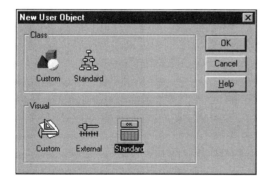

Figure 12-3
The New User Object dialog box.

Table 12-3

Selections in the New User Object Dialog Box

New User Object Button	Object Class
Class	
Custom	NonVisualObject class
Standard	One of the NonVisualObject subclasses, such as Transaction
Visual	
Custom	UserObject control class
External	A special window control using a DLL (Dynamic Link Library)
Standard	One of the window control classes, such as PictureButton

Next, the Select Standard Visual Type dialog box appears (Figure 12-4). It lists all of the standard window controls. In terms of the PowerBuilder object-class hierarchy, they are the subclasses of the DragObject class. Select "PictureButton," as shown in the figure, and click OK.

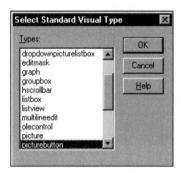

Figure 12-4

The Select Standard Visual Type dialog box.

PowerBuilder now drops you into the User Object Painter, as shown in Figure 12-5. In the painter is a PictureButton, waiting for you customize it.

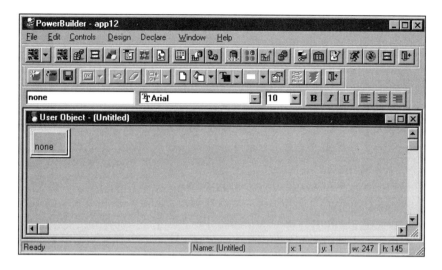

Figure 12-5
The User Object Painter, with a new PictureButton object.

The User Object Painter is very much like the Window Painter, except that in this case, you cannot add any new controls to the painter. You may work only with the one control, the PictureButton, that is already there.

The next few steps transform this basic PictureButton into a Close button. I described exactly the same steps in Chapter 2, in somewhat more detail, as a Window Painter exercise.

Double-click the new button to open its property sheet. In the General tab:

1. Erase the word "none" that appears in the Text space so that the button will have no text label, only a picture.

2. In the Enabled File Name space, specify the name of any Windows bitmap (.BMP) file to serve as the button's icon. I have used TUTEX-IT.BMP, which is supplied with the PowerBuilder tutorial.

3. Checkmark the Original Size option.

4. Click OK.

The button now contains the bitmap that you inserted. Now right-click the button and select Script from its pop-up menu to open the Script Painter. Type in this script for the button's clicked event:

```
Close(Parent)
```

Click Return (to User Object Painter) on the PainterBar. Back in the User Object Painter, resize the user object to match the size of the picture. The user object is now complete.

To save and name the new object class, select File | Save from the menu. In the Save User Object dialog box, type in "u_pb_closebutton" for the name and click OK. For this type of user object, I follow a two-prefix naming convention, as many others do: first the prefix "u_", indicating a user object, followed by a second prefix (in this case "pb_") indicating the control type that it is derived from. PowerBuilder saves u_pb_closebutton in your application's library (.PBL) file.

Select File | Close from the menu to close the User Object Painter. Your application's object class hierarchy now has a new user-defined class called u_pb_closebutton. It is a subclass of the PictureButton class.

USING THE CUSTOM CONTROL IN A WINDOW

The new object class, u_pb_closebutton, is a new custom control. Placing it on a window is pretty much the same procedure as with any ordinary control.

In the Window Painter, open the window on which you want to place the Close button. Click the User Object button on the PainterBar's drop-down object palette. (Be careful! Do not click the PowerBar's User Object button, which looks identical, but which opens the User Object Painter!)

The Select User Object dialog box pops up, as shown in Figure 12-6. It lists all of your user objects. In the figure, there is only one: u_pb_close-button. Select it, and click OK. Then in the Window Painter, click the location on the window where you want the button to appear. Figure 12-7 shows the result.

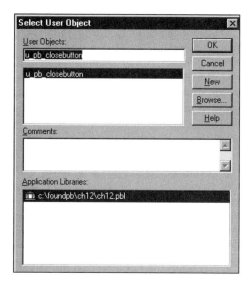

Figure 12-6

The Select User Object dialog box, for placing the control on the window.

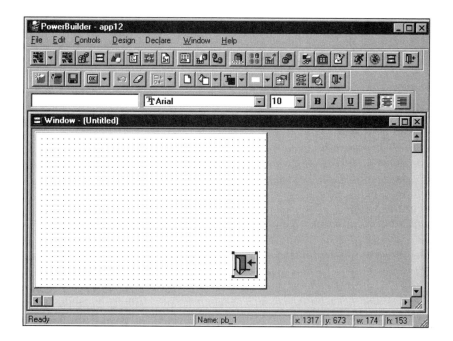

Figure 12-7

A new window, with the Close button user object on it.

There is no need to write a clicked script for the button on the window. The u_pb_closebutton comes already programmed, which is the whole point of using it. You could add still more programming to it, which is a topic I will take up later.

You can repeat this process any number of times, placing the Close button user object on any number of windows, old and new.

EXAMPLE: THE JIGGLE BOX — A USER OBJECT WITH A NEW OBJECT FUNCTION

Another example that I showed in the last chapter is a "jiggle box" object. It's a subclass of the StaticText control, to which I have added one new object function, uf_jiggleme, which jiggles the box up and down.

In Figure 12-8, the "jiggle box" is the box on the right. Its name is uo_st_jiggleBox. The clicked event on the button jiggles the box by calling the object function:

```
uo_st_jiggleBox.uf_jiggleme(20,50)
```

The uf_jiggleme function requires two parameters. The first (20) is how many times to jiggle. The second (50) is how far to jiggle.

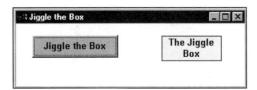

Figure 12-8
The "Jiggle Box" — Click the button and the box jiggles.

CREATING THE JIGGLE BOX OBJECT CLASS

The steps for creating the new object class are much the same as they were to create the Close button: Open the User Object Painter and click the buttons to create a new standard visual object. In the Select Standard Visual Type dialog box (Figure 12-9) select "statictext." (In the Close button exercise you selected "picturebutton" at this point.)

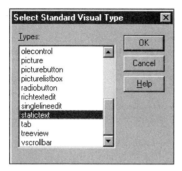

Figure 12-9

Selecting "statictext" from the Select Standard Visual Type dialog box.

At this point, the User Object Painter opens with the StaticText control in it. Using the property sheet, modify the properties of the control: its size, the text that it displays, its color, and so forth. Now it's time to add the custom object function, uf_jiggleme, to it.

DEFINING THE UF_JIGGLEME FUNCTION

A StaticText object, like every object in the PowerBuilder hierarchy, comes with a ready-made set of functions, such as Move and Hide. When you create a subclass of StaticText, the subclass inherits all of these functions, of course. And, in addition, you can define new functions of your own, such as uf_jiggleme.

To define the function, select Declare|User Object Functions from the menu, as shown in Figure 12-10. A dialog box pops up listing user-defined functions for this user object — there are none yet. Click New. This opens the New Function dialog shown in Figure 12-11. Fill in the dialog as you see in the figure to define the uf_jiggleme function and its two integer arguments: *ai_how_many_times* and *ai_how_far*. Click OK to enter the Function Painter, which is essentially the same as the Script Painter.

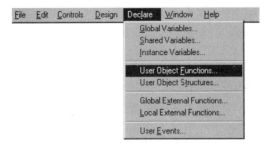

Figure 12-10

Selecting User Object Functions from the User Object Painter menu.

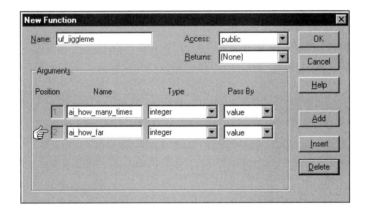

Figure 12-11

Defining the parameters for the uf_jiggleme function.

Type in these lines of code for the uf_jiggleme function:

```
Integer li_x,li_y,n
li_x = This.X
li_y = This.Y
FOR n = 1 TO ai_how_many_times
   This.Move(li_x,li_y+ai_how_far)
   This.Move(li_x,li_y)
NEXT
```

Click Return (to the User Object Painter) on the PainterBar to close the Function Painter. You have now finished defining the new user object. Select File | Save to save the object. Name it "u_st_jigglebox" and click OK. Then close the User Object Painter.

USING THE U_ST_JIGGLEBOX OBJECT IN A WINDOW

To begin using the new u_st_jigglebox object, create a new window. The process is no different than the one we walked through for u_pb_close-button: In the Window Painter, click the User Object button on the PainterBar. Select "u_st_jigglebox" from the list of user objects, and place it on the window. That creates the box shown in Figure 12-8.

PowerBuilder will name the box "st_1" because it is a control descended from the StaticText class. You should rename it "uo_st_jigglebox."

Wait a minute! Didn't we just name it "u_st_jigglebox"? No. The uo_st_jigglebox you placed on the window is actually a brand new object class, a descendant of the u_st_jigglebox, which in turn is a descendant of StaticText:

```
StaticText          (built-in object class)
  u_st_jigglebox    (subclass defined in User Object Painter)
    uo_st_jigglebox (subclass defined by placing it on the window)
```

Every time you place a control on a window, you are in fact defining a new subclass, which inherits all the features of its ancestor, but to which you can add new features such as event script programming.

As for the button shown in Figure 12-8, it is an ordinary CommandButton, not a user-defined object, with the one-line clicked script shown earlier:

```
uo_st_jigglebox.uf_jiggleme(20,50)
```

Making Objects Smarter

Before we create any more user-defined objects, I'd like to address another important issue: how to make your objects "smarter" by adding additional programming and other features to them. In the Close button example, we wrote a script for its clicked event. In the Jiggle Box example, we added a new function, uf_jiggleme. By doing so, we made the objects smarter than the ordinary PictureButton and StaticText objects that they are derived from.

An object, you will recall, is an encapsulation of variables and programming. Some of the variables and programming are hidden (private) within the object, making them inaccessible to the outside world. In order to allow the outside world to send messages to it, an object provides functions, events, and properties. The functions, events, and properties are themselves variables and programming, but they are "public" components of the object, and not hidden within it.

Table 12-4 shows the components of a built-in PowerBuilder object such as a PictureButton or a window. The hidden built-in variables and programming are hidden even from us application developers, so we tend not to think about them very often. But they definitely exist. They include, for example, the variables and programming that come into play when an object redraws itself on the screen after you move aside some other object that has been obscuring it.

Table 12-4

The Components of a Built-in PowerBuilder Object

	Programming	*Variables*
Hidden (Private)	Hidden built-in programming	Hidden built-in variables
Public	Built-in functions	Properties
	Built-in events	

When you create a new object class, it inherits all of these components from its parent class. Within the new object class, you can not delete the components inherited from its parent. However, PowerBuilder gives us great power to enhance the object further by adding more components to it. The new components are nothing more than additional variables and programming, some of it private and some of it public. In particular, you can define

- **Instance Variables** — You can add more variables to an object by declaring instance variables for it. When you declare an instance variable, you can specify whether it should be hidden or public. I will show how in just a moment. A public instance variable becomes a user-defined property of the object.

- **Functions** — You can create user-defined functions, and declare them to be hidden or public.

- **Events** — You can write the programming for any of PowerBuilder's built-in events. You can also create user-defined events. Events are always public components of the object.

Table 12-5 shows how these elements supplement the object's inherited variables and programming. Figure 12-12 illustrates how they fit into the concept of an object as presented in the last chapter.

Table 12-5
The Components of a User-Defined Object

	Programming	**Variables**
Hidden (Private)	*Hidden built-in programming	*Hidden built-in variables
	*Private and protected user-defined functions	*Private and protected instance variables
Public	*Built-in functions	*Properties
	*Built-in events (user-programmed)	*Public instance variables (user-defined properties)
	*Public user-defined functions	
	*User-defined events	

The uf_jiggleme function is an example of a public user-defined function, and you already know how to create those. You also know how to create user programming for built-in events: Every time you write a clicked script for a button, or any other event script, that is what you are creating. As for the rest of them, such as private functions, protected instance variables, and user-defined events, let's go through how to create each of them now...

INSTANCE VARIABLES: PRIVATE, PROTECTED, PUBLIC

I introduced instance variables back in Chapter 4 as one of the four scopes of variables: global, shared, instance, and local. An instance variable is one that is associated with an object instance, where an object might be an application, a window, a user object, or a menu.

What I did not say in Chapter 4 is that an instance variable also has one of three access levels: *private, protected,* and *public.*

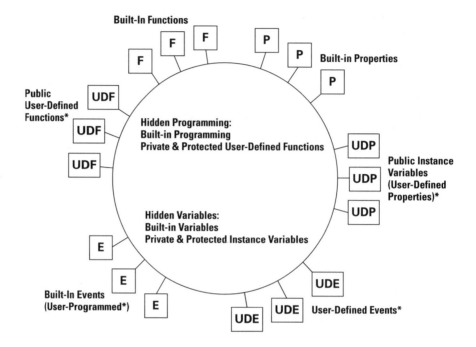

Figure 12-12

Adding new components to an object to make it smarter. Items marked with "" are created by the user (that is, the programmer).*

Private and *protected* variables are hidden variables. They are visible only to the programming within the object. (They are also visible to objects contained within the object, such as the controls within a window.) *Public* instance variables are visible to programming outside the object.

Private and protected variables are virtually the same. A distinction arises between them only when you derive a further subclass from your original user-defined object class. Both types of variables are inherited by the subclass, of course. But the two types behave differently. Any new programming added to the subclass can see and change its ancestor's protected variables, but it cannot see or change the private variables. Private variables are hidden from an object's descendant classes.

You declare instance variables by selecting Declare | Instance Variables from the menu. This menu choice is available in many painters, including the Window Painter, the User Object Painter, and the Script Painter. It opens the Declare Instance Variables dialog, into which you type your declarations, such as

```
Private:
    Integer    i1
    Real       r1, r2
Protected:
    Integer    i2
    String     s1, s2, s3
Public:
    Integer    i3
```

As you can see, by preceding a block of declarations with "Private:," "Protected:," or "Public:," you are specifying the access level of the variables.

An alternative syntax places the access level on the same line as the variable declaration:

```
Private    Integer    i1
Private    Real       r1, r2
Protected  Integer    i2
Protected  String     s1, s2, s3
Public     Integer    i3
```

Any programming outside an object can refer to an object's public instance variables, but it must use dot notation to do so. Here's an example that changes the value of the public instance variable *i3* of object A:

```
A.i3 = 255
```

Notice that you use exactly the same syntax to change the value of an object's properties:

```
A.BackColor = 255
```

Public instance variables behave very much like properties. They are in fact "user-defined properties."

You can fine-tune the access to a public or protected variable further by adding "access modifiers" to its declaration. The four "access modifiers" are PrivateRead, ProtectedRead, PrivateWrite, and ProtectedWrite.

For example, suppose that you modify the declaration of a public instance variable *i4* with PrivateWrite:

```
Public:
    PrivateWrite    Integer    i4
```

Because this variable is public, all objects can see it. However, because of PrivateWrite, only the object that owns the variable can change its value. The variable's read-access is public, but its write-access is private.

USER-DEFINED FUNCTIONS: PRIVATE, PROTECTED, PUBLIC

You define a new function for a user object by selecting Declare|User Object Functions from the User Object Painter menu and then clicking New from the Select Function in the User Object dialog box that follows. This opens the New Function dialog. Figure 12-11 showed how to fill this dialog out to define the arguments for the uf_jiggleme function.

On this same dialog box, you can select an access level for the function. There are three choices: private, protected, or public. These three terms have the same meaning as they do for instance variables. The default, which you see selected in Figure 12-11, is public.

Select public to create a function that is not unlike the object's built-in PowerBuilder functions, which can be called from anywhere in the application using the dot notation syntax:

```
objectname.functionname (parameters)
```

From scripts inside the object itself, you do not need the object prefix, and you can use simply

```
functionname (parameters)
```

Select "private" or "protected" to create a hidden function — that is, a function that cannot be called from outside the object, only from scripts within the object. As with instance variables, the distinction between private and protected becomes apparent only in subclasses derived from this user-defined object: New code added to a subclass can call its ancestor's protected functions, but not its ancestor's private functions.

Suppose you create a user object A and define for it two functions: F1, a private function; and F2, a protected function. Any script in object A can call F1 or F2:

```
F1()    // call the private function
F2()    // call the protected function
```

Now suppose you create a user object B as a subclass of A. When you write a new script for B, it can call F2 but not F1:

```
F1()    // this gives a syntax error: B's scripts cannot call F1
F2()    // this is okay: B's scripts can call F2
```

This does not mean that subclass B did not inherit the private function F1. F1 is there but is not visible to new programming added to B. From B's perspective, F1 with its programming is very much like the Powersoft-supplied built-in programming shown in Figure 12-12: It's there, it's operating behind the scenes, but it's not directly accessible to the programmer. Any programming that calls F1 must have been added back during the development of the parent object A.

The decision whether to make a function or an instance variable private or protected is a subtle one. It depends on how you plan your application's object class hierarchy.

USER-DEFINED EVENTS

In addition to writing scripts for the events that PowerBuilder attaches to an object, you can create new events — user-defined events — for an object, name them yourself, and write scripts for them.

To add a user-defined event to a user object, select Declare|User Events from the User Object Painter menu. This menu choice, like the one for defining instance variables, is available in other menus too. It opens the Events dialog box, shown in Figure 12-13, which lists all of the events for the object. At the top of the list are the built-in events, which you cannot modify and are grayed out. At the bottom of the list you can add new user-defined events by typing in an event name and, optionally, assigning it an event ID. Figure 12-13 shows how you could define three new events, named mousemove, mouseenter, and mouseexit, and assign the event ID "pbm_mousemove" to the mousemove event.

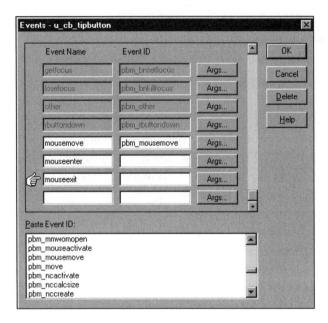

Figure 12-13
The Events dialog box.

The event name is how you will refer to the event in the future. The event ID is PowerBuilder's internal name for the event. You can give the event any name you want, except of course one that is already in use. For the event ID, you are restricted to picking one from the list at the bottom of the dialog box or leaving it blank. Scroll to the event ID you want and double-click it to select it. If you do assign an event ID to a user-defined event, PowerBuilder will detect the event and run your event script when it occurs.

Consider, for example, the event ID pbm_mousemove. This event fires on an object whenever you move the mouse pointer over the surface of it. (It fires a lot, because even the tiniest movement of the mouse pointer causes the event to occur.) PowerBuilder detects the event because Microsoft Windows detects it and notifies PowerBuilder. In Windows the event is called WM_MOUSEMOVE; pbm_mousemove is the PowerBuilder equivalent. In Figure 12-13 we are asking PowerBuilder to notify our user object when this event fires by firing the event that we have named mousemove. We plan to write a script to respond to that event in the future.

The list of possible event IDs is quite long. Windows fires a great many events on our objects. PowerBuilder picks up these messages and adds a few of its own, but it allows only a handful of them to surface as the built-in events that we normally work with. By creating user-defined events, you can tap into the larger world of Windows and PowerBuilder events. Most of these events are not described in the PowerBuilder documentation. All that's provided is a cross-reference between the Windows name for an event (WM_MOUSEMOVE) and its PowerBuilder name (pbm_mousemove). You must acquire and refer to the documentation for the Microsoft Windows Software Developer's Kit (SDK), or some other source, for more information.

By not assigning an event ID to a user-defined event, you can implement a custom event that is not detected by Windows or PowerBuilder. Through PowerScript programming, you can write scripts that determine when the event should occur and fire it at the appropriate time. The event can be anything, such as a business-process event. ("Inventory quantity is low; time to reorder.")

(There is one other possibility: You can assign an event ID to one of 75 Windows custom events, which PowerBuilder names pbm_custom01 to pbm_custom75. Prior to version 5.0 of PowerBuilder, this was the only way to do custom events; you were not allowed to leave the "Event ID" column blank in Figure 12-13. In version 5.0, this alternative is useful only if other programs outside your application will be firing custom events on your application's objects.)

In Figure 12-13 I define two custom events: mouseenter and mouseexit. I want mouseenter to fire when the mouse pointer moves across an object's border into the object, and mouseexit to fire when the mouse pointer moves out of it. There are no Windows or PowerBuilder versions of these events, so we can't rely on PowerBuilder to fire them for us. But by careful programming of the mousemove event, we can determine when they occur, and we can write scripts that fire the events with lines of code such as this:

```
This.EVENT MouseEnter()
```

This runs the object's mouseenter script we have written.
Let's look at the complete example.

Arguments and Return Values on Custom Events

When you click the Args button next to an event in the Events dialog box, an Event Declaration dialog box pops up. In it, you can define arguments to be passed into the event script and a return value to pass out of it. We used event arguments and return values for built-in events back in Chapter 10. They play an essential role in DataWindow events such as ItemChanged.

The Event Declaration dialog is virtually identical to the Function Declaration dialog that you use to set up a user-defined function (Figure 12-11). For a noncustom event (one with an Event ID), you can see the arguments and return value, but you can't change them. For a custom event, you can see and change them, just as you do for a user-defined function. In fact, there is very little difference between a custom event and a user-defined function.

EXAMPLE: BUTTON TIPS — A WINDOW WITH SMART OBJECTS AND USER EVENTS

This example shows how to implement "button tips," messages that pop up describing buttons on a window. Figure 12-14 shows the finished product, a window with four buttons. When you move the mouse into Button 2, the tip, "This is the second button," pops up as shown. In a real application, of course, the button labels and their tips would be more informative.

This example demonstrates the use of user events and other techniques that I have described in the last couple of chapters.

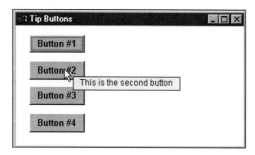

Figure 12-14

A window with button tips. When the mouse pointer enters a button, a message pops up describing it.

PowerBuilder implements this feature for its toolbar buttons — the feature is called "PowerTips." Many other Windows products offer the same feature. There is no easy way to implement this feature for CommandButtons and PictureButtons, however. You must resort to fancy work with objects, events, and scripts.

The four buttons on the window are not ordinary CommandButtons. They belong to the object class u_cb_tipbutton, a user-defined subclass of CommandButton that I created using the User Object Painter.

For the u_cb_tipbutton class, I defined three new user events — mousemove, mouseenter, and mouseexit — using the steps described earlier and illustrated in Figure 12-13. At this point, I can write scripts for the three events. PowerBuilder will run the mousemove script automatically, since it is tied to the PowerBuilder event pbm_mousemove. But mouseenter and mouseexit are custom events, and I have to figure out when to fire them myself. How do you do it?

There are several approaches to the "mouseenter/mouseexit" problem. Here is my approach: I notice that as you move the mouse across the surface of the window, PowerBuilder fires a steady stream of pbm_mousemove events. While the mouse is moving in an empty part of the window, the events fire on the window itself. While the mouse is moving inside a control, they fire on the control but not on the window. When the mouse moves out of the control, they resume firing on the window.

Thus, the first time mousemove fires on a button, that firing can trigger its mouseenter event. The next time that mousemove fires on the window, that firing can trigger the button's mouseexit event. There will have to be scripts on the window and on the buttons to accomplish this. The button scripts can figure out when to trigger mouseenter. The window scripts can figure out when to trigger mouseexit. (This approach would prove to have some flaws in more complex windows, such as when the buttons are enclosed inside other controls, which would require more programming.)

Here are the scripts for the u_cb_tipbutton class. First, its instance variables:

```
Public:
    String    is_tip = ""
Protected:
    Boolean   ib_mouse_in = False
```

The mouseenter script:

```
ib_mouse_in = True      // now the mouse is in this object
```

The mouseexit script:

```
ib_mouse_in = False     // the mouse is no longer in this object
```

The mousemove script:

```
IF NOT ib_mouse_in THEN
    This.EVENT MouseEnter()
END IF
```

The variable *is_tip* will hold the tip string for each of the four buttons, such as "This is the second button." It starts out as an empty string.

The variable *ib_mouse_in* is True while the mouse pointer is inside the button and False otherwise. As you can see, the mouseenter and mouseexit scripts set its value.

The mousemove script executes frequently as you move the mouse around inside the object. If *ib_mouse_in* = False ("IF NOT ib_mouse_in") when it runs, then the mouse has just now moved into the object. So the script calls the mouseenter event script.

That's the entire programming on the u_cb_tipbutton object class.

In the Window Painter, after placing each of the four buttons on the window, I added a little more programming to each of them. This is not an uncommon technique with user objects: You develop most of their features in the User Object Painter and then add a little more to their event scripts in the Window Painter.

This is Button 2's constructor event script, which assigns a value to the button's public instance variable *is_tip*:

```
This.is_tip = "This is the second button"
```

This is Button 2's mouseenter script, a one-line script that calls the window function wf_mouseenterscontrol. I'll describe that function in a moment:

```
Parent.wf_mouseenterscontrol(This)
```

This line of code could not be added to the mouseenter script in the User Object Painter, because in that painter you cannot use "Parent" to signify the window containing the button. In fact, there is no direct way for a script in the User Object Painter to address the window that will ultimately contain it. This is a common issue with user objects, and there are a couple of common techniques to overcome it. In this example, here's the technique I've used: In the User Object Painter, create a custom event, such as mouseenter; in the Window Painter, write a script for the custom event after placing the object on the window. In the Window Painter, the script has access to "Parent" and all the other features of the window, which the User Object Painter does not.

The window has these instance variables:

```
Protected:
 Boolean ib_mouse_in_control = False
 u_cb_Tipbutton  iu_mouse_control
```

The variable *ib_mouse_in_control* is True when the mouse pointer is moving inside one of the buttons and False when it is not. When ib_mouse_in_control = True, the object variable *iu_mouse_control* is the button containing the mouse: Button 1, Button 2, Button 3, or Button 4.

The window has a mousemove script, which determines when the mouse exits from a button. Although we had to add mousemove to the u_cb_tipbutton user object as a user-defined event, that's not necessary for windows that already have a built-in mousemove event. This is the window's mousemove script:

```
IF ib_mouse_in_control THEN    // the mouse is inside a control
   wf_mouseexitscontrol()      // this function triggers mouseexit
END IF
```

When the window's mousemove event fires, the mouse pointer is moving somewhere in the window outside its controls. If the event fires while *ib_mouse_in_control* = True, then the mouse has just exited from one of the buttons. In this case, the script calls the window function wf_mouseexitscontrol, which will fire the mouseexit event on the button.

The window has two window functions: wf_mouseenterscontrol and wf_mouseexitscontrol. You create window functions in exactly the same way as user object functions, starting by selecting Declare|Window Functions from the Window Painter menu.

Here is the source code for the wf_mouseenterscontrol function:

```
Integer   ix, iy    // x and y coordinates for the tip box
String    ls_tip    // the tip to be displayed

ib_mouse_in_control = True      // the mouse is now inside a control
iu_mouse_control = au_control   // remember which control it is

ls_tip = iu_mouse_control.is_tip
ix = iu_mouse_control.x + (iu_mouse_control.width * 4 / 5)
iy = iu_mouse_control.y + (iu_mouse_control.height * 4 / 5)
uo_st_tipbox.uf_showtip(ls_tip, ix, iy)
```

Here is the wf_mouseexitscontrol function:

```
iu_mouse_control.EVENT MouseExit()
ib_mouse_in_control = False
uo_st_tipbox.uf_hidetip()
```

The wf_mouseenterscontrol function is called by each button's mouseenter script. It sets the variable *ib_mouse_in_control* to True, since the mouse is now inside a button, and it sets the object variable *iu_mouse_control* to whatever button has the mouse. The variable *au_control* is passed as an argument into the function. If you look back at the button's mouseenter script, you'll see that *This* — that is, this button object — is passed in.

The last four lines of the function deal with displaying the pop-up tip — *iu_mouse_control.is_tip* is the text for the tip. Since *is_tip* is a public instance variable of the button, you can access it as a property. The calculations for *ix* and *iy* determine where in the window the tip box should appear. The tip box is a control named uo_st_tipbox, and it's usually invisible. As we shall see, it has two functions, uf_showtip and uf_hidetip, which make it visible and invisible. When you call uf_showtip, as the last line does, you must pass it the text you want to display, as well as the position (*ix* and *iy*) where you want the box to appear.

The wf_mouseexitscontrol function is called by the window's mousemove script. It fires the mouseexit event on whichever button the variable *iu_mouse_control* contains. It sets the variable *ib_mouse_in_control* to False, since the mouse is no longer inside a button. And it calls uo_st_tipbox's uf_hidetip function, which makes the tip invisible.

The control uo_st_tipbox, which is the text box in Figure 12-14 containing the message "This is the second button," is a smart object. Its object class is u_st_tipbox, which I created as a subclass of the StaticText object. The u_st_tipbox object has two user-defined functions, uf_showtip and uf_hidetip. This is uf_showtip:

```
This.Text = as_tip
This.x    = ax
This.y    = ay
This.Show()
```

The variables *as_tip*, *ax*, and *ay* are the parameters passed into this function when it is called: the tip text string, the x-position, and the y-position for the object, respectively. The first three lines of code transfer these variables into the object's properties. The last line makes the object visible.

The uf_hidetip function is even simpler. It makes the object invisible:

```
This.Hide()
```

This example has illustrated a number of techniques:

- **Object-oriented design** — Everything is encapsulated within three types of objects — the window, the buttons, and the text box. There are no global variables or global functions. The objects work together by sending messages to one another.

- **User events** — mousemove, mouseenter, and mouseexit.

- **User-defined object functions** — such as wf_mouseenterscontrol and uf_showtip.

- **Public instance variables** — Notice how the variable *is_tip* looks like a variable to the scripts inside the u_cb_tipbutton object and looks like a property to outside objects.

- **Polymorphism** — When the wf_mouseexitscontrol function fires the MouseExit method, it does not know which button it is sending the message to. But all buttons can receive this event, and each can respond to it in its own way.

Custom Visual User Objects

Now let's return to the discussion of the different types of user-defined objects. So far we've seen examples of new controls created as subclasses of existing controls such as CommandButtons. In PowerBuilder, these are called *standard visual user objects*. PowerBuilder calls another similar type of user-defined object a *custom visual user object*. I prefer to think of this latter type as a "compound control" or a "piece of a window." It is several controls grouped together to form a new type of control.

EXAMPLE: THE PROGRESS METER

Figure 12-15 shows a window with a progress meter. It's not important what the OK button does when you click it, but the processing, whatever it is, takes a long time. Maybe it's doing a series of FETCHes in a loop, to update 12,000 rows in a database table. And while it's doing it, the progress meter shows how far along it is. It shows progress numerically — "4451 of 12000 - 37%" — and graphically, by the length of the expanding bar.

Figure 12-15
A window with a progress meter.

The progress meter is a user object named u_progressmeter. It is not a simple single-control object like the buttons and such that we have built up to now. Instead, it is a collection of controls — rectangles, lines, and text controls — combined into a single object.

To build such an object, open the User Object Painter and click the New button. In the New User Object dialog box, click "Visual Custom" —

in past examples, we've selected "Visual Standard," as shown in Figure 12-3 — and click OK. The User Object Painter opens in a style virtually identical to that of the Window Painter, as you can see from Figure 12-16.

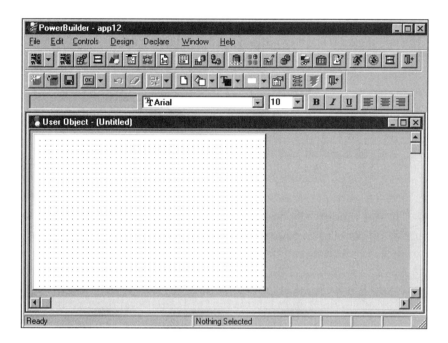

Figure 12-16
The User Object Painter, when designing a custom visual object. It is virtually identical to the Window Painter.

You design this user object just as you would design a window in the Window Painter. You can stretch the design surface bigger or smaller, place controls on it, and add event scripts to them. You can make the user object smarter by defining instance variables, user object functions, and user events.

Figure 12-17 shows the completed design of the progress meter user object, which I saved and named u_progressmeter. As for its programming, it turns out that none of the controls inside the object require any event scripts. This is just as well, since most of the controls are rectangles and lines, which don't have events and therefore can't be programmed.

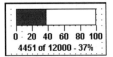

Figure 12-17

The completed design of the progress meter user object.

There are two public user object functions that the outside application can call to control the progress meter: uf_initialize, which initializes the meter (that is, resets it to zero), and uf_advance, which advances the meter to a new value.

You call the first function, uf_initialize, with a single parameter:

```
uo_progressmeter.uf_initialize(al_finalcount)
```

In the window (Figure 12-15), the control is named uo_progressmeter. Its object class is named u_progressmeter. The parameter *al_finalcount* is the final count, the number that is equivalent to 100 percent. In Figure 12-15, *al_finalcount* is 12,000.

Here is the source code for the function uf_initialize:

```
ir_finalcount = al_finalcount
uf_advance(0)
```

The first line stores the final count in the instance variable *ir_finalcount* so that the uf_advance function can use it later in its calculations. The second line calls uf_advance to set the meter to zero.

The second function, uf_advance, also takes a single parameter:

```
uo_progressmeter.uf_advance(al_count)
```

The parameter *al_count* indicates how much progress the process has made. For example, if the final count is 12000 and the current value of *al_count* is 6000, the progress meter will display "50%."

Here is the source code for uf_advance:

```
Integer li_percent        // percent complete
Real     lr_ratio         // ratio complete (between 0.0 and 1.0)
lr_ratio = al_count / ir_finalcount
li_percent = Round(lr_ratio * 100, 0)
```

```
st_text.Text = String(al_count)     + " of "   + &
               String(ir_finalcount) + " - " +    &
               String(li_percent)   + "%"
r_innerbox.Width = r_outerbox.Width * lr_ratio
```

The function modifies the properties of two controls inside the object: the Text property of st_text, which is the StaticText control that says, in Figure 12-15, "4451 of 12000 - 37%"; and the Width property of r_innerbox, which is the expanding rectangle.

 In the sample application for this chapter on the CD-ROM, you will find a little more programming than I have shown here. For example, you don't really want to update the progress meter 12,000 times. That would be terribly time-consuming. So the uf_advance function has additional logic to do an update only at one percent intervals.

Placing the completed user object on a window, as shown in Figure 12-15, is no different than for the other visual user objects that we have seen: In the Window Painter, click the User Object button on the PainterBar's dropdown control palette, select "u_progressmeter" from the list, and click the point in the window where you want the object to appear. PowerBuilder named the control uo_1. I renamed it uo_progressmeter.

The clicked script on the OK button does something like this:

```
Long i
uo_progressmeter.uf_initialize(12000)
FOR i = 1 TO 12000
   uo_progressmeter.uf_advance(i)

      (... some complex processing goes here ...)

NEXT
```

Custom Class (Nonvisual) User Objects

Of the five types of objects you create with the User Object Painter (Figure 12-3), three are visual:

Custom Visual

External Visual

Standard Visual

and two are nonvisual:

Custom Class

Standard Class

So far all of our examples have been visual objects. They end up as controls on windows, where the user can see them and interact with them. Now let's consider nonvisual objects which, since the user does not see them, tend to be more abstract.

THE BENEFITS OF NONVISUAL USER OBJECTS

Nonvisual user objects are useful because they let you encapsulate application operations into objects, making them easier to develop, manage, and maintain.

For example, in the chapter on data entry techniques, Chapter 10, we did a lot of work on a window for entering new orders for customers. At several points in the process, various scripts perform operations on the customer table. One script validates that the customer ID entered in a new order is valid. Another performs a customer credit check. A third updates the customer balance due with the amount of each new or changed order.

What if we collected all these code fragments and encapsulated them into a single object, called nv_customertable? We remove all of the SQL statements that access the customer table from the DataWindow's event scripts and place them all into this object. Any access to the table would require calling one of several custom functions on the object, such as these:

```
nv_customertable.uf_isvalid(custid)       // validate customer ID
nv_customertable.uf_creditcheck(custid)  // do a credit check
nv_customertable.uf_updatebal(custid, amount)  //update balance
```

Is this approach an improvement? At first it might not be much of one, but as your application gets more sophisticated or undergoes major revisions, I suspect you'll be glad to have all customer handling encapsulated. If there is a major change to the customer table's structure, or to the means of accessing it (for example, if it's moved to a different database server from the order table's), it will be much easier to isolate the programming changes necessary if they are isolated to a single object. The object is reusable and can be shared by other windows that have similar needs. Also, adding special refinements is easier, such as skipping the second SELECT if the user enters two orders in a row for the same customer.

Convinced? Here are some other ideas for nonvisual user objects:

- Encapsulating all the security management for an application into a single object.

- Encapsulating all the error handling into a single object. PowerBuilder already provides an object, the error object, which handles certain aspects. You might create a smarter subclass of the error object that is more sophisticated.

- Encapsulating business functions, such as managing inventory or updating stock market prices.

- Encapsulating access to remote computer systems, such as another subsidiary's accounting system.

In this chapter we will walk through at a couple of basic examples of nonvisual objects. Chapter 17, "The Application Infrastructure," will show more sophisticated examples and describe an application that relies heavily on nonvisual objects.

EXAMPLE: THE USAGE TRACKER OBJECT

As an example of a nonvisual user object, this chapter's sample application includes nv_usagetrack, a "usage tracker" object. This object accumulates runtime information about the application. Figure 12-18 shows a display of the information: recent activity and window usage statistics. In this application, the nv_usagetrack object is tracking when each window opens and closes and calculating statistics from that. But it would be easy to extend it to track just about anything, such as the number of transactions processed by the progress meter.

INSTANTIATING A NONVISUAL OBJECT

Visual objects are instantiated when you open them, or when you open the object that contains them. For example, when you open a window, you are instantiating the window object and also instantiating all the control objects, such as buttons, that the window contains.

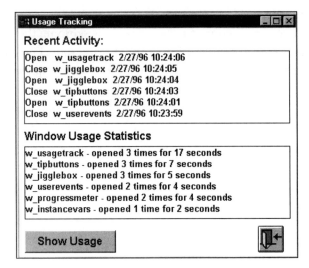

Figure 12-18

Usage tracking — a nonvisual object keeps track of application activity.

You don't open a nonvisual object but, of course you must instantiate it somehow. You instantiate a nonvisual object by declaring an object variable for it and using the PowerScript command CREATE.

In the sample application for this chapter, the object is declared as a global variable so that all windows and every other object in the application can see it:

```
nv_usagetrack gnv_usagetrack
```

The object class is named nv_usagetrack, and this application will use an instance of it named *gnv_usagetrack*.

The application's open script instantiates the object:

```
gnv_usagetrack = CREATE nv_usagetrack
```

You always instantiate a nonvisual object with this command:

```
<instance name> = CREATE <class name>
```

If you want to "de-instantiate" the instance, use the DESTROY command. You might do this in the application's close script, or at any time that you no longer need the object:

```
DESTROY gnv_usagetrack
```

After the object is instantiated, the other objects in the application work with it by sending messages to it (Figure 12-19). As always, the messages can be functions, properties, and events. Typically, most of the messages will be function calls. The nv_usagetrack object has several functions that are called by the window and control scripts in the application. When any window in the application opens, its open script calls the function uf_windowopens:

```
gnv_usagetrack.uf_windowopens(This)
```

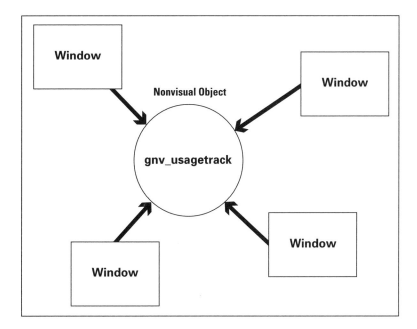

Figure 12-19
The windows in the application send messages to the "usage tracking" nonvisual object.

Each window's close script calls the function uf_windowcloses:

```
gnv_usagetrack.uf_windowcloses(This)
```

The programming for these two functions stores information about window opens and closes, such as the name of the window, the date, and the time in the object's instance variables.

The clicked script for the Show Usage button in Figure 12-18 calls two other functions on the nv_usagetrack object:

```
gnv_usagetrack.uf_getrecentactivity(li_num_log_items, ls_log)
gnv_usagetrack.uf_getstatistics(ls_win_names, li_num_opens, &
                                ll_seconds)
```

The function uf_getrecentactivity returns (in the multiline string *ls_log*) the list of recent activities. The function uf_getstatistics calculates and returns (in the arrays *ls_win_names*, *li_num_opens*, and *ll_seconds*) the window usage statistics.

CREATING A NEW NONVISUAL OBJECT CLASS

You create a new nonvisual object class with the User Object Painter in the same way as the visual objects we've shown earlier. In the New User Object dialog box (Figure 12-3), click Custom Class and then OK. When the User Object Painter opens, it looks the same as for a custom visual object as shown in Figure 12-16. The only difference is that the window title says "inherited from nonvisualobject" after the words "User-Object - (Untitled)."

The painter interface is misleading, because you cannot add controls to the object or in any way change its visual appearance. The only thing you can do to the object is add programming to it: user-defined functions, instance variables, user events, and so forth. In designing the object nv_usagetrack, I used the Declare|Instance Variables menu choice to declare the arrays that maintain the activity history and statistics. Then I used the Declare|User Object Functions menu choice to write the four public functions described earlier:

- **uf_windowopens** — notifies the object that a window is opening.
- **uf_windowcloses** — notifies the object that a window is closing.
- **uf_getrecentactivity** — returns a list of recent activity items.
- **uf_getstatistics** — returns arrays of statistics.

I also added some private functions to support the public ones. If you would like to see the source code for this object, please refer to the sample application that accompanies this chapter.

Standard Class (Nonvisual) User Objects

"Custom class" user objects, such as nv_usagetrack, are subclasses of the generic object class NonVisualObject, which is part of PowerBuilder's object class hierarchy (Table 12-1). You can also create subclasses of specific nonvisual object classes, such as Transaction and DynamicDescriptionArea. This allows you to create "smarter" versions of these objects.

EXAMPLE 1: A SMART TRANSACTION OBJECT

Let's go through the exercise of building a smarter transaction object. Begin by creating a new user object, and in the New User Object dialog box (Figure 12-3) click Standard Class and then OK. This pops up the Select Standard Class Type dialog box shown in Figure 12-20. It shows the PowerBuilder object classes that you can derive a subclass from. All of them are subclasses of the NonVisualObject class, but each serves a specialized purpose. I described Transaction, DynamicDescriptionArea, and DynamicStagingArea in Chapter 7, in the discussion of database programming. The next example will show how to use a DataStore. Others on the list will be described in later chapters. For now, select "transaction" from the list and click OK.

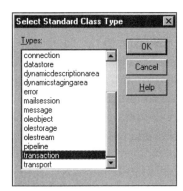

Figure 12-20
The Select Standard Class Type dialog box.

The User Object Painter looks and works as it has in the past (Figure 12-16), except that the title will say "inherited from transaction." As with the previous nonvisual object example, you cannot draw anything on the design surface. You may only add programming, such as functions and instance variables.

Let's add a function named uf_connect to the object which will connect the transaction object to a database. Select Declare|User Object Functions from the menu and click New in the Select Function in User Object dialog box. Define a public function named uf_connect with no arguments that returns a Boolean value — it will return True for success or False for failure:

```
This.DBMS       = "ODBC"
This.Database   = "Video Store DB"
This.UserId     = "dba"
This.DBParm     = "Connectstring='DSN=Video Store DB'"
This.AutoCommit = True
CONNECT USING This;
IF This.SqlCode <> 0 THEN
MessageBox("Error on Connect",                          &
      "SQL Code: "       + String(This.SqlCode)    +   &
      "~nError Code: "   + String(This.SqlDbCode)  +   &
      "~nError Message= " + This.SqlErrText,            &
      stopsign!)
   Return False
END IF
RETURN True
```

This script is very similar to those presented in Chapter 7 for defining the transaction object's properties and connecting to the database. The major difference is that the pronoun *This* replaces a transaction variable such as *trans1* or *sqlca*.

After defining the uf_connect function, you might define other functions, such as uf_disconnect to disconnect the transaction object from the database. Many other improvements are possible, such as functions to return the status of the object, options to connect to the database in different ways, and functions that log activity. You can add such functions now or return to add them later. When you are finished, save the object with the name nv_trans_smart and close it.

There are two ways to use the smart transaction object. The first way, which follows the technique shown earlier for nonvisual objects, is to declare an object variable for it and create it:

```
nv_trans_smart trans1  // declare trans1, an instance of
                       // nv_trans_smart
trans1 = CREATE nv_trans_smart  // instantiate the object trans1
trans1.uf_connect()  // call the function that does the CONNECT
```

Typically you'd put the first line in the global variable declarations and the other two lines in the application's open event.

The other approach is to make the built-in PowerBuilder variable *sqlca* an instance of the nv_trans_smart class. By default, *sqlca* belongs to the Transaction class, and PowerBuilder automatically declares and instantiates it for you (see Chapter 7):

```
Transaction sqlca          // never type in these two lines...
sqlca = CREATE Transaction //...PowerBuilder does them automatically
```

To make *sqlca* a member of the nv_trans_smart class instead of the Transaction class, open the Application Painter and click the Properties button on the PainterBar to open the application object's property sheet. The Variable Types tab is shown in Figure 12-21. There are five built-in global variables, of which *sqlca* is one. As you can see, the variable type (object class) for *sqlca* is "transaction." But you can change it to "nv_trans_smart" or to any other subclass of the Transaction class that you have defined. Thereafter, *sqlca* is a smart transaction object. You don't need a declaration statement or CREATE statement for it. To connect it to the database, you can call the user-defined *uf_connect* function:

```
sqlca.uf_connect()  // call the function that does the CONNECT
```

From this simple exercise, it may be hard to see the benefit of smart transaction objects. But as your applications and your database connections become more complex, it will be easier to maintain and enhance your application using these objects. The transaction functionality is encapsulated in its own object and not buried in scripts such as the application's open event script.

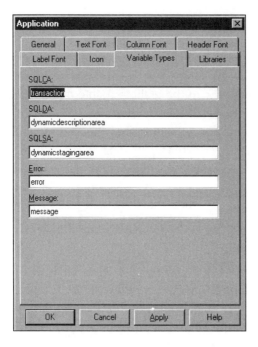

Figure 12-21

The Variable Types tab of the application object's property sheet.

EXAMPLE 2: A DataStore Object

The *DataStore* object is an especially interesting nonvisual object. A DataStore object is a nonvisual DataWindow control. It offers all of the data handling features of a DataWindow control, including most of the functions, events, and properties. You can assign a DataWindow object to a DataStore; retrieve data rows into it; filter, sort, update, and print the data rows; and so forth.

The big difference between a DataStore object and a DataWindow control is that a DataStore, being nonvisual, is always invisible at runtime. Also, since it's not a control, you do not place a DataStore into a window. Instead, you instantiate it at runtime by issuing a CREATE command.

The DataStore is useful when you want the power of a DataWindow but have no need for a visual display. You might use a DataStore, for example, to print a report. Or you might use it to transfer data through the middle tier of a three-tier application.

Designing a DataStore object is similar to designing a smart transaction object: Open the User Object Painter and click the New button. Select "Standard Class" from the New User Object dialog box (Figure 12-3). In the Select Standard Class Type dialog box (Figure 12-20), select "datastore." PowerBuilder opens the new DataStore object in the User Object Painter. As with other user objects, you can enhance this object by defining user object functions, writing event scripts, declaring instance variables, and so forth.

Unlike any other type of nonvisual user object, a DataStore has a property sheet, which you open by clicking the Properties button on the User Object PainterBar. Figure 12-22 shows a DataStore named nv_ds_orderlist, overlaid with its property sheet, being designed in the User Object Painter. The property sheet displays only one tab with only one property: the name of the DataWindow object to be associated with this DataStore. In Figure 12-22, the DataWindow object d_orderlist has been assigned to the DataStore nv_ds_orderlist. This DataWindow object lists video store orders in a style suitable for printing as a report. For a look at the printed report, see Figure 14-14 in Chapter 14.

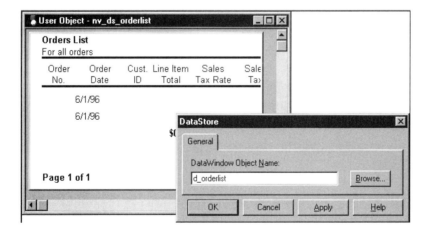

Figure 12-22
A DataStore and its property sheet in the User Object Painter.

At runtime, your application must execute a CREATE command to create an instance of the DataStore object, as we've seen for other types of nonvisual objects. This CommandButton script creates an instance of Figure 12-22's nv_ds_orderlist DataStore, naming the instance *lnv_ds_orderlist*:

```
nv_ds_orderlist lnv_ds_orderlist
lnv_ds_orderlist = CREATE nv_ds_orderlist
```

Like DataWindows, most DataStore objects begin operation by connecting to *sqlca,* or to some other transaction object, and then by retrieving rows from the database. You could write the code for these steps in the DataStore's constructor event:

```
This.SetTransObject(sqlca)
This.Retrieve()
```

Thereafter, you manipulate the DataStore with function calls and other programming. This code continues the CommandButton script that created *lnv_ds_orderlist*. It sets a filter on the DataStore, modifies the report's title, prints the report, and destroys the instance:

```
String ls_filter      // the filter expression
String ls_filterdesc  // description of filter, for report title

ls_filter = "orderdate >= date('1/1/1996') and custid = '1040'"
lnv_ds_orderlist.SetFilter(ls_filter)   // set the filter
lnv_ds_orderlist.Filter()               // apply the filter
ls_filterdesc = "For orders on or after 1/1/96 for customer 1040"
lnv_ds_orderlist.object.reportdescription.Text = ls_filterdesc
lnv_ds_orderlist.Print()    // print the report
DESTROY lnv_ds_orderlist    // destroy (dis-instantiate) it
```

You will find a running version of this example, along with error handling and a demonstration of other DataStore techniques, in the sample application for this chapter on the CD-ROM.

Other Subclasses Created with the User Object Painter

From Table 12-3 or Figure 12-3, you can see that we have covered four of the five types of object subclasses that can be created with the User Object Painter. There is one other: external visual user objects, which are created typically by and for C++, but which you can also utilize in PowerBuilder as a control. For more information on these, please refer to the PowerBuilder documentation.

Subclasses Created with Other Painters

From Table 12-2 you can see that there are four types of subclasses not created with the User Object Painter:

1. **Window** — subclasses of the Window object class, created with the Window Painter

2. **Application** — subclasses of the Application object class, created with the Application Painter

3. **Menu** — subclasses of the Menu object class, created with the Menu Painter

4. **Structure** — subclasses of the Structure object class, created with the Structure Painter

WINDOW SUBCLASSES

If you have been working with PowerBuilder for awhile, either by following this book's exercises or by working on your own, you have no doubt created many subclasses of the Window object class by now, without even realizing it!

Whenever you design a new window in the Window Painter, you are actually creating a new subclass of the built-in PowerBuilder Window object class. When you run the application and open the window, you are creating an instance of that subclass. This is illustrated in Figure 12-23 for a window named w_1. There will never be an instance of the Window class itself, only instances of its subclasses.

If you think carefully about the definition of objects, you will realize that every new window that you design must be a new object class. Suppose that you design two windows and add a little bit of programming to each, perhaps to their open scripts. Since each window will presumably have different programming, they cannot belong to the same object class. By definition, all instances of a single object class have identical programming, and, therefore, two objects with different programming must be from different classes.

(By the same line of reasoning, you can deduce that every control placed on a window must be a new object class. So if you have four

CommandButtons on a window, each button has its own object class. Each object class will be a subclass of CommandButton.)

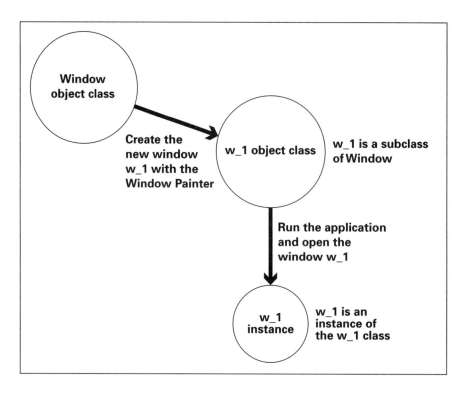

Figure 12-23
A Window object subclass and an instance of it.

In the normal course of things, the window subclass and its instance have the same name. PowerBuilder automatically declares an instance variable for each window subclass, as if you were to say

```
w_1  w_1  // "w_1" is an instance of object class "w_1"
```

If you like, you can add a declaration of your own in order to give the instance a different name:

```
w_1   lw_instance    // "lw_instance" is an instance of class "w_1"
Open (lw_instance)  // instantiate the window (create the instance)
```

Explicitly declaring your window instances becomes important when you want to open two or more instances of a window at the same time.

Each instance must have a different name:

```
w_1   lw_instance1, lw_instance2 // declare 2 instances of class w_1
Open(lw_instance1)    // open (instantiate) the first instance
Open(lw_instance2)    // open (instantiate) the second instance
```

Here's a similar example that uses an array to open five windows. By using an array, you avoid having to know in advance how many simultaneous instances there will be. This script also offsets each window slightly from its original position, because otherwise all of them would pile directly on top of one another:

```
w_1    lw_instances[]  // declare an array of window instances
Integer i              // declare a counter variable

FOR i = 1 TO 5         // loop to create five windows
   Open(lw_instances[i])
   lw_instances[i].x = lw_instances[i].x + 100 * (i - 1)
   lw_instances[i].y = lw_instances[i].y + 100 * (i - 1)
NEXT
```

You can also make subclasses of your window subclasses, to any depth. For example, you could make another window class w_2 as a subclass of w_1. Of course, inheritance comes into play here, and any changes you make to the parent window will be inherited by all of its children.

To create a subclass of an existing window, click the Inherit button in the Select Window dialog box when you open the Window Painter. Or select File|Inherit from the Window Painter menu. I will explore this topic in the next chapter.

MENU SUBCLASSES

As with windows, every menu you design with the Menu Painter is a new subclass of the Menu class. You can make sub-subclasses using the Inherit button or making the File|Inherit menu choice in the painter.

APPLICATION SUBCLASSES

Every new application is a subclass of the Application class. However, there is no ability to create sub-subclasses of the Application class, because there is no Inherit button or menu choice in the Application Painter.

This turns out to be a limitation of sorts. Chapter 17 will explain why this is so and show how to use nonvisual user objects to work around it.

STRUCTURE SUBCLASSES

I described structures in Chapter 4. There is not much more to say about them here, except to say that every type of structure that you define is a subclass of the Structure class that is built into the PowerBuilder object class hierarchy.

A structure is a fairly unintelligent object. It has properties — the elements that you define for it — but neither functions nor events. And you can't take one of your structures and create new subclasses of it. If you have a need for these abilities, you should consider using a nonvisual object instead.

What's Next with Objects?

This chapter is the second of three explaining object-oriented techniques. We have covered a great deal of ground so far, explaining how to create user-defined objects, how to make them "smarter," and how to add them to a PowerBuilder application.

I've saved the best for last! The next chapter explores the most powerful and interesting object-oriented feature: Inheritance.

13 Inheritance

*I*nheritance is one of the most powerful and important features of object-oriented programming. It is certainly the one feature that can yield the biggest rewards, if you plan its use carefully.

Chapter 11 gave a brief definition of inheritance along with a quick example. But inheritance is a much larger topic than that.

This chapter has two parts: The first part explains the mechanics of inheritance — how you set it up, and what it can and cannot do. The second part offers practical ideas and examples of how to put inheritance into practice in PowerBuilder applications.

The Power of Inheritance

When you create a subclass of an object, the subclass inherits all of the properties, functions, and events of its ancestor. If you make further modifications to the ancestor, the subclass inherits them also, unless the modification is to a feature that the subclass has overridden.

Inheritance gets really interesting when multiple subclass levels are involved. Consider the windows in an application. Suppose that the subclasses run only one level deep, meaning that every window is derived directly from PowerBuilder's window class:

```
Window    - a class in PowerBuilder's built-in hierarchy
   w_1    - subclass of Window
   w_2    - subclass of Window
   w_3    - subclass of Window
   w_4    - subclass of Window
```

This is exactly what you get, if you click only the New button and never the Inherit button, whenever you open the Window Painter to create your windows (Figure 13-1).

Figure 13-1
Opening the Window Painter. To create a subclass of the window class, click New. To create a subclass of a subclass, click Inherit.

Each of the four new windows inherit all the features of the PowerBuilder window class. But since the window class never changes, the inheritance is not at all dynamic.

Suppose instead that each window is a subclass of the one before it:

```
Window              — a class in PowerBuilder's built-in hierarchy
   w_1              — subclass of Window
      w_2           — subclass of w_1
         w_3        — subclass of w_2
            w_4     — subclass of w_3
```

You can get this arrangement by clicking the New button when you open the Window Painter to create w_1, but clicking the Inherit button to create each of the other windows (w_2, w_3, and w_4) from the window preceding it.

This scenario is very dynamic. Every little change you make to w_1, or to w_2 or w_3 for that matter, propagates itself to the deeper subclasses. If every window in your application is derived in some way from w_1, a little change to it can have a profound effect on the entire system.

Before we get too ambitious, however, it's wise to get a better understanding of how inheritance works.

The Mechanics of Inheritance

Let's continue to work with a window example. Figure 13-2 shows three windows: w_1, w_2a, and w_2b. Windows w_2a and w_2b are each a subclass of w_1. This is their object class hierarchy:

```
Window          – a class in PowerBuilder's built-in hierarchy
  w_1           – subclass of Window
      w_2a      – subclass of w_1
      w_2b      – subclass of w_1
```

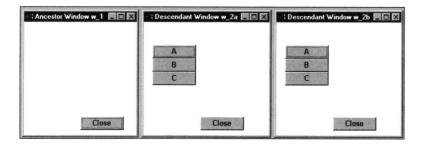

Figure 13-2

Three simple windows. Windows w_2a and w_2b inherit features from w_1.

The inherited windows w_2a and w_2b have different titles, along with additional buttons that their w_1 ancestor does not have.

If we make changes to w_1, the other two windows should inherit them. The changes will be to the properties, functions, and events. Let's look at each of these, beginning with properties.

If you would like to follow along as an exercise, you will find these three windows in the sample application for this chapter on the CD-ROM.

> ## Resetting Properties
>
> You might change your mind about w_2b overriding w_1's properties and prefer that it inherit them once again. To make that happen, select EditIReset Properties from the Window Painter menu for w_2b. If you select a control first, then EditIReset Properties resets just the control. If no con- trol is selected, the menu choice resets the window properties.
>
> Unfortunately, you cannot pick which properties an object is to reinherit — the menu choice always resets all of them.

INHERITING PROPERTIES

Before making any changes to w_1, change a few properties of w_2b: Make it wider, make it green, and move its Close button to the top. Now make a different set of changes to w_1: Make it taller and narrower, make it blue, and move its close button to the left. All of these are changes to the windows' properties.

Window w_2a inherits all of w_1's changed properties. Window w_2b, however, inherits only one of them: It grows taller. The reason is, a subclass never inherits a change to a property that it has already overridden. Since you changed the width property of w_2b when you made it wider, overriding the value it inherited from w_1, changing the width of w_1 no longer has any effect on w_2b.

Inheritance plays no role when you change the windows at runtime. The windows shown in Figure 13-2 are instances, displayed as they appear when the application is running. They are not the object classes, which you work with in the development environment. If a script turns w_1 red at runtime, the other windows do not inherit that change.

INHERITING EVENT SCRIPTS

Windows w_2a and w_2b inherit any change to an event script belonging to w_1. Once again, however, there are ways to override that behavior so that inheritance does not take place.

Inheriting a Window's Controls

When you derive a new window as the descendant of another, it inherits all the properties, functions, and events of its ancestor. But it also inherits much more: all of the controls of the ancestor and all of the properties, functions, and events of those controls.

In the descendant, you can move and resize the controls, and you can modify their properties, functions, and events. However, you cannot remove an inherited control. On the other hand, you can make it invisible which, from the end user's point of point of view, is the same as removing it.

A similar situation arises with inherited menus. A menu contains MenuItems, which are the individual choices within the menu. When a menu is derived from another menu as a descendant, it inherits all the MenuItems. You cannot delete an inherited MenuItem, but you can make it invisible. Chapter 15 will describe menus and MenuItems in more detail.

Write this script for w_1's clicked event:

```
MessageBox("Clicked script for w_1",      &
           "Run by " + This.ClassName())
This.BackColor = RGB(255, 0, 0)   // turn the window red
```

When you run w_1 and click the window, the message in Figure 13-3 appears. When you click OK, the window turns red.

Figure 13-3
The message for w_1.

Windows w_2a and w_2b inherit the script. When you click w_2b, the message pops up and the window turns red. Because of the ClassName function call in the script, the message displays the name of the window, "w_2b," as shown in Figure 13-4.

Figure 13-4
The message for w_2b, inherited from w_1's clicked script.

EXTENDING AN ANCESTOR SCRIPT

If both the ancestor class and the subclass have a script for the same event, what happens? Does the subclass script override the ancestor script, or does it run in addition to it? The answer is, you can have it either way. By default, it runs in addition to the ancestor script.

Here's a clicked script for w_2b. It's very similar to the script it inherits from w_1:

```
MessageBox("Clicked script for w_2b",     &
            "Run by " + This.ClassName())
This.BackColor = RGB(255, 255, 0)   // turn the window yellow
```

Now w_2b has two clicked scripts: this new one of its own and the one it inherited from w_1. When you run the application and open w_2b, you'll find that the descendant script extends the ancestor script: When you click the window, first the w_1 script runs, displaying the message in Figure 13-4 and turning the window red. Then the w_2b script runs, displaying the message in Figure 13-5 and turning the window yellow.

Figure 13-5
The message for w_2b, which appears after or in place of the inherited message.

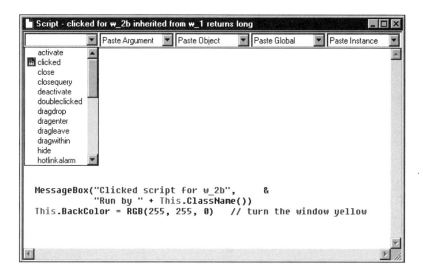

Figure 13-6
Working in the Script Painter in a descendant object.

It's important to know, when you are writing an event script, whether or not it has an ancestor. The Script Painter has a few features to help:

- **"Inherited from" in the title bar** — The Script Painter title bar warns you when the window is the subclass of another. Figure 13-6 shows the Script Painter editing w_2b's clicked script. Notice how the title bar tells you that w_2b is inherited from w_1. This does not necessarily mean that w_1 also has a clicked script, but it serves as a warning that it may.

- **The color-coded Select Event list** — When you pull down the Script Painter's Select Event list, as shown in the top left of Figure 13-6, icons appear next to events that have a script written for them. The icons are color coded: white for a descendant script only, purple for an ancestor script only, and two-color for both. In Figure 13-6, the clicked event has the two-color icon.

- **The Design | Display Ancestor Script menu choice** — When you choose this option from the menu, the Script Painter shows you the ancestor script in the dialog box shown in Figure 13-7. If there are multiple levels of inheritance, the dialog box's Ancestor and Descendant buttons will be available for stepping through the scripts at each level.

Figure 13-7

The Display Ancestor Script dialog box.

Overriding an Ancestor Script

The descendant script can override the ancestor script — that is, run in
place of it. To have it do that, select Design|Override Ancestor Script from
the menu, as shown in Figure 13-8.

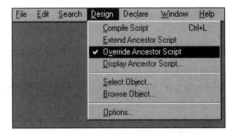

Figure 13-8

The Script Painter's Design menu, with Override Ancestor Script selected.

Running the Ancestor Script at the Conclusion, or in the Middle, of the Descendant Script

When the descendant script overrides the ancestor, the ancestor script does
not run. By executing the CALL command in the descendant script, however,
you can force the ancestor to run. This is the technique to use if you want
the ancestor to run after, or at some point during, its descendant script.

For example:

```
MessageBox("Clicked script for w_2b",    &
           "Run by " + This.ClassName())
This.BackColor = RGB(255, 255, 0)   // turn the window yellow
CALL Super::clicked
```

When you run the application and click window w_2b, the descendant script runs first, then the ancestor. The end result is that the window turns red.

The word "Super" in the CALL statement means "my ancestor." *Super* is a PowerScript pronoun, like *This* and *Parent*. The word "clicked" is the name of the ancestor script to run. You can run any of its scripts, not just the one you are working on.

Instead of using the *Super* pronoun, you can name the ancestor explicitly:

```
CALL w_1::clicked
```

This approach is necessary if there are several ancestor levels and for some reason you need to pick one of them in particular. (Although I would suspect, in this case, that you are making things overly complicated.)

INHERITING FUNCTIONS

A subclass always inherits all functions from its ancestor: built-in PowerBuilder functions, such as Move and Resize, and user-defined functions, such as window functions, menu functions, and user object functions. Although the descendant inherits all of these, it might not be able to "see" them all.

Suppose you define a window function named wf_InitPosition for w_1. It moves the window to an initial position in the center of the screen:

```
Long ll_screen_width     // screen width,  in PowerBuilder units
Long ll_screen_height    // screen height, in PowerBuilder units
Environment   env        // the environment var type is a special
                         // built-in PowerBuilder structure
GetEnvironment(env)      // fill the structure with environment info
ll_screen_width  = PixelsToUnits(env.ScreenWidth,  XPixelsToUnits!)
ll_screen_height = PixelsToUnits(env.ScreenHeight, YPixelsToUnits!)
This.Move((ll_screen_width  - This.Width)  / 2, &
          (ll_screen_height - This.Height) / 2)
```

The open script for w_1 calls the function

```
wf_InitPosition()
```

When you run the application and open the windows, not only does w_1 move to the center, so do w_2a and w_2b, since they inherit the function and the open script.

(If you need to center the window only when it first opens, this is the hard way to do it. The easy way is to open the Position tab in the window's property sheet in the Window Painter and center the window there.)

Let's say you want to be able to move w_2a to the center any time you click its "A" button, in case the window moves from its original position. Can a clicked script in w_2a call w_1's wf_InitPosition function?

```
wf_InitPosition()
```

The answer is yes, as long as wf_InitPosition is declared to be a public or protected function of w_1. You make this choice in the Access field when you first define the function, as shown in Figure 13-9. To change it later, select Design|Function Declaration from the Function Painter menu. If the access is protected, the function is visible to all of the object's descendants. If the access is public, it is visible to outside objects as well. If the access is private, however, only the ancestor's scripts can call the function; an attempt to call it from a descendant script causes a syntax error.

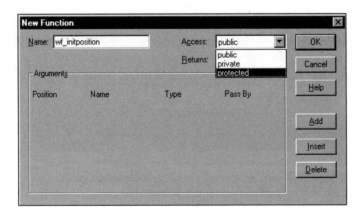

Figure 13-9
Setting the function's access type: public, private, or protected.

OVERRIDING AN ANCESTOR FUNCTION

If you declare a function in the descendant with the same name as an ancestor function, it overrides the ancestor function. There is no extend-or-override option for functions as there is for scripts. Override is the only option.

Let's say that this is the wf_InitPosition function for window w_2b, overriding the one it inherits from w_1:

```
This.Move(0,0)  // move the window to the top-left corner
```

When you open w_2b, its open script, which calls wf_InitPosition, runs. Even though that script is inherited from w_1, it is w_2b's version of the function that it calls, not w_1's. So the window moves to the top-left corner of the screen.

If you must call w_1's overridden function from the descendant, use the Super pronoun:

```
Super::wf_InitPosition()
```

Only the window's scripts and functions can call a function this way. Its control's scripts cannot, because for the control, *Super* is a control on the ancestor, not the ancestor window. As a workaround, you can declare a new window function and call it from the control:

```
wf_SuperInitPosition()
```

This new function can use the *Super* pronoun to call the original function:

```
Super::wf_InitPosition()
```

I'm sure that by the time you've gone through all this, you'll wish that you'd given the two functions different names to begin with.

OVERRIDING AN ANCESTOR'S BUILT-IN FUNCTION

If you create a user-defined function, such as a window function, and give it the same name as one of PowerBuilder's built-in functions, it will override that function. This is the same principle as overriding an ancestor's user-defined function. From an object-oriented point of view, there is no difference between user-defined function and a built-in one.

For example, you can define a window function to replace the Move function. Your version could accept *x* and *y* parameters in pixels, instead of in PowerBuilder Units. Figure 13-10 shows its definition. Here is its code:

```
Long    ll_x_in_units, ll_y_in_units
Integer li_return
ll_x_in_units = PixelsToUnits(al_x_in_pixels, xPixelsToUnits!)
ll_y_in_units = PixelsToUnits(al_y_in_pixels, yPixelsToUnits!)
li_return = Super::Move(ll_x_in_units, ll_y_in_units)
RETURN li_return
```

Don't forget the "Super::" when you call the built-in Move function. Otherwise you'll drop into an infinite loop, as the new Move function calls itself recursively.

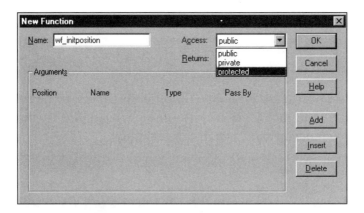

Figure 13-10
Declaring a new Move function to override the built-in Move function.

Personally, I make it a policy not to do this. It seems to me to cause more confusion than good to rewrite PowerBuilder functions. Why not name your function something else, like wf_Move, and call that instead of Move?

OTHER INHERITANCE MECHANICS

The examples so far have been limited to window inheritance, with only two levels of subclass: window to w_1 to w_2a/w_2b. The mechanics for inheritance in other objects, such as controls, menus, and user objects, are exactly the same. So are the mechanics when there are multiple subclass levels. Examples of these cases appear later in the chapter.

Regenerate

In PowerBuilder, inheritance is not one hundred percent automatic. You have to do part of it manually, by performing a process called *regenerate* or *rebuild*.

As you know, a descendant object should inherit changes made to its ancestor. When you change an ancestor, PowerBuilder must fit those changes into the descendant. Some of the changes might be complex, such as revising the definition of an ancestor function that the descendant calls. Some might cause errors, such as deleting an ancestor function that the descendant calls.

This is the step that PowerBuilder does not do automatically: When you change an ancestor, PowerBuilder does not review the impact on its descendants. When you run the application and open a descendant, the famous "unexpected results might occur." Frequently you will get a cryptic error message such as, "Unresolvable external <object name> when linking reference...."

So integrating an ancestor's changes into its descendants is your job. Fortunately, it's not as hard as it sounds. It entails a simple operation called "regenerate."

There are several ways to do a regenerate. The most thorough way, and the one that I use most often, is to open the Library Painter and select either Design|Incremental Rebuild or Design|Full Rebuild from the Library Painter menu. Either of these choices regenerates descendant objects from their ancestors. The incremental rebuild processes only those objects that need their inherited features refreshed — that is, descendants whose ancestors have been changed. The full rebuild processes all objects, whether or not they have changed ancestors. In either case,

PowerBuilder processes objects in object-hierarchy order, rebuilding ancestors before their descendants.

The process does more than just regenerate the part of an object that it inherits from its ancestors. It does a complete rebuild of the object, including a recompile of all PowerScript source code. Therefore, you may get errors that have nothing to do with inheritance. For example, you may get a message that a script references a global variable that no longer exists. That's why a full rebuild might pick up problems that an "incremental rebuild" would bypass, because an incremental rebuild does not process every object.

To regenerate a single object, click it in the Library Painter's tree display to select it. Then click the Regenerate button on the PainterBar. To regenerate more than one object, use control-click to select them before clicking the Regenerate button. If you use this technique, it's up to you to be sure to regenerate ancestors before their descendants.

Yet another way to regenerate is from the Browser. This technique lets you regenerate a selected section of the object hierarchy. The Browser has three tabs that show object classes that you have added to the hierarchy: Menu, User Object, and Window. Any object that may need regenerating will appear in one of these three tabs. Let's walk through the process of regenerating a window. The process for menus and user objects is quite the same.

1. Open the Browser and click the Window tab.

2. Right-click any window name on the left-side list and click the Show Hierarchy choice on the pop-up menu to turn on (checkmark) this feature.

3. At first, no descendant windows appear on the list, only windows derived directly from PowerBuilder's window class. Double-click each window to display its immediate descendants. Double-click each descendant as it appears as well, since it may have descendants in turn. Figure 13-11 shows the expanded hierarchy for the Video Store application.

4. Click any window to select it, and then click the Regenerate button in the Browser dialog box. PowerBuilder regenerates the selected object and all the objects on the tree below it.

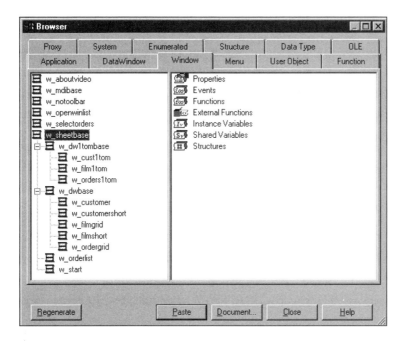

Figure 13-11
The object class hierarchy for the windows in the Video Store application.

Objects and Inheritance: Practical Examples

One of the axioms of object-oriented programming is that you should spend a lot of time up front carefully planning your object hierarchy before doing any development. You should devise a set of ancestor classes called *base* classes, and determine how to derive your other objects from them as subclasses. You should make the most of inheritance to shorten the initial development time and to make the application easier to maintain in the long run.

It's easy enough to say all that, but how do you get started? Do you create an elaborate structure of classes and subclasses, or should you try to keep things simple? How can you determine what ancestor objects your application will need before you've designed the descendants?

The answers to these questions are subjective. You will be able to develop your own approaches through experience and by observing the work of others.

The last two-and-a-half chapters explained the theory of objects. The remainder of this chapter puts it into practice. The CD-ROM that accompanies this book contains a sample application, the Video Store. I developed it with an object hierarchy that could serve as a model for your own applications. If not, it should at least suggest a type of foundation that would work well for you.

OBJECTS IN THE VIDEO STORE APPLICATION

Many parts of the Video Store application demonstrate object-oriented principles such as encapsulation and inheritance. Consider these features in particular:

- Windows
- DataWindow objects
- Visual user objects
- Menus
- Nonvisual user objects

This chapter covers windows, DataWindow objects, and visual user objects. Chapters 15 and 17 will cover menus and nonvisual user objects.

A WINDOWS OBJECT CLASS HIERARCHY

The windows in the Video Store are organized into this object class hierarchy:

```
Window              PowerBuilder's built-in window class
    w_sheetbase     base class for all sheet windows
        w_start     ...and other visible windows
        w_dwbase    base class for single-DataWindow windows
            w_customer  ...and other visible windows
```

```
w_dwltombase         base class for 1-M DataWindow windows
    w_orders1tom     ...and other visible windows
w_mdibase            base class for MDI frame windows
    w_mdivideo       visible MDI frame for the application
```

The "visible windows" are those that you actually see at some point while running the application. The "base class windows" are never seen. Their purpose is to serve as ancestor classes from which to derive the visible windows. Every visible window is a subclass of one of the base classes.

The Video Store application is an MDI (Multiple Document Interface) application. This means that you can open many windows at once, as depicted in Figure 13-12. The windows are called *sheets*. All sheets open within a large container window, entitled "Video Store Application," which is called the *MDI frame*. Only one window, w_mdivideo, is an MDI frame. All the others are sheets. (A few windows belong to a third group — dialog boxes — and are not part of this discussion.)

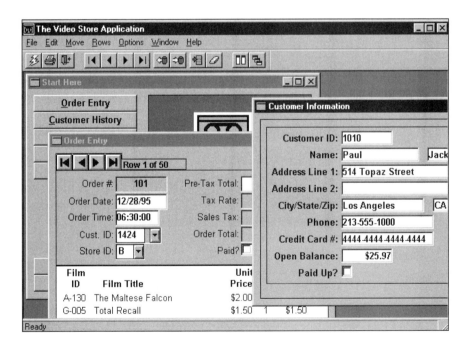

Figure 13-12

The Video Store application.

THE BASE CLASS FOR SHEET WINDOWS

All sheet windows have certain behavior in common. They all, or almost all

- Have a Close button
- Are light gray
- Write a time-stamped message to a log file upon opening
- Write another message to the log file when closing
- Have a menu associated with them (See Chapter 15.)

This is enough shared behavior to justify encapsulating it into a window, w_sheetbase, and deriving all sheets from this common base class. The window isn't much to look at, as you can see in Figure 13-13. But it is the common ancestor of many diverse descendants, such as w_start, shown in Figure 13-14.

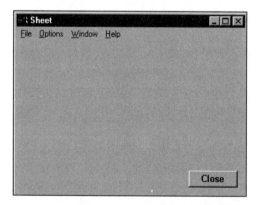

Figure 13-13
The w_sheetbase window, the "base class" for all sheet windows.

Having w_sheetbase as a common ancestor for all sheet windows has many benefits. For example, at some point in the future we plan to add a security check that takes place before each window opens. Rather than add code to every window's open script, we will need to add it to only one place: the open script of w_sheetbase.

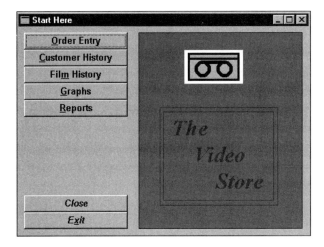

Figure 13-14
The window w_start is a subclass of w_sheetbase.

The Close button in w_sheetbase has the standard clicked script:

```
Close(Parent)
```

The window's open script is this single line of code. It calls a function that writes a line to the log file, a text file that records application activity:

```
gnv_logmanager.uf_writetolog("Opening window "+This.ClassName(), 0)
```

I will explain the nonvisual object gnv_logmanager and its function, uf_writetolog, in Chapter 17.

The window's close script is nearly identical:

```
gnv_logmanager.uf_writetolog("Closing window "+This.ClassName(), 0)
```

If you don't need some of this functionality in a particular window, it's easy enough to turn off. You can always make the Close button invisible or override the open and close scripts with other scripts.

As you create new sheet windows for an application, you will be tempted from time to time to make them direct subclasses of the window class, not subclasses of w_sheetbase. Especially very simple windows — you might believe they don't need even the small amount of sophistication that w_sheetbase brings.

Avoid the temptation! Make a rule that every window, no matter how unimportant, must be a descendant of the common ancestor. You will get benefits from following this rule. If you break the rule, the exceptions will probably become nuisances someday.

THE BASE CLASS FOR ONE-DATAWINDOW WINDOWS

Many sheet windows, such as w_customer, the Customer Information window shown in Figure 13-15, contain a DataWindow. Since they are sheets, these windows must be descendants of w_sheetbase. But they also have enough additional features in common to warrant another base class to unite them, w_dwbase. The window w_dwbase is a subclass of w_sheetbase and the parent class of w_customer and other windows with DataWindows:

```
Window                  PowerBuilder's built-in window class
    w_sheetbase         base class for all sheet windows
        w_dwbase        base class for single-DataWindow windows
            w_customer  Customer Information window
            w_filmgrid  Film List window
            w_ordergrid Order List window
            ...etc...   ...other windows containing a DataWindow
```

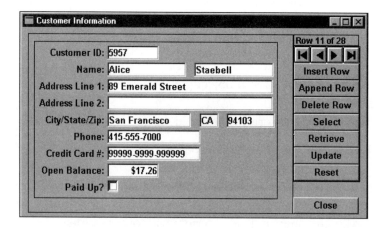

Figure 13-15

The w_customer window, a sheet with a DataWindow.

In Figure 13-16 you see something that the user never sees, the window w_dwbase. It contains three controls: a DataWindow control that is not yet attached to any DataWindow object; a StaticText control, where messages like "11 of 28" will someday appear; and a User Object control, which in turn contains the many navigation buttons. It also has a menu associated with it that includes DataWindow-oriented choices: Edit, Move, and Rows

Figure 13-16

The w_dwbase window, the base class window for all sheets with one DataWindow.

The DataWindow control is a "smart DataWindow." That is, it is a subclass of the regular DataWindow control class, created with the User Object Painter and containing a great deal of extra functionality.

Later I will explain each of these controls in greater detail, along with how they connect together in w_dwbase. For now, let me point out the single greatest benefit of w_dwbase: how quickly you can derive a fully functional new window from it.

1. In the Window Painter, inherit a new window from w_dwbase.

2. Right-click the DataWindow and pick a DataWindow object for it.

3. Save the new window.

You're done! The buttons, the menu, and the "11 of 28" display will be fully functional, no matter what DataWindow object you choose. The w_dwbase object class is that smart!

THE BASE CLASS FOR ONE-TO-MANY DATAWINDOW WINDOWS

Some windows in the Video Store, such as the Order Entry window in
Figure 13-17, contain two DataWindows linked in a one-to-many relationship. Chapter 19 on the CD-ROM explains the internal mechanics of such
a window. From an object-class perspective, this family of windows is
implemented with a new base class window named w_dw1tombase:

```
Window                        PowerBuilder's built-in window class
    w_sheetbase               base class for all sheet windows
        w_dw1tombase          base class for 1-M DataWindow windows
            w_orders1tom       Order Entry 1-M window
            w_cust1tom         Customer 1-M window
            w_film1tom         Film 1-M window
```

Figure 13-17
A window with two linked DataWindows.

THE BASE CLASS FOR MDI FRAME WINDOWS

The Video Store application, like many applications, has a single MDI
frame window. This window, named w_mdivideo, is the large window that
appears in Figure 13-12 with the title "Video Store Application" and that
contains all the sheets.

As you will see in Chapter 14, an MDI frame window behaves quite differently than a sheet. Therefore, I did not make w_mdivideo a subclass of w_sheetbase. Since there is only one such window, it hardly seems necessary to make a special parent class for it. Nevertheless, I did. Its parent class is named w_mdibase:

```
Window                    PowerBuilder's built-in window class
    w_mdibase             base class for MDI frame windows
        w_mdivideo        visible MDI frame for the application
```

The window w_mdibase encapsulates general behavior that I like an MDI frame to have, but that is not specific to the Video Store. The reason for it is that I will develop many applications, not just the Video Store. It will be beneficial to use w_mdibase as the common ancestor of every application's MDI frame window.

A "SMART DATAWINDOW" CONTROL

By almost any measure, the DataWindow control is the smartest object in PowerBuilder. Nevertheless, it's a good idea to develop your own custom DataWindow control that's even smarter.

If you design every DataWindow in an application from scratch, much programming will be duplicated in each: the navigation, Retrieve, and Update programming described in Chapter 8, and much of the general data entry programming described in Chapter 10.

It will save time to plan and develop a "smart DataWindow" control using the User Object Painter. Derive this control from the regular DataWindow control. Add to it all the general-purpose programming common to all DataWindows. Save it as a base object class, and derive all other DataWindows in the application from it as subclasses.

In the Video Store application, I named the smart DataWindow control u_dw_base — that is, "the DataWindow user object that is the base for all others." To create a custom DataWindow control, open the User Object Painter, select New and then Standard Visual object, and finally pick DataWindow from the list of controls. That brings you into the User Object Painter with a DataWindow control. Now you can enhance it with custom properties, functions, and events.

Figure 13-18 shows the smart DataWindow control in the User Object Painter. It never looks like more than an empty box because there's no point in placing a DataWindow object into it. DataWindow objects are added later, in the Window Painter, when you've placed this control on a specific window in the application.

In the User Object Painter, all the development work involves making choices from the Declare menu: Declare|Instance Variables, Declare|User Object Functions, and Declare|User Events.

Figure 13-18

The "smart DataWindow control," u_dw_base, in the User Object Painter.

Smarter Functions

Many of the user-defined functions serve as smarter versions of built-in DataWindow functions. For example, the DataWindow control has a Retrieve function, which retrieves rows into the DataWindow from the database. The smart DataWindow control has a user-defined function uf_Retrieve. It calls Retrieve, but it also performs several other chores that are part of my application's standard Retrieve process:

1. Perform an Update before the Retrieve to post existing changes to the DataWindow rows to the database before they are erased and replaced with the new rows.

2. Call the Retrieve function.

3. If no rows were retrieved, display a warning message.

4. Update the StaticText control, if there is one, that displays the row count ("Row 1 of 28").

5. If any step causes an error, call the application's standard error handling routines (Chapter 17) to process it.

I have added many functions such as uf_retrieve to the user object to serve as smarter alternatives to standard DataWindow functions. Figure 13-19 illustrates the relationship between the smarter functions and their standard counterparts. Although nothing prevents you from calling a standard function directly, it is always better to call the smarter version.

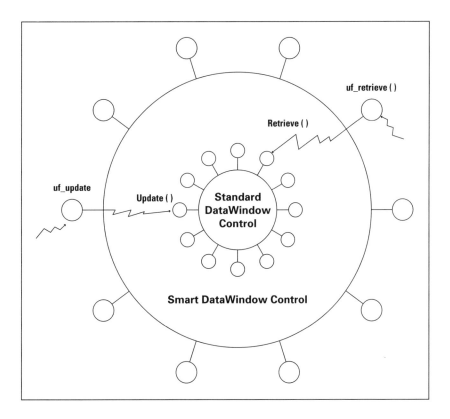

Figure 13-19

The user object's user-defined functions enhance the DataWindow control's standard functions.

BASIC FUNCTIONS

In the smart DataWindow, I've added functions for these basic DataWindow operations:

- **uf_navigate** — Move to another row by calling a function such as ScrollNextRow. An integer argument specifies how to move. That is, uf_navigate(1) is move to the next row, uf_navigate(2) is move to the next page, and so on.

- **uf_insertrow** — Insert or append a new row by calling the InsertRow function.

- **uf_deleterow** — Delete a row by calling the DeleteRow function.

- **uf_retrieve** — Retrieve rows into the DataWindow by calling the Retrieve function.

- **uf_update** — Update the database with changes by calling the Update function.

These functions implement the techniques I described in Chapter 8. As I have explained for uf_retrieve, they do more than the built-in functions that they call. For example, they all call the application's standard error handling routines if an error occurs.

SPECIAL EVENTS

In Chapter 10, I described common data entry tasks and how to write the programming for them — field-oriented processing, row-oriented processing, and update-oriented processing. Figuring out where to put the programming was as much of a challenge as writing it.

To simplify data entry programming, I've added user-defined events to the smart DataWindow:

- **FieldProcessing** — Place your field-oriented processing code here.

- **RowProcessing** — Place your row-oriented processing code here.

- **UpdateProcessing** — Place the update-oriented processing code for a single row here.

- **UndoUpdateProcessing** — Place the code that undoes the update-oriented processing for a single row here. This event fires if an update fails and ends with a ROLLBACK. In many cases, it is not needed.

In the user object itself, the scripts for these events are empty, except for some comments explaining when to use them. You add code to the scripts in its descendants after you've placed the control on a particular window. Only at that point do you know what data the control will contain, and therefore what processing it requires.

Throughout the user object, other events and functions trigger these events whenever necessary. For example, the script for RowFocusChanged triggers the RowProcessing event. So do the uf_deleterow and uf_update functions.

The smart DataWindow might fire the UpdateProcessing event multiple times in the course of a single update. The user object's UpdateStart event script calls a user-defined function, uf_updaterowloop. This function is a loop that identifies every row in every DataWindow buffer flagged for INSERT, UPDATE, or DELETE and triggers the UpdateProcessing event for it. I explained the logic of this loop in Chapter 10, but by using the smart DataWindow control, you're freed from having to code it yourself.

PUBLIC INSTANCE VARIABLES

As you know, public instance variables act as user-defined properties for a user object. The smart DataWindow has many of them, mostly to allow you to control the overall behavior of the special processing. Here are a few examples:

- **ii_initpopulate (Integer)** — specifies how to populate the DataWindow when its window first opens. Set it to one of these values:

  = **0**   to leave the DataWindow empty

  = **1**   to leave it empty, except for one new empty row

  = **2**   (default) to call the uf_retrieve function to retrieve rows into it

  = **3**   to call uf_retrieve and then add a new empty row

- **ii_safetyupdate (Integer)** — specifies whether an update should automatically occur prior to closing the window and prior to a retrieve:

  = **0**   do not do an update; lose any changes

  = **1**   do the update, post changes to the database before losing them

= 2   (default) pop up a dialog box asking the user whether to do an update

- **ib_updatebyrow (Boolean)** — specifies whether to automatically perform an update every time the user departs from a new or modified row. The default is False, which requires calling uf_update in some manual way, such as by clicking an Update button.

- **ib_valrequiredfields (Boolean)** — specifies whether to automatically validate that all required fields have been filled in a new row. As I explained in Chapter 10, required-field testing is the most common type of row-oriented processing. By setting this variable to True, which is the default, you have no need to write custom programming to perform it.

- **ib_ufupdate (DWBuffer) and il_rowupdate (Long)** — specify the buffer and row number that should be processed by an UpdateProcessing or UndoUpdateProcessing script. These scripts are written at the descendant level and will need to know these pieces of information.

The user object assigns default values to most of these variables when it declares them. For example:

```
Integer  ii_initpopulate = 2
Integer  ii_safetyupdate = 2
Boolean  ib_updatebyrow = False
Boolean  ib_valrequiredfields = True
```

You can override these values at any time in a descendant control to implement the behavior you require for a particular window. You might, for example, write this constructor script for a descendant control:

```
Integer  ii_initpopulate = 1
Boolean  ib_updatebyrow = True
```

THE FINISHED OBJECT

The completed version of u_dw_base has additional properties, functions, and events that I have not described here. For example, functions uf_filter and uf_sort perform filtering and sorting. You will find u_dw_base in the Video Store sample application on the CD-ROM, where comments appear to describe all features, including instructions on how to use them.

USING THE SMART DATAWINDOW

To use the smart DataWindow, u_dw_base, place it on any window. In the Window Painter, do this by clicking the User Object button from the PainterBar's dropdown object palette (not the DataWindow button). Click the spot in the window where the user object should appear. Then double-click it to open its property sheet and assign a DataWindow object to it.

At this point, you have a fully functioning DataWindow that already performs a little more work than a regular DataWindow. For example, when you run the application and open the window, it will automatically perform a retrieve. When you close the window, it will ask you whether to update any changes to the database, if any.

By further modifying the control in the Window Painter, you can further enhance it for this window's particular purpose. Most of the time, you will want to consider writing scripts for the new events, such as FieldProcessing, RowProcessing, and UpdateProcessing. You might also want to write a constructor script to override the default values of the control's instance variables. Usually, this constructor script should be set up to run before its ancestor's constructor script, using the "Design | Override Ancestor Script" and "CALL Super::constructor" techniques described earlier in this chapter.

In the Video Store application, I have placed u_dw_base on only two windows: w_dwbase (Figure 13-16) and w_dw1tombase (Figure 13-17). These windows, as I described earlier, are the ancestors for every other window in the application that contains one or two DataWindows. They contain PowerScript code that weds the DataWindow control to the navigation buttons and menu that you see in Figure 13-16. All final windows, such as the w_customer window shown in Figure 13-15, inherit the u_dw_base DataWindow control by way of w_dwbase or w_dw1tombase.

THE DATAWINDOW CONTROL PANEL

The DataWindow Control Panel is the set of buttons shown in Figure 13-20. The buttons perform basic DataWindow functions. In the Video Store application, the control panel is a custom visual user object named u_navbuttons. Although it has multiple buttons, it is a single user object, which makes it convenient to place on any window that needs it. In Figure 13-15 and Figure 13-16 you can see u_navbuttons placed on windows.

Figure 13-20

The user object u_navbuttons, a control panel for a DataWindow.

In the User Object Painter, each button has a simple clicked script, usually no more than one or two lines long. The scripts invoke the user-defined functions for the smart DataWindow object, u_dw_base, described earlier. For example, here is the script for the Next Row button, the third button on the top row:

```
idw.uf_Navigate(1)
```

The variable *idw* refers to the smart DataWindow control. The script calls the user-defined function uf_navigate, which is smarter than calling the standard function ScrollNextRow:

```
idw.ScrollNextRow()
```

As I explained earlier, uf_navigate provides error handling and other benefits.

The scripts in the user object cannot address the DataWindow control directly by name. For example, the DataWindow control in Figure 13-16 is named dw_1. However, in the User Object Painter, as you design u_navbuttons, this script would cause a syntax error:

```
dw_1.uf_Navigate(1)
```

No control named dw_1 lives in the u_navbuttons object, after all, and the User Object Painter has no way to go searching for it.

Therefore, the user object scripts use the variable *idw* instead. It is declared as a public instance variable of u_navbuttons:

```
u_dw_Base  idw
```

You might attempt to use "DataWindow" instead of "u_dw_Base" as the variable type:

```
DataWindow  idw
```

Unfortunately, that would cause a syntax error on lines such as "idw.uf_navigate(1)" — a DataWindow control does not support the function uf_navigate; only its descendant u_dw_base does.

When you place u_navbuttons on a window, as in Figure 13-16, then the user object and the DataWindow control are visible at the same time. So in the Window Painter, you can write a constructor script for the user object that assigns *idw* to a DataWindow control:

```
idw = dw_1
```

It is essential that you write this constructor script in the Window Painter, and not in the User Object Painter.

At runtime, when you open this window or any of its descendants and click a button, it will perform its operation upon *idw*, which has now been tied to the DataWindow control dw_1.

DESCENDANTS OF U_NAVBUTTONS

The regular version of u_navbuttons, shown in Figure 13-20, is probably not suitable for every window. A given window might not need all its buttons, or it might need them arranged in a different shape. For example, you might need only the four scroll buttons shown in Figure 13-21, which is another user object named u_navbuttons1.

Figure 13-21
The u_navbuttons1 object, a descendant of u_navbuttons.

This user object, u_navbuttons1, is not a completely new user object. Instead, it is a descendant of u_navbuttons. As a descendant, it contains the full set of buttons shown Figure 13-20. However, in the User Object Painter, I made most of the buttons invisible and shrank the user object to a smaller size.

In Figure 13-17 you see a window with u_navbuttons1 embedded on it twice. The constructor script of each instance ties its *idw* variable to a different DataWindow control.

You might derive any number of descendants from u_navbuttons — u_navbuttons1, u_navbuttons2, and so on — each with a different shape and a different set of visible buttons.

OTHER BASE OBJECT CLASSES

I have described three types of objects that serve as "base object classes:"

- **Window base classes** — w_sheetbase, w_dwbase, and w_dw1tombase
- **A DataWindow control base class** — u_dw_base
- **A DataWindow control panel base class** — u_navbuttons

These few objects are the ancestors from which many other objects in the Video Store application are derived. The descendants inherit many valuable properties, functions, and events from them, allowing you to avoid redundant code.

Summary

Through these examples I have shown how you can set about constructing an object class hierarchy, and you should have gained an appreciation of its value. I will extend the concept in later chapters: Chapter 15 will show a menu object class hierarchy, and Chapter 17 will show nonvisual object classes.

You might choose a completely different hierarchy for your own applications. It is very likely that you will want to have more base classes, or fewer, or a completely different set of them. The important thing is to devise the hierarchy up front, before getting too far into the detailed development process. A small amount of up-front planning can save an enormous amount of work later on.

IV Building An Application

14 More About Windows

Windows have played a role throughout this book. With so much experience, you may believe that you are quite a windows expert at this point. Not true! At least, not yet.

There are six types of windows in PowerBuilder. Almost all of our examples so far have been of a single type, called the "main type." This chapter explains what else you need to know about windows, starting with the six types.

Two of the window types play major roles in most applications:

- MDI frames (and MDI frames with MicroHelp)
- Response windows (dialog boxes)

The last half of this chapter is dedicated to these two, with detailed examples of how to use them.

The Six Types of Windows

The six types of windows are

- Main
- Child
- Popup
- Response

- MDI Frame
- MDI Frame with MicroHelp

In the Window Painter, select a window's type in the General tab of the window's property sheet, shown in Figure 14-1. The six types are listed in a dropdown list in the lower-left corner.

Figure 14-1

The "Window Type" dropdown list in a window's property sheet.

Each type of window has distinct characteristics, except for "MDI Frame" and "MDI Frame with MicroHelp," which are essentially the same. Table 14-1 lists and compares their features. There is a column for another type of window, a *sheet*. A sheet is a main, popup, child, or response window, when opened as the child of an MDI frame. I will describe sheets in more detail shortly.

Table 14-1

Characteristics of the Six Window Types

Window Characteristics	Main	Popup	Child	Response	MDI	Sheet
Relationship to the application environment						
Is the child of a parent window	No	Yes	Yes	Yes	No	Yes
Can open other windows of each of the six types	Yes	Yes	Yes	Yes	Yes	Yes
Can be the parent of other windows	Yes	Yes	No	Yes	Yes	No
Modal	No	No	No	Yes	No	No
Can get focus (i.e., can become the active window)	Yes	Yes	No	Yes	Yes	Yes
Can be opened from the application object	Yes	Yes (1)	No	Yes	Yes	No
Can be opened inside an MDI frame as a sheet	Yes	Yes	Yes	Yes	No	Yes
Minimizes to an icon at the bottom of the screen	Yes	Yes	No	N/A	Yes	No
Relationship to its parent window						
Closes when its parent closes	N/A	Yes	Yes	N/A	N/A	Yes
Hides when its parent is minimized	N/A	Yes	Yes	N/A	N/A	Yes
Floats on top of its parent, and can move outside its parent's frame	N/A	Yes	No	Yes	N/A	No
Contained completely within its parent	N/A	No	Yes	No	N/A	Yes
Minimizes to an icon within its parent	N/A	No	Yes	N/A	N/A	Yes
Design features						
Can be minimized, maximized, and resized	Yes	Yes	Yes	No	Yes	Yes
Can have a title bar	Yes	Yes	Yes	Yes	Yes	Yes
Must always have a title bar	Yes	No	No	No	Yes	Yes
Can have a menu	Yes	Yes (2)	No	No	Yes	Yes
Must always have a menu	No	No	No	No	Yes	No
Can have a toolbar	No	No	No	No	Yes	Yes

continued

Table 14-1 *(continued)*

Window Characteristics	Main	Popup	Child	Response	MDI	Sheet
Design features						
Has a design surface with controls	Yes	Yes	Yes	Yes	Yes (3)	Yes
Can have a status area (MicroHelp)	No	No	No	No	Yes	No

(1) When the application object opens a popup window, the window has no parent and behaves likes a main window.

(2) A popup window should have a menu only if it also has a title bar. Although there is a way to add a menu to a titleless popup window, it appears to be an accidental feature and behaves erratically.

(3) Although you can place controls on an MDI frame, I recommend that you do not. I will explain this further later in the chapter.

Parents and Children

Most windows in an application have parent-child relationships with other windows. The decision about which of the six types to choose for a window is based on how the window must behave: as a parent, as a child, both, or neither.

You should be quite familiar with parent and child windows by now. Consider a dialog box, as in Figures 14-12 and 14-13. The dialog box is a child window, and the window that opens it is its parent. Another example is a window within a window, as in Figures 14-3 and 14-4. The container window is the parent, and the inner window is its child.

One of the six window types is called *child*. However, it is not the only type that can be a child of another. In fact, every type except the MDI frame can be a child. (Table 14-1 indicates that a main window cannot be a child. However, when you open a main window as an MDI sheet, it becomes a child.)

When you open a window using a PowerScript function such as Open, you specify which other window, if any, should be its parent. In some cases you don't specify a parent, but PowerBuilder determines if it needs one. You'll see this in the examples later in the chapter.

MODAL WINDOWS

Sometimes, the child window grabs complete control of the application while it is open. Such a window is called a *modal* window. Most dialog boxes are modal windows. While a modal window is open, all other windows in the application, although they may be visible, are not accessible. You can see them, but you cannot click to them or switch to them. All you can do is respond to the modal window. (You can also switch to other programs running under Windows that are not part of your application.) After you close the modal window, its parent and the other windows become active once again.

In PowerBuilder, only one of the six window types is modal: the response window. All other types are modeless. (*Modeless*, or *nonmodal*, is the opposite of *modal*.) Therefore, you will tend to make your dialog boxes response windows. Although you can have a modeless dialog box, in this book all the dialog boxes are modal, and I use the terms *dialog box* and *response window* interchangeably.

WHEN TO USE THE SIX TYPES

Let's go through each of the six types of windows and see, from a practical viewpoint, why you would use each.

MAIN WINDOWS

Most of the windows in an application should be main windows: windows with DataWindows, windows with buttons that lead you through the application, sheets in an MDI frame. I would use a main window for each of these. It's not that other types cannot do the job, but that the main window is best suited for most ordinary tasks.

If your application consists of only one window, that, too, should be a main window.

POPUP WINDOWS

The popup window is very similar to the main window, except that it has a special relationship to its parent. In particular, the popup window always stays on top of its parent, even when it (the popup) is not the active window. (See Figure 14-2.) This is a special ability, since we are used to the active window floating above all others.

A popup window can be useful as an instruction sheet, walking users through the steps as they work on a main window underneath.

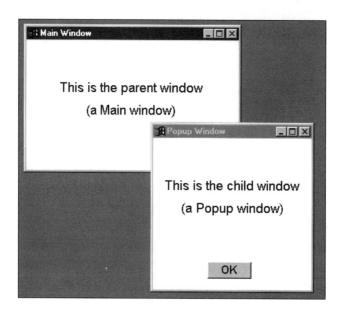

Figure 14-2
A popup window, overlaying its parent.

CHILD WINDOWS

I don't use the child window type much. Essentially, it allows you to implement something much like "MDI sheets," which I'll describe soon, without the need for an MDI frame. Since there's no particular reason to avoid MDI frames, there is nothing very compelling about the child window type.

Like a popup window, a child window maintains a close relationship to its parent. Unlike a popup window, which floats outside its parent, the child window remains inside the frame of its parent, as shown in Figure 14-3.

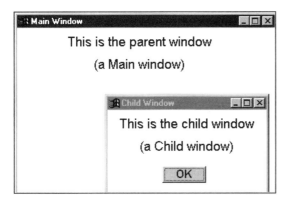

Figure 14-3
A child window, embedded within its parent.

RESPONSE WINDOWS

As I've mentioned, the response window is the only one that is modal. So you'll probably make most of your dialog boxes response windows. As you know, PowerScript provides the MessageBox function to produce simple dialog boxes. When MessageBox can give you the dialog box you want, there is no need to design a window for it. But for more complex interactions, such as asking the user to type in a range of dates for a report selection, you'll need to design a response window.

Later in this chapter I'll demonstrate several examples of response windows that implement familiar application functions. I will show how to create them and how they pass information back to their parent windows.

MDI FRAMES AND SHEETS

An *MDI frame* is a window whose main purpose is to be a container for child windows, called *sheets*. Figure 14-4 shows an example. The MDI frame is the large container window, entitled "The Video Store Application." It holds a menu, a toolbar, and four sheets, such as the one labeled "Films."

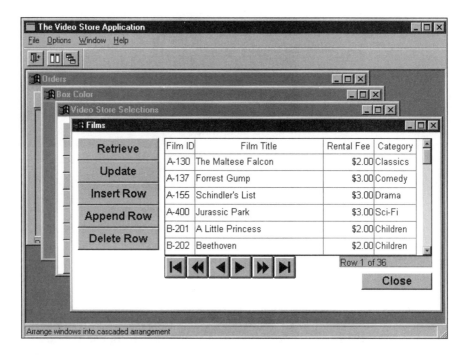

Figure 14-4
An MDI frame with four child sheets, in a cascaded arrangement.

MDI stands for *Multiple Document Interface.* It should be a familiar style to you, since almost all popular Windows products, including PowerBuilder itself, are MDI applications. All of your applications should be MDI applications too, except for the very simplest ones. An MDI application requires that one window be the MDI frame.

MDI FRAMES WITH AND WITHOUT MICROHELP

The MDI frame in Figure 14-4 is actually an "MDI frame with MicroHelp." The "MicroHelp" refers to the status bar, that quarter-inch gray bar running along the bottom of the window. The status bar displays messages. In Figure 14-4 the message describes a toolbar button I had just clicked: "Arrange windows into cascaded arrangement." In PowerBuilder, such a message is called *MicroHelp.* An "MDI frame without MicroHelp" would not have the status bar, but it would be identical in all other ways. That's the only difference between the two window styles. For most applications, I think you'll want the MDI frame with MicroHelp.

Displaying a Message in the Status Bar

There are many situations in which PowerBuilder will automatically display a MicroHelp message in the status bar line. In addition, if you want to place a message there yourself, call the SetMicroHelp function:

```
w_mdi.SetMicroHelp("")
```

The Open Function and Its Variations

Every window is opened by a script called the Open function, or some variation of the Open function. You learned about the Open function way back in Chapter 2. Here it is in its simplest form, opening a window named w_boxcolor:

```
Open(w_boxcolor)
```

The Open function can open any of the six window types. Thus w_boxcolor might be a main window, a popup window, a response window, or any of the other types.

There are four variations of the Open function. Each takes multiple arguments, most of which of are optional:

```
Open(winvar, winclass, parent)
OpenWithParm(winvar, msgparm, winclass, parent)
OpenSheet(winvar, winclass, parent, pos, arrange)
OpenSheetWithParm(winvar, msgparm, winclass, parent, pos, arrange)
```

The four functions are very similar, and each offers some special feature:

- **Open** — Open a window, the no-frills approach.
- **OpenWithParm** — Same as Open, but with an extra argument, the "parameter." It is a message, passed from the script to the new window. You as the programmer determine the type and contents of the parameter, and you write the script on the new window that interprets it. I'll show examples later in this chapter, especially in the section on dialog boxes.
- **OpenSheet** — Same as Open, but opens the window as an MDI sheet, the child of an MDI frame window.

- **OpenSheetWithParm** — Same as OpenSheet, but with the same extra parameter that OpenWithParm offers.

These are the arguments:

- *winvar* (window variable, required) — a window variable for the new window
- *winclass* (string, optional) — the name of the window's object class, such as "w_orders"
- *parent* (window variable, optional for Open and OpenWithParm, and required for OpenSheet and OpenSheetWithParm) — a window variable identifying the parent of the new window
- *msgparm* (string, number, or PowerObject variable, required) — a "message parameter" for the new window. The parameter can be anything you want. It's usually a string, a number, a structure, or an object. Typically, you will write an open script for the new window that interprets and responds to the parameter.
- *pos* (integer, optional) — the number of the menu item to which you want the name of the new window added. If *pos* = 0 or if *pos* is omitted, the window name will be added to the second menu item from the right, which is traditionally the Window menu choice, as Figure 14-6 demonstrates.
- *arrange* (enumerated data type, optional) — how to set the size and position of the new sheet: Cascaded!, Layered!, or Original!
- **return value** — returned by each of the four Open functions, 1 for success and -1 for failure.

All of this is a lot to digest, so let's look at some examples.

EXAMPLE 1: A SIMPLE OPEN

```
Open(w_boxcolor)
```

This example opens the window w_boxcolor. Since the *winclass* argument is omitted, w_boxcolor is not only the window variable but also the name of the window object class. In other words, in the library (.PBL file), there must be a window object with the name w_boxcolor.

Since the *parent* argument is omitted, the window must be a type that has no parent (main or MDI frame), or else the window calling the Open function will become the parent. There is one special case, a minor one: If the window calling Open is a child-type window, the child window's parent will become the parent of the new window.

When you call Open from an MDI frame, the new window opens as a regular window outside the frame, not as an MDI sheet. If you want a sheet, call OpenSheet instead.

EXAMPLE 2: OPEN WITH A WINDOW CLASS

```
Window w1, w2              // window object variables
Open(w1, "w_boxcolor")
Open(w2, "w_boxcolor")
```

This example opens two instances of the w_boxcolor window. Opening multiple instances of the same window is a most common reason for including the *winclass* argument. The simpler format in Example 1 can open only a single instance of the window at a time. For a better understanding of the object-oriented principles at work here, please refer to Chapter 12.

EXAMPLE 3: OPEN WITH A LOCAL WINDOW VARIABLE

```
Window w                  // local window object variable
Open(w, as_winname)
```

A common use for the two-argument Open call is to write a function like the one above, and pass the window class name as a string argument *as_winname*. If you name the function *f_openwindow*, for example, you might call it like this:

```
f_openwindow("w_boxcolor")
```

You can call the function any number of times to open many windows, including duplicate instances of the same window.

Since *w*, used to open the window, is a local variable, it ceases to exist when the function terminates. A problem that might arise is that there is no easy way later to control the window. For example, have a separate script try to close the window in this way:

```
Close(w)
```

If the windows are sheets in an MDI frame (and therefore the function above calls OpenSheet instead of Open), there is one way to control sheets opened with a local variable: By calling the function GetActiveSheet, you can attach a window variable to the active (topmost) sheet in the MDI frame. For example, if *w_mdi* is the MDI frame, this script closes each open sheet within it, one at a time from top to bottom:

```
Window w                          // window to be closed
DO WHILE True                     // loop to close each window
   w = w_mdi.GetActiveSheet()     // get the topmost window
   IF NOT IsValid(w) THEN EXIT    // no more sheets — all done
   Close(w)                       // close the window
NEXT
```

If there are no open sheets, GetActiveSheet returns an invalid window variable. Therefore, you should typically call the IsValid function immediately, as shown above, which returns True if the window variable is valid and False if it is not.

EXAMPLE 4: OPEN WITH AN ARRAY OF WINDOW OBJECT VARIABLES

```
Integer n                         // # of open windows
n = UpperBound(wins)              // size of array = # of open windows
Open(wins[n+1], "w_boxcolor")     // open one more window
```

This script, like the others, opens the w_boxcolor window. However, the window variable, *wins*, is an array, declared as an instance or global variable:

```
Window wins[]                     // an array of open windows
```

Because *wins* is a variable-size array, it can have any number of elements, so you can use it to open any number of windows:

```
Integer n                         // # of open windows so far
n = UpperBound(wins)              // size of array = # of open windows
Open(wins[n+1], "w_boxcolor")     // open one more window
Open(wins[n+2], "w_orders")       // open the order form window
Open(wins[n+3], "w_films")        // open the film list window
```

This is the most flexible technique for opening the sheets of an MDI frame, in which case you would use the OpenSheet function instead of Open. Among other benefits, it makes it easy to keep track of the windows later. For example, this simple loop closes all the open windows:

```
Integer i                         // window counter
Integer n                         // # of open windows
n = UpperBound(wins)              // size of array = # of open windows
FOR i = 1 TO n                    // do each window
   Close(wins[i])                 // close the window
NEXT
```

If your application has no need to keep track of what windows are open, you will find it simpler to use the local variable technique described in Example 3 than to use this array of windows technique.

EXAMPLE 5: OPENWITHPARM

```
OpenWithParm(w_ordersforcust, "4534")
```

This example opens the window pictured in Figure 14-5. The window has been designed to show all rows in the orders table. But in this case, the script wants the window to show rows for a single customer only, customer 4534. To pass "4534" as a parameter to the window, the script calls OpenWithParm.

There are other ways, besides OpenWithParm, to pass information from a script to a window. For example, you could use a global variable, although I don't recommend it. Since OpenWithParm is provided for message-passing, it makes sense to use it and not to use other techniques.

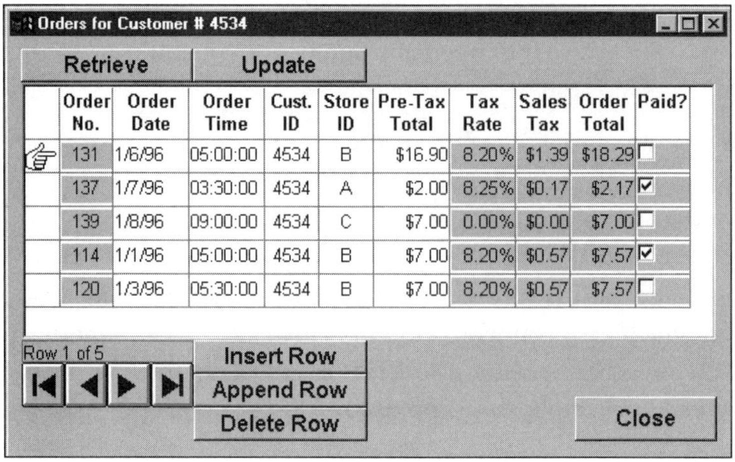

Figure 14-5

Orders for a selected customer in a window opened with OpenWithParm.

The OpenWithParm function places the parameter into a variable named *message* which, like *sqlca* and *error*, is a built-in global variable. The *message* variable is a structure, and one of its properties, *message.StringParm*, can hold a string value. In our case, the value of *message.StringParm* will be "4534."

There must be some programming in the window w_ordersforcust, probably in its open script, that picks up the parameter and makes use of it. When using this message-passing technique, you should interrogate the *message* variable as soon as possible in the PowerScript code for the new window, just in case some other function of your application changes its values to something else. Here is the script. It fetches the string value from *message*, adds it to the window's title, and passes it as a retrieval argument to the DataWindow's Retrieve function:

```
String   ls_custid            // customer #
ls_custid = message.StringParm  // get value passed by OpenWithParm
This.Title = This.Title + " for Customer # " + ls_custid
dw_1.Retrieve(ls_custid)       // supply cust # retrieval argument
```

The DataWindow will retrieve and display only rows for customer 4534. See Chapter 9 for more information about retrieval arguments and the Retrieve function.

EXAMPLE 6: A SIMPLE OPENSHEET

```
OpenSheet(w_films, w_mdi)
```

This example opens the window w_films as a sheet within the MDI frame window named w_mdi. In Figure 14-4, w_mdi is the frame, and w_films is the topmost of the four sheets.

This OpenSheet call is simple enough, but I prefer using a pronoun such as *This* instead of explicitly naming w_mdi. It makes the programming more generic and reusable:

```
OpenSheet(w_films, This)
```

You can't always use *This*. It depends on where the script is located. For example, if the script is on a button in another sheet, use "ParentWindow(Parent):"

```
OpenSheet(w_films, ParentWindow(Parent))
```

Parent is the button's parent, which is the sheet. The ParentWindow function returns the sheet's parent, which is w_mdi.

If the script is located in w_mdi's menu, then use the pronoun *ParentWindow*:

```
OpenSheet(w_films, ParentWindow)
```

EXAMPLE 7: OPENSHEET'S OPTIONAL ARGUMENTS

```
OpenSheet(w_films, ParentWindow(Parent), 0, Original!)
```

When you call OpenSheet without its optional fourth argument, *arrange*, PowerBuilder chooses a size for the new sheet that fits the size of the MDI frame. I usually prefer that the window retain the size that I set when I created it. The Original! argument opens the window in its originally designed size.

The third parameter, *pos* = 0, adds the window's name to the list of open windows under the Window menu choice. You're probably familiar with the Window menu choice and how it displays a numbered list of open windows from PowerBuilder and other products. The menu is shown in Figure 14-6.

Figure 14-6
The OpenSheet function adds the sheet names to the Window menu choice.

EXAMPLE 8: OPENSHEETWITHPARM WITH ALL SIX ARGUMENTS

```
Integer n                    // # of open windows
n = UpperBound(wins)         // size of array = # of open windows
OpenSheetWithParm(wins[n+1], "4534", "w_ordersforcust", &
                  ParentWindow(Parent), 0, Original!)
```

This script opens the window shown in Figure 14-5, listing orders for customer 4534, as a sheet in the MDI frame.

This example takes the Open call to its limit, but it doesn't introduce anything that we haven't seen before. The array of windows (*wins*) is drawn from Example 4. Passing the customer number "4534" as a parameter is from Example 5. "ParentWindow(Parent)" was explained in Example 6. The last two parameters, 0 and Original!, were explained in Example 7.

MORE ABOUT OPENSHEET

You've seen how OpenSheet and OpenSheetWithParm open a window as a sheet in an MDI frame. These are the only two functions that can open a sheet. If you try to use the Open function instead, the new window will open outside the frame, not as a sheet within it.

Of the six types of windows, which can be opened as a sheet? Four types can: main, popup, child, and response. Only an MDI window itself cannot be opened as a sheet.

All sheets have the same characteristics, which are listed in the last column of Table 14-1. PowerBuilder ignores the characteristics of the window's original type when that window becomes a sheet. Thus, a sheet is always modeless, even if you designed it to be a response window. It always has a parent, the MDI frame window, even if you designed it to be a main window. It can become the active window, even if you designed it to be the child window type.

Therefore, it really doesn't matter which of the four window types you choose for a sheet window. I tend to choose main, which is the default for new windows. It's a small benefit, but a main window is the easiest to test independently from the MDI frame.

MDI Applications

Most PowerBuilder applications should be MDI applications. That is, you should design them with an MDI frame window that opens other windows as sheets.

If your application consists of only one window, which might be the case if you develop a utility, the MDI style is not necessary. A one-window application has what is known as a *Single Document Interface* (SDI).

If your application consists of multiple windows, as most do, you can try a non-MDI approach, but you will quickly find it unsatisfactory. For example, you could create an application as a collection of main windows. But if more than a couple of main windows are open at once, it will be difficult for the user to find them. They will not be collected together within a frame, so they will tend to get lost behind spreadsheets and word processing documents and whatever else is open.

If you program things so that only one window can be open at a time, things will be simpler, but the user will probably consider your application restrictive and inflexible. Most people today are familiar with the MDI style and prefer it. If they are not familiar with it, they soon will be.

User Interface Design Conventions

One of the benefits of the graphical user interface, including the MDI style, is that published conventions exist for how a product should look and how it should function. Since all of the best software products follow the same conventions, most of them have a similar look and feel.

You will want your application to follow these conventions too. That will make learning easier for your users, because much will be familiar to them.

There are several documented versions of the design conventions. For all versions of Windows, including Windows 95, I rely on two books. One is Microsoft's work, *The Windows Interface Guidelines for Software Design*, published by Microsoft Press (1995). The other is *About Face: The Essentials of User Interface Design*, by Alan Cooper, published by IDG Books Worldwide (1995).

In PowerBuilder certain features, such as toolbars and MicroHelp, are available only with the MDI style.

Considering all of these things, I think you'll agree that the MDI style is best for all but the very simplest applications.

The Components of an MDI Application

What should be part of an MDI application, and what should be avoided? Here are my recommendations. Some are based on the standard conventions, and others are just my opinions and preferences.

THE MDI FRAME WINDOW

An application should have only one MDI frame window. More than one is never needed. You should create an MDI frame with MicroHelp. I usually name it w_mdi or w_mdiframe. The application open script opens it, so it is the first thing the user sees. If there is a sign-on window, it's okay to open that prior to, and separate from, the MDI frame.

THE "START SHEET"

When the MDI frame opens, it in turn opens a sheet. I call it the "start sheet" and name it w_start or w_main. Figure 14-7 shows the start sheet for the Video Store application. The buttons on the sheet lead the user to the important application modules.

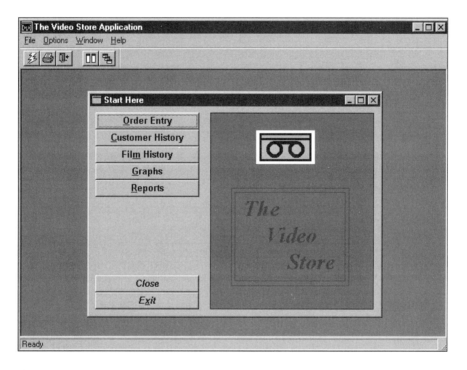

Figure 14-7
The "Start Sheet."

Because I place the start sheet in the middle of the screen, it grabs the user's attention. This is the "in your face" style. The user doesn't waste time hunting through the menu for features.

Of course, your application is likely to need more than the few buttons visible in Figure 14-7. But at first, you should present only a few. As you click them, others appear, revealing features a little at a time. For example, clicking the Reports button exposes the set of choices that you see in Figure 14-8. The right half of the start sheet is designed to display many different sets of buttons. It is, in effect, a menu tree implemented with buttons.

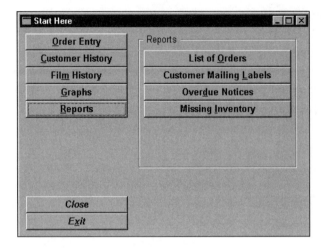

Figure 14-8
When you click the Reports button, more buttons appear.

BUTTON PANELS ON THE START SHEET

How do you implement the start sheet's invisible/visible buttons trick, with different button panels occupying the same space? There are several ways to do it. For example, all the buttons could be there on the window on top of one another all the time. Scripts could make them visible and invisible as needed.

I chose instead a different technique: When you don't see the buttons, they are not there. There are no invisible buttons hiding in the window. They are stored in the application's library as custom visual user objects. For example, the panel with the report buttons is a user object named u_reportbuttons.

A PowerScript function named OpenUserObject adds a user object to a window, and a corresponding function named CloseUserObject removes it. They are the key to the process. Here is the script for the Reports button:

```
IF IsValid(iuo_visible) THEN   // there is a visible U.O. already
   This.CloseUserObject(iuo_visible)  // close it
END IF
p_logo.Hide()                           // hide the picture
This.OpenUserObject(iuo_visible, "u_reportbuttons", &
                p_logo.X, p_logo.Y)
```

The object variable *iuo_visible* controls the user object. It is declared as an instance variable:

```
DragObject  iuo_visible    // user object being displayed
```

Why "DragObject?" Because the OpenUserObject function requires a DragObject, or a descendant of DragObject, as its first variable. If you review the object hierarchy (Chapter 11), you'll see that DragObject is the ancestor class of user object controls, as it is of all other controls.

The first few lines of the script call CloseUserObject, because many user objects will share the same space and share the same *iuo_visible* variable: u_reportbuttons, u_graphbuttons, and others. If another user object is already on display, the IsValid function returns True and the script closes the old one before it opens the new one.

"p_logo" is the name of the "Video Store" picture control that occupies the right half of the sheet in Figure 14-7. The Hide function makes it invisible.

The OpenUserObject function retrieves the user object from the library and places it in the window. The last two arguments of the OpenUserObject call — p_logo.X and p_logo.Y — position the new object at the same *x* and *y* coordinates that the now-hidden picture occupies.

MULTIPLE SHEETS

Most of the buttons on the start sheet open windows. There is also a File|Open menu choice that opens still more windows. A window stays open until the user closes it, but in the meantime the user can open any number of other windows, as was depicted in Figure 14-4. So the application is truly MDI.

The File|Open menu choice pops up a dialog box with an alphabetical list of windows, shown in Figure 14-9. It might be convenient for more experienced users. As a bonus, the list box lets you pick and open more than one window at a time, if you hold down the Control key while clicking. The list is a ListBox control. It has properties ExtendedSelect and MultiSelect, which allow multiple items to be picked

To open multiple windows, I use the array-of-windows technique that I explained earlier, in the section "The Open Function and Its Variations," Example 4. The local variable technique in Example 3 would do just as well.

Figure 14-9
File|Open displays a list of windows.

With an array of windows, the users can open any number of windows at any time in any order. They can open two or more instances of the same window. This is a wonderful feature for comparing two orders side by side, for example.

The start sheet is limited to one instance only. I do not use the array of windows to open it. I use the variable w_start. To make it easy to return to the start sheet at any time, there is a Start Here toolbar button — the first button, with the lightning bolt icon. It reopens the sheet if it's closed or brings it to the surface if it's buried.

Allowing so many sheets open at once, including duplicates, may be much too haphazard for your taste. With some groups of users, so much power can cause more harm than good.

If that's the case in your organization, it's simple enough to exercise more control. For example, the GetActiveSheet function tells whether there is a sheet open. If there is, you can prevent another from being opened. To avoid duplicate instances of the same window, simply remove the *winclass* argument from the OpenSheet function call. If an instance is already open, PowerBuilder will bring it to the surface instead of opening a second instance.

THE MDI CLIENT AREA

Inside an MDI frame window, the white space where the sheets appear is actually a control. Whenever you make a window an MDI frame,

PowerBuilder automatically creates this control. It is called the *client area*, its name is always mdi_1, and it belongs to the object class "MDIClient." You may have noticed MDIClient in the object tree hierarchy back in Chapters 11 and 12.

Like any control, mdi_1 has properties and functions. (It has no events.) Back in Figure 14-7, you saw that the start sheet opens centered within the client area. The two-line script that centers it relies upon the Width and Height properties of mdi_1:

```
w_start.X = (mdi_1.Width - w_start.Width) / 2
w_start.Y = (mdi_1.Height - w_start.Height) / 2
```

Most of the time, you don't have to worry about mdi_1. But you do in one special case: If you place one or more other controls, such as CommandButtons, in the MDI frame window, it becomes necessary to write a lot of code to set the size of mdi_1 and to resize it whenever the user moves a toolbar or resizes the frame. When there are no controls in mdi_1, PowerBuilder takes responsibility for managing its size, but as soon as you add controls, PowerBuilder hands that responsibility over to you. It turns out to be a lot of work to support what is a nonstandard user interface design anyway — typically, an MDI window should be empty, except for its sheets. I recommend that you avoid placing buttons and other controls in your MDI window.

MENUS AND TOOLBARS

PowerBuilder requires that an MDI frame window always have a menu. Optionally, it can have a toolbar as well. You design the menu and toolbar using the Menu Painter and then, in the Window Painter, assign them to the MDI frame window.

The menu and toolbar appear when the MDI frame opens. A sheet might have a menu and toolbar also. When such a sheet is active, its menu replaces the MDI frame's menu and its toolbar will appear in addition to the MDI frame's toolbar.

Chapter 15 will describe these procedures.

Cooperating Sheets

When you open multiple sheets, they operate independently of one another. Sometimes, however, you want a relationship among the sheets to work together, so that work you do in one affects the display in the others.

Figure 14-10 shows an example. It includes three sheets — Order Entry, Customer Information, and Film Information — which I have trimmed somewhat to fit on screen. As you scroll through orders and line items in the order entry sheet, the other two sheets automatically change to display the related customer and film.

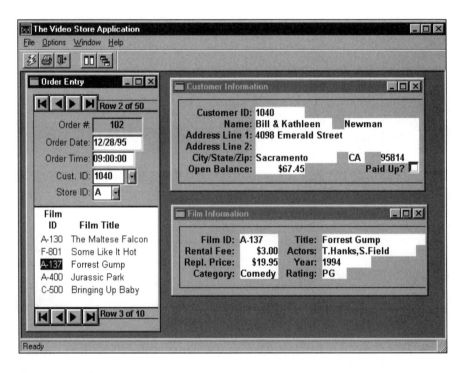

Figure 14-10
The Customer and Film windows are linked to the Order Entry window.

Getting sheets to cooperate like this requires a little bit of PowerScript, but it's pretty straightforward. The object-oriented way to do it is to have a user-defined function on the Customer window that can locate a customer. The Order window calls the function whenever it displays a new order, passing the customer number as a function argument.

The Film window has a similar function, which the Order window calls as you scroll through line items.

Let's walk through the scripts for the customer linking. The scripts for film linking are virtually identical. The Order DataWindow has a RowFocusChanged script, which runs whenever you arrive at a new order. It gets the customer number (custid) from the DataWindow and calls the function wf_findcustomer on the Customer window (w_customer):

```
Long    ll_row                          // row #
String  ls_custid                       // customer #
ll_row = This.GetRow()                  // get new row #
ls_custid = This.Object.custid[ll_row]  // get new cust #
w_customer.wf_FindCustomer(ls_custid)   // update cust window
```

This is the wf_findcustomer function. The customer number is passed into it as the argument variable *as_custid*:

```
Long    ll_row      // row # where the customer is found
String  ls_find     // the expression for the Find() function
ls_find = "custid = '" + as_custid + "'"
ll_row = dw_1.Find(ls_Find, 1, dw_1.RowCount())
IF ll_row <= 0 THEN RETURN False   // not found
dw_1.ScrollToRow(ll_row)            // display the found customer
```

The Find function locates a row in a DataWindow. Its first argument is a search expression, which in this case might be something like

```
custid = '1040'
```

The second and third parameters are the first and last row numbers in which the search is to be performed. Since the RowCount function returns the total number of rows, the script searches all DataWindow rows.

FIND OR RETRIEVE?

The function looks for the customer only among the rows already retrieved into the DataWindow. This approach works fine if you always retrieve all rows, but if you are doing partial retrieves, a different approach is needed. If the Find call fails, then the function should call Retrieve to try to fetch the row from the database.

REFERENCING THE CUSTOMER WINDOW

There might also be a problem with the RowFocusChanged script. This line might fail:

```
w_customer.wf_findcustomer(ls_custid)
```

Earlier I described the technique of opening MDI sheets using an array of window object variables. If you use that technique, then the variable w_customer is never assigned to an open window, and any attempt to use it crashes the application.

To solve the problem, you must ask the MDI frame to provide you with the array element for the customer window, and you must use that instead of w_customer. In the Video Store application, the MDI frame's array of windows is a public instance variable named *iw_sheets[]*. The MDI frame, which is named w_mdivideo, provides a function wf_getmdiSheet, which returns the array index for the sheet you need. Here's the revised RowFocusChanged script:

```
Long       ll_row       // row #
String     ls_custid    // customer #
Integer    li_sheet     // customer sheet #
w_Customer lw_cust      // customer window
li_sheet = w_mdivideo.wf_getmdiSheet ("w_Customer")  // get sheet #
IF li_sheet <= 0 THEN RETURN              // no such sheet
lw_cust = w_mdivideo.iw_sheets[li_sheet]   // get the customer window
ll_row = This.GetRow()                     // get current row #
ls_custid = This.Object.custid[ll_row]     // cust # being displayed
lw_cust.wf_findcustomer(ls_custid)
```

The variable *lw_cust*, which points to the customer window, must be declared as a "w_customer" variable, not as a "Window" variable. If you declare it as "Window," you will get a syntax error, because "Window" does not have a function named wf_findcustomer.

Here is the MDI frame's wf_getmdiSheet function. You pass it a window name as an argument (*as_winclass*), and it returns the array index for that window:

```
Integer i                    // sheet counter
Integer n                    // # of sheets
n = UpperBound(iw_sheets)     // # of sheets in the array
FOR i = 1 TO n                // check each sheet
```

```
    IF IsValid(iw_sheets[i]) THEN  // only if window is still open
       IF iw_sheets[i].ClassName() = as_winclass THEN   // found it!
          RETURN i                      // return the window #
       END IF
    END IF
NEXT
RETURN 0           // sheet was not found
```

The line that calls the IsValid function is essential. It returns True if the sheet is still open and False if it has been closed. After a sheet closes, it still continues to occupy an element in the *iw_sheets* array. But any attempt to reference that element, such as the ClassName call on the next line, will cause a runtime error.

MORE COMPLEX COOPERATION

If only a few sheets are involved, you can get them to cooperate just fine using the technique described above. One sheet can communicate with the others by calling custom window functions.

If many sheets are involved, and if they open and close in different combinations at different times, things can get out of control. Managing the large number of window functions, including figuring out when to call them, becomes frustrating. A more complex environment calls for a more sophisticated technique.

A technique that I like is to create a custom nonvisual object. The nonvisual object sits behind the scenes, coordinating the activities of the sheets. Figure 14-11 illustrates this approach.

 In the sample Video Store application on the book's CD-ROM, there is a nonvisual object named nv_dwlinker. It implements, in a generic and extensible way, multiple DataWindow linking, such as that pictured in Figure 14-11. Instead of sheets talking directly to one another, they send messages to the object. The object routes the messages to all other sheets that are interested.

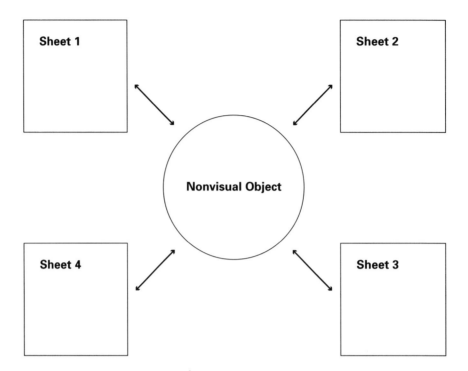

Figure 14-11
Using a nonvisual object to coordinate communication among many sheets.

Rather than walk through source code, I'll give you an overview of the principles at work. The nonvisual object provides functions such as these, which the sheets call to communicate:

- **uf_signin** — When a window opens, it calls this function to notify the object that it is ready to receive messages.

- **uf_ididsomething** — When a window does something, such as when the Order Entry window scrolls to a new order, it calls this function (or maybe one with a more descriptive name). This function is central to the whole operation. It interprets what has happened and in a loop sends a message to the other windows (all of them or some of them, depending on the situation) telling them to do something in response.

- **uf_signout** — When a window closes, it calls this function to tell the object to stop sending it messages.

Each window must provide a special function, too:

- **wf_DoSomething** — The nonvisual object's uf_IDidSomething function calls this window function to tell the window what to do. For example, it might send a message asking the window to find and display a customer or film.

This is fun object stuff!

Dialog Boxes

A dialog box is almost always a response window, because response windows are the only modal type of window. Furthermore, response windows look like dialog boxes, with the thicker frame that is the Microsoft Windows convention.

Because a dialog box is a window and not some special kind of PowerBuilder object, there's not much to learn about them that you don't already know. The Window Painter offers all the commonplace dialog box controls, such as

- Fields (SingleLineEdit, MultiLineEdit, and EditMask controls)
- Buttons (CommandButton and PictureButton controls)
- Pick lists (ListBox and DropDownListBox controls)
- Check boxes and radio buttons

To open a dialog box, call the Open or OpenWithParm function. Never call OpenSheet for a dialog box; otherwise, it will open as a modeless child sheet within an MDI frame.

COMMUNICATING WITH THE DIALOG BOX: THE MESSAGE VARIABLE

The only new issue with a dialog box is how it passes the user's responses back to its parent window. How does the parent window find out, for example, whether the user clicked OK or Cancel to close the dialog box?

In the section on "Cooperating Sheets" I described how windows can communicate with one another using custom window functions. That works for dialog boxes too: The dialog box could call a function on its parent window to pass information to it. Or the parent could call a function on the dialog box window to extract the information. Or you could do without window functions and pass the information through global variables, although that defies object-oriented principles. Any of these approaches work. However, PowerBuilder makes it especially convenient to use yet another technique: using a function, CloseWithReturn, which passes the information back in the *message* variable.

We've seen the *message* variable already. It's the "Parm" part of the OpenWithParm function, described earlier in this chapter. Like the *sqlca* variable used in database transactions, the *message* variable is automatically defined by PowerBuilder as a global nonvisual object. PowerBuilder provides it as a convenient container for passing messages.

The *message* variable has properties, which hold the contents of the message. Three of the properties are LongParm, StringParm, and PowerObjectParm. You can change or read them as you can any object properties:

```
message.LongParm = 1         // add a long integer to the message
message.StringParm = s       // add a string to the message
message.PowerObjectParm = x  // add an object, such as a window
                             //    or structure, to the message

l = message.LongParm         // retrieve a long int from the message
s = message.StringParm       // retrieve a string from the message
x = message.PowerObjectParm  // retrieve an object from the message
```

To understand exactly how to use the *message* variable with a dialog box, let's explore a few examples. These examples demonstrate not only the *message* variable but a number of other dialog box implementation issues as well.

DIALOG BOX EXAMPLE 1: SELECTING ROWS FOR DATAWINDOW DISPLAY

Figure 14-12 shows a window, Orders Grid, and a dialog box, Select Orders. When you click the Select button on the Orders Grid, it opens the dialog box.

In the dialog box, you type in criteria for selecting orders. In the figure, I have typed in the criteria for "Orders dated 1/1/96 or later for customer 1040." When you click OK, the dialog box closes and the Orders Grid window locates and displays the rows matching the criteria.

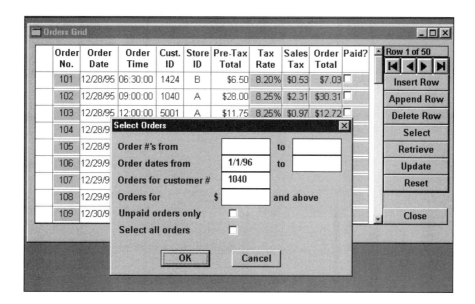

Figure 14-12

The Select Orders dialog box.

The Select Orders dialog box is a response window named w_selectorders. The Orders Grid window is a main window, perhaps opened as a sheet in the Video Store MDI frame. Within the Orders Grid window is a DataWindow control named dw_1, which displays the order rows. We have seen this window, or a very similar one, in Chapter 10.

Three main scripts are at work in the select-orders process:

1. The script on the Select button. It opens the dialog box window. After the dialog box window closes, the script uses the dialog box values to locate and display the specified order rows.

2. The script on the OK button. It collect the values from the dialog box controls and closes the dialog box, passing the values back to the Select button script.

3. The script on the Cancel button. It is simpler than the OK button, closing the dialog box without passing back values.

Also critical to the process is a structure variable that will contain all the values from the dialog box. The structure is named *s_selectorders*, and these are its elements:

```
s_selectorders.b_ok               // True="OK", False="Cancel"
s_selectorders.b_selectall        // whether to select all orders
s_selectorders.l_fromorderno      // "from" order #
s_selectorders.l_toorderno        // "to" order #
s_selectorders.d_fromdate         // "from" date
s_selectorders.d_todate           // "to" date
s_selectorders.s_custid           // customer #
s_selectorders.dec_fromamount     // "from" $ amount
s_selectorders.b_unpaid           // True= unpaid orders only
```

The application declares three instances of this structure: The dialog box window has one named *istr_response*, an instance variable. The Orders Grid window also has one named *istr_response* (same name, separate instance), also an instance variable. The Select button script has one named *lstr_response*, a local variable. The declarations are all similar. The instance variables, for example, are declared with this line:

```
s_selectorders   istr_response
```

The script for the Select button begins by opening the dialog box.

```
OpenWithParm(w_selectorders, istr_response)
```

The reason for using OpenWithParm, and not Open, is to pass into the dialog box the values the user typed in during the last visit. When the dialog appears, therefore, it will not be empty. Users can see their previous selections and use them as a starting point for entering new values — a nice touch. The values are passed to the dialog box in the structure variable, *istr_response*. I'll show soon how they got into the structure variable.

When the user fills in the dialog box and clicks the OK button, the script in Listing 14-1 runs. For simplicity, I show the code for only two of the many fields: the "from-date" field, which contains "1/1/96" in Figure 14-12, and the customer number, which contains "1040." The actual script is much longer, since it has similar code for six more fields and check boxes.

Listing 14-1

The clicked script for the OK button on the Select Orders dialog box

```
Date     ld_fromdate      // "from" date
String   s                // field value to be validated
String   ls_custid        // customer #

//  Validate the user-supplied values

s = sle_fromdate.Text
IF s = "" THEN
   SetNull(ld_fromdate)
ELSE
   IF not IsDate(s) THEN
      MessageBox("Sorry","Bad date")
      sle_fromdate.SetFocus()
      RETURN
   END IF
   ld_fromdate = Date(s)
END IF

s = sle_custid.Text
IF s = "" THEN
   SetNull(ls_custid)
ELSE
   ls_custid = s
END IF

//  Place the results into the structure variable

istr_response.b_ok       = True       // "OK" is clicked
istr_response.d_fromdate = ld_fromdate  // "from" date
istr_response.s_custid   = ls_custid   // customer #

//  Close the dialog box, passing the responses back to the parent
//  as a structure within the message variable

CloseWithReturn(Parent, istr_response)
```

The script begins by validating each field and by transferring its value from a control, such as sle_fromdate, to a local variable, such as *ld_from-date*. No validation is required for the customer number. For the from-date, the script uses the IsDate function to confirm that the text typed in is indeed a date and not nonsense like "abcde" or "2/31/96."

The next step is to place the values into the structure, *istr_response*. The script also sets the structure element *b_ok* to True. The Cancel button will set *b_ok* to False, and that is how the parent window will determine which button closed the dialog box.

The last line of the script is the CloseWithReturn call. This function is an extension of the Close function, in exactly the same way that OpenWithParm is an extension of Open. Like Close, the CloseWithReturn function closes the *Parent* window. You pass it an additional argument — *istr_response*, in this case — and PowerBuilder places that argument into one of the properties of the *message* variable:

- If the argument is a string, PowerBuilder places it into *message.StringParm*.
- If the argument is a numeric value, PowerBuilder places it into *message.DoubleParm*.
- If the argument is an object, such as a structure, PowerBuilder places it into *message.PowerObjectParm*.

Since the argument *istr_response* is a structure, PowerBuilder places it into *message.PowerObjectParm*. Back in the parent window, a script will retrieve the structure from this property, as you will see.

The Cancel button's script is much shorter:

```
istr_response.b_ok = False          // "Cancel" is clicked
CloseWithReturn(Parent, istr_response)
```

When you click Cancel, anything else you have typed into the dialog box is ignored.

The CloseWithReturn function call closes the dialog box window. Immediately, the script on the Orders Grid window, which had opened the dialog box, resumes execution. I showed one line from that script, the OpenWithParm call, earlier. Listing 14-2 shows the entire script.

Listing 14-2
The script for the Select button on the Orders Grid window.

```
String    ls_filter            // the filter expression
String    ls_segment           // part of the filter expression
s_selectorders lstr_response    // structure variable

OpenWithParm(w_selectorders, istr_response)

IF not IsValid(message.PowerObjectParm) THEN RETURN
lstr_response = message.PowerObjectParm
IF not lstr_response.b_ok THEN RETURN
```

```
istr_response = lstr_response   // save the response for next time

ls_filter = ""                  // no filter expression yet
IF not IsNull(lstr_response.d_fromdate) THEN  // there is from-date
   ls_segment = "orderdate >= date('"                      &
                + String(lstr_response.d_fromdate) + "')"
   ls_filter  += ls_segment + " and "
END IF
IF not IsNull(lstr_response.s_custid) THEN     // there is cust. #
   ls_segment = "custid = '" + lstr_response.s_custid + "'"
   ls_filter  += ls_segment + " and "
END IF
IF ls_filter <> "" THEN                        // there is a filter
   ls_filter = Left(ls_filter, Len(ls_filter) - 5) // remove "and"
END IF

dw_1.SetFilter(ls_filter)
dw_1.Filter()
```

After the script calls OpenWithParm, the script's execution is suspended, waiting for the modal child window (the dialog box) to close. When the dialog box closes, the script resumes.

The first concern of the script is how the user closed the dialog box. Was the OK button clicked, or the Cancel button? However, there is a third possibility, and it's a dangerous one to overlook. You can close the dialog box without clicking OK or Cancel: You can double-click its control box, for example, or press Alt+F4. These actions bypass the scripts that set up the *message* variable, leaving *message.PowerObjectParm* undefined. Any attempt to use PowerObjectParm then causes a system error. To avoid crashing, the script tests PowerObjectParm with the IsValid function:

```
IF not IsValid(message.PowerObjectParm) THEN RETURN
```

The IsValid function tells you whether or not an object variable is currently assigned a value. If it returns False, the *message* variable is unassigned, and there is nothing further to do. If it returns True, the *message* variable is okay, and the script can extract the structure from it:

```
lstr_response = message.PowerObjectParm
```

The next thing to check is whether the user clicked Cancel. We added the element *b_ok* to the structure for this very purpose. If *b_ok* is False, then the user has clicked Cancel, and there is nothing more to do:

```
IF not lstr_response.b_ok THEN RETURN
```

If the script proceeds beyond this line, then the user must have clicked OK.

The next line of the script preserves the structure in an instance variable:

```
istr_response = lstr_response    // save the response for next time
```

The next time the user clicks the Select button, the OpenWithParm call at the top of Listing 14-2 will pass this structure to the dialog box. The dialog box has a window open script that retrieves the structure from *message* and populates the window's fields with the structure's elements.

The bottom half of the script constructs a filter expression from the elements of *lstr_response* and places it into the variable *ls_filter*. For the values shown in Figure 14-12 the filter expression will be

```
orderdate >= date('1/1/96') and custid = '1040'
```

Every filled-in field in the dialog box contributes part of the expression. The OK button script placed a null in the structure element of each empty field, so the script in Listing 14-2 tests each element with IsNull before adding it to the expression.

Listing 14-2 shows the handling for only the from-date and the customer number. The actual script has similar code for all the other dialog box fields.

The script concludes by calling the SetFilter and Filter functions, which instruct the DataWindow to filter and display only the selected records.

Using SetFilter and Filter works if the DataWindow has already called the Retrieve function to retrieve all rows from the database. For large tables, however, you would never retrieve all rows. In that case, a different set of steps must be taken:

1. Construct an SQL WHERE clause, instead of a filter expression.
2. Call the SetSqlSelect function, instead of the SetFilter function, to change the DataWindow's SELECT statement, adding the WHERE clause to it.
3. Call the Retrieve function, instead of the Filter function, to fetch the matching rows from the database and display them.

The next example will show a script that performs these steps.

DIALOG BOX EXAMPLE 2: SELECTING ROWS FOR A REPORT

The first example used a dialog box to select rows for DataWindow display. The next example is similar: using a dialog box to select rows for a report. Since a report and a DataWindow are the same thing, there is little difference in how the dialog box works. But some differences exist in the overall process.

Note the List of Orders button in the Video Store application's start sheet (Figure 14-8). When you click it, it prints the report shown in Figure 14-14. But before it does, it first presents a dialog box in which you can specify which orders to print, as shown in Figure 14-13. This is the same dialog box that we used in the previous example, the response window w_selectorders.

Notice in Figure 14-14 that the report title includes a description of the selection criteria specified by the user. This is a nice user-friendly touch, and I'll show how the report-printing script puts it there.

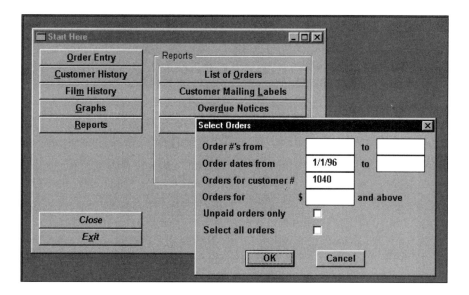

Figure 14-13

When you click the List of Orders button, a dialog box pops up so that you can specify which orders to print.

Orders List
Order date 1/1/96 and later, Customer # 1040

Order No.	Order Date	Cust. ID	Line Item Total	Sales Tax Rate	Sales Tax	Order Total	Store ID	Paid?
117	1/2/96	1040	$9.95	8.50%	$0.85	$10.80	D	☐
125	1/4/96	1040	$13.95	0.00%	$0.00	$13.95	C	☐
149	1/10/96	1040	$11.45	8.25%	$0.94	$12.39	A	☐
			$35.35		$1.79	$37.14		

Page 1 of 1

Figure 14-14

The printed report, with a description of the selection criteria in the title.

As Chapter 18 explains, a report is actually a DataWindow, and the DataWindow must be contained within a window. The window is named w_orderlist, and it doesn't look much different than the report itself. However, in the Video Store application the user never sees this window. The window stays invisible throughout the process.

In the Window Painter, you make the w_orderlist window invisible in its Window Style dialog box. When the List of Orders button calls the Open function to open the window, the window in fact opens and its scripts run, even though it is invisible. Here is the Open function call:

```
OpenSheet(w_orderlist, w_mdibase)
```

The w_orderlist window has a DataWindow control in it, which contains the report in Figure 14-14. The DataWindow control's constructor script does all the work: It opens the dialog box, constructs an SQL SELECT WHERE statement, retrieves the DataWindow rows, prints the report, and closes the window. The script is shown in Listing 14-3. You will recognize its similarity to Listing 14-2.

Listing 14-3

The script for the DataWindow constructor event

```
String    ls_desc          // report description
String    ls_origsql       // the original SELECT statement
String    ls_segment       // part of a WHERE clause
String    ls_sql           // the new SELECT statement
```

```
String    ls_where              // the WHERE clause
s_SelectOrders lstr_response    // structure from dialog box

This.SetTransObject(sqlca)      // associate sqlca with the DataWindow
Open(w_selectorders)            // display the dialog box
IF not IsValid(message.PowerObjectParm) THEN GOTO AllDone
lstr_response = message.PowerObjectParm
IF not lstr_response.b_ok THEN GOTO AllDone // did they click OK?

ls_where = ""                               // no WHERE clause yet
ls_desc = ""                                // no description yet
IF not IsNull(lstr_response.d_fromdate) THEN
    ls_segment = "orders.orderdate >= '"                    &
        + String(lstr_response.d_fromdate,"yyyy-mm-dd") + "'"
    ls_where += ls_segment + " and "
    ls_desc  += "Order date " + String(lstr_response.d_fromdate)
    ls_desc  += " and later,"
END IF
IF not IsNull(lstr_response.s_custid) THEN
    ls_segment = "orders.custid = '" + lstr_response.s_custid + "'"
    ls_where += ls_segment + " and "
    ls_desc  += "Customer # " + lstr_response.s_custid
    ls_desc  += ", "
END IF
IF ls_where <> "" THEN                       // there is a WHERE clause
    ls_where = Left(ls_where, Len(ls_where) - 5)  // remove "and"
END IF
IF ls_desc <> "" THEN                        // there is a description
    ls_desc = Left(ls_desc, Len(ls_desc) - 2)    // remove final ", "
END IF

IF ls_where <> "" THEN                       // there is a WHERE clause
    ls_origsql = This.GetSqlSelect()         // get the orig SELECT
    ls_sql = ls_origsql + " WHERE " + ls_where  // add WHERE to SELECT
    This.SetSqlSelect(ls_sql)                // apply SELECT to DW
    This.Object.reportdescription.Text = ls_desc
END IF

This.Retrieve()             // retrieve the rows
This.Print(True)            // print the report

AllDone:
cb_close.POST EVENT clicked ( ) // close this window on an error
```

Rather than walk through Listing 14-3 line by line, I'll just point out how it differs from Listing 14-2:

- Because this script is on the DataWindow control, it can refer to the DataWindow as *This* instead of as "dw_1."

- Because this is the DataWindow's constructor script, it includes the call to the SetTransObject function, which must be executed before any other DataWindow activity takes place.

- The script constructs a WHERE clause from the structure variable, not a filter expression. The syntax for a WHERE clause is different, especially in the date semantics:

```
WHERE orders.orderdate >= '1996-01-01' and orders.custid = '1040'
```

- There are some additional ins and outs to getting the WHERE clause to work, some of them depending on your database server product and on the DataWindow's original SELECT statement. The syntax shown here works for SQL Anywhere and SQL Server.

- In addition to building the WHERE clause in the variable *ls_where*, the script also builds a user-friendly description of the criteria in the variable *ls_desc*:

```
Order date 1/1/96 and later, Customer # 1040
```

- The line that begins *"This.Object.reportdescription.Text"* makes this string part of the report title. You can see it near the top of Figure 14-14. When designing the DataWindow object ("This.Object"), I added this text object to the header band and named it *reportdescription*. Initially, *reportdescription* = "All orders." This line of code changes its value to the value of the variable *ls_desc*.

- The script changes the DataWindow's SELECT statement, adding the WHERE clause to it, by calling the SetSqlSelect function (alternatively, you could change the This.Object.DataWindow.Table.Select property); it then calls the Retrieve function to execute that SELECT.

- The script calls the Print function to print the contents of the DataWindow as a report.

- Because the window's sole purpose was to print the report, and that has now been done, the last line of the script closes the window.

THE TROUBLE WITH THE CLOSE FUNCTION

The script closes the window in an unusual way. Typically, you would call the Close function:

```
Close(Parent)
```

However, Listing 14-3 is a constructor script, and it runs while the window is in the process of opening. If you close a window while it is opening, the window closes, but there is an unwanted side effect. Back in the parent window, the OpenSheet function call will return the value –1, indicating failure. If you write the OpenSheet script to test for an error — as you should do — then it will display an error message:

```
IF OpenSheet(w_OrderList, w_mdibase) <> 1 THEN  // test for error
    ... (display an error message) ...
```

If OpenSheet (or Open) returns a –1, there is no way to write the code to determine whether this is a legitimate error or it was caused by an open/constructor Close after the report printed.

A solution is to postpone the closing of the dialog box:

```
cb_close.POST EVENT clicked()  // close this window on an error
```

This executes the clicked script on a Close button on the window. That script closes the window in the usual way:

```
Close(Parent)
```

Using POST EVENT defers the clicked script until PowerBuilder has completed all pending work: the open event, the constructor events, and returning a success code, 1, to the parent window's OpenSheet script. Only after all these things happen does the Close take place.

This is a tricky business, but I find I run into this sort of problem often, especially when I try to do a lot of work in a window's open and constructor scripts. It's good to know the workaround.

PRINTING THE REPORT FROM A DATASTORE OBJECT

An alternative approach to this example would be to use a DataStore object instead of a window and DataWindow. With a DataStore, you would avoid the problems of how to keep the window invisible and how to close the window at the conclusion of the process. A DataStore object is a nonvisual DataWindow. Chapter 12 explained how to design a DataStore and showed a script to print a report from one. It's a simple exercise to combine the DataStore techniques from Chapter 12 with the dialog box techniques shown above. For a complete, working version, please refer to the Video Store sample application on the CD-ROM.

DIALOG BOX EXAMPLE 3: ASKING FOR A DATABASE PASSWORD

Often you want a dialog box to prompt for a user name and password, either to sign on to the application or to connect to the database. Figure 14-15 shows such a dialog box.

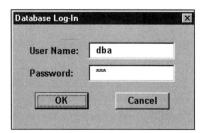

Figure 14-15
Prompting for a user name and a password.

The design and programming of this response window are similar to what was shown in the previous examples. The most significant difference is that when you type in the password, it echoes with "***" as a security precaution. You implement this feature in the Window Painter, where the password field is a SingleLineEdit control. Open its property sheet and checkmark its Password property, as shown in Figure 14-16.

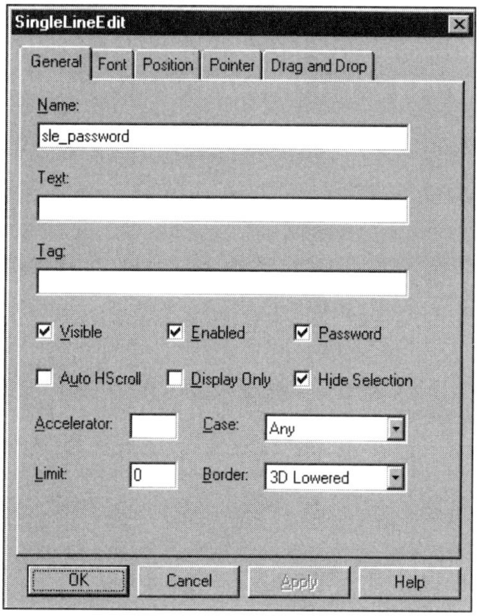

Figure 14-16
Setting the Password property of the password SingleLineEdit control.

Listing 14-4 is a script that uses this dialog box as part of the database connection process. It might be part of your application open script. It retrieves four *sqlca* properties — UserId, DBPass, LogId, LogPass — from the dialog box. The others it gets from PB.INI. In this case, the UserId and LogId are both the same user name, and the DBPass and LogPass are both the same password. That might not be the case for all databases.

Listing 14-4
A database connection script, using the Database Log-In dialog box.

```
Boolean lb_ok        // whether user clicks "OK" on dialog box
String  ls_section   // section in INI file with connection profile
s_dblogin  lstr_response    // structure for returning
                           // the dialog box results
//   The structure of s_dblogin:
//       b_ok              // True="OK", False="Cancel"
//       s_name            // user name
//       s_password        // password

//   Get some sqlca properties from the dialog box, w_dblogin .

Open(w_dblogin)
```

```
lb_ok = IsValid(message.PowerObjectParm)      // did it return values?
IF lb_ok THEN                                 // yes, it did
   lstr_response = message.PowerObjectParm     // get dialog results
   lb_ok = lstr_response.b_ok                  // did they click OK?
END IF
IF not lb_ok THEN                             // user did not click OK
   MessageBox("Error on Connect to Database"                &
      "Unable to connect to the database "       +    &
      "without a valid user name and password.",       &
      StopSign!)
   RETURN
END IF

// Transfer the dialog box results into sqlca

sqlca.UserId   = lstr_response.s_name
sqlca.DBPass   = lstr_response.s_password
sqlca.LogId    = lstr_response.s_name
sqlca.LogPass  = lstr_response.s_password

// Get the remaining parameters for the database connection
//   by reading them from an INI file.

ls_section = "Profile Video Store DB"
sqlca.DBMS       = ProfileString("PB.INI",ls_section,"DBMS","")
sqlca.Database   = ProfileString("PB.INI",ls_section,"Database","")
sqlca.ServerName =    &
            ProfileString("PB.INI",ls_section,"ServerName","")
sqlca.Lock       = ProfileString("PB.INI",ls_section,"Lock","")
sqlca.DBParm     = ProfileString("PB.INI",ls_section,"DbParm","")

CONNECT;                              // connect to the database
sqlca.DBPass    = "********"          // scramble the passwords
sqlca.LogPass   = "********"
IF sqlca.SqlCode <> 0 THEN MessageBox( ... etc... )  // it failed
```

Near the conclusion of the script are two lines that scrub the passwords from *sqlca:*

```
sqlca.DBPass    = "********"      //  Scramble the passwords
sqlca.LogPass   = "********"
```

Since *sqlca* is a global variable, I see it as somewhat of a security risk to carry these values around throughout the duration of the application. The database needs them only during the CONNECT. End users can't get at variable values. However, a rogue programmer could add a function to the application that transfers these values to a text file somewhere, so that as various users run the application, the programmer would accumulate everyone's passwords.

(I admit that there are plenty of other ways that a rogue programmer could do damage to a system, and this may seem like a very small hole to plug. But the way I see it, it makes sense to plug even the little holes when we spot em.)

The PowerBuilder Application Template

Whenever you create a new application, as you did in Chapter 2, PowerBuilder offers to "generate an Application template." When you select File|New from the Application Painter, the question in Figure 14-17 pops up. If you select Yes, PowerBuilder creates a small application for you.

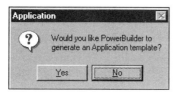

Figure 14-17

This question appears when you create a new application.

The application consists of one MDI frame window, one sheet window, and a menu and toolbar for each. It also includes two dialog box windows: one to manage toolbars, and one Help|About box. In the menu, the File|New choice can open multiple instances of the sheet, as you see in Figure 14-18.

The sheet is nothing more than an empty window, so the layout shown in Figure 14-18 is pretty much the limit of this application's functionality. However, this might be a good starting point for you, and you can begin adding your own application's features on top of it — if so, the template has saved you about an hour of work. Even if you don't use the template as your starting point, it can be a useful thing to explore to learn how to accomplish basic tasks. (Although nothing appears in it that's not covered in much more detail in this book.)

The template does nothing with DataWindows, nonvisual objects, or inheritance, which are valuable tools in a more sophisticated application. Also, there is no error handling, so you will probably want to go into the code and add it for things such as the OpenSheet function call.

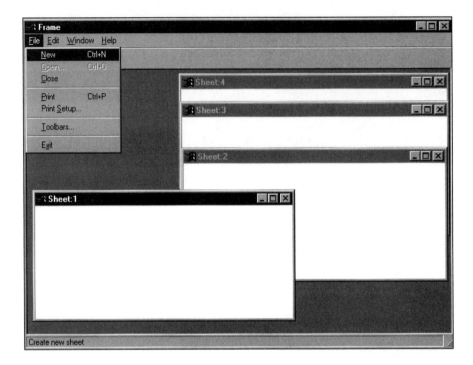

Figure 14-18
Running the application template.

Summary

This chapter has covered a lot of ground, showing that there is more to windows than first meets the eye:

- The six types of windows
- The variations of the Open function
- The MDI style of application
- Cooperating sheets
- Dialog boxes

Mastering these techniques is essential for PowerBuilder application development.

15 Menus and Toolbars

*T*his chapter explains how to design menus and toolbars, and how to integrate them into your application.

Menu Basics

Figure 15-1 shows an example of a simple PowerBuilder MDI frame window with a menu. A couple of selections have been made from the menu, displaying some of its lower-level choices. The choices in a menu are called *MenuItems*. The MenuItems are arranged into groups in a hierarchical structure.

In Figure 15-1, the menu has ten MenuItems displayed. It might also have others that appear when you click other choices. The four choices along the top — One, Two, Three, Four — are called the *menu bar*. When you select "One" from the menu bar, the next three choices appear — Five, Six, Seven. These are called a *dropdown menu*. When you select "Six," another set of choices appear — Eight, Nine, Ten. These are called a *cascading menu*. The total collection of MenuItems is called *the menu*.

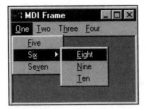

Figure 15-1
A menu and its MenuItems

The user sees a menu in one of two ways:

1. As a window-based menu
2. As a pop-up menu

Figure 15-2 shows a *window-based menu.* A window-based menu is associated with a window, and it is located just below the window's title bar. When the window opens, its menu appears automatically. At first you see only the menu bar, but dropdown and cascading menus appear as you make choices.

Figure 15-2
The menu bar.

Figure 15-3 shows a pop-up menu (Five, Six, Seven). A pop-up menu pops up somewhere on the screen, usually on top of a control or icon that you have just clicked or right-clicked. The pop-up menu in Figure 15-3 appears when you click the star icon. You make a pop-up menu appear by calling the PopMenu function from a script. A pop-up menu looks and acts a lot like a dropdown menu, except that it's not attached to a menu bar. Cascading menus can drop down from it.

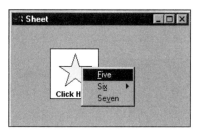

Figure 15-3
A pop-up menu.

Creating a Menu: the Menu Painter

Your application can include any number of menus, just as it can include any number of windows. You design a menu using the Menu Painter, give it a name, and store it in a library (.PBL file) along with windows and other objects.

When you click the Menu Painter on the PowerBar, the familiar Select dialog box pops up. (See Figure 15-4.) You can select an existing menu and modify it by clicking Open, or you can create a new menu by clicking New. You can also create a new menu subclass from an existing menu by clicking Inherit. Once you've made your selection, the Menu Painter opens, as shown in Figure 15-5.

In Figure 15-5, I have already typed a number of MenuItems into a new menu. There are five menu bar items: File, Edit, Options, Window, and Help. Under File, there is a dropdown menu with six items: New, Open, Close, Print, Printer Setup, and Exit.

Most of what you do in the Menu Painter is add and arrange MenuItems and set their properties. A MenuItem's properties are arranged into the tab pages that you see on the right side of the painter in Figure 15-5: General, Style, Shortcut, and so forth. The tab pages are a MenuItem's property sheet, but unlike elsewhere in PowerBuilder, this property sheet is always available. You don't have to open it by double-clicking or right-clicking something.

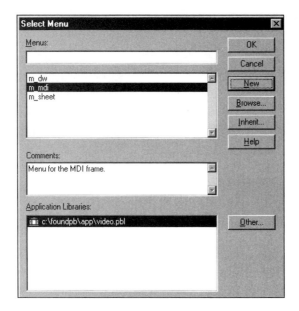

Figure 15-4
The Select Menu dialog box.

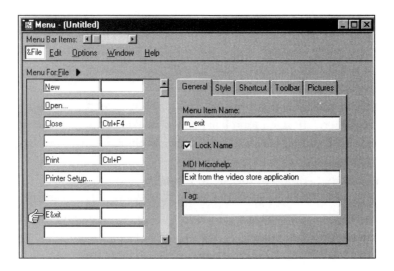

Figure 15-5
The Menu Painter.

Here is how to work with the Menu Painter:

SELECTING A MENUITEM

You select a MenuItem by clicking it. In Figure 15-5, "Exit" is the selected item, as indicated by the pointing finger. After clicking on the item, you can type in or change its text. For example, you could change "Exit" to "Quit."

INSERTING A MENUITEM

To add a new MenuItem to the end of the list, simply click the space at the end of the list. On the menu bar, that means clicking the gray area to the right of the last choice (Help).

To insert a new item to the left of, or above, another item, click an item and then click the Insert button on the PainterBar.

MOVING A MENUITEM

To move a MenuItem to a different position in its menu bar or dropdown menu, first click the Move button on the PainterBar and then click and drag the item to its new position. There is no way to move a MenuItem from one dropdown menu to another, or from the menu bar to a dropdown menu, or vice versa. There is also no way to copy a MenuItem.

DELETING A MENUITEM

To delete a MenuItem, select it and click the Delete button on the PainterBar. When you delete an item, PowerBuilder deletes its dropdown and cascading menus too.

DISPLAYING A CASCADING MENU

To add a cascading menu to a dropdown MenuItem, or to see its existing cascading menu, select the dropdown item and click the Next Level button on the PainterBar. The cascading menu appears in place of the dropdown menu. Cascading menus can run many levels deep, but good user interface design suggests no more than one level below the dropdown. To return from a cascading menu to its parent menu, click the Prior Level button on the PainterBar.

Scrolling across the Menu Bar

The scroll bar above the menu bar items lets you scroll left and right, if you have too many items to fit in the Painter window. When you run the application, Windows will wrap the menu bar onto multiple lines, if necessary, to hold a lot of items. It's bad design, however, to have too many items.

Accelerator Keys

To assign the accelerator key for an item, type an "&" in front of a letter in the item's name. In Figure 15-5, there is an "&" in front of the "x" in Exit. When you run the menu, the "&" does not appear, but the "x" is underlined. The "x" represents the accelerator key for Exit, which means that when this menu appears, you can select Exit by pressing "x" on the keyboard.

In Figure 15-5, you can see that every menu choice has an accelerator key. It appears as an underlined letter for the nonselected choices. Be careful not to assign the same accelerator key to more than one item in a group.

In the menu bar, accelerator keys operate even if the menu is not active, if you press Alt and the key. For example, Alt+F is File, Alt+E is Edit, and so forth.

Shortcut Keys

Shortcut keys make a choice from the menu, even when that choice isn't visible. In Figure 15-5, Ctrl+F4 is the shortcut for File|Close, and Ctrl+P is the shortcut for File|Print. These keys work even if the File dropdown menu isn't open. If you do open the dropdown menu, the shortcut keys are listed to the right of the items, as you see in Figure 15-6. To assign a shortcut key to a MenuItem, select the item, click the Shortcut tab in the Menu Painter, shown in Figure 15-7, and fill it in.

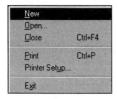

Figure 15-6
The dropdown menu, with shortcut keys and separation lines.

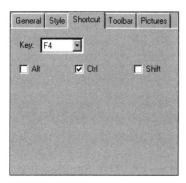

Figure 15-7
The Shortcut tab page in the Menu Painter.

SEPARATION LINES

To add a separation line between two items, insert a MenuItem between them and type in a single hyphen, the "-" character, for its text. You can see the separation lines in Figure 15-5, above the Print and Exit items. Figure 15-6 shows how they look at runtime.

MENU ITEM NAME

The "Menu Item Name" (on the General tab page, Figure 15-5) is an item's PowerBuilder object name, the name by which you will refer to this item in a script. By default, PowerBuilder assigns the name by adding the prefix "m_" to the menu text. For example, the "File" choice gets the name "m_file." If you change the text, PowerBuilder will change the name. A name change can wreak havoc with your existing scripts, however, so you should tend to leave the Lock Name property checkmarked so that PowerBuilder no longer changes it.

MDI MICROHELP

In the Menu Painter's General tab page (Figure 15-5), type a brief description of the MenuItem into the MDI MicroHelp field. When you run the application and highlight this menu choice, the description will appear in the window's status bar, if there is one. For more about the status bar and MicroHelp, refer to Chapter 14.

TAG

You are free to type whatever you want into the General tab's Tag field. PowerBuilder never looks at the Tag; it's provided for you as the developer to use however you choose. You could type a description of the MenuItem into it, or you could implement some developer-defined property. Some people use it to specify security access rights to the MenuItem.

CHECKED, ENABLED, VISIBLE

Using the Checked, Enabled, and Visible properties on the Menu Painter's Style tab page, shown in Figure 15-8, you can change the appearance of a MenuItem. Figure 15-9 shows the dropdown menu, with New checked, Close disabled ("grayed out"), and Printer Setup invisible.

When you use these three properties, you usually plan to change them at runtime. You can do this from a script. For example, this PowerScript line disables the Edit|Paste menu choice in the menu named m_main:

```
m_main.m_edit.m_Paste.Enabled = False
```

To implement the Checked property fully, you'll need some PowerScript code that toggles the checkmark on and off at runtime as the user selects the MenuItem. Writing this one line of code for the MenuItem's clicked script does the job:

```
This.Checked = not This.Checked
```

The PowerBuilder documentation lists a MenuItem's properties and functions and how to use them. To use a property or a function, you must specify the MenuItem's menu-tree path in dot notation: m_main is the name of the menu, m_edit is the Edit MenuItem, and m_paste is the Paste menu item. So m_main.m_edit.m_paste is Paste under Edit in the menu named m_main.

Figure 15-8
The Menu Style tab page.

Figure 15-9
*The dropdown menu, with New checked, Close disabled ("grayed out"),
and Printer Setup invisible.*

SHIFT OVER/DOWN

If the Shift Over/Down property on the Style tab page (Figure 15-8) is
checkmarked, then this MenuItem, no matter where it appears in the list,
will jump to the far right or bottom of the list at runtime, but only if this
menu is inherited from another. This feature is important when you add
new items to an inherited menu, as I will explain later.

MENU MERGE OPTION

The Menu Merge property, on the Style tab page, applies only to menu bar
items. It specifies what role a MenuItem should play during an OLE operation, when Windows merges your application's menu with the OLE server
product's menu.

TYPE OPTION

The Type Option is a property on the Style tab page. Pick one of three choices from the dropdown list: Normal, Exit, or About. Typically, you should set your File|Exit or equivalent menu choice to Type Exit, your Help|About or equivalent to Type About, and everything else to Type Normal. This property plays a role only during in the Apple Macintosh environment, where these features are handled differently than under Windows.

TOOLBAR AND PICTURES TABS

Use the Menu Painter's Toolbar and Pictures tab pages to add a button to the toolbar that corresponds to this MenuItem. I'll talk about Toolbars and how to set them up later in this chapter.

PREVIEWING THE MENU

To see how your menu will look at runtime, select Design|Preview from the Painter menu, or click the Preview button on the PainterBar.

SAVING THE MENU

As in other PowerBuilder painters, you save your work by selecting File|Save or File|Save As from the menu. If you close the painter without saving your work first, PowerBuilder will offer to do a save. The first time you save it, you must give it a name. The typical convention is to begin the name with the prefix "m_" — for example, "m_main" — just as windows begin with "w_". The menu is an object stored in the library (.PBL) file.

Displaying a Menu

To use a menu, you must assign it to a window or pop it up from a script.

ASSIGNING A MENU TO A WINDOW

To assign a menu to a window, open the window in the Window Painter. Open the window's property sheet by selecting Edit|Properties from the menu. In the General tab page, fill in the menu name in the space provided, as shown in Figure 15-10.

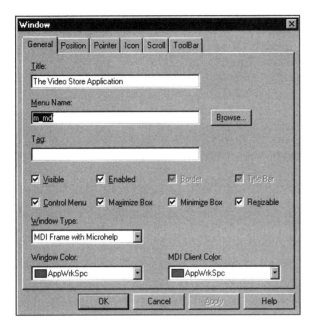

Figure 15-10

Assigning the menu to a window in the window's property sheet.

MDI frame windows are required to have a menu. For main and popup windows, a menu is optional. For child and response windows, a menu is not allowed.

When you run the application and open the window, its menu will also appear. You will see the menu bar across the top of the window, just below its title bar, as I've shown in Figure 15-2.

MENUS FOR MDI FRAMES AND SHEETS

Menus and windows have a special relationship in an MDI environment. When you open the MDI frame, it displays its menu, as you would expect. When you open a sheet inside the frame, the sheet's menu appears, not at the top of the sheet, but at the top of the frame, replacing the frame's menu. When many sheets are open, the frame will display the menu for whichever sheet is active. As you hop from sheet to sheet, the menu changes. When you close all the sheets, or when the active sheet has no menu associated with it, then the frame's own menu reappears.

POPPING UP A MENU

To open a pop-up menu, a script must call the PopMenu function. In Figure 15-3, the pop-up menu appears when you click the star, which is a picture control. This is the control's clicked script:

```
m_onetwothree.m_one.PopMenu(w_mdi.PointerX(), w_mdi.PointerY())
```

This says, "pop up the menu that is the dropdown menu for the menu bar item named m_one in the menu named m_onetwothree." The menu named m_onetwothree is the one shown in Figure 15-1. The MenuItem One in its menu bar is named m_one. One's dropdown menu contains the items Five, Six, Seven, and that it is the dropdown menu that pops up.

The two arguments in the PopMenu function call are the x and y coordinates where the menu should appear. The arguments that I have supplied cause it to appear at the mouse pointer's position, which is the natural place for it. The PointerX and PointerY functions return the position of the mouse pointer with respect to some object. That object in this case is w_mdi, the MDI frame window.

A menu contains an entire tree of choices, and with PopMenu you can display at any section of the tree. In Figure 15-3, I chose to display the part of the tree below the "One" choice — Five, Six, Seven. This script would pop up the part below the "Six" choice — Eight, Nine, Ten:

```
m_onetwothree.m_one.m_six.PopMenu  &
    (w_mdi.PointerX(), w_mdi.PointerY())
```

This script would display the top of the tree, the menu bar choices — One, Two, Three, Four — vertically arranged:

```
m_onetwothree.PopMenu(w_mdi.PointerX(), w_mdi.PointerY())
```

There is one catch. The menu referenced in the PopMenu, m_onetwothree, must be the menu associated with the currently active window; otherwise, the script can't "see" it. It's often the case that the window's menu will not contain the menu you want to display as a pop-up. In that case, you must add two more lines to the script before calling PopMenu:

```
m_onetwothree  m
m = CREATE m_onetwothree
m.m_one.PopMenu(w_mdi.PointerX(), w_mdi.PointerY())
```

These two lines instantiate an object variable for the menu and use it in the PopMenu call. This is similar to how we've used nonvisual objects in other chapters.

MenuItem Scripts

So far, you have learned how to create menus and display them, but these menus don't really do anything yet. File|Open doesn't open anything, and File|Close doesn't close anything. There's one more important step: writing scripts for the MenuItems.

Writing a script for a MenuItem is very much like writing a script for any other object. In the Menu Painter, select an item, and then click the Script button on the PainterBar. This opens the Script Painter.

A MenuItem has two events: clicked and selected. The clicked script is the more important of the two. It is the one that runs when you choose the item from the menu, typically by clicking it with the mouse. The select script runs when you highlight the item — for example, as you use the arrow keys to scroll through the items — whether or not you select it. The select script is useful for special purposes, such as context-sensitive help.

In this book, when I mention a MenuItem's script I am referring to its clicked script, unless I say otherwise.

Here is an example of a MenuItem script, one that implements the Window|Tile menu choice for w_mdi, an MDI frame:

```
w_mdi.ArrangeSheets(Tile!)
```

REFERRING TO A WINDOW IN A MENUITEM SCRIPT

Most MenuItem scripts do something to a window. The Window|Tile MenuItem is a good example. It tiles the sheets in an MDI frame. Therefore, most of your scripts need to refer to a window in some way.

It's easy to refer to a window if you know its name. In the example above, the window's name, w_mdi, is coded right into the script.

Unfortunately in many cases you won't know the window's name, or it might be one of several names. For example, you might design a menu and attach it to five or six different windows. You can't hard-code a window's name in that menu's scripts, because you don't know which window it will be at runtime.

In most of these situations, you can use the pronoun *ParentWindow* instead.

THE *PARENTWINDOW* PRONOUN

ParentWindow is a "PowerScript pronoun," akin to the pronouns *This* and *Parent* that we've seen in other chapters. *ParentWindow* can be used only in menu scripts. It refers to the window to which the menu is attached.

This script implements a File|Close menu choice, to close the window to which the menu is attached:

```
Close(ParentWindow)
```

REFERRING TO THE MDI FRAME

Some operations must operate on the MDI frame. If the menu is attached to a sheet in the frame, how can it reference the frame? This odd-looking script does the trick, closing the MDI frame, which for most MDI applications is how you implement the File|Exit menu choice:

```
Close(ParentWindow(ParentWindow))
```

This script is made confusing by the fact that the word "ParentWindow" is used for two different things in the PowerScript language: The *ParentWindow* pronoun is the parent window of a menu, and the ParentWindow function returns the parent window of a child window. In the script above, the "ParentWindow" on the right is the pronoun. It refers to the menu's parent, which is the sheet. The "ParentWindow" on the left is the function. When you plug a sheet into it as an argument, it returns the MDI frame. Thus the Close function closes the MDI frame.

Things gets trickier still. What happens if you attach the same menu (or its descendants) to the MDI frame and to its sheet windows? As you will see, this is quite a common thing to do. In that case, how do you implement a File|Exit by closing the MDI frame? While the menu is attached to the frame, you do it like this:

```
Close(ParentWindow)
```

But from the sheet, it's like this:

```
Close(ParentWindow(ParentWindow))
```

The latter script crashes when run from the frame's menu, because the frame has no parent window.

Here's how to write a File|Exit script that works in both cases:

```
Window  w                // the frame or sheet window
w = ParentWindow         // this might be the frame or the sheet
IF IsValid(ParentWindow(w)) THEN   // it's a sheet
   w = ParentWindow(w)            // this is the frame
END IF
Close(w)                 // close the frame
```

The IsValid function tests whether the window w has a parent. If so, it returns True; if not, it returns False. If the window has no parent, the window is a frame. If the window does have a parent, the parent is the frame. By the end of the script, the w variable is the frame, and the Close function closes it.

Some functions, such as ArrangeSheets, don't require this trick:

```
ParentWindow.ArrangeSheets(Tile!)
```

Whether ParentWindow is the frame or a sheet, ArrangeSheets knows what it must do. It always tiles all the sheets in the frame.

REFERRING TO THE "CONTROL LAST CLICKED"

If a menu script operates on a control, and if you can hard-code the names of both the control and its window, use "dot-dot" notation to refer to the window:

```
w_orders.dw_1.Retrieve()   // retrieve rows into the DataWindow
```

It is much more of a challenge for a menu script to refer to a control when its name can't be hard-coded — for example, when the script must operate on whatever control was "last clicked."

Consider the pop-up menu in Figure 15-11. I designed this one to pop up when you right-click a control, like the pop-up menus in PowerBuilder painters. The menu choices are the standard Windows clipboard operations: cut, copy, and paste. When you select one, a MenuItem script performs that operation on the control. Which control? The control that popped up the menu. In Figure 15-11 it might be one of the four SingleLineEdits, or it might be the DataWindow.

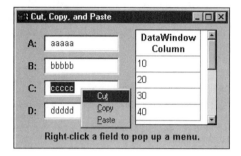

Figure 15-11

A control-based pop-up menu.

Unfortunately, there's no function available that can tell the MenuItem script an essential piece of information: which control on the window popped it up, or which control was last clicked. It is necessary for a script on each control to somehow pass that information to the menu.

Each control's RButtonDown script pops up the menu (RButtonDown is the right-click event):

```
m_cutcopypaste  m
m = CREATE m_cutcopypaste
m.iwo_parentcontrol = This
m.m_edit.popmenu(w_mdi.PointerX(), w_mdi.PointerY())
```

I explained most of this script earlier, when I described how to use the PopMenu function. The third line, however, is new:

```
m.iwo_parentcontrol = This
```

This line tells the menu "m" that *This* control popped it up. The variable *iwo_parentcontrol* is one of the menu's public instance variables. You can declare instance variables for a menu, just as you can for windows and other objects, and they are visible to all of the menu's scripts. Here is the declaration:

```
Public:
    WindowObject  iwo_parentcontrol
```

A WindowObject variable holds a reference to a control of any type. If you refer back to the object class hierarchy in Chapter 11, you'll see that the WindowObject class is the ancestor class of every control's object class.

So the menu knows which control popped it up: It is *iwo_parentcontrol*. The script for the Cut MenuItem is almost this simple:

```
iwo_parentcontrol.Cut()   // cut the value to the Windows clipboard
```

But I said *almost*. There is a Cut function in PowerScript, and it does operate on SingleLineEdit and DataWindow controls. Unfortunately, it does not work on WindowObjects, so iwo_parentcontrol.Cut() causes a syntax error.

The cut script must do a little more work. It must determine the type of control the WindowObject holds, and it must transfer it to a variable that is acceptable to Cut. This is the cut script that does work:

```
SingleLineEdit sle   // SingleLineEdit control to cut from
DataWindow     dw    // DataWindow control to cut from

CHOOSE CASE iwo_parentcontrol.TypeOf()   // what kind of control?
   CASE SingleLineEdit!                  // it's a SingleLineEdit
      sle = iwo_parentcontrol            // get the SLE control
      sle.Cut()                          // cut the value
   CASE DataWindow!                      // it's a DataWindow
      dw = iwo_parentcontrol             // get the DW control
      dw.Cut()                           // cut the value
END CHOOSE
```

The scripts for Copy and Paste are nearly identical.

The Menu as an Object

A menu is an object, and everything we said about objects in earlier chapters applies to menus. If you refer back to Table 12-1 in Chapter 12, you'll see that the menu object has a place in the object hierarchy, right next to the window object. In fact, from an object-oriented point of view, a menu is very similar to a window.

Every time you create a new menu in the Menu Painter, you are actually defining a new subclass of the menu object class. (We have said exactly the same thing about windows and the window object class.) The name you give to the menu — m_mdi, for example — becomes the name of the subclass. The new subclass inherits all of the functions, properties, and events of the menu class, and so it is not incorrect to refer to it as a menu object.

THE MENUITEM AS AN OBJECT

Within a menu, each MenuItem is also an object. A MenuItem has the same relationship to its menu object as a control has to its window object: A window object contains the control, and the menu object contains the MenuItem. A MenuItem script can see and manipulate its menu's instance variables.

However, there is something odd about the MenuItem object: It doesn't have a special class in the PowerBuilder object hierarchy. Oddly enough, the MenuItem and the menu object belong to the same object class! Maybe it should be called the "Menu/MenuItem class" instead of simply the "menu object class."

In practice, this means that menu objects and MenuItems provide all of the same functions, properties, and events. Experimentation indicates that this is true. However, the mechanics of the Menu Painter don't let you get to all of them. For example, there is no way to get to the menu object's event scripts. There is no way to define instance variables or user-defined functions for a MenuItem. The differences between menu objects and MenuItems are summarized in Table 15-1.

Table 15-1

Object-Oriented Features of the Menu and MenuItem Objects

Object Feature	Menu Object	MenuItem Object
Built-in functions	Yes	Yes
Built-in properties	Yes	Yes
Built-in events	No	Yes
User-defined functions	Yes	No
Instance variables	Yes	No
User-defined events	No	No

Are the menu and the MenuItem really the same kind of object? Yes they are, if you look at it in this way: Each is a single item, but each can also be a container for an entire tree of menu choices. The fact that the menu object contains the entire tree, whereas a MenuItem contains only a segment of the tree, does not make them substantially different.

MENU OBJECT INHERITANCE

When you create a menu, you are creating a new subclass. By clicking the Inherit button on the Select Menu dialog box (Figure 15-4), you can create subclasses of that subclass. As always, the subclass inherits all of the functions, properties, and events of its ancestor, and you can modify and augment them.

There is a limitation to what you can do to an inherited menu. It has to do with your ability to add and delete MenuItems:

In the descendant menu, you cannot delete any of the ancestor's MenuItems. You can, however, make them invisible, which effectively deletes them from the user's point of view. You also cannot rearrange the order of the ancestor's MenuItems, except by setting the Shift Over/Down property that I'll describe in a moment.

You can add a new MenuItem, but you can add it only to the end of the list — that is, to the right of all the ancestor's menu bar choices, or below all the ancestor's choices in a dropdown or cascading menu. The Menu Painter will not allow you to insert a new MenuItem between a pair of ancestor items, or above or to the left of them.

Nevertheless, there is a way to get the new descendant items to appear in between the ancestor items: by turning on the Shift Over/Down property on one or more ancestor items. You can see this property in the Style tab page in Figure 15-8. You can set this property in the ancestor or in the descendant menu. When it's checkmarked, that item jumps to the far right or bottom of the menu at runtime, leaping over the new descendant items.

There is a practical need for Shift Over/Down. Suppose that the ancestor menu has these four familiar MenuItems:

```
File  Edit  Window  Help
```

Further suppose that in the descendant menu you add two new MenuItems, Data and Rows. PowerBuilder forces them to the right side of the menu:

```
File   Edit   Window   Help   Data   Rows
```

Once you've checkmarked the Shift Over/Down property on Window and Help, the new choices fall into their proper position:

```
File   Edit   Data   Rows   Window   Help
```

It doesn't look this way in the Menu Painter, but it does when you run the application, or when you select Design|Preview.

The Exit choice in the File dropdown menu is another that should have the Shift Over/Down property selected so that it always drops to the bottom of its menu.

Of course, there are limits to what Shift Over/Down can accomplish. Some descendant menu arrangements are impossible to construct, and when you have descendants of descendants, things can get quite out of hand. I'll show an example of these problems, and a solution, a little later.

Toolbars

You can add a toolbar to your window, but only if it is an MDI frame-type window. Figure 15-12 shows an MDI frame with a three-button toolbar. The buttons are equivalent to the File|Exit, Window|Tile, and Window|Cascade menu choices, respectively.

Figure 15-12
An MDI frame with a toolbar.

The toolbar has a very close relationship with a menu. You define a toolbar in the Menu Painter. The toolbar is part of the menu. There is no such thing as a standalone toolbar, at least not in PowerBuilder. Each toolbar button must be the equivalent of some choice in the menu and serves as a shortcut to that menu choice. You can assign a toolbar button to an invisible menu choice, if you want the user to think that the button has no menu equivalent.

ADDING A BUTTON TO THE TOOLBAR

To create a toolbar button for a MenuItem, use the Toolbar and Pictures tab pages. On the Pictures page (Figure 15-13), you specify the toolbar button's picture. On the Toolbar page (Figure 15-14), you specify its other properties.

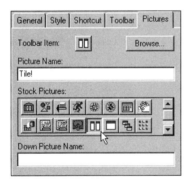

Figure 15-13
Selecting the picture for the toolbar button.

The quickest way to set up a toolbar button for a MenuItem is to fill in the Picture Name box on the Picture tab page. You can type in the name of a picture (.BMP, .RLE, or .WMF) file, perhaps of your own design, or you can select a picture from the scrolling list of over 400 "stock pictures." In Figure 15-13, I have assigned the stock picture named "Tile!" to a toolbar button for the Windows|Tile MenuItem.

You can also assign a "Down Picture Name" that will be displayed when the toolbar button is depressed.

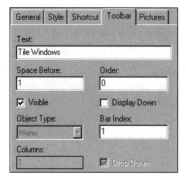

Figure 15-14
The Toolbar tab page.

On the Toolbar tab page (Figure 15-14), you specify additional properties of the toolbar button:

- **Text** — Type in the PowerTip text for the button. A *PowerTip* is the yellow description box that pops up on a toolbar button when you touch the mouse to it.

- **Space Before** — Type in a number greater than zero to insert some space into the toolbar, separating this button from the button to its left. For the Tile button, the value is 1. Note the separation between the Exit and Tile buttons in Figure 15-12.

- **Order** — Type in a number greater than zero to specify where to place this button in the toolbar in relation to other buttons. The default, zero, arranges the buttons in the same order as their corresponding menu choices.

- **Visible** — Specify whether the button should be visible or invisible initially. You can control this, and the other properties, from a script at runtime.

- **Display Down** — This property, when checkmarked, causes the button to stick in its pushed-in position when clicked. It is useful only with a MenuItem which has its Clicked property turned on.

- **Bar Index** — By placing a number into the Bar Index box for each toolbar button, you can divide the toobar into multiple "dockable" segments. At runtime, you can move each segment to a different part of the screen by dragging it with the mouse, independently of the other segments.

■ **Object Type, Columns** — These properties play a role in setting up dropdown toolbar buttons, which are described in the next section.

DROPDOWN TOOLBAR BUTTONS

You've seen dropdown toolbar buttons in PowerBuilder, such as the toolbar palette of controls in the Window Painter. You can add similar dropdown buttons to your application's toolbars.

Figure 15-15 shows an example. The user has clicked a dropdown button on the toolbar, and a palette of four buttons has appeared. These four buttons are equivalent to the four choices under the Alignment choice in the menu bar.

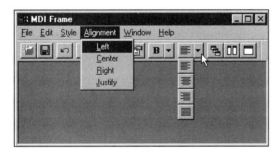

Figure 15-15
A dropdown toolbar button.

(Figure 15-15 shows both the menu and the toolbar palette dropped down at the same time. This is unusual. Usually, you will see one or the other, but not both.)

The set of dropdown buttons must correspond to a dropdown or cascading menu somewhere in the menu tree, such as the Alignment dropdown menu in Figure 15-15. Select the parent MenuItem (for instance, Alignment) and, in its Toolbar tab page, change Object Type from Menu to MenuCascade. Also, make sure that Drop Down is checkmarked to instruct PowerBuilder to arrange all toolbar buttons for the dropdown MenuItems into a dropdown toolbar palette. (You must define a toolbar picture for each of those MenuItems in the usual way.)

In the "Columns" choice, you specify how many columns to arrange the dropdown buttons into. In Figure 15-15, Columns = 1.

THE TOOLBAR AT RUNTIME

When you run the application, the toolbar appears when its menu appears, if you have set up at least one button for it. As you move the mouse across the toolbar buttons, their PowerTip text appears beneath them. At the same time, the MenuItem's MicroHelp text (not the PowerTip text) appears in the status bar below, if the window is an MDI frame with MicroHelp.

The menu object has several properties for controlling the toolbar items from a script. For example, the ToolbarItemVisible property can make the button visible or invisible.

THE FRAMEBAR AND THE SHEETBAR

I explained earlier how an MDI frame displays a menu: It displays its own menu when no sheets are open, or when a menuless sheet is active. But if a sheet has a menu, the sheet's menu replaces the frame's menu while that sheet is active.

Toolbars work a little differently. If both the frame and the sheet have menus with toolbars, one toolbar does not replace the other. Instead, both toolbars appear. Figure 15-16 shows what this effect looks like. The menu bar you see in the figure is the menu for the Customer Information sheet. The top toolbar, called the *FrameBar*, belongs to the MDI frame's menu, even though that menu is hidden. The bottom toolbar, called the *SheetBar*, belongs to the Customer Information sheet's menu. The situation with one menu and two toolbars is the exactly same as in the PowerBuilder development environment, where two toolbars — the PowerBar and the PainterBar — often share the screen.

Sometimes PowerBuilder creates two separate rows, as in Figure 15-16. Sometimes it places them side by side in a single row, if they fit the width of the screen.

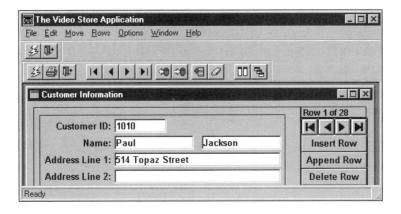

Figure 15-16
Two toolbars — the FrameBar and the SheetBar.

You can change the appearance of the toolbars interactively or with PowerScript commands. Interactively, you can click and drag a toolbar to a new location. You can also right-click either toolbar to pop up the menu shown in Figure 15-17. From this menu, you can make a toolbar visible or invisible, move it to a new location, or make the buttons bigger to show text descriptions on them. You should be familiar with these techniques from the PowerBuilder development environment. It's nice to have them in our applications too!

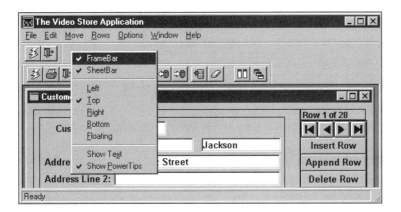

Figure 15-17
The pop-up menu for adjusting the toolbars.

In my applications, the FrameBar and the SheetBar together are usually redundant. As you can see in Figure 15-16, all the FrameBar buttons are also on the SheetBar. So I often execute this script line, perhaps when the first sheet opens, to hide the FrameBar:

```
This.ToolbarVisible = False
```

"*This*," in this case, is the MDI frame window, and its toolbar is the FrameBar.

Putting Theory into Practice: the Video Store Menus

The Video Store application provides an example of how you might structure the windows, menus, and toolbars in your own application.

Although the Video Store application has many windows, it has only three menus. Furthermore, the menus are related as ancestors and descendants of one another in the object class hierarchy. The three menus are

1. **m_mdi** — the menu associated with the application's MDI frame window

2. **m_sheet** — the menu associated with every sheet window in the application, except for those windows that contain a DataWindow. This menu is a subclass of m_mdi and therefore inherits all of its MenuItems, properties, and toolbar items.

3. **m_dw** — the menu associated with every sheet window that contains a DataWindow. This menu is a subclass of m_sheet and therefore inherits all of its MenuItems, properties, and toolbar items.

Every window in the application — except response windows (dialog boxes) — has one of these three menus associated with it. Window inheritance makes the job of assigning menus to windows easy. In the Video Store application, every window with a DataWindow is a descendant of a window named w_dwbase. The menu m_dw is tied to w_dwbase, and so all of its descendant windows inherit that menu. Every other sheet window is a descendant of a window named w_sheet, and the menu m_sheet is tied to it. So all of w_sheet's descendants inherit that menu. There is only one MDI window, named m_mdivideo, and m_mdi is its menu.

Just as window inheritance makes development easier, it makes sense to take advantage of menu inheritance too. All three menus have many MenuItems in common. In fact, each menu is a superset of the one before it. This kind of situation has "inheritance" written all over it.

This is the menu bar for m_dw, the largest of the three menus:

```
File   Edit   Move   Rows   Options   Window   Help
```

Listing 15-1 shows the complete tree for this menu. The numbers along the left margin indicate in which of the three menus an item first appears. For example, File and File|Open appear in m_mdi. File|Print and Window first appear in m_sheet. File|Print|Report and Edit appear only in m_dw.

Listing 15-1

The MenuItem tree for the menu m_dw. Items marked with (T) have toolbar buttons.

```
1    File
1        Start Here (T)
1        Open
2        Close
1        ────
2        Print
2            Screen
2            Window (T)
3            Report (T)
1        Printer Setup
1        ────
1        Exit
3    Edit
3        Cut, Copy, Paste
3    Move
3        First Row (T), Prior Page, Prior Row (T), etc.
3    Rows
3        Retrieve (T), Update (T), Reset
3        Insert Row (T), Append Row, Delete Row (T)
3        Filter, Sort
1    Options
1        Database Connections
1        System Administration
1        Preferences
2    Window
2        Tile (T), Cascade (T), Layer, etc.
1    Help
1        Contents, Search, Help, About
```

In this menu hierarchy, each subclass has more MenuItems than its parent. There are two ways to implement this:

Alternative 1: The ancestor class has the fewest MenuItems. Each descendant adds more items.

Alternative 2: The ancestor class has all the MenuItems, but many of them are invisible. Each descendant makes more of the items visible.

Alternative 3: The ancestor class has all the MenuItems, and all are visible. All descendants are derived directly from it. In each descendant, various items are made invisible. One of these descendants is attached to the MDI Frame window. The other descendants are attached to the various sheets.

The first approach seems most intuitive. Typically in an object class hierarchy, the descendants are smarter than their ancestors. With PowerBuilder menus, however, one of the other two approaches might be necessary.

It turns out, for example, that there is no way to get the Window MenuItem to fit into its correct position in the menu bar if you follow only alternative 1. The limitations of the Shift Over/Down property become insurmountable. (Try it.) With alternative 2 or 3, there's no problem.

In the Video Store application, I used a combination of alternatives 1 and 2. In applications with more complex menu schemes, you'll probably be drawn toward alternative 2 or 3.

I constructed the first menu, m_mdi, with this menu bar:

```
File  Options  Window  Help
```

The Window choice is invisible. When the MDI frame opens, and before a sheet opens, there is no need for the user to see Window in the menu.

The second menu, m_sheet, inherits m_mdi's items, makes Window visible, and adds new items, Close and Print, under File.

The third menu, m_dw, inherits m_sheet's items, adds three new items — Edit, Move, and Rows — to the menu bar, and slides Options, Window, and Help to the right. It also adds a new item, Report, under File|Print.

At each level, some menu items contribute toolbar buttons as well. You can see the complete toolbar for m_dw in Figure 15-16. It includes a set of VCR buttons for navigating through a DataWindow.

Summary

When you run an application, its menus and toolbars appear to be simple features, without much complexity. But now that we've looked at them in depth, you can see that there is a lot more to them behind the scenes. PowerBuilder offers a wealth of functionality for menus and toolbars, and there should be plenty to work with here, enough to satisfy almost anyone's needs.

Libraries, Applications, Projects, and Executables

This chapter describes three PowerBuilder painters:

- The Library Painter
- The Application Painter
- The Project Painter

We've talked about the Library and Application Painter in past chapters. This chapter covers them in more detail. The Project Painter is a new topic. It has one very important purpose: to convert your application into an executable version so that you can deploy it into production.

The Library Painter

A library is a file, with the extension .PBL, in which PowerBuilder stores the components that make up an application. Depending upon the size and complexity of an application, you might decide to organize its objects into more than one library. (See "Planning a Multiple-Library System" later in this chapter.)

With the Library Painter, you can inspect and manage the contents of a library. To open the Library Painter, click the Library button on the PowerBar. Figure 16-1 shows the three component libraries that make up the video store sample application: VIDEO1.PBL, VIDEO2.PBL, and VIDEO3.PBL. They reside in the directory c:\foundpb\video.

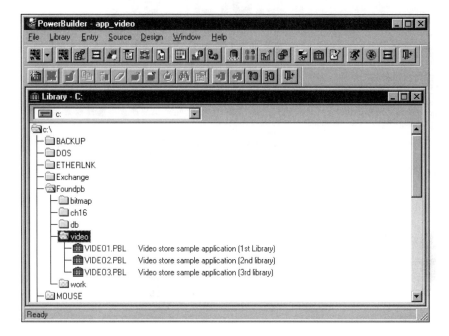

Figure 16-1
The video store sample application PowerBuilder libraries (.PBLs).

The Library Painter displays .PBLs in a tree style like you find in the Windows File Manager, Windows Explorer, and other products, and extends it to show you the internal contents of any .PBL file. In Figure 16-2, the contents of the third library, VIDEO3.PBL, are displayed.

At first the painter shows the contents of the current library. Double-clicking a directory or .PBL toggles how it is displayed, showing or hiding its contents. If you double-click VIDEO1.PBL, its contents will appear.

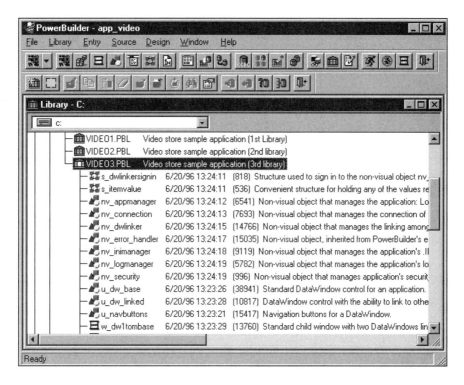

Figure 16-2
The video store sample application PowerBuilder libraries (.PBLs) with VIDEO3.PBL expanded.

You will see eleven types of objects in a library:

- Applications
- Data Pipelines
- DataWindows
- Functions
- Menus
- Projects
- Proxies
- Queries
- Structures
- User Objects
- Windows

Keeping the Library Painter Open

I often open the Library Painter at the beginning of a work session, and keep it open throughout, even though I spend most of my time in other painters. The Library Painter is very convenient. It provides an excellent bird's-eye view of the application. It's usually faster to open another painter from the Library Painter, by double-clicking an entry in the tree display, than to open it from the PowerBar.

You can configure PowerBuilder to open the Library Painter automatically upon startup. To configure it this way, add "/p library" to the start-up command. In Windows 95, right-click the icon or item you use to launch PowerBuilder, select Properties from the pop-up menu, and add "/p library" to the Target field on the Shortcut tab page. In Windows 3.1, single-click the PowerBuilder icon in Program Manager, select File|Properties from the menu, and add "/p library" to the Command Line field. This is my PowerBuilder startup command, which uses Windows 95 long file names:

```
"C:\Program
    Files\Powersoft\PowerBuilder
    5.0\PB050.EXE" /p library
```

These are the major objects that make up an application. There are other types of objects that the Library Painter does not display, such as controls, MenuItems, and scripts. They are also stored in the .PBL, inside the major objects. To see the controls and scripts inside a window, for example, you must open the window in the Window Painter.

LIBRARY PAINTER FEATURES

The next several pages describe the features of the Library Painter. None of these features is very difficult, but almost all of them are useful. It's good to know where to find them.

SELECTING AN ITEM

Many of the choices in the Library Painter menu require that you first choose an item from the tree that is displayed. To choose an item — a directory, a library, or an object — click it with the mouse. The selected item is highlighted, as the library VIDEO3.PBL is in Figure 16-2. You can also use the movement keys on the keyboard, such as the up and down arrow keys, to scroll from one item to another.

Only in the Library Painter!

There are a number of features that probably belong in other painters but for some reason are found only in the Library Painter. Many people, myself included, have spent fruitless hours searching for them elsewhere. Here are the most important features that are hiding here:

- **Entry|Copy** and **Entry|Move** — Copy or move an object, such as a window or DataWindow, from one library to another.

- **Entry|Delete** — Delete an object from a library.

- **Entry|Print** and **Entry|Export** — These functions provide documentation for objects in a library. For example, Entry|Print can print all the scripts in a window, among other things.

- **Entry|Search** — Search for text within one or more objects.

THE LIBRARY MENU

These functions under the Library menu operate on a library. For most of them, you must first select the library by clicking its name in the painter tree.

The choices in the Library menu also appear when you right-click a library name in the painter tree.

- **Library|Create** (same as Create Library on the PainterBar) — Create a new library.

- **Library|Delete** — Delete a library.

- **Library|Select All** (Same as Select All on the PainterBar) — Select all the objects in the library, in order to perform an operation such as Entry|Copy on the entire group of them.

- **Library|Optimize** — Reduce the size of a library and improve the speed of access to a library by removing the empty space left by deleted objects and by rearranging the order in which objects are stored. You should perform this operation on your libraries from time to time during the development project.

Using the Pop-Up Menu

Many of the most popular menu choices also appear in the menu that pops up when you right-click an item in the painter tree. For example, Figure 16-3 shows an object's pop-up menu, which combines choices from the Entry and Source menus.

- **Library | Build Runtime Library** — Used with multilibrary systems to turn some libraries into DLLs or PowerBuilder dynamic libraries. See "Deploying Your Application" later in this chapter for a discussion of these alternatives.

- **Library | Print Directory** — Print the list of objects in a library.

- **Library | Properties** — Open the library's property sheet. Here you can change the library's comments.

Figure 16-3
The pop-up menu for an object in the painter tree.

THE ENTRY MENU

The Entry menu functions operate on an entry — that is, on an object in a library. For most of them, you must first select the entry by clicking its name in the painter tree.

Renaming an Object

There is no Entry|Rename menu choice to rename an object. Renaming an object is a multistep process: (1) Open the object in its painter. (2) Select File|Save As from the menu to save a copy of the object with the new name. (3) Return to the Library Painter and select Entry|Delete from the menu to delete the version with the old name.

There is also no version of the Entry|Copy menu choice that makes a copy in the same library. To accomplish this, you must open the object in its painter and select File|Save As to save it as a copy.

Some of these functions can operate on more than one entry at a time. There are several ways to select more than one entry. One way is to "control-click" them — that is, hold down the Ctrl key on the keyboard while clicking entries with the mouse. Another way is to select the library and then choose Library|Select All from the menu.

The choices in the Entry menu also appear when you right-click an entry name in the painter tree.

- **Entry|Edit** (Same Edit on the PainterBar, or as pressing the Enter key) — Opens the selected entry with the appropriate painter. For example, if this choice is clicked with the window "w_dw1tombase" selected, this window painter will be opened and "w_dw1tombase" will be automatically loaded.

- **Entry|Copy** (Same as Copy on the PainterBar) — Copy an entry to another library.

- **Entry|Move** (Same as Move on the PainterBar) — Move an entry to another library.

- **Entry|Delete** (Same as Delete on the PainterBar, or pressing the Delete key) — Delete an entry.

- **Entry|Export** (Same as Export on the PainterBar) — Create a text file with the complete source code of an entry in a special description language. The file includes not only the PowerScript source code that you have written and stored within the entry, but also the hidden source code that PowerBuilder creates to describe every object and property within the entry.

Troubleshooting with Export and Import

Sometimes I have used export and import as the troubleshooting tool of last resort, when I have seriously damaged an object. When you export an object, you get a source code text file that thoroughly describes the object's contents and properties. By carefully editing the text file and re-importing it, you can recreate a version of the object that, hopefully, is fixed.

I have used this technique to change the ancestor object from which a descendant object is inherited.

- **Entry | Import** (Same as Import on the PainterBar) — Create a new entry by reading its description from a text file, such as a text file created by Entry | Export.

- **Entry | Regenerate** (Same as Regenerate on the PainterBar) — Regenerate an entry by refreshing the features that it inherits from its ancestor objects. As explained in Chapter 13, you should regenerate all descendant objects after you modify an ancestor.

- **Entry | Search** (Same as Search on the PainterBar) — Search for a text string within the properties, scripts, and variables of an entry. When you select Entry | Search, the dialog box in Figure 16-4 pops up. Figure 16-5 shows the result of searching for "CLOSE" in every window of VIDEO1.PBL.

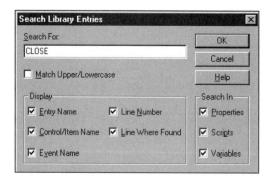

Figure 16-4

Options for searching libraries.

The meaning of the Properties and Variables options in Figure 16-4 is somewhat fuzzy. The Properties option searches such things as regular property names, such as "BackColor," and instance variable names. The Variables option searches the names of function argument variables and global variables, but not instance variable names. Both options search internal parts of the object's definition, which the Entry|Export function also shows you but which you otherwise don't normally see, as well as the PowerBuilder code that you type in.

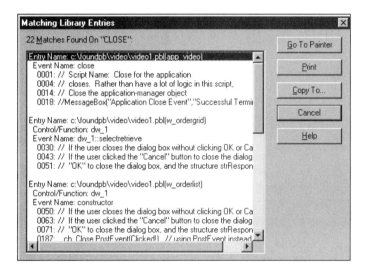

Figure 16-5
Results of searching for "CLOSE" in VIDEO1.PBL.

- **Entry | Print** — Print a detailed description of an entry. A dialog box pops up (Figure 16-6) so that you can specify how much information you want to print. For example, you can select whether or not to print a window's scripts and whether or not to print its controls' scripts. The printout is a convenient way to document your objects.

- **Entry | Properties** (Same as Properties on the PainterBar) — Open an entry's property sheet. Here you can change the entry's comments.

Printing to a File

The Entry|Print choice prints the documentation for one or more objects on the printer. How can you output it to a text file instead? The first thing to try is Entry|Export, which produces a text file very similar to Entry|Print that may be suitable for your needs.

If not, there is no PowerBuilder feature to output Entry|Print to a file, but there is a general way in Windows to redirect almost any printed output to a file.

In the Windows Control Panel, use the Printers dialog box to install a Generic/Text

Only printer, if you don't have one installed already. Click the Connect button on the dialog box to connect the printer to the port named "FILE:".

In PowerBuilder, make sure that this special printer is selected: Choose File|Printer Setup from the menu and select "Generic/Text Only on FILE:" from the list of printers.

Now, when you select Entry|Print, Windows will prompt you to type in a file name and will direct the output to that file.

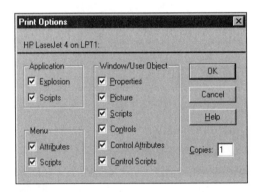

Figure 16-6
Options for printing an entry.

THE SOURCE MENU

The Source menu functions provide project-team source control for your library — the ability, among other things, to make sure that two people don't try to edit the same object at the same time. PowerBuilder has a rudimentary level of source control capability built into it. To get more, you can install ObjectCycle, the Powersoft source control product that's bundled with PowerBuilder. Or you can integrate a third-party source control product, such as Intersolv's PVCS, into PowerBuilder.

Many of the choices in the Source menu are disabled until you connect to an external source control product. A few are always available. They let you "check out" an object by copying it from the main library to another library where, presumably, only one person can modify it. Later, you "check in" the object by copying the modified version back into the main library. While you have an object checked out, the original version of it remains in the library, but other people are restricted to read-only access to it.

These are the choices that are always available after you have selected an object in the painter tree. Some of these choices also appear when you right-click an entry name in the painter tree:

- **Source | Connect** — Connect to a third-party product for source control.

- **Source | Check In** (Same as Check In on the PainterBar) — "Check in" an entry.

- **Source | Check Out** (Same as Check Out on the PainterBar) — "Check out" an entry.

- **Source | Clear Check-Out Status** (Same as Check Status on the PainterBar) — Clear the check-out status of an entry without checking it in.

- **Source | View Check-Out Status** — View a list of checked-out entries.

THE DESIGN MENU

These functions operate on the tree of directories, libraries, and objects that the painter displays.

- **Design | Expand/Collapse Branch** — (Same as double-clicking a directory or library name in the tree, or selecting it and pressing the Enter key) Open the directory or library and display its contents. Or, if it is already open, close it. This menu choice appears only when a directory or library is selected in the tree.

- **Design | Select Device** — Change the drive whose tree is displayed. In Figure 16-2, the C: drive is displayed. The dropdown list box at the top of the painter window also displays and can change the drive.

- **Design | Incremental Rebuild** — Regenerate the objects in the application that require it; that is, those for which an ancestor object has been modified.

- **Design | Full Rebuild** — Regenerate all objects in the application, beginning with ancestor objects and continuing through descendent objects.

- **Design | Migrate** — Convert an application created with an earlier version of PowerBuilder, such as 4.0, to the 5.0 format. The internal structure of .PBL files changed between versions, and one version of PowerBuilder cannot read another version's .PBLs unless you convert (migrate) them first.

- **Design | Options** — Open the Library Painter's property sheet, which has two tab pages: General and Include.

THE GENERAL TAB PAGE

Figure 16-7 shows the Library Painter property sheet's General tab page. It offers these options:

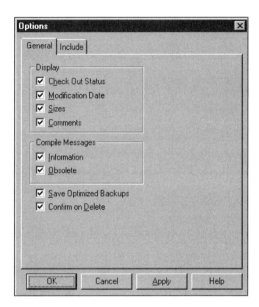

Figure 16-7

The property sheet's General tab page.

- **Display options** — What information to display on each line of the painter tree. Figure 16-8 shows the tree with every option turned on.

    - **Check Out Status** — an icon that indicates which objects are checked out. In Figure 16-8, the icon appears next to d_filmgrid, a checked-out item.

    - **Modification Date** — the date and time that the object was last modified.

    - **Sizes** — the size (number of bytes) of the item, in parentheses.

    - **Comments** — the comments. Select Entry|Properties from the menu to change the comments.

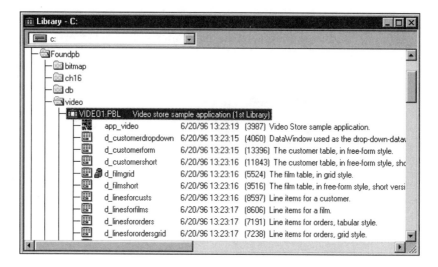

Figure 16-8

The painter tree, with all display options.

- **Compile Messages** — what types of problems the PowerScript compiler should display as errors.

  - **Information** — whether to display warning messages that are not fatal, but may cause run time problems. Database errors, such as a reference to an unknown table name, are an example.

  - **Obsolete** — whether to display warning messages about function calls that are obsolete. Many functions in PowerBuilder 5.0 have been carried over from past versions for compatibility, but have been replaced by newer techniques. They still work in 5.0, but Powersoft plans to eliminate them in future versions.

- **Save Optimized Backups** — whether to make a backup copy of the original library file, giving the backup file the extension .BAK, when you select Library|Optimize from the menu.

- **Confirm on Delete** — whether PowerBuilder pops up a confirmation dialog box when you use Entry|Delete to delete an object.

THE INCLUDE TAB PAGE

Figure 16-9 shows the Library Painter property sheet's Include tab page. It lists the eleven types of objects that the Library Painter displays. At first, all of them are checkmarked. By checking and unchecking items, you can restrict the types of items appearing in the painter tree.

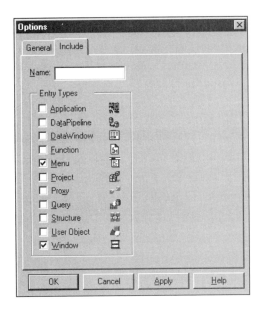

Figure 16-9
The Design | Options | Include tab page with only windows and menus selected for display.

The Application Painter

The application object is a small but essential part of an application. Every application must have one and only one application object. This object and its open event script are the only parts of an application that PowerBuilder requires.

In spite of the key role the application object plays, you don't spend much time working in the Application Painter. In fact, a key objective of Chapter 17 is to devise ways to keep functionality out of the application object!

Nevertheless, the Application Painter includes features that you can't find anywhere else. So you will no doubt be clicking the Application button on the PowerBar to visit here at least a few times during your project.

THE WHERE-USED HIERARCHY

Like the Library Painter, the Application Painter can display the objects of an application in a tree arrangement. (See Figure 16-10.) It is quite a different arrangement than the Library Painter's, however. The Application Painter shows them in a where-used hierarchy.

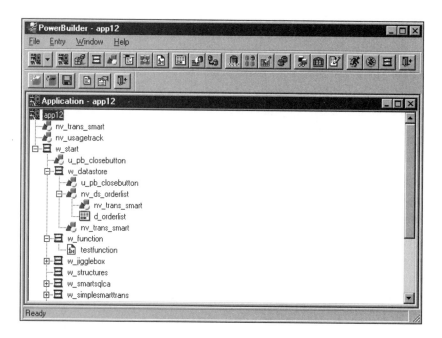

Figure 16-10

The Application Painter.

At first, only the application object is showing. Double-click it, and the objects it references, in its scripts or in its properties, appear below it: nv_trans_smart, nv_usagetrack, w_start, and so on. Double-click w_start, or click the "+" symbol to the left of it, and the objects it references appear: u_pb_closebutton, w_datastore, w_function, and others. Double-click each object, and soon you will open up the entire hierarchy of what uses what.

To edit an object by launching its painter, click the object to select it, and then press the Enter key.

If an asterisk (*) appears after an object's name, it indicates that the object is inherited from another. Click the object to select it, and select Entry|Inheritance Hierarchy to see its ancestors.

Unfortunately, the hierarchy has its limits. There are certain where-used relationships that the Application Painter fails to detect. For example, in Figure 16-10, the window w_start appears beneath the application object app12, because app12's open script contains this statement:

```
Open(w_Start)
```

The Application Painter "sees" this reference to w_start and adds it to the tree display. Consider, however, this alternative script, which works just as well:

```
Window w
Open(w, "w_Start")
```

Because the reference to w_start is now in a literal string, the Application Painter does not see it as it scans the script looking for object references. The painter does not attempt to interpret the contents of literal strings, just as it would not attempt to guess at the contents of variables. Therefore, the display of the where-used hierarchy is severely truncated, as you can see in Figure 16-11. It no longer displays w_start, and thus it cannot display anything further down on the chain.

Figure 16-11

The Application Painter can't see the window.

The video store sample application suffers from the same shortcoming. Its MDI frame window opens all of its many sheets, except one, using a similar indirect referencing technique. Therefore, the Application Painter shows very little of the contents of this extensive application.

OTHER APPLICATION PAINTER FEATURES

Other features of the Application Painter are found in its menus:

THE FILE MENU

- **File | New** (Same as New on the PainterBar) — Create a new application object, either in an existing library or in a new library.

- **File | Open** (Same as Open on the PainterBar) — Open a different application object.

- **File | Close** (Same as Close on the PainterBar) — Close the Application Painter.

THE ENTRY MENU

- **Entry | Edit** (Same as selecting an item in the painter tree and pressing the Enter key) — Open the painter that edits the selected object.

- **Entry | Inheritance Hierarchy** — Display the ancestors of an object. This menu choice is active only when you select an item with an asterisk (*) in the painter tree.

- **Entry | Script** (Same as Script on the PainterBar) — Open the Script Painter for editing the application object's event scripts: open, close, idle, and SystemError. From within the Script Painter, the Declare menu choice can define the application's shared and instance variables, application functions, and application structures.

- **Entry | Properties** (Same as Properties on the PainterBar) — Open the property sheet for the application object, or for whatever object is highlighted in the painter tree. The next section describes the application object's property sheet.

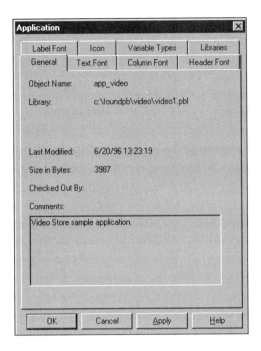

Figure 16-12
The application object's property sheet.

THE APPLICATION OBJECT'S PROPERTY SHEET

Figure 16-12 shows the property sheet for the video store sample application. These are its tab pages:

The General Tab Page

This page displays library information about the application object and lets you add to or modify its comments.

The Fonts Tab Pages

There are four of these pages: Text Font, Column Font, Header Font, and Label Font. Use them to change the default fonts used by various design elements in PowerBuilder

The Icon Tab Page

On this page you specify an icon for the application. When you run the application and then minimize it, this is the icon that Windows presents for it.

In the Window Painter, you can also assign an icon to a window. If the main window (the MDI frame window, typically) and the application both have icons, the window's icon takes precedence when you run and minimize the application. The application's icon appears only when the window has no icon of its own and in the Windows Program Manager.

The Variable Types Tab Page

This page shows the variable type used for each of PowerBuilder's five built-in global variables. You can change the types to use an object class type that you have developed. Figure 16-13 shows the default settings.

In other chapters, I've discussed how and why you might want to change a variable type. Chapter 12 gave an example of changing *sqlca* from "transaction" to "nv_trans_smart," a smart transaction object. Chapter 17 on the CD-ROM describes changing *error* from "error" type to "nv_error_handler," a custom error handling object.

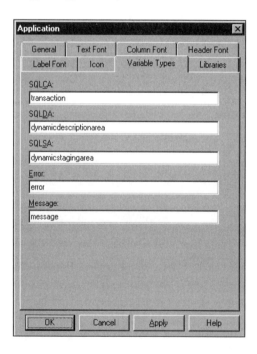

Figure 16-13

The Variable Types tab page.

The Libraries Tab Page

On this page you specify the library search path, which is the list of libraries the application searches for objects it needs. Figure 16-14 shows how to set up the video store application to draw objects from three libraries: VIDEO1.PBL, VIDEO2.PBL, and VIDEO3.PBL.

Planning a Multiple-Library System

You can organize the objects that compose an application into more than one library. In fact, it's probably a good idea to do so, especially for large applications.

Breaking up a library into two or more libraries is a straightforward process. In the Library Painter, select Library|Create to create the new libraries. Then select objects in the old library to move to the new one, and use Entry|Move to move them.

Next you must open the Application Painter on the application object and open its property sheet. Click to the Libraries tab, shown in Figure 16-14. At first you will see only one library, the application object's library, in the Library Search Path. You must add the names of the other libraries, separated with semicolons. You can type them in by hand, or click the Browse button to select them.

This Library Search Path tells the application where to search for the objects that it refers to. It is similar to the directory search list (the "path") that the operating system uses to search for program files. In Figure 16-14, all three libraries are in the same directory, but they could just as well be in different ones.

There are no restrictions on how many libraries you can have, or which objects should go into which libraries, or what order the libraries should occupy in the search list. There are guidelines, however:

- The PowerBuilder documentation recommends that a library not grow bigger than 800 KB nor contain more than about 60 objects, for performance reasons. As your library approaches this number, you should consider breaking it up.

- On the other hand, you shouldn't have a lot of very small libraries. If the library search list is long, performance will suffer as the application searches for its objects.

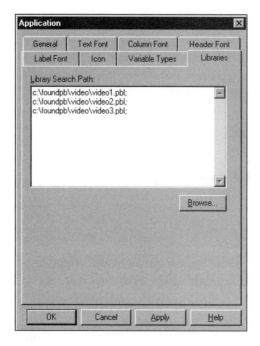

Figure 16-14
Specifying the library list for an application.

- For the best performance, you should arrange the libraries in the search list into "most frequently used" order, since the application always searches through them in the order listed.

- If a set of objects are general-purpose utilities that will be used by more than one application, it makes sense to separate them into one or more utility libraries that can be maintained independently of any one application and added to the search list of many applications.

Deploying Your Application

Deployment is the process of migrating your application from the PowerBuilder development environment to the end user's production environment.

Up to this point in the book, we have described all the steps involved in developing and testing your application in the PowerBuilder development environment. At this point, here is what you have:

- **.PBL files** — These are the PowerBuilder libraries containing the objects that make up your application. The objects are such things as windows, DataWindows, and menus.

- **Resources** — These are the icons and bitmaps that your application uses — for example, pictures on PictureButtons, pictures on toolbar buttons, the icon assigned to the application, and icons assigned to windows. They will be individual files with these extensions: .BMP, .CUR, .ICO, .RLE, or .WMF.

We have not made too big a deal of resources in past chapters. In fact, we didn't even call them "resources," which is the term that the Project Painter uses to describe them. We've just used them as we needed them, placing pictures on PictureButtons and so forth. But now that we're talking about deploying the application, we must pay special attention to them. Resources are parts of the application that don't get stored in the .PBL, and so we must take care that they get transferred somehow to the end user's system. Otherwise, the end user will have blank PictureButtons and toolbar buttons.

Besides .PBLs and resources, you may have set up other files and elements that your application requires. The most common examples are .INI files and database connection configurations. You must set up copies of these files on your users' system, someplace where the application can find them.

Deploying the application consists of two main steps:

1. **Building the executable** — Use the Project Painter to convert the application to an executable.

2. **Installation** — Transfer the converted application files to the end user's system. There are some other files that you must also transfer, and some additional setup to be done.

BUILDING THE EXECUTABLE (THE PROJECT PAINTER)

The Project Painter is the part of PowerBuilder that converts the .PBLs and resources into executable files. Its name, "Project Painter," is a bit of a misnomer. A PowerBuilder project has nothing to do with "project management" as we usually think of it, with tasks, schedules, and responsibilities. A PowerBuilder project is actually nothing more than the set of specifications for creating an executable. "Executable Painter" would have been a more accurate name for it.

Let's do a quick walk-through of how to convert the video store application. After that, I'll explain some of the options and details.

Begin by making sure that the video store's application object, which is named "app_video," is the current application. The Project Painter always operates on the current application.

Click the Project button on the PowerBar to open the Project Painter. This opens the Select Project dialog box, listing any projects you have already created in this library. (You might not have any.) Click the New button to create a new project.

The Select Executable File dialog box pops up. Type in the filename of the executable you want to create — "video.exe," for example — and click the Save button. This drops you into the Project Painter, which is shown in Figure 16-15.

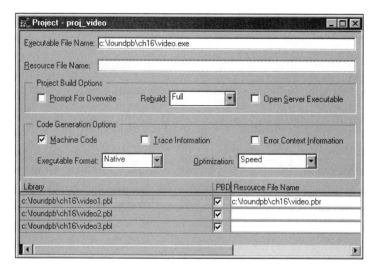

Figure 16-15
The Project Painter.

The top of the Project Painter shows the name of the executable to be created: C:\FOUNDPB\CH16\VIDEO.EXE, in this case. The middle of the painter offers various conversion options. The bottom of the painter lists the .PBL files that contain the application's objects: VIDEO1.PBL, VIDEO2.PBL, and VIDEO3.PBL. (If you are following along and your screen lists only VIDEO.PBL, don't worry — there are several variations of the application on the CD-ROM, some with everything in one .PBL. The three-PBL version is in the CH16 directory.)

Figure 16-15 shows all of the default choices. I have made only one change: In the Resource File Name column in the lower right, I have typed in "c:\foundpb\ch16\video.pbr" across from "video1.pbl." This .PBR file is a simple text file listing all the resources that the application needs. Here's what VIDEO.PBR looks like:

```
first18.bmp
last18.bmp
left18.bmp
logo.bmp
right18.bmp
video.bmp
video.ico
```

I will explain the requirements and options for .PBR files shortly. For now, let me make just a few points: VIDEO.PBR lists resources — that is, every bitmap and icon used by the application. Although you could supply a full path for each bitmap file, the more common practice is to omit the directory path from the .PBR file, but to add it to your system's search path. And it doesn't much matter which "Resource File Name" space I typed "c:\foundpb\ch16\video.pbr" into; my decision to type it next to "video1.pbl" was fairly arbitrary.

If you are following along, you must create a similar VIDEO.PBR file and type its name into a "Resource File Name" space.

Next, select File|Save from the menu and save the project as "proj_video." The project is just another PowerBuilder object, like a window or a menu, stored in the .PBL file. You can create multiple projects with different names if you want to set up various executable configurations.

Now it's time to create the executable: Click the Build button on the PainterBar, or select Design|Build Project from the menu. PowerBuilder scans the .PBL and .PBR files and creates executables. Depending on the size of your application and the options you've selected, this may take a while. For the video store application, it takes a few minutes.

Here's what it creates:

- **VIDEO.EXE** — the executable program file
- **VIDEO1.DLL** — the executable version of all the objects that were in VIDEO1.PBL, plus the resources that are listed in VIDEO.PBR
- **VIDEO2.DLL** — the executable version of all the objects that were in VIDEO2.PBL
- **VIDEO3.DLL** — the executable version of all the objects that were in VIDEO3.PBL

A .DLL file is a Windows "Dynamic Link Library" file. Like any library, it contains reusable code modules and objects. When you run VIDEO.EXE, it starts the application and loads objects as needed from the .DLL files to open and use them. But you can't run it yet! There's more to be done, which is coming up in the "Installation" section that follows.

By the way, these PowerBuilder-generated .DLL files do not have the same internal format as standard Windows .DLL files produced by C++ and other compiler products. Therefore, only a PowerBuilder application can use them.

THE MACHINE CODE OPTION

The Project Painter offers numerous options. One of the most important is the Machine Code option, which is a checkbox near the middle of Figure 16-15. When this option is checkmarked, PowerBuilder compiles your application into true machine code instructions. When it is not checkmarked, PowerBuilder it compiles into "p-code," which is a proprietary coding system requiring a run-time driver.

Machine code is almost always the preferred option, since it produces an executable that runs faster (in some cases, much, much faster) than the p-code alternative. The disadvantages of the machine code option are that PowerBuilder builds the executable more slowly, and it can't do it at all if you're running PowerBuilder on a 16-bit (Windows 3.1) platform. The machine code option is available only if you're running PowerBuilder on a 32-bit platform (Windows 95 or Windows NT), although it is capable of building 16-bit executables (selectable via the Executable Format option). So your end-users can be running on any platform.

.EXE, .PBD, AND .DLL OPTIONS

The quick Project Painter exercise just described built one .EXE and three .DLL files from the three .PBL files. This is not the only possibility. You will always get exactly one .EXE. But for each .PBL you have a choice:

■ By checking its PBD column, as I have done for each .PBL in Figure 16-15, you convert it to a .DLL. Each .DLL will have the same name as the .PBL and be placed in the same directory. (The PBD column is mislabeled, in my opinion. It should be labeled "DLL" instead since it controls the building of .DLL files. Or maybe it should be labeled "PBD/DLL.")

■ By not checking its PBD column, you instruct PowerBuilder to add the .PBL's objects to the .EXE.

Thus you have a lot of combinations: At one extreme, you can check-mark nothing in the PBD column. This choice results in one large .EXE and no .DLLs. At the other extreme, you can checkmark all of them, which gives you a small .EXE and as many .DLLs as there are .PBLs. Or you can place checkmarks in any combination, adding some .PBLs into the .EXE and converting the others to .DLLs.

There is no way to fine-tune which objects go into which .DLLs. Each checkmarked .PBL becomes one .DLL, and all of its objects go into it. If this arrangement doesn't suit you, it's a simple matter to open the Library Painter, create new .PBLs, and copy the objects according to the organization that you want.

I have been describing the machine code option, in which the Project Painter builds an .EXE and .DLLs. With the p-code option, you get an .EXE, but instead of .DLLs you get files with the extension .PBD (PowerBuilder Dynamic library). A .PBD is the PowerBuilder p-code equivalent of a .DLL. Everything else I've said, however, about how PowerBuilder converts .PBLs to .DLLs, is also true about the conversion of .PBLs to .PBDs.

You do have to take some care, because there is a case in which PowerBuilder will exclude an object in the build process. If you check-mark the PBD option for a library, PowerBuilder copies all of its objects into the .DLL or .PBD. However, if you don't checkmark the PBD option, PowerBuilder copies an object from the .PBL into the .EXE only if it has a "direct reference." If the object is "dynamically referenced," PowerBuilder ignores it, and that object doesn't make it into the executable. This is a bad thing! Table 16-1 summarizes these possibilities.

Table 16-1

.PBL Conversion Options

Is the PBL Checkmarked for PBD/DLL	How Is the Object Referenced	Where Does PowerBuilder Put the Object
Yes	Either way (direct or dynamic)	In the .PBD/.DLL
No	Direct	In the .EXE
No	Dynamic	Nowhere!

What's a "direct reference," and what's a "dynamic reference"? A direct reference is anywhere you've hard-coded the name of the object, without enclosing it in quotation marks, somewhere in your application. For example, this script makes a direct reference to the window object w_orders:

```
Open(w_orders)
```

If you use a quoted string or a string variable to name the object, you have a dynamic reference, such as this reference to w_orders:

```
Window w
Open(w, "w_orders")
```

Another example: Using the Window Painter to assign a DataWindow object to a DataWindow control makes a direct reference to the DataWindow object. Making the assignment in a script, like this, is a dynamic reference:

```
dw_1.DataObject = "d_filmgrid"
```

The Project Painter can only "see" a direct reference. For whatever reason, it transfers only objects that have direct references into the .EXE, rather than transferring all the objects that are in the .PBL.

At run time, any attempt to reference a missing object causes an "Unknown Object Type" system error.

You have one more way to get a DataWindow object into an .EXE, .DLL, or .PBD: Add a line referencing it to a resource file (.PBR) that is part of the Project Painter specification. Earlier, I showed .PBR lines describing .BMP and .ICO files. Here's one that describes a DataWindow object d_another from a library VIDEO4.PBL:

```
video4.pbl(d_another)
```

THE RIGHT WAY TO DO IT

Having explained all this, I should point out that for most applications, you should probably checkmark the PBD/DLL option for every .PBL, as shown in Figure 16-15. The .EXE will be a small kernel with no objects. This scenario creates the most flexible run-time application in terms of memory management and probably the fastest performer as well.

RESOURCE FILE OPTIONS

As I mentioned before, resources are the icons and bitmaps that your application uses, such as pictures on PictureButtons. During development, they are individual files with these extensions: .BMP, .CUR, .ICO, .RLE, or .WMF. Your application's .PBL objects contain pointers to them — that is, they store the names of these files. The .PBL does not contain the graphic images themselves.

To deploy the resource as part of the application, you have two choices:

1. **The .PBR file option** — Add the resource's file name to a .PBR file, such as VIDEO.PBR described earlier, and place that .PBR file into one of the Resource File Name fields in the Project Painter. In this case, PowerBuilder copies the resource image itself into the .EXE or one of the .DLLs or .PBDs, making the .EXE/.DLL/.PBD that much bigger, but making the application a little easier to distribute.

2. **The direct transfer option** — Copy the resource file (the .BMP file, or whatever) to the end user's system, so that the user has the exact same file that you have.

You don't have to make the same decision for all resources. You can throw some into a .PBR and directly transfer others.

If you go the .PBR route, you don't have to list them all in a single .PBR. You can separate them into multiple .PBR lists, as long as every .PBR is in a Resource File Name field somewhere in the Project Painter. This allows you to place some resources into the .EXE (note the Resource File Name field under the .EXE name in Figure 16-15) and distribute others across the various .DLL/PBDs.

In the example in Figure 16-15, I listed all resources in a single .PBR, VIDEO.PBR, and placed them all into VIDEO1.DLL.

There is no requirement that a resource end up in the same .EXE/.DLL/.PBD file as the object that references it.

Be careful when you type the .PBR filename into the Project Painter! PowerBuilder does not complain about a misspelled name or a .PBR file that it can't find. It just ignores it and fails to add your resources to the executable without giving you any warning!

As we saw with .PBL objects, there is a peculiar twist or two to the placement of resources. For one thing, PowerBuilder adds a resource to the .EXE file if any object in the .EXE makes a direct reference to the resource. But PowerBuilder doesn't do the same for dynamically referenced resources, nor for resources that are directly referenced by some object in a .DLL or .PBD. Table 16-2 summarizes the possibilities.

Table 16-2

Resource Options

Is the Resource in the .EXE's PBR?	Is the Resource in a .PBL's .PBR?	Is It Directly Referenced by an .EXE Object?	Where Does PowerBuilder Put the Resource?
Yes	—	—	In the .EXE
No	Yes	—	In the .DLL/.PBD
No	No	Yes	In the .EXE
No	No	No	Nowhere

The "Nowhere" case in Table 16-2 is not as dangerous for a resource as it was for a .PBL object. It just means that you have chosen the "direct transfer option" for it.

At runtime, the deployed application searches for resources as it needs them. Suppose, for example, that the user opens a window with a PictureButton. The window object itself does not contain the bitmap image (nor does the PictureButton). Instead, it contains the resource's original filename, as it did back in the development environment. Let's say that the file name is FIRST18.BMP. While opening the window, PowerBuilder searches for the bitmap in the following sequence:

- First it searches the .EXE, to see if the bitmap image was placed there.
- Second it searches the .DLLs or .PBDs, to see if the bitmap image was placed in any of them.
- Third it searches directories in the user system's search path, searching for a file with this name.
- If all of these searches fail, the window opens with no bitmap image on the PictureButton.

Once more, there's an odd twist. If the original reference to the resource is a full path name, such as "c:\foundpb\ch16\first18.bmp" instead of simply "first18.bmp," that's exactly what the deployed application will look for. If the user happens to have that file in a directory with the same name, it'll find it. But it will also find it if you used the .PBR option and stored the resource in an .EXE/.DLL/.PBD — *but only if* you include the resource's full path name in the .PBR. The rule is, the .PBR entry for a resource must exactly match the way the application's objects reference it.

A peculiar by-product of this becomes apparent if you reference a resource dynamically in a script, using a path name:

```
pb_1.PictureName = "c:\foundpb\ch16\first18.bmp"
```

and you add the path name to a .PBR in the Project Painter:

```
c:\foundpb\ch16\first18.bmp
```

Then the script will find the bitmap image, even though it references a directory name that does not exist in the end user's system. The image is stored in the .EXE/.DLL/.PBD with the full path name, and that becomes its name for search and retrieval purposes.

Identifying Your Resources

If you're like me, you don't keep careful track of your resources while developing your application. Maybe they're all together in one directory, or maybe you've misplaced a few. So when it comes time to create a .PBR file listing them, where do you get the list?

Here's a tip: Do a global search in the Library Painter. In the Library Painter, expand a library and choose Library|Select All. Then choose Entry|Search and search for ".BMP". PowerBuilder will show you every reference to .BMP files in this library. Repeat the search for each resource extension: .BMP, .CUR, .ICO, .RLE, and .WMF. Then repeat the process for each of the application's libraries.

INSTALLATION

Now that we have an .EXE file and maybe some .DLL, .PBD, and resource files, all that's left to do is move them to the end user's computer, right? Well, no, there's more:

- **Other External Files** — You might have other external files that you've integrated into your application. You must transport them to the user's system too, and you must make sure that they are in a place that's accessible to the deployed application. One example is .INI files, which I've described in other chapters. Another is help files.

- **PowerBuilder Deployment .DLLs** — The .EXE built by the Project Painter, whether machine code or p-code, can't run on its own. It makes calls to routines found in some of PowerBuilder's own .DLL files. Therefore, you must transfer these .DLLs to the end user's system, and place them in a directory that's part of their search path. Which .DLL files are required depends on the end user's platform. Refer to the PowerBuilder documentation for a list of them.

- **Database Connection** — The end user will need the same, or similar, database drivers and database configurations that you do in order to connect the application to the database. I described these in Chapter 5. You will find more detailed information in the *Connecting to Your Database* manual. You may need to purchase additional licenses from the database vendor to connect end-user workstations to the server.

Summary

As you can see, the Application Painter, the Library Painter, and the Project Painter are the three most important tools for organizing, compiling, and deploying your application.

The Bonus Chapters

*T*he CD-ROM that accompanies this book contains five additional chapters. They cover PowerBuilder topics of specialized interest.

Chapter 17: The Application Infrastructure

This chapter applies the object-oriented techniques of Chapters 11–13 to the real-world problems of building business software. We show how to develop a collection of powerful, reusable objects that will serve as the infrastructure for just about any application. The chapter demonstrates and describes objects that perform file management, error handling, application startup, and more.

Chapter 18: Reports

Report development is probably the most mundane and "unglamorous" part of any programming project. But it's also an essential part, often consuming a large share of the project hours. It can't be ignored.

In PowerBuilder, you use the DataWindow Painter to design and print reports. It's easy to produce a very simple report, but often things get complicated, especially when you are new to PowerBuilder. This chapter shows how to design many common report styles, such as mailing labels, form letters, and envelopes. It also demonstrates the procedures for managing printers and print jobs.

CHAPTER 19: MORE DATAWINDOW TECHNIQUES

This chapter covers many advanced DataWindow topics:

- Master-Detail DataWindows
- Nested Reports
- The ShareData Function
- Update Two or More Tables from a Single DataWindow
- Graphs
- Crosstabs
- Blobs and Graphics
- OLE (Object Linking and Embedding)
- DataWindow Query Mode
- Dynamic DataWindows

CHAPTER 20: MORE TOOLS

This chapter introduces a number of miscellaneous PowerBuilder features:

- Debug
- Adding on-line help to your application
- Tags
- Drag and Drop
- The Data Pipeline
- DDE (Dynamic Data Exchange)
- The Text File Editor

CHAPTER 21: SQL: A BRIEF INTRODUCTION

Although most developers have heard of SQL, the Structured Query Language, and understand the role it plays in client/server computing, many people come to PowerBuilder with no actual experience using the language. For readers who are new to SQL, this chapter provides a brief introduction to its most important commands. It also gives an overview of the PowerBuilder tools for constructing, testing, and saving SQL commands, such as the Data Administration Painter and the Query Painter.

Upgrading from 4.0 to 5.0

*T*his book describes PowerBuilder version 5.0. But what about the previous release, version 4.0? Some readers might already be familiar with that version or might be called upon to upgrade a 4.0 application to 5.0. This appendix outlines what's new in PowerBuilder 5.0 and explains the process of migrating an application from 4.0 to 5.0.

What's New in PowerBuilder 5.0?

As in every upgrade of PowerBuilder, version 5.0 introduces hundreds of new features. A few are major, and there are a lot of minor ones as well. In total, they add up to a major upgrade.

Here's the big stuff.

SUPPORT FOR WINDOWS 95, WINDOWS NT, WINDOWS 3.1

PowerBuilder 5.0 runs on Windows 95, Windows NT 3.51, and Windows 3.1. Versions for Apple Macintosh and UNIX are due in the months to come. If you are working on one of the Windows platforms, you can develop applications that will run on the others. For example, you can develop an application on Windows 95 and deploy it for Windows 3.1. There are some limitations when you are developing on Windows 3.1; for example, the machine-language compile option is not available.

WINDOWS 95 LOOK AND FEEL

Powersoft has reorganized the PowerBuilder user interface to make it consistent with Windows 95 standards. Most menus, toolbars, and dialog boxes have been rearranged. If you are an experienced 4.0 developer, this will be a little disorienting at first as you hunt for familiar menu choices and attribute check boxes. It doesn't take too long to catch on, and when you do I think you'll agree that the new arrangement is much more logical.

The most important user interface changes in the development environment are:

- **Tabbed dialog boxes** — Many dialog boxes now contain tab pages. Tab pages are very effective at organizing a dialog box with a large number of choices, such as the dialog for setting a window or control's properties.

- **Property sheets** — Property sheets are a particularly prevalent type of tabbed dialog box. A property sheet contains all the properties of an object together in one place. (The old term "attribute" has been replaced by the term "property.") Windows 95 itself makes heavy use of property sheets, so PowerBuilder is being consistent by providing them too.

- **Custom toolbars** — Version 4.0 gave you a certain amount of control over toolbars. You could add or delete buttons from them and move them to different parts of the screen. Version 5.0 extends this flexibility. You can now define entirely new toolbars. You can also "dock" two or more toolbars side by side across a single row.

- **Dropdown toolbar palettes** — Some toolbars were getting too crowded, such as the dozens of control buttons on the Window PainterBar. Version 5.0's solution is to introduce dropdown toolbar palettes. When you click a dropdown button on the toolbar, a palette of additional buttons appears in a manner similar to the way menus work. This space-saving feature allows version 5.0 to add new functions, such as align/space/size controls to the toolbar, making them much more convenient. Version 4.0's ColorBar has been eliminated. Its functions are now consolidated into two dropdown buttons on the Window PainterBar.

Not only are these features available in the PowerBuilder development environment, but you can add them to your application as well. There is a new tab control that adds tab pages to any window. You can dock toolbars side by side. And you can add dropdown palettes to your toolbars. These new features work on any platform, including Windows 3.1.

Machine Language Compilation

You can now compile your application into a machine language executable. You don't need to go through a big learning curve to start doing this — it's a single checkmark in the Project Painter.

Previous versions compiled scripts into p-code, an intermediate form of object code that does not run as fast as true machine language. You still have the option to do p-code compiles in version 5.0. The machine language option actually translates your PowerScript programming into Watcom C++, and then the Watcom compiler (bundled with PowerBuilder) compiles it into machine code.

This feature has attracted a lot of attention, but you shouldn't expect too much from it. Sure, if you have a script that does nothing but a million integer subtractions, it will run much faster in machine language than in p-code. But many of the bread-and-butter components of an application will not run any faster at all. For example, your windows will probably take about the same amount of time to open — unless your window open scripts do a million integer subtractions! DataWindow Retrieves and Updates, and other SQL operations, rely on the speed of the database server. Machine language compiles won't speed them up.

Distributed Objects

You can now develop three-tier (or *n*-tier or multitier, as some people call them) applications with PowerBuilder. That is, you can divide your applications into two or more partitions and run those partitions on separate computers.

Powersoft has implemented three-tier application partitioning as a straightforward extension of its object-oriented features. In a version 4.0 application, you might have had a user interface object — that is, a window — send messages to a nonvisual object to perform services for it. Both the window and the nonvisual object would be part of a single program running on a single workstation. With 5.0, the two can be separated, with the window object still on the workstation but the nonvisual object on a server machine. The objects send the same messages to each other, but now the messages travel across the network.

PowerBuilder Foundation Class (PFC) Library

The PFC library is an object class library. In other words, it is a collection of prebuilt object classes from which you can derive the objects for your applications. Building an application using a class library as a base has always been a good idea. Version 4.0 offered such a framework library, called AppLib, which was much less extensive than version 5.0's PFC. Using PFC as the foundation for your applications is an excellent alternative to developing such a library yourself or purchasing one from a third-party vendor.

DataWindow.Object Notation

With previous versions of PowerBuilder, scripts that manipulate DataWindows were cluttered with strange functions and cumbersome syntaxes. To retrieve a column value, you had to choose among GetText, GetItemString, GetItemNumber, and several other choices. To change a value, you called the SetItem function. To read or change a column's color or other property, you had to do battle with the Describe and Modify functions.

PowerBuilder 5.0 streamlines all that by introducing a new "DataWindow.Object" notation similar to the dot notation used in other parts of PowerScript. For example, here's how you fetch a value from the "zipcode" column in the DataWindow dw_1's tenth row in PowerBuilder 4.0:

```
z = dw_1.GetItemString(10, "zipcode")
```

In PowerBuilder 5.0, you do it like this:

```
z = dw_1.object.zipcode[10]
```

The old functions, such as GetItemString and SetItem, are not entirely obsolete. They are still part of the PowerScript language, and they still operate in the same way as before. In fact, in some situations, although not all, they run faster than the DataWindow.Object alternative.

RICH TEXT EDIT

PowerBuilder 5.0 adds support for rich text, which is text with formatting — mixed fonts, boldface, italics, color, tab stops, and the like. You can add a Rich Text Edit control to windows and design DataWindows with a Rich Text Edit presentation style.

OBJECT BROWSER

The Object Browser is a tabbed dialog that provides a complete list of the objects available to your application, including their properties, events, functions and other features. The Object Browser replaces two version-4.0 dialog boxes: Browse Objects and the Class Browser. Those old dialog boxes were hard to find and clumsy to use. The new Object Browser is always close at hand because there's a button for it in the PowerBar. It has a clear, consistent organization that makes it easy to find information. By clicking the Document button on the Browser, you can print the documentation for an object or export the documentation to a file.

ADDITIONAL OLE 2.0 FEATURES

PowerBuilder 5.0 extends the support for OLE 2.0 in several ways. It now supports OLE automation so that you can control OLE server products from a script. You can embed OCX controls into your application and also build new objects that inherit the features of OCX's. (An OCX is an OLE control. It is the successor to the VBX control supported by PowerBuilder 4.0.) There is a new OLE 2.0 DataWindow presentation style. And PowerBuilder applications, nonvisual objects, and DataWindows can act as OLE servers.

COMPONENT GALLERY

The component gallery is a collection of ready-made OCX controls, such as meters and calendars. You can drop them into your windows, user objects, and DataWindows.

OBJECTCYCLE

ObjectCycle is a full-featured version control system that is bundled with PowerBuilder 5.0. Up until now, most large development teams have relied on third-party products to provide version control for their PowerBuilder projects.

POWERSCRIPT EDITOR ENHANCEMENTS

The PowerScript editor has a number of appealing enhancements. The most striking is color coding. As you type, the editor colors each word as it recognizes it. Commands are green, comments, blue, quoted strings, brown, and unfinished quoted strings, red. You can change the color scheme if you like. I find that the colors help me to avoid many common typing errors.

The editor automatically controls indenting. For example, it inserts a tab on the next line following an IF-THEN. It removes a tab when you type the END IF.

You can move or copy text by dragging it with the mouse. Mark a block of text by dragging the mouse across it. Then click and drag to move it, or control-click and drag to copy it.

These editor enhancements might seem modest at first, but they might turn out to be the features that you are the most thankful for. Like me, you probably spend more time in the editor than in any other part of PowerBuilder, and little improvements here can be a big advantage.

OTHER FEATURES

There are many other little features that you will notice scattered through-out PowerBuilder 5.0. For example, it always drove me crazy that, in the global/shared/instance variable dialogs, pressing Enter closed the window instead of inserting a new line. In PowerBuilder 5.0, it works the way it should. I'm sure there are many pleasant surprises like this in store for you, too.

Here are a few other little things. Of course, any one of them might be a very big thing for your project:

- Watcom SQL 4.0 has been upgraded to 5.0, and its name has changed too. It's now called SQL Anywhere.

- A new painter, the Table Painter, takes you directly to the "Alter Table" part of the Database Painter.

- The new Run Window button on the PowerBar runs a single window without the need to run the entire application. This feature was available in previous versions as a function key-press, but many people overlooked it.

- The syntax for calling a function has been extended. By adding new keywords such as EVENT, DYNAMIC, and POST to the function call, you can call an event instead of a function (EVENT), defer validation of the function until runtime (DYNAMIC), and defer execution (POST). Please refer to Chapter 11 for the syntax and other details. To call an event, you might prefer to use this new syntax instead of calling the old TriggerEvent and PostEvent function.

- "Function overloading" is now allowed. This is the ability to call a user-defined function in different ways — that is, with a different number of arguments or different types of arguments.

- There are many new object types in the object class hierarchy. Consult the Object Browser to see them.

- "Attributes" are now called "properties," to be consistent with Windows 95 terminology.

- The Preference Painter is gone. This version 4.0 feature accumulated all of your PowerBuilder configuration settings into a single dialog box. In version 5.0, these settings are distributed throughout the various painters. You will find most of them in version 5.0's many property sheets.

Migrating an Application from 4.0 to 5.0

The format of PowerBuilder .PBL files (library files) has changed between version 4.0 and 5.0. Therefore, you must convert your libraries to the new format before you can begin using them in 5.0. Until then, you'll get an error message when you try to access the library's components. PowerBuilder calls the conversion process *migrating*.

To migrate a library or group of libraries, attempt to open an application object within it. PowerBuilder will display a dialog box offering to migrate it for you. The dialog box recommends making a backup copy before proceeding, and so do I. If you don't have a backup copy, click Cancel and make one. Otherwise, click OK to proceed.

When you click OK, PowerBuilder converts the library and its objects to the 5.0 format. At the same time, it regenerates and recompiles each object. At the conclusion, you will probably see a dialog box listing Compile Errors. On this dialog box I have made the mistake of clicking the Print button to print the errors and then the OK button to close it. The printout turned out to be truncated, because most of the messages extended beyond the right margin of the page and the Print function just chopped them off instead of wrapping them onto the next line. So instead of Print, you should click the Copy To button to copy the error messages to a text file.

OBSOLETE DATAWINDOW FUNCTIONS

There are a number of obsolete DataWindow control functions in version 5.0:

- SetActionCode
- GetSqlPreview
- GetUpdateStatus
- DBErrorCode
- DBErrorMessage
- GetClickedColumn
- GetClickedRow
- GetMessageText

They still work as they did in version 4.0. However, there are new techniques that you should use in place of them. The migration process flags the functions as errors, and so does the PowerScript compiler. Perhaps in a future release of PowerBuilder they will no longer work at all. Therefore, you should convert each of them to the new technique. Table A-1 shows how.

Table A-1

Replacement Techniques for Obsolete Functions

Replace 4.0 Function Call:	*With This Technique in 5.0:*	*In These Event Scripts:*
SetActionCode(n)	RETURN n	Clicked DBError ItemChanged ItemError PrintPage RetrieveRow RetrieveStart UpdateStart
GetSqlPreview(s)	s = sqlsyntax	DBError SQLPreview
GetUpdateStatus(r,buf)	r = row buf = buffer	DBError SQLPreview
ec = DBErrorCode()	ec = sqldbcode	DBError
s = DBErrorMessage()	s = sqlerrtext	DBError

c = GetClickedColumn()	IF dwo.Type = "column" THEN
	    c = Integer(dwo.ID)
	ELSE
	    c = 0
	END IF
		Clicked
		DoubleClicked

r = GetClickedRow()	r = row	Clicked DoubleClicked
s = GetMessageText()	s = text	Custom Event for pbm_dwnmessagetext

All of these functions are obsolete because in PowerBuilder 5.0 event scripts now have new arguments and return values that supersede them. The action performed by SetActionCode is now performed by concluding an event script, such as ItemChanged or RetrieveStart, with a RETURN statement. The information that GetSqlPreview and the other functions in the table were designed to provide is now provided by script arguments. The script arguments are *sqlsyntax, row, buffer, sqldbcode, and sqlerrtext, dwo,* and *text*.

The replacement for GetClickedColumn includes an IF...END IF statement. The reason is that the *dwo* argument passed to the Clicked or DoubleClicked script is an object variable. It represents the object that has been clicked. If you click in some part of the DataWindow control that is not a column, such as an empty region outside the DataWindow object, *dwo* will not be a column. If *dwo* is not a column, then it might not have an *ID* property and the reference to *dwo.ID* causes a system error. (This was not a problem with the GetClickedColumn function, which returns 0 in these situations.) Testing *dwo.Type* before *dwo.ID* avoids the system error.

Curiously, although GetSqlPreview is obsolete, its companion SetSqlPreview is not. In other words, do not attempt to replace,

```
SetSqlPreview(s)
```

with

```
sqlsyntax = s
```

The PowerBuilder compiler will accept the replacement, but it doesn't work because the sqlsyntax argument is passed by value, not by reference! In some cases, removing the functions might require more than a simple replacement. For example, an ItemChanged script might not call SetActionCode directly. It might call a function that in turn calls SetActionCode on the DataWindow control, like this:

```
dw_1.SetActionCode(1)
```

You can't simply replace this line with "RETURN 1," since a RETURN value might have no meaning, or some other meaning, to the function. Therefore, you'll have to add logic to pass the code back to the ItemChanged script somehow, so that it can conclude with "RETURN 1."

CONCLUDING A CLOSEQUERY EVENT SCRIPT

The way to conclude a window's CloseQuery event script has changed in version 5.0. PowerBuilder does not flag the old technique as an error — it just doesn't work any more. So you'll have to track your CloseQuery scripts down and change them yourself. Otherwise you'll have windows that compile and run, but that don't behave the way you intend.

In version 4.0, you set *message.ReturnValue* = 1 in the CloseQuery script to keep the window open. To allow the window to close, you set *message.ReturnValue* = 0 (or don't set it at all, since 0 is the default).

```
message.ReturnValue = 1    // keep the window open
message.ReturnValue = 0    // let the window close (the default)
```

In version 5.0, PowerBuilder ignores *message.ReturnValue*. Instead, you should conclude the CloseQuery script with "RETURN 1" or "RETURN 0" to indicate what to do next.

```
RETURN = 1   // keep the window open
RETURN = 0   // let the window close
```

FOR ADDITIONAL ASSISTANCE

For additional information about migrating an application to version 5.0, please refer to the Word documents named techmigr.doc and pb5micra.doc, in the \support\docs directory of the PowerBuilder 5.0 installation CD-ROM.

PowerBuilder 5.0: a Good Investment

Whenever a new release of a software product comes out, there are always those who ask, "Is it worth the price of the upgrade?" For PowerBuilder 5.0, I believe the answer is yes for most companies. PowerBuilder 5.0 might be essential if you are moving to Windows 95 or Windows NT and want to make the most of the 32-bit environment. Even if you're not, there are probably enough productivity improvements in version 5.0 to make it a worthwhile investment.

B How to Use the CD-ROM

*T*he accompanying CD-ROM contains a number of resources that you will find valuable:

- The entire text of *Foundations of PowerBuilder 5.0 Programming* in easy-to-use hypertext form
- The additional "bonus" Chapters 17–21
- Sample files with all the libraries, source codes, and databases used in this book.

For information on how to install and use the additional chapters and the sample files, please view or print the text file README.TXT, which is in the CD's root directory. This file might also contain additional information that was added to the CD after this book went to print.

The remainder of this appendix explains how to install and use the hypertext version of the book.

Installation Instructions for the Hypertext Book

To install the hypertext book from the CD, follow these steps:

1. Put the CD in your CD drive.
2. From Windows Program Manager (or File Manager) select File|Run.
3. Enter *d*:HYPERTEXT\SETUP (where *d* is the drive letter of your CD drive).

This creates a program group named "IDG Books" and the *Foundations of PowerBuilder* icon. Double-click the icon to start the hypertext viewer program.

How to Use the Hypertext Viewer

The viewer used for this CD is Microsoft Multimedia Viewer, which is used in many multimedia products, such as Microsoft Bookshelf. On the viewer's toolbar are the following buttons. To select an option, click on the appropriate button or press the underline letter.

<u>C</u>ontents   Move to the contents page.

<u>I</u>ndex   Display a list of key words and phrases.

Go <u>B</u>ack   Return to the previously viewed page.

His<u>t</u>ory   Display a list of the most recently viewed pages and select one to return to.

<u>S</u>earch   Perform a full-text search for any word or phrase used in the text.

Text References Within the Hypertext Book

Within the text, certain words and phrases are highlighted in red or blue.

A red highlight means there is a glossary definition for the term. When you click on the term, a pop-up window appears that contains the definition. When you click anywhere else or press Escape, the pop-up window disappears. (You may also use the Tab keys to select a highlighted term and press Enter to display the reference.)

A blue highlight is a reference to another page document. When you click on a reference to a figure, table, or listing, a new window opens that contains the figure, table, or listing. When you click on a reference to a chapter or sidebar, the screen changes to the first page of the chapter or sidebar.

SEARCHING THE HYPERTEXT BOOK

When you select the Search button, a dialog box appears. Using this dialog box, you may search all of the book, or selected sections, for any word or phrase. To search the entire book, simply type the word or phrase in the Search by Word box and press Enter or click on OK. To search only specific sections, select the parts to search in the Topic Groups box.

You can do more complex searches by using the keywords AND, OR, NEAR, and NOT to narrow the search; click the Hints button for some samples.

To limit the search to the topics selected on a previous search, select the Options button and check List of Previous Topics Found.

To limit the search to topic titles only, select the Options button and check Topic Titles Only.

SEARCH RESULTS

When a search has completed, the Search Results dialog box is displayed. You can use this dialog box to review all the "finds" of your search. All topics containing the searched text are listed. You can scroll through this list to look for likely areas to view.

Click the GO TO button to display the topic. The Search Results dialog box stays open on the top of the document so you can move easily from place to place within the list, reviewing all references to the searched text. In the document, the text found is highlighted wherever it appears.

The Previous Match and Next Match buttons move within a topic, stopping at each highlighted find.

The To Search button returns to the Search dialog box.

The Cancel button closes the Search Results box, leaving the current topic on display.

THE INDEX TO THE HYPERTEXT BOOK

The Index box provides a list of all indexed key words and phrases. Type the first character or characters of a word or phrase and the list will move to the first entry that matches the characters entered. Click OK to select a key word.

If only one topic contains a reference for the key word selected, that topic will be displayed immediately. If more than one topic is referenced, a dialog box listing all related topics is displayed. Select the topic desired and click OK. Click TO Index to return to the index list, or click Cancel to close the dialog.

Index

IDG Books Worldwide License Agreement

3. <u>**Other Restrictions.**</u> You may not rent or lease the Software. You may transfer the Software and user documentation on a permanent basis provided you retain no copies and the recipient agrees to the terms of this Agreement. You may not reverse engineer, decompile, or disassemble the Software except to the extent that the foregoing restriction is expressly prohibited by applicable law. If the Software is an update or has been updated, any transfer must include the most recent update and all prior versions.

4. <u>**Limited Warranty.**</u> IDG warrants that the Software and disk(s) are free from defects in materials and workmanship for a period of sixty (60) days from the date of purchase of this Book. If IDG receives notification within the warranty period of defects in material or workmanship, IDG will replace the defective disk(s). IDG's entire liability and your exclusive remedy shall be limited to replacement of the Software, which is returned to IDG with a copy of your receipt. This Limited Warranty is void if failure of the Software has resulted from accident, abuse, or misapplication. Any replacement Software will be warranted for the remainder of the original warranty period or thirty (30) days, whichever is longer.

5. <u>**No Other Warranties.**</u> To the maximum extent permitted by applicable law, IDG and the author disclaim all other warranties, express or implied, including but not limited to implied warranties of merchantability and fitness for a particular purpose, with respect to the Software, the programs, the source code contained therein and/or the techniques described in this Book. This limited warranty gives you specific legal rights. You may have others which vary from state/jurisdiction to state/jurisdiction.

6. <u>**No Liability For Consequential Damages.**</u> To the extent permitted by applicable law, in no event shall IDG or the author be liable for any damages whatsoever (including without limitation, damages for loss of business profits, business interruption, loss of business information, or any other pecuniary loss) arising out of the use of or inability to use the Book or the Software, even if IDG has been advised of the possibility of such damages. Because some states/jurisdictions do not allow the exclusion or limitation of liability for consequential or incidental damages, the above limitation may not apply to you.

7. <u>**U.S. Government Restricted Rights.**</u> Use, duplication, or disclosure of the Software by the U.S. Government is subject to restrictions stated in paragraph (c) (1) (ii) of the Rights in Technical Data and Computer Software clause of DFARS 252.227-7013, and in subparagraphs (a) through (d) of the Commercial Computer — Restricted Rights clause at FAR 52.227-19, and in similar clauses in the NASA FAR supplement, when applicable.

IDG BOOKS WORLDWIDE REGISTRATION CARD

Title of this book: Foundations™ of PowerBuilder™ 5.0 Programming

My overall rating of this book: ❏ Very good [1]   ❏ Good [2]   ❏ Satisfactory [3]   ❏ Fair [4]   ❏ Poor [5]

How I first heard about this book:

❏ Found in bookstore; name: [6]

❏ Advertisement: [8]

❏ Word of mouth; heard about book from friend, co-worker, etc.: [10]

❏ Book review: [7]

❏ Catalog: [9]

❏ Other: [11]

What I liked most about this book:

What I would change, add, delete, etc., in future editions of this book:

Other comments:

Number of computer books I purchase in a year: ❏ 1 [12]   ❏ 2-5 [13]   ❏ 6-10 [14]   ❏ More than 10 [15]

I would characterize my computer skills as: ❏ Beginner [16] ❏ Intermediate [17] ❏ Advanced [18] ❏ Professional [19]

I use ❏ DOS [20] ❏ Windows [21] ❏ OS/2 [22] ❏ Unix [23] ❏ Macintosh [24] ❏ Other: [25]_____
(please specify)

I would be interested in new books on the following subjects:
(please check all that apply, and use the spaces provided to identify specific software)

❏ Word processing: [26]

❏ Data bases: [28]

❏ File Utilities: [30]

❏ Networking: [32]

❏ Other: [34]

❏ Spreadsheets: [27]

❏ Desktop publishing: [29]

❏ Money management: [31]

❏ Programming languages: [33]

I use a PC at (please check all that apply): ❏ home [35] ❏ work [36] ❏ school [37] ❏ other: [38] _____

The disks I prefer to use are ❏ 5.25 [39] ❏ 3.5 [40] ❏ other: [41]_____

I have a CD ROM: ❏ yes [42]   ❏ no [43]

I plan to buy or upgrade computer hardware this year: ❏ yes [44]   ❏ no [45]

I plan to buy or upgrade computer software this year: ❏ yes [46]   ❏ no [47]

Name: _____ Business title: [48] _____ Type of Business: [49] _____

Address (❏ home [50] ❏ work [51]/Company name: _____)

Street/Suite# _____

City [52]/State [53]/Zipcode [54]: _____ Country [55] _____

❏ **I liked this book!** You may quote me by name in future
   IDG Books Worldwide promotional materials.

My daytime phone number is _____

IDG
BOOKS

THE WORLD OF
COMPUTER
KNOWLEDGE

☐ YES!

Please keep me informed about IDG's World of Computer Knowledge. Send me the latest IDG Books catalog.